American Sociology Series

KIMBALL YOUNG, GENERAL EDITOR

American Sociology Series

Social Problems and Social Policy
JAMES M. REINHARDT, PAUL MEADOWS, *and* JOHN M. GILLETTE

Sociology, A Study of Society and Culture, Second Edition
KIMBALL YOUNG

Isolated Communities
OSCAR W. JUNEK

Administration of Public Welfare
R. CLYDE WHITE

Fundamental Concepts of Sociology
(Gemeinschaft und Gesellschaft)
FERDINAND TONNIES
Translated and Supplemented by Charles P. Loomis

Crime and Its Treatment
ARTHUR E. WOOD *and* JOHN B. WAITE

Population Problems, A Cultural Interpretation
PAUL H. LANDIS

The Family
ERNEST W. BURGESS *and* HARVEY J. LOCKE

Rural Sociology
LOWRY NELSON

Social Work, An Introduction to the Field
HERBERT H. STROUP

Minorities in American Society
CHARLES F. MARDEN

World Population and Future Resources
Edited by PAUL K. HATT

Social Problems and
Social Policy

James M. Reinhardt

CHAIRMAN, DEPARTMENT OF SOCIOLOGY
UNIVERSITY OF NEBRASKA

Paul Meadows

PROFESSOR OF SOCIOLOGY
UNIVERSITY OF NEBRASKA

John M. Gillette

LATE PROFESSOR OF SOCIOLOGY
UNIVERSITY OF NORTH DAKOTA

American Book Company

NEW YORK   CINCINNATI   CHICAGO   BOSTON   ATLANTA

DALLAS   SAN FRANCISCO

To Our Distinguished Colleague

Joyce Oramel Hertzler

Preface

This book attempts to deal realistically and in a straightforward manner with some of the major problems that confront our society today. The authors recognize that social problems arise out of complexes of changing conditions which create conflicts in ideals and between divergent interests and activities. Since, from the authors' point of view, social problems are generally deeply rooted in institutional behavior and related to human experience, an intelligent approach to an understanding of social problems requires some knowledge of institutional behavior and history.

This book carries over a considerable amount of material from an earlier publication, *Social Problems in a Changing Social Order*, and the present authors are deeply indebted to the late John M. Gillette not only for material contributions but also for invaluable counsel during the planning stages of this book.

The authors have been guided throughout by a social philosophy which hold that an understanding and a solution of modern social problems are best achieved through democratic processes in which the group acts in concert in the interest of the general welfare. Hence, the strong emphasis on national and social policies.

James M. Reinhardt
Paul Meadows

Contents

Contents

CHAPTER 1

The Nature and Field of Social Problems

Character and Significance of Social Problems

Social conditions and problems. Social problems rise out of social conditions. Social conditions exist wherever and whenever a relationship obtains between two or more human beings. Simple society occurs where people live in face-to-face relations with one another. Society becomes complex and impersonal when institutions and extensive organizational machinery develop, so that relationships between persons are established and operated through and by means of such institutions and organizations. "Social problems" is an abstract term to cover the general features of troublesome situations appearing or coming to public attention in either simple or complex society. Social problems become concrete when we are face to face with some particular situation. We need to guard ourselves against overemphasizing the idea that social problems occur very much more frequently in a large, complex society than in small, simple ones. First, we know that social problems arise in simple societies such as the family and small community; and, second, these small societies exist everywhere and penetratingly ramify, like tissue cells, throughout all of the greater society.

Since social conditions constitute the background of social problems, it is appropriate to study such conditions along with social problems. Considered in the broad sense, the ultimate goal of all societal study and investigation is the description and analysis of social problems. (See below.) The study of social conditions leads to an understanding of such conditions and social relationships and should develop an intelligent capacity for detecting the causes of maladjustments. And from this understanding, it is hoped, prediction and control will emerge.

1

The nature of social problems.   A social problem is a situation for the appearance of which no one individual or a few individuals are responsible, which threatens injurious results for many persons, and the removal or control of which is completely beyond the ability of one person or a few individuals. The moral responsibility for meeting such situations or solving social problems is thus placed upon society at large, if not for their appearance, at least for their control. We thus have at least three well-defined characteristics of a social problem: (1) It is largely social in origin, that is, it has a group bearing. (2) It is social in its results. (3) The responsibility for it is social.

Stated otherwise, a social problem is a collective difficulty which the total public or some constituent group of the public thinks exists. It is likely that no two persons or publics have exactly the same conception of a given problem-difficulty because of differing information, insight, attitude, interest, and character. In like manner differing publics, such as political parties and factions, wets and drys, capital and labor, Negroes and whites, may differ concerning the causal conditions of any given problem and regarding the remedial measures to be applied. We thus discover that a large subjective element of personal judgment is necessarily present in social problems, or at least in our conception of them.

Some of the inherent features of social problems are clear when we view them as conflicts between social interests and maladjustments of social institutions and organizations.

(1) *Disadjustment.*   Society is constituted of interest groups or publics, such as political parties, churches, employers, labor, professions, or as interest groups representing steel, oil, automobiles, agriculture, each of which, in turn, is made up of persons whose economic or other concern leads them to organize to promote their common interests. These interest groups are institutionalized; that is, they become relatively permanent patterns for making social adjustments. The members of each group adjust themselves to their group and to the larger society or other publics through their own public. The various publics may get out of adjustment with other publics and with total society. Thus, farmers were in a bad way for years because of disadjustment between agricultural interests as a public and other publics.

(2) *Conflict.*   Social adjustment often involves social conflict, as when organized interests oppose measures proposed for the

benefit of society as a whole or suggested for the removal of socially injurious conditions. This is a conspicuous occurrence in our present big society. In state legislatures and Congress, when bills are proposed to correct the evils of monopoly, inflation, housing, repressed voting, and the like, powerful pressure groups, or lobbies, beset these legislative bodies and often prevent the passage of anything like adequate remedial laws.

Social problems as disadjustments. All social problems are disadjustments. Many of them, probably, are maladjustments, or bad adjustments. All misadjustments which are necessary to evolution or progress must be "good" for society, although they may seem to be "bad" at the time or for the persons concerned. Such are unemployment, due to mechanization of industry and agriculture, and family disorganization which may be attendant upon family evolution. Since all disrupting social changes *look* bad, while some of them may *be* good or necessary, we will call them disadjustments.

Social disadjustments may be personal, between persons, such as criminal actions, family disagreements, racial friction, and some insanity. Much of it is impersonal because it is in the nature of collisions between groups, organizations, and institutions.

Practical and scientific social problems. The differences between social problems and those of general or "pure" sociology, as objectives of investigation, are largely fictitious. The distinction between them commonly made is one of research aim rather than of research method. The following paragraph establishes the questionable nature of this distinction. The substitution of "social disorganization" or "social pathology" for "social problems" is a somewhat artificial attempt to appear more definitely scientific, for neither has definite boundaries. In fact, all the problems remain just as they were for the public to face.

Consideration of a social problem should be quite as scientific, both in spirit and in method, as that of a so-called scientific problem. If the student collects the data objectively, tabulates, compares, organizes, and interprets them scientifically, drawing only the conclusions warranted by the facts, his procedure is scientific. The only difference between a scientist who devotes his attention to social problems and one who considers general sociology is that of considering practical utilization of results. Sometimes the one is called "applied" and the other "pure" sociology. The former is supposed to have a practical aim, the latter's aim to be void of any necessary application. Yet the distinction is more or less fictitious and barren, for every "pure" scientist believes his work will prove useful to mankind, if not soon, then sometime; and the applied scientist may have as his primary aim to be thorough and scientific at every step of his work, with little interest as to how and when the results may be applied. The idea that the so-called pure scientist is of a higher order of scientific being than the applied scientist is one that only the superficially minded presently entertain.

The practical importance of social problems appears in the fact that statesmanship in every calling of life meets them and is forced to devote much attention and effort to their consideration. The social burden of pauperism, poverty, criminality, delinquency, insanity, feeble-mindedness, blindness, deafness, separation and divorce in families, neglect of children, vice, drunkenness, and war touches officials, legislators, educational administrators and teachers, ecclesiastical organizations, lodges, civic associations, labor groups, corporations, homes, communities, and nations. No one escapes the burden, and those in charge of administering these affairs cannot dodge the responsibility of having to deal with the victims and perpetrators of social disadjustments.

Since any science deals with nothing more nor less than a set or series of intellectual problems, the solution for which is sought in the course of the science, and since every social problem is an intellectual and so a scientific problem, it is obvious that a consideration of the problems of society is also an approach to scientific sociology. Again, a competent consideration of social problems admits us to the very heart of sociology, as was previously pointed out. This fact is true because attention to the causes of social problems reveals those factors which account for social movements and activities. There is no better method of securing an understanding of how things come to pass in society than by a thorough study of the origin and development of its various problems.

It is the practical rather than the scientific import of social problems which captivates the interest of the larger number of persons. Illustrating this from college life, the writers have found that, in their own department, courses in applied sociology draw much heavier enrollment than the more strictly theoretical and scientific courses. This, doubtless, is due to the fact that such courses touch what are likely to be regarded as the most vital interests. They give concrete consideration to widely discussed issues close about us. Just as the defects and diseases of our bodies attract and hold attention more than the normal characteristics and development, so it seems that pathological and exceptional sociological conditions provoke our curiosity and study more than do the normal.

Causal factors in social problems. The accompanying table on causes of poverty is an illustration of the complexity of causation in social problems, the tendency of problems to overlap, and their commonness from problem to problem. The items under each of the three classes could be multiplied, but these are sufficient for illustrative purposes.

TABLE 1

Potential Causes of Poverty

In the person	In the physical environment	In the social environment
Hereditary	Soil	Economic system
Constitution	Temperature	Distribution of wealth
Malformation	Humidity	"Business cycle"
Temperament	Precipitation	Unemployment
Capacity	Air conditions	Technological conditions
Acquired	Catastrophes	Accidents
Prenatal		Social institutions
Postnatal		Government
Habits		War
Character		Education
From disease		Family
From accident		Community
Sense-organ defects		Caste and class
Attitudes		Religion
		Relief systems
		Communication systems
		Amusement
		Customs

A few brief remarks on the table will clarify the points at issue.

1. The causal conditions are surprisingly numerous. They are found in the person, in external nature, and in the social environment. Not all are likely to be present in a given problem, and those present vary from problem to problem. This scheme of causes of poverty would fit that of crime about as well and also would be applicable to most of our problems.

2. It is evident that social problems provide a large basis of common causal factors. They emerge out of a common soil of socio-cultural life and the conditioning natural environment in which hereditary human constitutions develop.

3. It follows that social problems are interrelated and interdependent. It is the particular combination of factors which makes problems different.

Interrelationship of social problems. Since social problems are social in their nature, that is, reflect and pertain to a collective situation in some manner, it is rational to infer that they sustain a somewhat necessary relationship to one another. We can suggest only some of the major interrelations.

1. Many problems are interdependent. They are not interfunctioning, as we commonly think of that term, but interconditioning. That is, they act on one another as causes, in the sense that they are mutually and cumulatively promotive and provocative. Thus, the more there is of unemployment or blindness or feeble-mindedness, for instance, the more of crime and poverty there is likely to be. The reverse also is true, that increasing crime and poverty may result in the increase of blindness and mental deficiency.

Thus, there is a kind of cumulative co-operation or consort between some or many of our social-problem conditions. They tend to beget each other and to foster and encourage one another. This is a very important fact and should always be considered when plans are made to administer either preventives or "cures" to any or most of the social problems.

2. Social problems may have a common origin. Inasmuch as two or more problems may arise out of a given social situation, they are likely to have common causal conditions. A natural catastrophe, such as flood or earthquake, may produce dependency, crime, sickness, and other unfortunate results. The same may be true of a social emergency such as a strike, a depression, or a war.

3. Still, a social problem may have a single cause. The Galveston storm (1900) gave rise to a most menacing social situation in that city. The San Francisco earthquake (1906) and subsequent fire precipitated a like situation upon that city. Of course the larger society in each case was touched by these occasions and responded to them, but the problems were primarily those of a local group or society. The Missouri floods of 1951 were a natural calamity which swept over and affected portions of

several states; this constituted an emergency problem for many separate communities, for the states affected, and also for the nation.

4. Certain social problems may have a more or less common approach as to analysis and as to the methods of treatment. This is particularly true of problems arising relative to the defective classes, especially in so far as the hereditary features play a part. Hereditary transmission is the same, we suppose, in all cases and may, therefore, be thought of as common. But the care and disposal of defectives of the various classes are similar only up to a given limit.

5. There is a similarity in social problems in that each of them is produced by a plurality of causal conditions. Scarcely ever is a problem accounted for by just one kind or set of conditions, except, perhaps, in the case of floods, earthquakes, and other catastrophic occurrences of nature, which, as we noted, set up a train of social difficulties. It is important to note that this multiplicity of causes involves the thought that each social problem is likely to root back into all the different kinds of conditions and fields of society. To try to class social problems into divisions so that one class is produced by one set of causes and another by another is at once superficial and scientifically groundless. Nearly every problem is to be accounted for by referring it back to "social" causes, economic causes, cultural causes, and hereditary, physical, and governmental causes. Classes and divisions of problems, therefore, can represent no more than the recognition of the fact that some one set of conditions is more weighty as a cause than some other set.

Genesis of Social Problems

Reasons for appearance. Social problems have their history: their origins and development. Evidently there was a time in human history when they did not exist. That was at the very beginning of human association, when society was so vague, undefined, and simple that problem conditions had not yet arisen. And during thousands of years, no doubt, if problem conditions existed, there were no persons sufficiently intelligent to see them; and so, practically, there were no problems. Consequently, we must think that they arose with the coming of a more complex society.

Social problems have been the result particularly of the development of certain social and cultural conditions: (1) differentiation and multiplication of social interests and functions; (2) development of an analytical insight into the causative interdependencies and interworkings of the parts of society; (3) the increased possibility of social disturbance by the physical environment, as a result of dwindling resources by reason of an expanding population; (4) the accelerating frequency of social change by reason of the rapid multiplication of scientific discoveries and mechanical inventions; (5) a growing ability to recognize the hereditary nature of many of our defective individuals; and (6) the development of humanitarian sentiments and the recognition of the worth of human life and the rights of the common man.

Multiplication of interests and social organs. One reason for the existence of a larger array of perplexing situations at present than in early or earlier society is not far to seek, namely, the growth in the number and kinds of human interests and the consequent multiplication of functions and social agencies by which they may be realized. The principle that the greater the number of parts in a machine or an organism, such as the animal body, the greater the opportunity and probability of disadjustment among parts holds equally good for societies. In the industrial and business world thousands of kinds of goods are made and sold which were not known formerly. Since the manufacture of each kind of goods requires a social organization or structure and since the sale may demand another special organization, it is readily understood how very rapidly social differentiation has been taking place in that one phase of society. In manufacture, transportation of goods, financing of businesses, and distribution of commodities the industrial world is many times more complicated than it was before the Industrial Revolution. And what has transpired in this field in the direction of specialization has also been taking place, only in lesser degrees, in government, religion, education, publication, and other great social realms. Thus, there is increased opportunity for a collision of interest with interest and function with function. There may be too little functioning of some organs and too much of others. The resulting complexity constitutes a labyrinth in which one or more unknown or uncertain causative factors are concealed. Society has become a jungle in which the less civilized and less altruistic members of the group may hunt and prey upon the weak and the unprotected. Even well-meaning individuals may, on occasion, start activities entailing destructive consequences which they cannot foresee and, once begun, they do not know how to check.

The rise of particular kinds of societies or conditions is a prolific source of dislocations and disadjustments. Eskimos have no "housing problem," pygmies no "labor problem," and Bedouin Arabs no "rural problem." These problems in their full-fledged state have to await the arrival of a society which is differentiated into city and country, and in which concentration of population in large cities, high land values, and developed commercialism have occurred.

Insight. Again, there is a tendency for social problems to multiply in proportion to the development of our power to make a scientific analysis. Scientific problems are the result of a developed insight into the constitution and working of nature. Such insight is the product of a long cultural development and is still undergoing growth and improvement. Human beings lived in society for a much longer time before there was any social insight than they have lived in it since the beginnings of such insight. It was relatively late in the history of social thought that a competent analysis of social interests and structures was made. It required advanced societies, such as Babylonia and Greece in the ancient world, for the production of social philosophers and legislators capable of tracing the operation of social cause and effect. But even such great minds as those of Hammurabi and Aristotle had not mastered the intricacies of society. Today the work of analysis is in full sway, more and more the minutiae of social interworkings are revealed, and more insistently do the possibilities of conflict, breakdown, and malfunctioning come to light. Issues which formerly were regarded as simple are broken up into several issues, and the number of problems is multiplied.

We used to discuss rural communities as if they were all alike. Now we recognize a multiplicity of rural-community types, different sets of geographical conditions in the various portions of our nation being recognized as important although not sole causes. Our growing knowledge not only multiplies the kinds of natural conditions but also our perceptions of how they influence man and society. Likewise our recognition of hereditary types of human beings has grown. Thus, psychiatrists no longer talk of "insanity" but of "insanities," knowing there are diverse forms of insanity. Mental hygienists also recognize many types and stages of feeble-mindedness. Probably the greater portion, if not all, of these new types are products of enlarged scientific knowledge and powers of discrimination rather than of hereditary differentiation.

Civilization. This term, in its broad sense, means a society having a variety of contents and processes, but in this setting it signifies the recent stage of development of higher societies. So used, we may say that social problems are inherent in civilization, and that by its very nature civilization begets such problems in great number and frequency. Why this is true is worth examination, although we already have denoted it by implication and indirection.

Briefly, the reason is found in the fact that ideas are dynamic and that, as they multiply and are put to use, they act as great moving forces in society. Every idea tends to act itself out through the organism. The multiplication of ideas and their inculcation in human beings is, in principle, like scattering explosives about. This multiplication of ideas is much more rapid than we are likely to conceive. Those acquainted with the evolution of prehistoric man and the appearance of culture on earth are aware that during millenniums of time new ideas and techniques appeared very infrequently. With the increase of cultural evolution, new ideas appeared more and more frequently, so that today among our advanced peoples new ideas are derived perhaps at the rate of hundreds of thousands a year. We have some hard facts from the records of our patent office to show this. Our patent office issues patents and trade-marks at a rate of over 45 thousand a year. The average yearly number of new patents and certificates of registration issued in the nine years 1941–1949 was 46,350; of patents alone it was 29,507; and of trade-marks alone it was 8777.[1] But these covered only some of the new ideas relative to material things, and we must believe that new ideas in other fields were somewhat proportionally numerous.

Some great inventions of machines and processes have produced revolutionary effects. We ascribe the Industrial Revolution to the invention of a few important machines. We are now in the midst of a mechanical and scientific revolution even more significant in its consequences. The introduction of just one machine alone, the motor vehicle, has resulted probably in more numerous and far-reaching changes than did the French Revolution. It made new vocations and places for millions of men and women. It destroyed many old lines of employment, such as trucking, draying, and transportation of passengers by horse-drawn vehicles. It unsettled and shifted about millions of inhabitants. The suspension of its manufacture would throw

[1] *U.S. Stat. Abstract*, 1950, p. 450.

millions into unemployment and turn a large portion of them into dependents. One of its effects on American farming has been to reduce the number of horses from about 21.5 millions to 6.3 millions between 1918 and 1947, and thus undermine the market for the farmer's hay and oats. The automobile has greatly changed the standards and modes of living and the outlook on life of millions of persons.

There are other illustrations. The refined Bessemer and other processes of making steel have greatly reduced the cost of steel and improved its quality; and structural work has been revolutionized, as seen in bridge building, erection of skyscrapers, machines, and railways. The development of a process for cracking and refining oil has produced cheaper oil products, especially gasoline, making it available for gas-driven motors. This has been a condition of the universalization of motor vehicles. Such is the result of the application of new ideas and processes of science to industry and life.

The introduction of new ideas has affected profoundly the points of view and standards of peoples. This fact is registered in the transition from one set of ideals and objectives of life to another. Thus, we have such contrasting goals of effort and interest as the head-hunting of Malays and becoming a millionaire today; the gladiatorial combats of Roman times and modern bull fights, football games, and pugilistic prize-fights; the standard of slavery as the estate of the masses of people and "free labor" contract and democratic aspirations and participation in social life; the divine sovereignty of rulers over the masses and the sovereign power of the latter over the former.

Not all the results arising from such revolutionary inventions and practices are problematical. Fortunately by far the greater portions of ensuing social changes are highly beneficial. Still, out of the multitude of social changes which they engender, there arise some structural and functional disadjustments which we call social problems.

Evolutionary revolution. The larger proportions of social changes are small and simple, and they resemble osmosis in the fields of physics and organic life. There is a long, slow, and sometimes insidious transformation and spread in the habits and standards of the masses of people, and their cumulative effects on individuals and classes may be widespread and deep-rooted. The gradual expansion of applied science and the use of mechanical devices in agriculture, the widening practice of sex license with the frequent accompaniment of venereal disease, the growing frequency of natural marriage and companionate marriage finally may become so common as to have very observable and serious consequences which society is compelled to consider and to deal with. When these conditions have arrived at a point where society is forced to deal with them or at least to give them adequate attention, they will have developed into the social-problem stage.

Human valuation. In a manner, the appearance of social problems awaited the rise of a general and popular valuation of human life. Individuals dodged death and practiced self-preservation in backward societies, mothers loved their children and protected them, sibs retaliated when their own members were plucked off by outside sibs. But a high general appreciation of the worth of human life, of the lives of fellow men of all classes and descriptions is a late comer in cultural history. According to E. A. Ross, even the Chinese place a low value on life. A campaign to save children, to reduce child mortality, would likely be resented by the Chinese masses because the population is great in proportion to the resources. In certain portions of our country it is not considered a heinous offense to lynch a man. In China and portions of the United States the lives of certain classes of persons are scarcely worth saving. To ward off death and to salvage life among them is not a social problem. Many of the whites in the South would say there is no Negro problem with them. They say the white man has solved the problem there. The Negro is "put in his place" and is kept there. Since his place in society is determined for him, there is no question about his position, future, or deserts. Everything is settled.

Altruism. It is one thing to be able to see the cause of social disadjustment, and another to want to check or relieve it. The desire to obviate and cure social misery could not appear until considerable altruism, or reflective sympathy, and humanitarianism had developed. Sympathy of the unreflective sort existed early in society. Savages alleviate the hunger of one another so long as anyone has food. Food was administered communistically among some of our American Indian tribes. So long as members of a kinship group had food, others had a right to partake of it. The whole group went up or down together. It was a feast or a famine. The group did not reflectively and foresightedly study the matter of production and preservation of food or anything else for a season's duration. Famine and disease devastated

Indian life, and it was not known how to go about controlling them. Reflective and foresighted sympathy was out of the question. In so far as we seek today to solve our problems, the solution rests on sympathetic insight into the complex human situation.

Number of social problems.   Several statements are necessary to illuminate the discussion of the number of social problems. First, the number varies according to our placement of emphasis on major or minor problems, the latter being many times more numerous than the former. There might be, for example, anywhere from twenty to forty major problems and hundreds or even thousands of secondary and tertiary ones.

Second, in so far as social problems are disadjustments of persons to social structures and of structures to one another, their number would obviously increase with the growing complexity involved in social evolution. In principle, the increase would be the cumulative product of the number of parts. The maximum number of different ways to relate three parts is 6 ($1 \times 2 \times 3$); to relate five parts, 120; six parts, 720; and seven parts, 5040. Obviously, there may be many possible modes of disadjustment between parts. Since persons are more numerous than social structures, the maximum number of possible disadjustments theoretically is almost infinite. But our social problems do not actually multiply that rapidly during social evolution, for there are many duplicating factors. However, the principle has considerable applicability.

Third, a growing understanding of society increases the discovery of new social problems. There was no problem of child labor in the time of Alexander ·Hamilton, for he advocated high tariffs so that the stimulated industries would give labor to women and children. Were he living today, he would most likely oppose child labor. Few persons of his time saw its harmfulness to body, mind, and morals, and its deprivation of play and other recreation which we today believe so essential to full personality development. Slavery was complacently tolerated by civilization until a sympathetic understanding of human nature and a wide altruism had come into existence.

Are all social problems reducible to one?   This question is interesting to scientists but is not of great practical importance, as our discussion of it will make clear. The late professor C. A. Ellwood wrote a book, *The social problem* (1915), in which he argued that the one great social problem for humanity was to learn how to live amicably and without conflict. His contention was supported scientifically. But for practical purposes, this one big problem has to be broken down into many smaller problems in order for us to be able to understand them and perhaps to control their causal conditions. The one big problem is so gigantic and intricate as to be elusive when it comes to finding methods of bringing about universal co-operation and harmony. We are in the position of the astronomer facing the study of the immense universe. He may vaguely grasp it as a total entity, but in dealing with it he must study its structures one by one, its galaxies, its nebulae, planetary systems, suns, meteors, asteroids, star dust, and all the rest. His total universe of matter and so-called "empty" space is known only fragmentarily and is largely a generalization or abstraction. By the same token, we can scarcely know the total Great Society and its one great social problem. Rather, we must study its parts and learn to treat its problems.

This book deals with a large number of social problems. It does not claim to consider them all. It repeatedly recognizes the plurality of problems in its treatment of the great problems. The reader is invited to discover, multiply, and "solve" other problems up to the limit of his capacity and interest.

Solution of Social Problems

Need for scientific procedure. A social problem is a situation, confronting a group or section of society, which promises or inflicts injurious consequences that can be handled only collectively. The solution of a mathematical problem consists in supplying the missing factor. For scientific purposes, the solution of a social problem may be regarded as comprising the discovery of the causes of the situation which constitutes the problem, and the demonstration of the method of procedure for restoring the situation to its normal state. In mathematics there are set rules to be followed in working out the solution of a problem. If one has intelligence enough to understand and follow the rules, the rest is easy, and the correct answer is assured. This is not the case regarding social problems. There are no certain rules to be followed step by step in the discovery of the solution. Our best recourse is to employ scientific methods rigidly at every step in the analytical procedure. Yet, because of uncertain factors always present, we never can be sure that our conclusions are more than approximations of the truth.

In the discovery of causes we proceed to unearth every kind of influence which has a bearing upon the production of the undesirable results. There can be no cut-and-dried way to accomplish this task except to make a very thorough canvass of the whole situation so as to be sure that nothing vital to the situation has escaped the investigator. This procedure does not mean that useful schedules for collecting causal facts may not be employed. It does mean that every problem attacked is likely to be unique and to have individualistic traits which differentiate it from other problems. Furthermore, it is even true that no two problems in the same field, as in that of crime let us say, are ever exactly the same at successive times or in different locations. This is due to the fact that the combinations of social elements making up society at different times and places are never exactly alike.

The search for controls. Anything like a competent solution of a social problem depends upon the discovery of controls or means of readjusting the causative conditions. There can be, of course, only an intellectual solution of a problem where the causal conditions are beyond control. In a sense, where conditions are outside the bounds of control, there is no problem to be solved, in the practical or applied meaning.

The astronomer's problems concerning the material universe are only intellectual or purely scientific, because he can do nothing about it. Sun spots may be bad for health, rainfall, production of crops, or induce other undesirable results, but we are powerless to prevent them. The astronomer may know what causes them and how they produce results in our society which are destructive or harmful, yet he can do nothing to alleviate our woes. In so far as the producing conditions of cancer are unknown, it is a problem only in the scientific sense. Cancer may cause much trouble, but there is no practical solution for cancer problems until scientific workers have established the cause of the disease and have shown how it may be controlled.

In a sense there are practical social problems only in situations where we think or know that the determining, producing conditions are within the range of influence and control by society. In that sense, were divorce, vice, or poverty known to be outside the limits of human influence, they would not constitute social problems—only inevitabilities.

Controls limited. There are inherent difficulties in the solution of social problems which are due to difficulties of control. In none of the problems is there complete control. This lack of complete control may be because: (a) Some problems are occasioned by such fiats of nature as droughts, floods, tornadoes, earthquakes. (b) Others have heredity as a causal factor, and the exact nature of its processes are as yet little understood. (c) Society has not the right to treat human beings like guinea pigs, consequently limits to the solution of human problems are inevitable. (d) The conflict of social interests is often so pronounced as to block the application of preventive and curative programs which otherwise might be effective in solving the problem. For instance, the redistribution of wealth might, at least temporarily, put an end to the problem of poverty, but the vested interests of various sorts, the rights of property, the belief in the doctrine of the incentives of individualism, and the like, all defeat its realization.

Are Social Problems Social Diseases?

Social degeneration.   What social problems, if any, represent social degeneration? Biologically, degeneration means a gradual and fundamental impairment of an organ, perhaps rendering it vestigial, as in the case of fishes' eyes in the Mammoth Cave. In medicine, degeneration means breaking down an organ by chemical changes in its essential substance so that it functions poorly or not at all. Only by analogy could social degeneration represent a chronic, continuous breaking-down of social structure or social institutions, manifesting itself in malfunctioning. In Spengler's *Decline of the West*, the fundamental idea is that degeneration is inherent as a final stage in every culture. We have long heard of the decline of peoples, nations, and their cultures, and of their eventual disappearance. Some publicists broadcast that our nation and times are degenerate, but they do not offer substantial proofs.

In order to pronounce on a case of supposed degeneration, we would need to possess criteria and standards for judging which of the social changes represent degeneration, and we would also need appropriate devices for their estimate and measurement. Not only do we not have these criteria and devices, but, further, we have scarcely begun to think about inventing and constructing them. Instrumentalities fit for criteria and measurement are treated in the following paragraphs. But it is certain that such a simple and universal institution as the family cannot be proved to be undergoing degenerative changes, although it is profoundly affected by the times and is undergoing pronounced transformation.

Social pathology.   To know whether social problems represent diseased or pathological conditions depends, first, on defining normal and abnormal society. The *mean* of a series of variables, such as mean stature, mean temperature, mean income, is often used as the normal. But the mean is only a device for comparing different sets of variables and may coincide with not a single one of the variables. It is possible to conceive that a series of social conditions, or variables, extending over many years or areas might fluctuate all about the mean without any one coinciding with it and without any of the conditions being abnormal. The mean income of a group might tell us nothing about the poverty of a large section of the inhabitants. Consequently the mean is not a competent index of normal society. We shall likewise have to discard the *median* and the *mode* (although the mode is the better criterion of normal social phenomena), because they are too narrow and do not inherently indicate the normal or abnormal.

Some measure of deviation of social variables from the average, such as the *standard deviation* and the *intraquartile*, might serve as more available statistical instruments for determining abnormal or pathological social conditions. But it would be necessary to agree on how far conditions may fluctuate from the mean without being considered abnormal. The measure of deviation in itself does not represent abnormality; it serves only as a device which might be made to indicate it. Thus, in a given population the mean income is $2500 a year and the standard deviation is $500. "Normal" incomes, accordingly, would range from $2000 to $3000. Incomes above or below these would then be called abnormally high or low. But in the case of both these devices we are compelled to decide as rationally as possible on the justification of the yardstick. In other words, it is our good sense, or scientific sense, which measures the fitness of the measuring stick and, consequently, what is normal and abnormal in society.

Social problems cover several situations which rightfully should not be classed as pathological. First, those situations brought about by natural events, such as floods, droughts, and earthquakes, appear not by the impairment of the social structure but specifically by events in nature which are legally named "acts of God." Second, the growing pains or birth pangs of social evolution brought on by more or less necessary social transformations are not symptoms of social disease. These are obviously distinct from disadjustments of static society. Technological unemployment, public support under mothers' allowances, health problems created by declining rates of population increase due to birth control, standards of health, rising divorce rates which affect the family—all may be thought of as examples of developmental social disadjustments. Third, the utopian views for society which make many present social conditions *seem* problem situations are the ideals by means of which we evaluate, find defects in society, and so proceed to improve it. But few persons have such ideals that are well founded, and it is only in their minds that the specified kind of social problems arises.

It remains a question as to whether or not the other classes of social problems should be called pathological. The term "social pathology," if scientifically determined, might serve a valuable purpose. But it has not been so defined, and it therefore is probably more useful for popularizing information than for promoting scientific research.

The Field and Usefulness of Social Problems

It is observed that human society is the stage on which social problems as dramatic figures appear, act out their course of events, and disappear, or, peradventure, stay on as unwelcome guests. Social problems may arise because of conditions in society itself, in human beings, or in the physical environment, or out of disadjustments between some or all of these. But, just because they are in their very nature social situations, they are, and must be, social problems. It seems worth while to try to visualize the field of social problems and their relation to society.

The field. It is a convenience in scientific investigation to think of the phenomena pertaining to nature, man, and society as composed of various fields. Each science or subject has a field of events and facts appropriate to it. On this field the scientist and the student can concentrate attention more effectively than if they tried to cover all events in the universe. The study of social problems thus constitutes a field of events with which society has to deal. Other studies may also deal with these events; but, since every study treats them from its own point of view and for its own purposes, they keep pretty much out of each other's way. Let us note some of the features of the field of social problems.

1. Social problems lie close to the center of social life. The habitual, daily, routine, conventional activities of life fortunately make up the greater part of life. Often, however, they are broken across by social breakdowns, disturbances, dislocations, and the appearance of very troublesome classes of persons. At least these

problem situations attract as much attention as the numerous and important daily tasks and jobs. A "crime wave" gets more space in the news columns day by day than does teaching, or making steel, or legislating, or farming. The depression aroused us to greater emotional heights than a decade of prosperity or normalcy. We have to attend to the poor, unemployed, insane, robbers, and increasing divorce cases because we think they carry a menace.

2. Social problems range all over society and run the gamut of social affairs. There is no social holy of holies, where social problems may not intrude; there are no social institutions or organizations which are exempt from their invasion. The "breakdown of the family" occurs in numerous ways and by reason of many causes. The race problem in the guise of race prejudice and friction exists all over the United States and is appearing in Africa and elsewhere. Bootlegging and hijacking were expressions of a more or less general breakdown of our political system in its attempt to realize the spirit of the Eighteenth Amendment. The various failures of the industrial system of this nation, as well as of other nations, affected every business and class of persons, "ruined" farming, bankrupted thousands of banks, caused owners to lose millions of homes, threw out of employment and made dependent many millions of our steadiest and most deserving citizens, broke characters, wills, and ambitions, and touched every other range of social life.

3. The study of social problems constitutes the heart of sociology as a science. If all scientific treatises in the field of sociology were weighed and measured and their contents gauged, it would certainly demonstrate that, in quantity at least, the problem situations, both intellectual and practical, make up the bulk of all their considerations. Even so-called "pure" or theoretical sociology more and more devotes itself to these practical problems of society. There are great treatises, called *Principles of sociology* or just *Sociology*, which concentrate their attention on social problems. To extract these problem features from scientific sociology would be to tear out the latter's vitals.

The reason for this is evident: social problems lie close to the heart of society itself and at times absorb pretty much all serious social consideration. In so far as social problems are pathological, they are phenomena to be explained scientifically, and therefore they belong quite properly to scientific sociology.

4. Social problems seem to be closely associated with develop-

ing civilization and to be coextensive with that civilization. To many students of society who are enlightened as to recent trends, society takes on the appearance of a great jungle in which the strong and the cunning prey upon the weak and the ignorant, where might makes right, and where principles of justice and right do not prevail. This position seems erroneous, yet there is so much to it that we recognize that the multiplication of problems with the unfolding of society must inhere either in the nature or in the increasing defects of civilization itself.

Usefulness of social-problem studies. What has been said regarding the field of social problems suggests the importance of the utility attached to their consideration. Certain further brief suggestions as to this utility may be mentioned.

1. Such a study does much to deepen our insight into the nature and workings of human society. As an illustration regarding the value of research in another field, consider the germ theory of disease, which is young—only a little over a half century old. Yet the knowledge that many diseases are spread by the transmission of kinds of germs from person to person, directly or indirectly, has not only revolutionized public health but perhaps has set the practice of medicine forward more than has any previous discovery pertaining to diseases. It has led physicians, biologists, and other scientists to a wide and intensive investigation of various pathological traits of human beings and animals, and it has brought a greatly increased understanding of the human physical organism. In like manner the research and thought devoted to understanding the conditions which account for the various social problems, pathological or otherwise, have increased our insight into the nature and intricacies of society.

2. The study of social problems promotes our social economy. It is a highly utilitarian study because it is pointed to an understanding of a problem situation and the consideration of means by which the situation may be improved. Some of the proposed remedial measures are likely to be purely theoretical in the sense of being hypothetical and impractical. Nevertheless, there is bound to be a goodly residue of practical and highly useful ideas bearing on improvement. This very old social world has learned more by the slow process of trial-and-error than in any other way and has stored up all it knows that is useful. Sometimes, especially when the world was young, men stumbled accidentally onto useful discoveries, without having made a preceding guess. More and more, however, in all ranges of thought and action

men began to think in advance about how to improve the situation in which they were interested; then they tried out their advanced guess. Sometimes the guess worked, but more often it failed. Yet, through a constant accumulation of good guesses, a great storehouse of useful information has been amassed.

In like manner our social problems are tinkered with, with a good deal of guessing as to causes and cures. Some of the guesses prove to be accurate, with useful results; the majority of the hypotheses, however, are failures because not enough is yet known. We are becoming more and more scientific, however, in making our hypotheses and consequently getting closer to the truth. In this volume the student may discover some unscientific guessing, because there is a lack of scientific information and insight about some of the problems discussed. It is left to the readers of this volume to exercise their critical intelligence, to locate the bad guesses, and to discover the good ones which should be followed. Much of the study should be useful because it is well-founded; the remainder will, perhaps, serve as a practice field for the exercise of the critical faculties of those who read and ponder.

Having reviewed the field and utility of social problems, it is well to regard somewhat directly the society whose problems are to be considered and in the midst of which social problems arise. Let us briefly recall the nature of society and observe the relation between it and social problems.

Important Features of Society

Society. Society is the various forms of interaction between conscious human beings. The situation must be such that the persons are aware of one another and modify their behavior through this awareness.

The simplest human expression of society is the personal-contact association, such as family, tribe, neighborhood, playground, and other small local groups. In these, individuals are in close contact, are aware of one another, and respond in attitude and behavior in some expressive manner. The most meager society exists where one person is aware of and is influenced by another who, in turn, is not conscious of the former. The fullest expression of the personal group perhaps is found in a co-operative community enterprise, where all meet, discuss, plan together, and organize to realize their common purpose.

The larger society consists of impersonal relationships between human beings; animal society never rises to this level. Society is such a system of relationships between persons that their activities cannot be explained except with reference to that system. In the larger societies and groups the relationships are brought into existence and maintained by artificial means rather than by face-to-face contacts. Societies consist of both complete and incomplete groups. Complete groups are comparatively independent and self-perpetuating, such as families, cities, states, nations, and world society. Incomplete groups, such as trade unions, political parties, clubs, lodges, and sororities, are not self-sufficient but act with reference to other interests.

Ecological adjustment. Every large society has a geographic setting and is conditioned by the physical factors surrounding it, such as climate in its manifold constitution, soil, topography, plants, and animals. Human society cannot exist without reference to nature; but while geographic conditions are absolutely necessary for the existence of society, they are not sufficient to account for it completely. Man has built up a social mechanism and a system of achievements by the use of which he may employ nature for his purposes, "control" it for his advantage, and even protect himself against its direct attacks. This idea is continued further in a later connection, and it will be found that some of our social problems emanate from nature.

Interdependence. Society is a system of interdependence. It is a situation of mutual dependence of persons and conditions, and of activities and functions on one another. Some of the principal kinds and features of this interdependence will be briefly noted.

1. *Interdependence of function and structure.* This interdependence is perceived in biological organisms; for example, the human body consists of multitudes of organs, each with its special function. Each one functions for the whole body rather than only for itself, although it is helped by the function because the organism to which it belongs is aided. Eliminating or crippling one part destroys or cripples the whole organism. Maintaining all the structures in good working form promotes the welfare of all and of each. Any permanent social group, large or small, exemplifies this principle. The more mature members of the family are interdependent and interfunctioning personalities, each with a job or a role. All big structures of society, such as manufacture, trade, banking, farming, medicine, law, school, and government, are

functional; service agencies which are necessary for the existence of society and the welfare of each are determined by what all do and are. If for long any one of them functions badly, society becomes defective and all are injured thereby.

2. *Interdependence of condition.* This interdependence is observed where an area of a nation or a section of the population experiences a considerable and significant condition or event. A crop failure in one large area disturbs in various ways, some functional and others nonfunctional, the other areas of a nation. Or, the prevalence of a contagious disease in one section of the population causes anxiety at once in other sections, with the result that preventive agencies are set to work.

3. *Interrelations of dependency.* The helpless condition of individuals calls out protection, care, and maintenance by others, or by the group, or by society. Some of this protection and maintenance may be the outcome of inherited impulses and emotional drives, as perhaps when a mother cares for her child. Much of it, however, is the outcome of developed sentiments and standards which drive highly developed groups into action. For example, there appears to be a compensation in satisfied feelings of justice for assisting needy classes of people generally.

Interdependence of function and of condition reveals mutual causation. Activities and conditions in society act as operating causes and effects relative to one another. Social causes are interrelated conditions, and there are no magical or mysterious "forces" in the situation at work which provoke results or bring things to pass. But there is always a little time lag between the occurrence of the causal condition and the social effect. Thus, prosperity causes increased marriage and divorce, but neither of these speeds up immediately with the arrival of prosperity.

Perhaps this fact of interdependence in society is one of the most significant factors in accounting for present-day social problems, if not also for those at every other stage of social development. Human society has developed, however, to such a gigantic scale of multitudinous interlocking and interdependent factors that this complex meshwork of cause and effect has gained the ascendance over other causative conditions. The more intricate and delicately adjusted a machine becomes, the greater the disturbance produced by the breakdown or disadjustment of any of its parts.

Communication. Communication is the heart of society. Society is a process or system of intercommunication. There is no associational fact prior to communication between persons, and association proceeds so long as communication continues. This condition is apparent in the case of small personal groups and crowds. It is obvious when we think through the processes going on and the relations obtaining in the larger society. Trade, for example, begins only after responsible business parties are brought into contact with one another, either personally or by mechanical agencies, and trade agreements are made. Then traffic covered by the agreement is carried on by a series of communications, such as advice concerning shipment and arrival of goods, payments by checks, drafts, or by other goods. Carrying on government with the exercise of authority is pretty much a process of communication from top to bottom. In case of a function performed manually, such as carrying rural mail or operating as a forest ranger, the function rests back upon the directing agency, or it is a form of communication.

It is important to recognize communication as the condition of interdependence in society. The cause-and-effect relation that constitutes interdependence either is communication or rests upon it. You may modify my conduct, let us say, by getting in contact with me so that I imitate what you do or take suggestions from you. Or, middlemen get together and organize effectively to control selling prices of their merchandise, and so affect the cost of living of consumers. Or, we all get influenza by setting up contacts among ourselves either closely or distantly through the stratosphere. Therefore, in human society the dislocations and disadjustments which occasion social problems may be resolved into matters of social give-and-take in the nature of communication.

Co-operation, competition, and conflict. For brevity, these terms are placed together, although at once a graduated series is seen in them. They all exist in society. Although they appear to be set off from each other, they are or may appear together in one society. A harmonious family of parents and children is an illustration of a small group doing teamwork together to maintain and advance the welfare of the family group. The children may compete with one another to gain the approval of parents and in their play strive to "beat" or win, and the parents even may become rivals for the affections of their children. Unfortunately, some families have bickerings, strifes, brawls, and "rows." In the great arena of world society, all the processes of society are witnessed in war between nations. Nations co-operate in war; men, armies, and nations compete for place and honor; the world society is rent in conflict.

Some of the social problems may be based largely on deficiency in co-operation and on the appearance of conflict. Thus, the family problem of disorganization may arise through the loss of mutual confidence of husband and wife, or through the failure of co-operation between various members of the family due to personality conditions. Poverty may result from strife between various economic factors.

Continuity. The history of peoples, nations, and civilizations reveals the fact that human society is a continuous process. It is presumed that a continuity of personal contacts has existed from the first human beings to the present generation, whether six thousand or a million or more years ago. This contact doubtless has been like a meandering stream that flows and spreads through sandy areas and finally breaks up into multitudes of scarcely visible threads of water, most of which are absorbed in the sands or sink underground, the continuity being visibly maintained by just one tiny rivulet. Many entire peoples have disappeared during human history, yet the stream of human contacts has persisted.

Social continuity may be spoken of in terms of culture or social heredity. Culture is the sum total of human achievements, the surplus and reservoir of human experience, existing at any given time in any given society. Culture, in this broad sense, is constituted of all the social patterns or ways of behaving and reacting employed by people; it is made up of ideas, sentiments, and overt practices. All material products of human hands are represented because, first of all, they were inventions, ideas, and plans that were made or conceived by human minds. The achievement, the culture part, is immaterial, psychical. It is this part that passes down from mind to mind. If all material structure and goods were destroyed, culture would remain, and men could rebuild and replace the material things. All institutions, likewise, are achievements and quite as much inventions as are machines. Institutions embody ideas and plans by which organizations realize human desires. This is true also for books, paintings, doctrines, religions, philosophies; the ideas and sentiments embodied in them are cultural achievements.

In thinking of social continuity as social heredity, it is necessary to emphasize the process side. Biological heredity is a process by which traits are transmitted from generation to generation of organisms by means of the germ plasm. This is a physical process. In social heredity it is immaterial achievements or culture which is transmitted; the transmission is not by the germ plasm but by way of minds and communication. The ideas invested in achievements of all sorts are passed on from mind to mind in the series of human generations. "Culture" is the content of social heredity. Another term for this content is sometimes used, namely, "social tradition" or "traditions."

Social continuity maintained by means of social heredity is due to two circumstances. First, there is a building-up, generation by generation, of a greater cultural surplus that becomes the working capital in all social undertakings and that roots back into the more or less remote past. The principles of agriculture; principles of the machine in the guise of lever, wheel, axle, and the like; methods of writing and recording measurements and numbers; cosmogonies, or theories of how things came to be; and many other sets of ideas began in neolithic times in Europe and Asia five to eight thousand years ago. By them we are tied back to and connected with the ancient past in a very vital manner.

Second, as the old members of society die and pass away, their places are taken by the young who are born and develop in the midst of that society. Population is kept up by physical reproduction, but society is maintained by means of the socialization of the young. The children and youth have to be indoctrinated, acculturized, trained, and educated by the older generation in order that they may fit into the level of cultural and social development and be able to carry on.

Social problems may arise in connection with social continuity, and the acculturizing process may have a bearing on social prevention and remedy, but the need for thought about discontinuity in industry or education and about our dependence on proper training to keep society stabilized and progressive should be emphasized.

Social change, evolution, and progress. Anything that becomes different in society represents social change. This may be in custom, fashion, fad, religion, government, farming, brick making; that is, it may occur in anything and anywhere. New departures in the family group, or rural neighborhood, or village, or city are social changes. Social change is more frequent in modern society than it was in primitive and ancient societies. Our pace is more rapid, and we have more things which may undergo variation. In one sense, change is inevitable and desirable; in another sense, change is infrequent and social order and stability are desirable. Groups and institutions require only sufficient change to render them good and effective agencies. Social change, therefore, is not an end in itself; it is only a means of realizing satisfactory objectives.

Social evolution is an aspect or result of social change. The principle of evolution and growth may be represented as essentially one and the same. Growth ordinarily is quantitative and qualitative; it is an increase both in size and in modes of functioning. It involves increasing complexity and specialization of parts and structure, advancing interdependence, and consequent intensification of unity. We see this in plant, animal, and human growth. It is observed in social evolution. It is apparent that social continuity is maintained while social evolution takes place. There is a tendency to conclude that social evolution always means improvement or progress. Probably this conclusion is generally true. It is theoretically conceivable that evolution might take place with a resulting social injury. Theodore Roosevelt classed trusts as "good trusts" and "bad trusts." Some trusts might have bad social effects, notwithstanding the fact that they are wonderful evolutions of social mechanisms. A community or nation might grow enormously in wealth, and yet that wealth might be so badly distributed as to be a curse to the masses.

Social progress is not continuous, as is social change. A change may occur in family, farm neighborhood, city, state, nation, or world society. It is only when we think of society abstractly that we are likely to infer that social progress is constant and continuous. It may be true that somewhere in the world or in our nation progress is occurring always in some little section or in some phase of the Big Society, but the total society is not making progress in all its parts all the time.

It is neither possible nor desirable that change should obtain in everything all the time. We could not live, could not adjust ourselves to, or find our way in, society if all social conditions changed from moment to moment or from day to day, or probably from year to year. We must recognize that we do not live for progress. We live in order to live and to enjoy life. So long as life is satisfactory, social change is undesirable. Progress, like change, is merely a means to life and betterment. It is agreeable to be thought of as "progressive" individuals, clubs, communities, or nation. Such an estimate means only that we are "open-minded" and ready to accept or promote social change, and so make advancement, when it promises to be beneficial.

Change, evolution, and progress have a direct bearing on social problems. For one thing, some of our problems may be the penalty society is paying for securing progress. Possibly the pangs suffered in and from the Civil War are to be viewed as our inevitable contributions for abolishing slavery. We may have to regard the elimination of villages now going on in that way. Again, changes in society are involved in settling problems. The idea of progress is a criterion for initiating and promoting "cures" and "solutions." Social progress is social betterment.

Ethics and Human Nature

All social relationships possess an ethical character; that is, they have a moral quality. This is due to the fact that social relations are established when the actions of one individual of a group or society have an effect upon some other individual. Society has built up and maintains a body of moral rules or norms, such as right and wrong, justice, rights, and the like. These principles are operative in preserving the sanctity of persons, property, order, and social welfare generally. Consequently, when our activities affect another person in any way they are liable to have a bearing on his rights and privileges, that is, have an effect on his property, person, and orderly relationship to others.

Since groups and societies constitute a network of relationships between individuals and institutions, since they are the interdependencies or functioning of individuals as such or by way of organizations, since they almost wholly consist of persons affecting or being affected by one another, it is difficult to conceive of any human action that touches others which is not of ethical import. A person may think his farm or his store, his bank or his profession is entirely his own affair, and that he is free morally to run it as he chooses; but in a compact society like ours he cannot carry out his idea. A farmer does not farm for himself in the sense that he consumes all his own produce and does not depend on others for anything. He sells most of his produce in markets, which are social affairs, and with the proceeds he purchases all the kinds of goods he needs from marketing firms of various kinds. Thus, the farmer is a social functionary and hence is at all times in moral contact with the rest of society.

The solutions proposed for social problems must be viewed

relative to their ethical import. "Cures" must not violate the rights of the individuals concerned and must conserve the general welfare. This principle must be observed in administration, so that the social order is preserved and social change is brought about when desirable.

Human nature. Many allegations are made concerning what human nature will and will not do. Writers assert that it is and is not changeable, that it is not responsible for war, vice, drunkenness, and other undesirable phenomena. Some publicists make it a factor in social progress, while others say progress is impossible because human nature is always the same. It is important to get a scientific background of the concept.

Human nature is both born and developed, hereditary and acquired. Note the factors with which we are born: human form as distinct from subhuman form; maximum brain capacity, that is, a level beyond which the individual could by no possible means go; dynamic drives, impulses, and "instincts" so far as there are any; and at least some of our unit reflexes. These are foundations of human nature; the first two of them may not be modified, and the last two may be modified by experience and training. In general we say that this hereditary human nature has not been changed essentially since present men took form some thirty thousand years ago; that is, not since Cro-Magnon man appeared in Europe. However, we do organize our reflexes and impulses in new ways and inhibit them by means of experience and training. Anger, hate, love, fear, and other emotional factors are strengthened, weakened, and modified by discipline.

The personality of the little child is embryonic in comparison with what it will be when the individual becomes an adult. The psychical side of personality is the impressive one, for it is the development of this which differentiates personalities at the various culture levels. The psychic factor consists of the ideas, beliefs, desires, sentiments, patterns, and skills which individuals learn and carry as the cultural content of the mind. Personality is socially derived and capitalized by culture. The personality of modern man differs profoundly from that of a savage. The biological inheritance and equipment may be similar; but the modern man as philosopher, scientist, artist, or skilled mechanic is what he is because of what society has achieved, stored up, and made available for his development. Eliminate the cultural element and none of us would be other than a savage at the very foot of the personality ladder.

Thus it appears that human nature is hereditary and acquired, unchangeable in some respects but highly modifiable in other respects and in most respects. So, in directing our thought to social problems and social progress, we have a ground for hope that so far as human nature goes the case is not hopeless. It appears that our biggest undertaking is to build a fit social environment. If that can be accomplished, it is pretty certain that human nature will respond, fit into the new order smoothly and harmoniously, and live and work in it efficiently and happily.

QUESTIONS

1. (a) What is a problem? (b) a life problem? (c) a social problem? (d) What are the traits of a social problem?
2. (a) Distinguish between a social and a scientific problem. (b) Of what importance may social problems be to scientific sociology?
3. Why could not social problems have presented themselves to early man?
4. Show how the following factors might give rise to problems: (a) high value of human life, (b) altruism, (c) multiplication of social structures, (d) ability to see causes of bad conditions.
5. Can there be a social problem, or a problem of any nature, where there is a lack of ability to control the producing conditions?
6. (a) Are social problems to be classed as symptoms of social degeneration? (b) What else might they be?
7. (a) Can you draw a distinction between social degeneration and normal society? (b) Might a problem indicate pathological social conditions without also reflecting social abnormality?
8. (a) Distinguish between single and multiple causes of a social problem. (b) In how many different fields of causal conditions may multiple causes be distributed? (c) What is the bearing of this on classification of social problems?
9. (a) Are all social problems reducible to one? (b) What would be the difficulties in trying to treat one big social problem?
10. (a) Is there any difference between social conditions and social problems? (b) between disadjustments and maladjustments?
11. (a) What is the relation of society to social problems? (b) Would the relation between any given problem and society be the same as that of any other problem?
12. (a) Distinguish between social problems as intellectual and as practical problems. (b) Which does "pure" sociology mostly deal with, supposedly? (c) How close is the study of social problems to the center of sociology?
13. (a) Is "civilization" anything other than society at any given stage of development or a certain stage? (b) Is there a ratio between the

development of civilization and the appearance and number of social problems?

14. (a) Of what scientific and practical import is the study of social problems? (b) What is the probability of the success of "solutions" for social problems that have not yet been tried out in actual social experience? (c) Might a "solution" outlive its usefulness?

15. (a) Develop reasons for thinking society is a co-operative enterprise. (b) Discuss qualities without which co-operation would be impossible.

16. How do you account for the intense co-operation during war as compared with that during peace?

17. (a) Is conflict an inevitable social characteristic? (b) Give illustrations of conflict in neighborhood, church, family, nation, the Big Society.

18. (a) What is interdependence? (b) Is there interdependence between the parts of the solar system? (c) How does interdependence in society differ from that in the solar system?

19. Distinguish between interdependence of function and of condition in the family, village, nation, world.

20. (a) Is change as inherent in society as in matter and nature? (b) What evidences social change? (c) Could Washington now get about safely in a city, were he to return? (d) Is all change progressive? Why?

21. (a) What is meant by "ethical"? (b) Why must all human conduct have an ethical quality? (c) Is society made up of conduct, or are all social relations conduct relations?

22. In what ways do geographic conditions place limits on and condition human society?

23. (a) What is social continuity? (b) On what is it based and by what made possible? (c) Is it absolute or relative?

24. (a) What is human nature? (b) personality?

REFERENCES

BENNETT, J. W., and TUMIN, M. M., *Social life*, Part IV. New York: Alfred A. Knopf, 1949.

BOGARDUS, E. S., *Sociology*, Ch. 1, "Social Groups." New York: The Macmillan Company, 1934.

CHAPIN, F. S., *Cultural change*, Ch. 2, "The Accumulation of Culture." New York: Appleton-Century-Crofts, 1928.

COOLEY, C. H., *Social organization*, Ch. 1, "Primary Groups" and Ch. 6, "The Significance of Communication." New York: Charles Scribner's Sons, 1909.

DAVIS, BREDEMEIR, LEVY, *Modern American society*, Ch. 26. New York: Rinehart and Company, 1949.

DAVIS, KINGSLEY, *Human society*, Chs. 1, 3, 4, 6. New York: The Macmillan Company, 1949.

DAWSON, C. A., and GETTYS, W. E., *Introduction to sociology*, Ch. 10, "Social Interaction between Culture Areas." New York: Ronald Press, 1948.

GILLETTE, J. M., "Nature and limits of social phenomena," *Social Forces*, VIII (June, 1927): 561–571; and "Community concepts," *ibid.*, IV (June, 1926): 617–629.

HERMAN, A. P., *An approach to social problems*. Boston: Ginn and Company, 1949.

LAPIERE, R. T., *Sociology*, Chs. 1, 4, 7, 10, 12. New York: McGraw-Hill Book Company, 1946.

LEE, A. M. and ELIZABETH B., *Social problems in America*. New York: Henry Holt and Company, 1949.

LUNDBERG, GEORGE A., *Foundations of sociology*, Ch. 4, "Sociological Laws." New York: The Macmillan Company, 1939.

LUNDBERG, GEORGE A., "Societal pathology and sociometry," *Sociometry*, Feb., 1941: 78–97.

MACIVER, R. M., *Society, its structure and changes*, Ch. 18. New York: Rinehart and Company, 1947.

ODUM, H. W., *Man's quest for social guidance*, Ch. VII, "Social Change and Social Problems." New York: Henry Holt and Company, 1927.

ODUM, H. W., "Notes in the technicways in the contemporary society," *American Sociological Review*, June, 1937, 11: 336–346.

OGBURN, W. F., and NIMKOFF, M. F., *Sociology*, Ch. 26, "The Social Effects of Invention." Boston: Houghton Mifflin Company, 1946.

SUTHERLAND, R. L., and WOODWARD, J. L., *An introductory sociology*, Ch. 4, "Nations and Classes." Philadelphia: J. B. Lippincott Company, 1948.

YOUNG, KIMBALL, *Sociology*, Ch. 3, "The Nature of Culture." New York: American Book Company, 1949.

CHAPTER *2*

The Democratic State and the Public Interest

Democracy and Society

Root meaning of "democracy." There are almost as many meanings of *democracy* in common circulation as there are users of the word. Naturally some of these meanings are more legitimate and scientific than are others. The Greek roots from which the word is built are *demos*, "people" (masses *vs.* classes), and *kratos*, "rule" (government by the masses or common people). The Greek Herodotus (fifth century B.C.) said he understood *democracy* to mean the "multitude's rule." Thucydides (B.C. *c.* 471–400) wrote: "We are called a 'democracy,' for the administration is in the hands of the many and not of the few." Cicero, the Roman orator and writer (B.C. 106–43), wrote: "If, finally, all power is vested in the people, the state is democracy." Our American President Lincoln said that "government of the people, by the people, for the people" is the essence of democracy.

Principles of democracy. Light is thrown on the significance of *democracy* by a statement of its telic principles, or purposes. It involves: (1) the right of the masses of people to participate in the essential satisfactions of life which have been wrought out by past ages; and (2) their right to control the societal agencies by which these satisfactions are made available. By "essential satisfactions" are meant all the things necessary to an adequate standard of living in the given age. In ours, this would include: ample clothing, food, housing, medical care, educational opportunities, avocations, travel, leisure, etc. Further meaning is evident in the statement in the second proposition: the right of the people to control the societal agencies by which the satisfactions are made available. Without these ideas, democracy is as empty

33

of power as an automobile without gas or an army without fighting instruments.

Pure and complete democracy.   Pure or complete democracy would consist of an equal sharing of all things by all people. Perhaps it has never existed in any society. Probably even few American families could boast of such equalitarianism. It may well have been approximated on occasion in certain religious communistic sects.

Critics often say that such a conception of pure democracy is a most fanciful utopianism, that it is indeed chimeric. They contend that people are not all equal by nature in any physical or mental respect; which, of course, we concede. The physical anthropologist has the greatest difficulty in finding a sufficiently large number of persons closely alike in head structure, skin color, form and color of hair, conformation of face, nasal index and form of nose, or other physical characteristics so as to be able to build anything like a concept of a valid race. Comparisons of the mental qualities of individuals by whatever method reveal marked differences, even within a wide range of capacities accepted as normal. Moreover, it has not been shown that fitness for democracy is positively correlated with any of these differences.

Perhaps the best action democracy could take would be to check the formation of artificial and unfair barriers in the socio-economic system which would prevent individual capacities from developing to their maxima. This is all that equalization of opportunities would and could mean, nothing more. Thus, democratization of society would consist in the removal of obstacles built up in the social structure so that all might be able to utilize opportunities to the degree made possible by their inherent capacities. The large number of persons (but small proportion of the population) who are defective mentally, say below 70 IQ, might well be provided for altruistically, if we would preserve our democratic humanitarian outlook.

Examples of equalization of opportunity.   Society has been busy during the ages in gradually extending opportunities to the masses regarding many kinds of satisfactions. We note a few.

Education: For ages after writing began, the priestly class held a monopoly on education. But gradually that function was extended to a greater proportion of the population, and in recent times the more advanced nations have made schooling compulsory for those under a certain age. In some regions the further step has been taken toward setting up equalizing funds to provide schooling for the underprivileged and high-school training for rural farm youth.

Discussion: In many lands freedom of speech, of publishing new ideas, and of meeting together in groups is greatly restricted. The more dictatorial a nation, the stronger the taboo on these essentials of democracy. Tyranny cannot stand up under the bright glare of general information and criticism of public acts. Fascist and Communistic governments are good illustrations of this. During the German *Blitzkrieg,* Britain allowed large freedom of discussion and criticism of the governmental conduct of the war. Probably our greatest problem in this connection is to secure a press and radio that are wholly free from the restraints placed upon them by powerful pressure groups or by the government itself.

Political participation: From absolutism in government of the "divine right of king" theory to widespread political participation was a revolutionary stride. Step by step until recently the civilized nations extended the right of the masses to take part in conducting matters of state. In most advanced countries, the franchise has been given to practically all adults irrespective of sex and race. Furthermore, in the United States any native-born person of specified age may aspire to the highest office. Naturalized foreign-born persons may, if elected or appointed, hold any office in our national government except the Presidency. Of course, we must recognize that we have far to go to make our democratic declarations 100 per cent true. We still have racial and other prejudices to overcome. These deny political and other kinds of equality to persons of color. Yet we may legitimately hope for their ultimate conquest and control.

Medical care: Equal opportunities to keep or attain good health would be a tremendous blessing. We have done much to extend medical care to the poor, the underprivileged, the helpless in mind or body. Our low national mortality rate constitutes one kind of evidence of this. The numerous provisions for medical care in our cities and states are another index. But the great difference in death rates among states and races indicates that large numbers of our citizens are still poorly cared for. We stand in need of large applications of some sort of socialized or collectivized medical care, including attendance by physicians and accessibility of hospitals.

Freedom from slavery: Slavery has been prevalent in the long course of history. As soon as war on a considerable scale arose during social evolution, large masses of captives were conserved as a labor force by the conquerors. Many of the ancient nations had recourse to this practice. The slavery of the Roman Empire passed into the serfdom of the Middle Ages and feudal times, a kind of mediation between slavery and freedom. The rise of commercial cities and the factory system offered opportunity for "hired labor, and many serfs and villeins thereby escaped from their feudal lords." So "free labor" arose. Men became free to travel about for work and to enjoy the fruits of their labor. But vestiges of the slave system remained as a curse upon modern peoples, and it was not until the last century that Britain and the United States abolished slavery. But free labor, unlike slavery, does not insure work and a living. The vast bodies of the unemployed who must live below decent standards of living and must be assisted by governmental resources are a standing testimony to the need for a greater economic democracy that will afford them the opportunity to work and to live in reasonable comfort and security.

Religion: Democracy in religion would consist of freedom of belief; toleration of other religious or nonreligious beliefs; and control, by the masses of believers, of the ecclesiastical organization through which they secure their doctrines and opportunity to worship. But ecclesiastical organizations vary from almost pure democracy to absolutism regarding their control over the masses of church members. Within recent centuries persecution of persons for their "heresies" and intolerance of those of differing faiths have abounded. It is a black page of history. But the separation of state and church in this country, one of the greatest steps ever taken toward freedom, made it possible for all men to believe as their consciences dictated.

Our national democracy. In a very significant sense, the United States is one of the most democratic of nations. First, as to the social attitudes and atmosphere, as compared with older European nations, our country is free from hard-and-fast class distinctions and is distinguished by a pronounced atmosphere of equality of persons, so far as "whites" are concerned. In most European countries there is a somewhat rigid pyramidal arrangement of a considerable number of classes, each of which is expected to keep its place. Those above look down upon the lower classes as inferiors, and those below look up to those above as superiors. Here in the United States we have no kingly or nobility class and no "soil" or peasant class at the other extreme.

The various socio-economic classes mingle quite freely without much show of considering matters of class rating and levels.

Second, our governmental agencies are about as democratic in all ranges and levels—local, state, national—as we will find. It is representative government, as expansive areas make necessary; there is the widest participation in all governmental functions, privileges, and rights. Our greatest failure, here, is in the field of race prejudice. Of course there are serious industrial impediments to the working of our representative democracy. These are being recognized by a growing proportion of our citizens and are being discussed. Perhaps the youth of today will learn how to remove them.

Why this democracy? The reasons for our democratic society and state are fairly well known. We can think of three main sources of our democratic ideas and practices. First, the struggle of the original thirteen colonies to maintain self-government, as against the arbitrary rule of governors sent from Europe, gave the colonial legislators an experienced understanding of the problem and of the means and methods by which self-government was to be attained. Those were the men who drafted our Constitution. Second, some of the founders of our national government, such as Jefferson and Madison, were students of the liberal political philosophy which had been developed in France and England by such men as Rousseau and John Locke. The doctrines of inborn inalienable rights and equality were pronounced and appear in our Declaration of Independence and our Constitution. Third, an abundance of land to be had almost for the taking was a most influential factor. Men might go always to the West and become landowners. This opportunity accomplished three important things for democracy: (a) Attainment of property by everyone made everyone feel equal to everyone else. Here was the birth of the democratic atmosphere, largely a West Appalachian episode, for there was the seemingly limitless wilderness. (b) This led to the establishment of democratic state governments in the Middle and Far West, universal manhood suffrage, and the right to hold office. In turn, since there was a great movement of population from the Eastern Coast states to the West in search of "freedom," the older states were driven to liberalize their governments to help hold their people. Thus, the state governments of the older regions were liberalized. (c) Since many laborers in the East went to the West to settle on land, employers were forced to pay better wages to hold their workers. This migration, instead of high tariffs, was the largest factor in accounting for the high wages of industrial workers at that time.

Democracy a moral issue.   In seeking to justify democracy we are forced to resort to moral reasons. We have seen that it is a matter of recognizing equality of opportunity because of human considerations. We saw that it cannot be grounded on evidence from the physical and mental structure of man that all men are born equal or else acquire equality. Ideas of equality arise gradually in the course of a developing social order. Democratic aspirations do not emerge full-grown but increase slowly, as man's rational and ethical personality is heightened and widened. Human rights are society-made and accumulate with the ages. They are moral concerns. We develop a protective consciousness about our rights. After we come to enjoy them, we feel a lowering of dignity and worth, a deep sense of injustice if they are threatened or lost. Expanding democracy is the realization and recognition of the validity of men's aspirations toward self-direction and self-realization in a society of rights and duties. Democracy means, implicitly, the right of all normal persons to self-realization. The most pertinent and effective arguments in behalf of democracy are based on the justice of that claim and the injustice of its denial. Where might alone makes right, as under the natural selection of the jungle and, avowedly, in totalitarian states, the force of moral claims and arguments is unavailing or absolutely disclaimed and denied.

Democracy and the State

Forms of the state.   There have been and are today many forms of political control: tribal, city-state, feudal, national, republican, imperial, and dictatorial. The first was based on the idea of blood kinship. The city-state was necessarily small, being composed of the inhabitants of the nuclear city and the environs which the city was able to control. Feudal states were relatively small and chaotic, the ruling power being no stronger than the military might of the king or overlord, a freebooter among freebooters. Republics are comparatively recent, the Athenian and Roman being about the first. Imperial and dictatorial states are old. Witness the Greek oligarchies and the empires of Persia, Alexander, Rome, and the like in ancient times.

The state more than government.   The state comprehends a larger section of a total society than mere government. Government is central, important, and conspicuous. It legislates, it administers, it adjudicates. But behind and underneath government are the attitudes and beliefs of the citizens about government and the business of the state, customary law, and public opinion. In the long run the form the state takes, as denoted by the kind of governmental powers it exercises, is the result of the beliefs and aspirations of the people who constitute the citizenry. Other things being equal, a people that believes earnestly in democracy will struggle for and ultimately establish a democratic state. But a people who have a tradition for being dominated and arbitrarily ruled by autarch or oligarch will supinely submit to having their rights determined for them. Exceptions to this statement are small democratic nations and peoples who are engulfed and subordinated by overwhelming military force.

The state as most authoritative social institution. For one thing, the state is a social institution among other social institutions. Several of the fundamental and far-reaching institutions have a history that runs back even to preliterate days, such as the state religion, family, economic division of labor, judicial systems, and the like. Today they stand apart in our thought and function much more clearly than they did in their beginnings.

For a second thing, the state has come to be the most authoritative social institution. Not so long ago, it was religion which dominated men's lives as against everything else. A few centuries ago, the church claimed leadership over men's souls and over the state as a political instrumentality. Our form of government set a wholesome example to the world in separating state and church, freeing government by the state from religious restrictions, and setting religion free from state interference. Other nations have adopted the plan. In being set free, the state has become more and more authoritative over many fields of co-operative activity. Our examples of "equalization of opportunity" are largely illustrations of the results obtained by the extension of governmental control in important domains of society. We state it as a principle: *The state has come to be, and perforce must be, the controlling agency over every societal situation and condition which fundamentally affects and determines our common rights and interests.*

Authoritative state functions. A few statements will indicate, in principle, what these are to be. The old statement of governmental functions as "essential" and "nonessential" is not worth much, because the nonessential functions of one age have often come to be regarded as essential by a later age. The protection of persons and rights is bound to form a large portion of governmental functions. Rights of persons and of property are classed here. Regulation of infrasocietal matters opens up wide and numerous functions. Woodrow Wilson said:

"The hope of society lies in an infinite individual variety, in the freest possible play of individual forces: only in that can it find the wealth of resource which constitutes civilization. . . . It should be the end of government to assist in accomplishing the objects of society. There must be constant adjustment of governmental assistance to the needs of a changing social and industrial organization. . . . [This] is not interference: it is the equalization of conditions. . . . All combinations which necessarily create monopoly [natural monopolies], which necessarily put and keep indispensable means of industrial or social development in the hands of the few, and those few not the few selected by society itself but the few selected by arbitrary fortune, must be under the direct or indirect control of society."[1]

But there are things outside natural monopolies which require regulation. To quote Woodrow Wilson again:

"By forbidding child labor, by supervising the sanitary conditions of factories, by limiting the employment of women in occupations hurtful to their health, by instituting official tests of the purity or quality of goods sold, by limiting the hours of labor in certain trades, and so on multitudinously, government has assisted equity."[2]

Holding general or public welfare as the criterion, we may generalize thus: *It is the business of the state to undertake to do what other agencies will not or cannot do; and to undertake to do anything which it can do better than other agencies.* On the one hand are many functions like regulating foreign and interstate commerce, coining and regulating the value of money, maintaining police and court systems and armed forces, establishing national parks and highway systems. On the other hand are functions such as passing antitrust laws, maintaining public waterworks, establishing and maintaining bureaus of standards and measurements, public health agencies, national and state systems of public works and

[1] Woodrow Wilson, *The state* (Boston: D. C. Heath and Company, 1918), pp. 633–636.
[2] *Ibid.*, p. 636.

relief, setting up yardsticks for regulating public utilities such as the Tennessee Valley Authority, and soil and forest conservation.

Government: The Democratic State at the Crossroads

Inevitability of a changing state.   Why should anyone expect the state to remain static and unmodified when it is an intimate and vital part of a socio-cultural system that is swept by vast and frequent tidal perturbations? No other age has begun to approach ours in frequency of socio-economic disturbances, which in turn are largely outcomes of scientific discoveries and inventions of tremendous significance. Continental populations are sometimes thrown into bewildered migratory movements. Millions experience serious occupational dislocations. Unemployment results on a scale which stuns the imagination. A mighty diversification and a specialization in industry and other societal activities ensue. World struggles and transformations bombard society by shock after shock. The business world is profoundly disturbed and staggered, our foreign and domestic markets are undermined, our finances and our stock markets are disarranged, and our farming populations become restless and disadjusted. In the 1930's our government was besieged by bankers, industrialists, farmers, and the unemployed for relief. Later, we fought a colossal war and were called on to bear the major share of financing the world. To meet such situations, government must be as resilient as rubber, as resourceful as the mother of a big family on a small income, as pliable as a plastic figure, and as adjustable as a chameleon. If it endures at all, it is fortunate; and it is bound to change.

Impact of world events on our state.   Our relatively free system of government and our people have been subject to strains from several directions. A brief summary of these factors is enlightening.

World revolutionary movements: Since the beginning of this century national revolutions have grown in frequency and scope, especially across the Atlantic to our east. China has changed its ruling regime, the Russian government was overthrown in 1917 by Communists, a "loyalist" movement was defeated in Spain, India sought independence with final success, and the peoples to the east and south of that country are undergoing revolutionary movements. South America has had numerous revolutions, but they have not affected the world greatly. The Italian government was overthrown by Mussolini and his Fascists, and the German government by Hitler at the head of the Nazis. Italy and Germany set up forms of state which made their appeal to some of our citizens. Some of our "big business" officials admired autocracy so much that they longed for an American Mussolini or Hitler to "put labor in its place." Fascism and Nazism were scourges which shook the world and set governmental patterns which still live and have their influence.

War and war organization: The United States has fought two world wars in this century and has had to organize huge military forces for them. Recently we had over 13 million individuals under military call. There has been a vast pressure on civil government by the military. Military organization is necessarily autocratic organization. The incorporation of millions of young people into such an organization tends to replace democratic self-decision by passive willing. There is the temptation to set up great military leaders in political places. Taxes to maintain a world defense and potential offense become a burden. Gradually pressure is exercised for more and more autocracy in government. Our state cannot escape unscathed.

The fifth-column menace: Fifth columnists from or directed by Communist Russia exercise insidious influences throughout the world. They have overthrown the independence of several nations, are striving for dominance in Italy and France, and are manifest in this country. Our Declaration of Independence favors revolution against tyranny, but Jefferson would recoil from revolutions against our government by people under orders from foreign powers and probably would class these fifth columnists as spies and traitors. By crafty and incessant effort they gain control of organizations and commit them to Communism. They might even infiltrate into the national government and inflict creeping paralysis. The Communist state is a form of state with which our democratic state has to compete and by which it is influenced.

A threat to the democratic state arises from within. It is the indifference of the citizenry to political affairs which manifests itself at elections in minority voting. Including and since the election of 1928, less than half of the eligible voters turned out to vote at the elections except that of 1944. The same obtains for state and local elections. In some municipal elections important issues are decided by a small fraction of eligible voters. Whether or not minority voting is a general tendency would require critical investigation, but it does operate on an extensive scale.

Perhaps bad government makes for this indifference, and perhaps a reform in government would remove this indifference.

Readjusting the State to the Age

To discuss successfully the readjustment of the state to the age would require one or more large volumes. We can merely briefly and partially indicate the larger aspects of the problem.

Trend toward "peoplizing" government. This trend has been noticeable in national, state, and local government for a long time. We state our idea of democracy as the right of the masses to the essential satisfactions of life, and their right to control the means of distributing these satisfactions. Several amendments to the Federal Constitution have been made in this direction, such as giving suffrage to Negroes and to women, and the popular election of United States Senators. A further trend appears to be likely, namely, dispensing with the electoral college and electing the President by popular vote. In a number of our states and cities direct legislation and the recall have been put to use. In the same trend has been the liberalizing construction of the general-welfare clause of the Federal Constitution, both by Congressional enactment and by judicial interpretation. A large task of the future is to train all our citizens to realize the importance of guarding their rights and of making use of the means of control they now have.

Trend toward assuring masses economic security. Rather large advances in assuring economic security for the masses have been made by government and by private employers. Such security involves the state either explicitly or implicitly. Let us note a few facts.

Direct economic security is furthered by government in such measures as workmen's compensation, unemployment insurance, assistance to the aged, and pensions not only to veterans of wars but also to workmen at retiring age. The national government has put into effect the Security Act, and individual states have done much along various lines. And we may expect a further extension of the national security system. Health has economic features, and health security is being provided for by government in increasing amounts.

Welfare provisions for workers have been and are being provided by many employing firms. Some are granted voluntarily, and some under union pressure. Various great corporations now provide retirement pensions for employees, and the coal industry has set up a hundred-million-dollar-a-year welfare fund for its miners. In the immediate future, welfare plans are likely to be widespread in the larger industries.

Looking toward a balanced economy.   No state can be stable when its economy is unbalanced. Ours has been beset by cycles of depression and prosperity almost from its beginning. Both national and other levels of government have been put to the test by such great depressions as that of the 1930's. More and more governments are extending assistance to the unemployed and the poor, and governments went into the red for many billion dollars during the last great depression to do so. Now governments stand in dread of the recurrence of depressions. So do businessmen. All hope there will be none, and there are social devices to prevent it. A balanced economy would greatly relieve government, the state, and business. It would be a blessing to humanity, almost as great as that of the abolition of war. During war, the state controls the economy as a necessity, but after war has ceased it takes off most controls. Foresighted economists and statesmen believe we must stabilize production, so that labor will be continuous, and stabilize the value of money, so that prices will cease to shift up and down, creating uncertainty and ruin. The trend in that direction must be made more complete. One of the great sectors of our economy, farming, is being stabilized by a government guaranty of support-prices for farm products.

An economy of abundance in the offing.   Noted economists have long advocated an economy of abundance as the goal of democracy. Reputable publicists now assert that such an economy has arrived. They are close to the truth, in view of our total national wealth and income, but far in error when we regard the way in which these are distributed. We may have enough to go around, but it fails to get around democratically. Our national income is now said to be some 25 billion dollars a year. An equal division of this among our 38 million families would give each family an income of $5900 a year. It would be much less than that, however, because the cost of production has to be allowed for. The way the national income was distributed among the 33.3 million families of 1942 was far from equalitarian. Less than a tenth of them received $5000 or more yearly. Almost 8 million families, or nearly 21 in a hundred, were on incomes of less than $1000. If the minimum of the larger amount meant abundance, all families on the lower income level were in dire need. Seven tenths of the families were under the abundance level, and most of them had to practice rigid economy. A democratic realization of the division of wealth and income would go far to make the economy of abundance a reality.

A planned society. The results of competent study call for planning of national scope. Yet we scarcely know what to plan for, whether for a "normal" or "new" social order. Then, too, many natural events (floods, droughts, pests) and man-made happenings (great inventions, foreign wars, etc.) may sharply modify the operation of any plan.[3] But, after all, planning is still our most intelligent procedure, after we have ascertained the facts; and we must resort to it, always with a view to mending the weaknesses when they appear.

We must expect that national affairs and international conditions will demand the most efficient planning of which we are capable. Conditions now struggle against and with each other, as do the many climatic countercurrents and elements in producing our weather—pacific and stormy. We cannot hope to mend the weather, but we can hope to improve the co-ordination of living and business conditions so as to make them operate in a more rational and co-operatively helpful manner. Just what the exact and detailed plan will be can only be told after the investigators have done their work.

To carry into operation anything like the total national planning will, of course, involve much regimentation. A large portion of the selfish and highly irrational *laissez faire* of the present will be banned. Business will have to take directions and sometimes be put in a strait jacket. Labor and capital will be prevented from wasteful conflict; profits, prices, and wages will have to be co-ordinated. Farmers and miners may be told what and how much to produce. Much resentment, struggle, and resistance is to be anticipated. To many thoughtful people this seems to be the only way to save our collective lives and individual entities. To them the alternative appears to be the collapse of modern society through self-destruction. On the other hand, such over-all and drastic planning would not leave much of the former democracy.

Laissez faire. Anything like pure individualism has become practically impossible. Democracy must have individualism, the

[3] *Cf.* J. M. Gillette, "An examination of criteria for determining normal society," *American Sociological Review*, Aug., 1937: 501–507; and "Can we plan successfully for normal society?", *Sociology and Social Research*, Nov.–Dec., 1939: 103–110.

promotion of the good of individuals as its objective; but it is against individualism as expressed in *laissez-faire* libertinism in business and in conduct affecting others. The business of government is to free individuals from oppression and to protect them from injury and exploitation. Artificially organized repression and exploitation are things it must attack and prevent. The claim of "big businessmen" that *they* make prosperity and that government makes or continues depressions by interference with business is empty in the face of the prolonged and repeated efforts of business to appropriate government to its own ends. If business knows enough and has power enough to make prosperity, it must bear a large measure of responsibility for depressions. Seemingly unknown to themselves, businessmen are the puppets of the capitalistic economic system and helplessly participate in what the system brings about.

Conditioned democracy. So we see that our democracy is most likely to be hedged about and highly conditioned. But it has always been conditioned. There have been limits set to the distance we might go toward injuring others in the exercise of our freedom. More and more we have discovered that living in the Great Society calls for governmental control and limitations on us in running factories, mines, railways, dairies, waterworks, driving in cities and in the country, and in other matters. What we are now called on to face is an extension of those controls, not an entire change in the nature of government.

There is a real dilemma here. Yet many firmly believe that intelligent control does not necessarily entail the elimination of democracy. They hold that if we preserve the democratic outlook and attitude in our legislation and administration of laws, so that the rights and aspirations of the masses, the common men, are duly regarded and furthered, we will preserve the essence of democracy. We shall still be free to discuss issues, conduct campaigns, vote for our favored candidates for office, hold office, aspire to the highest offices, and generally participate in the conduct of local, state, and national affairs. We shall still be free to assemble for political and other purposes, to print and publish the important facts about public affairs, to broadcast what is fit and beneficial, and to listen to the broadcasts. We shall still rule in the Great Society from the bottom up and not be ruled from the top down, as is the case in autarchies. On the other hand, we must not overlook the probability that the rigid controls of the planned state and its economy will mean that public discussion and "free" elections will be largely empty gestures.

Our national democracy: irresponsive. Our national government is irresponsive to the wishes of the citizens in several ways. (1) The three separate and almost independent legislative, administrative, and judicial branches often do not promote but block effective government. Woodrow Wilson said that the only existing unifying agency is the political party in power, which supposedly unifies by officering all departments. (2) The four-year executive term allows the citizens, if they desire new policies, no way to gain them during its existence. (3) A divided political situation may exist, the executive being of one party and one or both houses of Congress being of the other. We need an amended Constitution to provide that both houses of Congress shall be of the same party for the given period. We need an amended Constitution to make the administration responsible to the popular will, something like the parliamentary system which obtains in Great Britain. There the government falls when there is a vote of lack of confidence, a new election is held, and the citizens then elect those who will carry out their will. (4) National legislation at the command of powerful and unscrupulous pressure groups has voided the power and rights of great masses of unorganized citizens. Multitudes are not truly represented but are misrepresented by their Senators and Representatives, a case of "taxation without representation."

Relation of national, state, and local governments. In our country the relation of local, state, and national governments is somewhat peculiar, and we have some political problems pertaining to their co-ordination and interfunctioning. The efficiency of our politico-social life is affected accordingly. Our national government is federal rather than unitary. The nation is sovereign in matters specified in the Constitution. Sovereign powers not so reserved are possessed by the various states and commonwealths. These states are not administrative units of the national government. This distribution of sovereignty is perplexing to foreigners and in some respects is a grave limitation on national activities. There has been a twofold tendency to democratize the national government by means of (1) amendments to the Constitution and (2) by an expansion of the operation of its sovereignty through amendments and interpretations by Federal courts of elastic provisions in the Constitution. The twenty-two amendments have expanded and guaranteed a long

list of personal rights, emancipated Negro slaves, recognized
political parties in the choice of Presidential electors, and provided for income taxes, the popular election of Senators, and
woman suffrage. Jurisdiction over various interstate affairs has
been assigned to the nation by court decisions.

Common and differential problems. The operation of local,
state, and national governments creates somewhat different functions, demands co-ordination of such functions so that there shall
not be overlapping and waste, and may conceivably require a
somewhat different point of view where all approach the same
problem. We have seen that the national government executes
tasks, for all, peculiar to it alone. The states also do some things
that the localities do not undertake, such as legislation for all,
superintending local government in some cases, maintaining a
militia, regulating marriage and divorce, and so on. To local
government fall multitudes of functions required by people
living in compact communities, such as providing police protection, pure water, and lighting systems; supporting schools;
maintaining sidewalks and streets; establishing sanitary agencies
such as drainage and sewers; inspecting milk and food, and the like.

However, it is likely that all levels of government may at
times have to face one and the same problem, such as questions
of education, health, poverty, and crime. The national government chiefly publishes information about schools and education,
statistics and results of special investigations, information which
will prove useful to the country at large. The states establish
school systems and determine what the function of each unit
and level of public education shall be. The localities carry out
state provisions, vote taxes to support local schools, and operate
such schools. Regarding poverty, the nation formerly did
little save gather and publish statistics about the number, care,
and support of the poor in institutions in the various states.
However, it is having to consider unemployment, sickness, old
age, and other factors which produce poverty, and it has legis-
lated on some of these matters. It appropriated billions of dollars
to insure employment to those made idle during the 1930's and
even to feed and clothe the nation's indigent. Sooner or later it
must face the problem of the distribution of wealth and income
and deal with it. The states carry on a large work for the poor,
the defective, and other dependent classes, chiefly by way of
legalizing provisions and supporting public institutions for them.
They also frequently do something for noninstitutionalized in-

dividuals, such as finding homes for neglected and dependent children and subsidizing the care of unmarried mothers. On the localities falls the direct burden of providing for the poor, the unemployed, and, chiefly as yet, the feeble-minded.

Law as an Agency of the State and Society

The modern state has a legal foundation, and it regulates many social affairs by law. It would be quite impossible to give a fair account of the state without considering law. By "law" we understand the collection of principles and rules which society has worked out to further co-ordination of its individuals and parts and their orderly adjustment to one another. These rules or laws may be unwritten and embodied in what is known as the "common law." Or they may be written and appear as constitutions and charters or as session laws, codes, and ordinances. Law is man-made or society-made. It is a part of culture, the accumulation of political thinking and acting during centuries.

The need for law. The fact that a social structure or function exists is not conclusive proof that it is needed or contributes to the social good, since social evils, such as prostitution and slavery, may appear as social institutions. But law is needed by society. It is one of the fundamentals of social order. Plato in his *Laws* laid down two propositions regarding the necessity for law.

First, individuals living in a complicated and intricate society are unable to recognize the principles of right and justice so as to make them effective for adjustment between themselves without embodiment in the form of conventionalized rules. We have thousands of personal and property adjustments to make in the course of our living together, some intricate and far-reaching in their effects, and we require guideboards and highway signs for our own and others' safety. Ways of acting and adjusting must be standardized to prevent confusion and destruction. There must be ordered ways of relating the sexes, holding property, assessing taxes, passing on the highways.

Second, laws are a support and stimulus to the morally weak to do right and deal justly. Without the restraining effect of laws, thievery might be more common than it is. Such practices as wife-beating and slavery might drop out of social practice as a consequence of the development of intelligence and finer sentiments without being legally forbidden, but formal statutory enactments serve to hasten their abolition. Law is a crutch. It does not cure social or moral lameness, but it helps many of the lame to walk. One may go wrong in spite of the law, but it is a restraining influence on a large proportion of persons who otherwise might misconduct themselves.

Functions of law.   Some of the things said concerning the need for law would be as pertinent if applied to functions. But beyond those, there are a number of social services legal rules perform.

First, law helps establish normal social relations and duties by defining them. For instance, traffic regulations define what drivers are to do in passing others on the highways, streets, and junctions and where and how they are to park. Traffic laws standardize social relations. Of the thousands of vehicles hourly passing Michigan Boulevard and Jackson Street, Chicago, all except a few ignorant of the rules and some lawbreakers proceed exactly alike. Law is both positive and negative, as it forbids certain actions and commands others. It establishes or helps establish a social order in which security and freedom of self-expression within legal limits are realized.

Second, it helps to stabilize society. It provides a given order of relationships. Functioning in an ordered way, as at the street crossing in Chicago, is social order. Social structures are so built. Law binds us as contemporaries into a social order. It also articulates us with the past by means of the continuity of law so that there is a continuity in the social order. It lays a foundation for the future and foreordains that the society of tomorrow will be much like that of today.

Third, human adjustments are facilitated by law, because modes of activities are defined and charted. We can make the busy traffic crossings more expeditiously, on the average, when the rules of the road are well defined. Thus, law lays the basis for utilizing human energy directly and efficiently with a minimum of waste.

Fourth, law lays the foundation for liberty by assisting to build an ordered society. It crystallizes the principles of order in constitutions and codes. Without order there would be neither security nor liberty. The great codes of the past—the Mosaic, that of Hammurabi, the Roman and Napoleonic codes—provided orderly societies which were the stepping stones to new departures. Social orders are changed by the amendments of codes, and liberty grows by such amendments.

Limitations and problems.   Limitations in law may constitute social problems, and beyond these are other problems related to law and its enforcement.

First, the tendency of law is to become inflexible. Democracies require elasticity, since they are a process of realization. Society of our type demands flexibility. New conditions call for new adjustments. Petrified constitutions and codes help produce disadjustments. The comparative inflexibility of law is largely due to two factors: (a) The influence of the legalist who regards law as final, as an end in itself, possessing merit in spite of what society thinks or needs. Law is an agency, a tool, not an end in itself, and it must be kept adjusted to new needs. (b) The iron hand of precedent in rendering judicial decisions. Precedent has a large and worthy place in society and court decisions, but constructive and scientific thinking and research must be guides to decisions relating to human welfare. We want to know what past jurists thought about the application of a law, but their decisions should not be binding, any more than what the first chemists thought about a given chemical element or its reaction should bind the scientific conclusions of today's chemists.

Second, there may be legislation by untrained and often ignorant legislators, or by politically minded individuals who resort to "log rolling" and value the "pork barrel" more highly than they do the public welfare. Consequently there are many immature and positively pernicious laws—legislation which is not needed and which is detrimental.

Third, there may be commercialization and "corporationization" of lawyers and, hence, of judges, since only lawyers become judges. Many lawyers have been retainers of big corporations and business interests for so long a time that they have contracted the corporation point of view, regard the interests of corporations above everything else, and throw their influence and decisions on their side as against public needs. Instances are known where supreme courts of states have had to be educated on certain issues to prevent their rendering reactionary decisions.

Fourth, there is a multiplicity of laws. The minds of society, legalists, and jurists are burdened by almost innumerable laws. According to estimates, there are over 2,400,000 in the United States, of which 400,000 are obsolete. Growth of population, differentiation of every phase of society, especially in the economic field, and refinement of ideas about life and its requirements help to account for the growth of law. Certainly no one mind can master or systematize the field of law, and many kinds of legal specialists may well spell social confusion. An increase in the number of laws appears inevitable, but two attitudes would be helpful: systematic restraint in passing laws, and codification of laws already passed, the latter serving as a systematizer for the various kinds of codes.

Political Parties

Political parties in the United States are vital parts of the democratic state and government. They were not thought of when the Constitution was adopted, and no organized parties appeared during Washington's administration.[4] The present method of choosing Presidential electors, adopted in 1804, reflects the rise of organized political parties in the first years of the nineteenth century.

Functions. In a political system in which people elect officers and help determine policies for the conduct of government, political parties serve useful purposes. First, they are agencies for selecting officials for governmental positions. They formulate issues and present them to the voters, those elected supposedly being representative of party convictions. When the issues are numerous, however, as in national elections, it is impossible to say what issues represent the mandates of the voters.

Second, under our system of government, political parties are means of unifying our rather separate and independent departments: legislative, executive, and judicial. A party may get these departments to pull together smoothly to realize some given policy.

Third, parties act as agents of interest groups. These groups determine the policies and platforms of the parties, the various planks being representative of different interests. These interests furnish candidates for office who will further their issues and points of emphasis.

Fourth, parties serve as educators of the voters on public issues. In so far as arguments of all sides are heard, considerable information is obtained and a judicial attitude is developed.

Fifth, parties organize and express public opinion and public will. They are instruments by which the public mind is made up and makes itself known on questions at issue.

The problem of political parties. Parties are a problem in so far as they fail to serve the public and seek to defeat the public will. Let us consider wherein parties may prove to be obstacles.

First, parties gradually become traditional. Voters continue

---

[4] *Cf.* O. G. Libby, "Political factions during Washington's administrations," *Quarterly Journal University North Dakota,* III: 293–318.

to vote the party ticket because it is the party, not because of its continued services. The "Grand Old Party" receives a loyalty and reverence because of the great things it once did. The majority of voters are party-blind and cling to their party with the same automatism as that with which they eat, drink, and dress. Party leaders cultivate this habit of the people and are able to manipulate parties because of that fact.

Second, political parties encourage the unscrupulous office-seeking politician. Such an individual is the real demagogue since he is willing to advocate any measure in order to get into office. Possessing a good front and a persuasive tongue, he is able to attract voters to their detriment.

Third, political parties foster control of parties by "big interests." "Big businesses" should have a voice in government proportionate to their importance. But, unfortunately, they frequently wield an influence far beyond their deserts. By contributing heavily to party funds, they obligate party managers to block regulatory legislation or to advance that which is highly favorable to them. Presidents have been known to have their hands tied by campaign-fund pledges made by party managers prior to the election.

Fourth, political parties promote multiplex and cumbersome platforms. National party platforms are extensive documents which are made up of many subjects containing numerous subdivisions. So many more issues are raised than are discussed during a campaign that it is impossible to determine which issues have been accepted and which rejected by the voters. The situation is one which confuses the masses of voters, perhaps sometimes designedly.

Fifth, political parties decoy voters by raising false issues. Parties which control the government during depressions and other times of embarrassment, or when grave perplexing problems exist which should receive consideration, designedly raise false issues in order to draw public attention away from the real situation. The grip of the interests, party self-preservation impulse, and party office-holders' fear of losing their positions are underlying causes of the ruse.

Obvious correctives. Certain correctives of these difficulties have been suggested. First, educate voters about issues and governmental problems. Second, simplify platforms and reduce them to a few clearly stated issues. Third, secure the nomination only of suitable men. Fourth, train the voters to regard parties as tools, to be prized as long as they are useful and to be discarded when they become inefficient, thus undermining false loyalty.

Governmental Readjustment

Human government is undergoing constant readjustment in the more advanced nations and occasionally in the less advanced. Governmental problems are being solved in some cases, and in others they are in process of solution. Very few certain and sure solutions are furnished by provisions. The method is largely one of trial-and-error, taking steps, proving them, modifying the plans, and trying again. Let us consider a few of the influences at work which prompt changes and readjustments.

Influence of technology on government. "Technology" means the application of scientific techniques and methods of procedure. The growth of technology in the last few decades has been enormous. Its influence on government has been indirect and direct, the latter occurring when technical methods are carried out in governmental administration. We may list the technological influences on government.

First, technology stabilizes governmental functions. Government must be assured and steady in order that the many technological operations in various departments of life may occur regularly and smoothly. When a nation is almost wholly agricultural, as ours was a century ago, the means of communication might be broken by war, Indian outbreaks, and the like without vitally affecting national affairs. Farmers were practically self-sufficient. Now, however, a break in railway, mail, telegraph, telephone, and airways produces havoc and loss. Internal war, strikes, and natural catastrophes paralyze intercommunication with resulting famine and suffering.

Second, technology differentiates governmental functions. Growing technology differentiates society and creates new goods, callings, and duties. Government is obliged to respond to consequent new calls for regulation and assistance. Building highways, developing parks, forestation, establishing air-mail lines, and working out standardized methods for industrial processes are a few of the multitudes of new duties government has recently taken over.

Third, this growth of technology and the assumption of new governmental duties necessarily increase the burdens of government. A greater proportion of the population is pressed into governmental service. Between one and two per cent of our national population are engaged in some governmental occupation. There is a resulting increase in the need for revenues and the pressure for more taxation.

Fourth, government itself is being transformed into a large-scale technical business. Note the technical implications of these: providing public health service; testing water, foods, and drugs; studying the chemistry of soils; improving stock and animal breeding; standardizing tests for steel, oil, and many other products; testing road materials and inventing improved materials and methods of road building; collecting, tabulating, and studying statistics; making physical and cultural anthropological investigations; reckoning tides for thousands of places; gathering weather data, reporting them, and developing the science of weather prediction; running a postal business employing a quarter of a million persons; prosecuting cases and judging the law. Good and efficient government increasingly requires training in science, invention, business, and the professions.

Solution of governmental problems. The solution of problems of government is no more difficult than the solution of economic and social problems in general. The former is conditioned by the latter. When we have solved the problems of poverty, crime, feeble-mindedness, and the like, we can easily secure good and competent government. If business is dishonest, we will have people bribed in government. If business keeps breaking down at times, as it now does, we may expect government to flounder, get into debt, and prove inadequate for emergencies. Lincoln Steffens, an eminent reform journalist, believed that we will continue to have corruption in government so long as we allow the causes of corruption, namely, private ownership and operation of public utilities. Some well-known economists believe that an equalization of wealth would solve the economic, crime, and poverty problems, and that with these removed government would prove adequate. Other students of affairs believe a government by commissions of experts and technologists would bring good government, since government is so largely technological. It is rather apparent that government would be greatly improved if governmental processes were largely committed to such commissions, provided a working device were secured through which such commissions were (a) kept in close touch with public opinion and (b) freed from the obfuscating influences of special interests on political appointees.

Thus we conclude that the reform of government awaits the

reform of many other conditions. It is not likely to be realized far ahead of the setting-up of a better economic and social world generally. We must expect to go on trying to improve government as we try to improve other conditions. Society develops all together, all parts and institutions moving upward together, interacting, sometimes one lagging a bit, then another, but all gradually emerging as co-partners in a great enterprise. We have grounds for being hopeful of gradual improvement in government, as in other affairs, because we recognize that there has been improvement in the past. What we have attained is the result of thousands of years of occasional gains and frequent setbacks, and future history may follow the same plan.

To the statement that reform is impossible because human nature is always the same, we reply that human nature is a composite and that it has both developed and changed. Human nature is the resultant of natural capacities developed and molded by society and culture. The human nature of a civilized man is something bigger and finer than that of his savage ancestor. He has developed ideas, sentiments, and refinements which his savage ancestor could neither conceive nor appreciate. He inhibits and directs his inborn impulses and drives according to the patterns of his age and social demands. His patterns of action have changed from age to age, and his nature and personality have been transformed accordingly. He has taken on scores of inhibitions and restraints and is likely to accumulate others according to the changes in the situation. Human nature has been made and will continue to be made. Reforms in the state and elsewhere are possible because human nature is plastic and because society and culture change and evolve.

QUESTIONS

1. Is there evidence that the concept *democracy* originated with the ancient Greeks?
2. What two essential principles of democracy are there?
3. If put into execution, would those principles realize "pure democracy"?
4. Is there anything in the hereditary nature of man to make the realization of complete democracy difficult or impossible relative to "normal" men?
5. Since the rise of civic society, what have been some of the significant trends toward realizing greater equalitarianism?
6. What would constitute real democracy regarding (a) education, (b) medical care, (c) religion?

7. Is there justification for thinking the United States has realized a larger degree of equality than other nation-states?

8. (a) Have the frontier and abundance of land been influential in working out a democratic spirit in this country? (b) What prevented other nations and peoples who have gone through pioneering stages and possessed abounding natural resources from developing the same level of democracy?

9. Why is the basic argument in behalf of democracy bound to develop along moral lines?

10. What evolution has taken place in the forms of the state?

11. What features are there in the state which are not primarily those of government?

12. Why is the state obliged to be the most authoritative social institution?

13. How did Woodrow Wilson characterize the authoritativeness of the state?

14. What are some of the inevitabilities that the democratic state must undergo transformation?

15. How would the rise of totalitarian states be likely to influence our own nation-state?

16. Are we justified in speaking of our socio-economic system as "democratic capitalism"?

17. (a) With what dilemma has our "democratic capitalism" been faced? (b) Does the "defense program" promise to abolish it?

18. How has the development of an "economy of abundance" complicated the economic system?

19. (a) If you were a responsible national statesman, would you advocate governmental expert planning? (b) "total national planning"?

20. Is there indication that *laissez-faire* government is outmoded?

21. If our democracy must be conditioned, must the conditioning lie along the line of greater regimentation?

22. Is greater regimentation in government consistent with maintenance of freedom of speech, of assembly, of press, and of worship?

23. What is law? What is its relation to society and government?

24. (a) Why do the masses of people need laws? (b) Illustrate the need for law by the most intelligent and well-meaning persons.

25. Illustrate how law promotes the following social requisites: (a) human liberty; (b) social order; (c) social adjustments; (d) social continuity and structure.

26. What factors account for the inflexibility which law often shows?

27. What results for government arise from (a) multiplicity of laws; (b) untrained and ignorant lawmakers?

28. (a) What is a political party? (b) How early under our Constitution did parties begin?

29. What needed functions do political parties perform for our nation?

30. (a) What indicates that parties are interest groups? (b) What of the proposal to place representation on an interest rather than a territorial basis?

REFERENCES

ALLEN, ROBERT S., *Our sovereign state.* New York: Vanguard Press, 1949.

BARR, P., "Is labor learning democracy?", *Christian Century,* LIV: 261–263, Oct. 13, 1937.

BEARD, C. A. and MARY, *Rise of American civilization,* Ch. 27, "Towards Social Democracy." New York: The Macmillan Company, 1927.

BEARD, C. A. and W., *American leviathan: The republic in the machine age,* Ch. 1, "Government in a Technological Society." New York: The Macmillan Company, 1930.

BECKER, C., "Dilemma of modern democracy," *Virginia Quarterly Review,* Jan., 1940: 11–27.

BENEŠ, E., *Democracy today and tomorrow.* New York: The Macmillan Company, 1939.

BRYSON, LYMAN, *Which way America? Communism, fascism, democracy, socialism.* New York: The Macmillan Company, 1940.

CATTELL, J. M., "Science and democracy," *Scientific Monthly,* XLVI: 80–88, Jan., 1938.

CHASE, STUART, *Idle money, idle men.* New York: Harcourt, Brace and Company, 1940.

COHEN, J., and TRAVERS, R. M. W., *Educating for democracy.* New York: The Macmillan Company, 1939.

HEIMANN, EDUARD, *Communism, fascism, or democracy?* New York: W. W. Norton and Company, 1938.

HUDSON, J. W., *Why democracy?* New York: Appleton-Century-Crofts, 1936.

ICKES, H. L., "Crisis of democracy," *N.E.A. Journal,* 28: 33–34, Feb., 1934.

KERN, J. D., and GRIGGS, IRWIN, *This America,* Parts II, III. New York: The Macmillan Company, 1942.

LEDERER, EMIL, *State of the masses.* New York: W. W. Norton and Company, 1940.

LEIGHTON, J. A., *Social philosophies in conflict.* New York: Appleton-Century-Crofts, 1938.

MERRIAM, C. E., "Assumptions of democracy," *Political Science Quarterly,* 53: 528–549, Sept., 1938.

MERRIAM, C. E., *New democracy and the new despotism.* New York: McGraw-Hill Book Company, 1939.

MERRIAM, C. E., and GOSNELL, H. F., *American party system.* New York: The Macmillan Company, 1940.

MOSCA, G., *Ruling class.* New York: McGraw-Hill Book Company, 1939.

MOUSLEY, E. O., *Men or leviathan?* New York: W. W. Norton and Company, 1939.

MUIRHEAD, J. H., *Man versus the state as a present issue.* London: George Allen and Unwin, 1939.

MUMFORD, LEWIS, *Faith for living.* New York: Harcourt, Brace and Company, 1940.

NOYES, C. E., "Economics of freedom," *The Nation*, Dec. 7, 1940: 555–558.

NOYES, C. E., "Nazi challenge to democracy," *The Nation*, Sept. 14, 1940: 207–210.

VAN DRESSER, P., "New tools for democracy," *Harper's Magazine*, 178: 397–403, March, 1939.

VON HAYEK, F., "Freedom and the economic system," *Contemporary Review*, 153: 434–442, April, 1938.

WALLACE, H. A., "Racial theories and the genetic basis for democracy," *Science*, 89: 140–143, Feb. 17, 1939.

WILSON, WOODROW, *The State.* Boston: D. C. Heath and Company, 1918.

CHAPTER 3

Resource Utilization and the Social Interest

Balance and Imbalance in Human Social Adjustment[1]

The human struggle for adequacy. Wherever life is found, there also is an environment. All forms of life enter into instrumental relationships of sustenance, end-seeking, and survival with their environment. A century ago Charles Darwin was insisting that in the struggle for existence the price of survival is adaptability, adjustability, and plasticity. Those forms of life capable of rapid adjustment have had, in organic evolution, better chances of surviving. Mobility, intelligence, a developed nervous system—these have been the attributes of superiority.

In these characteristics the uniqueness of the human animal has become a commonplace observation. No species has mastered more drastically changing or varied forms of environmental necessity than has man, and no animal is more widely distributed across the earth than is he. His inherent behavior (intelligence, among other things) and his acquired behavior (culture) have enormously enhanced the chance of his survival although they have not assured them. The demands of man's physiographic environment ("the natural landscape") have been countered ("balanced") with the possibilities of a man-made environment ("the cultural landscape").

The primary human search seems to have been for the establishment of an equilibrium with the environment of a given time and place. In part, such an adjustment has been achieved by man, as by other animals, through biological methods, such as excessive fertility, migration, and conquest. In part, balance has come through "technology": the creation of cultural equipment

[1] Adapted by permission of the editor from an article with this title by Paul Meadows appearing in *Social Forces*, 22 (May, 1944): 415–419.

and behavior patterns which have mediated man's relationships with natural conditions in glaringly different parts of the world. The history of human society is, thus, a record of this changing balance.

The persisting human problem has been one of order. Human behavior, like that of all forms of life, is a continuing adjustment process. The demands of the inorganic and organic environments call for techniques of adjustment. These adjustment techniques—tools, equipment, medicines, foods, groups, ideas, philosophies, sciences—are learned and transmitted.[2] They pattern the behavior of man in nature as well as in society. Collectively, they constitute the culture of man. They make society possible. Human society, thus, is an interlocking and intricate system of learned or cultural behavior patterns which have grown out of man's attempt to organize his life adjustments to his physical and social worlds. His adjustment processes and patterns are his human resources in an unfriendly environment. The utilization of such resources yields adequacy or balance. Their inhibition and frustration bring inadequacy or imbalance.

By environment is meant, in the present context, all physical factors and conditions which are external to man, which impinge upon him and condition his behavior, and which register effects on his society. It includes plants, animals, the geographic factors of soil, topography, and climate, the earth, our solar system and galaxy, and all the other cosmic forces which operate throughout the universe. We may call this complex of conditions *nature*.

Relation of man to physical environment. There are outstanding theories regarding the way man is related to nature.[3] It is possible for us to consider only two of the most opposed theories.

First, there is the position that nature is the absolute master of man in the sense that it is the determining factor in his behavior. Man's courses of action as well as those of the society he builds are exclusively and completely decided by the geographic conditions. So whenever man acts individually or collectively, the activities are called out by nature and immediately adjusted directly to it. It is conceded that man may think he is master of

[2] The theme outlined here is developed more fully in L. L. Bernard, *An introduction to sociology* (New York: T. Y. Crowell Company, 1942), Ch. 29; also Bernard, "A classification of environment," *American Journal of Sociology*, 31 (1925–1926): 322 ff.

[3] *Cf.* A. J. Todd, *Theories of social progress* (New York: Henry Holt and Company, 1918), Ch. 9.

his destiny, but this is only one of his many delusions. It is held that nature always dominates him and that he follows its dictates in all particulars.

In a certain large way this position is true. Man certainly is bound into and articulated with the great system of nature much as the wheel, the gear, and the shaft are articulated into the machine. Man is placed upon the earth, the earth in the solar system, that system in our galaxy, and that galaxy in the system of celestial galaxies, and so on *ad infinitum*. There is nothing man can do about this. When, however, we come to view the situation near by, that is, man's connection with things right around him in nature, there is ground for questioning this absolute theory.

Second, opposed to this, not as an extreme theory but as a scientific rational conception, is the idea that civilized man has a conditioned relation to nature. We shall treat this idea at some length later. In this connection it is sufficient to say that by the use of his culture and social organization man is able to modify and control some of the more direct thrusts of nature. In this way he mitigates and mollifies experiences that otherwise would be very bitter and menacing.

Objective of nature's influences.   There are two objectives of nature's influence on man. First, men as individuals, living apart from one another as mere units, would receive all the thrusts of nature merely as individuals. In certain cases we think this obtains now, and we shall consider shortly some of these influences.

Second, society, or men in organization and mass movements, may receive and mediate the thrusts of nature. Individuals may move when nature speaks, but they are moved because nature speaks through the collectivity. Or, on the contrary, they may not move at all as individuals because the social group forbids their movement. The concept is expanded and illustrated later.

Individuals as objectives of nature.   There are many illustrations of the way the influences of nature seem to terminate in the individual.[4]

1. The effect of altitude is registered immediately in the individual. It is not altitude itself, of course, but the conditions which accompany it. The rarity of the atmosphere is the affecting factor. The supply of oxygen becomes less and less with elevation above sea level. An ample supply of oxygen is essential to life.

---

[4] For a fuller discussion of these points, *cf*. Ellsworth Huntington, Part I: "Society and its physical environment," in Jerome Davis, and H. E. Barnes, eds., *Introduction to sociology* (Boston: D. C. Heath & Company, 1931).

2. Extremes of temperature affect human beings directly unless they are protected artificially. A person could not live in Canada or in northern United States the year around without clothing or houses because he would freeze or chill to death. At the opposite extreme, it is found that a torrid climate is debilitating and that it is difficult for persons from temperate zones to become acclimated and perform work successfully. The excessive heat seldom kills people, but it does slow them down.

3. Moisture affects individuals directly, although differently. Some seem to require air with a large amount of moisture in it, while others require dry air. A dry desert air would greatly discommode some, and an ocean atmosphere would enervate others.

4. Air currents of considerable velocity may make life disagreeable for unprotected persons, by impeding their movements or by projecting dust and other objects into their eyes. Winds of great velocity, as seen in tornadoes and hurricanes, are often destructive of life.

Zones of efficiency. Ellsworth Huntington believes he has demonstrated that zones of climatic efficiency are distributed over the face of the earth.[5] Thus, the larger portions of the United States, southern Canada, northwestern and western Europe, and Great Britain are regions of highest efficiency and mental achievement. The proof is so complicated and there are so many uncertain factors that the results are not certain. Further, it appears that the zones are largely those of cultures. Those of today are different from those in the time of Babylonia, Egypt, Greece, and Rome. Centers and areas of civilization shift from age to age. A high efficiency area in one age may be a low one in another. Thus, in successive eras Egypt and Greece, Greece and Rome, and Rome and northwest Europe and Great Britain represented high and low efficiency zones.

Society as the objective of nature. Originally, the sole environment of man was external nature, but modern civilized men live in a double environment—a physical one and a social one. It is the latter that has been built in around man, and between him and nature. Many of his behavior reactions are directed toward and upon the social environment, which receives and mediates many of the influences exerted by nature. Let us note some of the ways in which nature influences collective man.[6]

[5] Cf. Ellsworth Huntington, *Civilization and climate* (New Haven: Yale University Press, 1924).

[6] Cf. A. Goldenweiser, *Anthropology* (New York: Appleton-Century-Crofts, 1937),

1. Mass movements of population follow nature's topography. Those who are acquainted with the old trails of the American Indians know that they followed natural features. Thus, in the swamp regions of northern Minnesota the trails were sinuous, threading ridges between lakes and swamps. We know that some of the routes used by prehistoric men of Europe coincided with those of more recent men. The great river ways, the mountain passes and valleys, and lowlands along the shores of the sea have always been the highways used by migrating peoples. In the United States and Canada, the population movements westward, in settling the continent, likewise have utilized and been directed by mountain gaps, rivers, valleys, lakes, and lake shores in their spread over the land. The location of routes of canals and railways also have followed the easy paths of nature.

2. Topography helps determine where people will live. In settling a new territory, migrants spread over the land in obedience to topography, provided its different areas are equally fertile. Level and slightly undulating surfaces are attractive because they are easily tilled and traversed. Mountains and hills are avoided until crowding population or attractive natural resources create a demand or necessity. Of course, armies march and conduct campaigns where topography favors, and the latter may determine the success of military operations.

3. Topography, along with fertility and climate, determines density of population. The great densities are not on mountainsides and plateaus but in level, fertile valleys and plains and at junctures of land and sea or rivers, where commerce is easy. The valleys of the Nile, Indus, Tigris, and Euphrates, the Yangstze, the Danube, Rhine, Rhone, and Thames, the Hudson, Mississippi, and others have been and are the populous areas of the world. Part of this is due to topography and much to climate, fertility, and location features. We are likely to underrate location as a determinant of population density. The difference, however, between the population density of inland states, like Kansas and North Dakota, and that of shore-line states, such as Rhode Island and Ohio, is largely the result of location. The inland states are not immediately accessible to international highways of trade.

4. Mass population movement is mindful of climate. Climate

Ch. 5; W. D. Wallis, *Introduction to sociology* (New York: Alfred A. Knopf, 1927), Ch. 9; C. Wissler, *Man and culture* (New York: T. Y. Crowell Company, 1923), Ch. 15.

is a great complex of temperature, humidity, precipitation, wind, and seasonal factors. Migrating peoples generally head for regions of mild and congenial climates, and such areas are first settled. Civilization arose in mild climates and has moved toward more rigorous climatic areas as necessity dictated and as man's inventions helped him to circumvent nature. The settlement of the United States has followed largely, though not exclusively, the same trend. The desirable climatic features of southern California have been the chief factor in causing it to be more populous than the northern sections of the state. California and Florida are the climatic Meccas of our citizens.

5. Climatic conditions also regulate and determine the pursuits and life activities of man. Climate is decisive regarding crops; they can be grown only where climate permits or encourages them. Particular kinds of crops require certain kinds of climatic conditions. This is seen and illustrated in the different crop areas of our own nation, such as cotton, tobacco, corn, small-grain, and citrus-fruit areas. To a much lesser degree climatic conditions affect the production of farm animals. It is likewise true that certain kinds of manufacture are favored by special climatic combinations.

6. The recreational life of peoples responds to climatic features. Northern populations, because of long, severe winters and an abundance of snow, indulge in sleighing, skiing, skating, curling, and tobogganing; these sports are impossible to the people of southern states. On the other hand, the latter revel in an outdoor life with its games, sports, and social activities that are quite impossible to the former during a large part of the year. What the Eskimo does for fun would not be attractive or possible to the Floridian, and what the latter does would not be understood or sought after by the former.

How Man Influences and Adjusts Himself to Nature

Methods of adjustment. Nature has been buffeting, cajoling, heaping insults on, and putting problems to man ever since he appeared. During most of this time man has been at a decided disadvantage in the contest. For most of his existence he has been as the subhuman animals—dumb, driven, and helpless. Had it not been for his superior brain endowment, along with his erect posture and free hands, he would have remained chained by nature. Because of superior endowments, however, he at last built up achievements and a social organization which have partially emancipated him. By means of cultural surplus and social organization he is able to do three useful things: (1) Protect himself in many ways against the thrusts of nature. (2) Adjust himself to nature more advantageously. (3) Manipulate and "control" nature within limits in many useful directions. We confess that this control is limited and partial. Nevertheless it is a momentous accomplishment.

Man's adjustability and cultural control. Man is like other animals in requiring food, warmth, and protection from deadly animals, storms, and cataclysms of nature, all of which are physical environmental factors. These are ultimates without which man could not exist, and so far man draws on nature relative to them. Man is unlike other animals, on the contrary, in at least two respects. First, he has a much greater ability to adapt himself to the varying conditions of nature. He can live in practically every kind of region and under every known climatic condition. Animals are creatures of restricted habitats. The dog is probably the only animal that can accompany man almost everywhere. Second, man possesses a greater power over nature than do animals. Some of the latter can build dwellings, dam water, manufacture food, weave, rear food plants, and domesticate animals; but their efforts are comparatively limited. In general, their power over the environment is feeble. Lester F. Ward, a great sociologist, formulated the difference between man and animals in this way: *Man transforms the environment; animals are transformed by the environment.*[7]

Culture conditions nature. The culture historian and the enlightened geographer recognize that the effects of nature on society and man are not fixed and absolute, but change from age to age.[8] In this connection two points should be discussed.

First, the effect which geographical conditions will have depends on the level of culture and of social organization that man has attained. The influences of nature become less and less immediate and more and more mediate or indirect. Prolonged zero temperature would have utterly destroyed nude and unprotected early man, but our great surplus of achievements makes it possible for us to dwell within the Arctic Circle. Formerly peoples had "natural barriers" which separated and protected them from other peoples. Today, however, great nations have nothing like

[7] *Cf.* L. F. Ward, *Psychic factors of civilization* (Boston: Ginn and Company, 1893, 1903).

[8] On this phenomenon of variability, *cf.* Kimball Young, *Sociology: A study of society and culture*, 2nd edition (New York: American Book Company, 1949), Ch. 4.

absolute geographical boundaries, because our communicating and transporting agencies surmount and transcend all barriers. There are no boundaries to the British Commonwealth of Nations as a political entity.

Second, culture is the active factor and nature the passive factor in inducing new ideas, mechanical and industrial inventions, discoveries, modes of behavior, and ways of social response. Nature never made an idea and never will make one. Only men's brains, capitalized by accumulated experience and stimulated by nature or by existing achievements, create ideas. Our American Indians faced and saw the same environment that white men confronted, but they did not get the same ideas from it, if they got any at all. They looked at forests, coal deposits, rich alluvial land, but did not "see" lumber, utilization of coal for heat and motor power, and farms. White men saw those things because the level of culture of nations from which they came suggested use in those directions. Man puts meaning into nature as he develops civilization, and men of lower cultural and social development are unable to decipher those messages. Nature today is pretty much what we make it.

The cultural perspective. A further illustration of the development of a cultural surplus gives a perspective of different developmental levels and of the time element.[9] This is the perspective of the growth of culture in Western society. Most of our forebears were savages. If man has lived a million years, during some 985,000 years of that time he was a savage with few and crude cultural tools. During another five or ten thousand years he was a barbarian with a larger surplus but feebly developed and crude. Civilization, as a high stage of development, has been a very recent comer, being only a few thousand years old. The content of culture has expanded enormously during the very recent part of the civilized stage. In fact, the great expansion has come in the scientific and industrial fields during the last century and a half.

Aspects of Particular Problems of Adjustment

Production of material goods as objective. Self-preservation is the first law of nature. A considerable part of organic efforts to

[9] *Cf.* F. S. Chapin, *Cultural change* (New York: Appleton-Century-Crofts, 1928); V. G. Childe, *Man makes himself* (London: Watt and Company, 1936); M. Fairchild, and H. Hart, "A million years of evolution in tools," *Scientific Monthly*, 28 (Jan., 1929): 71–79; F. Cooper-Cole, *The long road: From savagery to civilization* (Baltimore: Williams and Wilkins, 1933).

live is devoted to securing food, and after that clothing and housing. Efforts devoted to the latter are particularly the functions of human beings, especially in the more advanced levels of development. The efforts of human beings to obtain material goods are at first the rather random and unsystematic actions of individuals. Later on, some sort of co-operative activities of persons in hunting and fishing develop. These efforts are followed by a more systematic pursuit of material goods, by agriculture, mining, lumbering, and the use of various forms of motor power. Today there are over two billion living human beings. In order to support these, and to enable them to adjust themselves to nature, especially those dwelling in the more developed nations, we require the labor of millions of workers who are engaged in the extractive industries. The extractive industries are the first steps in the productive adjustments.

Waste and efficiency. It has required ages to develop human beings and society up to a stage of efficiency in making the necessary productive adjustments. In many respects, the level of efficiency which is desirable has not yet been attained in most of our productive undertakings. Were our natural resources unlimited, we would not have to consider either efficiency or waste, except perhaps to satisfy our esthetic tastes and pride in workmanship. But because of past waste, narrowed resources, and expanding world population, we are faced with the need for conservation and avoidance of waste of nature's goods. On the average, over long periods of time, our adjustment problem is to avoid waste and to become efficient up to the nth power.

The idea of waste is a relative one.[10] What we regard as waste is not waste among savages, because they have not developed standards of efficiency in use. Our pioneers, in clearing land of forests and in making farms, destroyed billions of feet of timber which now would be almost invaluable; but then the action was necessary and useful. The rich "live riotously" and "waste lavishly" what seems to the poor and to the unemployed to be fabulous wealth. Such action, too, is a form of social waste, as is the destruction of natural resources which violates our technological standards and the democratic needs of society.

[10] On the concept of "waste" *cf.* Stuart Chase, *Tragedy of waste* (New York: The Macmillan Company, 1925); H. Hoover, ed., *Waste in industry* (New York: McGraw-Hill Book Company, 1920); W. N. Palekov, "Waste: Report of committee of eliminating waste in industry," *New Republic*, 27 (July 6, 1921): 159–161; W. C. and H. S. Porritt, *Water—wealth or waste?* (New York: Harcourt, Brace and Company, 1939); G. T. Renner, *Conservation of national resources* (New York: John Wiley, 1942), Ch. 1.

Let us consider a few examples of waste, chiefly in the productive field, remembering that waste will be illustrated more fully in later connections: A man hunting for a job which society should find for him, or doing in two hours what he could easily do in one. Production of nonessentials—baubles. Charging the consumers prices which are many times the cost of production. Duplicating one another's work, as in stores of the same kind and by delivery cars with identical goods covering the same streets, thus multiplying costs to consumers. Billing goods by the long route rather than by the short one. Shipping materials to distant points and receiving the same kind of materials from those points for local consumption. Using up more of any natural resource, such as timber, coal, iron, or soil, than is required to produce such goods when measured by the technical developmental level of the age. Killing birds which are useful in destroying crop pests and are nondestructive of crops. Shooting game birds or animals ruthlessly or beyond limits.

Variability in problems of adjustment.   These problems of adjustment to nature vary from age to age and from time to time, due to developing and changing needs and standards of society.[11] The problem of food production of hunting tribes was far different from that of settled agriculturists and required distinguishing undertakings and technical devices. It is evident, likewise, that the objectives and modes of realization in the horse-power and steam-power ages, and in the stone and steel ages, were widely differentiated. Our present American farmers who produce for world markets and make use of a highly mechanized mode of production are compelled to develop a system of concepts and establish systems of adjustment to the land that are almost diametrically opposed to those of the farmers of 1800. Again, we see demands for changing procedure within shorter spaces of time. Farmers, miners, and lumbermen alike have had to make new adjustments to nature, as the result of the incidence of wars and the development of the business cycle.

We notice also that the adjustment problem varies from nation to nation or people to people. Thus, Great Britain views its relations to the land, to agriculture, far differently from the way we have viewed it. Because of a proportionately greater industrial development and smaller agricultural domain, its chief effort

11 *Cf.* G. I. J. Dixon, "Land and human migrations," *American Journal of Economics and Sociology*, 9 (Jan., 1950): 223–234; W. Vogt, *Road to survival* (New York: Wm. Sloane Associates, 1948); A. G. Keller, *Societal evolution* (New York: The Macmillan Company, 1931).

has been spent on manufacture and foreign trade, while, until recently, our main work has been agriculture, with manufacture and the export of manufactured goods in second place. Or, were we to compare our nation to China or to India relative to agriculture, mining, and lumbering, we would discover differing modes of adjustment.

Wasteful Utilization of Resources

Soil destruction.   Wasteful use of soil is of two kinds: absolute and relative.[12] Erosion represents the first kind, the soil being absolutely destroyed by being transported elsewhere. This may be accomplished by wind or water, the latter being the more destructive agent, although in many sandy regions heavy winds displace much soil and often uproot crops. The areas of greatest erosion by water are on mountainsides and hillsides. Formerly, mountainsides were usually covered with forests and thus were protected by roots, moss, shrubs, and grass from the rush of water after rains or in the case of melting snow. The removal of this ground cover has been one of the sins of "civilization." Fields on hillsides likewise erode badly. The preventives of erosion are: (1) reforestating mountains, (2) seeding steep hillsides to grass and extending drainage ditches laterally to check a downhill rush of water, and (3) promoting grass sod on sandy lands.

Relative soil waste takes place by means of soil depletion. This occurs when the same crop is grown on the same field year after year, thus exhausting the particular soil properties required by the given crop. Soil depletion is likely to occur in new regions where extensive farming is practiced, such as the spring-wheat areas; but it may and does occur in the small-field areas of the South where the cropper system abounds. Under the one-crop system, the yield is greatly reduced, often as much as 50 per cent or more. It is a backward and wasteful method of farming.

Soil improvement and utilization may occur in several ways.[13] First, there may be crop rotation and diversification, the latter being the means of accomplishing the former. This method prevents soil depletion and serves to rebuild the soil after depletion. When rotation is practiced for a few years, the soil is restored to nearly its original fertility.

[12] *Cf.* A. F. Gustafson, et al, *Conservation in the United States* (Ithaca: Comstock Pub. Co., 1929), Part I.

[13] For a full discussion of these methods, see H. H. Bennett, *Elements of soil conservation* (New York: McGraw-Hill Book Company, 1947).

Second, fertilization will restore the worn-out soil. Scientific tests have shown that the application of fertilizers under certain conditions may double or even treble the crop yield per acre.

Third, the adjustment of kinds of crops to various kinds of soil advances production. The discovery of the varieties of soil requires soil surveys. Up to 1940, our nation had made a detailed survey of about half our agricultural land, thereby leading all other countries in the proportion thus mapped out.

Since the beginning of man, society has adjusted itself to nature in obtaining a food supply, much more largely by the use of plant substances than in any other way. Today the major portion of the world's food is derived from plants. Plant culture, therefore, is a fundamental and vital method of social adjustment. Farming may appear to be largely an individual affair; but it is in reality a great social undertaking, one of the great functions operated by the larger society, on which all have to depend.

The wastage of forest resources. During most of man's existence he has been a forest animal and has depended on forests for protection, food, fuel, and housing. Only in recent times has any considerable portion of humanity become divorced from forests, and then only indirectly. The direct and indirect dependence is still great.[14]

1. The uses to which forest materials are put have multiplied with social evolution. Before the advent of fire as a human utility, forests furnished protection and edibles. After the advent, they supplied fuel also, and still later, housing. With the development of advanced societies, the modes of utilization are limited only by man's inventive ability and by competition with more advantageous materials.

2. The rapidity with which our forests have dwindled makes the conservation of forests an important issue. Our original forest acreage of 822 millions has decreased to one of 462 millions, and our total board footage from over 5 trillions to something like 1.75 trillions.

3. The necessity of importing forestry products is growing apace. We are now dependent on outside resources for a large share of our wood pulp. This growing dependence on outside

---

[14] The extent of our continuing dependence on the forests is seldom recognized. For a more detailed statement, see B. P. Kirkland, "Place of forests in the farm economy," *1940 Year Book*, Department of Agriculture, *Farmers in a changing world* (Washington, D.C.: Government Printing Office, 1940): 533–540; also R. Marshall, *People's forests* (New York: Random House, 1933).

sources demands that we discover the sources of our wastage, which we shall briefly discuss.

"Forest mining" is a term applied to our methods of forest destruction in logging operations. Forest area after forest area has disappeared because we have allowed and sanctioned this practice. Let us take a case from northern Minnesota that happened about 1920. It was an area of some two square miles of the finest white and red (Norway) pine, with a sprinkling of other forest trees. The commercially valuable pines were logged off, and all that remained of young pines and other timber was destroyed in the process of logging and by thorough burning of brush. Nothing remained but completely denuded sandhills. Not a living plant of any kind was to be found afterwards over most of the area. Northern Minnesota is now a standing witness to this kind of destruction in its millions of acres of cut-over land with its mute vestiges of charred and rotting trunks of white birch and other valuable trees.[15]

Destructive fires, largely of human origin, cause a tremendous annual loss. The extent of this destructiveness appears when we consider that of the 22.5 million acres of forests "used up" annually, 3 million are consumed by fires.

There is wastage in cutting and in manufacture at every step of the way, from the raw material to the finished product. This wastage is so extensive that approximately only 50 per cent of the original material gets to the consumer. The lost values are apparent when we consider that "the destructive distillation of a cord of this waste product will yield: 50 bushels of charcoal; 11,500 cubic feet of gas; 25 gallons of tar; 10 gallons of crude wood alcohol; [and] 200 pounds of acetate of lime."[16]

Wastage also appears in the high cost of lumber, due to the long hauls made necessary by the destruction of near-by forest supplies. One by one the great forest areas of New England, the Great Lakes, and the South have been destroyed or essentially depleted. Our chief lumber supply now is from the Pacific Coast. A forest famine results when the cost of lumber becomes so high that it limits use; that point was reached long ago in this country.

Restoration and prevention. Our country had a campaign for the "conservation" of natural resources when Theodore Roose-

---

[15] Cf. P. G. Beck, and M. C. Forster, *Six rural problem areas*, F. E. R. A. Research Monograph I (Washington, D.C.: Government Printing Office, 1935).

[16] Chase, *op. cit.*, p. 258.

velt was President, the conservation of forests being uppermost.[17] Since then, ideas and techniques have been developed for accomplishing it. The more consequential things to be done are:[18]

1. We must prevent and lessen forest fires. Of destructive forest fires which destroy billions of board feet annually, 84 per cent are started by human beings. Hunters, tourists, logging crews, railway engines, and the like are responsible. Evidently both education and legislation are needed as preventives. The organized, systematic work of government forest rangers is of first-rate importance and very effective.

2 Much of the destruction of billions of board feet of lumber per year comes from insects and diseases that afflict trees and from windfalls largely the result of such enemies. Something is now done under state and national forest control to prevent such inroads, but it is insignificant as compared with what needs to be done

3. The national government has promoted investigation of wastes in manufacture of wood products and methods of obviating them. In certain places a good deal has been accomplished in this direction, but the undertaking is still in its infancy.

4. If we want to produce our own forest supplies, we must drive much harder for reforestation and the establishment of forests than we are now doing. Our annual planting of trees amounts to about 1.5 million acres, while we cut and waste 22.5 million acres. We destroy by fire more than eight times the acreage which we annually set to young trees. It should be remembered that it requires from 50 to 75 years for most trees to become commercially valuable. Reforestation is an undertaking for generations; and federal, state, and local governmental units must co-operate to speed it up.

5. Co-operation between private owners and the government should be stimulated. Forest mining is not indulged in by some of

[17] For a history of the conservation movement, cf. Gustafson, op. cit., Introduction; G. Pinchot, Fight for conservation (New York: Doubleday and Company. 1910); Theodore Roosevelt, Autobiography (New York: Charles Scribner's Sons, 1920), Ch. 11; C. H. Van Hise, and L. Havemeyer, Conservation of our natural resources (New York: The Macmillan Company, 1935); Renner, op. cit., Ch. 5.

[18] For a more complete discussion of these points, cf. K. Glover, America begins again (New York: McGraw-Hill Book Company, 1939); C. J. Hynning, State conservation of resources, National Resources Committee (Washington, D.C.: Government Printing Office, 1939); Stuart Chase, Rich land—poor land (New York: McGraw-Hill Book Company, 1936), Chs. 13–16; National Wildlife Federation, Conference on education in conservation (Washington, D.C.: National Wildlife Federation, 1939); Vogt, op. cit.

our best and most progressive owners. Great railway systems are taking scrupulous care of their forests and are resorting to reforestation. Laws that drive logging men to use destructive methods should be modified, and penalties should be imposed for violating fair laws.

6. We should proceed to develop substitutes for forest material to a greater extent than ever. The use of steel, aluminum, other metals, and cement as substitutes for wood appears in the construction of bridges, buildings, railway cars, machines of various sorts, and in other ways.

The wastage of mineral, coal, oil, and gas resources. This is the age of metals, also of concrete, of rubber, of oil, or of the automobile, or of any other prominent or dominating factor, according to the viewpoint from which the discussion proceeds. The foregoing are all economic factors because they enter into and so largely condition our whole industrial and commercial life. But they are much more than economic factors; they are sociological because they are woven intimately and significantly into the fabric of our total societal life. They enter into our very thoughts and ways of life. By means of them society has been revolutionized in the last hundred years. Without them, society would revert to its rather primitive condition, as in the days of Washington and Jefferson. Consequently they are wonderful agencies of adjustment to nature, and we must consider them in that connection.

Our interest in these factors at this point is not only economic or technological. Those angles must be left to the economists and technologists.[19] We are interested in the supply of these agencies in so far as they promise to affect our collective existence. We want to know how long they will last, what wastes affect their duration, and what intelligent preventives and savings society might adopt. Again, we must resort to selected samples to serve our purposes.

Iron has been in use by mankind for some 3400 years. Its utilization began in the Egyptian and Babylonian regions, and from there it spread to Europe and the rest of the world. The invention of steel was a great advance, and its later production by the Bessemer process reduced its cost and so widened its use. Today steel is the prime element in all great buildings, bridges,

[19] *Cf.* the excellent coverage of the purely economic aspects of conservation by A. C. Bunce, *Economics of soil conservation* (Ames: Iowa State College Press, 1942).

dams, railways, and machines of most kinds. Our modern society is so dependent on it that its exhaustion would spell ruin. Our intimate dependence on steel is seen in the fact that the index of steel production is regarded as a good barometer of economic conditions.

We are interested first in the supply of iron and its duration. Sometimes a very dark picture is painted regarding this. Its supply is limited, but there is no menace of an immediate iron famine. As in the case of most other natural resources, the duration of the iron supply is difficult to estimate because it is conditioned by so many variables. Among these factors are the following:

1. The known supply of iron ore fluctuates with time, not only because it is being lessened by mining but also because it is being increased by the discovery of new iron-ore deposits. The discovery of the great Mesabi range increased the iron supply of the United States manyfold. New supplies are being discovered in the Americas and elsewhere from time to time.

2. The available supply of iron is being enlarged by the discovery of new processes of recovering the metal from ore-bearing rocks. Of the original 80 billion tons within the United States, only 4788 million tons, 6 per cent, were available, because then only calcareous ores could be recovered. More recently, the previously unavailable ores found in siliceous rocks, which could not be recovered unless the proportion was at least 50 per cent, have been made available by the discovery of a recovering process from such rocks bearing a lower percentage of ore.

3. The duration of the iron supply is lengthened by the use of substitutes such as stone, cement, aluminum, and other substances.

4. The supply is conserved by the use of metallic irons. This means the re-use of iron by breaking up and melting down old stoves, machines, and other outworn utilities.

5. Our supply is also conserved by the introduction and use of preservative and protective devices. Painting steel structures and machines preserves them against rust. The production and use of "rustless steel" and other alloys is a wonderful preservative, tending to make steel imperishable. Sheds for farm machinery, car barns for cars and engines, and garages for automobiles are examples of protective devices which prolong the life of machines.

6. Waste is eliminated by the discovery of processes which will

make a pound of iron go as far as several pounds went previously. Thus, a German scientist has produced a steel that is several times lighter and stronger than that we commonly use.

7. Finally, if the maximum of building and construction work is reached, it is to be expected there will be a reduction in the mining, production, and consumption of iron. When all the houses, cities, and bridges that mankind needs get built, new material will be required only for replacement purposes.

Three natural elements as forms of motor power are important to us: coal, oil, and natural gas. These elements furnish heat and energy for our various purposes. Their importance in today's economy may be inferred by considering what our societal life would be without them. Coal was not a great item in social life before the eighteenth century. Oil and natural gas began to be important only within the last few decades. Today we little realize how much our many utilities have revolutionized collective life.

The real advent of coal usage came with the invention of the steam engine, although coal had been used previously for heating and smelting. The engine made coal the great and universal driving power for machines. Coal became the dynamic heart of the factory system and the prime creator of the Industrial Revolution. It has competitors now, but it still remains the master motor power and supplier of heat.

When we consider the wastes and variables, we find that the duration-time of our coal resources is much shortened.[20] (1) There is a tendency to increase the rate of consumption. (2) There are certain large wastages in mining coal, such as leaving large supporting pillars of coal; leaving thin beds of coal unmined; the destruction of upper beds of coal by the cave-in of earth after lower beds have been mined; and the throwing away of slack. In the case of anthracite, it is estimated that these wastages equal as much as one and a half times the amount mined. For bituminous coal it is reckoned that 50 per cent is so wasted. (3) New coal fields occasionally are discovered, thus enlarging the supply. How long this will continue is of course speculative, but it will end sometime.

From all this complex of variables we may safely draw the conclusion that our coal supply is likely to endure for many

[20] The problem of estimates of reserves is extremely thorny. Estimates must be tentative because of continuous changes in technology and of the discovery of new areas. *Cf.* National Resources Committee, *Technological trends and national policy* (Washington, D.C.: Government Printing Office, 1937).

hundreds of years, probably, at least, until scientists have discovered adequate substitutes.

The problem of conservation of a resource is one of exercising control. There can be no conservation where there can be no control of conditions. Some of the factors we have mentioned are susceptible to a degree of control. The rate of consumption can be modified by better methods of consumption, as by means of better engines, more scientific firing of engines, improvements in mining processes so that larger percentages are reclaimed, and utilization of slack. Improvement of coal engines and stoves is highly desirable. Locomotive engines are said to transform not more than 4 or 5 per cent of the coal they consume into power. Contrast this with the Diesel engine, which utilizes about 15 per cent of the oil it uses. Our domestic stoves and furnaces deliver about as small a proportion of the coal they consume into our houses in the form of heat. In the production of coke our old type of beehive coke ovens give no return for a large part of the coal they use. They should be replaced by the new type, which saves the by-products, such as oils, tars, and the like. The value of these products may be seen from the statement that besides the 1500 pounds of coke the Ford Company gets from a ton of bituminous coal, it reclaims 8000 cubic feet of gas, 10 gallons of gasoline, 20 pounds of ammonium sulphate, 30 gallons of crude light tar, 3 gallons of creosote oil, 2 gallons of crude lubricating oil, and 10 pounds of grease. One might well ask if it is not a "crime" to use up our coal merely by letting it "go up in smoke."

Many engineers believe that it would be economy to liquefy our coal; others believe it would be economical to transform the coal into electricity at the mines and transmit the electricity over wires, thus avoiding heavy transportation, storage, and handling costs. Both forms of transformation are being experimented with and put to use, and we may sometime witness the use of the new products in place of the "black diamond."[21]

The significance of oil in the life of today is seen in its widening use for an increasing number of purposes and in the place it occupies in world affairs. It is oftentimes an international issue.[22] The United States has become an automotive nation, and other

[21] The problem of new sources of power and of their control is discussed in Ch. 4 of this book. Also, see C. C. Furnas, *Storehouse of civilization* (New York: Bureau of Publications, Teachers College, Columbia University, 1939); and E. Hodgins, and F. A. Magoun, *Behemoth: The story of power* (New York: Junior Literary Guild, 1932).

[22] *Cf.* the suggestive article, "Aramaco," dealing with the Arabian-American oil development, in *Fortune*, March 28, 1949: 62 ff.

nations are rapidly becoming such. In 1929 we produced 84 per cent of all the automobiles in the world; and in 1931, 79 per cent. Wealth invested in motor-vehicle businesses runs into many billions of dollars. Millions of persons live by means of them. Autos are responsible for the existence of our great national highway system, for great shifts and fluidity of population, and for our multiplying contacts, broadening the horizon of millions by travel and causing tremendous changes in the ways of living of urban people. They are responsible also for profound transformations in sex, family, and moral relationships. Oil enters into all this as a conditioning factor.

It is difficult to arrive at a very satisfactory estimate of our own national oil supply, to say nothing of trying to estimate the world supply. In the early 1920's we were informed and warned that our supply would last only four or five years. Since then we have increased our rate of consumption severalfold, but we can also believe that the day of reckoning has been postponed.[23] We must rest our case with the estimates made from authoritative sources.

How long we may depend on making use of oil as the dominant source of automotive power is not determinable because of the existence of a list of variables: (1) We increase our rate of production, which of course means consumption, very rapidly. (2) New fields are being discovered all over the world, which increase the supply. (3) Improved processes of making and refining oil make certain essential forms more plentiful. (4) Driving deeper wells enlarges the supply. Wells may be sunk more than twice as deep as formerly. (5) Improved consuming agencies, especially furnaces and engines, serve the same purpose. Automobile engines have been very inefficient, and greatly increased efficiency is possible. (6) New forms of energy may be discovered which will serve as substitutes for oil. A consideration of such variables makes it evident that no accurate forecast of the duration of the oil supply can be made.

The future supply of oil will be much greater than the present supply if it becomes possible to eliminate or reduce the wastes which obtain. Some of the principal wastes are the following: (1) The greatest waste of oil occurs in mining. Probably not more than one fourth of the supply in the earth is brought to the top. This loss of 75 per cent will likely be scaled down since the trend is in that direction. (2) The multiplication of wells over an oil

[23] Cf. Gustafson, op. cit., Ch. 16; Vogt, op. cit., is much less optimistic.

pool, sometimes to the extent of one per town lot, as at Signal Hill, California, is a most wasteful method of mining. Nothing short of pooling interests by the many landowners can overcome this. (3) Where the natural gas is allowed to escape, less oil can be recovered from the underlying pool by reason of lessened pressure. The remedy is in blocking the escape of the gas or replacing it by air pumped in from the surface. (4) Permitting water to seep into oil wells is a destructive factor which may be greatly mitigated by careful engineering. (5) Inefficient engines and consumption plants are great sources of waste. An engine that will utilize 25 per cent rather than 5 per cent of the gasoline is perhaps possible.

The extensive use of natural gas is only a few years old. Previously the gas was allowed to escape into the air or was lighted to make a public spectacle. By billions of feet, consumption in this country increased at least twentyfold. During the same time customers increased at least twelvefold.

The reasons for this great and new development are as follows: (1) Extensive fields of gas along with oil were discovered. The gas areas are largely coincident with oil areas. (2) The invention of new and practical means of manufacturing and laying gaspipe makes possible the transmission of gas thousands of miles, with almost no loss. (3) The rapid introduction of gas for industrial purposes occurred. Industry now consumes over 80 per cent of the natural-gas supply. (4) Natural gas is being substituted for artificial gas, for purposes of domestic consumption.

It is impossible to make a fair estimate of the amount of natural gas that is wasted. Most of it has been wasted thus far, and it would be safe to place this loss in billions of billions of cubic feet. This wastage is important not only because of the large monetary value involved, but also because of two other considerations. One is that this destruction represents a large proportion of our very precious terrestrial supply of energy. Until we have found substitutes for coal, oil, and natural gas in abundance, it is rather tragic to allow so much useful energy to escape. From another direction, that of the consumers, this destruction results in higher consumer costs.[24]

The utilization of water resources. Water power is transformed into electric power, or what we call hydroelectric power. It is an advantageous form of power, because after the initial

[24] On the general problem of the relationship between wastage and economic costs, cf. Bunce, ob. cit., Ch. 7.

outlay of capital its economy of operation is great. Our chief concern is the fact that it is a substitute for coal and oil, and so conserves the supply of natural energy. But so far as belonging to the people goes, in the sense that it is more intrinsic to the earth, it belongs to them no more than do coal and oil. It just happens that water power comes usually from public, not from private, waters. In that sense it is more public than are the other factors.

The problems connected with water power concern, first, the development of all possible sources of such power so as to conserve oil, coal, and forest supplies; second, the distribution of ownership of hydroelectric power and the regulation of rates in such manner that the consumers receive all to which they are justly entitled. These questions have been the core of the controversy which has been going on in the various river basins of the country and on the floor of the Congress. Although there is some confusion as to whether regional resource development should take place through administrative co-ordination of governmental and private agencies or through a public corporation modelled after the Tennessee Valley Authority, there is complete agreement on the wisdom of multiple-purpose dams serving jointly the needs of irrigation, power generation, flood control, and river transportation.[25]

The Planned Use of Resources: Conservation[26]

Throughout this discussion of wasteful utilization of resources one question has been insistent. What is the best *economic* use of our natural resources?

The economic use of resources is hardly the only aspect of the problem, as we have sought to show; certainly the word "best" takes us into the realm of social as well as economic values. Certainly "best" requires social judgment. And social judgment is a process of anticipating consequences flowing from action: a process which emphasizes actions and consequences involving,

[25] For a general survey of this problem, *cf.* National Resources Committee, *Regional factors in national planning and development* (Washington, D.C.: Government Printing Office, 1935); also the committee's pamphlet series, *Regional planning;* likewise the committee's report, *Energy resources and national policy* (Washington, D.C.: Government Printing Office, 1939); David Lilienthal, *TVA: Democracy on the march* (New York: Harper and Brothers, 1944); H. W. Odum, *Understanding society: Principles of dynamic sociology* (New York: The Macmillan Company, 1947), Ch. 4, 5, 35.

[26] The following pages are adapted from Paul Meadows, "Some sociological aspects of land-use policy," *Social Forces*, 24 (December, 1945): 231–235; used by permission of the editor.

requiring, implying, and affecting other human beings. The best economic use of natural resources, then, is a peculiarly human problem.

As a human problem, resource utilization is hinged on a single observation: it affects the institutional pattern of human beings, the pattern of their settlement, organizations, community services—the quantity and quality of their community life. Thus, the U. S. Forest Service, in its report to the Land Planning Committee of the National Resources Planning Board, stated emphatically: "Effectiveness in forest land use obviously means effectiveness with respect to man's organized living and economic affairs."[27] This principle of effectiveness for organized living outranked all others in the Forest Service's list of "basic principles governing formulation of a comprehensive forest plan." "All land capable of growing forests and for which no other higher social or economic use or need exists or can be foreseen should be maintained in or restored to a forest cover for the twofold purpose of conserving its soils, and of deriving from it products and services of social and economic importance most readily obtained through the agency of trees."[28] This human or social touchstone, then, remains at the center of considerations, regardless of the policy. "Best" economic resource utilization may call for a policy of abandonment, or utilization for the purpose of providing supplementary income, or survival at all costs, or modifications in the operations or organization of the economic unit.[29]

If, then, "best" economic use and control of land require some initial acts of social judgment, what are some instances of the latter? Five social criteria of land-use policy, in the form of propositions, are suggested here.

Resource utilization and social stability.   In the first place, it is from the social point of view desirable and necessary in planning land use to attempt to stabilize utilization patterns.

Problems of resource utilization must be viewed in their setting of human ecology. Man is an ecological factor, like all other animals. One outstanding human distinction from other members of a given "biome" is that he succeeds usually in upsetting, more

[27] *Forest land resources: Requirement, problems and policy*, Part VIII of the Report of the Land Planning Committee, National Resources Planning Board (Washington, D.C.: Government Printing Office, 1935), p. 3.

[28] *Ibid.*

[29] Adapted from S. E. Johnson, "Farm-management problems in an era of change," *Yearbook*, U. S. Department of Agriculture, 1940: 489 ff.

than does any other ecological factor, the balance of climate and climax, of nature and numbers, of scarcity and satisfaction. Yet man strives for a balance with nature. Certainly he does not survive long in a condition of imbalance. Continuous and tenuous imbalance terminates, unless restored, in an impoverished and impossible social existence. Stability in a balanced ecological interaction is a prerequisite to continuity and expression of all the human arts.

This problem is not insoluble. Of course, here as elsewhere, technical skills outstrip social mastery. But technically, land-use planning, particularly as contemplated by the Forest Service, for example, starts with a balanced community. Thus, Dean Jeffers has written: "The owner or administrator of a forest property is dealing with a balanced community in nature. The forest is also a balance in the total community of plants and people and other factors."[30] He adds: "It is the business of the forester to maintain the balance of the resources in the wild lands under his control." Ecological stability in order to achieve and preserve social stability, then, becomes a primary criterion of planning.

Of course, this criterion of action is not a universal favorite. One thinks of the disastrous "cut-out-and-get-out" policy of American private forest operations. But devastating exploitation is not confined to forestry. Thus, two British writers, to cite a quotation which is at hand, voice a common attitude of modern industrialized agriculture. "A decline in the proportion of the population engaged in agriculture is . . . an inevitable concomitant of economic progress and an improving standard of life; and it is impossible to lay down *a priori* grounds any limits to the extent to which this proportion may eventually decline."[31] But some students of rural economy cannot contemplate this scene with composure; somehow, as they see the situation, we must manage to conserve human resources; with the fate of this undertaking they identify the future integrity of human society and individual expression.[32]

Certainly if a utilization policy is stated in the large terms of resource management, stability as a criterion and as a goal of action is both initial and ultimate. The Forest Service report to

[30] D. S. Jeffers, "Multiple use of wild lands in the Rocky Mountain and Intermountain region," *Journal of Forestry*, 41 (September, 1943): 630.

[31] Viscount Astor, and B. S. Rowntree, *British agriculture* (London: Longmans, Green and Company, 1938), p. 50. Quoted by permission.

[32] *Cf.* O. E. Baker, R. Borsodi, and M. L. Wilson, *Agriculture in modern life* (New York: Harper and Brothers, 1939), *passim*.

the Land Planning Committee held forth this prospect: "By restoring forests to these areas [*e.g.*, cut-over lands] and organizing them for sustained yield a stable base of raw materials can be provided for existing and new wood-using industries; and the communities founded on such industries can plan safely for a long life."[33] Elsewhere the assertion is made, with respect to timber management: "The use of timber from the public forest should be planned as fully as possible to stabilize the industries and communities dependent partly or wholly on forests."[34] The famous Copeland report of the Forest Service stated the case firmly and succinctly thus: "Permanent forests support permanent communities."[35]

If stability be the essence of a wise rural economy, are there principles of action which can serve as guides? The following principles have been suggested by a member of the Bureau of Agricultural Economics:

"(1) Forestry efforts should be harmonized with a changing and evolving form of rural economy; (2) forests should be used to help develop and maintain the best possible kind of stable rural economy; (3) a program to rebuild depleted forests would help stabilize rural economy and could help pay our debt to forest communities; (4) wise forest use depends in large part upon a more stable general economy." . . .[36]

Resource utilization and the total situation. This emphasis on an over-all co-ordination of land use suggests the second major social criterion of land-use planning. It is desirable and necessary to approach the problem of stabilizing land-use patterns in terms of the total situation.

The structure which comprises the community of man and nature is not swung on half hinges. Life has an integral relatedness; relations tend to be internal, so that what affects one affects all, and the part can never be abstracted from the whole. Perhaps the social whole is not greater than the sum of its parts, but the part can never be understood apart from the whole. This totality of things is just as necessary a phase of land-use policy as it is of any other policy.

In saying this the intention is not to imply that students of land use are unaware of this organic quality of relations. Quite

[33] *Forest land resources* . . . , *op. cit.*, p. 5.
[34] *Ibid.*, p. 80.
[35] *A national plan for American forests*, Document #12, 73rd Congress (1933), p. 108.
[36] E. Foster, "A plan to help stabilize rural economy by the wise use of forest resources," *Journal of Forestry*, 39 (September, 1941): 796.

the contrary. Thus, the total-situation approach, with its accent on the integration of factors, is made by the ecologist. Clements and Chaney in their study of the Great Plains wrote: "Every sequence of events following fire, overgrazing, cultivation, lumbering, road-building or other conversion of the vegetative cover is in the fact made up of interlocking series, in which change or diversity at any one point may affect the entire process and its outcome."[37] Totality is a key word in the field of good management. For example, one finds it in Kirkland's list of the principles of good management: "(1) stabilization of ownership, (2) rebuilding the timber stands to their former productivity, (3) providing patterns of taxation and ownership tenure that will eliminate economic pressure for excessive exploitation, (4) providing for community benefits from near-by forests, (5) utilizing employment possibilities."[38]

Totality is the central theme of "multiple-use management," a very common phrase in the literature of forestry, for example. Thus, Sparhawk and Show, of the U. S. Forest Service, wrote in the Copeland report: "A major aim of public policy is to bring about multiple-purpose management of the private forest lands on which several values exist."[39] Dean Jeffers' list of "soil principles of wild-land use" displays totality as a guiding criterion of planning: "the maintenance of the plant life-soil cycle"; "the greatest good for the greatest number on the long run"; "sustained yield"; "soil-use productivity"; "diversification"; "conservation."[40] Finally, the total situation is an absolute imperative in land classification, as the following itemization by the Land Planning Committee of factors important in classifying land as submarginal shows: soil fertility, population density, market accessibility, costs of clearing the land, feasibility of mechanization of operations, extent of erosion, presence of topographic barriers.[41]

Resource utilization and ownership. We are no less without sociological guides when we turn to the next and more controversial proposition bearing on the social aspects of resource

[37] F. E. Clements, and R. W. Chaney, *Environment and life in the Great Plains* (Washington, D.C.: Carnegie Institution, 1936), p. 49.

[38] B. P. Kirkland, "Place of forests in the farm economy," *Yearbook*, U. S. Department of Agriculture, 1940, p. 542.

[39] *A national plan . . .* , *op. cit.*, p. 90.

[40] Jeffers, *op. cit.*, p. 628 ff.

[41] *Maladjustments in land use in the United States*, Part VIII of the Report of the Land Planning Committee, National Resources Board (Washington, D.C.: Government Printing Office, 1935), p. 13.

utilization. It is desirable and necessary to approach the problem of stability in terms of ownership.

In the literature of forestry, agricultural economics, and rural sociology, ownership appears as the nub of the problem of stabilization. If a system of property is viewed as a set of human relations, especially as a key of human privileges and responsibilities, then it must be fairly clear that the stability of utilization can never exceed but will inevitably be a function of the stability of ownership.

The most exhaustive study of this problem is without doubt the Copeland report. The judgment of this study is blunt and outspoken: "Experience here and abroad does not indicate that private owners on their own initiative and unassisted will utilize the land for timber growing or even maintain a forest cover to the extent that is desirable or necessary."[42] The reasons are weighty: "lack of knowledge as to how to use the land effectively for forestry; the belief that other uses will be more profitable; lack of financial resources; lack of assurance that such use will yield a profit; or even a well-founded belief, in many instances, that it will not; desire to liquidate their investment and lack of interest in the land after the timber has been removed."

The prospects that private management will ever achieve a reasonable and socially responsible program of conservation are not at all reassuring. The Copeland report is equally adamant on this point. "Owing to the almost complete removal of the forest capital from about 40 per cent of the privately owned forest land and to a very material reduction on an additional 30 per cent, less than 280 million acres out of the 396 million acres of privately owned forest land in the United States is capable of being organized into sustained-yield forest properties from which annual returns can be expected immediately."[43]

It is perhaps not within the purview of this chapter to enter into all the consequences which flow from this considered conclusion. In part, these consequences involve some program of public responsibility, whether along the lines of public co-operation, public regulation, or public acquisition. One suspects that increasingly the line of public action will proceed toward acquisition, chiefly by default. At least this realistic if tragic *dénouement* has developed in the forest areas east of the Great Plains. There is little reason to doubt that this kind of future

[42] *A national plan* . . . , *op. cit.*, p. 944.
[43] *Ibid.*, p. 983.

awaits the great western forests also. In the meantime a full complement of public powers has already matured, measures which are designed to introduce into an unsettled and ruinous social situation a modicum of stability. These measures include: rural zoning, co-operative grazing associations, differential taxation, subsidies, credits, covenants restricting disposal or use of land, social conservation districts, land classification, and so on.[44] Nor are precedents lacking for the taking of these initial, and for that matter subsequent, steps, according to the Office of the Solicitor of the U. S. Department of Agriculture.[45] One student of the problem of resource ownership and stability has urged: "Instead of waiting for the slow development of regulation, it seems reasonable to draw from the experience of the past to plan consciously for a type of decentralized but centrally co-ordinated administration which will produce efficient results in a democratic manner."[46]

Resource utilization and economic costs. Resource planning never gets far away from the problem of economic costs. Perhaps the necessity which underlies this fact is just. "The gravest mistake," according to Siegfried von Ciriacy-Wantrup, "would be the creation *ad hoc* of some sort of 'cost-free' land economics in order to make proposed actions appear economically desirable when they are not, although these actions may be of great social value from other aspects and may deserve consideration for that reason."[47] A fourth proposition, then, may be formulated: It is not always desirable and necessary to state the problem of stability of resource utilization in terms of economic costs.

This proposition shares the same ground, on this point at least, with the Copeland report. "It can be admitted at the outset that forestry will not always, under all circumstances, show a cash profit to the owner, whether he be an individual or the public."[48] In resource planning it is sometimes necessary to see matters *sub specie eternitatis*. Fortunately, from this kind of economic calculus, a perspective, perhaps a "perspective by

[44] *Cf.* V. W. Johnson, and H. Walker, Jr., "Centralization and co-ordination of police power for land-control measures," *Journal of Land and Public Utility Economics*, 17 (February, 1941): 17 ff.

[45] *Cf.* C. H. Stoddard, Jr., "Pattern for public regulation of private forests," *Journal of Forestry*, 40 (May, 1942): 371 ff.

[46] *Ibid.*, p. 373.

[47] "Economic aspects of land conservation," *Journal of Farm Economics* (May, 1938): 472.

[48] *A national plan* . . . , *op. cit.*, p. 111.

incongruity," as Kenneth Burke suggests,[49] emerges. This is what former Chief Forester Silcox had in mind when he wrote in his letter transmitting the Copeland report: "In recommending forest use for all suitable land not needed for other purposes, it has been the position of the Forest Service that idle acres are a symbol of economic short-sightedness."[50]

Economic short-sightedness is not uncommon in our society, of course. If its blight on the forest lands is stressed here, it is because the problem being considered here for purposes of illustration is forest land-use policy. To be sure, from the standpoint of economic costs, the behavior of the forest industries shows little resemblance to so-called "sound" economic principles. No other industry does business on the basis of the liquidation of its capital to the extent that the forest industries do. The upshot of "cut-out-and-get-out" is inescapable. "The capital has been consumed currently instead of continuing to support industry and promote human sustenance."[51]

Examination of the reasons for the utilization of submarginal lands reveals no pious devotion to the sacred principles of economic costs. The reasons for cropping submarginal soils, as formulated by the Land Planning Committee, show that fact plainly enough.[52] The reasons include: shifts in comparative advantage due to settlement of new and more productive areas and to deterioration by erosion; inadequate understanding of the character and productive capacity of the land; exceptional prices in exceptional times, the availability of poor land for poor people. Likewise, the ills resulting from the use of submarginal lands, as listed in the same study, can hardly be regarded as purely economic ills.[53] Among them are: "(a) small incomes and consequently low plane of living, (b) low level of community life and morals, (c) financial difficulties of local government units, (d) waste of individual and social effort, and (e) the exploitation of people who are ignorant of the facts and conditions in these areas." Not all the costs are economic; there are nonmensurable, serious human costs.

It is, then, not too much to ask that when the objectives of land-use action are established economic costs must not be

[49] Cf. K. Burke, *Permanence and change* (New York: New Republic, Inc., 1935): p. 118 ff.
[50] *A national plan* . . . , *op. cit.*, p. 4.
[51] *Ibid.*, p. 895.
[52] *Maladjustments in land use, op. cit.*, p. 2.
[53] *Ibid.*, p. 14.

allowed to loom too large. One admires the clarity and boldness of the thinking incorporated in the Forest Service report, which in recommending measures to safeguard the public interest in private forests stipulated a number of noneconomic objectives, objectives which do not pay too much attention to the conventional accounting demands of our not too economic industrialism.[54]

Resource utilization and social conservation. A final proposition expressing the social stake in resource utilization may serve as a recapitulation of all the preceding considerations. It is desirable and necessary from a social point of view to stabilize utilization in terms of the psychology and logic of conservation.

The criterion is, after all, the substance of any socially oriented remarks which may be made on this general theme. Perhaps this sentence from Marsh and Gibbons will make the point sufficiently clear. "Forest-resource conservation offers one important means of maintaining a balanced rural economic and social structure in the parts of the country which will grow timber, through utilizing all the land productively for the purposes for which it is best suited, maintaining private industries in perpetuity, and holding a reasonable part of the population in the country in a healthy, diversified rural life."[55]

Unfortunately for social action, "conservation" is a direction rather than a directive. It is, moreover, a weasel word. To some it means wasting less; often it means management; sometimes, the adjusting of production to effective demand; frequently, replacement or the maintenance of the present level of productivity or even the rehabilitation of a former or higher level of productivity. A very usable conception of conservation is that of E. C. Weitzell: "the maintenance of a specific level of productivity for an infinite period of time."[56] If land use may be said to determine the institutional patterns of a people, from a social point of view here is a social criterion of land-use policy which is eminently satisfying.

It goes beyond the conventional categories of physical conservation and urges "a method or methods of land utilization which will return a maximum net income without depleting

---

[54] *A national plan . . . , op. cit.*, p. 59.
[55] R. E. Marsh, and W. H. Gibbons, "Forest-resource conservation," *Yearbook*, U. S. Department of Agriculture, 1940, p. 458.
[56] "Economics of soil conservation. I. Individual and social conservation," *Journal of Land and Public Utility Economics*, 19 (August, 1943): 340.

or impairing the productivity of the basic resources in the long run. . . . "[57] The problem of utilization is seen not as one of improving productivity but as one of maintaining a specific desired level. This statement of the issues throws into a new light the question of costs. Costs consist of those expenditures "which would be necessary to maintain" a given level of productivity. Likewise, this conception of conservation forms the basis of a more generous theory of entrepreneurship, for the latter, "to be consistent with the social interest, is not merely a matter of merely maximizing income over the span of one or more generations, but one of maximizing *the income of society in perpetuity*."[58] The heart of resource policy, then, appears to be a matter of time preference.[59] A time preference to conserve must replace a time preference to consume. The complicated problems of social evaluations in resource policy come to consist mainly in a social-psychological awareness, one in which a time preference rising from the future edge of experience dominates the time preference of the present indicative and the past imperfect.

QUESTIONS

1. What practical difference does it make whether we regard the environment as determining or conditioning human society? Can you illustrate the difference? Distinguish between direct and indirect influences of the natural environment on man.
2. Illustrate the following statement: Culture conditions nature; nature conditions culture.
3. Under what circumstances are we led to consider the necessity of efficiency in our utilization of resources?
4. What do we mean by "resources"? What do we mean by "the wasteful use of resources"? Does the definition of "waste" really make any difference?
5. What is the distinction between the absolute and the relative waste of soil?
6. Explain why it is difficult to establish limits upon the reserves of our natural resources. Does this difficulty have any significance for the conservation movement? Explain.
7. List the various forms of waste of our forest resources. Can any of this waste be reduced or eliminated? Explain.
8. In what ways is the problem of the best economic use of our natural resources also a social problem?

[57] *Ibid.*
[58] *Ibid.*, p. 343.
[59] *Cf.* also A. C. Bunce, "Time preference and conservation," *Journal of Farm Economics* (August, 1940): 542.

9. What are the social criteria to be considered in land-use policy? Are these criteria any more urgent in the consideration of forest management than in our utilization of other resources?
10. What are some of the difficulties in establishing public regulation of privately owned resources? Does conservation always require regulation? Explain.

REFERENCES

BENNETT, H. H., *Elements of soil conservation*. New York: McGraw-Hill Book Company, 1947.

BUNCE, A. C., *Economics of soil conservation*. Ames: Iowa State College Press, 1942.

CHASE, STUART, *Tragedy of waste*. New York: The Macmillan Company, 1925.

CHASE, STUART, *Rich land—poor land*. New York: McGraw-Hill Book Company, 1936.

Copeland Committee Report, *A national plan for American forests*, Document #12, 73rd Congress. Washington, D.C.: Government Printing Office, 1933.

GLOVER, K., *America begins again*. New York: McGraw-Hill Book Company, 1939.

GUSTAFSON, A. F., et al, *Conservation in the United States*. Ithaca: Comstock Pub. Company, 1929.

MARSHALL, R., *People's forests*. New York: Random House, 1933.

National Resources Committee, *Energy resources and national policy*. Washington, D.C.: Government Printing Office, 1935.

PORRITT, H. S., *Water—wealth or waste?* New York: Harcourt, Brace and Company, 1939.

RENNER, G. T., *Conservation of national resources*. New York: John Wiley and Sons, 1942.

U. S. Department of Agriculture, *Farmers in a changing world, 1940 Yearbook*. Washington, D.C.: Government Printing Office, 1940.

VAN HISE, C. R., *Conservation of natural resources in the United States*. New York: The Macmillan Company, 1910.

VOGT, W., *Road to survival*. New York: William Sloane Associates, 1948.

CHAPTER 4

Technology and Social Adjustment

Culture Change Through Technology: The Airplane

Search for a symbol. Certainly no one would deny that ours is a technological culture. One way of describing it is to say it is an aviation age. It is a singularly effective symbol of culture change through technology. Ours is a culture which must be and is becoming "air-conditioned." This change in the face and spirit of contemporary civilization, still in process and in prospect, may be seen from at least four points of view.[1]

An aerographic conception of the earth. In the first place, the aerial dimension of modern man is bringing him to a new—an aerographic—conception of his earth.

This new orientation to the earth can be seen in the new maps. A map is a picture of space. Historically, the map shows the widening knowledge of the globe which comes from exploration, pioneering, industrialization. Sometimes map-makers falsify the facts, consciously or unconsciously. "Attention is necessarily directed," General McClellan of Civil War fame once wrote, "to the erroneous maps in our possession." An Air Corps general can make the same comment about most of our present-day global maps. We became accustomed, in pre-air days, to flat Mercator projections. They showed us a hemispheric, two-dimensional picture, nicely patterned into isolated continental systems of land masses and bodies of water. Such a picture, always artificial, is obsolete and misleading now.

Antoine de Saint-Exupéry has well said: "The airplane has unveiled for us the true face of the earth."[2] In pre-aviation days, bounded by land and water, the distortions of a Mercator map

---

[1] Adapted by permission of the editor from Paul Meadows, "Aerial dimension," *The Technology Review*, 50 (January, 1949): 154 ff.

[2] Antoine de Saint-Exupéry, *Wind, sand, and stars* (New York: Reynal and Hitchcock, 1939). Quoted by permission of Harcourt, Brace and Company.

were rather unimportant. Aeronautically, however, a new global picture has become imperative. For example, a map which focuses on the North Pole and arranges land and water systems around that center—polar rather than Mercator projection—is of revolutionary value to air-minded people. It not only lays out new routes of world travel—the Great Circle route of Northwest Airlines, for instance—but it reveals a new earth.

A monospheric map corresponds with aerial reality. The aerial dimension must deal in time-distance advantages—the only kind it has over surface transport—and these come from adherence to the rule of the shortest distance between two points. It may be some time before northward flights across the top of the globe are economically feasible on a mass scale, but such flights bespeak the logic of the air. The time-shrinkage of the earth—no point more than fifty hours away, we are told—is more than a by-product of the airplane: it is literally the geographical revolution which William A. Burden once said is contained within the airplane itself.[3]

Aerial travel has revealed to us not only a new earth but a new heaven. We have come to understand that the atmosphere has a topography of its own: the survey of the "surfaces" of the air, so to speak, has become a task no less dramatic, and far more daring probably, than has been the study of the land or the sea.[4] "Everything is queer in the upper reaches," comments Saint-Exupéry. Stratosphere flight, supersonic aviation, global weather—these problems call for skills at least as learned, planning at least as comprehensive, teamwork at least as extensive, and heroism at least as bold as reported in the annals of land and sea explorations. Better still, the work has just begun.

"Aviation," according to Charles Hurd, journalist and aviation specialist, "is recasting our maps, rewriting our geographies, and upsetting our sense of direction."[5] His reference is not merely to the fact that aviators are, like the cowboys of the 'seventies and 'eighties along the Chisholm Trail, pointing northward. He refers rather to the fact that, unlike surface transport, aerial travel has no absolutely necessary discontinuities. The continuities of the air come only in part from the absence of aerial

[3] W. A. Burden, "American air transport faces north," in H. W. Weigert, and V. Stefansson, eds., Compass of the world (New York: The Macmillan Company, 1944), p. 137 ff.

[4] Few people have sensed this fact so well as the late French airman-writer Antoine de Saint-Exupéry, op. cit., to whom frequent reference is made in these pages.

[5] Charles Hurd, "World airways," in Weigert and Stefansson, op. cit., p. 109.

barriers; they arise also from the fact that, as British geographer James Fairgrieve has pointed out,[6] the northern lands, grouped around the Pole, along the Great Circle route and north of 30°, are fairly continuous. They are likewise the lands of greatest

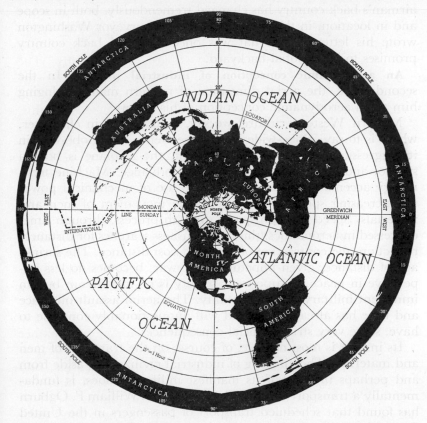

Figure 1. A Polar Projection Map. The weakness in this map is that distortion of geographical shapes increases in geometric ratio as one goes away from the North Pole.

human settlement and industrial development. An air map of the world does not divide the air into parts; the aerial component of modern civilization is one unit, boundaryless and universal.[7] The modern aviator, like Saint-Exupéry's friend Mermoz, who flew the trans-Andean air mail in the early days, is engaged in

[6] James Fairgrieve, "Geography and world power," in Weigert and Stefansson, *op. cit.*, p. 190 ff.

[7] *Cf.* Keith Hutchinson, *Freedom of the air* (Washington, D.C.: Public Affairs Pamphlet, #93, 1944).

throwing bridges across the world—the Sahara, the Andes, the Seven Seas.

In 1755 George Washington wrote back home: "I herewith send you a small map of the back country." The American airman's back country has changed tremendously, both in scope and in location, in the two centuries since surveyor Washington wrote his letter. And what was once a global back country promises to be a global backyard.

An aerodynamic conception of industrial society. In the second place, the aerial dimension of modern man is bringing him to an aerodynamic conception of his society.

Modern Western culture, we say, is industrial in character, which is to say, globe-wide in its dependence and globe-wise in its aggression. A global product itself, the airplane is both a symbol and an agent of technological advance. Machine technology accents speed and power: the use of mechanical power for increasing speed of movement. the movement of men and materials. Speed through space, through process, through time; expressed in aeronautics, this consciousness searches for distance-reduction, the contraction of time-and-cost distance. The shrinkage of distance, given impetus by the war, becomes no less imperative in peace. A supersonic society is no idle dream but an imminent military and civil reality. The aerial assault on space and time has already had, and will unquestionably continue to have, some very striking social consequences.

Its impact is most notable, of course, on the transport of men and materials. The air wing of industrial civilization, aside from and perhaps in spite of its manifest military values, is fundamentally a transport vehicle. Thus sociologist William F. Ogburn has found that scheduled transport of passengers in the United States showed an annual rate of growth in passenger-miles of 30 per cent for the 1930 decade.[8] He has estimated that by 1953 between six and eight million passenger-miles will be flown. He extrapolated air-cargo data and suggested that very probably fifteen to twenty times as much cargo would be flown in the first few years after the second World War as was carried in the prewar years. His forecast for international travel for the decade of the 'fifties sees from 650 thousand to a million passengers. Aerial transportation not only makes possible the opening-up of new markets in distant areas but stimulates, partly as a result

[8] *Cf.* W. F. Ogburn, *Social effects of aviation* (Boston: Houghton Mifflin Company, 1946), pp. 118–120.

of the new markets, business activity. It will undoubtedly, Ogburn holds, speed up already existing trends in marketing: special orders, specialty goods, direct selling from producer to retailer, creation of national markets, the quickening of business transactions.

The new dynamic embodied in aviation has certain inevitable effects on technological change. Enough evidence has been accumulated concerning the processes of technological innovation for predictions to be made intelligently. Modern industrialism not only builds on the foundation of past inventions in a given field but also promotes the transfer of a technology from one field to another. Concretely, aviation would have been altogether impossible without the internal combustion motor, but with the aid of the aerodynamics learned from the utilization of the gasoline engine, technologists have gone on to develop jet propulsion; an age of rocketry is without question in the offing.

In the same manner the aerial technologies have been put at the disposal of other technologies: war, mining, agriculture, forestry, conservation, and so on. Aerial surveying for mineral deposits, flying in supplies and flying ore out, transporting workers, these and many other uses will make the employment of aviation indispensable in the development of new mines and mining areas. The airplane has already proved its usefulness in dusting and spraying fruits, vegetables, trees; in sowing seeds, in mosquito and rust abatement; in soil surveys; in river-valley development work; in wild-life inventory and predatory control; in forest fire-fighting. Already airplanes have taken off the cream of land-borne and water-borne transportation: "sooner or later," as Charles Hurd has observed, "they will dip down into the milk."[9]

No less dynamic have been and will be the effects of aviation on certain human aspects of industrial civilization. The interchanges of cultural items through trade and the exchange of cultural ideas through travel can hardly be stopped, though they may be postponed by iron curtains dropped here and there on the globe. Industrial culture, like water, will seek its level, and in an aerial civilization it is a rising level of industrial art and aspiration. Death rates will go up from war and accidents, but they will be pulled down by air-transported medicines, food supplies, and knowledge. Population will continue to flow, as it

[9] Hurd, in Weigert and Stefansson, *op. cit.*

always has, along the lines of travel, and new settlements will be opened up along the air routes. The cultural dominance of the great cities will inescapably widen; indeed, it has already. New threats to public health from air-borne causes and new problems for medical research are emerging. The airplane is already competing with the automobile as a mode of recreation, and the spectator and participant public in competitive sports is yearly being enlarged. Sadly enough, aerially-mediated crime —smuggling, disposal of stolen goods and of criminals—must be debited against the airplane.

The hastening tempo of existence in the air age is both an index and the agency of the evolution of industrial civilization. Sociologists are fond of saying that a society is coterminous with the limits and speed of communication. An aerodynamic society is beginning to discover, how literally, perhaps also how magnificently, true that statement is!

An aeropolitical conception of the state.   In the third place, the aerial dimension of modern industrialism is leading to a transformation in the contemporary thinking about the state—to an aeropolitical conception of the state.

Sociologist Hornell Hart has worked out an interesting correlation between the speed of transportation and the size of empire: the faster the transport, the larger the empire. Whether this association is or will continue to be true, it should be quickly apparent that in the field of political behavior the airplane has magnified the discontinuities of the earth's surface, the land and water boundaries of the nation-state. The aerial maps may not show them, but there are in point of fact all kinds of boundary lines staking off the sky's dimensions. Air routes are not merely commercial; they are perhaps even more significantly political and military.

In 1902 Paul Fauchille, French jurist, remarked: "The air is free. The states have no authority over it in time of peace or in time of war other than that which is necessary for their own preservation."[10] However, the First World War made another thesis more urgent, and in the Paris Convention of 1919 the first clause read: "The high contracting parties recognize that every power has complete and exclusive sovereignty over the air space above its territory." Freedom of air passage and the establishment of what was then called "international airways" was made con-

---

[10] Quoted by Hutchinson, *op. cit.*

ditional upon the consent of "the states flown over." That this work still involved tremendous problems to be solved—in spite of the International Civil Aviation Conference which met in Chicago in November, 1944 with 54 nations attending and despite the "agreements" of that conference—may be seen in the fact that a world system of airways is not yet and perhaps will not for a long time be an actuality.

The difficulty is only partly economic. General Baranov, then head of the Soviet Air Force, took occasion in 1927 to explain that the development of a network of airlines "is one of the most powerful methods in the struggle for new markets."[11] The struggle for airways is highly competitive, company against company, nation against nation. But the economic subtly shades into the political, and "the freedom of the air" becomes a weapon of the political state no less than did "the freedom of the sea."

The influence of Admiral Mahan on our thinking about the importance of the air is very marked.[12] Mahan's doctrine of sea power posited a "fleet-in-being," backed by a merchant marine and a sea-faring people. Similarly, the contemporary doctrine of air power, aside from the verbal battles over sea versus air power, builds on the Mahan pattern. The modern political state, if capable of a military and industrial establishment of any size, cannot avoid seeing the advantages in a commercial air-transport system able to back the air fleet if and as it may be aided and abetted by an air-faring people.

In many ways so modern a thing as German geographer Haushofer's "geopolitics" has already been rendered *passé* by the plane. His geographical and political creed, more or less followed by the Nazis and being increasingly adopted by many Americans, was thoroughly dominated by what Eugene Staley has so appropriately called "the myth of the continents."[13] The flat Mercator maps are mainly responsible for Haushofer's belief in the continental system of isolated land masses neatly arranged in a descending order of importance around the Asiatic "heartland." Haushofer to the contrary, today in the aerial age he who controls the polar approaches controls the world, and that fact brings spaces all over the great globe itself into vulnerable relationship with each other. The whole concept of buffer states

[11] Quoted by Burnet Hershey, *Skyways of tomorrow* (Headline Series, #47, 1944), p. 42.

[12] *Cf.* John Stuart, *Wings over America* (Washington, D.C.: Public Affairs Pamphlet, #114, 1946).

[13] *Cf.* Weigert and Stefansson, *op. cit.*, p. 89 ff.

needs a polar reorientation. Likewise, the myth of hemispheric defense must sooner or later come to terms with the highly lethal strategies of monospheric offense *via* air.

General Arnold, reviewing American aviation history, put the aeropolitical conception of the nation-state on a time scale which, unfortunately, too few people really understand. "In this spectacular conquest of time we have already on the horizon the techniques which, when realized, will cause us to measure distances in terms, not of miles, but minutes."[14] The power and the vulnerability of the modern state which this fact implies, particularly in an age which must be called atomic as well as aerial, can only give mature minds a painful pause.

An aeropsychic conception of human living.   Finally, the social impact of aviation technology is succeeding in crystallizing, perhaps none too perfectly, an aeropsychic conception of the human being and his way of living. It is impossible to catalogue all the ways in which the airplane is entering, or is likely to enter, into the symbolism and themes of air-minded people, but a few examples may perhaps illustrate the variety.

The airplane is the symbol of, and a challenge to, an outward projection of the human personality. The urge to travel, to see foreign lands and places, is intensified by aviation at the same time that flying makes easier such fulfillment. This outward-bound psyche is sometimes regarded as a mode of escape; possibly it is. "You feel," wrote Anne Morrow Lindbergh, "no longer rooted to the earth."[15] This Daedalus-Phaëthon mythology, now a technological reality, seems nevertheless not to have escaped the Greek fate. The escaping pair of wings is still earth-bound.

There are other psychocultural effects. Thus, the airplane, new instrument of space conquest, becomes a domicile for the human being. In his *Flight to Arras*, Saint-Exupéry echoes this feeling: "All that tangle of tube and wiring has become a circulating network. I am an organism integrated into the plane. . . . The plane is my wet-nurse. . . . Suckled by the plane, I feel a sort of filial affection for it."[16] A note of sadness and tragedy often enters into the human spirit in flight; the sadness and tragedy of war. The bomb bursts at Los Alamos, Hiroshima,

[14] *Air Force*, 29 (November, 1946): 13.

[15] Anne Lindbergh, *Listen! the wind* (New York: Harcourt, Brace and Company, 1938). Quoted by permission.

[16] Saint-Exupéry, *Flight to Arras* (New York: Reynal and Hitchcock, 1942). Quoted by permission.

Nagasaki, and Bikini have added unhappy overtones to this motif.[17]

Some writers find hope in a gradual assimilation of the airplane as a machine. John Masefield, in a letter describing his first flight, wrote, "I was glad to have done it—though I felt that it belongs to this generation, and not to mine." There is much evidence, both from wartime pilots and peacetime airmen, that an air-conditioned generation is coming into its own. Thus, Saint-Exupéry, perhaps the most articulate of them, put it this way: "Contrary to the vulgar notion, it is thanks to the metal, and by virtue of it, that the pilot rediscovers nature." He added: "The machine, which at first blush seems a means of isolating man from the great problems of nature, eventually plunges him more deeply into them." Yet he confessed that the emotional and intellectual life of modern man will take time. "We shall have to age somewhat before we are able to write the folksongs of a new epoch."[18] Meantime, there is for our guidance that curse pronounced by Selden Rodman's Inventor in his invocation to the Earth-Mother, a curse upon all who will use wings for "any ambition higher than bold design and art to freely cruise."[19]

Technology and Social Change

When mechanization takes command. The preceding review of cultural change through aviation technology illustrates not only the social effects of technological innovations but even more pointedly what happens in a society when mechanization takes command. The rule of modern industrial culture is one of mechanization. For mechanization not only transforms the surfaces of contemporary living but stirs its depths. Modern people have encountered and have deliberately sought to encounter the machine in every area of their existence.[20] Mechanization involves both the application of power to an end tool and the adaptation of human institutions and the human environment to a machine economy.[21]

[17] *Cf.* Harrison Brown, *Must destruction be our destiny?* (New York: Simon and Schuster, 1946).

[18] Saint-Exupéry, *Wind, sand, and stars, op. cit.*

[19] Selden Rodman, *Airmen* (New York: Random House, 1941).

[20] *Cf.* Siegfried Giedion, *Mechanization takes command* (New York: Oxford University Press, 1948). Certain sections of this discussion of "Technology and Social Change" appeared in *The Technology Review*, 53 (January, 1951): 150 ff., and are reprinted by permission.

[21] *Cf.* A. J. Todd, *Industry and society* (New York: Henry Holt and Company,

Neglecting for the moment the scientific-technical base for this drive toward mechanization, we might examine the social sources of the mechanization of the means of human satisfaction. In other words, what do people anticipate from the increased utilization of machine technology? In general, the answer is social progress. The measure of the good life is popularly regarded as a mechanical one: the establishment of controls over the human environments. The motives for mechanization, then, can be found in the values deriving from the use of the machine:

1. Higher plane of living.
2. Lengthened life span.
3. Decrease in the hours of labor.
4. Increase in the total demand for labor.
5. Gradual disappearance of class system based upon land ownership and patents of nobility.
6. Expansion of consumer choice.
7. Technical mastery of the environment.
8. Encouragement of co-operative thought and action.
9. Esthetic excellence of machine forms.
10. Transposition of the realm of order from absolute political institutions to a new type of order in which power, economy, objectivity play a more decisive part.
11. Decline of a supernatural frame of reference.
12. Use of machines and machine products for an increasingly varied ego expression and sense of power.
13. Stimulation of research, exploration, discovery, travel, and invention.
14. Shrinkage of space and time distances, resulting in a greater human interaction.
15. A social philosophy—instrumentalism—which proposes to exploit the logic and methods of science-technology in the solution of all types of human problems.[22]

To be sure, the widening exploitation of machine technology is not likely to be regarded universally as an unmixed blessing. The report of the Subcommittee on Technology to the National Resources Committee listed certain major "findings" in their survey of technological trends:

1. The large number of inventions made every year shows no tendency to diminish. On the contrary, the trend is toward further increases.

1933); Lewis Mumford, *Technics and civilization* (New York: Harcourt, Brace and Company, 1935).
[22] Based on Todd, *op. cit.*, Ch. 1.

2. Although technological unemployment is one of the most tragic effects of the sudden adoption of many new inventions (which may be likened to an immigration of iron men), inventions create jobs as well as take them away.

3. No satisfactory measures of the volume of technological unemployment have as yet been developed, but at least part of the price for this constant change in the employment requirements of industry is paid by labor since many of the new machines and techniques result in "occupational obsolescence."

4. The question whether there will be a larger amount of unemployment during the next period of business prosperity rests only in part on the introduction of new inventions and more efficient industrial techniques. The other important elements are changes in the composition of the country's production . . . the growth of population, changes in the demands for goods and services, shifts in markets, migrations of industry, hiring-age policies of industries. . . .

5. Aside from jobs, subtracted or added, new inventions affect all the great social institutions: family, church, local community, state, and industry.

6. A large and increasing part of industrial development and of the correlated technological advances arises out of science and research.

7. Advance of many aspects of industry and the correlated technologies is dependent upon scientific research and discovery.

8. Though the influence of invention may be so great as to be immeasurable, as in the case of gunpowder or the printing press, there is usually opportunity to anticipate its impact upon science since it never comes instantaneously without signals.

9. While a serious obstacle to considering invention in planning is lack of precise knowledge, this is not irremediable nor the most difficult fact to overcome. Other equally serious obstacles are inertia of peoples, prejudices, lack of unity of purpose, and the difficulties of concerted action.

10. Among the resistances to the adoption of new inventions and hence to the spread of the advantage of technological progress there is specially noted those resistances arising in connection with a scrapping equipment in order to install the new.

11. The time lag between the first development and the full use of an invention is often a period of grave social and economic maladjustment. . . .[23]

Clearly, then, an age of technological change may expect, whatever else it contains by way of fulfillment or frustration,

[23] National Resources Committee, *Technological trends and national policy* (Washington, D.C.: Government Printing Office, 1937), p. ix.

technological change to be in a real sense a social process itself. Technology is fundamentally a new, a modern methodology of social adjustment. The fundamental equilibrium which may be established at any one time in a given system of techniques is precarious. Innovations seem to start chain-reactions of change in many seemingly unrelated areas of social living. What problems, therefore, arise from the functional interdependence of technological inventions?

The problem of interrelated change. Students of modern technology are deeply impressed by the manner in which inventions in one area of modern life are linked with inventions in other areas. This technological symbiosis or mutual dependence is indeed the very ground for the general concern with the problem of technology and social adjustment, for technology is not merely itself a mode of social adjustment but, even more significantly, it is a cause of new social adjustment. In a most thorough study of agricultural technology and social change an interbureau committee of the federal government suggests this very point as follows: "Scientific advances in agriculture constantly release labor at a time when employment opportunities are no longer open in urban industry. . . . Lacking other alternatives, the surplus hired men of agriculture swell the ranks of migratory farm workers, apply for direct relief, or find some shelter in subsistence farming, too often in the poorer localities."[24]

Ogburn and Nimkoff have suggested a classification of sequences and concomitant variations of technology and society which summarizes these problems of interrelated change.[25]

A. A major material invention may have multiple effects: *e.g.*, radio exerting influences on recreation and entertainment, transportation, education, religion, business and industry, government, and so forth.

B. A single invention may have a long series of consequences flowing from it: *e.g.*, the cotton gin resulting in new forms of labor, clothing, industries, styles, class relationships, and so forth.

C. A given social condition may represent the net result of a number of converging inventions: *e.g.*, the declining birth rate linked to the factory system, the automobile, changing occupational patterns, smaller homes, social mobility, and so forth.

[24] U. S. Department of Agriculture, *Technology on the land* (Washington, D.C.: Government Printing Office, 1940), p. 5.

[25] W. F. Ogburn, and M. F. Nimkoff, *Sociology* (Boston: Houghton Mifflin Company, 1940), Ch. 24.

D. A cluster of inventions may have far-reaching derivative effects: *e.g.*, atomic-energy conversion and medicine, power, international organization, military strategy and defense, and so forth.

E. Social inventions may require physical inventions for their facilitation or control: national defense and military communication, aviation, organizational innovations.

Interrelated change and cultural growth. A fruitful way to describe this fact of an interrelated series of changes is to formulate the principles of culture growth.

In the first place, interrelated change is accumulative in character. A physical invention or group practice introduced into the culture requires additional inventions for its integration or incorporation into the life of society: the case of the automobile necessitating legislation, roads, governmental agencies, safety education, and so forth.

In the second place, interrelated change is elaborative in character. A new invention must be improved; it must be made more dependable, flexible, sensitive to control; it is called on to perform additional tasks; it may be thrust into novel situations requiring new technics and technical skills. Aviation is a first-rate example.

In the third place, interrelated change is accelerative in character. Ogburn and Nimkoff have called this tendency "the exponential principle."[26] As the stock of existing technology and technics enlarges, the rate of discovery and invention becomes faster and faster. The pattern of increase is like that of the compound-interest curve. Again, interrelated change is irregular in character. Growth in one area of social life tends to be more rapid than in other areas. The differential rate of borrowing, the fact that inventions are not of equal significance, the blocking of the development of one area of society by the vested interests of another, these are a few of the many factors which create disuniformity and strains in culture change.

Finally, interrelated change is integrative in character, though not necessarily so. The elaboration of a given culture complex— *e.g.*, transportation—may create a bulge in the over-all culture pattern of a given society, thereby causing enormous social disorganizations. The latter, however, become challenges calling for response, in the Toynbee phraseology; new devices must be found which will fit the fast-changing complex into the total

[26] *Ibid.*, p. 791.

pattern of the culture. This work of integration in a machine society can never be complete. It may, indeed, be a perennial source of dissatisfaction. Yet it is likewise the perennial necessity which mothers invention. An inventive civilization survives by its inventive wit.

Technological Change and Social Policy

Social policy is a self-conscious search for a more adequate social adjustment. It is, in other words, a search for new physical or social inventions. In a changing culture it is an inevitable and ceaseless search. In American society it has several major foci of interest.

The problem of anticipated change. In the first place, a changing culture needs some way of anticipating the pattern and the rate of change. This need is dictated by the principles of culture growth outlined in the preceding paragraphs.

Unhappily, as Gilfillan has shown, the record of successes in the field of prediction is slight and not reassuring.[27] Most certainly for dependable generalizations we must look forward to an intensified scholarly research in the future. However, the *predictability* of social change is based upon the following experiences. (1) Trend lines can be established and extrapolated, as the statisticians say. Any single invention is "a multitudinous collection of little ones."[28] (2) Embryonic inventions have a slow curve of growth; mature inventions a fast curve. (3) Inventions have causes; cause-and-effect relationships can be formulated; invariant relationships have predictive value. Known bodies of fact and law, assumed future events (*e.g.*, the onset of television), pressing social or economic or political need form the causal bases for prediction. (4) The presence of experimental curiosity and analytical summaries of failures and successes of previous predictions establish grounds for anticipating predictive formulas. (5) Finally, time will often elapse before the full effects of an innovation have matured. This period provides an excellent opportunity to study and forecast other inventions which the present innovation requires or will make necessary.

The problem of anticipated change is aggravated not merely by the lack of scholarly studies, but even more by the presence of

[27] National Resources Committee, *Technological trends . . . , op. cit.,* Section II, p. 15 ff.
[28] Gilfillan in *Technological trends . . . , op. cit.,* p. 18.

certain harmful social attitudes. Sentimental optimism, wishful thinking, the popular resistances offered by tastes, customs, and laws, preoccupation with material profit, and a total unconcern with social consequences, all these factors have delayed systematic efforts to solve the problems of anticipated inventions and their usually unanticipated consequences.

The problem of resistance to proposed change. In the second place, social policy must reckon with the many ways in which individuals and groups, even the total culture, inhibit the process of change.

Paradoxically, these resistances often spring from a social philosophy about change itself. Hornell Hart in a comprehensive catalogue has outlined these failures and blockages in social attitudes as follows:[29]

A. *Self-satisfied Attitudes:*

1. Fatalistic optimism: "Progress is inevitable; all we need to do is to accept and use it."
2. Aggressive culture conceit: "Progress has been and will be the peculiar achievement of our people, or race, or our nation; we should spread our culture over the rest of the world."
3. Conservative exploitation of past progress: "We have arrived; the progress of the past has brought us to the present ideal state of affairs, which may now be used and enjoyed."
4. Proud opposition to changes from past achievement: "Let well enough alone; whoever attempts to modify the wonderful institutions devised by our forefathers should be repressed or punished."
5. Changelessness: "What has been good enough for all my ancestors is good enough for me; let it remain as it always has been."

B. *Pessimistic Attitudes:*

1. Sentimental pessimism: "The good old days are never to return; let us mourn them."
2. Fatalistic despair: "Inevitable disaster impends; get what you can out of life before the crash comes."
3. Cyclicalism: "Civilizations rise and fall in waves or cycles. At present we are past the crest of a culture wave and are on the decline into a new dark age. All we can do is to recognize this fact and adjust ourselves to it."

[29] Hornell Hart, *Technique of social progress* (New York: Henry Holt and Company, 1931), pp. 4–5. Reprinted by permission.

C. *Reconstructive Attitudes:*
  1. Repristination: "Let us go back to the old days and restore the glory that is departed."
  2. Panacean alarmism: "Unless we act quickly civilization will perish; come and help put into operation the one essential remedy."
  3. Meliorism: "Progress is the fundamental trend, but it is subject to reverses . . . these reverses may be mitigated and even eliminated. . . ."
D. *Agnostic Attitudes:*
  1. Anthropological positivism: "Progress and regress are subjective, and therefore unscientific terms."

The possibility that this catalogue is not an armchair listing of hypothetical cases is suggested by a careful study of resistances to several historic social innovations. Theodore K. Noss investigated the opposition to seven social changes, all accepted eventually by the American people: parcel post, postal savings, rural free delivery, bobbed hair, woman suffrage, simplified spelling, hookworm treatment.

Noss concluded: "As the change cannot be adopted until society agrees to accept it, enough time intervenes between the introduction and social acceptance for organized resistance to appear. The first to oppose the innovation are those who conceive of it as interfering with their interests in society. Under this threat special-interest groups become more self-conscious. The members of the group turn to each other for consultation and support. This interaction serves to consolidate the group internally and partially to isolate it from the larger society, but at the same time the members imaginatively identify themselves with society, especially with the social good. Typically, they exaggerate the importance of their group function and may call themselves the cornerstone of the social welfare. As they do not desire the social innovation themselves, they may believe that the public does not desire it. . . . If they dislike the proponents, they may castigate them as public enemies. . . . They may predict that social destruction will be the end result of the adoption of the innovation. As a result of their interaction, they develop what they call the 'truth' of the situation which they endeavor to promulgate with what means they have at their command."[30]

[30] T. K. Noss, "Rise of active resistance to social innovation," *Bulletin of the Society Social Research* (December, 1949): 9.

In a similar review of the resistance to technological innovations in several industrial fields—transportation, communication, power, metals, textiles, agricultural machinery, building—B. J. Stern reported to the National Resources Committee the following finding. "From the results of this study it is apparent that the psychological factors of habit, fear, desire for personality equilibrium and status, and the tendency of groups to coerce their members to conformity are latent predisposing factors toward resistance to change."[31]

The problem of free basic research. In the third place, social policy must reckon with the need for maintaining free but well-financed programs of basic research (or so-called "pure science"). Change in a technological culture is dependent on the elaboration of scientific discovery and its subsequent linkage with technical application.

How important this problem is may be suggested by two illustrations. The first is the development of atomic-energy research. Some scientists feel strongly that with the army and the F.B.I. in virtual if not actual control of atomic-energy research, uninhibited international research and communication, except in a very limited way, have been throttled in recent years. Says Dr. Condon of the National Bureau of Standards: "Prominent scientists are denied the privilege of traveling abroad. Physicists are not allowed to discuss certain areas of the science with each other, even as between individuals working on closely related phases of the same subject. They can only communicate through official channels, involving censorship of their communications by Army officers without knowledge and so without competence."[32]

This situation is usually defended in terms of security. But the motivations which lead to a dominated and fettered science involve far more than security risks. An instructive example is the story of German science during the days of the Nazi regime. As detailed by Samuel Goudsmit, the Gestapo-ridden science of Hitlerite Germany fell prey to several easily imitated mistakes. These included (1) complacency, (2) deterioration of interest in pure science, (3) regimentation in the administrative controls over research, (4) the hero worship of individual scientists, (5) the stifling secrecy of national security measures, (6) the failure

---

[31] National Resources Committee, *Technological trends* . . . , *op. cit.*, p. 59.
[32] For a fuller discussion, *cf.* Paul Meadows, "Leagues of frightened men," *Prairie Schooner* (Summer, 1949): 75 ff.

to maintain open and widely used channels of communication among scientists themselves, (7) fanatical nationalism, and (8) doctrinaire dogmatism.[33]

Scientific research is a type of industrial work. To put the problem of free basic research in its simplest form, social policy must find and preserve ways of protecting and stimulating the workmen, of providing them with tools, of securing the conditions of their work, and of encouraging organized attacks on meaningful problems.[34]

The problem of monopoly of applied science. In the fourth place, social policy must reckon with the widespread practice of withholding basic discoveries from public use or of releasing them at prohibitive costs: the problem of "vested interests."

An interesting case in point is the housing industry. Mr. Thurman Arnold, then Assistant Attorney General, testifying before the Temporary National Economic Committee in July, 1939, called attention to five types of building-trade restraints:[35]

> There is, in the first place, the price-fixing by producers of building materials. This device takes such forms as patent-holder monopolies, zone pricing systems, the cutting-off of raw materials supply, and harassing lawsuits. There are, in the second place, the restrictive practices of the distributors, such as the fixed mark-up between the prices they pay the manufacturers and the price at which they sell. A third type of restraint is practiced by the contractors: through the use of bid depositories, of contract-estimating bureaus, and of closed markets from which they exclude outside contractors. A fourth type of restrictive practice is found among the building-trades unions: the refusal to supply labor where the contractors' ring wishes labor withheld or the refusal to permit the use of new materials or new methods. Finally, legislative bodies likewise engage in restriction through such devices as the licensing of contractors, the rating of bidders according to some purposely vague standards, and municipal ordinances designed to curb competition.

[33] Cf. Samuel A. Goudsmit, Alsos (New York: Henry Schuman, 1947).

[34] Cf. Paul Meadows, "The industrialization of social research," trans/formation, I: 2 (1951): 110–114.

[35] Thurman Arnold, "Restraints of the building trades," Verbatim Record of the Temporary National Economic Committee (Washington, D.C.: Government Printing Office, 1939), pp. 458–461. The literature on cartels brings out a considerable body of illustrations of monopolistic or restrictive use of empirical science. Cf. G. W. Stocking and M. W. Watkins, Cartels in action (New York: Twentieth Century Fund, 1946); Stocking and Watkins, Cartels or competition? (New York: Twentieth Century Fund, 1948); W. Berge, Cartels: Challenge to a free world (Washington, D.C.: Public Affairs Press, 1944).

These restraints, according to Arnold, have had certain very undesirable economic effects.

> 1. They have kept prices from dropping when purchasing power dropped; and when purchasing power rose, they have raised prices still faster. 2. They have harassed, boycotted, and eliminated competitors able and willing to reduce prices. 3. They have kept the industry horizontally split into groups whose separate contributions to the final product are so limited that no single group can get increased volume by lowering prices. Thus they have created a situation where the incentive of each group is to raise prices in order to obtain for itself the greatest share of any new money available for housing. 4. They have handicapped the use of prefabricated materials and thwarted the development of methods of mass production in the industry. 5. Finally, and most important, these practices have prevented experiment in housing design, materials, and methods of construction.

Housing is merely one of a multitude of examples of the manner in which advancements in the field of applied science, or technology, have been hamstrung by restrictive practices. It is a familiar story in American history. Thus, in 1912 before the Oldfield Hearings on Patents, Louis Brandeis, later Supreme Court Justice, declared:[36]

> These great organizations are constitutionally unprogressive. They will not take on the big thing. Take the gas companies of this country; they would not touch the electric light. Take the telegraph company, the Western Union Telegraph Co., they would not touch the telephone. Neither the telephone nor the telegraph company would touch wireless telegraphy. Now, you would have supposed that in each one of these instances those concerns if they had the ordinary progressiveness of Americans would have said at once, 'We ought to go forward and develop this.' But they turned it down, and it was necessary in each one of those instances, in order to promote those great and revolutionizing inventions, to take entirely new capital.

A similar and more recent testimony is offered by the Inventors' Guild.[37]

> It is a well-known fact that modern trade combinations tend strongly toward constancy of processes and products, and by their nature are opposed to new processes and new products originated by independent inventors, and hence tend to restrain competition

[36] Quoted by Stern in *Technological trends . . .* , *op. cit.*, p. 63.
[37] Quoted by Stern, *ibid.*

in the development and sale of patents and patent rights; and consequently to discourage independent inventive thought.

Social policy—an unfinished business. Finally, it is wise to remember that social policy with respect to proposed or anticipated innovations and their consequences is necessarily an unfinished—even unfinishable—business.

On this matter the recommendations of the Subcommittee on Technology of the National Resources Committee are not only enlightening but even more relevant now than when they were formulated in the middle 1930's.[38]

1. The reports herewith presented reveal the imminence of a few very important inventions that may soon be widely used with resultant social influences of significance. Since these inventions may deeply affect planning it is recommended that a series of studies be undertaken by the planning boards, with the aid of such natural and social scientists as may be needed, on the following inventions. . . .

2. A special case of the influences of invention is technological unemployment. It is recommended that a joint committee be formed from the Department of Labor, the Department of Commerce, the Department of Agriculture, Bureau of Mines, Interstate Commerce Commission, Social Security Board, and the Works Progress Administration with such other co-operation as may be needed, for the purposes of keeping abreast with technological developments and ascertaining and noting the occupations and industries which are likely to result in unemployment. It is recommended that such information be made available through the appropriate departments to the industry and labor likely to be affected.

3. In view of the findings regarding the importance of technology and applied science, it is recommended that the federal government develop and more specifically that there be set up in the respective departments science committees with the definite function of investigating and reporting at regular periods on the progress and trends of science and invention and the possible and economic effects flowing therefrom as they affect the work of the departments and of the agencies to whom they render service. . . .

4. Since the patent laws have considerable influence on the rate of technological progress, it is recommended that the whole system be reviewed by a group of social scientists and economists. This review, unlike others dealing with specific reforms, technical

[38] *Ibid.*, p. XI.

operations, scientific aspects, or ethical implications should be concerned with the articulation of the patenting process with the fundamental processes of human progress and the types of economic systems. From such basic relationships the better adaptation of the system to changing conditions can be worked out in the necessary detail.

5. It is recommended that the Science Committee of the National Resources Committee, with the co-operation of other scientists that may be needed, make an investigation of the adequacy of the reporting of inventions and of discoveries in applied science and advise on the feasibility (a) of more balanced coverage, (b) of selecting those more socially significant, and (c) of assembling of such data in some central location or locations.

6. The most important general conclusion to be drawn from these studies is the continuing growth of the already high and rapidly developing technology in the social structure of the Nation, and hence the hazard of any planning that does not take this fact into consideration. This pervasive interrelationship so clearly manifest throughout the pages of this report points to one great need, namely, a permanent over-all planning board. Such a board is needed to give breadth of consideration to the variety of factors which affect specific plans.

It is a sad irony that the very agency which made these highly significant recommendations has long since been chopped off by a Congressional economy ax!

The important implication of these recommendations is their emphasis on the totality of factors involved in the processes of technological change. A recent study of this problem reached the same conclusion.[39]

> Problems of technological change have been treated as part of the labor problem, the land problem, the cycle problem, or the problem of social disorganization. Changing patterns of labor and utilization were treated as such with little attempt to isolate the shifting state of the arts and segregate its effects or devise policies to treat it apart from other causes of difficulties. . . . The total examination of the field of technological change will require a team approach. Only by combining the work of economists, sociologists, psychologists, political scientists, and other specialists can the total cost and total effect of any given change be measured. . . . After the efforts of these specialists are combined, we will have the relevant data for the kinds of decisions that are attempted in modern social organizations. To combine these

[39] Yale Brozen, "Social implications of technological change," Social Science Research Council Items, 3 (September, 1949): 33–34.

efforts, however, will require the invention of a structure for merging them.

Technology and Social Conflict

One of the most urgent problems in the appraisal of modern technology is its impact on human conflict. Has it measurably increased or decreased the probability of conflict in social relations? What are the potentialities for social control—in other words, for social policy? This issue, it might be pointed out, is a general problem, existing long before the advent of the atomic bomb, though unquestionably the latter has aggravated the situation.

Conflict as a social process.[40]   Conflict is a process: that is to say, it is a series of stages leading from one condition to another. These stages can be typically denoted and expected. They emerge in any and all the occasions of human interaction. Industrial technology has radically changed the character of each of these steps in the conflict process. Human behavior from contact to conflict is typically somewhat as follows:

1. Contact;
2. Emergence of differences;
3. Awareness of differences;
4. Belief in the exclusive (irreconcilable) nature of differences;
5. Decision to eliminate, or coerce, the opposing differences (by this time called "interests");
6. Action calculated to realize this definition of the situation; and
7. Establishment of equilibrium.

Technology has entered into every one of these stages, hastening the transition from one to another.

The collapse of isolation.   Industrial technology, with its progressive development, has broken down the walls of human isolation. Immobility—induced by the barriers of space, time, fear of the unknown, dread of the stranger, love for the past or the next world—has yielded to the technicways of mechanical invention in communication and transportation. "Men on the move" are the dramatic symbols of an age which has given wings to feet and speech.

This breaking-up of vicinal isolation, together with the mental mobility which it created, has sent men on great voyages of discovery of their world. The 16th century discovered "the environ-

[40] Adapted by permission of the editor from Paul Meadows, "Technological change and human conflict," *The Personalist* (Autumn, 1948): 396 ff.

ment." The 17th and 18th centuries explored it. The 19th century harnessed it. The 20th century promises to exploit it. Like a spring thaw, this release of the human mind has outpoured in many directions. For example, human migrations have taken place on a hitherto unparalleled scale. Some 60 million Europeans left their homes, beginning in the first part of the 19th century, to settle new lands.[41] Again, some of this emancipation has been expressed in broad and fast-flowing channels of communication. Here the rates have been amazingly accelerated.[42] Thus, printing: the 15th century could boast of some 30 thousand printed items; the 20th century can point to over 17 million separate volumes. Radiocasting had 60 thousand outlets near the close of World War I. Before the start of World War II, radio communication had over 21 million outlets in the United States alone. About 58 thousand movie theaters carry the film productions of the world, almost two thirds of which are shipped from Hollywood.

Technology has lent expressiveness to the human spirit. It has overcome the time factor in human contacts. It has achieved incredible swiftness through space. It has become the obedient servant of the masses, diffusing the intentions and contentions of human minds to all men. The frequency and the variety of human contacts responded to the tempo set by technological culture. Who can say that this process will cease, or even slow down?

Technology and social differentiation. Socially, human differences have not been diminished by increased contact but have been multiplied. It is true, of course, that the basic types of human interests and functions are fairly stable. Men have always and everywhere been religious, economic, familial, political, esthetic, and so on. But within these areas of human expression they have manifested tremendous variability. "Cultural variation" is the bargain which the anthropologist drives when we exchange questions and answers within this field. Human experience is unique. No amount of cultural ritualization can eliminate the singularity of a man's interaction with his environment, for the human organism is selective, and so is his habitat.

Modern technology is an impressive monument to this human uniqueness. The craftsmanship of the human species, unap-

[41] *Cf.* Donald Taft, *Human migration* (New York: Ronald Press, 1936), Ch. 3.
[42] See the factual data assembled by J. W. Albig, *Public opinion* (New York: McGraw-Hill Book Company, 1939).

proached by even the most intelligent of man's infra-human "poor relations," is the very genius of his cultural prowess. The whole, wide, rich range of culture bears witness to this "instinct of craftsmanship." We call the human craftsman by such names as discoverer, inventor, technological expert, technician, sage, technological adviser, artist; the words change, the song does not.

All the talk of human standardization as a result of machine technology must be qualified by this fact. For machine technology has incredibly multiplied the specialization of human functions, the division of labor, the variability of interests, the extent of differences. "The machine," as we like to simplify matters, has broken the mold of uniformizing human traditions and "neophobia," and it has put the human species on a thousand revolving stages to enact its dramatic rendezvous with meaningfulness. The world is a factory; but it is also a playhouse, a hospital, a laboratory, a church, a library, a school, a home, for specialization within *mechanical* technology has also made possible specialization in all the other cultural technologies.

Moreover, the technological differentiation of human interests and functions has pulled us out in many directions. It has shifted us from localism to cosmopolitanism; from the sacred to the secular; from the provincial to the national and international; from locality and blood groups to special-interest groups; from primary society to secondary or derivative society.[43] Man has become under industrialism a highly multivalued creature. Only the destruction of his technological culture can change the involvements of that fact.

Technology and ideological irreconcilability. But in all this shuffling and reshuffling of the cards of human destinies, the stakes have become higher and higher, and deliberately so. Men, made different, act differently. They become aware of their differences, justify them, sentimentalize them, strive to make them irreconcilable and immortal. They come to see their differences through the glasses of exclusion. They set their sights on the far hills of exclusive realization.

This shift in human thinking is the work of ideology and the ideologists.[44] Just as the provincial conflicts of the medieval and

---

[43] *Cf.* Paul Meadows, "Dictatorship and the derivative society," *Free America* (Spring-Summer, 1946): 7 ff.

[44] *Cf.* Karl Mannheim, *Ideology and utopia* (London: Paul, Trench, Trubner, 1936).

early modern period had their mercenaries, so the world conflicts of our own day have their paid hirelings. Janizaries have
been replaced by ideologists, and primary fealties by secondary
apologetics. Fragmented world-views become supported by
segmental rationalizations, and the towering spires of passionate
imperialisms are strengthened and adorned by the flying but-
tresses of idea-systems, slogans, and stereotypes.

This conduct is no accident. It is linked to the train of events
which we call industrialization. Advancing technology calls for
sophistication, but it does not canalize sophistication; instead, it
is given impetus everywhere. In so doing, the conflicting ideologies of man move from violence, through intimidation and
fear, to fraud: from force to fraud, as Lester F. Ward would put
it.[45]

This re-orientation is apparent in many of the competing as
well as conflicting ideologies of our time. One finds it in the
ideologies of war. In terms of strategy and tactics, there is probably not much difference between tribal conflict and global
warfare; in terms of technics, of course, vast contrasts exist. But
the real distinction lies deeper: in the words, myths, slogans,
stereotypes, idea-systems of nationalism and imperialism. In one
century it is the "White Man's Burden"; in another, it is the
Herrenvolk or the "Greater East Asia Co-Prosperity Sphere."
The logic becomes more subtle, more intricate, more involved,
perhaps more persuasive, if for no other reason than that it is
more fraudulent. In a world of differences, we refine our philosophies of differences, and we call them ideologies. Henceforth,
ideological irreconcilability is wedded to the strategy and the
tactics of group annihilation or, more simply, to the strategy of
terror.[46]

Technology and human insecurity. Unfortunately, we pay a
terrific price for this behavior—not in terms of other men's costs,
for they do not matter (so we think), but in terms of our own.
The conflicts of the external social universe become the mirror
of the self, and the personal imbalances of insecurity and fear
are the tribute money we pay for the privilege of technological
exploitation of our physical and social worlds.

[45] Lester F. Ward, *Dynamic sociology* (New York: Appleton-Century-Crofts, 1883),
Vol. II, p. 503 ff.

[46] For illustrations of this fact, *cf.* Edmund Taylor, *Strategy of terror* (Boston:
Houghton Mifflin Company, 1940). Also *cf.* the powerful discussion by Aldous
Huxley, *Science, liberty, and peace* (New York: Harper and Brothers, 1946).

Of course, we hardly have to be reminded that man has always been victimized by his fears. "In the beginning was fear," says Lewis Browne, "and fear was in the heart of man, and fear controlled man."[47] A thousand vestiges in religion and art and family life bear testimony to this truth.[48] And yet, can we say that technology has been guiltless in provoking this fear? Prehistoric man lived in a world of the unseen, the supernatural. That world had to be coerced. Magic is our name today for early man's wish-fulfilling "controls" over that world.[49]

But this primitive system of technology only fed fuels to the flames of his fears, as the ritual prayers and ceremonies of his "rites of passage" show. In like manner, man's newest technology, scientific industrialism, plays on his fear. He has the tools, the instruments, the technical processes of this new technology. But does he understand them? Do the technological experts care whether he does or not?[50] Indeed, is not his altogether too frequent reaction one of ambivalence: either to rush barbarian-like into this his newest temple and vent his spleen and spite on its technics, or else to retire in humble but ignorant awe of its marvels and mouth the mumbo-jumbo of "natural laws" or the "divine hand of Providence"?

At any rate, few people can deny the great increase in human anxiety.[51] "Be not anxious about tomorrow" was an injunction of an agricultural society which knew little about business cycles, cut-throat competition, iron-curtain communication, or imperialistic rivalries. It is hardly a fitting social philosophy for the vast, congested, poorly articulated, diseased, impersonal, swift, expensive, wasteful, megalopolitan culture-centers of the twentieth century!

[47] Lewis Browne, *This believing world* (New York: The Macmillan Company, 1932), p. 27. Quoted by permission.

[48] For a fuller discussion of this theme, in terms of the history of art, *cf.* T. H. Robsjohn-Gibbings, *Mona Lisa's mustache: A dissection of modern art* (New York: Alfred A. Knopf, 1947); also Paul Meadows, "Case against the rebel painters," *The Technology Review*, 51 (February, 1949): 220 ff.

[49] *Cf.* C. H. Toy, *Introduction to the history of religion* (Cambridge: Harvard University Press, 1924).

[50] *Cf.* the development of this theme by J. Ortega y Gasset, *Revolt of the masses* (London: G. Allen and Unwin, 1932).

[51] This is a moot point which can hardly be demonstrated statistically. However, for general logical and psychological demonstration, *cf.* Karen Horney, *Neurotic personality of our time* (New York: W. W. Norton and Company, 1937); J. M. Reinhardt, *Social psychology* (Philadelphia: J. B. Lippincott, 1938); and Erich Fromm, *Escape from freedom* (New York: Farrar Strauss, 1941).

Obsolete modern man? The future of atomic energy is perhaps the most dramatic symbol of the impact of technology on human conflict. So tremendous have been the anxiety and confusion created by this suddenly announced conquest of a new source of power that one critical observer, Norman Cousins, has declared that it has made modern man obsolete.

Few people have been able, though many have sought to do so, so clearly to put the cultural issues raised by atomic energy as Cousins. "We can put on blinders; we can laugh it all off as just a false alarm; we can claim that talk of an Atomic Age is sheer fancy; we can protest that the threat of the destructive use of atomic energy is exaggeration, overstatement, hysteria, panic. But all the manufactured calm and scorn in the world cannot alter the precise fact that the atomic bomb plus another war equals global disaster. Nor that the crisis is fast approaching and may be upon us within a few years unless we act now to avert it. Nor that this crisis is created not only by the explosive atom but by inadequate means of controlling international lawlessness. Nor that control is inoperative without power, that power is dangerous without law, and that law is impossible without government."[52]

Perhaps as phenomenal as the atom bomb itself (or its derivative, the hydrogen bomb) has been the powerful excitement of the atomic scientists. Unused to discussion of social policy, they suddenly found themselves confronted with a social problem of the utmost urgency. More so than most men they have seemed qualified to testify on the relationship of atomic energy to human conflict. This they have done on every possible occasion. The theme of their reactions is nowhere expressed more poignantly than in their widely read symposium, *One world or none*.[53] "The nations," they wrote, "can have atomic energy, and much more. But they cannot have it in a world where war may come."[54]

[52] Norman Cousins, *Modern man is obsolete* (New York: The Viking Press, 1949), p. 48. Quoted by permission.

[53] D. Masters, and K. Way, eds., *One world or none* (New York: McGraw-Hill Book Company, 1946). Quoted by permission.

[54] *Ibid.*, p. 78. Further discussion of this theme may be found in: J. R. Newman and B. S. Miller, *Control of atomic energy* (New York: McGraw-Hill Book Company, 1948); A. J. Coale, *Problem of reducing vulnerability to atomic bombs* (Princeton: Princeton University Press, 1947); P. M. S. Blackett, *Fear, war and the bomb* (New York: McGraw-Hill Book Company, 1949); B. Brodie, ed., *Absolute weapon: Atomic power and world order* (New York: Harcourt, Brace and Company, 1946); H. Hart, "Social science and the atomic crisis," *Journal of Social Issues*, Supplement Series, #2, April, 1949.

QUESTIONS

1. Using aviation as an example, distinguish between the direct and the indirect effects of technological change on society.
2. What do people anticipate from the increased utilization of machine technology?
3. Show how social invention may require physical inventions; how a given social condition may be the result of a number of converging inventions.
4. To what extent is it possible to predict the social consequences of an invention? Why? Illustrate.
5. What are some of the various types of attitudes a "vested interest" may have toward a proposed technological innovation?
6. Describe the social psychology of resistance to innovations.
7. What are some of the consequences of the acceptance of the idea that scientific research is a type of industrial work?
8. In terms of the restrictive practices which occur in industry, show why a social policy toward technological change is so difficult to formulate and realize.
9. Using the process of social conflict for illustration, evaluate the proposition that industrialism has speeded up and extended human conflict.
10. Has technology increased or decreased human insecurity? Explain your answer.

REFERENCES

BERGE, W., *Cartels: Challenge to a free world*. Washington, D.C.: Public Affairs Press, 1944.

BRODIE, B., ed., *Absolute weapon: Atomic power and world order*. New York: Harcourt, Brace and Company, 1946.

BROWN, HARRISON, *Must destruction be our destiny?* New York: Simon & Schuster, 1946.

BUSH, V., *Modern arms and free men*. New York: Simon & Schuster, 1949.

COALE, A. J., *Problem of reducing vulnerability to atomic bombs*. Princeton: Princeton University Press, 1947.

COUSINS, NORMAN, *Modern man is obsolete*. New York: The Viking Press, 1947.

FLEDDÉRUS, M. L., and VAN KLEECK, M., *Technology and livelihood*. New York: Russell Sage Foundation, 1944.

GIEDION, S., *Mechanization takes command*. New York: Oxford University Press, 1948.

GOUDSMIT, S. A., *Alsos*. New York: Henry Schuman, 1947.

HART, HORNELL, *Technique of social progress*. New York: Henry Holt and Company, 1931.

HUXLEY, ALDOUS, *Science, liberty and peace*. New York: Harper and Brothers, 1946.

MEADOWS, PAUL, *Culture of industrial man*. Lincoln: University of Nebraska Press, 1950.

MUMFORD, LEWIS, *Technics and civilization*. New York: Harcourt, Brace and Company, 1935.

National Resources Committee, *Technological trends and national policy*. Washington, D.C.: Government Printing Office, 1937.

NEWMAN, J. R., and MILLER, B. S., *Control of atomic energy*. New York: McGraw-Hill Book Company, 1948.

OGBURN, W. F., et al, *Social effects of aviation*. Boston: Houghton Mifflin Company, 1946.

STOCKING, G. W., and WATKINS, W. M., *Cartels in action*. New York: Twentieth Century Fund, 1948.

CHAPTER 5

Economic Insecurity and Social Policy

The Nature of Modern Economic Insecurity

Risk in human life. If, as the Darwinian analysis holds, life is a struggle for existence, not the least important element in making it a struggle is the presence of risks. Man has been by natural necessity a risk-taker. Indeed, the evolution and elaboration of human culture may be interpreted as a search for controls over the emergents and emergencies of the human environment.[1] "The struggle of human progress has been a battle for security."[2] Control over the areas of insecurity has been sought through physical and social technology. Though the institutions of society and physical technology have varied from time to time and from society to society, they have achieved in most cases some modicum of equilibrium with the risk-giving milieu.

However, such equilibrium as may be achieved at any given time is a precarious one, for it must submit to the buffeting of an unpredicted environment and to the new adjustment problems created by an advancing technology. Security tends to be a goal rather than an actuality. Indeed, it would appear that the very pursuit of progress leaves a pathway strewn with insecurities. This fact is most clearly seen in contemporary industrial society. Modern industrial people live in and through the operations of a market economy, where price is king and income is the key to major satisfactions. The protective resources which spell security for modern men are contained in their possession of income. Ours is a civilization knit together by a cash tie. Security is measured

---

[1] This theme was developed in Ch. 3 of this text.
[2] Abraham Epstein, *Insecurity: A challenge to America*, 2nd rev. ed. (New York: Random House, 1938), p. 3.

by adequacy of income. Interruptions of income, insufficient income, loss of income, herein lie the real economic and social insecurities of modern industrial people. Hence, security must be found, if it is found at all, in the assurance and adequacy of income. And social policy, if there is to be a social policy at all, must aim at income assurance and adequacy.

In this respect modern industrialism is sharply different from other human cultures. In both primitive and feudal societies, for example, the pattern of reciprocal responsibility served to cushion the shocks of risk.[3] The serf and his lord, the primitive tribesman and his group mutually re-enforced one another in periods and moments of insecurity. But in individualistic cultures such as our own, this reciprocity is lacking. The individual is his own guardian of security. Prodded and armed by fear and foresight, he must be—in the individualistic tradition—the protector of his own citadel. However, the repeated and repeatable failures of *laissez-faire* individualism have sent modern industrial societies off in search of other methods of insurance against insecurity.[4] These roads seem to point in the direction of collective measures to ensure adequacy. These measures are contained in one basic principle: that of "reducing risks by sharing them."[5]

This principle is known under many names, but the family name is "social insurance." Whether it is the private group or the state which is the vehicle of action, the demand is for the distribution of risks through the sharing of costs. On this foundation have been built all the private and public programs for collective insurance which have become so integral a phase of modern civilization. And in all of them one goal-condition predominates: income security. Security in a cash culture is defined in large part by the individual's or group's dependable access to resources in the form of income.[6]

Types of risk factors.   Socially speaking, most of the risks in income security seem to be linked to a few basic contingencies: death, sickness and disability, unemployment, and old age.[7] Rubinow has called them "The Four Horsemen of the Apoca-

[3] *Cf.* M. S. Stewart, *Social security* (New York: W. W. Norton and Company, 1937), pp. 16–17.
[4] *Cf.* I. B. Rubinow, *Quest for security* (New York: Henry Holt and Company, 1934), Part II.
[5] Stewart, *op. cit.*, p. 17.
[6] *Cf.* E. M. Burns, *American social security system* (Boston: Houghton Mifflin Company, 1945), p. 6.
[7] *Cf. ibid.*, Ch. 1.

lypse."[8] These contingencies operate in varied ways. Sometimes they affect only the breadwinner of the family, sometimes the members of his family.[9] Although a considerable body of actuarial wisdom can be built up about their incidence, the individual must always be looked upon as a special case. For example, death rates offer no specific promises to a given individual; nor do sickness and disability rates, nor the changing volume of unemployment. All that the individual can hope for himself is that his resources will prove to be adequate for the demands upon him, for security is nothing else than a balance between these two facts of his life.

Illusory security devices. The individual can seek a balance between resources and demands by a fearful foresight which accumulates reserves in cash or credit or commodities. Unhappily he can never accurately forecast the intensity or the extent of the demands. The blanket of resources is always in hazard of not providing coverage. He can adjust his standard of living at an irreducible minimum, can trim the sails of his style of living, and can inhibit his consumer wants. But such anchors to windward are no sure safeguard in a hard-slugging storm. The individual can depend on the good-will and sympathy of friends and relatives, which may be a good security so long as they are not besieged by the same troubles as himself. He can rely upon the comforting philosophy that nature and society move in regular and recurring cycles; in so doing, of course, he is not wise to forget that the pattern of such cycles is more easily discerned for those in the past than for those in the future. He can be stoical and fatalistic and thus recover psychologically if not economically from the shock. Or he can identify himself with messianic and utopian movements which offer pie in the sky or a place in the sun. He can join a crusade, Townsend-like, which may not be realistic actuarially but which can be unquestionably satisfying emotionally.

Essentials of security. Without suggesting at all that risks can be eliminated, the proponents of a social policy for economic insecurity do insist that they can be calculated and that through collective efforts their costs can be reduced. This belief, actuarially sound, is embodied in property-loss insurance, life insurance, market-hedging operations, market analysis and forecast, and in the practice of individual and group reserves. Such

[8] *Cf.* Rubinow, *op. cit.*, Ch. 2.
[9] *Cf.* Epstein, *op. cit.*, p. 51.

collective measures are not regarded as substitutes but as supplements for individual foresight and planning. However, they do assume that the most careful and conscientious sketch of the future is limited by the perspective of the individual and by his skill. The collective sharing of perspectives, of skills, and of ideas brings the reduction of risks. Security can mean nothing more certain than this; indeed, no security plans in existence or in contemplation—except those of the lunatic fringe—conceive of anything beyond this possibility.

Social Sources of Economic Insecurity

Unemployment as an illustration. In order to describe the manner in which economic insecurity of the individual arises, unemployment, which is his most severe risk, may be taken as an example.

Of all the contemporary social problems in America it can hardly be gainsaid that employment is the most pervasive and probably the most critical. Upon the skill with which modern society solves this problem everything in our civilization literally depends. Students of social pathology have demonstrated over and over again that the causation trail of our major disorganizations leads inevitably back to some aspect of modern mass employment. To see why this is true it is necessary to understand a few salient characteristics of modern industrialism.

The American economy a technological culture. The focus of any culture tends to be on its economic arrangements.[10] An economy is the cultural organization which develops around some central mode of economic activity. Industrialism is a cultural system which has been built up around the machine technology. It is a system of technics involving the use of machines in production. There is an internal core consisting jointly of specialized machines and tools, knowledge of processes and exchange problems, and a group of human beings disciplined for industrial work. There is an outer pattern of relationships requiring a minimal concentration of men and machines in a type of group production called the factory. In addition, a co-operative organization of the physical and social productive factors is needed to process resources and to market products. This entails a community organization which supplies living quarters and which demands behavior patterns and controls

[10] *Cf.* Paul Meadows, *Culture of industrial man* (Lincoln: University of Nebraska Press, 1950), Ch. 2.

for the human beings responsible for business and industrial functions—the city, in other words.[11]

Industrial technology, as we have known it in the United States, plainly requires and has acquired a mass organization. The work of extracting, processing, transporting, merchandising, consuming the products of "the machine" has assumed a mass scale. Perhaps the most direct way to bring out this fact is to cite our changing labor force. In 1890 it consisted of 22.2 million persons; this was slightly less than 25 per cent of the total population. In 1949 it was 53 millions, or 40 per cent of the people. By 1960 it is estimated that it will be about 64 millions. As a perspective on this increase it is helpful to remember that in the interval between the Civil War and the Second World War the population more than doubled, but the labor force more than trebled. Within this pattern of manifest bigness another pattern, fitted to the same scale, emerged: the large-scale enterprise. The Temporary National Economic Committee was advised in 1938 by a United States Department of Commerce economist that six per cent of all corporations control 86 per cent of the nation's corporate wealth.[12] Moreover, one half of the workers of the United States are in enterprises where there are 250 or more workers. Nine tenths of one per cent of the employers hire 50 per cent of the workers.[13]

Another aspect of employment in industrial America is its tendency toward economic dependency. The fact is, "the majority of people under the present economic system are economically dependent upon a minority who own and control the machinery of production and distribution. The majority depend upon someone else for the opportunity to make a living, which explains their economic subordination."[14] The extent of this dependence is brought out in the following table.[15]

[11] On the importance of the urban community for industrial economy, *cf.* Ch. 7 of this text.

[12] On this problem of the concentration of employment in a small number of enterprises, *cf. Big business: Its growth and its place* (New York: Twentieth Century Fund, 1937).

[13] Dr. W. L. Thorp, Hearings before Temporary National Economic Committee, 75th Congress, Third Session, *Investigation of concentration of economic power*, December 1, 2, 3, 1938. Part I, pp. 102–103.

[14] *Cf.* G. S. Watkins, and P. A. Dodd, *Labor problems* (New York: T. Y. Crowell Company, 1940), p. 217. Quoted by permission.

[15] *Cf.* Watkins and Dodd, *op. cit.*, p. 217; also A. H. Hansen, "Industrial class alignments in the United States," *Journal of the American Statistical Association*, 17 (December, 1920): 422; T. M. Sogge, "Industrial classes," *ibid.*, 28 (June, 1933): 199 ff.

TABLE 2

The Trend Toward Economic Dependency in Employment in the
United States: 1900–1940
(Occupation Groupings of All Gainfully Employed Individuals Expressed in
Percentages of the Total Number Employed)

Class	1900	1920	1940[a]
Total Number Employed (in 000's)	29,073	41,614	52,000
Dependent Class			
Total	51.9%	60.7%	65.0%
Farm laborers	7.0	5.6	5.5
Industrial wage-earners	35.4	42.4	38.0
Servants	5.0	3.1	4.0
Low-salaried group	4.5	9.6	17.5
Independent Class			
Total	39.6%	34.2%	31.0%
Farmers and working children	28.0	20.0	15.0
Proprietors and officials	6.2	7.6	7.0
Professional group	5.4	6.6	9.0
Unclassified	8.5	5.1	4.0

[a] Estimates for 1940 are crude estimates, made by free-hand curves. Adapted from Watkins and Dodd, *op. cit.*, with permission.

A final aspect of employment in industrial America is the mass character of its maintenance. Before the First World War unemployment was more or less taken for granted. Today, however, especially since the depression years of the 1930's, a chronic deficiency in the total demand for labor has come to be regarded as a disastrous thing for society. Hence, public expectation is centered on the urgent need for full employment. As Henry A. Wallace observed: "There can be no lasting full employment in any one group or area of our national life unless there is lasting full employment in all."[16] The mass character of the maintenance of employment has been described by Sir William Beveridge, who has been a long-time specialist in these matters, as follows: "The need for a new attack on the problem of unemployment cannot be denied today, except in a mood of unthink-

[16] Henry A. Wallace, *Sixty million jobs* (New York: Reynal and Hitchcock, 1945), p. 36.

ing optimism. The attack must be on three lines. There is unemployment due to chronic or recurrent deficiency of demand. There is unemployment due to misdirection of demand. There is unemployment due to the degree to which the labor market remains unorganized and to the manner in which particular industries respond to demand. The reduction of unemployment to a harmless minimum requires, therefore, measures of three kinds: measures to ensure sufficient steady demand for the products of industry; measures to direct demand with regard to the labor available; measures to organize the labor market and to assist the supply of labor to move in accord with demand."[17]

The mass character of unemployment. Thus far it has been urged that one of the most important phases of industrial society is mass employment. A corollary of this thesis can now be examined: mass unemployment is likewise and by the same token a very critical phase of modern economy. An industrial society employs men and women on a mass scale, and it disemploys them on that scale; it does so recurringly, continuously, chronically.

This fact has been suggested by a great many studies in the field of economic theory. Although not all unemployment is a resultant of business cycles, its role has never been minimized by students of the problem. Business-cycle theorists necessarily think in terms of the whole system, and whether the direction of their thought is capitalistic, socialistic, or communistic, mass unemployment appears to them as an inescapable concomitant of the mass action of the industrial system which has developed in the last two centuries.[18]

A further insight into the mass nature of unemployment is provided in the fact that any given sample of unemployed workers shows them to be representative of the whole labor force.[19] Every occupational type and social class in the economic system is touched by the processes of disemployment. The unemployed workers during the 1930's, for example, were rather evenly distributed among all the age groups in the labor force.

[17] W. H. Beveridge, *Full employment in a free society* (New York: W. W. Norton and Company, 1945), p. 109. Quoted by permission.

[18] *Cf.* Alvin H. Hansen, *Business cycle theory* (Boston: Ginn and Company, 1927); I. Fisher, *Booms and depressions: Some first principles* (London: Allen and Unwin, 1938); J. M. Keynes, *General theory of employment, interest and money* (New York: Harcourt, Brace and Company, 1936); A. C. Pigou, *Theory of employment* (London: The Macmillan Company, 1933).

[19] For example, *cf. Unemployment census*, 1937, U. S. Bureau of the Census, 1938; G. L. Palmer, and K. D. Wood, *Urban workers on relief* (Washington, D.C.: Works Progress Administration, Division of Social Research, 1936); J. N. Webb, *Transient unemployed* (Works Progress Administration, 1935); Nels Anderson, *Men on the move* (Chicago: University of Chicago Press, 1940).

Most of them were married. They were to be found uniformly in all the skill levels. They were evenly distributed among communities large and small. Most of them were employable.

Again, studies of unemployment directly confront the mass character of its causation. Earlier views regarded it as an incident, undesirable of course but inevitable, of industrial expansion. A widespread popular attitude held that to be without work was a sure sign of personal failure: "Some people won't work." Slowly, failures in the labor market or in the industrial demand for labor came to be appreciated as significant causes of unemployment. In recent years worklessness has been understood as a consequence of the failure of the whole economic system. Today there is a host of possible "explanations" for unemployment. A typical study groups the causal factors into "demand" and "supply."[20]

I. Demand Factors
    a. Industries of a particular region.
    b. Proportion of agriculture, manufacturing, commerce.
    c. Character of markets and products.
    d. Occupational requirements, degree of mechanization.
    e. Size of industrial units, character of segment.
    f. Seasonal fluctuations.
    g. Technological trends.
    h. State of business—boom or depressions.
II. Supply Factors
    a. Age and sex distribution.
    b. Economic, racial, residential density of the population.
    c. Social, economic, individual factors determining period of attendance at school.
    d. Character of general education.
    e. Training methods, etc., in industry.
    f. Immigrant labor supply; sources, agencies, skills, objectives.
    g. Adaptability and mobility of the working force.

This survey of unemployment as a most important segment of economic insecurity has sought to illustrate the social sources of modern insecurity. Its causes and occurrence are on a mass scale. Hence, mass measures to reduce and prevent this sort of economic insecurity are imperative.

Mass aspects of other risk factors. Unemployment is a major item in the economic insecurity of modern people. However, there are members of the labor force who are not able even

[20] Cf. L. C. Marsh, *Unemployment research* (New York: Oxford University Press, 1935), p. 41.

though willing to work: those who are physically incapacitated or have reached an age when industry supposedly cannot use them. The pattern of insecurity is the same here as in unemployment.

Physical incapacity may result from accidents or from sickness. Of course, not all accidents result in injuries, but the incidence of damaging accidents is high enough. Considering only industrial accidents, we find that some 24,000 of them annually cause death, about the same number cause permanent disabilities per year, and about 2,000,000 result in temporary time-loss injuries. One student has estimated that "for each accident-producing injury of any kind (regardless of severity) there are at least 10 other accidents."[21] If we consider only fatal accidents from all causes, we are confronted with an annual death rate that has ranged from 70 to 90 per 100,000 population for most years in the twentieth century. This rate will probably increase. One study concluded that if normal time losses were applied to deaths and permanent disabilities in industry alone, the total time loss would equal about 233,840,000 man-days, or the equivalent of full-time annual employment for 780,000 employees.[22]

Economic costs arising from accidents may be classified as direct or indirect. The former include payments for workmen's compensation and medical care, which may aggregate at least four billion dollars annually. On analysis these costs prove to be only about one fourth as great as the hidden costs: time and material losses to industry, human losses in physical and earning capacity and to the family of the worker. A classic statement of this problem reported a generation ago: "Three fifths of the victims of work accidents are heads of families and one third of the remainder contribute to the support of others. . . . In the great majority of instances, therefore, a serious work accident deprives a necessitous family of its sole and chief support. The immediate result, in the absence of systematic accident relief, is poverty and the long train of evils that flow from poverty."[23]

The loss of income from sickness is like the loss from injury. Both sickness and injury heap the burden of medical care on the worker's regular expenses of maintenance. Data collected by the

[21] E. L. Bowers, *Is it safe to work?* (Boston: Houghton Mifflin Company, 1930), p. 5.

[22] *Cf.* M. D. Kossoris, and S. Hjaer, "Industrial injuries in the United States during 1940," *Monthly Labor Review*, August, 1941: 327.

[23] E. H. Downey, *Workmen's compensation* (New York: The Macmillan Company, 1924), pp. 13–14. Quoted by permission.

United States Public Health Service in an unparalleled survey of the health of the American people showed that there is an average daily sickness of close to five and a half million persons. The following table suggests the rates of disabling losses which American people sustain from sickness.

TABLE 3
Rates of Disabling Sickness, All Causes

Type of Rate	Rate
Frequency:	
Illnesses per 1000 persons	172
Severity:	
Days per case	57
Disability:	
Annual days per case	9.8

Adapted from H. E. Barnes, *Society in transition* (New York: Prentice-Hall, 1940), p. 432; reprinted by permission.

Translated into work loss, sickness is responsible for over one billion man-days of absenteeism.[24] If it is remembered that there is a high correlation between illness and the volume of relief, between illness and the vitality and productivity of the nation, between inadequate medical care and poverty, we have a most important insight into the character and consequences of modern economic insecurity.

Finally, old age in an industrial economy represents the last but by no means the least of the anxieties and inadequacies of the modern income-earner. The American people are growing older. In 1920 there were only five million people 65 years and older. Today there are over 11 millions, totalling 7.5 per cent of the population. By 1980 we may expect about 19 millions, or about 14.4 per cent of the population. This shift would not create any serious problems if it were not for a few stubborn facts. Less than a fifth of our aged population can support themselves on incomes from investments and savings.[25] Over a fifth have no incomes, and over a third have incomes of less than $1000 a year. Social-security pensions go to only 1.5 million old people, old-age assistance payments to 2.5 millions. Chances of employment are very poor. Even during the war years only one third of those 65 and over were employed, many of them on farm jobs. The adoption of specific age limits in many industries means

[24] Medical and other costs of sickness are discussed in Ch. 15 of this text.
[25] *Cf.* "What to do about the old folks," *Newsweek*, March 20, 1950: 58 ff.

that many workers are turned loose at an age which in the past was regarded as "the prime of life." Analyses of family budgets have demonstrated over and over again that the possibility of personal surpluses set aside for old age is an idle hope for millions of income-earners.

Programs of Social Security

The over-all pattern of American social security. Thus far it has been suggested that the primary concern of social policy in the field of economic insecurity is "the assurance of income to some or all members of the population."[26] This view does not disregard those social services to health and welfare which do not provide cash-income security. Nor does social policy as outlined here mean that only government assumes the chief responsibility for such a guarantee. Supplementation by private industrial, labor, and community services is desirable and urgent. But cash-income security seems to be imperative in a society in which interruption to the continuity of private incomes occurs on the mass scale which has been indicated in these pages. Cash-income security in a cash-dominated culture appears to be the only logical alternative which an intelligent people can pursue!

For sake of convenience, the income-security programs which have evolved in American society are grouped into (a) those which are directed specifically at the risk of unemployment, (b) those which operate on the principles of social insurance, and (c) those which give assistance on the basis of need. They will be discussed in this order.

The methodology of employment security. Some of the methods of employment security recognize, properly enough, the inevitability of a certain amount of mass unemployment. Others are more sanguine in their expectations, stressing not only the reduction but the elimination of unemployment.[27] In the first category are (1) public works, (2) work relief, (3) unemployment compensation, (4) dismissal compensation. In the second group are (5) organization of the labor market, (6) apprenticeship and training programs, (7) employment regularization, and (8) planned resource development. The first group of methods is directed chiefly at "cyclical" and the second at "frictional" unemployment. Each method will be briefly identified.

[26] Burns, *op. cit.*, p. 6.

[27] This consideration of methods leans heavily upon a similar discussion in Philip Taft, *Economics and problems of labor*, (Harrisburg: Stackpole Sons, 1942), Chs. III, IV.

1. Public-works advocates are not in agreement as to the functions of their program. On the one hand, it is proposed as a means of checking the deflationary spiral of the business cycle, thus shrinking the volume of unemployment. On the other hand, it may be regarded as a means of redressing permanent deficiencies in the economy. The first view calls for cyclical deficit spending as a restorative measure, the second for compensatory deficit spending in order to augment private investment which has slumped, or is beginning to slump. The second view obviously is more preventive, at least in purpose. Either policy requires long-range planning and the flexible adaptation of public works to fluctuations in business indexes. Timed correctly, public works can make a real contribution to the cause of full employment.[28]

2. Another measure designed to ameliorate the effects of unemployment but not to prevent them is work relief. Actually an attempt to substitute work for relief in order to avoid the cruelty and unwise features of the latter, work relief is prompted by the desire to furnish useful employment for the needy unemployed. More costly than direct relief, it is less economic than public works because it is less well planned, less efficient, and not nearly so selective in its projects. However, it makes possible incomes at a time when income opportunities are negligible, and human and community values are conserved, even if at higher costs than might be desirable.[29]

3. Unemployment insurance, or compensation, is a comprehensive semipublic, semiprivate measure designed to relieve the excessive costs of unemployment but not to prevent them. First developed on a private basis through mutual associations, it became a compulsory national system in England in 1905. Its adoption has become widespread since then. It was incorporated into the Social Security Act of 1935 and became part of the whole social-insurance program of the United States. Although it is by no means a perfect system, the benefits which are possible from it are calculated to aid the worker during short-time work-

[28] For further discussion, cf. Alvin H. Hansen, *Full recovery or stagnation* (New York: Harcourt, Brace and Company, 1940); Arthur D. Gayer, *Public works in prosperity and depression* (New York: National Bureau of Economic Research, 1935); J. M. Keynes, *Means to prosperity* (New York: Harcourt, Brace and Company, 1933); J. M. Clark, *Economics of planning public works* (Washington, D.C.: National Planning Board of the Federal Emergency Administration of Public Works, 1935).

[29] Cf. Leah Feder, *Unemployment relief in periods of depression* (New York: Russell Sage Foundation, 1936); Edward A. Williams, *Federal aid for relief* (New York: Columbia University Press, 1939); A. E. Burns, and P. Kerr, "Survey of work relief policies," *American Economic Review* (December, 1937): 71 ff.

less periods. Unemployment compensation systems are storm
cellars, but they are vulnerable to a "big blow" in the form of
prolonged business depression.[30]

4. Dismissal compensation serves a purpose similar to that
of unemployment compensation. Consisting of a monetary payment to the worker, in addition to his wages or salary, upon
termination of employment without fault, it functions as a bridge
to another income opportunity. Although such payments are
usually low and uncertain and are made by only a few employers,
they are excellent public-relations devices and contribute to
the worker's morale.[31]

5. Labor markets may be local, regional, or national. Well-
organized, they avoid the hit-or-miss hiring practices of an earlier
phase of industrial development, when workers were employed
at the gate or by some other haphazard arrangement. Employment agencies, some of them private and fee-charging, others
public and free, have begun to introduce a modicum of order-
liness and comprehensiveness into labor markets. The entry of
the federal government into the labor-market field, in 1907 with
the Bureau of Immigration and Naturalization, led the way to
more systematic activity, first in the form of the United States
Employment Service as a division of the Department of Labor
during the First World War and later as a part of the Social
Security Board during the 1930's. As a means for bringing job
openings and job seekers together, it has never been as sys-
tematically developed and perfected as it might very well have
been. Traditional *laissez-faire* attitudes still dominate the American labor markets.[32]

6. It is becoming more apparent that one way to reduce the
load of unemployment and to prevent it lies in more thorough
preparation of the worker for the job or for several jobs. Job
preparation may be carried on through vocational schools or

[30] *Cf.* Social Security Board, *Social security in America* (Washington, D.C.: Government Printing Office, 1937); E. Wight Bakke, *Insurance or dole* (New Haven: Yale
University Press, 1935); Mary B. Gilson, *Unemployment insurance in Great Britain*
(New York: Industrial Relations Counselors, 1931); Ronald G. Davison, *British
unemployment policy* (New York: Longmans, Green and Company, 1938); Committee
on Social Security of the Social Science Research Council, *Abstract on unemployment
insurance legislation in European countries* (Washington, D.C.: Social Security Board,
1938).

[31] *Cf.* Everett D. Hawkins, *Dismissal compensation* (Princeton: Princeton University
Press, 1940).

[32] *Cf.* Shelby M. Harrison and Associates, *Public employment offices* (New York:
Russell Sage Foundation, 1924); Darrel H. Smith, *The United States employment
service* (Baltimore: Johns Hopkins Press, 1923).

through apprenticeship programs. The latter, it might be pointed out, play an unrecognized role in providing and stabilizing employment. The cause of vocational education has been greatly aided by the work of the federal government in the Smith-Hughes Act of 1917, the George-Deen Law of 1937, the Federal Committee on Apprenticeship, the defense vestibule schools, and the "G. I." apprenticeship provisions.[33]

7. Another technique for preventing frictional unemployment is known as employment regularization or stabilization. It means, simply, the provision of job opportunities in a given industry or plant throughout the year. This end might be realized through (a) the discovery of new uses of its products; (b) better sales promotion during slack periods; (c) diversification of products; (d) simplification of style; (e) price changes to stimulate buying in slack seasons; (f) rescheduling production on an annual basis. Economically difficult to achieve, employment stabilization is also subject to criticism on social grounds. However, it is particularly attractive to specialists in personnel administration. Its possibilities have probably not begun to be appreciated as yet.[34]

8. Planned resource development has come to have such a place in the maintenance of employment that no discussion of this problem can exclude it. It represents the collaboration of business and government in the discovery, research, and encouragement of enterprise in new and old resources. Its basic assumptions are twofold: that technological culture survives only through continuous expansion of its resource utilization and that only through such expansion will the ever-enlarging number of employable workers find suitable income opportunities. There can be no really honest opposition, particularly after the 1930's, to lodging larger responsibility in government for the maintenance of prosperous conditions. However, this responsibility can be despatched in more than one way. In the long run, from the standpoint of increasing employment opportunities it is undoubtedly best despatched through the many ways which are at the disposal of government in stimulating job-creating enter-

[33] For a discussion of apprenticeship in an industrial society, see Paul H. Douglas, *American apprenticeship and industrial education* (New York: Columbia University Press, 1921).

[34] *Cf.* Herman Feldman, *Regularization of employment* (New York: Harper and Brothers, 1925); *Lay-off and its prevention* (New York: National Industrial Conference Board, 1930); *Employment regularization* (New York: National Association of Manufacturers, 1940).

prises, public and private. Planned resource development, in this sense, offers the very best job security an industrial people could want, and without it there is little likelihood that any of the other measures sketched here will have much meaning.

Finally, it should be pointed out that the quest for employment security is more than a search for jobs; it is part of a pattern— the overwhelming contemporary desire for social justice. Inequalities of opportunity, the frustration of economic expectations by mass causes, the thwarting of equitable distribution in an economy of technological abundance, these are confusing dilemmas from which social tensions and political movements inevitably arise. They are the bases for the revolution of our times. "Under such circumstances multiple currents of discontent make their appearance in the social order, and disruptive, subversive forces become articulate. Active minds begin to speculate concerning the merits of alternative economic and social systems, messiahs of new milleniums appear on the national scene, and the pastures of other systems seem greener than our own."[35] Full employment, therefore, is an important but only an initial step along the road of a sound social policy.

The methodology of social insurance.   The use of the principles and methods of insurance in order to provide continuity of income for American families is due partly to a humanitarian impulse: to avoid the harsh and inadequate methods of aid of the early poor-law system. Social insurance is defended, as Burns has pointed out,[36] on the ground that benefits paid out have been paid for in part or in whole by the beneficiaries themselves. It is defended, moreover, on the ground that social-insurance payments are really a type of deferred pay and are indeed "a mere extension of the concept of payment for performance of work."[37] It is defended, in addition, on the ground that insurance principles and practices introduce the highly necessary element of predictability in the meeting of human contingencies. It is defended, finally, on the ground that eligibility for insurance benefits is determined solely by reference to the work record and not by need (or as the traditional phrase puts it, by "the means test"). These considerations have made social insurance popularly appealing to the mass of American wage-earners. Though it is a mass program, it is in the matter of administration a

---

[35] *Cf.* Watkins and Dodd, *op. cit.*, p. 1085. Quoted by permission.
[36] *Cf.* Burns, *op. cit.*, p. 31.
[37] Burns, *ibid.*

quick and almost automatic method of meeting specific contingencies. This fact has likewise occasioned a widespread approval of it.

The social-insurance program in the United States has been an imposing structure of services built around the major human risks: unemployment, disability, old age. Included in the system are: Old-Age and Survivors Insurance, Unemployment Insurance, Workmen's Compensations, Temporary Disability Benefits (as in operation in Rhode Island, New Jersey, California), and Veterans' Services—disability compensation, disability pensions, death awards to survivors of deceased veterans, and veterans' readjustment allowances.[38]

The methodology of public assistance. Public-assistance programs are drawn up and administered in terms of public aid to "needy" persons. They are based on the concept of the right to draw benefits under certain specified circumstances.[39] There are two major forms: special and general. Under the Social Security Act three specific groups of needy persons are recognized: the aged, dependent children, and the blind. Services to these groups comprise what professional social workers call "the categorical aids." General assistance is a sort of residual program, supplementing all the others. Before the depression years, that is, before the passage of the Social Security Act, general assistance was the chief social policy in this country. Usually known as relief, it is operated on a highly individualistic case basis, in which professional techniques are employed to determine the nature and extent of the need. Neither the benefits provided nor the cases covered can compare in volume or adequacy with the special public assistances or with the social insurances.

The administrative interrelationships of security services. American social services are administered by various governmental units—federal, state, and local—which share in their financing and management. The result is a complex and involved system. Burns has distinguished six different patterns of administration and financing: wholly federal, jointly state and federal, state and larger units of government, wholly state, state and local, and purely local. The following table, adapted from Burns, suggests the over-all pattern.[40]

---

[38] These programs are discussed at length and expertly by Burns, *op. cit.*, Chs. 4–10.

[39] For further discussion, *cf.* Ch. 15 of this text.

[40] Burns, *op. cit.*, p. 61. Used here by permission.

I. Wholly Federal:
   Old-Age and Survivors' Insurance; Railroad Retirement; Railroad Unemployment and Temporary Disability Insurance; Veterans' Programs; Workmen's Compensations.
   II. Federal-State:
   Unemployment Insurance; Old-Age Assistance; Aid to Dependent Children; Aid to the Blind.
   III. Federal-State-Local:
   Old-Age Assistance; Aid to Dependent Children; Aid to the Blind.
   IV. State:
   Workmen's Compensations; Disability Insurance; General Assistance; State ABC and AB; Disability Assistance; Veterans.
   V. State-Local:
   Concurrent ADC and AB; General Assistance.
   VI. Local:
   General Assistance.

By way of explanation and defense, it should be pointed out that this complicated system is, as Burns has said, "a mirror of the fact that America is a country characterized by great diversity of living conditions, economic interests, social attitudes and customs, and by a federal form of government. It reflects, too, the fact that the different circumstances which occasion interruption of private income present different types of economic and social problems."[41]

The extent and type of coverage provided by the American security system is suggested in Table 4.

Continuing Problems of Economic Security

Persisting negativism. Despite the impressive coverage of the economic contingencies affecting American families, every fresh appraisal of contemporary insecurities is met with denials and distractions. The handbook of the security negativists contains a few basic and oft-repeated formulas:

1. The proposal is unwanted.
2. It is unwarranted.
3. It threatens the integrity of (some unnamed or highly generalized sacred value or institution; demonstration is oratorical and emotional).
4. The beneficiaries of the proposals are unworthy.
5. It represents another instance of (radicalism, violation of states' rights, big government, intervention, creeping socialism, etc.).

[41] Burns, *op. cit.*, pp. 61–62.

TABLE 4

Beneficiaries under Social Insurance and Assistance Programs: 1947*

Program	Beneficiaries (000)
Old-Age and Survivors	1,978.3
Railroad Retirement	290.2
State Unemployment Ins.	621.4
R. R. Unemployment Ins.	77.8
Workmen's Compensation	. . . .
State Disability Ins.	22.5ᵃ
Veterans:	
Pensions and Compensations	3,271.9
Unemployment Allowances	464.6
Self-Employment Allowances	72.9
Old-Age Assistance	2,332.0
Aid to Dependent Children	1,059.9
Aid to the Blind	81.1
General Assistance	356.0
Grand Total	10,628.6

* Adapted from Burns, *op. cit.*, p. 48; based on data from Social Security Year Book and from Social Security Administration. Used here by permission.

ᵃ Data not available.

6. We are confident that the good sense of the American public will lead them to see the alien character of the proposal.

7. It violates the legitimate principles of government.

These forensic formulas appear and re-appear in every battle over any new security proposal: medical care, public housing, drainage-basin development, the extension of social security to citizens not now covered, and so forth. "Social insurance," asserted Dr. Edward Ochsner, well-known Chicago surgeon, "is the hybrid offspring of impracticable sentimentalism and political expediency."[42] His now familiar bill of particulars included such clichés as "undemocratic," "administrative, legislative, judicial (!) inefficiency and corruption," "actuarial unsoundness," "excessive costs," "deterioration of service," "character debilitation."

Interesting irrelevancies. Many of the negative value-judgments on security programs in this country are completely irrelevant. They are straw men set up in order to be toppled dramatically by great winds of oratory.[43] For example, pro-

[42] E. H. Ochsner, *Social insurance and economic security* (Boston: Bruce Humphries, Inc., 1934), p. 13.

[43] For an example of this straw-man technique, *cf.* Eric Johnston, "Social security

ponents of income security for American families do not argue that the state is all-wise and should be all-powerful, nor do they contemplate removing responsibility from the individual for the planning and conduct of his own life. It is never anticipated that social-security devices should replace full productive employment in the economy. The philosophy of income security is not explicitly or implicitly stated in terms of public competition with or elimination of private efforts. The general theory of social security is that every possible measure, public and private, which protects the nation and the individual against the deterioration of human resources and which promotes a community of mutual re-enforcement against contingencies must be sought, examined, and integrated into the life of the society. Any critical deviation from this task may be interesting, but it is irrelevant.

Historic perspective on income security. The evaluation of both existing and proposed income-security programs should bear in mind a simple historical fact. Social security is a new social institution in America. Like all other social institutions it aims at satisfying a set of universal needs. However, unlike such institutions as the family, religion, education, it is relatively new, emergent within the last generation. In theory and practice it represents a further application of the principle of insurance which has received an accelerated use by both business and labor organizations. The public-assistance phase of income security does not, of course, have the connection with work and wages which distinguishes social insurance. But both of them aspire to the same goal of a basic security and both are a far cry from the early system of public relief.[44] "Freedom from want" has become an essential American doctrine.

Administrative perfection. The social policy of the American people with respect to economic insecurity has been settled. As Burns has remarked: "Public social-security measures now form an important element in the institutional equipment of America, as of all major countries, affecting as they do the personal lives of millions of citizens and the pockets of millions of taxpayers."[45] Nevertheless, tensions about these measures continue to exist, and inevitably so.

---

in the post-war," *Social security in America* (Washington, D.C.: U.S. Chamber of Commerce, 1944): 3–7.

[44] *Cf.* Karl de Schweinitz, *People and process in social security* (Washington, D.C.: American Council on Education, 1948), Ch. 1.

[45] Burns, *op. cit.*, p. 442. Quoted by permission.

There is, for example, the problem of further extensions. Aside from the confused protestations of the negativists, there is the practical issue of the willingness of the economically secure to help finance the income security of those who are not. It is one thing to finance income security from the contributions of the beneficiaries themselves. It is quite another thing to transfer, through taxation, income from one group to another. Yet the existence of modern government presupposes the necessity of some transfer. So far as the extension of social-security services is concerned, the controversial point is one of limits. The settlement of this controversy depends upon the value-judgments of the public, not on science.[46]

But value-judgments, once made, must be scientifically and judicially executed. Hence another continuing problem of social security is that of administrative efficiency and professional effectiveness. The demand that income-security programs be abolished because there are weaknesses or failures might just as easily be applied to business enterprise itself. Yet the demand that these programs be efficient and effective is well within the circle of mature experience. However, it must be remembered that efficiency and effectiveness are not achieved by campaigns of terror or ridicule. Just as the businessman searches for increased efficiency through the extension of professional knowledge and technical competence, so must the public in its improvement of the administration and financing of its social-security programs. For this purpose an informed public opinion as to the nature of modern economic insecurity and as to the values and disvalues of various security techniques must work in partnership with a trained and professionalized corps of public-administration and social-welfare workers. Devices for the continuing safety of income-security programs must themselves be perfected, for this too is a part of the costs of security.[47]

[46] However, science may put a fund of tested information at the disposal of the public as part of the background for such value-judgments. On this particular problem of limits, cf. S. E. Harris, *Economics of social security* (New York: McGraw-Hill Book Company, 1941); L. Meriam, *Relief and social security* (Washington, D.C.: Brookings Institution, 1946); L. Meriam, K. T. Schlotterbeck, and M. Maroney, *Cost and financing of social security* (Washington, D.C.: Brookings Institution, 1950). For a careful evaluation of these and similar materials cf. Burns, *op. cit.* Consult also Committee on Economic Security, *Social security in America* (Washington, D.C.: Social Security Board, 1937).

[47] These problems are discussed over and over again in the issues of the *Social Security Bulletin, Public Welfare*, the *Annual Reports of the Federal Security Agency*, the *Social Work Year Book, Issues in Social Security*.

QUESTIONS

1. In what ways and for what reasons is risk different in modern industrial cultures from what it was in primitive or in feudal societies?
2. What is the underlying philosophy of social insurance? How does it differ from other security devices which the individual may have?
3. What is the primary justification for programs of social justice which center around income redistribution?
4. What are the social implications of the fact that employment and unemployment occur on a mass scale in our society? Explain the reluctance in the past to recognize the mass character of unemployment.
5. Cite examples to show that social responsibility for employment, if assumed, must start with the fact that unemployment is of different kinds.
6. Explain the importance of the "timing" of a public-works program.
7. Discuss the importance of planned resource development in an industrial system such as that of the United States.
8. What is the primary difference between general assistance programs and social insurance?
9. What are some of the charges made against the social-security system in this country? Evaluate both the motivations behind and the accuracy of these indictments.
10. What are some of the important further extensions of the social-security system?

REFERENCES

ANDERSON, N., *Men on the move*. Chicago: University of Chicago Press, 1940.

BOWERS, E. L., *Is it safe to work?* Boston: Houghton Mifflin Company, 1930.

BURNS, E. M., *American social security system*. Boston: Houghton Mifflin Company, 1945.

CLARK, J. M., *Economics of planning public works*. Washington, D.C.: National Planning Board, Federal Emergency Administration of Public Works, 1935.

DOWNEY, E. H., *Workmen's compensation*. New York: The Macmillan Company, 1924.

FEDER, L., *Unemployment relief in periods of depression*. New York: Russell Sage Foundation, 1936.

GAYER, A. D., *Public works in prosperity and depression*. New York: National Bureau of Economic Research, 1935.

HARRIS, S. E., *Economics of social security*. New York: McGraw-Hill Book Company, 1941.

HAWKINS, E. D., *Dismissal compensation*. Princeton: Princeton University Press, 1940.

PALMER, G. L., and WOOD, K. D., *Occupational characteristics of workers on relief in urban areas*. Washington, D.C.: Works Progress Administration, Division of Social Research, 1936.

PIGOU, A. C., *Theory of unemployment*. New York: The Macmillan Company, 1933.

RUBINOW, I. M., *Quest for security*. New York: Henry Holt and Company, 1934.

STEWART, M. S., *Social security*. New York: W. W. Norton and Company, 1937.

TAFT, PHILIP, *Economics and problems of labor*. Harrisburg: Stackpole Sons, 1942.

WALLACE, H. A., *Sixty million jobs*. New York: Simon and Schuster, 1945.

CHAPTER *6*

Problems of the Rural Community

General Aspects of the Rural Community

Scope and significance. "The rural problem" is of long standing. It was in 1910 that President Theodore Roosevelt appointed his famous Country Life Commission to make a thorough study of American rural life. That commission succeeded dramatically in focusing attention on the social and economic problems of this important segment of national life. Since then rural sociology, agricultural economics, and other rural studies have become almost universal disciplines in our schools. Thousands of books, articles, surveys, and field investigations have been published on these topics. National and state governments co-operatively have done much to help inform the general public about the problems of rural community life. From both a scientific and a practical point of view, the results of this vast field of information deserve study.

Many-sidedness of rural society. Like many other types of communities, the rural community presents many features. In the study of these one may now specialize in rural education, rural religion, rural sociology, agricultural economics, or rural social work, to mention a few major interests. The specialist in each of these tends to see the big problem in rural life in his segment of that life. This tendency is, of course, not peculiar to the rural field.

In a very significant sense it is almost impossible to speak of "the rural community." Variations are tremendous. For example, since social living reflects the prevailing regional economic base, one might say that there are at least seven types of rural community in the United States alone: Cotton Belt, Corn Belt, Wheat Areas, Range-Livestock Areas, Dairy Areas, Western Specialty-Crop Areas, General and Self-Sufficing

Areas.[1] Each shows differences in population, incomes and levels of living, group life and organization, degree of urbanization, and so forth.

Like the rest of modern society in recent decades, country life has been rather kaleidoscopic. The organizing for World Wars I and II and the dislocations afterwards have registered deep-seated effects on rural society. Then, certain scientific developments have had most revolutionary effects on social relationships. In some respects the automobile, the highway, and specialized agricultural equipment have unsettled and uprooted rural industries more than any other calling. These changes have taken place so incessantly and rapidly that it has been difficult to appreciate what the situation is or will be at any given time.[2]

The concept of the rural community. As an initial step in understanding rural changes and problems, it is wise to agree on our definitions. What do we mean by "the rural community"? At the turn of the century it was generally defined in terms of the "team haul."[3] Of course, this radius, defined by the horse and wagon, has immeasurably expanded with the coming of the automobile. Functionally speaking, the rural community refers to the clustering of people and activities and interests in a local area characterized by dispersed farmsteads ("the open-country neighborhoods") and villages. Statistically speaking, it consists of population aggregates of varying densities but under 2500 people. Agriculture in its many different phases is the predominant economic activity. The rural community, generally speaking, is an agricultural producing and trading area. There are, of course, rural villages which are functionally industrial in character, though these may have strong social and economic ties with the population on dispersed farmsteads.

Phases of rural-population aggregation. It is customary to distinguish between rural people living on dispersed farmsteads and those living in some kind of community cluster; the former are known as rural-farm, the latter as rural-nonfarm. In 1920

[1] *Cf.* C. C. Taylor, et al, *Rural life in the United States* (New York: Alfred A. Knopf, 1949), Chs. 20–27.

[2] *Cf.* National Resources Committee, *Technological trends and national policy* (Washington, D.C.: Government Printing Office, 1937), Section I, pp. 97 ff.; Mary L. Fleddérus, and Mary van Kleeck, *Technology and livelihood* (New York: Russell Sage Foundation, 1944), Ch. 3; United States Department of Agriculture, *Farmers in a changing world* (Washington, D.C.: Government Printing Office, 1940), *passim.*

[3] *Cf.* W. H. Wilson, *Evolution of the country community* (Boston: Pilgrim Press, 1907).

rural-nonfarm constituted 39 per cent of the total rural population; in 1930, 44 per cent; in 1940, 47.3 per cent; and by 1950, more than half. In terms of the total national population, these changes marked a shift from 18.9 per cent in 1920 to 20.6 per cent in 1940. Over half (53.7 per cent) of the total rural-farm population is concentrated in sixteen Southern states, whereas slightly over 50 per cent of the rural-nonfarm are found in the northern states (New England, Mid-Atlantic, and Midwest).

Of particular interest to the student of rural social life are the various kinds of rural community clusters. Estimates are at hand which indicate that, as of 1940, there were 58,818 hamlets and 19,359 villages, totaling 17,703,000 population. Four out of five people living in these rural community clusters live in the villages. About one half of American rural families live in dispersed farm dwellings. Each rural trade center averages from 80 to 500 families with about the same number scattered in the trade area surrounding the center. It has been estimated that there are about 35,000 trade-centered rural communities. Open-country neighborhoods, which are loosely knit and locally recognized areas, number about 24,000.[4]

Some population aspects of the rural community. Important in an understanding of the problems of the rural community are the facts about rural population patterns. As of 1940, children under 15 years of age constituted 31.6 per cent of the farm population, in contrast to 25.1 per cent of the urban community. There are, however, fewer persons in the economically and socially productive years 20 to 55. There has been a marked increase of persons 65 and older in rural-nonfarm communities; an increase of 26.2 per cent in the decade ending in 1940, which was twice the rate of growth of rural-nonfarm population as a whole![5] Increasingly, aging farmers retire to the villages and small towns. Unfortunately, this movement is not sufficient to provide enough farms for the younger rural population. The Bureau of Agricultural Economics estimated in December, 1944, that in the decade 1940 to 1950 there normally became or would become available only three fifths as many farms as there would be young men reaching 25 years of age. Here is one of the important reasons for the farm-to-city migration, of which we will speak later.

[4] *Cf.* Taylor, et al, *op. cit.*, Chs. 4, 5.
[5] *Cf.* J. H. Kolb, and E. de S. Brunner, *Study of rural society* (3rd ed., Boston: Houghton Mifflin Company, 1946), p. 54.

Rural reproductive rates are much higher than those for the urban areas. The net reproductive rate—a rate of 100 would represent 100 females reproducing 100 daughters growing to child-bearing age—for the urban area during the decade 1930–1940 was 75; for the rural-nonfarm, 115; for the rural-farm, 160. Although the rates for all three areas have dropped since 1905–1910, according to one estimate,[6] the rural-farm decline since then was only 17.9 per cent, the urban decline was 22.5; significantly, the rural-nonfarm drop was 23.3 per cent.

Trends in open-country neighborhoods. Changes in American transportation and employment have speeded up the decline of the open-country neighborhoods. They have decreased in number and activities, particularly in the older and more urbanized regions. They tend to disappear in the vicinity of villages and towns but to persist in isolated areas. Hamlet-centered neighborhoods have in recent decades managed to increase, due in large measure to the inability of villages to hold their status as trade centers. There has been a marked increase in the number and activity of suburban country neighborhoods. Throughout, the neighborliness bond has given way to the formal institutional or organizational group as the cement of social life. Indeed, in some parts of the country, notably in the Midwest, some actual gains in number and activity in open-country neighborhoods have been made, largely as the result of revitalization by certain interest groups, such as the county extension program in co-operation with the Farm Bureau.[7]

Trends in American villages. American economic culture has rendered its villages unstable and weak. A large number of studies uniformly point to loss and general decline, particularly in the incorporated villages.[8] Regardless of size, the rate of loss represented a decline for all villages. The causative factors are many. They include: competition of trade centers, particularly

---

[6] *Cf.* C. C. Taylor, *op. cit.*, p. 237. On rural population dynamics, *cf.* the penetrating and highly important work of O. E. Baker in Baker, Borsodi, and Wilson, *Agriculture in modern life* (New York: Harper and Brothers, 1939), *passim.*

[7] *Cf.* the excellent summary by Dwight Sanderson, *Rural sociology and rural social organization* (New York: John Wiley and Sons, 1942), p. 243.

[8] *Cf.* especially C. E. Lively, "Growth and decline of farm trade centers in Minnesota, 1905–1930," University of Minnesota Agricultural Experiment Station, Bulletin #287, 1932; S. C. Ratcliffe, "Size as a factor in population changes of hamlets and villages," *Rural Sociology,* VII (1942): 318 ff.; G. T. Trewartha, "Unincorporated hamlet: An analysis of data sources," *Rural Sociology,* VI (1941): 38 ff.; J. M. Gillette, "Some population shifts in the United States, 1930–1940," *American Sociological Review,* VI (October, 1941): 619 ff.

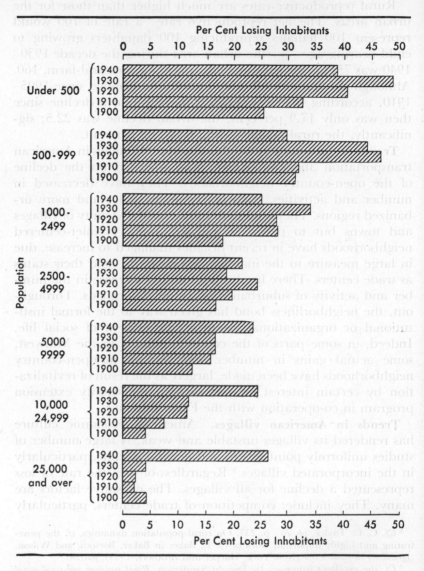

Figure 2. Per Cent of Incorporated Places Losing Population During Each of Five Decades from 1890 to 1940, by Class of Place

among the larger ones; changes in marketing organization and rural buying habits; changes in transportation and communication; shifts in type of farming. Generally speaking, it is almost a law of population that the probability of a place's losing inhabitants at any time varies inversely with the size of the population: the smaller the place, the greater the probability; the larger the place, the less the probability. This relationship is underscored in Figure 2.

A marked comparison appears between the trends of change in the unincorporated and the incorporated nonfarm communities, as the following table shows.

TABLE 5

Per Cent of Increase of the Rural Population of the United States, by Divisions and by Class of Population

Division	Farm 1930–1940	Nonfarm, 1920–1930	
		Incorporated	Unincorporated
United States..........	−0.00*	2.5	31.0
New England.............	−5.9†	14.2	37.3
Middle Atlantic...........	3.3	3.2	16.2
East North Central...........	2.9	1.0	31.9
West North Central...........	−7.1	−1.4	12.1
South Atlantic...........	1.7	8.2	41.7
East South Central...........	3.7	3.7	27.0
West South Central........	4.8	9.0	27.0
Mountain.................	−2.0	0.4	30.6
Pacific....................	11.6	−6.3	66.8

(Estimated from data of the 1940 census)

* − means decrease.

† The percentages for New England are almost worthless, since the classes of population are not well defined in most of the states.

This wonderful increase of unincorporated populations needs investigation. For the present we shall have to present the evidence, so far as there is any, and supplement it by more or less informed suggestions. The evidence and observations may be listed as follows.

1. Much of the increase is due to a rapid shifting and settlement of people in suburban clusters, thus building satellite villages around and near great urban centers. It has been shown that the unincorporated population in New York State lost

nearly 8 per cent during the decade ending 1900; gained 1.7 per cent between 1900 and 1910; increased 0.7 per cent during the next ten years; and expanded nearly 50 (49.6) per cent during the twenties.[9] Anderson traces also the rapid growth of rural populations in the urban counties of that state in contrast to the almost universal loss in the more rural counties. Thus, the rural population in the four New York City suburban counties gained 17 per cent between 1900 and 1910; 10 per cent during the next ten years; and 61 per cent during the decade ending 1930.[10] The rural-nonfarm and unincorporated inhabitants of those four counties grew nearly 70 per cent during the last ten years; while those on farms in the four counties lost 7 per cent; those in the villages of 2500 or less gained 57 per cent; those in the cities of from 2500 to 10,000 increased 34.5 per cent; and the urban population made a gain of 107 per cent.[11]

We also have an indication for the whole nation that growth of unincorporated populations is largely determined by urban population and urban growth. In 1930, the Middle Atlantic, East North Central, and South Atlantic divisions contained about 74 per cent of our national urban population and 56 per cent of the unincorporated inhabitants. During the ten years ending in 1930, 64 per cent of all urban increase and 54 per cent of all unincorporated increase were in those divisions. It seems that the development of systems of highways radiating from great cities and the accessibility of extra-urban regions made possible by motor vehicles have been largely responsible for these changes.

2. There has been a great multiplication of service stations and recreation centers along the highways throughout the nation. These appear as garages, filling stations, cafés, dance halls, cottages for tourists, and so on. There is likely to be a considerable number of persons continuously attached to these places to carry on the services demanded.

3. With the advent of automobiles and improved highways there also has been a rapid appearance of recreation, health, and retirement places in the more highly favored regions of the nation. Wherever the climate is favorable, such places spring up along the seacoast, on the shores of beautiful lakes, near the

[9] W. A. Anderson, *Population trends in New York State, 1900–1930*, 1932, p. 37.
[10] *Ibid.*, p. 10.
[11] *Ibid.*, p. 14.

streams and in the gulches of mountain regions, and even in the midst of deserts.

4. Some new farming districts, especially in irrigable regions, have opened and near-by villages have appeared as convenient service stations for agriculturists.

5. Changes in the laws of states regarding the classification of places might have a bearing. The loss of unincorporated population in New Jersey may be so explained. Had this not occurred, the per cent of gain in unincorporated inhabitants of the Middle Atlantic states would have been considerably larger.

6. There is considerable de-incorporating going on throughout the nation. By this means some places drop out of the list of incorporated places and join the ranks of the unincorporated. During hard times there is quite an inducement in this direction in order to lower the burden of taxation.

Estimates made from appropriate data of the 1940 census reveal what is taking place between central cities and village populations which lie within metropolitan districts but outside the central cities. The districts studied constitute seven twelfths of all metropolitan districts. Of these, 43 have central cities of 100,000 or more inhabitants and 38 have central populations of 50,000 to 99,999 each. The results show that the villages within the metropolitan area increased much more rapidly than the central cities. The villages comprised both incorporated and unincorporated aggregations, persons living on farms being excluded. In districts with great city centers, the unincorporated villages increased about fifteen times more rapidly and the incorporated villages only about ten times more rapidly than central cities. In the case of districts with smaller centers, the rate of increase of the former was five times that of central cities while that of incorporated villages was only a little over three times as fast.

In order to discover just what is taking place, an analytical estimate was made of the situation in four states where census material had become available. Probably much the same situation obtains in the other states. Only great city districts are missing because of a dearth of available data—two such districts are in Ohio. Table 6 presents the results of the study. These results were made possible by the fortunate discovery of a new and convenient method of estimating natural increase for various classes of state or national populations when the state rate is available.

Two attention points regarding the table are in order. First, the term "differential gain" is not entirely fit because it may represent either the sum of, or the difference between, "census" and the area from beyond its borders. Second, a comparison of the differential gains of the central and outside areas tells something about what is taking place between the two populations, but only a part. Thus, the central-area loss in Ohio just about

TABLE 6

Differential Gains in Metropolitan Districts of Specified States with Central City Having 100,000 or More Inhabitants: 1930–1940[12]

STATE	CENTRAL CITY					OUTSIDE OF CITY				
	Census Gain		Natural Increase		Differential gain	Census Gain		Natural Increase		Differential gain
	Thousands	Rate	Thousands	Rate*	Thousands†	Thousands	Rate	Thousands	Rate	Thousands†
Ohio: 6 districts	−4.7	−0.25	63.0	3.3	−58.3	81.7	13.3	31.9	5.2	59.8
Missouri: 2 districts	−6.5	−0.6	32.0	2.56	−38.5	91.2	13.1	26.3	4.43	64.9
Washington: 3 districts	11.8	2.0	14.3	2.44	−2.5	41.8	38.7	4.4	4.02	37.7
Tennessee: 4 districts	67.7	10.7	28.0	4.42	39.7	62.0	37.0	16.4	9.76	45.6

* Specific rates of natural increase were obtained by establishing the mean index number of the population classes, great cities, smaller cities, rural-non farm villages, and rural-farm and assigning to each class as its rate of natural increase such percentage of the mean state rate of natural increase for the decade in question as the weight of its ratio-index relative to the mean ratio-index entitled it to. Amounts of natural increase are derived by applying the mean decennial rate to the 1930 population. Because the number of children under five reported to enumerators is generally too small, consequent natural increase rates are understatements by 5 to 10 per cent.

† Minus sign means loss.

equals the outside-area gain by in-migration. It strongly suggests that the outside channeled off some or much of the population from the center. Of course, both areas gained inhabitants from afar and also lost migrants to distant regions. But the results are much the same as if just so many persons had moved over the inter-district boundaries in a body.

This shift outwards of city populations must signify at least two things. First, a desire to improve the economic condition by lessening rents, taxes, and other costs of living and sometimes

[12] J. M. Gillette, "Some population shifts in the United States, 1930–1940," *op. cit.*

engaging in "subsistence farming." Second, a change in attitude toward living in great centers. The auto and the highway have made it possible for city workers to live in the country, as it were, to enjoy more spacious surroundings, to have trees, gardens, plenty of sunshine, and fresh air. It is doubtless a part of the process of big-city decentralization now going on and is a significant sign of the times.

Social Economics of the Rural Community

The rural community is the scene of a group of the nation's major industries, those having to do with the producing, storage, transfer, and sale of raw materials, some of which are processed in rural areas, and much of which comes back as commodities for sale. Most, if not all, problems of the rural community are linked directly and indirectly to chains of events in the rural economy. It is very necessary, therefore, to pass in review some of the salient facts about the social economy of rural people.

The agricultural establishment. Slightly more than 30 million persons—almost 25 per cent of the national population—live on farms.[13] Many of them work at nonagricultural occupations. However, about one third are actively engaged in agriculture: in 1940, one out of every six persons gainfully employed was so occupied. There are about six million farms in the United States (as against 200,000 manufacturing establishments).[14]

American farms are highly differentiated. A group of rural economists have distinguished five major types.[15]

I. Large-scale Farms (totaling 58,313, producing over $10,000 per farm);

II. Family-Commercial Farms (totaling 2,973,192, producing from $600 to $9,999 per farm);

III. Part-time Farms (totaling 600,000, producing under $600, with operator 100 days off farm);

[13] A sample survey of the civilian population reported by the Census Bureau for April 1, 1948 indicated that the percentage of rural-farm had declined to 19.2. Moreover, the rural-farm population showed a net loss between 1940 and 1948 of 8.0 per cent, as against an increase of 20.5 per cent for the rural-nonfarm and of 13.8 per cent for the urban population. *Cf.* Bureau of the Census, *Current population reports*, Series P-23, No. 1.

[14] *Cf.* H. Barger, and H. H. Lansberg, *American agriculture, 1899–1939* (New York: National Bureau of Economic Research, 1942). However, about 30 per cent of agricultural products sold comes from no more than 250,000 farms! *Cf.* O. E. Baker, *Graphic summary of the number, size, and type of farms and value of products* (Misc. Pub. #266, United States Department of Agriculture, 1937): 68.

[15] M. R. Benedict, F. F. Elliott, H. R. Tolley, and C. Taeuber, "Need for a new classification of farms," *Journal of Farm Economics*, XXVI (1944): 694 ff.

IV. Residential Farms (totaling 600,000, producing under $600, with operator 65 years and over, working off farm less than 100 days);

V. Small-scale Farms and Unclassified (totaling 1,725,000, producing under $600, with operator under 65 years, working less than 100 days off farm).

In the last generation or so the number of farms has decreased, as the following table shows.

TABLE 7*

Number of Farms: 1910–1945

(in 1000)

Years	Number
1910	6,361
1920	6,448
1930	6,812
1940	6,097
1945	6,006

* Adapted from Kolb and Brunner, *op. cit.*, p. 93.

Parallel with this trend there has taken place a corresponding change in the pattern of ownership. It has been estimated that, as of 1940, the percentage of full owners amounted to 50.6; part owners, 10.1; tenants (of various types—cash, share, share-work, share-croppers, and others), 38.7; and managers, 0.6.[16] The growth in farm tenancy has been throughout the years large and increasing (though not consistently so). In 1880, slightly over one fourth of the farms were tenant-operated; in 1930, 42 per cent; in 1940, 38.7 per cent.[17] The factors causing the growth of farm tenancy may be listed as follows: (1) speculation and high land values, (2) the cropper system, (3) recurring economic depressions, (4) uneconomical credit and tax policies, (5) natural hazards, (6) specialized cash-crop production.[18] But whatever the complex of causes may be in any given area, the most important point socially is the fact that it is inevitably associated with undesirable social-economic conditions. Among the latter

[16] Lowry Nelson, *Rural sociology* (New York: American Book Company, 1948), p. 251.

[17] *Cf.* J. F. Timmons, "Tenure status of farm people, 1940," *Land Policy Review,* IV (1941): 29 ff.

[18] *Cf.* The President's Committee on Farm Tenancy, *Farm tenancy* (Washington, D.C.: Government Printing Office, 1937); R. R. Renne, *Land economics* (New York: Harper and Brothers, 1947), p. 438 ff.

one must include the following: (1) loss of soil fertility, (2) wind and water erosion, (3) population instability and insecurity, (4) inadequate community participation of farm tenants.[19]

One phase of change in the agricultural establishment has been the trend in the size of farms operated. The average farm comprises 175 acres, not a very good index of size in view of the fact that three fifths of all farms range from 20 to 175 acres, while 4 per cent of farms average over 500 acres and comprise 45 per cent of the total farm acreage in the United States.[20] Here again we see that the agricultural enterprise is typically small-scale; in the case of the average unit, it is not very significant in the total national economy. In terms of size, farm units have been increasing at the top and at the bottom of the ladder: the last two decades have seen a pronounced growth in the very large and in the small-scale farms. One recent study reports: "Each size group between 20 and 260 acres have decreased in importance during the decade of the 'thirties, whereas the number of farm units over 1000 acres in size increased by a fourth and the acreage of such units by a third."[21]

The agricultural labor force.   Employment in agriculture has over the last century experienced a steady and sharp drop. In 1850, 63.7 per cent of the gainfully employed were in agriculture; in 1910, 31.0 per cent; in 1940, 17.6 per cent.[22] Broken down into types of employment, the working force in agriculture was estimated for the middle 'forties thus:

TABLE 8

Estimated Working Force in Agriculture*

Type	Number
Commercial Farmers	3,300,000
Wage-workers	4,800,000
Unpaid family workers	4,200,000
Noncommercial farmers	2,200,000

*Adapted from W. Goldschmidt, "Employment categories in American Agriculture," *Journal of Farm Economics*, XXIX (1947).

[19] These conditions, and others originating also in the specific fact of farm tenancy, are treated in the President's Committee report, *op. cit.; cf.* also J. D. Black, and R. H. Allen, "Growth of farm tenancy in the United States," *Quarterly Journal of Economics*, LI (1937), 409 ff.

[20] Nelson, *op. cit.*, p. 253.

[21] Walter Goldschmidt, *As you sow* (New York: Harcourt, Brace and Company, 1947), p. 242.

[22] Taylor, *op. cit.*, p. 246.

The sizable aggregate of wage-workers in agriculture, totaling about one third of the working force, is rather surprising, especially in view of the cherished stereotype of the prevalence of individualistic, family-size farm enterprises. This situation is in large measure a result of the tremendous mechanization of agricultural operations and the commercialization of agriculture itself. The general relationship between industrially increased output on the farm and employment is brought out in the following table.[23] Unfortunately, though agricultural productivity

TABLE 9
Output per Worker: 1870–1940*

Year	Output	Employment	Output per Worker
1870	100	100	100
1890	189	145	130
1910	273	169	162
1930	345	153	225
1940	379	134	284

* Adapted from Barger and Lansberg, *op. cit.*, p. 253.

has almost doubled since 1910, agricultural wages have shown no notable increase, are in fact lower than that of any category of workers except hotel employees.[24] One should go further and point out that some of the most disadvantaged classes and areas in American life are to be found in the rural community. Thus, C. C. Taylor and associates have pointed out: "With 200,000 to 350,000 agricultural migrants in the United States, working for limited periods in harvesting intensified crops in certain areas of the country, conditions of gang labor . . . combined to exist in American agriculture."[25] Using an index based on low income, hired farm workers, farm tenants, farm families on poor land, and migrating farm families, this group of rural economists finds that disadvantaged farm people are concentrated in certain

[23] For a fuller account of mechanization in agriculture, *cf.* C. H. Hamilton, "Social effects of recent trends in mechanization of agriculture," *Rural Sociology*, IV (1930): 3 ff.

[24] *Cf.* Bureau of Agricultural Economics, 1946, *Agricultural outlook* (Washington, D.C.: Government Printing Office, 1946), p. 15.

[25] C. C. Taylor, H. W. Wheeler, and E. L. Kirkpatrick, *Disadvantaged classes in American agriculture*, United States Department of Agriculture, Federal Security Administration, and the Bureau of Agricultural Economics, co-operating, Social Research Report VIII (Washington, D.C.: Government Printing Office, 1938): 32.

areas: in the Old South, northern New Mexico, Arizona, the northern Great Plains, and scattered sections that include the Great Lakes cut-over country.[26]

The over-all mechanization tendency under way in American agriculture has led one careful and sympathetic student to summarize the evidence developed from an intensive study of an industrialized agricultural area in California as follows:

1. The industrialization of farm production is well under way and follows the general pattern of industrialization that has taken place in other branches of production.

2. The increased and ever-increasing machinery and equipment will make it possible to produce food in plenty with an ever-decreasing working force on the production end.

3. With industrialization has come a class system and a social pattern in agriculture that is essentially similar to those found in urban areas.

4. With only the rarest exception do any of the legal protections for wage workers in agriculture exist, though the agricultural industry has been and without doubt will continue to be allocated its share of total national income.

5. The conditions of farm workers, both social and economic, are substandard and not conducive to a healthy social order.

6. The number of wage workers is greater than the number of agricultural employers, while the farm operators who do not hire labor, and many who hire supplemental work done, derive their income from the value of the work they perform rather than from their entrepreneurial profits.

7. Farm policy has not been successful in halting the trend toward industrialized farming, and there is evidence to show that both price and labor policies have actually hastened the process.

8. Efficiency of operations, when measured by productive use of land or income returns to the farm-working force, is not greater on large-scale farm operations than it is on farms of moderate size capable of utilizing modern and small-size power equipment.

9. The rural values are generally translated into pecuniary terms and therefore social status and personal self-respect are in a very large measure determined by the financial condition of the individual.

10. Rural society under industrial conditions has not only excluded from social participation the wage-working group, but has effectively and in many instances advertently prevented the development of associations within the laboring group itself,

[26] *Cf.* also P. G. Beck, and M. C. Forster, *Six rural problem areas*, Research Monograph I, Federal Emergency Relief Administration (Washington, D.C.: Government Printing Office, 1935), *passim.*

thereby preventing it from developing a sense of, and capacity for, social belonging as well as from participating in community decisions.

11. The exclusion of labor from participation in the community is also the result of their poverty, poor living conditions, low educational opportunities, and the instability which results from the necessity of constant migration.[27]

Changing culture pattern of the rural economy. The industrialization and urbanization of American life have left a deep imprint on the rural economy and society. Summarily stated, they have led to such wide-ranging changes as (1) lessened rural isolation, (2) commercialized agriculture, (3) transition from hoe-culture to mechanized farming, (4) increase in part-time farming, (5) increase in the size of farm units and in the importance economically and socially of the large-scale farms, (6) decline in the movement of rural enterprisers up the agricultural ladder to farm ownership, (7) decreasing rural-urban differences socially and culturally, (8) increased emphasis on consumption (installment buying, urban merchandising standards and methods, urbanized folkways and interests).[28] The dichotomy between urban and rural is disappearing very fast in America.

A very revealing insight into the changing culture of the rural community may be found in the facts and factors of the mobile rural population. In a large and insecure stream, rural people have for three or four generations now left their homes, many of them urban-bound, others shunting back and forth through the rural community. Loss of rural population urbanward began in the 1870's, became a national phenomenon by 1910, reached its peak in the 'twenties, and is still disturbingly great.[29] In the period 1935–1940, more than half (53 per cent) of the farm population which moved went to another farm, 21.4 per cent to rural-nonfarm areas, the remainder to the city. A million farm families move annually. Tenants move two to six times as frequently as farm owners. The greatest proportion of new migration from rural-farm areas consists of the age group 15 to 19.[30]

[27] W. Goldschmidt, *As you sow, op. cit.*, p. 262. Quoted by permission.

[28] For a fuller discussion, *cf.* Taylor, et al, *Rural life, op. cit.*, Ch. 30.

[29] *Cf.* O. E. Baker, "Utilization of natural wealth," in *Recent social trends* (New York: McGraw-Hill Book Company, 1933), pp. 110–111.

[30] *Cf.* E. H. Bernert, *Volume and composition of net migration from the rural-farm population, 1930–1940*, Bureau of Agricultural Economics (Washington, D.C.: Government Printing Office, 1944). The gross economic loss of this movement— in terms of education, health, and other investments by the rural population—for

One very important background of this migration lies in a little-publicized fact about rural income. "In 1929, a fairly prosperous year, nearly half of the farms of the United States produced less than $1000 worth of crops; in the major cotton areas this group included 20 to 80 per cent of the farms."[31]

Deficits in rural social life. The variety of economic changes and trends which we have sketched here forms the background for a number of deficits in rural social living which ought to be noted. As compared with the city, the rural community is backward in culture. "Culture" is used here in the sociological or anthropological sense to include all the ideas and behavior patterns in society. Cities are the depositories of culture. The great institutions of almost every sort—places of higher education, libraries, museums, newspapers, theaters, businesses and factories, great churches and cathedrals, and seats of governments—are housed in cities. This is not necessarily because cities made or created them, but because cities are points and centers of distribution not only of material goods but of ideas, services, and influences. Incidentally it may be said that the great majority of pattern ideas and practices outside of agriculture and other extractive industries originate in cities.

The unequal distribution of, or opportunities of access to, cultural depositories and processes is a misfortune to country dwellers, from the point both of satisfactory living and of efficient work. The human mind transcends that of lower creatures because of man's great brain development. If given the chance, the mind is a great laboratory for working up ideas, and it finds the highest satisfaction in doing this. In order to be at its best, it requires constant and varied stimulation. It needs to be in touch with men and institutions where ideas abound and are exchanged. So stimulated, it develops, lives more fully, and realizes its broadest and best existence. Art, literature, music, and drama are not only fields of activity in which individuals may engage but also inspirations to high living and lofty ends for the realization of life. Culture is impersonal. It belongs to the whole of society. It should be the heritage of everyone to enjoy facilities for coming in contact with it and participating in the cultural process as fully as capacity permits.

---

the decade 1920–1930 has been estimated by O. E. Baker to exceed 20 billion dollars. *Cf.* Baker, Borsodi, and Wilson, *op. cit.*, p. 74.

[31] C. Goodrich, et al, *Migration and economic opportunity* (Philadelphia: University of Pennsylvania Press, 1936), pp. 130–131.

Rural society often is poorly equipped with certain important local institutions, such as church, school, government, and sociability facilities. It is far more a question of quality than quantity regarding school, government, and church. The one-teacher school with its average small number of pupils and great multiplicity of classes is not an efficient institution. The teacher may be immature and poorly trained. The curriculum may not be adjusted to the needs of farm life. The equipment may be meager. Opportunity for high-school training frequently is not attainable locally. The building may be ugly and the grounds bare. There are usually no facilities for carrying out projects. Much of the learning is formal, uninspirational, and perfunctory. Traditional academic bones rattle as they march through the educational process. There are, however, many good country schools. The foregoing statements regarding our backward schools are only a characterization of much that abounds in many places in our nation.

Many of the country churches could be described in somewhat the same terms as were the schools: small, undifferentiated edifices, poorly paid and poorly trained ministers, sermons and ministrations without social vision, infrequent ministrations because of "ministerial vivisection," Sunday school and music in keeping with other conditions. It is not surprising that the country church fights a losing battle. Often the rural church is not vitalizing, because it is itself devitalized and moribund.

Access to books is infrequent in the country as compared with cities. Direct and immediate library service is available for 98 per cent of urban people of Canada and the United States, while only 17 per cent of rural inhabitants have such service. The per cent for farmers is still less. Circulating libraries are good but incomplete substitutes.

Many agricultural communities are almost without sociability agencies, and residents have to travel outside or visit the neighbors to enjoy social advantages.

Farming regions generally are poorly supplied with certain kinds of welfare agencies. The availability of juvenile-court service to country populations is very much less than to urban inhabitants, even in the case of the county-court system: a ratio of 10 per cent to 100 per cent availability. The establishment of child-care agencies under federal stimulus has remedied the situation, although far from completely; in a state such as North Dakota less than half of the 53 counties possess such agencies.

Farming districts are short on such health agencies as medical inspection in schools, visiting school nurses, dental clinics, health centers, and hospitals. Physicians have deserted sparsely settled rural districts. Vital statistics lag.

In many farming communities recreation facilities for the young are backward or do not exist. Too often, farm work is supposed to furnish the growing boy and girl all the exercise they need. The object of play is commonly not understood, and play is apt to be regarded as a waste of time and energy.

If a comparison is made between the homes of farmers and those of the equivalent property and income class of cities, it is found that the homes of the farmers are, on the average, inferior. One sees in the country in all parts of the nation farm shacks which would be almost a disgrace in the worst city slum district. The redeeming feature is that farming people have plenty of pure air and sunshine, and room for the enjoyment of them; also, generally, an abundance of fresh, wholesome food. The conveniences in the home are likely to be inferior to those in the barn and field. Water piped into the house is found in less than a sixth of farm homes, bathtubs in a fifth, gas or electric light in 13 per cent, and power machinery in 15 per cent; but over 50 per cent have washing machines, 95 per cent sewing machines, 60 per cent sink and drain, 96 per cent screened windows, and 85 per cent an outdoor toilet. Farm homes with a telephone range from 11 per cent in the South Atlantic to 65 per cent in the West North Central states, the national farm average being 34 per cent. It is likely that the homes of farmers of the Northeast and the North Central regions of the nation are as well as or better supplied with telephones than are those of the masses of city dwellers.

The rapid changes which have appeared in many parts of the open country have been due to, or are associated with, several agencies or influences. These are the widespread adoption of the automobile by farmers, the increased accessibility to improved highways, the universal spread of the radio, and the increased power and stimulus of urbanism.

All these improvements together have now placed a large proportion of the farming inhabitants in touch with city and town life and attractions. They have facilitated greatly the urbanizing of the minds of country people.

These combined influences have greatly transformed social attitudes, contacts, and forms of organization and association.

Studies by J. H. Kolb in Wisconsin and by John Johansen in North Dakota have found that the old neighborhoods have disintegrated, many having passed out of existence. In their place wider associations and organizations are forming, some of which are clearly temporary in character. What the ultimate form of these associations is going to be is not yet evident. There is also a strong tendency among farmers to neglect the close neighboring with near-by neighbors, formerly practiced. Joy rides, pleasure trips, wider organizations, town attractions, passing on roads rapidly with a salute instead of stopping to talk as previously when driving horses have minimized the intimate and frequent visiting of former days.

Again, the changing culture pattern of the rural community is suggested in the decline of the rural village. There are ample reasons for considering village decline as a national social problem. It represents a shift in the population of a nation, due to the changing conditions at work within that nation. Too, the number of persons directly involved in villages and hence fighting a losing battle constitutes a significant portion of our nation's inhabitants. The total rural-nonfarm population, people living in villages, amounted to over 27 millions in 1940, which was over 20 per cent, or about one fifth, of our total population. The portion represented in the affected villages would be several million persons.

Finally, the life of the inhabitants of the villages which are losing population is adversely affected in nearly all social-economic directions. Businesses are failing, property values are disappearing, homes are being broken up, ambition and hope are waning, anxiety and worry are incapacitating life activities, and local institutions are disintegrating. The forces that are working out these results are beyond the control of the people involved, and the process goes on gradually, but inevitably. The number of families and persons and the amount of property involved far exceed the losses from the San Francisco earthquake or the Mississippi flood. The importance of the problem has been obscured by the fact that the afflicted villages are dispersed throughout the nation, and the process of decline is gradual and unobtrusive. To make an array, though necessarily a partial one, of the causes and of their possible control is a worth-while undertaking.

An absolute loss of farming people brings decline in the agricultural villages. Such populations decline by migration to towns and cities, by migration to other extractive areas, and by reduced rates of natural increase. So far, the widespread depopulation that exists is chiefly occasioned by migration from farms, and seldom by falling birth rates, although farm birth rates are falling. The specified reductions in farm population of the following states during the decade closing with World War II are to be explained by out-migration from farms: North Dakota 69,000; South Dakota 82,000; Nebraska 87,000; Kansas 101,000; Oklahoma 90,000; Iowa 69,000: total 498,000. The great social and cosmic forces behind such migrations hold little hope for control; in fact they have become intensified.

The social-cultural evolution of the last century has brought villages increasingly into competition with larger aggregations of population. Improved railways, rural mail delivery and parcel post, the coming of motor vehicles, federal aid to states for highways, the creation of good roads everywhere, and mail-order business are some of the agencies making for closer rivalry in business. As improved highways and motor vehicles appear, the doom of many villages is sealed. We cannot hope for a reversal of the process. They are all agencies making for so-called civilization and will not be denied.

Mining and lumbering villages depend for their existence on forest and mineral supplies. When mining and lumbering cease, these settlements decline and become "ghost towns" or disappear. In its nature, mining is destructive of mineral supplies. Mined-out veins, lodes, and pools are gone forever. There is no restorative. Hence gold, silver, copper, coal, zinc, and oil fields are strewn with wreckages of once-flourishing villages and cities. In this country, lumbering and dependent villages tell about the same story. We have imperial domains where forests have been mined out and destroyed and of cut-over land which carries a minimum of hope. We shall never resurrect the magnificent forests we have mined and burned nor the thousands of towns they once gave life to. We may plant new forests where some of them were, and new lumbering villages may appear in the dim future; but the great lumber age with its villages has gone forever.

This causal interpretation was first set forth by one of the writers in 1922.[32] It is substantiated in a concrete way by the study of C. E. Lively[33] in Minnesota and that of T. Lynn Smith

[32] Cf. J. M. Gillette, *Rural sociology*, 1922: Ch. 21; and 1936: Ch. 28.
[33] *Loc. cit.*, Growth and decline of farm trade centers in Minnesota, 1905-30.

in Louisiana. We reproduce a table from Lively's book on the factors of decline for 37 out of 68 case studies which gives additional data.

TABLE 10
Factors in the Decline of Villages

Immediate Factors in Decline (1905–1930)	Number of Cases
1. Loss of post office	22
2. Destruction of business establishments that were not rebuilt	5
3. Death of proprietor of business establishment	4
4. Breakdown of social unity due to decline of dominant institution, the church	3
5. Poor merchandising,—too few goods and poor service	2
6. Loss of county seat	1

Toward the Stabilization of the Rural Community

The problems of the rural community, as we have seen, have long been national problems. The attention of the nation was focused on them by the various agrarian movements of the nineteenth century.[34] Popular concern was powerfully stimulated by President Theodore Roosevelt's famous commission and by the subsequent Country Life Movement which got under way with the nation-wide discussion of the findings of the commission. The farm bloc which was formed in the years after the First World War and which was spurred on by President Harding's National Agricultural Conference in 1922 was able to spearhead a legislative drive that achieved—for better or worse—such measures as the Tariff Act of 1922, the Federal Farm Board, the Smoot-Hawley Tariff Act, as well as numerous credit and marketing legislations. By the 1930's agriculture had become accepted as a special national interest requiring a special public policy. Initially—and continuously—the heart of "the rural problem" has been the various phases of the farm-income situation. More generally stated, rural-community improvement must be seen, fundamentally and ultimately, as economic improvement.

[34] For a brief summary of them, cf. B. H. Hibbard, *Agricultural economics* (New York: McGraw-Hill Book Company, 1948), Chs. 27–32.

Farm income and rural-community welfare. The income capacity of the rural population has suffered rather severe disadvantages. Consider the following instances. Between 80 and 90 per cent of the entire agricultural output is food, yet the national per capita food consumption has remained very stable for the last forty years. Agricultural production has increased 50 per cent since 1899, whereas industrial production has gone up fourfold. The share of agriculture in the national income since the turn of the century sank from 21 to 12 per cent, but the share of manufacturing rose from 19 to 30 per cent.[35] Farm-product prices are very sensitive to changes in the industrial economy; however, the prices of the products farmers buy are relatively insensitive to changes in general economic expectations. Unlike industrial production, which is highly responsive to ups and downs in economic expectations, agricultural production in the aggregate responds very slowly, or not at all. As economist Theodore W. Schultz puts it, "When business contracts, agricultural production does not drop, while the prices received by farmers for their products move more slowly than the prices they pay for goods and services used. . . . "[36] This inverse relationship between trends in agricultural and industrial indexes has resulted in a paradoxical situation, well described by President A. W. Griswold of Yale University: "Hence the greater the expansion of the national income through industrialization, the smaller the portion of it received by farmers."[37]

Recognition of this disparity has been the essential principle of American farm policy since 1922. That year President Harding's National Agricultural Conference reported: "The manufacturer has in the past quickly adjusted his production to price recessions while the farmer has not. When farm production is so large that the product cannot be sold for prices that will maintain a reasonable standard of living on the farms, the supply is too large."[38]

Appreciation of this disparity has been the cornerstone of the various American farm programs since that time, especially

[35] *Cf.* H. R. Tolley, "Appraisal of the national interest in the agricultural situation," *American Economic Review: Papers and Proceedings, 1940:* 112–113.

[36] Theodore Schultz, *Agriculture in an unstable economy* (New York: The Macmillan Company, 1945), p. 132.

[37] A. W. Griswold, *Farming and democracy* (New York: Harcourt, Brace and Company, 1948), p. 6.

[38] Quoted by Wesley McCune, *Farm bloc* (New York: Doubleday and Company, 1943), p. 17.

with the advent of the New Deal in 1933. It is the underlying principle in the Agricultural Adjustment Act of 1933, the Soil Conservation and Domestic Allotment Act of 1936, the new Agricultural Adjustment Act of 1938, the Agricultural Marketing Agreement Act, and the establishment of the Federal Crop Insurance Corporation. The Agricultural Adjustment Act of 1933 formulated the current parity concept as follows: "It is hereby declared to be the policy of the Congress—(1) To establish and maintain such balance between the production and consumption of agricultural commodities, and such marketing conditions therefore, as well as to re-establish prices to farmers at a level that will give agricultural commodities a purchasing power with respect to articles that farmers buy, equivalent to the purchasing power of agricultural commodities in the base period." Subject to many different formulas and experimental programs, this general policy underlies the governmental attempt to stabilize rural community life in this country.[39]

It must not be forgotten, however, that instability of farm income is, despite varying parity formulas and measures, likely to continue, for two important reasons: changes in the demand for agricultural commodities and changes originating in agricultural production itself. To assist in anticipating and counteracting the former, Schultz, who is a prominent agricultural economist, has urged that compensating payments to farmers in periods of industrial unemployment and depression plus the long-range stabilization of the industrial-urban economy are vitally necessary to the rural community. For the latter he has stressed improvements in farm technology, crop insurance, and storage programs, along with soil-conservation measures.[40] These, he has argued, should provide the floor absolutely essential to an economy which has been in the last two generations so disastrously unstable.[41]

A program for agricultural labor. Another phase of rural stabilization concerns the status and outlook of agricultural labor.

[39] This policy is not without its contradictions. Comments Schultz: "What we have experienced in agriculture suggests that vigorous, enterprising farms and equally vigorous, well-designed governmental programs may be highly complementary." Schultz, *op. cit.*, p. 164. Quoted by permission.

[40] *Cf.* Schultz, *op. cit.*, pp. 212 ff.

[41] Students of rural economics realistically accept the necessity and desirability of a commercialized agriculture. Typical of their reaction to such counter-proposals as self-sufficient farming is the following comment: "A self-sufficient farm in our time is more likely to be a haunt of illiteracy and malnutrition than a wellspring of democracy." Griswold, *op. cit.*, p. 137.

American agriculture has been increasingly characterized, as we have seen, by overcrowded and underproductive employment. The mechanization hastened by the labor shortages of the second World War only underscored this condition. The virtual stagnation of the upward-bound stream of rural enterprisers from the status of tenancy to farm ownership is a very disturbing facet of this problem. The lack of protection and security of agricultural workers is not widely appreciated in this country. Nor has the outward-bound volume of rural migration, so unsettling in its effects on the rural community, spent itself, for various reasons. Foremost among the factors creating pressure for movement of people from the farms are: (1) labor-saving equipment, which is becoming more readily available; (2) the fact that agricultural earnings are still out of line with those in other enterprises; and (3) increasing efficiency in farm management, which has as one of its effects economizing on labor.

Most decidedly, then, a general equity program is urgent. Several suggestions have been made. They include:

1) minimum wages;
2) establishment of the right to organize and bargain collectively;
3) extension of the principles of social security (*e.g.*, unemployment insurance, old-age pensions, and so forth);
4) the development of an adult-education system patterned after the present Extension Service but freed from its apparent servitude to the Farm Bureau Federation;
5) creation of an employment service operated with the view to getting the workers jobs;
6) the development of community labor pools among farmers;
7) break-up of large holdings;
8) co-operative farming developments;
9) land purchase programs with federal aid.[42]

Social elements in rural community stabilization.   Rural stabilization is, of course, more than a matter of economics. Mark A. Dawber, well-known rural specialist, has expressed this point strikingly. "There are four major planks in the rural life platform; they are: people—land—agriculture—community."[43] As elsewhere in American society, these phases interact and inter-

[42] *Cf.* Goldschmidt, *As you sow, op. cit.*, pp. 264 ff.; M. R. Benedict, "Economic aspects of remedial measures designed to meet the problems of displaced labor," *Rural Sociology*, V (1940): 163 ff.

[43] In "Foreword" to D. E. Lindstrom, *Rural life and the church* (Champaign: Garrard Press, 1946). Quoted by permission.

penetrate. We have, however, in the present discussion taken the fairly realistic position that making a good living helps immeasurably to make a good life, for rural people as for anybody else. How important this fact is can be seen in certain aspects of the rural standard of living.

A standard of living is the level of expenditure maintained by a family or other class or group of people. Standards of living "rise" with the increase of income. This means chiefly that the scope of expenditure widens, so that more goods and services are used and commanded. Investigators of farm standards of living have much to say in behalf of the desirability of raising or widening standards. They undoubtedly are correct in their position. It would be a splendid thing if all farmers could enjoy more of the amenities and benefits of a high level of culture. However, since about 1922, the trend has been toward lower rather than higher standards of living for the masses of farmers of the United States. It is useless to advocate a campaign in behalf of higher living levels until the nation has solved the farmer's economic problem. Since we have already reviewed the economic situation and outlook for agriculture, we shall have to rest our case with that statement.

Four crucial areas of rural community stabilization are those of education, religion, homes, and health. In closing this general discussion of the rural community we can hardly do better than to consider them.

Students of rural education generally agree that school consolidation offers the greatest possibilities for improving rural schools. The chief benefits to rural life to be derived from consolidation are the following:

1. Stimulus in schoolwork which comes from larger numbers in school and class.
2. Organized play and games made possible by increased numbers.
3. Better-equipped teachers, specialization in teaching work, and improvement in superintendence due to an increased teaching staff.
4. A greater degree of scientific, vocational, and community-articulated education by reason of adequate buildings, grounds, and equipment.
5. The accurate grading of the schools, with consequent advantages to pupils and teachers and heightened efficiency.
6. The provision of a plant and facilities for community life and social-center activities, and the continued education of adults.

7. Increased comfort and sanitary safety for pupils and teachers.
8. Enlarged attendance and lengthened school year due to increased efficiency, fruitfulness of schoolwork, stimulus of numbers, and drawing power of gymnasium and athletics.
9. The improvement of local roads, bringing in outside talent for community programs.
10. The provision of much-needed opportunity for high-school work while giving the child the advantage of living at home.
11. The re-organization of the school to train really and constructively for farm life, with the resultant creation of the permanent, resident leadership from the lack of which the country is now suffering.
12. The eventual establishment of teacherages, thus securing a more permanent teaching staff that can identify itself with farm life and furnish some of the needed social leadership.

Many of our open-country schools have been inferior because local taxes were insufficient to maintain them properly. Especially during times of depression, in certain parts of the nation a large number of the farmers' schools have been closed for want of funds. Some of the state legislatures, during the winter session of 1933, favored closing the higher institutions of learning and using state educational funds for local farm and village schools. North Dakota provides funds to supplement low salaries of rural teachers and to pay tuition of farm boys and girls attending high schools outside their district.

Because the church is a voluntary institution and especially because of the competition among the multiplicity of religious sects, any solution for the church is beset with great difficulties. Inasmuch as the situation is vulnerable, however, it seems that some improvement might be made by developing churches in the following directions:

1. Consolidate churches, making possible larger and better-equipped plants, improved facilities, greater specialization and organization for the social work of the community, a wider and more secure economic basis for the support of pastor and community undertakings. This will make more attractive, more effective, and better churches and make possible pastors instead of mere preachers.

2. Modernize the training of ministers. This contemplates two things. First, reconstruct the curricula of theological seminaries so that the minister's mind comes to have the scientific and social approach. Second, specialize ministers for pastorates

among farming people, that is, for understanding farm problems in their economic and social aspects, and equip them with the methods and techniques to realize the farmer's social needs.

3. Pay ministers living wages, something that is not now done in the country generally. This will raise the grade of pastors, by making it possible for men of a higher type (by both capacity and training) to devote themselves to the service of farm life. This, together with the other improvements, will eliminate ministerial vivisection and the minister's division of his time among two or more churches, and it will allow a man to do a man's job with and for one community.

Home improvements. The difficulties met in considering the improvement of the farm home are numerous. Consider the force of these facts: First, 39 per cent of our farmers are renters, and the improvement of the home plant depends on the good will of the owner. Second, a large per cent of farmer-owners are marginal producers, and there is no surplus from which improvements can be made. Third, a much larger per cent of the farmers are without much education and do not appreciate the need for improvement. These are only some of the factors of the situation.

Consider how those conditions could be changed. Our present dominant system of farm tenancy places a premium on soil and farm-plant deterioration by the renter because it does not provide him an economic motive for making improvements. If he makes improvements and has to leave a farm, he loses the cost of improvements. British laws secure renters against such losses. As to marginal producers, little can be expected from them. A long process of education might be expected to raise the standards and demands of low-culture farming people who now do not appreciate improved homes.

The chief impediments to realizing adequate farm homes are poverty and the traditional patriarchal attitude of the farmer. The average farmer begrudges money that goes into dwellings and household equipment. Until his attitude is changed, many farms will have dwellings inferior to the economic ability of the owner-operator. The older generation will likely remain obdurate, but oncoming farmers could be trained to think of good dwellings as a necessary part of the farm plant.

The federal government provides limited financing of farm homes by way of Home Owners' Loan Corporation, Federal Housing Administration, Farm Security Administration, and the Rehabilitation Program, which is part of the Farm Security Administration. The HOLC is largely a refunding institution. Loans are conditional upon a pretty thorough repairing of the dwellings. The FHA makes loans up to 90 per cent of the cost of construction, thus making building possible with a cash advance of only 10 per cent. The plan of repayment is long-term amortization, with interest at 5 per cent, with an additional 0.5 per cent for administrative costs. The last-named agencies may build homes and equip farms for down-and-out farmers who are good investments; or buy out submarginal farmers and provide new farms, including construction of adequate farm and home buildings, on favorable terms.

Finally, there is the important matter of rural health. Judged by death rates, rural districts have been healthier than urban and they still are, although urban populations in some states have lower rates than rural. The greater deficiencies in health in eyes, ears, teeth, and throat of rural children are probably due to a greater lack of medical care and perhaps even to a less balanced diet than urban children experience. While the situation relative to rural health is generally satisfactory as we have regarded things, considerable improvements are possible and necessary. This has been shown by the experience of counties having full-time health units. The health experiments conducted by the Kellogg Foundation, the Rockefeller Foundation, the United States Public Health Office, and those reported by the Milbank Memorial Fund demonstrate that a well-manned rural health unit can overcome much of the inadequate medical care and can improve rural health. The greatest handicap of the rural community in this respect is the distance from physicians and hospitals. Really competent county health units and group medical programs can greatly reduce this isolation and lack, as widespread and increasingly popular efforts have shown. The interest in co-operative medical programs being displayed by such national rural groups as the Farmers' Union and the Farm Bureau Federation as well as by the variety of health services being provided by various governmental agencies, state and federal, will go a long way toward correcting this imbalance.

There are many roads to rural security, as we have learned in the last generation. The biggest problem remaining perhaps is to map them, study them, publicize them and encourage their use co-operatively by schools, churches, rural community councils, and governmental agencies.

QUESTIONS

1. Why is it important to distinguish between various types of rural community? Illustrate.
2. How may the trends in the population of rural communities be explained? Will they continue? Why?
3. Contrast the popular with the professional economists' conception of "the farm." Which of the two do you think federal and state legislators consider? Why?
4. What are the social or community consequences of farm ownership as against farm tenancy? Explain.
5. What evidence can be cited for the argument that agricultural workers are becoming "industrialized"?
6. In what ways is the culture pattern of the rural community changing? Why?
7. List some of the deficits in rural social life. Do you think that rural people would agree with your list? Why?
8. What are the reasons for the rural income since 1920? What was the proposal made by the National Agricultural Conference in 1922? What has been done about that proposal since then?
9. Why may we continue to anticipate instability of farm income?
10. What are the various "roads to rural security"? Are they all economic? In what sense is economic security basic to all the other programs of rural security?

REFERENCES

BAKER, O. E., BORSODI, R., and WILSON, M. L., *Agriculture in modern life*. New York: Harper and Brothers, 1939.

BECK, P. G., and FORSTER, M. C., *Six rural problem areas*, Research Monograph I, Federal Emergency Relief Administration. Washington, D.C.: Government Printing Office, 1935.

GILLETTE, J. M., *Rural sociology*. New York: The Macmillan Company, 1936.

GOLDSCHMIDT, W., *As you sow*. New York: Harcourt, Brace and Company, 1947.

HIBBARD, B. H., *Agricultural economics*. New York: McGraw-Hill Book Company, 1948.

KOLB, J. H., and BRUNNER, E. DE S., *Study of rural sociology*. Boston: Houghton Mifflin Company, 1946.

LINDSTROM, D. E., *Rural life and the church*. Champaign: Garrard Press, 1946.

McCUNE, W., *Farm bloc*. New York: Doubleday and Company, 1943.

NELSON, LOWRY, *Rural sociology*. New York: American Book Company, 1948.

President's Committee on Farm Tenancy, *Farm tenancy*. Washington, D.C.: Government Printing Office, 1937.

RENNE, R. R., *Land economics*. New York: Harper and Brothers, 1947.

SANDERSON, D., *Rural sociology and rural social organization*. New York: John Wiley and Sons, 1942.

TAYLOR, C. C., et al, *Rural life in the United States*. New York: Alfred A. Knopf, 1949.

United States Department of Agriculture, *Farmers in a changing world*, 1940 Yearbook. Washington, D.C.: Government Printing Office, 1940.

CHAPTER 7

Social Problems of the Modern City

The City as a Social Fact

The city, more than any other part of society, is the expression of the cumulative experiences of men in their attempt to live and work together. It is the intensification of association and interdependence, and the expression of the highest achievements of civilization. Cities exhibit all the social problems, save those peculiar to agricultural extractive pursuits. The larger share of a city's problems arises from, or centers about, the concentration and congestion of population. Many of these problems are treated elsewhere in this volume. Here we shall confine ourselves to those problems arising chiefly out of the massing together of humanity within small areas.[1]

Culture stage of origin. The determination of the cultural stage at which the city developed depends on the inclusiveness of the concept "city."[2] In the broadest sense, the dominating idea of *rural* is farming—agricultural extraction. All people whose occupation is not agricultural extraction, and who at the same time live in larger segregated groups, are urbanites.

The city, as we know it, came into existence whenever villages and towns became dominantly industrial and commercial. The hunting villages developed into agricultural communal aggregations. These have appeared almost everywhere, but they were made up of farmers. The rise of permanent market places,

[1] On the phenomenon of urbanism as an historic and sociological fact, see L. Wirth, "Urbanism as a way of life," *American Journal of Sociology* (July, 1938), 44: 1 ff. Certain parts of this chapter appeared in *The Standard* 37 (November 1950): 64 ff. Reprinted by permission of the editor.

[2] For various definitions of the city, see S. A. Queen, and L. F. Thomas, *City* (New York: McGraw-Hill Book Company, 1938), Ch. 1.

or towns, heralds the rise of cities. The retailers, the exporters and importers of goods, the craftsmen of various sorts, and the subsidiary-service functionaries constituted a population distinctively different from that of primitive agricultural communes. Such places appeared very late in the life of mankind. In terms of European history, the phenomenon of the town extends no further back than 2500 years. In Egypt and Mesopotamia it antedates the Christian era by some four thousand years. It is thus seen that of all the thousands of years which anthropologists now allege man has existed, urban phenomena cover only five or six thousand.[3]

Development of cities. Occidental civilization has seen two city ages: the "classic" period, that preceding the medieval or so-called "dark" ages, and the one during the last two or three centuries.[4] The ancient world had a few large centers of population and relatively few small ones. In the time of city-states, the state comprised a large urban population in the capital city and a larger rural one scattered in agricultural villages and a few towns. Thus, Athens was the center of Attica, Corinth of Achaia, Jerusalem of Judea, and Rome of ancient Italy. Industrialism, as we know it, had not appeared. Nevertheless, the cultural splendor of Athens was built upon the wealth obtained from its industrial and commercial life.

Rome went beyond the city-state stage of government. The great system of highways operated by the government seems to have brought into existence a high development of urbanism and travel. Imperial couriers covered 150 miles a day, and private travel from the Euphrates to the Thames was "swifter, safer, and more comfortable than ever again until well into the nineteenth century." Caesar found no real towns in Gaul, but "in the third century that province had 116 flourishing cities, with baths, temples, amphitheaters, works of art, roads, aqueducts, and schools of eloquence and rhetoric. Particular attention was paid to the water supply. That of Rome was better than that of London or Paris today. Most of the large cities, too, had more and better public baths than the modern capitals of Europe or the cities of America."[5]

[3] Cf. P. Geddes, *Cities in evolution* (London: Eyre and Spottiswoode, 1913); N. S. B. Gras, *Introduction to economic history* (New York: Harper and Brothers, 1922).
[4] Cf. R. Turner, *Great cultural traditions* (New York: McGraw-Hill Book Company, 1941), 2 vols.
[5] W. M. West, *Ancient world* (Boston: Allyn and Bacon, 1913), pp. 493–502.

Plainly the life of Rome was a city life. "We are to think of a few great cities, like Rome, Alexandria, and Antioch," with great populations "and with their rabble fed by the state. Then we must think of the rest of the empire mapped into municipalities, each a farming district with a town at its core."[6]

For five hundred years after the fall of Rome, Europe was essentially rural. The typical figures of society were the tonsured priest, the mailed horseman, and the field laborer bent with toil and hard fare. In the 11th century, cities again appeared; and the townsman, or burgher, was added to the other three figures. The rise of the medieval towns marks the appearance of new interests and forces. Feudalism had grown up out of military force in the persons of great freebooters and leaders. The new civilization was the product of trading, manufacturing, and business interests. Feudalism had been militant and aristocratic. The new order demanded peace and order and, in its measure of power and insight, worked for the elevation of the common people.

The modern city, proper, is only a century or so old—in some nations, only a half century or less—and expresses many new conditions. Let us see what some of these are.

Outstanding social characteristics. There is a group of qualities which differentiate cities, especially large ones, from farming and village populations. We shall have to mention and treat them in the most meager fashion.[7]

1. Industrialism, with labor and capital, instead of land, is the dominating feature. Cities are great industrial centers in which raw materials are shipped in, worked up into consumers' goods, and again shipped out to consumers. The process calls for great masses of labor and much capital. The massing of population gives rise to many pathological social conditions.

2. Family and home life are relatively less important in cities than among farmers. The city home is not a workshop or center about which the family life revolves. It lacks economic unity and function, as compared with the farm family. Many of its functions are absorbed by hotels, boarding houses, clubs, and eating places; and many interests bid for the attention and

---

[6] *Ibid.*

[7] For a more comprehensive discussion of urban social characteristics, *cf.* N. P. Gist, and L. A. Halbert, *Urban society*, 3rd ed. (New York: T. Y. Crowell Company, 1948), Parts IV-V; N. Carpenter, *Sociology of city life* (New York: Longmans, Green and Company, 1931); Queen and Thomas, *op. cit.*

time of the various members old enough to move about outside. The percentage of owned homes is much smaller than in rural districts. There is a greater percentage of single, divorced, and widowed persons.

3. Age distribution favors the city. It has proportionally fewer dependent persons on account of immaturity and decrepitude than the country. Thirty-eight per cent of those who lived on farms as compared with 24.2 per cent of those living in cities were under 15 years of age in 1940. At the same time, 14.3 per cent of farmers and 15 per cent of urbanites were 55 or over. Thus nearly 51 out of every 100 city people were in the vigorous, productive period of life as compared with only 47 in the country.

4. Urban people are relatively remote from nature. Surplus culture has intervened between them and nature. They are highly protected against the thrusts of physical environment. Production of material goods is one or several steps removed from that of raw materials. There is a high degree of artificiality of life, in the sense that artificial rather than natural things and processes are employed. Multitudes of children in great cities scarcely see the sun, step on soil, feel direct thrusts of the wind, or know what animals outside the zoos look like.

5. Racial and class divisions abound in large cities.[8] There is a spectacular juxtaposition of racial and nationality elements. The foreign-born segregate into colonies of their own kinds and stand aloof. Because the population differs in occupations and in ownership of wealth, urban society is stratified into many more or less defined economic and social classes.

6. Cities abound in antitheses and extremes.[9] Juxtaposed occur colossal wealth and extremest poverty, mansions and hovels, blacks and whites, browns and yellows, geniuses and idiots, creators and wasters, the learned and the illiterate, the pure and the vile, criminals and those of meticulous probity. There appears the strange paradox of the finest humanitarianism and altruism and the most brutal disregard for life and rights in business, factories, and on the street. The same man may give lavishly to schools and foundations and at the same time pay

[8] On the racial and class structure of the city, cf. W. L. Warner, and P. S. Lunt, *Social life of a modern community* (New Haven: Yale University Press, 1941); E. L. Anderson, *We Americans: A study of change in an American city* (Cambridge: Harvard University Press, 1937).

[9] For a study of these paradoxical extremes, cf. H. Zorbaugh, *Gold coast and the slum* (Chicago: University of Chicago Press, 1939).

his workers less than a living wage or dump them onto the public by closing his workshops without warning.

7. Cities are segregating and producing places of various pathological classes.[10] In 1923, commitments of criminals and delinquents were three times that in rural districts, 25.1 to 7.6 per 100,000 of the population. There is almost exactly twice the proportion of insane persons in cities as in rural districts. The poor, those who need public relief, are made in cities or congregate there. Depressions throw millions in factories and stores out of work. Technological unemployment is disproportionately heavy in urban places. Because of anonymity, residents and transients have greater protection for immoral practices, and are less loyal to marital vows.

8. Large centers of population tend to overstimulation.[11] The multitude of activities and interests press on the mind from every direction and make their seductive appeals. Sounds, sights, crowds, currents and movements, things to go to every moment, papers coming out hourly are invitations and excitants difficult to avoid. Probably the average person is overstimulated. Too many appeals may produce superficiality of thinking. Excessive stimulation breaks down nerve control and results in disintegration of personality. Unless there are sufficient counterchecks, frequent stimulation of ideas and exciting situations are conducive to crowd-mindedness.

9. Cities are centers of culture.[12] In them the cultural surplus of the ages is deposited and ready for absorption. They probably create culture more than do other communities. At least they are distributors of culture.

10. Communal activities are inevitably practiced in urban centers.[13] Necessity compels segregated persons in large number to co-operate in many ways. Safety of person, health, and property leads to police, fire, and health activities. Convenience

[10] On the social pathology of the city, cf. Queen and Thomas, op. cit., Chs. 17, 21; R. E. L. Faris, and H. W. Dunham, Mental disorders in urban areas (Chicago: University of Chicago Press, 1939); M. B. Clinard, "Process of urbanization and criminal behavior," American Journal of Sociology (1942) 48: 202 ff.

[11] On the psycho-cultural values of the city, cf. Theodore Dreiser, Color of a great city (New York: Boni and Liveright, 1923).

[12] Few studies have brought out this fact so well as Turner, op. cit.

[13] The city as a communal, symbiotic fact has been a primary concern of the urban ecologist. Cf. R. D. McKenzie, Metropolitan community (New York: McGraw-Hill Book Company, 1933); M. A. Alihan, Social ecology (New York: Columbia University Press, 1938); J. A. Quinn, Human ecology (New York: Prentice-Hall, 1950).

also may lead to large joint undertakings. The group must also look after the poor and neglected.

The city as an index of the culture. This brief review of the salient social traits of the city suggests that the urban community is a mirror of the total culture. It is not merely a characteristic place of residence but also the workshop of American society. The metropolitan areas of this nation contain the majority of industrial establishments, industrial wage-earners, and salaried workers. Most of the wholesale trade is centered in these areas. Indeed, they tend to be the managerial, service, and commercial distributing centers of the nation. They are likewise the foci of communication and transportation. "Half of all railroad passengers either begin or end their journeys in twelve metropolitan districts."[14] They are the heart of American cultural activity. For here is found "the cultural apparatus of modern civilized living."[15] Finally, the metropolitan and urban districts of America "play a major role in the national economy." For example, "a preponderant share of the public services formerly non-existent has fallen upon the shoulders of urban government."[16] The Urbanism Subcommittee of the National Resources Committee concluded that the urban community is, indeed, a measure of the maturity of the nation.

The city: uniformities and variations. It is, of course, inaccurate to talk about "the city" without reminding ourselves that cities, like human beings, exhibit huge variations.

To be sure, there are marked uniformities, the most noteworthy of which are the spatial patterns of American cities. Cities expand in the form of pulsations from their centers. The result is a pattern of concentric zones. This image of the city depicts five well-defined areas: 1. The "Loop," chief business, civic, social work, and culture center. 2. A "transition" district, where industry and business are entering and people are moving out. Those who live here are the poor; "slums" exist, and new immigrants live in "colonies." "Social problems" concentrate here: housing, poverty, vice, crimes. 3. Chiefly a workingman's family area and the second stand for immigrants on their development upward to higher social strata. It is a tenement district largely. 4. A zone which is the abode of business and professional

---

[14] National Resources Committee, *Our cities* (Washington, D.C.: Government Printing Office, 1937), p. 3.
[15] *Ibid.*
[16] *Ibid.*

families, a better type of residential district than the third area.
5. Commuters' zone, consisting of suburbs and satellite cities.

In much the same manner, the areas are classified relative to
the domestic situation. The "Loop" region is a nonfamily area
where single people live in hotels and boarding houses. Surrounding this is the "emancipated" family area, along highways between defined neighborhoods. Next is the "paternal" family

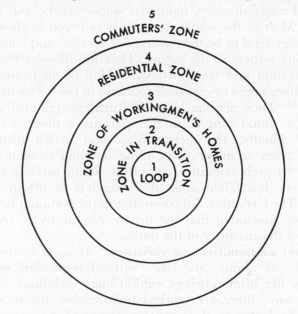

Figure 3. Idealized Form of a Great City

region of wage-earners, where the father is the head of the family.
Families are large, there is little divorce but much desertion.
Beyond this is the "equalitarian" family district of business and
professional people much addicted to apartments. Families are
small, and there are some divorce and desertion. The wife has
some interests outside the home. Last is the "maternal" area of
separate homes, small families, almost no divorce and desertion,
with the wife the head of the home for neighborhood purposes.[17]

[17] For evaluation of the zonal hypothesis, cf. M. R. Davie, "Pattern of urban
growth," in G. P. Murdock, ed., *Studies in the science of society* (New Haven: Yale
University Press, 1937); H. Hoyt, *Structure and growth of residential neighborhoods in
American cities* (Washington, D.C.: Federal Housing Administration, 1939); W.
Firey, *Land use in central Boston* (Cambridge: Harvard University Press, 1947);
Quinn, *op. cit.* The zonal hypothesis was originally presented by E. W. Burgess,
"Growth of the city," in R. E. Park, ed., *City* (Chicago: University of Chicago
Press, 1925).

Another way to describe the uniformities of modern cities is to call attention to the set of forces which seem to determine their life-ways. These forces are generally summarized under the term "urbanization."[18] The modern city is a creation of the industrial culture. Two well-known writers on urbanism have catalogued the social-economic forces creating and changing the urban community as follows: I. Industrialization; II. Commercialization; III. Mechanization of agriculture; IV. Psycho-cultural attractions of the city: adventure, freedom, anonymity, variety.[19] Working concomitantly, they uniformly bring technological and social changes to bear upon cities of all sizes and locations.

However, cities vary in many marked respects in their social and ecological responses to these changes. Some cities are very old, others very young; some densely populated, others dispersed; sprawling and large-scale, or small. Some are industrial cities, others residential, or commercial, or cultural. One city may have a single economic function, others many such functions. Some are linked together in great strings or conurbations or swarms —giant metropolitan regions; others are isolated by great distances. American cities manifest wide variations in their housing, social welfare, and educational and recreational standards and practices.

Yet, the city, whatever its size or quality of life, seems to create certain typical social problems. Noting a very large number of them, the Urbanism Subcommittee of the National Resources Committee selected the following problem situations as common and urgent:[20]

1. economic security of the working population;
2. the problem of size, congestion, optimum growth;
3. social welfare;
4. crime prevention and control;
5. leisure;
6. slums; substandard and inadequate housing;
7. land-use policies and planning;
8. transportation and other public utilities;
9. community organization and planning;
10. modernization of government.

[18] On this concept, cf. W. S. Thompson, "Urbanization," Encyclopedia of social sciences, XV: 189–192; H. Tisdale, "Process of urbanization," Social Forces, 20 (1942): 311–316.
[19] Cf. Gist and Halbert, op. cit., Ch. 5.
[20] Our cities, op. cit., p. 73 ff.

In what ways do these situations present problems? What kinds of social policies and procedures have evolved for their management?

Problems of Physical Change and Growth

Problems of the rate of growth. The urbanization of America has not only occurred recently but has also grown rapidly. In 1790, when the first census was taken, only 5 per cent of our people were urban. A century later about 40 per cent of the population were urban. By 1949 the figure stood at 59 per cent. To be sure, the rate has slowed down: the percentage of urbanization was 56.5 in 1930. The urban increase for 1930–1940 was 7.9 per cent; for the decade of the 'twenties it was 27.3 per cent.

The major point here, however, is the fact that the historic rate of growth has been very rapid. The consequence has been a characteristic lack of design, of anticipation, of control of the modern city. Its paradoxes abound.[21]

> The organization of its life is centralized and hierarchical, but its spatial pattern sprawls without design. The metropolis concentrates huge, mixed segments of population, but it fosters social distances among its people. Though it has been both responsible for, and the product of, an incredible multiplicity of interests, it has made the life of the average individual citizen plain and unattractive. A remarkable level of material success has been made possible, but the physical structure of metropolitan existence is shabby, costly, monotonous, and barren.
>
> The industrial city has been built upon the technological conquest of space, and yet its perennial problem is one of congestion. Its growth has been quickened by the economic calculations of profit and loss, but the city is an expensive investment with its assets frozen and its future bound by complicated credits and speculative ventures. There is a fantastic range of personal incomes and mass poverty amid scenes of tremendously rich operations. The city is the product of engineering, yet no engineering entered into its over-all expansion.

Problems of the limits of growth. Even before the development of the atomic bomb, it had become clear to many people that there were limits to the growth of the city. Lewis Mumford, an astute commentator on urbanism, has formulated these limits

[21] From Paul Meadows, *Culture of industrial man* (Lincoln: University of Nebraska Press, 1950), p. 33. Quoted by permission of the publishers.

as follows.[22] There are the physical limits of water supply, sewage disposal, traffic control, physical distance. There are the economic limits of increasing costs, frozen "price-pyramids" of land rents and mortgages, civic depletion, urban blight. There are the social limits of population density, complexity of organization, loss of social control, institutional impoverishment, and negative vitality. In fine, the modern city has come to terms with the familiar principle of diminishing returns.[23]

The report of the Urbanism Subcommittee is in substantial agreement with this view.[24]

> The American way of life has always assumed that there was no ceiling to our potential growth. With the marked slowing-down of our population increase and the apparent approach toward a stationary population and national maturity, we cannot reasonably expect a continuation of the unprecedented growth of American cities witnessed during recent decades. These changes, as yet not generally realized, demand a more prudent use and conservation of physical and human resources and the substitution in place of the philosophy and aspiration of bigness an aspiration of quality.

However, the committee did not find the answer to the problem of expansion (or overexpansion) in dispersion.[25]

> The concentration of so large a proportion of the urban population in extremely limited areas is wasteful of resources, time, and energy. The same would be true of undue dispersion. The Committee believes that the most desirable environment for the urban dweller and for the effective use of human and natural resources is more likely to be found somewhere between these two extremes.

Problems of urban-rural balance. The growth of the city has been made possible by many compensating losses in the rural community.[26] This relationship is generally described by the

---

[22] Lewis Mumford, *Culture of cities* (New York: Harcourt, Brace and Company, 1938), p. 235.

[23] That principle has been formulated thus: "At any given time and in any given condition of industrial technique there is likely to be a point, beyond which further increase in size gives little further increase in economy and efficiency." Alfred Marshall, *Industry and trade* (London: The Macmillan Company, 1927), p. 249. Quoted by permission of The Macmillan Company.

[24] *Our cities, op. cit.*, p. 73.

[25] *Ibid.*, p. 84.

[26] These losses were described in the preceding chapter of this text. Also, *cf.* Arthur Morgan, *Small community* (New York: Harper and Brothers, 1942).

term "urban dominance."[27] The city reaches outward for control of its rural hinterland, and the measure of its dominance is found in many things: urbanward migration, metropolitan trade centers, centralization of many institutional functions (*e.g.*, education, religion, government), the concentration of communication and transportation, metropolitan annexation of fringe communities, suburbanization, and so forth.

Achieving a rural-urban balance is of primary importance to both areas, for their needs are mutual and interpenetrating. Balance must be found in programs of economic and social rehabilitation and redevelopment for both areas. This philosophy is embodied in a number of social policies and movements. It is the core of "regional development."[28] "Regional," rather than the more limited "urban," planning starts with the assumption that the city and its environs constitute a working unit, with services and resources in both that are indispensable to both. The philosophy of balance is likewise incorporated in the idea of economic diversification.[29] Neither the rural nor the urban community has security in a single-industry economy, nor in domination by a single institution. Diversification yields flexibility and resourcefulness. The idea of balance is expressed in the movement toward "rurbanization"—model suburbs, garden cities, suburban homesteads, decentralized industries.[30] Finally,

[27] For a fuller discussion of the concept of "urban dominance," *cf.* B. MacKay, *New exploration* (New York: Harcourt, Brace and Company, 1928); J. A. Kinneman, *Community in American society* (New York: Appleton-Century-Crofts, 1947), Part II; R. D. McKenzie, "Concept of dominance and world organization," *American Journal of Sociology*, 33 (1927): 30 ff.; A. B. Hollingshead, "Dominance," in R. E. Park, ed., *Outline of the principles of sociology* (New York: Barnes and Noble, 1939), Ch. 12.

[28] J. O. Hertzler has suggested the term "regionalization" to describe the development of a sociological structure adjusted to and reflecting the area. *Cf.* his *Social processes* (Lincoln: Nebraska Book Company, 1950), p. 196 ff.; for further elaboration, *cf.* H. W. Odum, *Understanding society* (New York: The Macmillan Company, 1947).

[29] On the disastrousness of single-industry dominance, *cf.* H. W. Odum, *Southern regions of the United States* (Chapel Hill: University of North Carolina Press, 1936); H. W. Odum, and H. E. Moore, *American regionalism* (New York: Henry Holt and Company, 1938).

[30] *Cf.* J. E. Sanders, and A. J. Rabuck, *New city patterns* (New York: Reinhold, 1946); National Resources Committee, *Urban planning and land policies* (Washington, D.C.: Government Printing Office, 1939), Vol. II; Thomas Adams, *Outline of town and country planning* (New York: Russell Sage Foundation, 1930); H. M. Lewis, *Planning the modern city* (New York: John Wiley and Sons, 1943), Vol. II, Ch. 18; W. H. Blucher, "Significance of the greenbelt town," *Housing yearbook*, 1938; Walter Firey, "Ecological considerations in planning urban fringes," *American Sociological Review*, 11 (1946): 411 ff.

the idea of balance is suggested in the movements which seek a community of interest between farmers and workers, between agriculture and industry, between stabilized farm prices and stabilized industrial purchasing power.[31] In sum, the search for rural-urban balance represents the rejection of urban dominance, not merely because it is exploitive but because it is mutually lethal.[32]

Problems of the conditions of growth. The growth of the modern city has been not only rapid but disorderly, resulting in deteriorated and dangerous conditions of living for its people. These conditions may be summarily described as follows.

First, there is the problem of congestion. Cities not only concentrate people and buildings; they overconcentrate them. Overcrowding begins in the central areas, in the form of multiple housing and overpopulation per unit, crowding of lots, and blighted buildings. The human consequences are numerous: malnutrition, rapid propagation of disease, high mortality rates, loss of social control, and lack of community services. The economic costs are striking: higher protection costs, loss of tax income in blighted areas, the prohibitive expense of redevelopment and redesigning, deteriorated land values, misapplication of modern building technics, and violation of building codes.[33]

Second, there is the problem of inadequate, if not absolutely undesirable, land utilization. Both residential and commercial dwellings tend to be arbitrarily and haphazardly located. This fact means that the worst sites in the city provide dwellings for the most people; that real-estate speculation has hindered where it has not deliberately prevented rational land-use development; that building laws have little or no effect on either present structures or future construction; that modern engineering and architecture enter into the growth of the city in only an advisory or an *ad hoc* manner.[34]

[31] *Cf.* P. A. Waring, and C. S. Golden, *Soil and steel: Exploring the common interests of farmers and wage earners* (New York: Harper and Brothers, 1947).

[32] For documentation of this thesis, *cf.* C. C. Taylor, et al, *Rural life in the United States* (New York: Alfred A. Knopf, 1949); O. E. Baker, "Rural people," *Farmers in a changing world,* 1940 Yearbook, Department of Agriculture (Washington D.C.: Government Printing Office, 1940), pp. 827–847; H. W. Odum, *Understanding society, op. cit.,* Ch. 35.

[33] *Cf.* J. L. Sert, *Can our cities survive?* (Cambridge: Harvard University Press, 1942), Part II; P. Zucker, ed., *New architecture and city planning* (New York: Philosophical Library, 1944), Part II; M. R. Davie, *Problems of city life* (New York: John Wiley and Sons, 1932), Chs. 1, 3, and Part II; *Our cities, op. cit.,* Sec. 3.

[34] *Cf.* Lewis, *op. cit.,* Vol. I, Part II; Sert, *op. cit.,* Parts VII, IX.

Third, there is the problem of duplication on the fringe of the city of the same set of problem-situations which characterize its central areas. Their emergence on the country-city fringe is ironic, for movement to the periphery of the city is usually dictated primarily by the desire to escape similar situations in the central areas. An excellent study of a typical fringe area, around Flint, Michigan, has demonstrated the failure of these expectations.[35] In summarizing the reasons for the problem character of the fringe, Firey lists the following factors:

(a) It removes land from agricultural productivity.
(b) Platting becomes unguided, unco-ordinated, and generally in excess of effective demand, thus creating vast tracts of idle land, irregular settlement patterns, and tax-delinquent holdings.
(c) Taxes must increase in order to maintain the services necessary in such densely populated settlements; but such taxes commonly exceed the tax-paying capacity of both farmers and shop workers.
(d) Unregulated platting frequently permits tracts to be subdivided with no deed restrictions, thereby ruining adjacent subdivisions that may have started under high deed restrictions.
(e) Fringe dwellers are frequently ill prepared and ill informed about buying land, getting implements, and cultivating gardens.
(f) The fringe area boosts land values to the point at which it no longer pays to continue agricultural operations.

The rational answer to these problems of urban growth is contained in the philosophy and practice of urban planning. Since it would be wiser to consider the latter topic as a whole and not piecemeal, it will be postponed until this anatomy of the problems of the modern city is completed.

Problems of Physical Articulation and Social Organization

The mislocation of economic functions. By this is meant the failure of urban communities to see the need for a self-conscious program of industrial development which will assess the community's limitations and industry's contributions, both negative and positive. The goal of such foresightedness is one of fitting

[35] Cf. W. Firey, Social aspects of land-use planning in the country-city fringe: The case of Flint, Michigan, Bulletin Michigan State College Agricultural Experiment Station, 1946. On fringe problems in general, cf. Rural-urban fringe: Proceedings of the Commonwealth Conference (Eugene: University of Oregon Press, 1942); M. Rodehaver, "Fringe settlement as a two-dimensional movement," Rural Sociology, 12 (1947): 53 ff.; H. Hoyt, "Structure of American cities in the post-war era," American Journal of Sociology, 48 (1943): 777 ff.

industries "into a structure which will secure the maximum employment of the available labor supply, the minimizing of seasonal and cyclical fluctuations in the total employed pay roll of the community, the optimum use of the advantages of location from the standpoint of raw materials and markets, and a balance between the cost of community services to industry and the income derived by the community from industry."[36] How important these considerations are may be seen in the following comment. "A poorly balanced local industrial structure throws the entire industrial front out of joint by causing migration of labor, unemployment, lower wages, curtailed purchasing power, less trading business, lower living standards, high cost of relief, high taxes, tax delinquency, untenanted property, stagnation of building enterprises, obsolescence of community plant and depreciation of industrial equipment."[37]

Blockages in the urban flow. Urban society and economy is a great, fast-moving stream of life. Interruptions and inhibitions of human mobility are costly in time and money as well as human life. Regional studies of New York and its environs have suggested that congestion on Manhattan Island alone costs $500,000 a day and in the whole region approximately $1,000,000 a day.[38] Traffic fatalities show a high positive correlation with increase in the number of vehicle-miles and in the number of registered motor vehicles.[39]

The blockages are easily discerned. The most important difficulty is the rigid, nontechnological street-pattern of the average city. The typical American city is laid out on a gridiron of small-sized streets and highways which cross one another at right angles. Seeking out new facilities, locations, and speed, competing forms of transportation have enmeshed cities in endless delays, costs, and necessary redevelopment. Terminal facilities and traffic patterns are seldom adequate for the fast-increasing load which the new mobility has demanded. Past transit policies of piecemeal consideration, favoritism, and poorly limited franchises have left a heavy charge on the general public in the form of waste of time and of land, inconveniences and hazards, excessive cost of public services, overconcentration of population, speculative land operations, and so forth.[40] The

---

[36] *Our cities, op. cit.*, p. 61.
[37] *Ibid.*
[38] Lewis, *op. cit.*, Vol. I, p. 179.
[39] *Ibid.*, p. 176.
[40] *Cf.* Sert, *op, cit.*, Part X; Lewis, *op. cit.*, Vol. I, Part V.

fast-growing volume of private motor vehicles has only added to the ineptness and inefficiency of an undesigned transport system.

Obstacles to physical improvement. The modern city is under the constant obligation to modernize its physical structure and equipment. Technological change, rising standards of efficiency, safety, and speed, and increase in the total demand upon services call for adaptation of existing structures and the introduction of new ones.

The task is not simple, for it is complicated by inadequate governmental income, due to limitations inherent in real-property taxes, legislative restrictions on taxes and bonded indebtedness, and taxpayers' reluctance to add further burdens. The unwillingness and in some cases the legal inability to adopt scientific valuation and assessment procedures is a very real handicap. Furthermore, the powers of municipalities are carefully circumscribed by the restrictive provisions of state laws, by court decisions, by interpretations of the attorney general's office, and by unforesighted grants of power.[41] There is, moreover, the imposing barrier of overlapping governmental units, which present a bewildering maze of jurisdictions. The Urbanism Subcommittee summarized the situation in the 96 metropolitan areas thus:[42]

> Together with their over-layers of counties, townships, school districts, sanitary districts, sewer districts, library districts, health districts, park districts, forest-preserve districts, street-lighting districts, utility districts, water districts, and even mosquito-abatement districts—each of them a separate body politic and corporate—these communities present an odd picture of independent bailiwicks, performing related or even identical governmental functions with some degree of co-operation, but with a great degree of competition for municipal revenues, for administrative prestige, and for legal powers. Frequently, these districts are too small in area or have insufficient tax resources to support essential public services. All this governmental duplication, confusion, and localism are in sharp contrast to the obvious disregard of the network of urban boundary lines by epidemics which complicate urban health work, by criminals who are not stopped by city limits, and by city and suburban users of highways and transportation facilities who seldom know or care about the maze of political boundaries in metropolitan districts.

[41] *Our cities, op. cit.*, p. 66.
[42] *Ibid.*, p. 67. The Urbanism Subcommittee of the National Resources Committee has called attention to the various attempts and proposals to correct these weaknesses and deficits. *Cf.* pp. 79 ff.

But administrative obstructions do not tell the whole story. Among the obstacles to physical improvement are the attitudes of the people themselves. The modern city, unlike its medieval counterpart,[43] has long lost its organic quality, its sense of mutuality. This loss is reflected in part by the widespread apathy of urban people to urban reform. The British public-opinion organization, Mass-Observation, reported this mass withdrawal from involvement thus: "If 'Mass-Observation' has achieved anything in five years of hard work, it is that we have analyzed and documented the marked shrinkage in citizen interest at the mass level . . . degree of community feeling in massive urban population is much lower than has been supposed."[44] A similar judgment was arrived at by the American opinion-study agency, the Bureau of Urban Research. "Despite the official existence of city planning or zoning bodies in many localities, comparatively few municipal actions are influenced by the planning process. Planning for cities remains more an idea than an actively operative municipal service, for it reflects neither public understanding nor support."[45] For that matter, even the planning experts lack the broad, organic approach which is so important for the success of any sizable urban improvement. Thus, Robert A. Walker reported at the onset of World War II:[46]

Even in the larger cities many of the commissions confine their interest to zoning and public works. Planning technicians are pushing forward to a broader range of activities in some places, but with a few exceptions commission-members have not played an important part in recent developments. Planning commissioners are drawn primarily from business executives and from those professions closely identified with construction—realtors, architects, and engineers. The influence of zoning has also drawn a fairly high proportion of lawyers to the boards. Persons identified with labor, social welfare, education, etc. are rarely found. In general commission-members have a limited social outlook and a wholly inadequate grasp of planning.

This segmentation of the community is partly a result of its extreme occupational specialization, its sharp class cleavages,

[43] On this point, cf. E. Saarinen, City: Its growth, its decay, its future (New York: Reinhold, 1943).

[44] Tom Harrisson, "Human planning," The New Statesman and Nation, 22 (Sept. 27, 1941): 301–302.

[45] M. C. Branch, Jr., Urban planning and public opinion (Princeton: Bureau of Urban Planning, 1942), p. 1.

[46] R. A. Walker, Planning function in urban government (Chicago: University of Chicago Press, 1941), p. 333. Quoted by permission of the publishers.

its well-defined and socially distant ecological zones, differentiated and noninteractive ethnic groups, and the system of private property which limits and prevents planned action where it cannot markedly profit from it.

Yet it would be fatal to forget that after all the city *is* the people, as one famous architect and urban planner has said.[47] Moreover, a human orientation, even though blocked by conflicting interests and claims, must start with questions about the people themselves. Thus:[48]

> How many people is the locality to have in . . . 10 to 20 years? . . . Is it likely to become larger or smaller than it is now? What are and what will be the kinds of people—young or old, rich or poor, skilled or unskilled, people of long residence or new arrivals? Where are the people and their jobs located? . . .
>
> How many and what kinds of jobs will the area be able to provide, in view of resources of men, money, and materials? How much and what kinds of production will be desirable and attainable? . . .
>
> What kind of community do the people look forward to?

Problems of social integration.   Social pathologies, not peculiar to the city of course, nonetheless abound there. There are many reasons, inherent in the city situation itself, which encourage them.[49]

Urbanism fosters economic insecurities through its monetarization of human relations, its job dependence, its business irregularities, its industrial conflicts, and its rapid technological changes. Many urban people were born in the country and must adapt their life-ways to those of the metropolis; some never get over the initial "culture shock."[50] The urban landscape is a quick succession of changes—ecological, institutional, and psychological. Heterogeneity of the cultures and ethnic composition induce estrangement, distance, conflict. Mobility and massing of people, producing anonymity, encourage behavior experimentation and deviation. The city is a place of pressures: advertising, group promotions, fast tempo of living, "causes," and

[47] H. S. Churchill, *City is the people* (New York: Reynal and Hitchcock, 1945).

[48] *Action for cities: A guide for community planning.* Published under the sponsorship of American Municipal Association, American Society of Planning Officials, and International City Managers' Association. Publication No. 86. (Chicago: Public Administration Service, 1943.)

[49] *Cf.* Queen and Thomas, *op. cit.*, Ch. 21.

[50] *Cf.* Carpenter, *op. cit.*

"interests" push and pull urban individuals and organizations into joining, buying, selling, fighting, escaping.

The rates of urban disorganization are high, as data on divorce, physical and mental disease, social conflicts, and crime invariably show.[51] Social isolates, social deviants, antisocials, and social incompetents the city has in excess. For many reasons, therefore, the city has a peculiar and primary responsibility of achieving social integration and of supplying social services for its people.

These efforts are multi-dimensional; they consist of community co-ordination, community-service programs, and community planning. The last named, because it is more comprehensive and involved, will be discussed subsequently.

Community co-ordination refers to those steps taken to secure community agreement or consensus and to enlarge the areas of community participation. Consensus is aggravated by the segmentation of the city, which we have previously mentioned; yet it is made imperative by that self-same segmentation. Pressure groups, social tangent groups, differentiated interest groups, and bystanders must find a *modus vivendi*. This is the task of the community council. Consisting of delegates from a representative sample of the organized interest-associations of the city, the community council is in an excellent position to ascertain the social and physical needs of the city, to bring together a common fund of goals and good-will, and to draw up an advisory program of community action. The council may be organized for highly specific common tasks or for wide-ranging general programs. As described by the national Co-ordinating Councils, Inc., community councils "function as counseling, co-ordinating or planning groups, but not as agencies. . . . [They] work through the many organizations, agencies, and departments included in their membership. . . . A solution to each problem is sought through the agencies or organizations already rendering service in the general field of the problem in question. Through co-operative planning, through the pooling of ideas and resources a way is usually found to meet the needs which all agree are urgent."[52]

Providing community services is, in its most desirable form, a

---

[51] For a summary of the literature on urban social disorganization, *cf.* Gist and Halbert, *op. cit.*, Ch. 16.

[52] *Guide to community co-ordination* (Los Angeles: Co-ordinating Councils, Inc., 1941), pp. 9–10. On the work of the community councils in general, *cf.* Arthur Hillman, *Community organization and planning* (New York: The Macmillan Company, 1950); Morgan, *op. cit.;* Kinneman, *op. cit.;* Jesse Bernard, *American community behavior* (New York: Dryden Press, 1949),

matter of joint responsibility between public and private agencies and associations. It is a work of collaboration and should never be one of competition. Ideally, it should be a phase of the over-all community-planning process. Its purpose is to re-enforce, not supplant, existing institutions and agencies. It is an extension of the family, the school, the church, and the government into unserviced or underserviced areas of community living. Some of the programs of community services are aimed at children, others at youth, still others at adults in the community. Some are focused on health needs, others on recreation, on adult education, on social welfare, on cultural expression, on race relations, on housing. Most effective when it is indigenous to the city itself, utilizing thus the talents and support of both laymen and experts, community service is likewise most efficient when it is based on factually determined need and oriented around popularly selected goals. The measure of its success is not merely one of "cases serviced" but of consensus maintained and effort shared.[53]

How important is the work of community integration? Though not many would say it exactly as he has, few would repudiate the philosophy Baker Brownell has expressed in the following appraisal of the need for the integration of the social life of the modern community, large or small. "In this era of great cities, megalopolitan culture, and massive events we are likely to forget the human measure. The human scale, the quiet integrity of our finite powers, is ignored; and because we can pile events on events in mountainous accumulations by the use of mechanized energy, we assume that the human scope and range of life can expand to include them. But this is not true. Neither is it desirable. . . . Men have increased their control of the natural environment, it is true, but in so doing they have created a social and mechanical environment so out of scale with man that it is overwhelming. . . . To maintain human integrity against the mass of our own creations is the main problem."[54]

The Principles and Practice of Urban Planning

The philosophy of urban planning.   Planning is essentially the foresighted and co-operative adaptation of means to ends. As a social process, it involves succession of actions:

[53] On the nature and problems of these community services, cf. especially Wayne Mcmillen, *Community organization for social welfare* (Chicago: University of Chicago Press, 1945).

[54] Baker Brownell, "Preface," in Morgan, *op. cit.* Quoted by permission.

1. Appraisal of needs and agreement on goals.
2. Analysis of conditions which determine action.
3. Synthesis of needs, goals, and conditions.
4. Elaboration of a design for action.
5. Putting the plan into action.
6. Re-evaluation of needs and goals in terms of experience with the plan.

As a form of collective behavior, urban planning is based on the premise that forward-looking action can not only correct existing mistakes but can also prevent future ones. As a co-operative experience, it holds that a more adequate social integration of urban life can be achieved. The philosophy of urban planning stipulates that urban problems, like all social problems, do not come singly but in a network of relationships. Planning is, as Patrick Geddes said, an effort at simultaneity. The scope is limited by the needs but also by the human and physical resources for meeting the needs. Sometimes planning must be partial; at other times it may be comprehensive and total.

The idea of redevelopment. One phase of urban planning is the attempt through rehousing to check the spread of blight and at the same time make possible a more satisfactory living environment for city people.[55]

Two major alternatives are possible: slum clearance and vacant-land development.[56] These alternatives are really only two phases of the same thing. One process, slum clearance, involves buying deteriorated structures on their sites. The other means building in outlying areas and thus draining the slums of their inhabitants. Arguments can be marshaled on both sides. Proponents of rehousing on the old sites call attention to the fact that these areas are already intensively developed, that utilities are already present, that most of the people concerned probably prefer to remain near their work, and that housing projects in the outlying districts of the community tend, because of inadequate control, to duplicate and thus spread the conditions of blight. Opponents of slum clearance and redevelopment point to the prohibitive cost of the slum land, unless high rents or heavy subsidies prevail. They emphasize the physical and

[55] On the general philosophy of redevelopment, *cf.* Lewis Mumford, *City development* (New York: Harcourt, Brace and Company, 1945).

[56] The following paragraphs are adapted by permission of the editor from Paul Meadows, "Housing the American family," *Journal of Business of the University of Chicago*, 21 (1948): 80 ff.

geographic limitations on the type of housing which can be built and stress the existence of acute shortages of rental properties.

Three different solutions have been proposed. One method would pay the price asked for the slum land and would accept one or more of the results: higher rent, reduction in size and quality of the quarters, higher population density, reduction of construction costs, reduction of the carrying costs.[57] A second proposal is that housing programs should seek cheaper lands, whether on the fringe of the city or elsewhere. This solution opens the way for three possible results. Municipal boundaries could be extended, with or without full accounting costs. Undeveloped land would over a period of time incur expenses, whether or not there have been improvements. Again, there is a possible profit to be made on cheap land, a profit which would offset losses, if any, incurred in housing construction. A third proposal resembles the first, except that it is more positive and comprehensive and is unquestionably less expensive. It may be called a land-assembly program, or a program of government land acquisition.[58] Vesting the power to act in a municipal housing authority, the community would, through the use of police powers, of the right of eminent domain, and of taxation, assemble the land necessary for redevelopment. This land, thus secured, would be as available for rehousing as land at the fringe of the city. It would, moreover, insure controls over those elements of community life which, as has been pointed out, are as important to family living as the physical shelter itself.

The neighborhood formula. Another phase of urban planning, of interest to both public and private agencies, is oriented around the physical setting of the home—the neighborhood environment. The neighborhood, like the larger community itself, is an extension of the family, its larger living-room, so to speak. The family, therefore, has a stake in the integrity of that living space.[59]

A neighborhood formula has been evolved which satisfies the normal expectations of the family in this respect. The formula con-

[57] *Cf.* A. C. Holden, "Land problem in relation to housing," *Annals*, 190 (1937): 50 ff.

[58] *Land assembly program for urban redevelopment*, National Housing Bulletin 3 (Washington, D.C.: National Housing Agency, 1945).

[59] This paragraph adapted from Meadows, *op. cit.* The principles cited were formulated by C. A. Perry, *Housing for the machine age* (New York: Russell Sage Foundation, 1939), p. 50 ff. For further development of the neighborhood approach, *cf.* Lewis, *op. cit.*

sists of six "principles." The principle of size holds that the extent of the area should coincide with the needs of the families for elementary schooling and should be somewhat dependent on population density. The principle of boundaries calls for an arterial street pattern which facilitates the by-passing rather than the penetration of the neighborhood by through traffic. The principle of open spaces provides for a system of small parks and recreation spaces suitable to neighborhood needs. The principle of institutions sites stipulates that institutional and other services should be grouped around a central point, or common. The principle of local shops calls for business locations at traffic junctions and at the circumference of the neighborhood, adjacent to similar districts of adjoining neighborhoods. The principle of internal street systems holds that streets should be proportioned to their traffic load and not designed to encourage internal circulation within the neighborhood.

The neighborhood formula, then, aims at the development of community units, which have organic being, are capable of a certain amount of self-control and interaction, and are characterized by a high degree of safety and freedom.

Zoning and other land-use controls. Another phase of urban planning, also limited in scope, involves the use of zoning. Zoning is the imposition of restrictions on the type of land use and building for given areas of the city.[60]

Zoning is both an individualistic and a collective idea. On the one hand, by means of land-use restrictions the individual is protected against the tyranny of the city as a whole and against the aggressive designs of other individuals. On the other hand, through reasonable restrictions the city stabilizes property values, adds to its dignity as a place to live, and protects the security of its people. As defined by an Advisory Committee appointed by the then Secretary of Commerce Herbert Hoover, zoning means fundamentally "the application of common sense and fairness to the public regulations governing the use of private real estate. It is a painstaking, honest effort to provide each district or neighborhood, as nearly as practicable, with just such protection and just such liberty as are sensible in that particular district."[61] Rezoning is an inescapable corollary of urban planning, for the city is a creature of change.

[60] *Cf.* the excellent sociological evaluation of zoning in Davie, *op. cit.,* p. 59 ff.; also Lewis, *op. cit.,* Vol. I, Ch. 12.

[61] *Zoning primer,* by the Advisory Committee on Zoning, Department of Commerce (Washington, D.C.: Government Printing Office, 1926), p. 1.

The use of a master plan. Another phase of urban planning, systematic and comprehensive in character, involves the adoption of an over-all "map" of the present and the projected pattern of the city. In its most desirable form it should be a fairly flexible model of the future change of the city. It must be factually based and popularly understood, and it should be a constant source of advice and a frame of reference for any particular act of revision of the urban structure. It should always be a supplement to, never a substitute for, the official map of the city.[62]

The master plan is an attempt to bring into interrelationship and control the physical equipment, land uses, traffic pattern, and institutional pattern of the city. Its elements typically include plans for the

1. street and transport system;
2. civic centers and other public buildings;
3. system of parks and playgrounds;
4. zoning of land uses;
5. building code;
6. utility system;
7. housing, redevelopment, and neighborhood design.

The limitations of urban planning. However, in the nature of the case, city planning cannot be absolute and complete in its realization. There are possibilities and probabilities of various kinds of contingencies arising in the future of the city which will obfuscate or annul the best-made plans. Let us suggest some of the limitations to perfect realization, even to perfect planning.

First, real-estate interests may dominate in directing city growth. So far in our country new city projections have been made by real-estate men and development companies. Districts are laid out, the arrangement of streets and other groundwork arrangements are predetermined, and, finally, the district is taken into the city. These projections are often made without reference to the larger good of the city, but where the probability of profit is present. As long as this obtains, the direction of city growth is accidental.

Second, the erection of residential areas, parks, boulevards, civic centers, and so on is likely to be determined by aristocratic rather than democratic ideas. The "residential" district is the place where the wealthy live; and it gets protection, convenience,

[62] On the concept and use of the master plan, *cf.* E. M. Bassett, *Master plan* (New York: Russell Sage Foundation, 1938).

and comfort. Factories and businesses must not appear there. Where the great masses live is a matter of indifference. Parks, boulevards, good paving, sidewalks, protection from vice and from factory smoke are absent. The ruling powers are not concerned about the masses. Consequently the bulk of the citizens of the city are neglected in the plans.

Third, it is not entirely possible to forecast the population of urban communities, especially smaller places. Statisticians did not foresee that Los Angeles would double its population from 1920 to 1930, or that Manhattan Borough, New York City, would lose a half million people. The outlook for multitudes of cities of 50,000 or less is quite uncertain. Even were scientific forecasts made, it is doubtful if they would be accepted and money voted to carry out the foundational provisions for meeting distant demands.

Fourth, there are possibilities that new inventions and conditions will render future provisions inadequate or useless. New modes of communication and transportation, new sources of power, and new currents of population may tip over the best-laid plans.

Yet the issue is not "to plan or not to plan," for any act of urban problem-solving is a plan-act of some sort. Nor is there reason for pessimism. As the Urbanism Subcommittee of the National Resources Committee so ably reported:[63]

> The faults of our cities are not those of decadence and impending decline, but of exuberant vitality crowding its way forward under tremendous pressure—the flood rather than the drought. . . .

> If the assets of an urban-industrial civilization are not always set forth here as fully as its liabilities, this does not mean that there are not substantial gains to the Nation in the highly specialized activities of the cities, in the advantages of association, in the vast expansion of productive power, in the growth of centers of science, medicine, education, invention, religion, in high levels of attainment in artistic and cultural achievement. . . .

> All in all there has been more widespread national neglect of our cities than of any other major segment of our national existence. Whether this is to be attributed to the absorption of our best efforts by the demands of our commercial and industrial system, or by other pressing claims of national policy, it is evident that America must now set out to overcome the continual and cumula-

[63] *Our cities, op. cit.*, pp. vii, x.

tive disregard of urban policies and administration and take into account the place of the urban community in the national economy.

QUESTIONS

1. Contrast the cultural functions of "the city" with those of "the country." Do you think the contrast will continue to be as great in the future as in the past? Why?
2. What social characteristcs of the city encourage the growth of social problems there?
3. What problems have been created by the rapid growth of modern cities? Why? Were they inevitable?
4. How has the city had to "come to terms" with the principle of diminishing returns?
5. What are some of the ill effects on the city of its dominance over its hinterland?
6. In concrete terms, what is meant by "rural-urban balance"?
7. Is there any "solution" of the problems of congestion in the modern city?
8. Account for the social characteristics and problems of the urban fringe.
9. What are some of the obstacles to the physical improvement of the city?
10. Can the city achieve social integration? If so, how?

REFERENCES

ANDERSON, E. L., *We Americans: A study of change in an American city.* Cambridge: Harvard University Press, 1937.

BERNARD, J. S., *American community behavior.* New York: Dryden Press, 1949.

FARIS, R. E. L., and DUNHAM, H. W., *Mental disorders in urban areas.* Chicago: University of Chicago Press, 1939.

FIREY, W. I., *Land use in central Boston.* Cambridge: Harvard University Press, 1947.

GEDDES, P., *Cities in evolution.* London: Eyre and Spottiswoode, 1913.

GIST, N. P., and HALBERT, L. A., *Urban society,* 3rd edition. New York: T. Y. Crowell Company, 1949.

HILLMAN, A., *Community organization and planning.* New York: The Macmillan Company, 1950.

KINNEMAN, J. A., *Community in American society.* New York: Appleton-Century-Crofts, 1947.

HOYT, H., *Structure and growth of residential neighborhoods in American cities.* Washington, D.C.: Federal Housing Administration, 1939.

LEWIS, H. M., *Planning the modern city.* New York: John Wiley and Sons, 1943.

MACKAYE, B., *New exploration*. New York: Harcourt, Brace and Company, 1938.

McKENZIE, R. D., *Metropolitan community*. New York: McGraw-Hill Book Company, 1933.

MUMFORD, LEWIS, *Culture of cities*. New York: Harcourt, Brace and Company, 1938.

National Resources Committee, *Our cities*. Washington, D.C.: Government Printing Office, 1937.

National Resources Planning Board, *Urban planning and land policies*. Washington, D.C.: Government Printing Office, 1939.

QUEEN, S. A., and THOMAS, L. F., *City: A study of urbanism in the United States*. New York: McGraw-Hill Book Company, 1938.

SAARINEN, E., *City: Its growth, its decay, its future*. New York: Reinhold Publishing Corp., 1943.

SANDERS, S. E., and RABUCK, A. J., *New city patterns*. New York: Reinhold Publishing Corp., 1946.

SERT, J. L., *Can our cities survive?* Cambridge: Harvard University Press, 1942.

WALKER, R. A., *Planning function in urban government*. Chicago: University of Chicago Press, 1941.

CHAPTER 8

Population Changes and Social Problems

Population Change as a Source of Social Problems

The nature of population. In this chapter we shall consider human numbers as a source of social problems. Population—that is, human numbers—refers to the inhabitants of a given territory, whether the area is local, county, state, nation, or world. Numbers may be viewed as a biological fact, for human beings are subject to life-and-death processes just as are all forms of life. However, human population is not merely a biological fact, since human beings become conscious of one another and set up interacting responses. Their behavior becomes socially and culturally conditioned. Population, at the human level, then, is a socio-biological fact. In the following pages we shall try to show how changes in the aggregate of human beings arise and how these changes create problem situations.

The nature of population problems. Ever since Thomas Robert Malthus published his celebrated essay on population in 1798, discussions of population have sought to demonstrate the relationships between population changes and social phenomena. Malthus himself stressed the general relation between population size and food supply. Subsequent writers have called attention to a great many more phenomena. Though the so-called Malthusian formulas are still generally accepted, the present-day literature on population views the problems of population as much more complex and far-reaching than the simple ratio between numbers and subsistence.

Population problems arise out of the changes which occur

198

between the functional relationship between human numbers and certain physical and social factors. This functional relationship may be described in a pseudo-mathematical formula,

$$P = f \left(\frac{\text{physical resources} \times \text{economic culture}}{\text{level of living}} \right).$$

The size of the human aggregate in any area, thus, is dependent on the available physical resources as developed by the economy of the people in the area; but the controlling factor is the standard of living held by the people. For example, it is possible to reduce very greatly the physical resources of a people, as in war or drought, and disorganize the economy, as in depressions; yet the size of the population may not be appreciably changed, for the people may adjust to the new plane of living. Again, if there is a tremendous expansion of physical resources accompanied by a revolution in the economic arts, the level of living of the people rises; so likewise does the size of the human aggregate. Human numbers as such are not the critical source of population problems. Population becomes a problem when the functional relationship between numbers, on the one hand, and the physical resources, economy, and level of living, on the other, is changed.

However, it should be noted that only those changes in this relationship which create situations needing control, in other words, social problems, are to be regarded as population problems. Such changes alone as increase in population, decline in population, spatial shifts in population, pronounced changes in the age or sex distribution of the population are not in themselves problems of population. *They become problems only when they produce situations which people feel need to be controlled.* Specifically, these situations are any population changes which endanger the level of living of the people, or which impose new demands upon the economy, or which threaten to exhaust the physical resources, or which upset an accustomed or desired ratio between numbers and manpower, military, industrial, or ecclesiastical.

The nature of population policy.[1] Most forms of life are amazingly fecund. Indeed, there seems to be a rule that all species increase at such a rapid rate that, if not destroyed or checked in some way, the progeny of a single pair would in a relatively short

[1] Adapted by permission of the editor from Paul Meadows, "Balance and imbalance in human social adjustment," *Social Forces*, XXII (May, 1944): 416–417.

time cover the earth. Man is no exception to the rule. However, like other organic beings, he is subject to certain checks on these propensities: in his case—land, level of living, economic culture, counter-conception devices, and so on. As a result, in the long run nature and human numbers balance.

The iron law of numbers, as it may be phrased, means that a species can multiply up to the limit of the supporting power of their habitat. Among subhuman forms, numbers depend on physical resources available to them: $P = f (PR)$. In a general sense, this relation is true of man too. However, the historic development of culture has added other factors, as indicated in the previous formula: $P = f\left(\dfrac{\text{physical resources} \times \text{economic culture}}{\text{level of living}}\right)$.

Balance between human numbers and these factors of human existence can be achieved by manipulating any one of the items in the formula. New physical resources can be tapped; the economic arts can be revolutionized; the level of living, that is, the standards as well as planes of the population, can be changed; or the size of the human aggregate can be increased or decreased through heightened birth rates or death rates.

Human culture has freed man of the iron law of numbers which characterizes subhuman groups and which causes them to pay a terrific price in loss of numbers in order to survive. Culturally, human beings can live at any balanced relationship with their environment which they choose. They have four different policies which they can pursue. One is a *numbers* policy, wherein there is a control of ratio of births and deaths. A *resources* policy—using land in the most general sense, referring to the stock of physical resources—seeks through conquest, trade, soil rehabilitation, irrigation, and so forth to expand the resources to the population. An *arts* policy can concern itself with the technical and organizational methods of production and distribution of goods and services: this may mean technological or social or political revolution. Finally, a *consumption* policy may seek to control changes in the level of living through consumer education or propaganda, legislative additions to or subtractions from the purchasing power, increased productivity of the population, and so forth.

In other words, the man-land ratio may be cushioned by a number of devices—literally, population policies—which appear somewhat as follows:

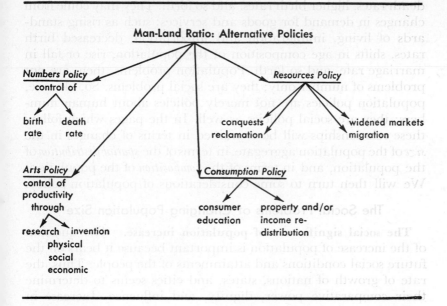

Man-Land Ratio: Alternative Policies

Numbers Policy
control of

birth   death
rate   rate

Arts Policy
control of
productivity
through

research invention
physical
social
economic

Resources Policy

conquests   widened markets
reclamation migration

Consumption Policy

consumer   property and/or
education   income re-
            distribution

These population policies may be summarized in this manner. Some of them may aim at control over the supply of goods and services which human beings need and want: by intensive soil culture, improved food preparation and preservation; increased productivity of land, labor, and machines; extension of frontiers; trade agreements and assistance (Marshall Plans, Point-Four Programs, and so forth); more efficient transportation, and so on. Other policies may aim at control over the demand for goods and services: by changing the habits of subsistence, rationing, taxation, redistribution of income, emigration, immigration, war, counter-conception, senicide, infanticide, disease, and so forth.

The variability of population problems. It should be clear from the foregoing discussion that the nature of population problems varies with the nature of population change. Variations in the man-land ratio as outlined produce stresses in human relationships which are felt as population pressure, scarcity situations, strain and unrest, optimism or pessimism about the future, and so forth. Changes in the man-land ratio may come from shortages or expansion of physical resources, such as in depletion of soil, exhaustion of minerals, biological disasters, discovery of new minerals, opening of new lands, increased productivity through mechanization, lengthened life span, lower death rates, higher birth rates, and so forth. They may come from changes in demand for goods and services: such as rising standards of living, immigration and importation, decreased birth rates, shifts in age composition of the population, rise or fall in marriage rate, and so forth. Population problems, then, are not problems of number only; they are social problems. So, likewise, population policies are not merely policies about human numbers; they are social policies as well. In the pages which follow these relationships will be examined in terms of changes in the *size* of the population aggregate, in terms of the *spatial distribution* of the population, and in terms of the *composition* of the population. We will then turn to some considerations of population policy.

The Social Problems of Changing Population Size

The social significance of population increase. The question of the increase of population is important because it bears on the future social conditions and attainments of the people. Thus, the rate of growth of nations, states, and cities seems to determine their comparative power, dignity, and influence. Increase in numbers also concerns the utilization and duration of natural resources. Thus, correlated with agricultural resources, increase determines the limits of subsistence and when they may be reached or exceeded. The increase of population of nations, especially of saturated or overpopulated ones, may lead to grave international issues. A nation which is already filled or overpopulated and which multiplies rapidly is likely to be viewed as a menace to other nations, either because of efforts to place excess individuals elsewhere as emigrants or because of possible seizure of additional territory for purposes of exploitation.[2]

There is no complete agreement as to what population pressure directly affects. However, the following situation appears to be true. During the early economic stages of society, the pressure of population increase is exerted directly upon subsistence or supply of food. But when the higher stages of social developments are attained, the family income has to be spread over so many things besides food that the strain becomes one between the income, or of spendable wealth and the standard of living. There are probably no Western nations in which the income of the masses is sufficient to cover expenditures for food alone in a

[2] On these points, *cf.* R. Mukerjee, "Population theory and politics," *American Sociological Review*, VI (1941): 784 ff.; and E. P. Hutchinson, and W. E. Moore, "Pressures and barriers in future migration," *Annals*, 237 (1945): 164 ff.

lavish manner. Even in low-income classes, the per cent of incomes of workers spent for family food is only 50 or 60 per cent of the family budget, the remainder going for rent, clothing, light, heat, and other commodities and services. Many persons and families actually skimp expenditures for food and are under-nourished, in order to satisfy the many other wants, such as automobiles and movies.[3] So, for our Western nations, we should think of population increase in relation to the income of the masses expendable for general living purposes. In that sense the further population increase of several nations is a grave question for them.[4]

A world saturation point?   Overpopulation among advanced people presses upon standards of living and reaches subsistence chiefly in that way. Among low-standard peoples, who form the bulk of the world population, the pressure is exerted on sub-sistence primarily. It is appropriate, therefore, to consider how long it will require world population to reach the limits of world subsistence.[5] Estimates of the time when the limits of subsistence of the different nations will be reached are difficult to make and of uncertain value. For one thing, advanced nations supplement their own food supply by importing certain foods. Again, the evaluation of subsistence as an item of the standard of living is difficult. Income that in a simple society is largely devoted to the purchase of food is spread over hundreds of other items. More-over, the attempt through the United Nations to achieve a balanced dietary program and diversified food supply in more backward countries may, barring devastating world war, prove to be a revolutionary development of this century.

Optimum population.   Quite different from the concept of maximum population is that of optimum population.[6] The first

[3] On the general pattern of family expenditures in the United States, cf. *How families use their incomes*, U.S. Department of Agriculture, Miscellaneous Publication No. 653 (Washington, D.C.: Government Printing Office, 1949).

[4] On this problem cf. W. R. Espy, *Bold new program* (New York: Harper and Brothers, 1950); and E. P. Prentice, *Food, war and the future* (New York: Harper and Brothers, 1944).

[5] It appears that a planetary ecology, so to speak, may be developing, partly through the efforts of the Food and Agricultural Organization of the United Na-tions. In addition to publications made available by that organization, cf. also W. Vogt, *Road to survival* (New York: Wm. Sloane Associates, 1948). An earlier but still useful though provocative study is that of E. M. East, *Mankind at the cross-roads* (New York: Charles Scribner's Sons, 1927).

[6] For a lengthy and illuminating discussion of this concept, cf. I. Ferenczi, *Syn-thetic optimum of population* (Paris: International Institute of Intellectual Co-operation, 1938).

idea expresses complete saturation; the second, satisfactory saturation. The latter would occur in a nation when its population had become as large as its resources could satisfactorily sustain according to the standard of a good life for the masses of its citizens. It contemplates, not the greatest population that may barely subsist within a geographical territory, but the greatest population that may live there and live satisfactorily. Important here is not only the standard of living which the people expect, but also the natural resources to which they have access (either locally or through international trade) as well as the technical and social organization of the productive arts which they have developed. An optimum population is a desired balance of nature and numbers; obviously, it will vary with the culture of nations. What is optimal for a religious, otherworldly culture, for example, is unspeakably bad for a technological society.

Overpopulation. This condition in a given habitat may be thought of as the result of the pressure of numbers on resources in spite of, usually because of, the level of living and the level of the arts. It is not ordinarily indicated by density of population. The Netherlands, for example, had a density of 690 people per square mile in 1940; China's density was 147, India's 195. But one could hardly say that all three countries were overpopulated. The latter countries are overpopulated because the economic arts and the physical resources are undeveloped and inadequate for the demand. Overpopulation is a measure not of numbers but of economic organization: mass demand outruns supplies made available by the economy. This imbalance is, of course, greatly aggravated by catastrophic shortages in supply brought on by famine and disaster; it is also intensified by high birth rates. One sore spot in the world-population picture today is the Orient, where more than half the people of the world live and where populations increase up to the limit of subsistence. Any slight decrease in high death rates there through sanitation, improved agriculture, or industrialization will greatly increase the population. India, for example, increased as a result of these factors by 51 millions during the decade ending in 1941. The answer to overpopulation seems to lie, therefore, in a systematic utilization of all the population policies. It is not enough to improve the arts or raise the level of living. Continuing high birth rates in overpopulated areas may well put to rout any efforts at an optimum population.

Lowering rates of increase.   The natural history of population change under conditions of industrialization seems to have two stages. In the first stage, industrialization brings higher levels of living and, consequently, lower death rates: the natural increase—that is, births over deaths—boosts the total population rapidly. In the second stage, as industrialization and its twin, urbanization, progress, high levels of living compete with reproduction. Social pressures, the independence of women, later marriages, and birth control cut down birth rates until they again approach death rates and the natural increase diminishes. Such populations grow more slowly and seem headed for a stationary or declining condition. Industrial Europe, the British Dominions, and the United States seem now to have reached this later stage. Japan is the only Asiatic country which has moved into this second stage of the cycle, if it is a cycle. The great reproductive areas of the world in the future seem most certainly to be in Asia and Africa. There the lowering of birth rates by later marriages or birth control and the shrinking of population by emigration do not appear to be at all likely. A declining rate of increase seems to be in prospect for the aging and industrialized countries of the West.[7]

Declining birth rates and shrinking populations.   The critical factor in the declining rate of increase of older industrial populations seems to be the birth rate. The following are some of the important conditions that inhibit births. They involve considerable unavoidable overlapping.

1. Postponement of marriage.

2. The presence of large percentages of foreign-born in the population.

3. The woman's movement, which has made many women independent of immediate marriage and made them intelligent about reproduction and the rearing of children.

4. Rising standards of living and social ambition. The modern world is characterized by rising standards of living. It costs more to keep a standard family today than it did formerly. It costs more to rear a child in urban populations than in the country, and more of the population is urban than formerly. Also, urbanism involves increased insecurity of living, family risks, social and career ambitions where children tend to be in the way.

---

[7] For a fuller discussion of this situation, *cf.* W. S. Thompson, *Population problems* (New York: McGraw-Hill Book Company, 1935); K. Davis, "World demographic transition," *Annals*, 237 (1945): 1 ff.; and G. I. Burch, et al, *Population roads to peace or war* (Washington, D.C.: Population Reference Bureau, 1945).

5. Increasing celibacy in certain populations.

6. Possible increased sterility. Voluntary sterility, somewhat identical with voluntary birth control, is widespread and increasing and some involuntary sterility is present, although it is not demonstrated that it is increasing significantly. Certain studies indicate that about 10 per cent of the small number of male cases investigated were sterile, probably from venereal disease. Other recent research finds that spermatozoa of certain males have defective heads, infertility being associated with this condition. Females, of course, would also be subject to sterility from venereal disease.

7. Prolongation of life, resulting in a larger proportion of aged persons in populations with consequent infertility.

8. Increasing use of contraceptives.

9. Causes of operating in prenatal life, such as recourse to abortion, producing a maternal mortality rate of 30 per cent. Regarding the relation between sex excitability and ovulation little is known, but it may conceivably have a bearing on the decline in the birth rate.[8]

10. Urbanism inhibiting births. In the United States, the ratio of children under 1 per 1000 females 15 to 45 is from 50 to 100 per cent greater in rural than in urban populations.[9]

America's declining rate of increase. We are familiar with the fact that our own national population has ceased to increase as it did a decade or two ago, but it is not common knowledge that the downward trend in rate of increase goes back nearly a century. Originally this nation gained inhabitants at a rate almost unrivaled in history. Within a relatively few decades after independence had been attained, we became a "leading" nation not only in natural resources but also in number of inhabitants. The population curve given in Figure 4 shows that by 1870 we were a people of about 40 million. But the curve of the rate of decennial population increase runs counter to that, running on a level until 1860, and then dropping to lower and lower levels until one of less than ten was reached for the decade 1930–1940. The average decennial rate of increase from 1790 to 1860 was 34.6 per cent, the lowest being 32.7 and the highest 35.9. Between 1860 and 1910 the average decennial rate of increase was

---

[8] *Cf.* L. Hogben, *Genetic principles in medicine and social science* (London: Williams and Norgate, 1931), pp. 186–189.

[9] *Cf.* J. M. Gillette, "Immigration and the increase of population in the United States," *Social Forces* (1926–27): 44.

24.1 per cent, the lowest being 20.7 and the highest 30.1. For the remaining decades down to 1940, the average rate descends to 14.0, the highest being 21 and the lowest, that of the last census decade, 7.2, one fifth that of the first seven decades.

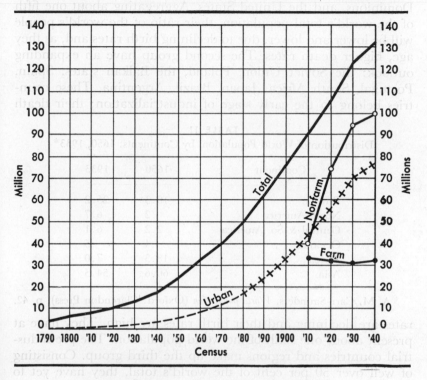

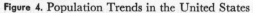

Figure 4. Population Trends in the United States

The Social Problems of Population Distribution

World pattern of distribution.   The distribution of population throughout the world and within a continent or a large nation occurs in a most irregular and peculiar manner. Populations pile up in particular places, as China, India, Rhode Island, New York City, and they decrease in others. World distribution appears somewhat as shown in Table 11 (p. 208).

The growth pattern of continental populations is marked by sharply rising curves since the middle of the eighteenth century, as Figure 5 shows (p. 209).

Growth potentials of world populations.   The growth rates of different areas of the world as they are depicted in this figure suggest certain possibilities for the future. In terms of growth potentials, world populations may be divided into three groups.[10] In the first group, the prospect is a stationary one. Here belong the peoples of Western Europe, the United Kingdom and the Dominions, and the United States. Aggregating about one fifth of the world's total population, their ratio of the world's people will be lower and lower, due to declining birth rates and, as they age, higher death rates. The second group have an expanding outlook: the Soviet Union, Poland, the Balkan states, Spain, Portugal, South Africa, Japan, Brazil, Argentina. These countries belong to the early stage of industrialization; their death

TABLE 11

Distribution of World Population, by Continents: 1650, 1933*

Continent	1650	1933
Europe	18.3	25.2
North America	.2	6.7
Central & So. America	2.2	6.1
Oceania	.4	.5
Africa	18.3	7.0
Asia	60.6	54.5

* A. M. Carr-Saunders, *World population* (Oxford: Clarendon Press), p. 42.

rates are declining and their birth rates are high. They have at present about one sixth of the world population. The pre-industrial countries and regions make up the third group. Consisting of well over 50 per cent of the world's total, they have yet to experience the rapid increase in population under conditions of industrialization.

World distribution and the quality of living.   Translating these data into appraisals of living conditions, we should note that the greatest pressure of numbers on subsistence is in the areas occupied by pre-industrial peoples. Given the present rate of increase, at the end of the present century the stationary countries will represent only 13.5 per cent of the world's total; the expanding nations and regions, about one fifth; and those in the pre-industrial category, over two thirds. The latter are constantly beset by the Malthusian checks of famine and disease; if present conditions persist, they will be even more menaced than they

[10] *Cf.* Kimball Young, *Sociology*, 2nd ed. (New York: American Book Company, 1949), pp. 198–209.

are now. Both the expanding and the pre-industrial countries are characterized by low income, inadequate diets, high death rates; they constitute more than half of the world's total. It is a situation of strong population pressure.

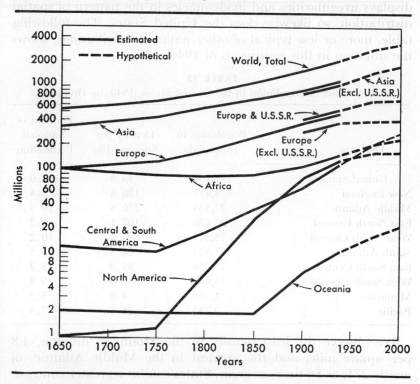

Figure 5. Estimated Population of the World and of Continental Areas, 1650–2000. (Adapted from Davis, *op. cit.*, p. 2, by permission of the Office of Population Research, Princeton University. Population data are given on a logarithmic scale.)

The alternatives are severely limited. Industrialization is by no means a simple and certainly not a quick solution.[11] Barriers obstruct the traditional resort to migration of excess population. Deliberate control over fertility runs counter to the mores of these peoples. Strong nationalist pressures are most certainly in prospect. Even the mild surrenders of national sovereignty by

[11] *Cf.* J. J. Spengler, "Aspects of the economics of population growth," *Southern Economic Journal*, XIV (1947): 123 ff.; Frank W. Notestein, "Problems of policy in relation to areas of heavy population pressure," *Demographic studies of selected areas of rapid growth* (New York: Milbank Memorial Fund, 1944).

the stationary countries are negated by intense nationalist demands of the saturated nations. In the race for food, numbers will surely add fuel to the fires of politics and incipient war.

Distribution as a potential problem. Just as world population displays irregularities and inadequacies in the pattern of spatial distribution, so likewise does the United States. The following table, more or less typical of other national distributions, shows the situation in this country as of 1940.

TABLE 12
Distribution of Population in the United States, 1940, by Divisions

Divisions	Population in Thousands	Density per Square Mile	Per cent of National Population
United States	131,668	43.8	100.0
New England	8,437	126.8	6.4
Middle Atlantic	27,539	270.8	20.9
East North Central	26,626	107.1	20.2
West North Central	13,517	26.1	10.2
South Atlantic	17,823	62.8	13.5
East South Central	10,778	59.9	8.2
West South Central	13,065	30.3	9.9
Mountain	4,150	4.8	3.3
Pacific	9,733	28.6	7.4

We observe the least density in the Mountain division, 4.8 per square mile, and the greatest in the Middle Atlantic, of nearly 271, or 56 times as great. States exhibit a greater contrast. In New England, the density of Massachusetts is 537, Rhode Island is 706, and Connecticut is 356. In the Middle Atlantic division, New York has a density of 280 and New Jersey of 552. Contrast with this the Mountain states, such as Nevada with a density of 1.0, Wyoming with one of 2.5, and New Mexico with one of 4.3. Thus, Rhode Island has a density about 706 times that of Nevada.

The more evident causes of this pattern of distribution are differences in natural resources; industrial and business opportunities; professional, educational, recreational, and social attractions; location; age or time element; and fortuitous choice and migration. Location is a more important cause than it is usually thought to be. It measures the possibility of development of certain kinds and, consequently, the number of inhabitants of a region. Thus, North Dakota has greater natural resources than Rhode Island, but it can not have more than a small measure of its density because the commercial outlet of sea and harbor, among other things, is lacking. Age and time may greatly increase densities, but they cannot offset the advantages of location.

Inequalities of distributions of populations within our nation are partly the outcome of "chance" governing individuals in

TABLE 13

Per Cent of Civilian Population Changing Residence, by Sex, Age, and Type of Migration, United States: 1940–1947, 1948–1949*

Sex, age	April 1940 to April 1947		April 1948 to April 1949	
	All types of migration	Type of Migration (from other state)ᵃ	All types of migration	Type of Migration (from other state)ᵃ
Civilians, 18 and over	57.0	3.4	19.1	10.9
Males				
18 plus	57.5	11.0	19.8	3.9
18–34	69.6	15.5	30.1	6.3
35–64	52.4	8.8	14.2	2.5
65 plus	37.9	5.2	9.5	1.8
Females				
18 plus	56.4	10.8	18.5	3.0
18–34	72.4	16.2	28.8	5.0
35–64	47.3	7.6	12.4	1.8
65 plus	38.5	5.0	9.9	1.6

ᵃ Includes those who moved into the country from abroad.

* Sources: Bureau of the Census, *Current population reports*, Series P-20, Nos. 14, 22, 28. Washington, D.C., 1948, 1949, 1950.

their efforts to locate so as to realize their aims. Among the appeals are resources, opportunities to get on, desire for comforts and attractions. There is no sure method of getting what they want. There is no guidebook to show just where people are most needed, and where they can do best for themselves. So people make guesses, play at trial-and-error, wander rather aimlessly and ineffectively, and pile up in too great numbers in some places. Besides this, there are vast changes going on at times in society. Great inventions and achievements unsettle the economic equilibrium, make a demand for more people in some places and fewer in others. There are regional depressions and waves of prosperity. Crops and industries operate seasonally and shuttle workers about from place to place. And war adds its force to the pressures on population movement. Table 13 shows the pattern of national mobility during the decade of the 'forties.

The Social Problems of Population Composition

Age pattern in the United States. By composition of population we refer to age distribution, proportion of the sexes, and ethnic texture. These have a bearing on the quality of population and the way it functions. They likewise establish certain social conditions under which the major institutions of society must operate. In the present connection social problems arising from changing age and sex distributions will be reviewed.[12]

By age distribution is meant the proportion of a population which is found in each of the various age classes. Only a few of the more important results arising from age distribution can receive attention here. First, let us illustrate actual cases of distribution in order to get a perspective of our national situation. Figure 6 shows the national distribution as to age. In 1940, note that 30.3 per cent of our inhabitants were under 15, that 49.9 per cent were between the ages of 15 and 44 that 15 per cent were between 45 and 64, while 4.8 per cent were 65 or over. Seventy years earlier, in 1870, the percentages for the same age classes in the respective order were 39.2, 45.8, 11.9, and 3.1. The curves for the different age groups show the proportions at each intervening census and tell us what has happened to each age-class in 70 years. The proportion of persons under 15 years of age decreased about 9 points, or 22.7 per cent, that of those 15 to 44 increased 4 points, that of those 45 to 64 increased 3 points, while that of persons 65 and over increased 3.1 to 4.8. There has been a long-time shift toward a population that has proportionally fewer children and youth and more elders.

However, the decade ending in 1949 produced, due in large measure to conditions produced by the war, some marked interruptions in these curves. "An outstanding feature of population change during this decade has been the very rapid growth of the

---

[12] Matters of race and nationality receive ample consideration in a separate chapter of this text.

child population. . . . The great increase in the number of children under 10 years old, about 6.8 million children, reflects primarily the fact that the number of persons born during the period 1941 to 1948 was larger than during the period 1930 to 1937. . . . In the population between 20 and 64 years old there

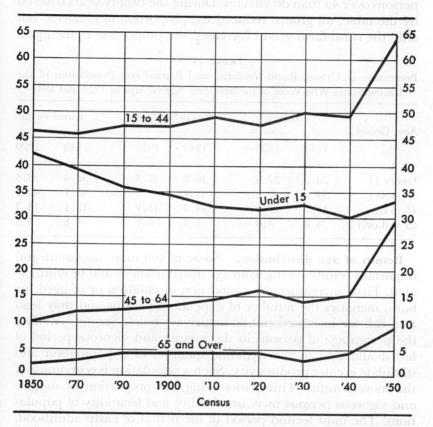

Figure 6. Age Distribution of National Population from 1850 to 1950, by Censuses

were increases in each 5-year age group. . . . These increases range from 425,000 or 37 per cent for the age group 20 to 24 years, up to about 1,353,000 or 23.1 per cent for the age group 55 to 59 years of age, and tended to be relatively larger with increasing age. The population 65 years old and over increased by almost two million persons."[13]

[13] Bureau of the Census, "Current population reports, population estimates," Series P-25, #21, May 27, 1949.

The way populations are distributed in city, country, and village in the United States is shown in Table 14. The farms have more children, fewer persons in the most vigorous and productive period of life, and a larger proportion of the aged than do cities; they have a larger proportion of children under 15 but fewer persons over 45 than do villages. During the twenty years covered by the table, all groups reduced the proportion of children, but only the rural-farm group increased the proportion of the aged.

TABLE 14

Percentage of Urban, Rural-Nonfarm, and Rural-Farm Populations of the United States Who Were of the Specified Age Groups in 1920 and 1940

Age Group	Urban		Rural-Nonfarm		Rural-Farm	
	1940	1920	1940	1920	1940	1920
Under 15	24.2	27.6	30.8	32.8	38.4	38.5
15 to 44	54.8	50.9	49.4	45.3	43.7	42.3
45 to 64	16.7	17.0	14.3	15.9	13.1	14.7
65 and over	4.4	4.5	5.5	6.1	4.8	4.5

Results of age distribution.   Some of the more apparent and important results arising from age distribution should be enumerated. First, increasing the proportion of children or of aged, or both, increases the number of dependent persons and may lead to a call for increased public or private relief. Second, swelling the percentage of persons in the mature and vigorous period of life should add to the dynamic qualities of a population and stimulate greater productivity. Such a population is economically the more fruitful. Third, increasing the proportion of mature and vigorous persons increases fertility and fecundity of populations. The most fecund period of life is that of early adulthood. The fertility of women ceases before the age of fifty. The younger children are neither fertile nor fecund.

Further results might arise from increasing the proportion of those in the ages of dependency, such as comparative provisions for education, pensions or other provisions for the aged, expenditures for protecting child life in the fields of health, child labor, recreation, and the like.

A population group may undergo transformation in age distribution, largely as a result of a declining birth rate. That happened to France after 1860. It is taking place in the United States now. The number of adults for each 1000 children under 16 has increased. In 1790 the number was 780; in 1900, 1580; in 1920, 1880; and it was estimated at 3400 in 1940. Thus we are coming to be a "nation of elders." This will bring about certain social and economic readjustments. The "deadline," the expulsion age for workers in industry, has been 40. This must advance, or society will have to carry an enlarged number of unemployed. Habits of consumption will be transformed. There will be a smaller proportion of youthful goods, more undertakers, and fewer baby carriages. Other things being equal, conservatism in business, politics, and social movements will increase; on the other hand, radicalism is a youthful trait. The direction of activities along recreational and cultural lines is likely to change.

Proportion of sexes. The proportion of sexes constitutes one of the foundations of morality. The ethical life of a people or community is likely to be the best when the sexes are about equal in number. An excess either way disturbs the socio-biological economy. An excess of males may lead to vice and immorality. It stimulates prostitution in some form. It may also prove a social-economic disadvantage. Males are deprived of home privileges, economies, and comforts. This is particularly burdensome in farming populations, where wives are a necessity as homekeepers. An excess of females may encourage promiscuity between the sexes. It certainly deprives females of the desired home and the privilege of rearing children, may lead to the dependency of some of them, and affects the economic status of males by placing women as competitors in many occupations.

Figure 7 (p. 216), showing ratio of males to females in the United States, gives a picture of the situation for the total population and the foreign-born inhabitants, from the beginning of statistics for each down to 1930. We note that males have always been more numerous than females in our national population, the ratio being about 101 to 106 males to 100 females. By comparing the curves of total population and foreign-born ratios, we see that the fluctuations in the total population are produced by those in the foreign-born group. The ratio of males to females among the foreign-born operates at a much higher level than among inhabitants at large. The range of variations is from about 115 to 130. Since 1910, there has been a rapid descent in the excess of males to the lowest point since 1870.

Preliminary estimates by the Census Bureau show a continuing decline from 1940. The sex ratio declined to 99.4 in 1946 and 99.1 in 1948. Comments the Bureau: "Since the leading factor accounting for this apparently increasing disparity in the number

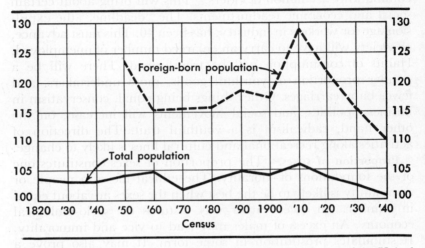

Figure 7. Ratio of Males to Each 100 Females in the Population of the United States: 1820–1940

of males and females is the difference in their death rates, an appreciable narrowing of this difference will be required if the number of males and females is to approach equality again." The Bureau goes on to point out that not all age groups had sex ratios lower than 100. "There were approximately 104 males for every 100 females in the population under 20 years of age. . . . In contrast, the sex ratio of the population 45 years old and over was only 97.1 and represents an excess of 605,000 women in this age range [in 1948]. . . . The trend toward numerical dominance of women in this age group is a result of the fact that rates of increase by age (in the 1940's) were substantially higher for females than for males 45 years old and over, averaging 20.1 per cent for females and only 13.7 per cent for males. The relatively lower mortality of females throughout the age scale and the rapid attrition in the number of foreign-born persons, half of whom were over 51 years of age in 1940, and somewhat more than half of whom were male, were the main factors producing this change in the relative numbers of men and women over 45."[14]

[14] *Population estimates*, May 27, 1949, *op. cit.*

Toward a Population Policy: Norms[15]

This review of some areas of population change will perhaps serve as the basis for a consideration of certain very urgent phases of modern population policy.

In the first place, it is generally agreed that a modern public population policy should aim at replacement. An analogy may be found in the work of the U.S. Forest Service in its advocacy of sound timber management: their policy is one of "sustained yield" through which timber practice will maintain for generations to come as fine and as plentiful a supply of lumber as exists at present. If this ideal is good for trees, it is no less sound for men.

In the second place, the mores seem to have established as a principle the individual value of voluntary parenthood. While strict cause-and-effect cannot be argued in this connection, it seems reasonable to suppose that the spread of the birth-control idea and practice is more the result of the desire for voluntary parenthood (or nonparenthood) than the cause. The many statistical studies which display causal correlation between improved economic and educational status and lower birth rates may well be offered at this point as evidence of the prudential check postulated by Malthus. Today the most cogent reason for the practice of birth control is not the one offered by the so-called Neo-Malthusians—that is, reduction of the general birth rate—but rather its advisability in individual cases. Mental hygienists are at one with family sociologists in support of the thesis that family stability is greatly strengthened by the ability to plan for the advent of babies.[16]

In the third place, from the standpoint of sociology a modern public population policy should be family-centered. This position was taken by the Swedish Population Commission, 1935–1938, when they were assigned the task of formulating a population policy for that country. Since all the motivations which may function at all in a population policy must operate within the framework of the family, it is important to achieve stability for this institution; this rule is especially desirable in view of the

[15] The following material is adapted from Paul Meadows, "Toward a socialized population policy," appearing in *Psychiatry*, 11 (1948): 193 ff.; and *Culture of industrial man* (Lincoln: University of Nebraska Press, 1950). Used by permission of the editors.

[16] For example, cf. J. K. Folsom, *Family and democratic society* (New York: John Wiley and Sons, 1934), Ch. VIII.

interlocking relationship between the family and all other social institutions. Replacement of the population must not be sought for at the expense of the exploitation of the family institution or personalities within the family.

In the fourth place, the desirability of merging both quantitative and qualitative population measures as necessary complements may be regarded as another principle of population policy. Altogether too frequently population enthusiasts proclaim one set of measures without reference to—and often in violation of—the other set. All children, born and unborn, legitimate or illegitimate, must be safeguarded, both by being planned for and by arriving and growing up in a suitable human environment. "If the nation's resources or the social ingenuity for redistribution cannot ensure such average conditions for all children, no additional children should be sought."[17]

In the fifth place, all population considerations should be fitted into the frame of reference known as optimum population. This concept will very likely always be more of a desideratum than a precise formula. Following Ferenczi, however, we may make two approaches in the search for an optimum population. Quantitatively, it implies a set of economic and social conditions which will allow each citizen an opportunity to satisfy his fundamental needs according to certain minimum standards. Qualitatively, it means a population program which, while guaranteeing the continued maintenance of a people, takes into account the eugenic as well as euthenic improvement of the population. Obviously, a fixed optimum is an impossibility.[18]

A final norm for a modern population policy is one of balance, particularly balance in the reproductive behavior of its various social classes, its urban and rural communities, and its different regions. It is, of course, common knowledge that there is no such balance today, and it is also a commonplace that the present imbalances constitute severe losses and unfair costs to the disadvantaged groups. A nation which replaces itself by means of the excessive fertility of its lower-income classes, its rural-farm families, and its isolated and economically disenfranchised regions does not occupy a very healthy position demographically or socially. A democratic society which will not replace its expansionist institutions and ideologies in the field of population by a set of institutions and ideologies which look toward stability

[17] A. Myrdal, *Nation and family* (New York: Harper and Brothers, 1941), p. 108.
[18] *Cf.* Ferenczi, *op. cit.*

can hardly claim longevity as a democracy. The frustrations which such a cultural lag engenders are not conducive to a democratic outlook and practice.[19]

Toward a Population Policy: Methods

In the field of population theory it is difficult to separate purely demographic proposals from those of a social nature: population policy and social policy show a tendency to merge at many points. The foregoing "norms" are implicitly if not explicitly norms for social action in most fields.

It is customary to distinguish between quantitative and qualitative methods of population policy. This distinction is not altogether necessary; in point of daily fact, it does not even exist. It is better to group population methods according to the specific types of problem which will be solved.

Means for correcting the decline in birth rates and for stabilizing and improving the quality of a people were grouped by the Swedish Population Commission under two headings: educational and socio-economic reforms. They are absolutely necessary to one another, and one alone would be self-defeating without the other. The first involves the instruction of the young and old in family values; the encouragement of and preparation for voluntary parenthood; birth-control information and technics; decreased child mortality; the stimulation of the marriage rate partly with the goal of bearing more children within marriage and partly to enrich the growth conditions of all children. The tendencies which eventuate in family limitation may be counteracted by means of socio-economic measures designed to guarantee the fundamental security of a people. In addition, working mothers must be protected; families in which children represent a disastrous economic risk must be aided; the physical environment of the child must be socialized (via nutrition and housing programs, adequate educational and work opportunities.)

These latter measures shade into those which are intended to solve the socio-economic problems of a people. These latter methods center on the general question of the ratio of human numbers and human resources: the man-land ratio. This ratio, it will be remembered, was formulated earlier in this chapter thus:

$$P = f\left(\frac{\text{physical resources} \times \text{economic culture}}{\text{level of living}}\right).$$

[19] This general thesis receives careful attention in Gunnar Myrdal's *Population: A problem for democracy* (Cambridge: Harvard University Press, 1940).

This pseudo-formula suggests the range of technics available for the relief of what is usually denoted as population pressure. This condition arises from (1) a decrease of supply, due to shrinkage of resources, failures in the economic culture or from (2) increases of demand, arising out of improved living standards or increases in numbers.

Each set of causes for population pressure suggests a corresponding compensatory action to relieve that pressure. Thus, measures may be taken to increase supply (PR × EC) by conquest, extension of frontiers, intensive soil culture, production efficiency, use of by-products, consumption economies, improved preservations. Again, measures may be taken to decrease demand (LL) by seeking to lower the habits of insistence (through propaganda usually), rationing, taxation, contraception, emigration, abortion, prudential checks. A democratic population policy will accent the increase of supply, but it will not neglect the possibilities of reducing demand. Anti-democratic population policies have opportunistically followed lines of action suggested in both groups.[20]

A final set of measures in a modern population policy are those having to do with the spatial distribution of people. During World War II the phrase, "migration—the fifth freedom," was not uncommon. Like most war phrases it has tended toward obscurity. The free international movement of people, of course, has been virtually nonexistent since the decade preceding World War I.[21] The immigration policy of most nations has been one of restriction by means of administrative control, either through exclusion or regulation. There was a tendency for a country with declining population, notably France, to have a predominantly favorable attitude toward immigration. Some smaller countries, especially the South American, confronted with certain technological needs have been inclined to welcome persons with technical skills. Control over movement has usually been exercised unilaterally. During the interwar period the International Labor Office encouraged bilateral and multilateral treaties and conventions, especially with reference to labor. The questions of the final disposal of displaced persons, refugees, have again raised the issue of multilateral agreements. There may be open

[20] For further discussion, cf. R. Mukerjee, "Population theory and politics," op. cit.

[21] Cf. Ferenczi and Willcox, International migrations (New York: National Bureau of Economic Research, 1929); also cf. Hutchinson and Moore, "Pressures and barriers in future migration," op. cit.

doors for goods in certain parts of the world, but not for people. This condition is unfortunate, especially in view of the fact that our historic method for the relief of the strains created by in-equalities in the global distribution of people and resources has been the transfer of populations. One thing is certain: the countries which are favored by a rich endowment of resources and technology and which refuse nationals of other countries must eventually face the prospect of hostility, repressed or overt.

Meantime, certain considerations govern the policy-making of people and areas characterized by conditions of overpopulation.[22] These considerations apply with equal force to whole countries and to regions within a country.[23]

1. Because of technological advance throughout the world, the proportion of the world's labor force that can profitably be used in the production of food and other raw materials is decreasing, and the share of the world's income that can be effectively claimed by the segment of the world's population employed in this way is steadily diminishing.

2. Conditions of farm living in general and peasant life in particular are conducive to large families. With the rapid spread of sanitation and other factors causing reduction of child mortality, peasant and plantation populations are generally characterized by ex-tremely high and rising rates of natural increase where checked by recurrent disasters or widespread abortion or infanticide.

3. The perpetuation of traditional folkways and mores inhibits the spread of family limitation. Political or economic conditions which induce a sense of indifference to the possibilities of eco-nomic progress have a similar effect.

4. Conversely, the following conditions are generally associated with the spread of family limitation: education, city life, industrial employment, employment of women outside the home in non-agricultural occupations, revolutionary social movements, popular participation in democratic processes, the spread of inventions and the advance of science.

5. Granted the prevalence of some or all of the motivating factors listed in the previous paragraph, extension of facilities or contra-ception or abortion will accelerate reduction in birth rates.

[22] There is not sufficient space to discuss the problems and methods of a national policy governing internal migration. An excellent discussion may be found in E. Beecroft, and S. Janow, "Toward a national policy for migration," *Social Forces*, XVI (1938): 475 ff.

[23] *Cf.* Lorimer, "Issues of population policy," in F. Lorimer, E. Winton, L. K. Kiser, *Foundations of American population policy* (New York: Harper and Brothers, 1940), p. 192 ff. Quoted by permission.

6. The possibility of constructive planning for overpopulated areas is enhanced by the fact that in many cases the same measures will cut three ways: (1) increase economic productivity, (2) reduce the frequency of births, and (3) make potential out-migrants more acceptable in other regions where there is more effective demand for their labor.

In concluding this discussion of population policy it may be said that the desiderata brought out in this chapter have been aimed at a socialized conception of population and at the destruction of the high value generally placed on the perpetuation of traditional population purposes and methods. The requirements of a sound population policy will vary from country to country, and for the American people from time to time and from region to region. In general, a "numbers" policy which places emphasis on the increasing rate of births regardless of the circumstances has been rejected in favor of a "family-centered" policy which respects personality and the conditions under which children are born and reared. Moreover, population policy cannot be separated from social policy in general.

QUESTIONS

1. What do we mean by "population problems"? Are they the same everywhere? Explain.
2. Why do discussions of population problems always find it necessary to go back to Malthus?
3. List the various ways in which problems of population emerge.
4. Distinguish between overpopulation, underpopulation, maximum population, and optimum population. What is the social significance of these distinctions?
5. Explain the differences between the social conditions in the Netherlands and in China, both of which have a high population density.
6. Can a country ever escape the limitations imposed by the Malthusian formula? Explain.
7. How do you explain the great increase in world population during the nineteenth and early twentieth centuries?
8. May we expect the present decline in death rates to continue? How long? Why?
9. What are the various meanings of the phrase "planned parenthood"? Are they equally "social" in purpose? In result?
10. How do changes in the social composition of the population affect the social problems of a people?

11. What do we mean by a population policy? What social criteria should be considered in the development of a population policy? Why?

12. Is the distinction between qualitative and quantitative population problems sound? Why?

REFERENCES

EAST, E. M., *Mankind at the crossroads*. New York: Charles Scribner's Sons, 1923.

FOLSOM, J. K., *Family: Its sociology and social psychiatry*. New York: John Wiley and Sons, 1934.

FERENCZI, I., *Synthetic optimum of population*. New York: Columbia University Press, 1938.

GINI, C., et al, *Population*. Chicago: University of Chicago Press, 1930.

GOODRICH, C., et al, *Migration and economic opportunity*. Philadelphia: University of Pennsylvania Press, 1936.

HIMES, N. E., *Medical history of contraception*. Baltimore: Williams and Wilkins, 1936.

LANDIS, P. H., *Population problems*. New York: American Book Company, 1948.

LIVELY, C. E., and TAEUBER, C., *Rural migration in the United States*, Research Monograph, Works Progress Administration. Washington, D.C.: Government Printing Office, 1939.

LORIMER, F., WINSTON, E., KISER, L. K., *Foundations of American population policy*. New York: Harper and Brothers, 1940.

MYRDAL, A., *Nation and family*. New York: Harper and Brothers, 1940.

MYRDAL, G., *Population: A problem for democracy*. Cambridge: Harvard University Press, 1940.

National Resources Committee, *Problems of a changing population*. Washington, D.C.: Government Printing Office, 1938.

THOMPSON, W. S., *Population problems*. New York: McGraw-Hill Book Company, 1935.

WILLCOX, W. F., *Studies in American demography*. Ithaca: Cornell University Press, 1940.

VOGT, W., *Road to survival*. New York: William Sloane Associates, 1948.

CHAPTER 9

Migration and Social Policy

Significance and Extent of the Problem

Among the many problems which have confronted our national society, those associated with migration have been regarded as of first-rate importance. Although the national significance of immigration has waned, certain aspects remain which deserve consideration.

A migration study. Migration is related to population problems, since it deals with movements of people and the increase or decrease of national populations. However, since the migrating people have been of different nativity and, sometimes, racial stocks, and since these involve biases akin to race prejudice, in this country we have often associated the treatment of immigration with that of race.

Human migration has passed through several developmental stages. In very primitive times, among small kinship groups, migration between groups was of small moment. Each group regarded itself as superior and other groups as strangely different, this being largely the result of differences in custom and religion. Certain unfortunate individuals might seek asylum in other groups. In this case, ceremonial rites of adoption were necessary for the privilege of living in the receiving group. Those rites were supposed to make the incoming individual a blood member of the group. At a later stage of development, when settled agriculture was their dominant pursuit, entire groups, sometimes very large populations, undertook a change of location. If they were sufficiently strong, other groups might be dislodged from their land, exterminated, or conquered and enslaved. Such movements as those of the East and West Goths, Vandals, and Huns, in the early Christian centuries, represent kinship group migrations of this sort. The migration of the Siouan peoples among our own American Indians from the southeastern to the northern plains region of our country during the last thousand years constitutes such a migration in this hemisphere. Among highly developed peoples, migration has become a movement of individuals, families, and sometimes small colonies from one nation to another. Where permanent settlement is allowed, some kind of naturalization process usually initiates citizenship, but temporary residence is commonly permitted.

An anthropological study. Migration touches the realms of both physical and cultural anthropology. The manner in which migration affects racial types and stocks through consequent miscegenation and marriage calls for the attention of physical anthropology. Cultural anthropology may consider among other things the results of the crossing of cultures through migration, the stimulus migration gives to cultural evolution, the selective effects of migration on culture, and migration as an agency for the spread and distribution of culture.

A general social study. Migration affects nearly every aspect of societal life. Because of this, it is scientifically impossible to deal adequately with it as a purely biological, eugenic, economic, or political matter. The problem is as broad as society itself, touching institutions and organizations of every sort, religion, state, industry, education, customs, manners, and language. It is also vital to neighborhoods and small communities when such areas are invaded and inundated by it. Samples of this are seen in city areas, such as old downtown Boston, and in agricultural areas, such as townships in certain counties of North Dakota. In both cases the old populations were displaced by immigrant colonizers. Migration may affect world society and be of international concern. The Japanese Exclusion Act disturbed international relations. Italy's method of cultivating and holding on to its emigrants in other countries has received international attention.

Disturbing social equilibrium. Migrations of people in large numbers, that is, relative to the populations affected, are unsettling factors in a society or societies. This has been observed already in dealing with matters of population. (See Chapter 8.) Here we want to register the thought in connection with immigration. It is evident that great migratory movements incite and create social changes and disturb the social order; great migrations may shift the center of gravity of the population of a continent or a nation, disturbing the political and economic balance. It easily may affect the labor supply of the receiving nation and so have an influence on wages and the standard of living of working populations. If the migrant population is of a different culture from that of the receiving nation, there may occur a transformation in the religious, political, and educational institutions and in the ideals, aspirations, and standards of a whole national society. An excessive migration in general or the migration of a particular race or from a particular country may raise questions of national policy and result in national immigration laws which place a strain on international friendships.

Extent of our immigration. The number of foreign-born at any given time is the resultant of the arrivals, departures, and deaths of alien migrants in the country considered. In 1940 the foreign-born population of the United States was about 12,650,-000, about 93 per cent being "white" and the remainder "colored," using common terminology. During the whole period from 1820 to June 30, 1950 we received a total gross foreign-born immigration of approximately 39,500,000. This is a tremendous number of people, and we are impressed with its significance when we remember that there are only ten nations in the world today having a population as great as or greater than that number.

Not all these migrants become permanent residents of our nation, since a large proportion return to their own home country or move to some other land. The percentage of "immigrant aliens" who live in this country for a time and then leave for other lands varies from year to year and for different decades. During the early decades of our national life, about 15 per cent of such immigrants departed to settle elsewhere. Later the percentage of departures increased until it was 50 per cent for the three years 1929–1931. It is the writer's belief that the average for our whole national history is about 30 per cent. If we apply this percentage to the total gross immigration that we have received, the result is a net immigration of 29,000,000.

The stream of immigration to this country gradually increased in size between 1790 and 1880, and then remained about the same size until the period of heavy restriction, beginning with 1924. By periods of years, the average annual immigration was as follows: (1790–1820) 9160; (1821–1840) 37,100; (1841–1900) 459,000; (1901–1920) 626,000; (1921–1939) 240,000. Regarded by single years, our period of greatest immigration was early in this century. In six different years between 1905 and 1914 over a million aliens arrived, the greatest number being 1,218,000 in

1907. Both gross and net immigration have suffered a decline since the passage of the quota measures. There was a decline in net immigration from an average annual number of 329,000 for the period 1921–1930 to an average annual loss of 40,180 persons between 1931 and 1936. The years between 1937 and 1947 showed an annual net gain of 49,074.

An immigration "saturation point." One measure of the gravity of problems of immigration is obtained by estimating the ratio of foreign-born to the national population. In 1800 there was a ratio of one foreign-born person to every 140 inhabitants. In 1810, the ratio was 1 to 66; in 1830, 1 to 49; in 1850, 1 to 10.5; in 1860, 1 to 7.8; and since then it has varied from 1 to 6.8 to 1 to 10.4, in 1940. It may be thought that when the ratio became stationary, about 1860, the saturation point had been reached. Justification for such a conclusion is found in the fact that, although both population and immigration greatly increased, the latter so adjusted itself to conditions here that the proportion of foreign-born persons remained practically stationary until exclusion laws obtained.

Kinds and nationalities. Practically all the races and nationalities of the world are represented in our foreign-born population, although accessions from many nations and certain racial stocks have been restricted, especially by recent legislation. Europe always has furnished by far the greater portion of our foreign-born.

We may note the significant changes in the sources of our immigrants:

1. Europe furnished from 81 to 93 per cent of all immigrants till 1921, and since then only 60 per cent. North and West European countries, including the United Kingdom, sent us 93 per cent of all during the first period indicated; 75 per cent in the second, ending in 1880; continued to decline to 41 per cent by 1901–1910; and then dropped to 32, less than one third, in the last decade. Meanwhile South and East Europe increased their contributions from six per cent in the second period to over half of all in the third, and continued to give us over one fourth in the fourth period.

2. As far as the United States is concerned, Asia has never been a large immigrant-exporting country, its largest contribution being 4.4 per cent in the second period.

3. American countries outside the United States have sent us important lots of immigrants at each period denoted, the largest

percentage being over 14 in the second and nearly 37 in the fourth. Canada and Newfoundland have been the chief contributors, with nearly 14 per cent of all immigrants in the second period and almost a fifth since 1921. Mexico sprang to the front after 1921, its donation being over 11 per cent of all after that date.

Shift from old to new immigration. The shift from West and North Europe to East and South Europe as sources of incoming migrants constitutes what is referred to as a transition from the "Old Immigration" to the "New Immigration." There was much false alarm regarding the probability of profound "racial" injury from this shift when it was assumed that the new immigrants were of inferior racial stocks as compared with the old. The newer scientific outlook discounts this doctrine. Yet we can realize that the transition may carry a menace, not to our heredity but to our socio-cultural system. South and East European countries generally have lagged far behind West and North European nations, culturally and socially. Indications of this are seen in their lack of public education, high rates of illiteracy, backward industry, low standards of scientific achievement, and a consequent inferior level of health and sanitation. The high mortality rates, especially among infants and young children, are the outcome of backward scientific developments. So, too, their political systems and spirit are different from ours, and those who come have often been slow to assimilate our outlook, attitudes, and standards.

The more important causes accounting for the shift from old to new immigration are as follows. (1) Modern communicating and transporting agencies penetrated East and South Europe, carrying news of opportunities and affording easy methods of migrating here. Agents of shipping companies and letters from friends already in this country were effective in stimulating migration. (2) On account of our enlarged population and consequent "exhaustion" of easily obtained land and a more crowded market, economic opportunities in the United States came more nearly to approximate those of West and North Europe. People in those lands, consequently, were less prone to take their chances with us. Nevertheless, our opportunities appeared to residents of South and East Europe as superior to theirs and so they came here in greater and greater numbers to improve their fortunes. (3) The demands for cheap workers in our expanding industries, during the period 1880 to the out-

break of World War I, called for the very sort of labor contribution which the poor peasants and poor urban dwellers of
Southern and Eastern European countries could furnish. This
economic "pull" from the United States must not be overlooked
when there are attempts to "blame" these newer types of immigrants for coming to our country.

The United States has been the great receiving nation for
emigrants from other countries, the sum of its accessions being
greater than that of all other Western nations. Between 1820 and
1924, European countries exported 55,500,000 migrants to other
large countries, 64.8 per cent coming to the United States. Some
other receiving nations are Argentina, Brazil, and Canada.
Between 1851 and 1926, Argentina received 5,741,653 immigrants. The migration to Brazil, between 1820 and 1929,
amounted to 4,339,000. That to Canada, from 1901 to 1930,
was 4,723,000, 33.4 per cent of which was from the United
States and 37.7 per cent from the United Kingdom. There is a
large recent emigration from Canada. Authorities report that
for the years 1921–1940 it was over a million, most of the migrants being native-born Canadians.

Causes of Migration

General causes of migration. Human migrations should be
studied in a critical and scientific manner in order to discover
their causes or reasons. It is exceedingly difficult to discern
which of the many causes of population movements are the most
important. It is apparent that the "reasons" for migrations vary
according to the stage of social development and, at a given level
of culture, according to socio-economic conditions.

Like other social changes, population shifts are motivated.
People migrate when they "want" to or "have" to move. Behind the internal promptings lie conditions in the environment
which force or entice them to act. The conditions may be either
geographical or sociological, the latter largely determining
modern movements, the geographical factors being perhaps
more important in the life of early man. The following causes of
migration are worthy of consideration.

1. In the simpler social stages of human existence when men
lived in small hordes of wandering, appropriating individuals,
the larger motive was the promise of a more abundant food
supply elsewhere. When the natural supply of food to be picked
up in one locality gave out, the group moved on more or less

aimlessly, being satisfied to settle down for a time where an ample supply of tubers, fruits, grains, animals, or insects was at hand. Droughts, famines, devastations of storms, and forests destroyed by fires set by lightning were doubtless influential natural disturbances. When human groups became larger, as the result of their hunting and fishing forays, the grounds and waters would be hunted and fished out, and droughts might dry up water and verdure on which animals lived, thus bringing starvation or forced migration.

2. Pressure from outside populations also set up population movements. When a large group got on the move to find a better food supply, it might come into conflict with other groups occupying the invaded lands. When a population was pushed out of its territory, it invaded that of other groups, and other population movements ensued.

3. Among modern peoples, the "reasons" for migration become exceedingly complex. Migrations are produced by natural geographic conditions, such as droughts and other catastrophes of nature, the exhaustion of natural resources, the effects of overpopulation, the greater economic inducements offered in other countries, military and governmental oppression, religious persecution, desire for travel and adventure, and cultural advantages abroad. Facilitating and stimulating the operation of these and other factors are improved transportation facilities, information sent back by satisfied emigrants, and campaigns for immigration by transportation companies and by industries desiring cheap workers. Probably the economic conditions constitute the largest single cause of migration.

Migration to the United States.   Immigrant movements of population to the United States are to be accounted for by the operation of all the conditions which produce migration in general; that is, the conditions of the natural environment, those of the social environment, and the special stimuli of particular interests.

We may think of three sets of conditions and causes which brought the waves of immigration to our shores.

1. Dissatisfaction with governmental or religious conditions in the homeland. During the colonization of our eastern coast regions these were important causes. The Puritan migration to New England and the later Roundhead migration to Virginia were due to political conditions and disturbances in England. The Huguenot exodus from France came because of religious

persecution. Of course, these political and religious factors were accompaniments and expressions of economic conditions. During the last century, there were waves of migrations of particular peoples due to both sets of factors. During the 1840's and 50's the Irish came in great numbers because of the British rack-renting system and bad crops. In the 1840's Germans left the "Fatherland" because of the victory of autocratic over democratic government. In this century the Jews left Russia in hundreds of thousands because of pogroms directed against them by the Russians—a racial-religious matter.

The United States has been an asylum for the oppressed and the persecuted. Multitudes have come here to realize a larger degree of liberty. Religious toleration, liberal government, "free" institutions, and a spirit and attitude of equality and fraternity as between individuals have constituted an appeal that scarcely could be equaled elsewhere. This attractive pull has been quite as effective as the repellent factors abroad.

2. Economic conditions here and abroad. It has been stated often that religious and political motives dominated in our earlier period of immigration, while economic motives have prevailed since our nation became industrialized. It is more probable that the economic motive always has prevailed, but that its goal or direction has undergone a change. Relative to this economic motive, it is seen that in the earlier period it was concerned chiefly with obtaining land, while later it has been directed to industrial pursuits, largely getting jobs in urban factories. From 1790 to 1820, when immigrants came at the average rate of 9000 a year, the economic objective of land was quite as dominating as was that for factory jobs after the Civil War. So long as our great domain of cheap land lasted, immigrants flowed into agriculture. Even as late as the 'eighties of the last century, securing land was a powerful attraction. The Dakotas and western Minnesota were populated largely by Scandinavians who settled on the land. But the supply of cheap land east of the Mississippi was pretty well exhausted by 1870, and the rapidly developing factories and mines then became the loadstone for immigrants.

The amount of immigration to this country and the economic history of the nation demonstrate two things: (a) economic conditions and motives are the most influential determiners of immigration, especially in later periods, and (b) economic conditions here are more directly determining than those abroad.

Both of these statements are proved by the fact that in the great waves of immigration the ebbs and flows are coincident, allowing for a lag, with waves of prosperity and of depression in this country. We have had serious depressions beginning with the following years: 1827, 1833, 1837, 1840, 1857, 1873, 1883, 1907, and 1930, to mention the more prominent ones. Each of these was preceded by years of prosperity, and the smaller currents of immigration coincided with periods of depression. These variations were more coincident with economic conditions here than with political or religious disturbances in other countries. The coefficient of correlation between economic conditions and migration, indicating the degree of agreement, is high, wherever tested. That of British migration to this country for the period 1870–1913 was 0.59, allowing for a lag of a year.[1] The coefficient would probably be greater were a lag of two or three months allowed for instead of a year.[2]

3. Promotional causes. Immigration to the United States, as well as to other countries, was promoted by various conditions of an especially stimulating sort. Shipping companies were known to have spread a network of agents over certain European countries to promote emigration and so secure passenger traffic. The opportunities and allurements of the importing country were painted in glowing colors, and many were stimulated to migrate who otherwise would have remained at home. Big employers of labor who desired cheap workers also sent agents abroad to secure laborers for their purposes. The importation of contract labor was illegal, but promotion was difficult to detect. Correspondence from and return to their own countries of satisfied immigrants greatly stimulated immigration. Millions of contacts were made every year in this way. The return home of a formerly poor and lowly person with evidence of wealth and importance in the new land was a moving argument.

Effects of Immigration

Many serious results might be expected from the admission of great volumes of foreign-born migrants. If 15 million foreign-born persons were set down at once in the midst of our population, the effects would certainly be cataclysmic, with outright

[1] Dorothy Swaine Thomas, *Social aspects of the business cycle* (New York: Alfred A. Knopf, 1927), pp. 148–149.

[2] Harry Jerome, *Migration and business cycles* (New York: National Bureau of Economic Research, 1926), pp. 90–95.

conflict and confusion. Generations would be required to restore equilibrium, and then our society and population would be fundamentally changed. By introducing the foreign stock over a series of years, somewhat gradually, the effects have been minimized and abrupt and catastrophic changes avoided. Nevertheless, we must expect to discover visible and sometimes grave results. The following brief and necessarily somewhat dogmatic treatment will serve to suggest some of them.

Effects on national stock. If possible, we should know the effects of immigration on our stock of people, that is, the biological, hereditary effects. Immigration is bound to bring intermarriage and intermixture of stocks. Where populations are similar, such intermixture can register only slight effects; but where they are racially dissimilar, as in cases of Mongoloids and Caucasians, or Negroids and Caucasians, decided physical changes will appear in the offspring.

Only during the last half century has much stress been laid on dangers to our national stock from immigration. Prior to 1880, our migrants were dominantly West European in origin. Then the so-called "New Immigration" set in. At about the time of the rise of the great migration to the United States from South and East Europe, there arose in Europe a school of dogmatic anthropologists headed by Comte de Gobineau, Houston S. Chamberlain, and others, which taught vehemently the absolute superiority of West and North European stocks over those of the South and East. This dogma later found followers in this country, such as Madison Grant, Lothrop Stoddard, and others, who directed it toward the "New Immigration." The dogmatic propaganda assumed various forms as it developed: Aryanism, Teutonism, Germanism, Anglo-Saxonism, and Nordic racial superiority. The peoples to whom these terms were applied were generally considered to be of the same general stock. They were accredited with definite and distinctive traits, such as fair complexion, light wavy hair, light eyes, tallness of stature, and dolichocephalism, or long-headedness. These characteristics were made the criteria of intelligence, initiative, courage, boldness, and adventuresomeness. Other peoples were charged with being inferior in those respects.

Later schools of anthropologists and geneticists have demonstrated the fictitious character of this dogmatism, and it is passing out. Still, it spread throughout the world rapidly, gained wide acceptance among scholars, scientists, and statesmen, and exercised a profound influence on legislation. Its revival in Germany (1933) was exhibited in the cry of the Hitlerites that Germany must belong to, and be dominated by, Germans and that the Jews must be suppressed, subordinated, and eliminated.

The newer immigrants are Caucasians (as are the so-called Nordics), but they belong to different subracial groups: Mediterranean, Alpine, and Slavic. This means only that in varying degrees they differ in head form, color of skin, hair, eyes, facial profile, stature, and bodily build. But these do not mean physical or mental inferiority. In health and strength they measure up to the average of "Old" immigrants.

There is no reason to think that the different racial stocks diverge fundamentally in mental capacity. With respect to racial varieties of the great racial division called Caucasian, certainly there is no evidence of differences among the several subracial stocks. In innate capacity there are no inferiors and superiors as between Alpines, Nordics, Semites, and Slavs. Further, our immigrant groups are nationalities rather than races anyway, and consequently they represent great mixtures of these various Caucasian ingredients. It is extravagant and unscientific to speak of Germans as being purely Nordic, Russians as purely Slav, or Italians as purely Mediterranean. To state that any particular degree of superior or inferior inborn mental capacity pertains to West or East European nationality is meaningless. What we do expect to find and what is found by mental tests are differences in intelligences, due to differences in levels of culture in the various nations. Further, a great deal of this difference among our immigrants is accounted for by their failure to know and to be able to use and understand the language in which the intelligence tests are given.

The propaganda embodied in the Nordic myth has done much damage by blocking mutual understanding and goodwill among our immigrant stocks and placing some of them at a disadvantage in getting adjusted to our type of culture and society. It has placed good people in a bad light and made them the object of a great injustice. It would be difficult to find one single feature to ascribe to its credit.

Effect on increase of national population. It has been a dogma in economics and sociology for decades that immigration on a large scale retards the natural increase of the native stock. This result is supposed to flow from competition for place, reduction of wages, lowering of standards of living, with consequent celibacy or restriction of the number of offspring. The writers tested this out statistically a few years ago and demonstrated that, at the time of the census of 1920, the rate of reproduction among the native stock was in inverse proportion to the percentage of foreign-born population. This was done for states and for divisions. The method of rank correlation was applied, and coefficients for weight of the foreign-born in the population and ratio of infants per 1000 native white women 15 to 45 years of age were estimated. Other coefficients to be mentioned later were likewise worked out.

The coefficient of correlation for the foreign-born and the native-white increase for the 48 states was −0.756, with a P.E. (probable error) of .04. For the 36 states having a foreign-born population equal to 5 per cent or more of their inhabitants, it was −0.57, with a P.E. of .075. This means that the greater the foreign-born element, the smaller the rate of increase among native whites. It forcibly suggests that the former is the cause of the latter.

There were also other significant correlatives to native fecundity. The coefficient of the latter with urbanism (the per cent of urban inhabitants in the population) for the 48 states was −0.85, with a P.E. of .03; with industrialism, −0.71, with a P.E. of .05; with per capita income, −0.82, with a P.E. of .03; with education, −0.64, with a P.E. of .06. All these are significant coefficients and serve to indicate that the reduction in the native-white increase is due to a complex of causes, of which the foreign-born are only one. It is apparent that urbanism in its broad sense—the city and all that goes with it—is an important influence in this field. By excluding the force of urbanism, the coefficient of foreign-born and native-white increase becomes −0.58. When the presence of the foreign-born is excluded, the coefficient of per cent of urban population in the state population and native increase is −0.61. It is likely that urbanism as a socio-cultural fact is the greatest cause of depression of the natural increase of the native stock.

So far, regarding the facts of correlation, the conclusion reached is that the pressure of the foreign-born on the native-white population does reduce the rate of increase of the latter. The depressive effect, state by state, is in proportion to the foreign weight in the population. Now, if this was true for the date 1920, it would likely be true of any other date. We should like to be able to make a statistical test of the historical influence of the foreign-born on the native increase, but this is impossible in terms of the test thus far indicated, because of the absence of the necessary age, sex, and nativity data in the early censuses. The best we can do is to use the ratios of the foreign-born in the total population and the estimated rates of increase of the old native-white stock for all the decades from 1790 to 1920. The resulting coefficient of correlation is −0.85, with a P.E. of .05. Standing alone, the result would appear insignificant, due to the fewness of terms in the series; but taken with the correlations for 1920, it appears to have some value. Corroborated as it is by the controlled coefficients of −0.58 alluded to, it is evidence that from the beginning of voluminous immigration the foreign-born inhabitants have acted as depressants, along with other features, on the natural increase of our native stock.

The exact extent to which our rate of natural increase has been impeded by immigration cannot be estimated. However, our knowledge is sufficient to warrant our saying that the statements that our population would have been as great or greater had we had no immigration are undoubtedly wild. The rate of increase of our population was falling before immigration assumed considerable proportions. The rate of increase in other nations in which immigration has not been an important factor has declined. Urbanization, education, rising standards of living, and other conditions of developing civilization inevitably would have decreased our rate of growth had there been no immigration at all.

Economic conditions and immigration. How immigration in great masses has affected economic conditions in our country is somewhat problematical. It is easier to discover the immediate than the remote effects. Let us review some of the immediate effects. (a) It has supplied labor power quickly. Critics assert, however, that we have never lacked a supply of native labor. (b) It has helped settle a wilderness in a century and also to exhaust the supply of natural resources. Formerly most of the immigrants went onto the land. (c) It displaced laborers and cut wages at times. Laboring people consider these effects injurious. Employers of the old type condone them. (d) It has tended to lower the standard of living of the masses of working people. Civilization is measured by standards of living. The fact that our standard has not been greatly lowered during normal times is due to wonderful natural resources and our inventiveness, which offset these possible influences of immigration.

The more remote results are less tangible. The big question is whether from the native's point of view it is better to develop a nation quickly by importing outsiders or more slowly by its own people. This supposes that foreign labor has speeded up the development. There are those who think our population would have grown as rapidly without as it has with immigration. This would have come from a greater reproductive rate due to noninterference of competitive and lower-standard imported laborers. Likewise, it is urged that it would have been better to keep our resources for the development of our own people, assuming that they would have lasted longer without immigration. Even if our population had increased as rapidly without immigration so that the resources would have been exhausted as quickly, our own people would have had the advantage.

In making the assumption that our population would have increased as rapidly without as with immigration, perhaps the fact is overlooked that our rate of national increase was declining before immigration assumed large proportions, and that the rate of other nations has declined without the pressure of much immigration. It remains evident that if our growth had been slower without immigration than it actually was, we could have used up our resources for ourselves at greater leisure, other things being equal.

What our standards of living without immigration would have been, there is no means of knowing. We must distinguish between the standard of living for the whole nation and that of the unskilled laborer. The wages of the latter have commonly been only a few hundred dollars a year. The benefits from mechanical inventions have passed to unskilled laborers in a greatly attenuated degree. We know that at times their incomes have been cut by immigration. The determination of how much better on the average it would have been without imported labor hinges on whether they would have reproduced much faster without it. Real wages for the masses are much higher in the United States than elsewhere. How much the unskilled worker participates in this needs determination. It is likely that he has shared in the benefits to a considerable extent.

Political life. Immigration has affected our political life in a number of ways. Our political institutions were inevitably influenced deeply by the introduction of multitudes of foreigners with divergent political backgrounds. Many of them were ignorant of republican government and its principles. (1) A large percentage have resided in our country permanently, without being naturalized, and have acted as a drag on political activities. Until recently, for those who have been naturalized, the process was one of conformity to time requirements only. We paid little attention to preparing them for citizenship, and the training that they received was accidental. (2) Our government, especially in cities, has often been corrupted by the ease with which the votes of masses of ignorant foreigners could be manipulated for political purposes. Political bosses have bargained with leaders of foreign colonies to vote them at election time at so much per head, the vote to be delivered en bloc. Complaisant judges speeded up naturalization to facilitate the process. Thus, to give an historical example, one New York judge issued 7000 papers in October, 1891, at the rate of about two a minute. Often enough the immigrant vote has decided city and state elections.

3. Illiteracy and ignorance of our language have been a hindrance to the understanding of our political requirements by foreign-born citizens. They were forced to depend for guidance on leaders, often of a questionable kind. They were not able to comprehend political speakers during campaigns or to read political news and discussions in the press. As a consequence, they often have been amenable to malignant political influences, to mass and gang control, and helped to swell enormously the unintelligent vote.

Although the federal government has made some attempt to direct immigration where it was needed, on the whole the migrants have been self-directed. This means that they have settled among their kinsmen and acquaintances whose language they knew and who might help them to get jobs and become adjusted. And these being dominantly in cities during recent decades, the cities have domiciled the bulk of immigrants.

Religion. At the beginning of our nation as an independent people, the religious belief was generally and predominantly Protestant. This was the belief of most of the foreign-born who settled here until the "New Immigration" from South and East Europe. The new immigrants came from Roman Catholic countries. Consequently, so far as the foreign-born element goes, together with their offspring, Protestantism has waned and Roman Catholicism has spread. This new immigration has also brought proportionately larger numbers of Greek Catholics from Russia and Greece, Mohammedans from Turkey and Southwest Asia, and Jews from Russia. Also in recent times there have been slight accessions from Oriental religions, such as Buddhists, Confucianists, Shintoists, and the like. And from the region of India have likewise come various Oriental mystical and philosophical cults bordering on religion, such as theosophy. The consequence of all this is to make our population very cosmopolitan in religious matters. The way it has affected our socioethical life seems to be a matter of opinion and dispute concerning which there is as yet little scientific evidence.

Benefits from immigration. We recognize that the destructive effects of immigration are of minor import. The vast majority of immigrants have been wholesome, industrious people. Their ways and customs have differed from ours, but they have generally become assimilated as most loyal and dependable citizens. At the time of our entrance into World War I, it was feared that those from our enemy countries might prove disloyal and cause political disturbances. But there was little disloyalty, and it is probable that 90 per cent of the foreign-born stock supported our government. The others caused little trouble. We can say the same for World War II.

Effects of Emigration

Effect on the countries. The homelands from which the millions of emigrants flowed have sustained various effects from the exodus. 1. Temporary relief from population pressure has resulted in such densely inhabited countries as Italy. Where the birth rate is high, the relief is likely to be only temporary, since improvement in living conditions invites an increase of births. Thus, emigration could not permanently relieve overpopulation in foreign lands unless people co-operated to restrict natural increase.

2. There was an exportation of an average of over 214 million dollars a year from 1922 to 1931 by our immigrants to their homelands.[3] Italy developed a national policy under which she encouraged emigration, kept loyalty to herself, and profited from remittances sent home from foreign lands. The amount thus received in 1921 was 168 million dollars. Commercial exports were only $9.28 per capita; but supplementing this by remittances received raised the per capita exports to $13.61.

3. The return of millions of immigrants who have lived in

[3] Charles Merz, *New York Times*, Dec. 18, 1932, Sec. 9:1.

the United States to their homelands, with their new ideas and methods of doing things, often superior to those at home, has been a considerable influence toward changing the culture of their countries. It has set up a demand for American ideas and machines and has helped to "Americanize" Europe.

4. Sometimes a country may be depleted and injured by excess emigration. This is asserted to have been the case with Ireland at one time. The United States has received more Irish than now live in all Ireland. New York is the largest Irish city. A book published in Ireland in 1908 asserted that Ireland was bleeding to death from migration to America and "unless it is soon arrested it will leave Ireland hopeless and pulseless."[4] Other writers have confirmed such an opinion.

Effect on the migrants themselves. Those settling in the United States have been deeply influenced by our society. We think generally the effects have been beneficial. They commonly have become property owners and/or self-supporting citizens, equal to any in the eyes of the law. Unfortunately, however, there have been untoward results. Often the newcomers, ignorant of our ways and language, have been preyed upon by unscrupulous residents of our country and mercilessly exploited. Naturally, also, some have failed to make the adjustment. This has not always proved to be the land of plenty. Many have been disillusioned regarding this land as one of speedy riches and unrestricted liberty.

Legislation Regarding Immigration

In the United States it is apparent that legislation regarding immigration has awaited the development of a distinct national consciousness about the problem. As in other matters, we do not call for governmental interference until the problem becomes pressing. Generally speaking, we may say that the chief reasons for immigration legislation have been: (1) the problems raised by the defective and pathological foreigners, (2) political and economic conditions brought on by great masses of foreign-born, (3) the "exhaustion" of our natural resources, and (4) the agitation of various organizations.

Developmental stages. Developmental stages in immigrant legislation are observable. In a rough general way they have been four:

[4] R. J. Kelly, *Effects of emigration*, quoted by W. W. Curtis, *Chicago Record-Herald*, Nov. 9, 1908.

1. Period of free immigration, 1782–1830. In this period, no problems of immigration became apparent. The continent was to be mastered, and the natural resources really seemed inexhaustible. Newcomers willing to help subdue the wilderness and develop the resources were welcome.

2. Period of toleration and some agitation, 1830–1882. The presence of the foreign-born exacted little pressure as yet. There was ample room, and the great industrial development begun during the Civil War gave cities great absorptive power. Yet voices began to be heard regarding the perils of immigration. The Molly Maguires in the East and the Chinese in the West stirred up uneasiness. The state of California besought the federal government to regulate Chinese immigration. Accordingly, in this period we find earlier efforts to limit immigration by prohibiting overcrowding on ships (1847) and by legalizing immigrant labor contract laws in Europe (1864), and later efforts directed toward Chinese immigration. The law of 1868 gave Chinese the right of voluntary entrance without naturalization, that of 1870 denied the right of naturalization, while that of 1880 empowered our nation to regulate, limit, or suspend Chinese immigration but not to exclude it. This laid the basis of later exclusion laws.[5]

3. National regulation by limitation and negative selection, 1882–1916. The few years centering in 1882 constitute a turning point respecting our attitude toward immigration. They saw the climax of the migration to this country from Northwest Europe and Britain. Also at that time the new immigration from Southeast Europe was becoming a mighty stream. Immigration had mounted to rather stupendous numbers in proportion to our population, the admissions for 1882 totalling 789,000. All this attracted attention, and people questioned the benefits of so great a movement. This resulted in a complex body of laws relating to immigration, the general import of which was limitation.

The arguments for a policy of restriction that developed are as follows: First, our supply of land and natural resources is becoming "exhausted," and it is wise to save the remainder for ourselves. Second, we must protect our own laborers against displacement by large importations of workers. Third, in the same manner the standard of living of our workers must be protected against the low-wage peoples from abroad. Fourth, there is the felt danger of swamping our type of culture and social

[5] *Cf.* Ch. 13 for a discussion of Oriental racial stocks.

institutions, especially free government, by foreign cultures and low-standard people. Fifth, large mass importations endanger our realizing our "optimum population," it being understood that such population signifies one which is sufficiently large to utilize to best advantage the natural and cultural resources of a nation. Sixth, machine production has displaced labor extensively and produced a situation in which the existing labor supply is more than sufficient to meet the demand.

Outright restriction of immigration was initiated and realized in the exclusion laws applied to the Chinese, beginning with that of 1882, for a period of ten years, which was renewed for a similar period in 1892 and indefinitely in 1902. The remaining laws were selective laws of an individual and negative character. They prohibited the admission of all sorts of defectives, diseased, antisocial, and potentially burdensome individuals, covering insane, impoverished, prostitutes, and even those holding certain views about government, such as anarchists. This was not done at once, but by piecemeal legislation. Meanwhile the administration of immigration laws was concentrated in one department, which was given greater authority and duties. Such laws eliminated the admission of the unfit, but they did not greatly affect the total sum of immigration.

4. Positive restriction and group selection, 1917 to 1930. By the time of our entrance into World War I, sentiment against unrestricted immigration had become pronounced. The demands of labor and others could not be evaded. The illiteracy law of 1917, which shuts out those who cannot read or write in any language, sought to limit immigration both quantitatively and qualitatively, being especially effective against the countries of Southeast Europe, where illiteracy is high. As we have seen in our statistical survey, immigration assumed astonishing proportions before World War I. That war practically eliminated importation of people, especially from Europe. However, the great floods of people that began to come in after the war, and the propaganda against Southeast European migrants so largely fomented by the outcome of the mental tests administered to our drafted men, aroused great hostility to immigration, especially from certain nationalities. The sentiment for restriction and group selection became overpowering and brought into existence the quota laws.

Quota laws. The first quota law, which was in effect between 1921 and 1924, aimed to restrict immigration and to exercise group selection by favoring Northwest Europe. Any European nation was entitled to send immigrants to the extent of 3 per cent of its native-born in the United States at the census of 1910. In 1924 the "national origins" law was passed. Instead of basing quotas on our foreign-born population, it sought to give weight to nationalities according to their cumulative descent from the beginning of the nation; but more particularly to give weight to native-born American stock. Thus, if the German stock here amounted to 16 per cent of the accumulated foreign stock, its annual admissions would be 16 per cent of the 150,000 immigrants permitted to enter our country annually. No quota nation would have a quota of less than 100. Because of the fact that methods of ascertaining nationalities according to origin were not sufficiently exact, the clause of the measure pertaining to national origins was suspended from time to time by Congress and did not go into effect until July 1, 1929. The quota is 2 per cent of the national-origins population as based on the census of 1920.

Compared with quotas under the previous law, Germany's allowance was cut from 51,000 to 26,000; that of the Irish Free State from 29,000 to 18,000; that of Norway from about 6500 to 2400; while the quotas of the following nations were increased: Great Britain and North Ireland from 34,000 to 66,000, and Italy from 3800 to 5800, these being in round numbers. Other national quotas underwent similar smaller changes. The so-called Japanese exclusion law was passed in 1924. The Japanese were not directly excluded, for the law merely declared the exclusion of all nationalities not eligible to citizenship in this nation. This law was largely the result of anti-Japanese agitation on the Pacific coast.

Administration. The law of 1924 vitally changed the administration of immigration laws by placing a part of the work of selection on our consular officers in quota nations. These officers became obliged to gather and examine evidence as to fitness of applicants for admission into this country and to issue visas indicating eligibility not to exceed the quota number of respective nations involved. The visas are presented by the holders at our ports of entry, the applicants for admission are examined by the inspectors, and the ineligible are turned back at the expense of the transportation companies bringing them over. The examination of applicants in foreign countries is limited to a scrutiny of evidence of fitness presented by the applicants. The desire of some that our consular agents should be empowered to make a thorough investigation of each case probably cannot be realized, as such an attempt would be resented by the different nations as invading their rights.

Quota law and social policy. There are two respects in which the national-origins law is fictitious and therefore unscientific and unjust. (1) According to the chief arguments for it in Congress, it discriminates in favor of Northwest Europe on biological or "racial" grounds. As we have seen, racial differences are physical and reveal no determinable mental or moral distinctions. (2) The attempt is made to assign quotas to various European nations according to their contribution to our population from 1820 to 1920. We are to think of such contributions, together with the present foreign-born, as Germans, Italians, Irish, etc. and give weight accordingly. There has been intermarriage, however, between all so-called "racial" stocks from the beginning. Nationalities have lost their identity and separateness. Nationality names may go down for generations unchanged, but the physical stocks disappear and are merged, diluted, submerged, and synthesized into American stock. There is no factual, scientific entity corresponding to the idea of "national origins."

On the other hand, there are two respects in which the chief object of the law is justified, although the reasons offered for its passage may have been unscientific. *First*, it gives appropriate weight to the native-white stock, including the original population of 1790. Natives were 85.5 per cent of the white population of 1920, 14.5 per cent being foreign-born. But a part of this proportion is assigned to nationalities and counts in determining and swelling immigrant nationality quotas. *Second*, Northwest Europe is favored as against Southeast Europe. This is probably justified as good social policy on cultural, though not on physical, grounds. If we are to select, we can best assimilate those whose ideas, beliefs, institutions, government, and educational level are most akin to ours.

In any case, the United States is not called upon now to solve the problems created by heavy waves of immigration. The problems lie elsewhere. They inhere in the prolonged cultural segregations that have characterized the lives of many "foreign" groups and the restricted transmission of group cultures that tend to perpetuate misunderstandings and suspicions. National policy needs to be directed toward a broad acculturation process out of which the best traits will find expression. The extent to which naturalization takes place by legal processes is not necessarily a measure of acculturation.

QUESTIONS

1. In what respects is immigration a population study?
2. (a) Is there any indication that immigration here ever reached a "saturation" point? (b) How long has the ratio of foreign-born to the total population been stable?
3. (a) Are migrations of people motivated phenomena? (b) Compare kind and number of stimuli to migration in primitive and in modern society. (c) Have political and religious disturbances abroad ceased to act as causes of emigration? (d) What are some promotional causes of emigration?
4. Are economic causes of immigration greater now than a hundred years ago?
5. What evidence, if any, is there that our population is vitally injured physically or mentally by crossing with immigrants?
6. What have been some of the baneful effects of large and rapid immigration?
7. What facts show that children of the foreign-born have a harder problem of adjustment than children of native-born parents or than foreign-born persons?
8. What would be required in order that emigration from an over-populated country permanently benefit that country?
9. (a) Give reasons for immigrant legislation in this country. (b) Are they all valid ones? (c) Why did our nation adopt restrictive measures?
10. (a) What is a "national-origins" population? (b) the "national origins" law of 1924? (c) How did the latter change selective emphasis?
11. (a) In what senses is this law fictitious? (b) In what sense is it justifiable?
12. (a) What is Americanization? (b) Give the relation of assimilation to immigration.

REFERENCES

ABBOTT, EDITH, *Immigration: Select documents and case records.* Chicago: University of Chicago Press, 1924.

ADAMIC, LOUIS, *My America.* New York: Harper and Brothers, 1938.

BOGARDUS, E. S., *Immigration and race attitudes.* Boston: D. C. Heath and Company, 1928.

BOGARDUS, E. S., *Mexican in the United States.* Los Angeles: University of Southern California Press, 1934.

BROWN, L. G., *Immigration.* New York: Longmans, Green and Company, 1933.

BROWN, F. J., and ROUČEK, J. S., eds., *Our racial and national minorities.* New York: Prentice-Hall, 1937.

DUNCAN, H. G., *Immigration and assimilation.* Boston: D. C. Heath and Company, 1933.

FAIRCHILD, H. P., *Immigration.* New York: The Macmillan Company, 1925.

GAVIT, J. T., "Americans by choice," *Survey,* Vol. 47: 815–23.

GETTYS, C. L., *Law of citizenship in the United States.* Chicago: University of Chicago Press, 1934.

GOODRICH, CARTER, et al, *Migration and economic opportunity.* Philadelphia: University of Pennsylvania Press, 1936.

Government publications:

    Abstracts of reports of the Immigrant Commission, 2 vols., 1911.

    Decennial censuses of the United States.

    "Europe as an emigrant-exporting continent and the United States as an immigrant-receiving nation," Hearings before Committee on Immigration and Naturalization, House of Representatives, 68th Congress, 1st session, serial 5-A, March 8, 1924.

    "National origins provision of immigration law," Hearings before Committee on Immigration, U. S. Senate, 70th Congress, 2nd session, on S. J. Res. 192, Feb. 4, 5, 8, 11, and 13, 1929.

HANKINS, F. H., "Problems of race mixture," *Racial basis of civilization,* Ch. VII. New York: Alfred A. Knopf, 1926.

HERSKOVITS, M. J., "Brains and the immigrant," *Nation,* Feb. 11, 1925: 139–141.

ICHIHASHI, YAMATO, *Japanese in the United States.* Stanford: Stanford University Press, 1932.

KUCZYNSKI, R. R., *Population movements.* New York: Oxford University Press, 1936.

MCKENZIE, R. D. *Oriental exclusion.* Chicago: University of Chicago Press, 1928.

MEARS, E. G., *Resident Orientals on the Pacific coast.* Chicago: University of Chicago Press, 1928.

SCHRIEKE, B., *Alien Americans.* New York: The Viking Press, 1936.

SEABROOK, WILLIAM, *These foreigners.* New York: Harcourt, Brace and Company, 1938.

TAFT, D. R., *Human migration.* New York: Ronald Press, 1936.

TAYLOR, P. S., *Mexican labor in the United States.* Berkeley: University of California Press, 1929–1933.

VAN VLECK, W. C., *Administrative control of aliens.* New York: Commonwealth Fund, 1932.

WILLCOX, W. F., ed., *International migrations.* New York: The Macmillan Company, 1931.

WIRTH, LOUIS, *Ghetto.* Chicago: University of Chicago Press, 1928.

YOUNG, DONALD, *American minority peoples.* New York: Harper and Brothers, 1932.

CHAPTER *10*

Social Change and Family Adjustment

Transitional Patterns of Family Living

Development. The history of family life is largely a history of the attitudes of the sexes toward each other. These attitudes have varied widely among different peoples throughout the world. Hence, there have been, and are at the present time, many types of family life. People everywhere have tended to look upon other and strange family practices as degraded or bad. Ethnocentrism is well illustrated in a people's views of their own family system.

In order to have an intelligent view of the family, it is necessary to think of it as an institution that has evolved out of human experience. This point of view is confirmed by an examination of various family systems that have developed under different environmental conditions. The effects of experience upon the familial habits of a people may be noted in the changing family life in the United States under the influence of a rapidly developing material culture. Some of the objective manifestations of these changes include a rising divorce rate, a declining birth rate, and the gradual transfer of economic and social functions from the family to other agencies.

The biological basis of the family is evident in its first important function of biological reproduction of the race. The lengthening period of infancy makes increasing demands upon the time and energy of the mother. This fact contributed, in early societies, to the establishing of a system of division of labor according to which the mother and children became the center of social life. The men did most of the roaming, hunting, and fighting, while the women performed domestic duties. The mystery connected with birth gave rise to certain beliefs about women which largely influenced familial habits among preliterate peoples. In time, the family practices that arose naturally out of experience became fixed in sentiment. Because they were sanctioned by the "gods," any deviation from them was viewed with harsh disapproval. There were relatively few offenders against the established codes for the reason that every child was brought up in them; his personality was shaped by them. Hence, the wishes of the individual as well as his forms of expression were limited by the cultural patterns of his group.

Functions of the family. The first important function of the family, then, is the reproduction and rearing of children. Yet there are others.

The second function arises out of the necessity of transmitting to the children the social heritage of customs, practices, skills, techniques, and beliefs of the society into which he was born. On such transmission depends the development of social organization. By such transmission are laid the foundations of personality of the child, whose most impressionable years are spent in the family circle.

The third function of the family is the control of sex behavior. Among the lower animals sex is regulated largely by biologically inherited instincts. Man, however, functions mainly on an acquired-behavior basis. It has been necessary, therefore, in the interest of social order and continuity, that certain basic impulses be held in check and to some extent redirected through institutionalized agencies.

The fourth function of the family is economic. In most societies the biological differences between men and women provide the basis of a division of labor between them. In turn division of labor gives rise to specialization, thus increasing the interdependencies among members of the family. Food must be secured, children cared for, enemies beaten off, the domesticated animals fed, fires kept, and clothing made. In the performance of these various tasks each contributes to the economic needs of all. The pattern of the services varies from one culture to the next, but the over-all economic function and mutual interdependence remain fairly constant.

Shifting family functions. The family as a social institution reflects the pattern of the culture as it exists in a given time and place. The family is interwoven with all the culture complexes of a society and is not independent of them. It is natural, therefore, that the transition to an industrial, monetary economy would bring a shift in the functions and nature of the family system. In general, the outstanding changes in the family of Western Europe and the United States, most markedly influenced by industrialization, have been the development of a highly dependent family system and the alteration of the major family functions. A secondary but tremendously important consequence of these changes is the fact that the instability of modern society is necessarily mirrored in the instability of the family.[1]

The early American families lived in small towns and in the open country. Land was usually plentiful, and contacts between people were confined, in the main, to small areas. School terms were short, and the curricula simple. Most of the food and clothing used by the family was produced and prepared in the home. Under these circumstances large families were desirable. Older children assisted in the major enterprises of the family, such as land clearing, road construction, crop raising, house building, food preserving, and cooking, while the younger ones helped with the chores. The comradeship of parents, brothers, and sisters seems to have been more common in the early American family than it is now. The family tensions caused by the monotony of a close and rigid rural existence seem not to have been so disturbing as are those today, engendered as they are by numerous and conflicting influences.

The rise of the factory system and of the city—of an industrial culture, in other words—changed this pattern of living. In part or in whole many functions of family living were transferred from the home to other agencies. Much of this transfer was a result of urbanization. Rural families have dwindled in number until now they constitute considerably less than half of the total.[2] In part this transfer of functions is due to technological change. The restaurant, the laundry, the bakery, the dairy, the tailor shop, the canning factory have taken over much of the work done in the home.[3] The family buys its services to a much greater extent than it produces them.

[1] Cf. E. R. Mowrer, *Family disorganization* (Chicago: University of Chicago Press, 1939); F. Alva Myrdal, *Nation and family* (New York: Harper and Brothers, 1941); C. C. Zimmerman, and M. E. Frampton, *Family and society* (New York: D. Van Nostrand Company, 1935); W. F. Ogburn, *Recent social trends* (New York: McGraw-Hill Book Company, 1933), Ch. 13; A. G. Truxal, and F. E. Merrill, *Family in American culture*, Part II (New York: Prentice-Hall, 1947).

[2] For further discussion, cf. Ch. 6.

[3] Cf. M. F. Nimkoff, *Marriage and the family* (Boston: Houghton Mifflin Company, 1947), Ch. 4.

Gainfully employed homemakers. The impact of industrialism and of its twin, urbanism, may be seen in the huge increase of homemakers gainfully employed outside the home. By "gainfully employed" is meant those who are engaged in commercially profitable production, whether as owners or as hired workers. Roughly, one out of every seven homemakers is employed in the labor force.[4] Increased specialization and mechanical routine in industry and business have greatly encouraged the use of women in business and industry. Also, most homemakers employed outside the home are there from necessity. Indeed, the families of women workers are not the standard ones of public thought.[5] The Women's Bureau in a special study of 6000 women workers reported about their families: "It is the broken and composite family in largest number . . . the family without a father, the family without a mother, the family with neither father nor mother, the family with relatives living with them."[6] For the women, employment outside the home spells crowding and congestion of family responsibilities in brief, after-work hours. For the children it means the loss of maternal care and supervision. In both cases it means the spawning of many irritating and often insoluble family situations.

Family functions and the cash nexus. The modern family, like everything else, is geared to the machine, and its fortunes reflect the vicissitudes of an industrial civilization. The most important economic tie the family sustains with industrial society is the money income from the job: the "cash nexus," as Carlyle called it. That tie is often very thin and weak, inadequate for the exacting burdens placed upon it. Thus, even in the prosperous postwar years, according to a report by the United States Treasury Department in 1948, a fourth of American families had a money income of less than $2000. In addition, there is the tragic possibility of unemployment, the most serious rupture in the security of the family. But employed or not, the family is completely dependent on services and commodities which must be purchased in the market. And all the advertising genius of present-day society is directed toward a tremendous increase in family demand for purchased goods. The gap between the family's expected standard of living and its actual plane of

[4] Nimkoff, *op. cit.*, p. 91.

[5] *Cf.* W. Goodsell, *Problems of the family* (New York: Appleton-Century-Crofts, 1928), Ch. 10.

[6] *Women workers in their family environment*, Bulletin 183, Women's Bureau (Washington, D.C.: Government Printing Office, 1941).

living—between promise and delivery, so to speak—becomes a source of tension. The good life is defined in terms of goods.

The decline of the secondary functions. The shifting family pattern has rendered the so-called secondary functions—education, religion, recreation, protection—even more secondary. The educational work of the family is done by specialists outside the family. Unfortunately, some of the most important instructional jobs—morals, sex education, conduct—are left to family members unable to compete with the school in expertness, efficiency, authority, or time. Religious functions have long been delegated to the church, which, however, will usually blame the family for any subsequent failures in the religious life of the child. The home is seldom the scene of the family's recreation. Indeed, recreation is a commodity, like clothing, bought and sold by commercialized agencies. Finally, the protective care of family members—sickness, old age, accidents, fire, crime—has been expertly institutionalized outside the family in such private and public agencies as the hospital and convalescent home, governmental aids and agencies, fire and police departments. The family is by all counts a consumer of purchasable and skilled services.[7]

Residual family functions. What, then, remains for the family? Its most important functions seem to be reproduction and the care of children and the provision of a money income sufficient to buy the services expected by a culture-patterned and high standard of living. The family situation reminds one of a chameleon placed on a Scotch plaid. It is well-nigh impossible for it to make good. There is, for example, the well-known fact that the reproductive function has long been declining. The falling birth rate, falling about 50 per cent in the last two generations, suggests that satisfying this expectation of society is less and less attractive and feasible. One can point to a number of reasons: the weakening of religious sanctions, the predominance of an individual pleasure pattern, the tensions and demands of a competition-success pattern of living, and a way of family life which has little place for children.[8] In general, the reasons center in the fact that children appear to large numbers of men and women in modern society to be an economic and emotional liability. The life of any individual today is so

[7] *Cf.* National Resources Planning Board, *Family expenditures in the United States* (Washington, D.C.: Government Printing Office, 1941).

[8] *Cf.* the excellent discussion of the role of these factors in our changing birthways by Paul Landis, *Population problems* (New York: American Book Company, 1948), Ch. 5.

intimately and intricately tied up with great collective movements and forces that "security" becomes a paramount consideration. Such a frame of values is a far cry from the family system as depicted in the annals of early America and as glowingly idealized in historic family traditions.

For a better understanding, then, of the problems of modern family living, we turn to the forces that have shaped present-day family culture.

Cultural Sources of Family Problems

The American family a composite formation. The manner in which social change induces family-adjustment problems may be seen in a review of the American scene. American culture, which is largely an extension of Judaeo-Christian cultures, is characterized by endless variety in its folkways and mores. This new society is a creation of many societies. In a sense, therefore, it is unwise to talk about the "American family." For family living in this country varies by region, occupation, religion, nationality, and race.[9] There is the southern family, the corn-belt farm family, the Jewish family, the German family, the Chinese family, and so on. These subcultures of America have interacted with one another and with certain predominant social forces common to all of them. Among these common social patterns which have in a sense directed the change and interaction of family life in this country may be included religion, capitalist industrialism, the frontier, the romantic complex, science, and democracy.[10] Each will be reviewed briefly in the following pages.

The Hebraic-Christian tradition. Earlier it was pointed out in this chapter that the story of the family is largely a history of the attitudes of the sexes toward one another. These attitudes are never "given," but learned. Americans have "gone to school" for their sex attitudes to a great, fused tradition, the Judaeo-Christian, transmitted to this country by the successive waves of European migration. As finally transmitted, this tradition insisted on the primacy of chastity, the necessity of virginity, the desirability of abstinence, the equal value of marriage and celibacy. The core of sentiment here is a dualism: the sinfulness of sex but likewise

---

[9] *Cf.* E. W. Burgess, and H. J. Locke, *Family: From institution to companionship* (New York: American Book Company, 1945), Chs. 2–6.

[10] *Cf.* A. G. Truxal, and F. E. Merrill, *op. cit.*, Chs. 3–10.

the necessity of sex.[11] This ambivalence toward the sex life, defined simultaneously as sinful and as desirable, established a moral code which was necessarily weak at the point of enforcement.[12] The gradual decline of religious controls over the sexual life of modern man and the emergence of a secular jurisdiction by no means strengthened the social discipline or removed the stigma of sinfulness. The much-popularized Kinsey report suggested, though it can hardly be said to have demonstrated, that the religious sex codes are considerably more revered than obeyed. A growing secularism, aided and abetted by science, has probably added to the confusion by replacing the older sinfulness with the concept of naturalness. The implications of this reorientation are still developing.[13] Long in revolt against the official code, a persisting folk tradition—unwritten laws, so to speak—has made its own particular contribution to the transitional sex code of modern Americans.[14] What is emerging, of course, is not immorality—except as severely judged by the ancient tradition—but a new sexual morality. It may be a long time before the new sex patterns are clearly and acceptably defined.

Capitalist industrialism. Many of the characteristic features of the American family system derive from the fact that the economic culture in this country is capitalistic industrialism.

Capitalism is an institutional complex embracing such well-known traits as private property for private profit, the sacredness of contracts, monetary economy, individualistic philosophy, and a machine technology.[15] It differs from earlier economic cultures

[11] *Cf.* Geoffrey May, *Social control of sex expression* (New York: William Morrow, 1931).

[12] On this point, compare J. K. Folsom, "Changing values in sex and family relations," *American Sociological Review,* II (1937): 714 ff.; T. M. Newcomb, "Recent changes in attitudes toward sex and marriage," *American Sociological Review,* II (1937): 659 ff.; M. L. Ernst, and D. Loth, *American sexual behavior and the Kinsey report* (New York: Bantam Books, 1948); Margaret Mead, *Male and female: A study of the sexes in a changing world* (New York: William Morrow, 1949), Chs. 14–15.

[13] Compare Havelock Ellis, "Sexual freedom today," *American Mercury* 4 (1937): 27 ff.; Hornell Hart "Sexual adjustment versus erotic anarchy," *Forum,* 97 (1937): 345 ff.; Bertrand Russell, "Our sexual ethics," *American Mercury,* 38 (1936): 36 ff.; "Family," Editorial, *Life,* March 24, 1947; E. H. Erikson, "Ego development and historical change," in *Psychoanalytic study of the child,* ed. by Anna Freud (New York: International Universities Press, 1947), Vol. II, pp. 359–396; Margaret Mead, "What is happening to the American family?", *Journal of Social Casework,* XXVIII: 323–330.

[14] *Cf.* R. B. Vance, and W. Wynne, "Folk rationalizations in the unwritten law," *American Journal of Sociology,* 39: 483–492.

[15] *Cf.* Werner Sombart, "Capitalism," *Encyclopedia of social sciences,* III: 195–208;

of the human family in many significant respects. Acquired status, contract rather than inheritance, production for profit rather than immediate use, this-worldliness in place of an otherworldly stewardship, and a pronounced secularism in values are primary traits of historic industrialism.

Capitalist industrialism needed for its development a special type of family culture.[16] Free, independent family members, mobile families, individualistic rather than patriarchal families, dependent not self-sufficient families, homes as consuming centers rather than productive agencies, these were essential to the new industrialism. It is a noteworthy fact that wherever capitalist industrialism has penetrated it has dissolved the family-centered culture ("familism") for the person-centered family ("individualism").[17]

A frontier society. The novelty of American family life springs in part from its frontier history. The frontier was not only the cutting edge of American civilization, it was the matrix of a whole new set of social values in American life.[18] At least five characteristic features of the frontier affected the American family culture. The mobility which it made possible was an acid corroding the older family bonds. The isolation which it enforced accented the companionship and personal dependence of men and women and of parents and children on each other. Its equalitarianism emphasized that personal achievement was the only thing that counted, not inherited family status. The individual choice of marital partners which it permitted released young people from dependence on the system of arranged marriages of early patriarchalism. Finally, the unbalanced sex ratio which the frontier created put a premium on women, encouraging greater economic independence, legal protection, and social freedom for them.

The romantic complex. In a sense, only modern peoples fall in love; in other societies they get married. "Falling in love" is a highly patterned behavior, disciplined by the glamour, emotional

---

Paul Meadows, *Culture of industrial man* (Lincoln: University of Nebraska Press, 1950), Chs. 2–3; W. E. Moore, *Industrial relations and the social order* (New York: The Macmillan Company, 1946), Chs. 2–4.

[16] *Cf.* C. C. Zimmerman, *Family and civilization* (New York: Harper and Brothers, 1947).

[17] *Cf.* such various accounts as W. I. Thomas, and E. Znaniecki, *Polish peasant in Europe and America* (New York: R. G. Badger, 1922); M. J. Levy, Jr., *Family in modern China* (Cambridge: Harvard University Press, 1949); Robert Redfield, *Folk culture of Guatemala* (Chicago: University of Chicago Press, 1941).

[18] *Cf.* E. R. and G. H. Groves, *Contemporary American family* (Philadelphia: J. B. Lippincott Company, 1947), Ch. 6.

intensity, individualism, and sexual eroticism of an inherited tradition—romanticism.[19]

Initially appearing among the European aristocracy in the late feudal period and later taken over by the rising bourgeoisie, the romantic tradition gradually fused a number of attitudes and reactions into a sexual code which functions both as the allure of modern marriage and as the source of its despair. The elements of the romantic mode of courtship and marriage are distinct. There is the belief in an "elective affinity" with whom one falls in love at first sight. Relationships with the beloved are typically intense emotionally and barren intellectually. The trivial is glorified, and each person seeks a monopoly of the other. An emotional infantilism which tries to recover the childhood security of the maternal presence is characteristic of romantic love. The utter unimportance in the last analysis of parental views is essential; in fact, parental disapproval is a sure cement.

This tradition, sketchily described here, has much in its favor. It accents companionship and personality values. It extends the sex impulses beyond the purely physical. It provides an appraisal of the sex partner, an appraisal overlain with some illusions, of course. It uniformly elevates the woman, thus compensating for certain contrary tendencies in the Hebraic-Christian tradition. And it is marriage-centered.

These decided assets are checked, however, by a few major liabilities. "To each his own!" is the romantic motto, but unfortunately some never find mates. The prospective marriage partner is not adequately judged in terms of family suitability but largely in terms of marital companionship: family success is less important than marital happiness. Few marriages can long maintain the erotic euphoria of romantic courtship. The romantic flexibility of courtship often sadly conflicts with the inflexible routines of marriage. Love may find a way, according to the romantic theme, but love is seldom enough.

The impact of science. Modern industrialism has influenced the contemporary family in so many ways that it is almost impossible to draw the contour lines of change. J. K. Folsom has grouped the influences under two major headings, mechanical and bio-social.[20] Mechanically, science—which is a disciplined search for change—has been responsible for a rising *standard* (if

[19] *Cf.* M. A. Elliott, and F. E. Merrill, *Social disorganization* (New York: Harper and Brothers, 1941), Ch. 23; F. E. Merrill, *Courtship and marriage* (New York: Wm. Sloane Associates, 1949), Ch. 3.

[20] J. K. Folsom, *Family and democratic society* (New York: John Wiley and Sons, 1943), Ch. 5.

not always a rising *plane*) of consumption. It has lengthened the space of mobility and quickened its speed. It has transformed the time and energy patterns of household routines. It has widened the scope and multiplied the variety of family recreations.

Bio-socially, science may be credited with lengthening the life span, reducing the volume of childhood sickness and death, correcting some of the causes of sterility, and aiding in preventing conception. It has helped shape a eugenic and euthenic human environment. It is in process of providing a new hygiene for sick minds, of re-orienting ethical values, and of fashioning new instruments of family service (*e.g.*, old age pensions, unemployment insurance, social case work, and so forth).

The democratic dogma. Finally, in outlining the social sources of modern family living, particularly in the United States, one cannot fail to mention the idea of democracy. Variously and often vaugely defined, democracy has tended to be for many people a way of voting rather than a way of organizing human society.[21] Historically, its form differs from one culture to another. In the case of the United States, democracy, considered as a doctrine, has championed the ideology of natural rights.[22] This *Weltanschauung* holds that all men have certain inalienable rights. The American Declaration of Independence and the American Bill of Rights were attempts to state and frame them in a setting of law. The natural-rights ideology has a strong equalitarian cast. By way of logical extension, it insists on the legal, educational, political, economic, and general cultural equality of opportunity for all people, regardless of age, sex, religion, or color. As a creed, it has shaped the relationships of men and women, parents and children, and families, and it has been a sanction for all the reforms and programs looking toward the improvement and control of family living.

Adjustment Problems of the Family Life Cycle

The family in terms of its life cycle. Like the individual, the family as a social group may be said to go through a life cycle: courtship, marriage, birthing, schooling, marriage of the children ("the empty nest"), recovery, retirement, death.[23] Each stage

[21] *Cf.* Meadows, *op. cit.*, Ch. 13.

[22] *Cf.* C. Brinton, "Natural rights," *Encyclopedia of social sciences*, XI: 299–302; G. Gurvitch, "Natural law," *ibid.*, 284–290.

[23] *Cf.* H. F. Bigelow, *Family finance* (Philadelphia: J. B. Lippincott Company, 1936), pp. 15–18; P. C. Glick, "Family cycle," *American Sociological Review*, XII (April, 1947): 164–174.

in the family cycle has its own peculiar adjustments to make. Failures or difficulties in these adjustments constitute what are generally called "the problems of the family." The problems of each stage vary considerably because families vary—in age, size, occupation, style of living, religion, region, and so forth. Not too much is known about the life-cycle patterns of the forty million American families; indeed, here is one of the most urgently needed areas of research in family sociology. However, sufficient information is at hand to suggest some of the typical problems apparently common to most families.

Problems of mate selection. People in Western culture "fall in love" as the customary preliminary to marriage. This romantic tradition is part of the Western tradition of individualism. Mate selection among moderns is a private affair, and it comes after a series of emotional attachments which serve as an apprenticeship for marriage. Unlike other cultures in which group methods and procedures direct the marital selection, individualistic romantic mating tends to be a matter of personal choice, of emotional and social considerations. And in this fact may be found the problems surrounding mate selection in modern society.

Among the difficulties and risks attending modern mate selection, there is, first of all, the problem of marriageability. Suitability for marriage tends to depend on personal attractiveness, on skill in mate attraction, on sexual normality, on the manner in which the individual "rates" in the "rating-dating" complex.[24] These factors condition his readiness and acceptability for marriage. There is, in the next place, the problem of marriage availability. There are situations in modern society in which imbalances in the sex ratio prevail, such as jobs with a predominance of women, communities with a predominance of men. An important difficulty is the lack of social opportunities for meeting persons of the opposite sex. Factors which delay the age of marriage—college training, war, depression—affect the volume of marriageable men and women. There is, in the third place, the problem of marriage values. High idealization or limited idealization may narrow the range of choice beyond the point of realization. Again, the tendency toward behavior patterns belonging to the opposite sex—for example, feminine behavior in men, masculine behavior in women—disturbs the

[24] For a fuller discussion of the rating-dating complex, *cf.* Willard Waller, *The family* (New York: Dryden Press, 1938), p. 230 ff.

attitudes toward marriage. Or, the conception of the role of marriage one has may emphasize its economic or social limitations, may accentuate its transient or nondurable features, thus causing a shying away from the marriage altar. Emotional disturbances, such as anxieties about sex, greatly aggravated by modern culture, may create a caution about marriage.

These problems do not represent insuperable barriers for young people, as the high percentage of married persons in American society demonstrates.[25] But they do suggest why more and more stress is being laid on marriage preparation, mental hygiene, sex education, organized youth programs, marriage clinics, and other social services for the family. Indeed, it would appear that a small-scale desertion of the earlier laissez-faire tradition of mate selection is under way. The widespread recourse to "advice to the lovelorn" columns, to testing and predicting marital success or failure, to clinical psychology, and church-sponsored study groups concerned with problems of friendship and courtship suggest the need for a more adequate preparation for the adjustment situations of marriage.

Problems of marital adjustment.   Living together in marriage is conditioned by the kind of personality which people bring to marriage. Indeed, nothing happens at a marriage altar to change basically the structure of the personality which the individuals have acquired up to that point. One might even assert that marriage seems to accentuate trends already present in the personality. This is one reason for believing that doses of good advice may really prove to be nothing more than a stimulating but temporary tonic.[26]

One must be careful in making generalizations. Certainly formulas simply cannot be proffered for all marital situations. However, a few cautious statements seem justified by the literature.[27] Marital adjustment seems to be much more influenced by

---

[25] The percentage of the population 15 years and over married stood in 1940 at 61.2. Bureau of the Census, *Marital status of the white population for states and larger cities*, 1940, Series P-15, #7 (Nov. 27, 1942). See also Bureau of the Census, "Characteristics of single, married, widowed, and divorced persons in 1947," *Current population problems: Population characteristics*, Series P-20, #10 (Feb. 6, 1948).

[26] O. S. English, and G. H. Pearson, *Emotional problems of living* (New York: W. W. Norton and Company, 1945); Karen Horney, *Neurotic personality of our time* (New York: W. W. Norton and Company, 1937); E. A. Strecker, *Beyond the clinical frontier* (New York: W. W. Norton and Company, 1940).

[27] *Cf.* J. K. Folsom, *op. cit.;* H. W. Mowrer, *Personality adjustment and family disorganization* (New York: American Book Company, 1935); E. R. Mowrer, *Domestic discord* (Chicago: University of Chicago Press, 1928); E. L. Koos, *Families in trouble*

the particular combination of personality traits possessed by both persons than by the presence of any single trait. Thus, neurotic symptoms in one partner may actually be compensated for by adjustability of the other. Or again, some personality traits usually prove to be quite unimportant, such as, for example, introversion or extroversion. The interactional combination, in other words, is more important for marital adjustment than the traits appearing in a single personality profile.

However, it is wise to remember that some personality traits are definitely loaded in the direction of happiness or unhappiness in general. Unhappy persons tend to have unhappy marriages; neurotic personalities, neurotic marriages. Conversely, mature and happy persons tend to have mature and happy marriages. For the most part, the more mature the socialization of behavior before marriage, the easier the adjustment in marriage. The traits of the personality in each case and their interactional combination seem to be more influential in determining marital success or failure than such extra-personality factors as economic status, income, occupation, education, religion, and so forth.[28] Very simply stated, the answer to marital success or failure seems to lie in the emotional and social maturity of the personalities.

Tensions are a natural phase of marital adjustment, just as they characterize all other human experiences. They may, of course, prove to be somewhat more acute in marriage than in other relationships, for marriage is the most intimate and inclusive social experience that people have. Tensions are the overt manifestation of frustration. We may group the frustrations of marriage into primary and secondary types.[29] The former include those that are essentially due to personality characteristics— temperament, response patterns, maturity. The latter embrace factors usually external to the personality ("extra-personal")— occupational, economic status, cultural status, "in-law" relationships, and so forth. Marital conflicts arise out of failure to resolve these frustrations. This fact suggests that some tensions may prove to be productive: if they succeed in liquidating false romantic idealizations, in revealing the depth of emotion of the partners, in defining the contours of the personality interests and

---

(New York: King's Crown Press, 1946); J. H. Levy, and R. Monroe, *Happy family* (New York: Alfred A. Knopf, 1938).

[28] *Cf.* Nimkoff, *op. cit.*, Ch. 14.

[29] For example, *cf.* Elliott and Merrill, *op. cit.*, pp. 670–700.

motives, and so on. Tensions which do not result in such insightful adjustment bring prolonged and often acute conflict.

Mild frustrations are often resolved by the natural rhythm of estrangement and reconciliation which begins in courtship.[30] They are usually susceptible to treatment by certain rational accommodative devices of the individuals themselves; such as, generosity, balance of mutual agreements (compromise), joint conferences, persuasion, and counseling with an outsider.[31] Frustrations which spring from the blocking of personality patterns call for a more expert care. They require—or should require—the help of a specialist in human-adjustment problems: the marriage counselor, the psychologist, the case worker, the psychiatrist, or other persons sufficiently trained in the skills of human guidance. It is a tragic fact that many marriages which end in divorce or desertion might very likely have "worked out" under trained guidance and care.

Problems of the middle stages. Bearing, schooling, rearing, and marriage of the children mark the major family interests of the middle stages of the family cycle. In terms of the husband's age, first births start, typically, around 24; it is completed at 30. The father will, on an average, be around 53 by the time his last child has married. It is true that some families never go through these stages of the life cycle. It is interesting to note that, as of 1940, among women married and past the period of fertility, 15.4 per cent (one in six, that is) had had no children. In 1890, the figure was 7.9 per cent (or one in twelve)! Four out of five husband-wife families, as of 1940, had no children under 18 living at home with them.

During these middle years which are the economically productive years for the husband the family responsibilities are at their heaviest. From two thirds to three fourths of the families have children to care for during this age period (that is, from 25 to 55 years). Moreover, after the husband reaches 45, on an average, he will be furnishing living quarters for one or more adults besides himself and his wife. Over half of these adults will be his own children over 18. These middle years present the greatest demands on the income earner. Unfortunately for most American husbands, the peak incomes they receive during their earning career come too late: they come, in other words, after the peak of their major expenses. In terms of the structure of family

[30] *Cf.* Waller, *op. cit.*, Ch. 11.
[31] For further discussion of these devices, *cf.* Folsom, *op. cit.*, pp. 450–465.

income in the United States, the family cycle creaks and groans at its most crucial stages. The following table illustrates this point.

TABLE 15

Median Family Incomes: 1939*

Age of Husband	Median Family Wage or Salary
Under 25	$ 861
25–29	1193
30–34	1393
35–44	1597
45–54	1626
55–64	1427
65 and over	1102

* Adapted from Glick, *op. cit.*, p. 172.

These are the years in which certain family needs are really pressing, among them shelter. Suppose we take home ownership as an index of the family income during this period. In other words, home ownership comes too late, so far as the children are concerned.

TABLE 16

Percentage of Families Owning Homes, by Age of Husband: 1940*

Age of Husband	Percentage of Families Owning Homes
Under 25	11.8
25–29	18.8
30–34	27.1
35–44	39.1
45–54	52.1
55–64	60.6
65 and over	68.5

* Adapted from Glick, *op. cit.*

In a cash-dominated society, family income is an ever-present factor in all family interaction. Although the problems of income were treated rather fully earlier in this book,[32] it may be helpful at this point to be reminded of the crucial character of family income for family life. Pre-1950 census reports by government

[32] See Ch. 5.

agencies indicated that for the prosperous year 1948, nearly 10 million of the nearly 40 million American families received less than half the national average of $4000 that year. About one fourth of the nation's families that year scrimped along on less than $2000. Of this less fortunate fourth, three out of four were headed by persons under 65 years of age. In general, the submerged third of the nation which the late President Roosevelt used to discuss has been reduced only fractionally. What they can do for a family budget in a period of high prices is a matter of some mystery to many people. Yet their problems are no different from those of any other families; they are simply more acute.

The broken family in the middle years. These middle stages in the family cycle are fraught with many risks so far as the family as a unit is concerned. These risks are generally suggested by the phrase, "the broken family." One out of five families is "broken" —by death, desertion, divorce, or separation. The largest cause is death, followed by divorce and desertion.

Death "breaks" the American family six times as frequently as does divorce and four times as frequently as does desertion. About three fourths of all such disorganized families have been dissolved by the death of the husband or wife. Widows are almost three times as numerous as widowers; on an average, death leaves about one half million wives widows per year. About two thirds of them are 45 years and over. One out of three has dependent children.[33] About half the widows have a life expectation ranging up to twenty years: a real problem in family finance! The extent of dependency on the surviving mother depends, of course, on her age. About two thirds of widows under 25 have dependent children. About three fourths of those between 25 and 44 have dependents. Almost 200,000 men are widowed annually; one third of them are left with dependent children.[34]

Desertion is a minor threat to family integrity, so far as the bulk of American families is concerned. About 50,000 desertions occur annually, most of them by the husband-father. Most desertions do not end in divorce; the marriage is either reestablished or else the wife does not sue for divorce. Deserters are of various types, having a variety of motives: some are intermittent, some gradual, some permanent.[35] Invariably, they

---

[33] *Cf.* Glick, *op. cit.*

[34] On sex differences in widowhood, *cf.* Nimkoff, *op. cit.*, pp. 613–618.

[35] *Cf.* E. E. Eubank, *Study of family desertion* (Chicago: Department of Public Welfare, 1916), pp. 37–49.

create economic and psychological adjustment problems for the family left behind, problems which require the aid of relatives, friends, and social agencies.[36]

The family problems arising from separation—"spouse absent from the home"—vary with the type of separation. About a million and a half women report to the census an absent spouse. Some of the latter are in institutions, others employed out of town, others in the armed forces, and some preparing to divorce. The consequences of separation tend to be in the nature of psychological and social hardships rather than economic; but they always suggest a certain amount of family disorganization.[37]

Divorce, so extensive in our society, is hardly the disorganizer of family life that it is usually reported to be. Divorce is the formal termination of a disorganized family; it comes as the last act in a cumulative series of tensions and conflicts. Occurring throughout the family cycle, it reaches a first peak in the fifth year of marriage and another in the eighteenth year. Data on the rate of divorce must be handled judiciously, as the following table suggests.

TABLE 17
Divorce in the United States: 1910–1940*

Year	Per 1000 population	Per 100 marriages	Per 1000 average for 10 yrs.
1910	.9	8.8	9.9
1920	1.6	13.4	16.0
1930	1.5	17.0	16.2
1940	2.0	16.9	20.6

* Adapted from Nimkoff, *op. cit.*, p. 626.

These data do not re-enforce the journalistic impression of a wild, leaping divorce curve. They do, of course, show a definite increase, practically a 100-per-cent increase in the last generation or so. However, they must be balanced against two facts: one, the very high remarriage rate, and the other, the very high percentage of the total population which is married.[38]

[36] For further discussion, *cf.* J. C. Colcord, *Broken homes: A study of family desertion and its social treatment* (New York: Russell Sage Foundation, 1919); E. F. O'Neill, "Report on a study of 100 cases of desertion," *The Family*, 10 (January, 1929): 287–291.

[37] *Cf.* William F. Ogburn, "Marital separations," *American Journal of Sociology*, 49 (January, 1944): 316–323.

[38] On the high remarriage rate, *cf.* Metropolitan Life Insurance Company, "Chances of marriage and of remarriage," *Statistical Bulletin*, 26 (May, 1945). The

Increase in the frequency of divorce in this country and abroad must be regarded as an expression of growing family instability. But it is only one of a number of such expressions, for behind divorce and family instability lie a great number of social "forces," changes, and conditions which act upon the family and which find expression in divorce and other symptoms of family disintegration. Most of these conditions are interwoven with our level and kind of "civilization" and are not to be regarded as superficial incidents. The following are some of the more important conditions and situations which underlie the family and help to account for its transformations and instability.

1. A democracy that insists upon the freedom of the individual and helps render family restraints distasteful.

2. A mobile population that serves to undermine the old moral and local restraints regarding sex and domestic relations.

3. Urbanization that multiplies personal contacts between sexes, heightens standards of living and increases expenditures for the home which may place a strain on marital ties, and provides stimuli and false situations that may lead to license and domestic disloyalty.

4. A heightened education that results in higher standards for married life and imposes new obligations.

5. New fields of achievement for women which render them less dependent economically and more free to break irritating and distasteful marital ties.

6. An undermined religious sanctity of marriage which once made it a sin to sever the bonds of matrimony.

7. The spread of the idea that marriage is a convenience for the satisfaction of sex wants and so may readily and legitimately be dissolved when it ceases to be mutually satisfactory.

8. The "woman's movement" in all of its many phases that has served to "emancipate" woman's mind from the old idea that her place in society and the home was that of subordination and personal service to the "superior" male and that has freed her to take up a career and work out life for herself.

9. The enormous multiplication of cultural, social, and recreational activities which tend to draw the members of the home away from it and so weaken the ties binding parents and children into a compact social unit.

10. The birth of the idea of divorce, the multiplication of the legal grounds of divorce, the laxity of many divorce courts in conducting hearings, and the lightening of the sense of marital obligation by the

---

percentage of men and women married in 1900 stood at 57.0 and 54.5 respectively; nearly a half-century later (1947), 64.2 and 66.2 respectively. *Cf.* Landis, *op. cit.*, p. 65.

consciousness that divorce is always possible—all have had a great influence on the family institution.

It may be true that the increase in divorce suggests increasing marital unhappiness. It means that more people are ready to separate by legal means. Where wives are economically dependent upon husbands, and where customs and law will not countenance divorce, marital unhappiness, if it exists, will not be likely to be revealed in court records to the same extent as where these conditions do not prevail. It seems doubtful if there is more marital misery in the West, with its comparatively high rate of divorce, than in the South Atlantic states, where in one state, South Carolina, until recently no divorces were granted. The high rate of divorce in the West may partly be accounted for by the larger economic independence of women and the comparative ease with which the legal separation can be effected.

Most of the studies dealing with the causes of disturbances in modern family life have been concerned with economic and cultural factors, such as the increased social and economic freedom of women; the improved legal status of women; the psychological influences of urban existence; crowded housing conditions; changed attitudes toward the rearing of children; the tendency for women to work outside the home, because of either necessity or inclination; and the decline of family functions through the increased activities of outside agencies. There is need, however, for more scientific study of such disturbing factors as sex incompatibility; differences in temperament and emotional life, due to early training or other factors; and general ignorance of the full significance of the marriage contract.

Whether or not we hold that the divorce problem should be "solved" will depend upon our conception of divorce. If we believe that divorce, as it stands, is necessary and if there is nothing of an abusive nature about it, then there is no divorce problem to solve. But if we think that divorce is altogether or largely unnecessary, that it represents indulgence, license, unrestrained impulse, abandonment of our finest sentiments and of our duties, conceding that a measure of divorce is justified, then we have a problem to think about and to try to find ways of solving, or at least of mitigating.

Problems of the later stages. The marriage of the children terminates "the middle years" of the family. This event typically occurs near the fiftieth year of the husband, about 25 years after the birth of his first child. Obviously the exact year at which these later stages begin depends upon the age of the husband at his marriage and at the birth of his last child, upon the independence of his married children, and upon his life expectancy. There is evidence that these last stages—recovery and retirement —are longer and are in prospect lengthier than in previous generations. A couple married in 1940 have a joint survival of 39 years. This means that such parents will live to see their children married and will have one fourth of their married life still to come after their last child leaves home. Two generations ago they would be fortunate if both of them lived to see their children married.

In 1900, when our total population was 76 millions, only 4.1 per cent were in the age bracket 65 and over. An agrarian, small community and young country could easily absorb into the normal family life its older people. The ebbing of the waves of immigration bringing over a young population and the life-saving achieved by modern medicine and sanitation have brought more and more of the total population into the older age brackets. The 1950 census indicates more than 11 million people 65 and over—7.7 of our population.[39] This proportion has doubled in the last half-century. What are the problems of the family during the later stages of its life cycle?

The economic difficulties of the aging family seem to be foremost.[40] About a fourth, never more than a third—even in wartime!—of those over 65 are employed. To be sure, Old Age and Survivors' Insurance, pensions sponsored by industry, savings and private insurance cushion the economic shocks of age. But the limitations both in the total number thus covered and in the size of benefits are well known. A related economic problem, housing, is likewise far from satisfactory. Alternatives are fairly limited: living with children or relatives, in institutions, in rented rooms or apartments, in nursing homes, and in the old family dwelling (if any). Each alternative has familiar difficulties. Moreover, the

[39] On some of the social and economic adjustments of an aging population, *cf.* the excellent discussion by Louis I. Dublin, "Our aging population," *Annual Forum*, New York Chapter of Chartered Life Underwriters; available from the Statistical Bureau, Metropolitan Life Insurance Company.

[40] *Cf.* N. P. Levin, "Statistical study of the economic and sociological significance of population age," *Journal American Statistical Association*, 23 (March, 1928): 41 ff.; R. Helton, "Old people and rising national problem," *Harper's*, 179 (October, 1939): 449–459; E. Kahn, and L. W. Simmons, "Problems of middle age," *Yale Review*, 29 (December, 1939): 349–363.

diminished need for space and the continued desire for privacy are paramount but thorny considerations.

The physical problems of the aging family are particularly distressing. The higher the age, the higher the sickness rate, especially for the chronic diseases. The latter entail considerable expense and specialized services, for which family income is often not adequate. A greatly expanded service by physicians, nurses, and nursing homes appears to be inevitable. Finally, the social problems of the aging family arise out of the diminished demand for their economic and social services. Few communities have studied these problems with care; those that have find a large number of creative and recreational opportunities for their aging families which are ordinarily neglected.

The recovery and retirement stages in the family cycle may not appear to be as urgent and as difficult as the earlier stages, and indeed in larger numbers of cases this is probably true. But a society with an aging population must learn to help its people to grow old, just as it seeks through education and community organization to help its young to grow up.[41]

Toward a Culturally Re-enforced Family System

The culturally dependent family system. Earlier in this chapter the manner in which the family is shaped by cultural forces was described. The various adjustment problems which appear in and dominate the successive stages of the family life cycle were outlined. The picture of the modern family which emerges is of a family system not only in trouble but in serious need. The source of its life and its problems lies in very large measure outside its own institutional framework. It is necessary, therefore, to review the many different kinds of attempts which are being made to assist the modern family achieve stability. These collective efforts may be grouped around the problems which characterize each stage of the family cycle.

Guidance for the unmarried. Education and guidance for marriage and family living have rapidly caught the imagination of community leaders in the last few years. School curricula, popular magazines, book publishers, professional associations, movies, youth groups are all channeling information to and making available advice and expert skill for modern young

[41] *Cf.* report on old-age institute sponsored by the University of Michigan by Tibbitts, *Adult Education Bulletin*, October, 1948; Ruth Cavan et al, *Personal adjustment in old age* (Chicago: Science Research Associates, 1949).

people. The thesis is that in modern society all careers require training; so likewise, marriage. Homemaking, however, is not merely a matter of housekeeping skill or of information about the birthing process. It must rather be conceived of as the development of mature personalities. How to choose a mate is an attractive question and more easily answered than how to become a mature person, but realistic family-life education is more concerned with the latter than the former.[42]

Families with marital troubles. Assistance for marriage difficulties is becoming increasingly though by no means adequately available through the services of professional specialists, skilled laymen, and published materials. Resolving marital tensions is rather simple when those tensions are secondary and do not involve personality motivations and their satisfactions. Being more complex in character, primary marital tensions call for specialized psychological skills. Unfortunately, many married couples seek to resolve these tensions by efforts both negative and positive in nature. Schematically, the techniques commonly used include the following.

A. Negative
　1. Escape patterns:
　　repression, intermittent conflicts and reconciliations, protest behaviors—alcoholism, infidelity, desertion, separation, and divorce.
　2. Temporary expedients:
　　compromise, balance-of-trade agreements, hortatory injunctions, change of residence or job, persuasion.
B. Positive
　1. Expressive responses:
　　joint participation in events and groups and activities of mutual importance.
　2. Counseling and guidance:
　　diagnostic information from a psychological specialist; directed interviews, involving prescriptions and proscriptions.
　3. Depth therapy:
　　use of services of psychiatric case worker, psychiatrist, clinical psychiatrist in order to achieve insight into motives, clarify roles, redefine values, and understand emotional complexes.

Perhaps the most useful point here is the realization by married couples that there are resources outside the family that

[42] See the excellent presentation of this thesis by Community Service Society of New York, *Family in a democratic society* (New York: Columbia University Press, 1949), Part I.

ought to be utilized. How to make this realization general is probably the most difficult problem of all, for it means that the individuals must themselves perceive the extent of their need. Unhappily, too, even yet there is a widespread reluctance to consult outside specialists in problems of emotional disturbance. There is, moreover, the regrettable circumstance that there are not as yet enough specialized services geographically and financially available for the many marriages in trouble.[43]

Services for the middle years. Modern society is responding to the family's problem of bearing, schooling, and rearing children with a number of programs designed to re-enforce the family structure. Thus, in some cases the community attempts, through birth-control clinics, to co-operate with fathers and mothers in the curtailment of the size of the family where certain family considerations seem to the parents to warrant it.[44] On the other hand, an impressive array of maternal and infant health programs in the form of grants-in-aid, improved hospitalization, hospital insurance, child-care institutes, and public health services seeks to encourage and assist families in the having and rearing of children. The extension of the education system, which is described in another chapter,[45] aims at achieving a better integration of the family and the school and thus promoting their mutual welfare.[46]

In the following chapter the great variety of collective efforts intended to promote child welfare is described. At this point, then, attention will be called only to two great family needs, both of them economic, in the rearing of children. One is concerned

[43] *Cf.* Koos, *op. cit.*, Ch. 8; also Reuben Hill, *Families under stress* (New York: Harper and Brothers, 1949).

[44] *Cf.* J. W. Riley, and M. White, "Use of various methods of contraception," *American Sociological Review* 5 (December, 1940): 890–904; R. K. Stix, and F. W. Notestein, *Controlled fertility* (Baltimore: Williams and Wilkins, 1940); N. Himes, *Medical history of contraception* (Baltimore: Williams and Wilkins, 1936).

[45] *Cf.* Ch. 12.

[46] On the various programs intended to assist families in the birth and care of children, *cf.* L. S. Hollingworth, "Social devices for impelling women to bear and rear children," *American Journal of Sociology*, 22 (July, 1916): 19–29; G. May, "Aid to dependent children," *Social Work Year Book* (New York: Russell Sage Foundation, 1941); the publications of the U. S. Children's Bureau; Alva Myrdal, *op. cit.;* W. S. Thompson, "Wage system and family survival," *Social Forces*, 4 (December, 1925): 399–407; National Resources Planning Board, *Problems of a changing population* (Washington, D.C.: Government Printing Office, 1938); O. E. Baker, "Effect of recent public policies on the future population prospect," *Rural Sociology*, 2 (December, 1938): 125–128; Gunnar Myrdal, *Population: A problem for democracy* (Cambridge: Harvard University Press, 1940); Paul Meadows, *Culture of industrial man*, *op. cit.*, Ch. 10.

with protecting the income of the family, the other with its housing. The income protection of the family may occur in three different ways. First, the money income needs to be increased: such is the motivation of the trade-union movement, minimum-wage legislation, aid to dependent children, and tax-financed social services ordinarily beyond the reach of the average family. Second, the money income of the family needs to be assured: this is the function of the emerging social-insurance system, workmen's accident compensation, employment offices, unemployment compensations, and so forth. Finally, the purchasing power of the family income needs to be stabilized: this is the idea behind the farm price program, the battle against inflation, the long-range efforts at reducing the costs of living through antimonopoly, antiwaste, and antimilitarism.[47]

The social support of the housing needs of the family is still far from adequate. But mention should be made of such activities as slum clearance through public housing, the facilitation of credit in order to stimulate home building (FHA), city planning, revised building codes, and innovations in building design and procedures.[48] The Twentieth Century Fund Committee on Housing, reviewing the housing needs of American families and calling attention to the ten-year backlog resulting from underbuilding, has outlined a seven-point program which bears repeating.[49]

1. A land-utilization program is vital: an extension of public regulation of land use; the regulation of speculative subdivision; the rationalization of zoning; and a foresighted assessment policy.
2. Industrial reorganization is indicated: encouragement of larger production organizations, of more highly productive industrial techniques, of more economical methods of materials distribution.
3. A reorganization of marketing is necessary: a flexible pattern of marketing which would take cognizance of such variables as sales, rents, size of community, investment, finance.

[47] Cf. Council of Economic Advisers, Reports to the President, 1947, 1948 (New York: Reynal and Hitchcock, 1948).

[48] Cf. Robert Lasch, Breaking the building blockade (Chicago: University of Chicago Press, 1940); J. P. Dean, Home ownership, is it sound? (New York: Harper and Brothers, 1945); Local community job under the housing act of 1949 (Housing and Home Finance Agency, Public Housing Administration, Washington, D.C., 1949); Paul Meadows, "Housing the American family," Journal of Business, 21 (April, 1948): 80–91.

[49] Miles Colean, American housing: Problems and prospects (New York: Twentieth Century Fund, 1944).

4. Attention must be focused on the financial problems of house-building: the simplification of mortgage procedures; less cumbersome and expensive long-term financing.
5. The expansion of public housing: through direct aids to private enterprise and through public construction.
6. Improvement and extension of rural housing.
7. The problems of maintenance and operation of housing must be met: through more liberal amortization procedures, more durable structural parts, and the elimination of outworn structures.

Problems of the later stages in the family cycle. These problems center on the re-integration of the family in its "empty nest" period, a time when its most direct ties with the community have been broken. Here the most significant contributions which can be made to the family are those which (a) ensure the continuity of family income, (b) cover the very decided increase in certain types of expenses, such as the medical, (c) scientific research which will make possible the more adequate treatment of the diseases of age, and (d) cementing the bonds of the family with the community.

In general, then, developing a culturally re-enforced family system means in part undoing the damages which the culture has inflicted on the modern family and in part overcoming the social isolation of the family which an individualistic culture has imposed upon it. In so far as the society can assist the family in doing these things, which it cannot do for itself, it promotes stability both for the family and for the social order.

QUESTIONS

1. Distinguish between the primary and the secondary functions of the family. What is the basis of this distinction?
2. Show the significance for the changing functions of the family of the "cash nexus."
3. Identify the outstanding social patterns which have directed the change and interaction of family life in this country.
4. Contrast the effects upon the family of the romantic complex and of science.
5. What are the difficulties of modern mate selection?
6. Discuss: "Nothing happens at a marriage altar to change basically the structure of the personality which the individual has up to that point."
7. Distinguish between primary and secondary frustrations in marriage. Is this a useful distinction? How?

8. What are some of the practical values of the analysis of the family in terms of its life cycle?
9. What are some of the implications of the fact that happiness in marriage seems to be a function of the maturity of personality?
10. What is meant by a culturally re-enforced family system?

REFERENCES

BIGELOW, H. F., *Family finance.* Philadelphia: J. B. Lippincott Company, 1936.

CAVAN, R., et al, *Personal adjustment in old age.* Chicago: Science Research Associates, 1949.

COLEAN, M. L., *American housing: Problems and prospects.* New York: Twentieth Century Fund, 1944.

FOLSOM, J. K., *Family: Its sociology and social psychiatry.* New York: John Wiley and Sons, 1934.

GLICK, P. C., "Family cycle," *American Sociological Review* (1947), XII: 164 ff.

HORNEY, K., *Neurotic personality of our time.* New York: W. W. Norton and Company, 1937.

HILL, R. L., *Families under stress.* New York: Harper and Brothers, 1949.

KOOS, E. L., *Families in trouble.* New York: King's Crown Press, 1946.

LEVY, J., and MUNROE, R., *Happy family.* New York: Alfred A. Knopf, 1938.

MEAD, M., *Male and female: A study of the sexes in a changing world.* New York: William Morrow and Company, 1949.

MOWRER, E. R., *Family disorganization.* Chicago: University of Chicago Press, 1928.

MOWRER, H. R., *Personality adjustment and domestic discord.* New York: American Book Company, 1935.

NIMKOFF, M. F., *Marriage and the family.* Boston: Houghton Mifflin Company, 1947.

TRUXAL, A. G., and MERRILL, F. E., *Family in American culture.* New York: Prentice-Hall, 1947.

CHAPTER 11

Society and the Child

"THE CENTURY OF THE CHILD"

A half-century of child welfare. In 1909, responding to a call from President Theodore Roosevelt, child-welfare workers from all over the nation met in Washington, D.C. in a "White House Conference on Children." Opinion was expressed that the then new century would prove to be "the century of the child." It was a remarkably clear-sighted and prophetic appraisal of the social forces already at work in the interests of American childhood. Probably no segment of American society has received the benefit of so many plans and programs as American children and youth.

The philosophy which prompts child-welfare work can be simply stated. "The treatment of the child may be considered as a forecast of social change because in the status and nurture of the child are expressed the knowledge and the hopes and the values of a people which they are building into the future society."[1] Adequate provision for the care and protection of children is important not only from an individual point of view but also with respect to the well-being of society generally.

The successive White House Conferences are themselves measures of the progress which has been made in this "century of the child." The first conference was primarily concerned with the *dependent child*. It set forth principles in this field which have guided social workers in all the years since. It resulted in the creation of the Children's Bureau in the federal government to speak for the interests of children. The second conference emphasized minimum standards of child welfare and focused na-

---

[1] L. K. Frank, "Childhood and youth," *Recent social trends* (New York: McGraw-Hill Book Company, 1933), Vol. II, p. 751. Parts of this present chapter appeared in Paul Meadows, "The century of the child," *The Humanist* (January, 1951): 27–31. Used by permission.

tional attention upon *child-labor legislation, maternity and infancy protection*, and *children in need of special care*. One of its by-products was the Sheppard-Towner Act, by which the federal government provides funds to aid the states in the care of mothers and infants. The third conference made available the most comprehensive diagnosis of the *needs of all children* and statement of goals for their protection which had ever been presented. The fourth conference, meeting as war approached, dwelt on the welfare of *children in a democracy* and sought to define objectives which would build toward democratic citizenship for children. It stressed the need to mobilize resources, federal, state, and local, in strengthening services to children. Plans for the fifth conference concentrated on studies describing how children could learn to live with others, how they could develop healthy personalities.[2]

Child welfare and the modern mind.[3]   Children in modern society have a position which is markedly different from that of children in earlier societies. Briefly, children in by-gone cultures were regarded as instruments, as means to other ends: as aids in the struggle for existence, as measures of prestige, as pawns against fate, as vehicles of group perpetuation. Often they were sacrificed for group values, as the well-known practices of infanticide, child selling, and child slavery suggest. The unqualified property right of the father in the child was no necessary boon to the child. Certainly the repressive discipline of a straight-laced and severe society is a far cry from modern social freedom. Bossard has shown how the arithmetic of reproduction, the child's economic contribution, the prevailing ideology of human rights, and the type of family system have been major determinants in the historic status of the child.[4]

In the American scene these four factors, operating in a manner much different from that in earlier cultures, have vastly changed the outlook of childhood in this country. The economic situation of the United States—our frontier history, freedom from tradition, mobility which loosened family bonds, the expectation that children will "do better" economically than their parents, the economic need for both girls and boys, and the "economic surplus" of American industrialism—put a premium on childhood. The colorful combination of humanitarianism, science,

---

[2] For a brief history of these conferences, *cf.* J. H. S. Bossard, *Sociology of child development* (New York: Harper and Brothers, 1948), Ch. 27.

[3] For a somewhat different treatment of this theme, *cf.* J. H. S. Bossard, "Child welfare and the modern mind," *Annals*, 182 (September, 1930): 1–5.

[4] *Cf.* Bossard, *Sociology of child development, op cit.*, Ch. 25.

and democracy created an ideological frame of reference very favorable to child development. Certain institutional characteristics of the American family—its relatively high status as a social institution, the small-family system, the gainful employment of women, the decline of the home as a productive center, the loss of family functions to other institutions—are likewise responsible for the emancipation of American childhood.[5]

In other words, the popular concern with the welfare of American children fitted into—because it is an outgrowth of—certain outstanding social forces in American life. Briefly, these forces are: (a) American industrialism, creating an economic surplus which could be tapped for the public welfare; (b) humanitarianism, engendering a systematic sense of social responsibility; (c) the social-service state, forming a methodology for the public interest through social legislation and social administration; (d) the democratic dogma, with its nucleus of beliefs in natural rights and personal integrity; and (e) science, developing new insights and new methods for the care and protection of the human being.

The natural rights of childhood. No better reflection of the modern mind, so far as childhood is concerned, can be found than in "The Children's Charter," formulated by the White House Conference on Child Health and Protection in 1930.[6]

I. For every child spiritual and moral training to help him to stand firm under the pressure of life.

II. For every child understanding and the guarding of his personality as his most precious right.

III. For every child a home and that love and security which a home provides; and for that child who must receive foster care, the nearest substitute for his own home.

IV. For every child full preparation for his birth, his mother receiving prenatal, natal, and postnatal care; and the establishment of such protective measures as will make childbearing safer.

V. For every child health protection from birth through adolescence, including: periodical health examinations and, where needed, care of specialists and hospital treatment; regular dental examinations and care of the teeth; protective and preventive

[5] Cf. ibid., Ch. 26.
[6] Cf. 1930 White House conference on child health and protection (New York: Appleton-Century-Crofts, 1930).

measures against communicable diseases; the insuring of pure food, pure milk, and pure water.

VI. For every child, from birth through adolescence, promotion of health, including health instruction and a health program, wholesome physical and mental recreation, with teachers and leaders adequately trained.

VII. For every child a dwelling-place safe, sanitary, and wholesome, with reasonable provisions for privacy; free from conditions which tend to thwart his development; and a home environment harmonious and enriching.

VIII. For every child a school which is safe from hazards, sanitary, properly equipped, lighted, and ventilated. For younger children nursery schools and kindergartens to supplement home care.

IX. For every child a community which recognizes and plans for his needs, protects him against physical dangers, moral hazards, and disease; provides him with safe and wholesome places for play and recreation; and makes provision for his cultural and social needs.

X. For every child an education which, through the discovery and development of his individual abilities, prepares him for life; and through training and vocational guidance prepares him for a living which will yield him the maximum of satisfaction.

XI. For every child such teaching and training as will prepare him for successful parenthood, homemaking, and the rights of citizenship; and, for parents, supplementary training to fit them to deal wisely with the problems of parenthood.

XII. For every child education for safety and protection against accidents to which modern conditions subject him—those to which he is directly exposed and those which, through loss or maiming of his parents, affect him indirectly.

XIII. For every child who is blind, deaf, crippled, or otherwise physically handicapped, and for the child who is mentally handicapped, such measures as will early discover and diagnose his handicap, provide care and treatment, and so train him that he may become an asset to society rather than a liability. Expenses of these services should be borne publicly where they cannot be privately met.

XIV. For every child who is in conflict with society the right to be dealt with intelligently as society's charge, not society's outcast;

with the home, the school, the church, the court and the institution when needed, shaped to return him whenever possible to the normal stream of life.

XV. For every child the right to grow up in a family with an adequate standard of living and the security of a stable income as the surest safeguard against social handicaps.

XVI. For every child protection against labor that stunts growth, either physical or mental, that limits education, that deprives children of the right of comradeship, of play, and of joy.

XVII. For every rural child as satisfactory schooling and health services as the city child, and an extension to rural families of social, recreational, and cultural facilities.

XVIII. To supplement the home and the school in the training of youth, and to return to them those interests of which modern life tends to cheat children, every stimulation and encouragement should be given to the extension and development of the voluntary youth organizations.

XIX. To make everywhere available these minimum protections of the health and welfare of children, there should be a district, county, or community organization for health, education, and welfare, with full-time officials, co-ordinating with a state-wide program which will be responsive to a nation-wide service of general information, statistics, and scientific research. This should include:

(a) Trained, full-time public-health officials, with public-health nurses, sanitary inspection, and laboratory workers

(b) Available hospital beds

(c) Full-time public welfare service for the relief, aid, and guidance of children in special need due to poverty, misfortune, or behavior difficulties, and for the protection of children from abuse, neglect, exploitation, or moral hazard.

FOR EVERY CHILD THESE RIGHTS, REGARDLESS OF RACE, OR COLOR, OR SITUATION, WHEREVER HE MAY LIVE UNDER THE PROTECTION OF THE AMERICAN FLAG

Stages in the child-welfare movement.[7] This perceptive appraisal of the rights and needs of children did not mature in a single day; it was, indeed, a long time coming. The earlier preoccupation with child welfare was with the dependent child. A

[7] For a fuller discussion of the history of the child-welfare movement, *cf.* Emma Lundberg, *Unto the least of these* (New York: Appleton-Century-Crofts, 1947).

consequence of an immature and rather heartless industrialism, child dependency was met by recourse to almshouses, apprenticeship, indenture, orphanages, and other generic devices which lumped all needy children into an undifferentiated mass. Gradually the idea developed that children have different kinds of needs which must be realized in different ways. Thus arose specialized institutions for the blind, the deaf, the mentally deficient, the reformatory, and various hospital services. Concurrently, the belief that wider and better coverage could be secured through co-ordinated efforts brought successively the charity-organization movement, children's aid and home societies, state boards of charities, juvenile protective associations, professionalized social services, and in our day departments of public welfare and the council of social agencies.[8]

Throughout this slow development a fundamental faith became dominant: "a belief in the possibility of controlling and directing social development through the care and nurture of children."[9] From simply saving children thrown upon the larger society for assistance, child-welfare work moved to an acceptance of specialized institutional agencies, to protective services (*e.g.*, the Children's Code movement), to the formulation of programs centering their efforts on the home situation of the child, and finally to the attempt to serve the interests of children in and through the larger social situation. Roughly, child saving has given way as a paramount motive to child development, a positive and wide-ranging conception of child welfare.

Problems of Life and Death

The arithmetic of child life. In earlier periods of history, the arithmetic of child life was very simple: have children, have many children, particularly boys. If children died, then "the Lord giveth, the Lord taketh away, blessed be the name of the Lord." This motivation has very nearly disappeared in industrial cultures. Although we have fewer children per family now, we keep more of them alive and for a longer period of time. Where birth rates have fallen, so likewise have the death rates. A primary problem of child welfare, then, is how to keep children alive

In England as late as the middle of the eighteenth century, fifty per cent of the population died before reaching the age of

[8] *Cf*. J. F. Steiner, *Community organization* (New York: Appleton-Century-Crofts, 1930).

[9] Bossard, *op. cit.*, p. 666. Quoted by permission.

twenty. In Prussia, at that time, seven tenths died before reaching ten years of age. In Russia, as late as the nineteenth century, only about a third of the child population lived beyond twenty years. In these dark ages of infant mortality epidemic diseases, inadequate diets, and undeveloped medical science were largely responsible for high mortality rates. The real curtailment in death rates in the industrial West began to take place around the turn of the present century. The speed with which these rates for different age groups fell can be seen very quickly in the following table.

TABLE 18

Average Annual Mortality per 1000 White Males of Selected Ages in the
United States: 1900–1910, 1930–1939*

Age	Deaths in 1901–1910	Deaths in 1930–1939
0	127.4	57.0
1	30.2	8.1
5	5.2	2.1
10	2.6	1.4
20	5.5	2.7

*Adapted from United States Abridged Life Tables, 1930–1939, U. S. Bureau of Census, 1942.

What factors lie behind this significant saving in child life? The mortality rate of children is very responsive to the general vitality of the environment; it is, indeed, "one of the most sensitive indices of the healthfulness of the environment."[10] Sanitation and medical care very quickly bring declines in infant mortality rates. Other factors should be mentioned, however: the way in which rising standards improve the chances of life; maternal education; the decreasing size of the family; improvement in feeding practices; hospitalization.[11] Special attention should be called to the effect of needed research in reducing the incidence of death from childhood diseases. In other words, as the controls over the environment of the child increase, so likewise do the chances of living!

[10] R. M. Woodbury, "Infant mortality in the United States," Annals, 188 (1936): 94–106.

[11] Cf. H. W. Green, Infant mortality and economic status (Cleveland: Cleveland Health Council, 1932); Paul H. Landis, Population problems (New York: American Book Company, 1948), Chs. 11–12.

Population changes and child welfare. A generation or more ago, anthropologist Robert Lowie wrote: "The conception of society as a structure segmented into age-layers . . . reveals genuine insight into sociological dynamics. . . . Its importance must be acknowledged as overwhelming."[12] What social effects are traceable to the change in the pattern of child mortality?

For one thing, this change has contracted the size of the childhood segment in the total national population. Declining mortality rates have not, contrary to what might be expected, increased the proportion of children in the total population, for birth rates have correspondingly declined. The long-range sequence of changes has been outlined by P. K. Whelpton as follows:

TABLE 19

Proportion of Population by Age Groups, for the United States: 1900–1945; Forecasts: 1950–1975*

Year	Per-Cent Distribution				
	Under 5 years	5 to 19 years	20 to 44 years	45 to 64 years	65 years and over
1900	12.1	32.3	37.8	13.7	4.1
1910	11.6	30.4	39.1	14.6	4.3
1920	11.0	29.8	38.4	16.1	4.7
1930	9.3	29.5	38.3	17.5	5.4
1940	8.0	26.4	38.9	19.9	6.8
1945	9.4	24.0	38.8	20.4	7.2
1950	8.3	24.6	38.3	21.1	7.7
1955	7.4	25.3	37.1	21.7	8.4
1960	7.0	25.0	36.3	22.6	9.1
1965	7.0	22.9	36.9	23.5	9.7
1970	7.0	21.7	36.6	24.5	10.3
1975	6.8	21.4	36.2	24.7	10.8

* Warren Thompson, and P. K. Whelpton, *Forecasts of the population of the United States*, 1945–1975. Bureau of the Census, Washington, D.C., 1947, p. 49. Forecasts based on medium fertility, medium mortality, no immigration.

This table suggests three facts of outstanding importance: first, the shrinking childhood segment should mean an expansion in the life opportunities for children per capita; second, the pro-

12 Robert Lowie, *Primitive society* (New York: Boni and Liveright, 1920; 1947, Liveright), pp. 314–315. Quoted by permission.

nounced increase of the "working" or productive section of the population should mean a continuing support for children;[13] and third, children and old people will increasingly become competitors for the national product.[14]

Continuing problems of child mortality. Child-life conservation is still handicapped by certain factors. For example, it is still a most acute problem in our colored population. Colored babies under one year suffer a death rate about 60 per cent higher than that of white babies; those in the first month of life die at a rate about 37 per cent higher; the still-birth rate is 85 per cent higher than that of whites.[15] Death from pneumonia and influenza, organic diseases of the heart, diarrhea, enteritis, tuberculosis, and acute poliomyelitis is still high compared to other lethal causes. Perhaps the most outstanding factor in this respect is the huge percentage (about 18 per cent of all childhood deaths) of deaths from accidental causes, chiefly automobile accidents.[16]

In general, then, many youngsters in the United States still die under circumstances that could be prevented. Many still do not receive the full benefits of existing knowledge and facilities in medicine and public health.[17] With a shrinking childhood segment, the nation's sympathetic attention to the problems surrounding its health and survival is most urgently needed.[18]

Types of Child-welfare Needs and Services

Determining the nature of need. In the nineteenth century, as we have seen, the conception of child-need was couched in terms of dependency; the problem was one of child-saving. In

[13] The population between the ages of 20 and 64 increased from 40 per cent in 1880–1890 to 57.7 per cent in 1940; the percentage will probably stand at 61–63 for the 1950's and 1960's. *Cf.* National Resources Planning Board, *Problems of a changing population* (Washington, D.C.: Government Printing Office, 1938), pp. 31–32.

[14] On these problems of an aging population, *cf.* E. V. Cowdry, ed., *Problems of aging* (Baltimore: Williams and Wilkins, 1942), Chs. 28–29; Talcott Parsons, "Age and sex in social structure," *American Sociological Review*, 7 (October, 1942): 604–617.

[15] *Cf.* L. I. Dublin, "Maternal and infant mortality rates in the United States— A forecast fulfilled," *Proceedings of the Third American Congress on Obstetrics and Gynecology:* 348–352.

[16] *Cf.* Metropolitan Life Insurance Company, "Golden age of child health," *Statistical Bulletin*, 27 (March, 1940): 1–3.

[17] *Cf.* Ch. 15.

[18] For further details, *cf.* Community Service Association of New York, *Family in a democratic society* (New York: Columbia University Press, 1949), Part II: "Health and the Family."

time child specialists came to appreciate, Bossard has suggested, "the economy of preventive work." Thus, child-saving "had to yield a large place to prevention and now both . . . are giving way to the larger and newer conception of child welfare."[19] Throughout these shifts there has been the central preoccupation with need. For our purposes "need" may be regarded as an inadequacy, whether felt by the child or not, which without correction means deprivation, now and in the future.

It should be quickly apparent that the variety of needs depends somewhat on the emphasis of the observer. Lengthy lists of needs are easily compiled. How extensive such lists can become—and how suggestive—is well illustrated by the report of the second White House Conference in 1919. The needs listed there included:[20]

I. Public Protection of the Health of Mothers and Children:
    maternity and prenatal centers; clinics for treatment during pregnancy; hospital facilities for complicated cases; adequate income to allow mothers to remain at home during the nursing period; education of the general public to the problems of maternal and infant mortality; complete birth registration; prevention of infantile blindness; children's health centers; dental and other clinics; adequate hospital facilities for children; state licensing and supervision of all child-caring institutions; general health education; proper physical school facilities; adequate playground and recreational facilities; adequate medical and nursing-school service; continuous health examinations and records; supervision to control communicable diseases; compulsory education until at least sixteen years of age; legal protection from exploitation, vice, drug habits, and so forth.

II. Standards for Children Entering Employment:
    establishment of age limits; compulsory education until at least sixteen and compulsory attendance during certain months; physical minimum certified by a physician.

III. Standards Relating to Children in Need of Special Care:
    statement of modern principles for the care of illegitimate children; individualized treatment of the physically and mentally deficient child; standards for juvenile-court organization and procedure; consideration of the special needs of rural children; the application of the scientific method in

[19] Laura Thompson, in Social work year book, 1929 (New York: Russell Sage Foundation, 1929), p. 72.
[20] Cf. Julia Lathrop, "Standards of child welfare," Annals, 173 (November, 1921): 1–8.

social work with children; and preventive, home-placement, case-treated work with dependent children.[21]

Since it is impossible here to examine this or any similar list in any detail, it has been found desirable to attempt to group child-welfare needs under the following headings.

I. Physically Handicapped Children:
Blind, partially seeing; deaf; hearing seriously impaired; defective in speech; crippled; tubercular; those with tuberculous tendencies; weak hearts; serious organic heart diseases; clinical and sub-clinical malnutrition.

II. Exceptional Children:
Children with behavior difficulties and with mental or nervous disorders; mentally deficient; epileptic; specially gifted children.

III. Exploited Children:
Child laborers; children exposed to vice, drug addiction, and so forth.

IV. Delinquent Children.

V. Dependent Children:
Those who are physically handicapped; illegitimate, foundling, abandoned; orphans; those whose parents are incompetent; homes broken by the death of the father.

The overlapping of these categories is apparent, but perhaps the classification will serve to reduce the task of describing the services which have evolved in the general field of child welfare.

Classification of institutional services.   The 1919 White House Conference properly and foresightedly called attention to the fact that not all child-welfare services should or even can be performed in or through special institutions. There is, indeed, a kind of institutional fallacy, reappearing frequently in public discussions, which holds that the "best" thing to do for a given child in trouble is to change his environment, to remove him from one and place him in another, presumably a better one. If regarded as an unswerving rule, it is a serious error which, among other things, misreads the record of professional experiences since the first World War. One critical observer has written: "In today's social thinking, a comprehensive child-welfare program includes (as one of its major divisions) . . . direct efforts to help parents and parent substitutes more adequately to care

[21] For further details and estimates, *cf.* the report of the Committee on Special Classes, in *1930 White House Conference, op. cit.*, p. 231 ff.

for and guide the growth of their children."[22] Such a philosophy not merely requires family guidance in parent-child relationships; it also entails the use of large-scale, collective measures to protect the family against the social, economic, and physical hazards which threaten the life and personality of the child. This latter point was of special concern to members of the 1940 and 1950 White House Conferences. The present discussion of "institutional" services for children, therefore, by no means refers only to their placement in institutions; it contemplates the whole array of services, both public and private, which through the use of social institutions proposes to assist children in need.

Substitute-care services. Some children need foster-care homes and institutions. They may be placed in a boarding home to which parents or an agency pay a stipulated sum for their care; or in a free home, to which no payment is made; or in a wage home, in which the child renders services for his care; or in an adoptive home. Use is usually made of the first three in the case of older children, of the latter for younger ones.

Placement in a home or institution is a difficult and delicate problem.[23] It requires—or should require—the skill of a specially trained worker; it is subject to state supervision. Placement in an institution rather than a home is ordinarily suggested for older children, for those who must be out of their homes temporarily but who have a strong emotional tie with their parents, for those who are adolescent and have repressive environments; for those who have behavior problems with which foster parents might not be able to cope; and those who are convalescent, who are physically or mentally handicapped. Substitute homes are often necessary for children of unmarried parents Although most illegitimate children remain with their mother or relatives, the majority of children placed for adoption are illegitimate. However, whether involving an illegitimate child or not, adoption poses both professional and judicial problems, is defined by law and supervised by professional workers, in the interest of the best possible placement and growth of the child. Social investigation of applications is essential; and the more careful the inquiry, the greater the protection of the child and society.[24]

[22] R. P. Bridgman, "Ten years' progress in parent education," *Annals*, 173 (November, 1931): 32.

[23] *Cf.* H. W. Stroup, *Social work* (New York: American Book Company, 1948), Chs. 4–5; H. W. Hopkirk, *Institutions serving children* (New York: Russell Sage Foundation, 1944).

[24] *Cf.* E. H. Baylor, and E. D. Monachesi, *Rehabilitation of children: The theory and*

Additional types of substitute-care services include the day nursery, receiving homes for foundlings or abandoned children and for problem-behavior children awaiting disposition by the court, institutions for the specially handicapped, and orphanages.[25] Important shifts which have occurred in substitute-care services for children involve: (a) the increase in the number of both public and private institutions; (b) the rising standard of supervisions, of licensing and inspection by the state; (c) the increase in trained personnel; and (d) the physical and financial improvement of these facilities. Much of this progress is due to the co-operative work between private child-care agencies—such as children's aid and home societies—and public administrative boards and institutions. Moreover, the spreading recognition of the necessity of social-case-work principles in the performance of these services has been a most significant salutary factor.[26]

Protective services. These institutional services for children are aimed at assisting (a) the emotionally disturbed child, (b) the child living in high-risk situations, and (c) the predelinquent child. L. J. Carr has outlined these responsibilities as (1) finding the children who need protection, (2) assisting the child with behavior problems, (3) screening the child living in the midst of high-risk situations, and (4) keeping the normals normal.[27]

Finding the child in need of protective services is not always easy. Usually the community or the family waits until severe behavior symptoms have already developed—until, in other words, it is impossible to avoid "doing something." There is the additional difficulty that most persons are not trained to recognize the preliminary distress signals of emotional disorder. The

---

practice of child placement (New York: Harper and Brothers 1939); Anna Freud, and Dorothy Burlingham, *Infants without families* (New York: International Universities Press, 1944); Dorothy Hutchinson, *In quest of foster parents* (New York: School of Social Work Publications, Columbia University Press, 1943); William Healy, et al, *Reconstruction of behavior in youth* (New York: Alfred A. Knopf, 1936), Chs. 11–21.

[25] *Cf.* "Day care of children," *Social work year book*, 1947 (New York: Russell Sage Foundation, 1947): 144–150; H. Kessler, *Rehabilitation of the physically handicapped* (New York: Columbia University Press, 1947); G. B. Mangold, *Problems of child welfare* (New York: The Macmillan Company, 1936), Ch. 10, 28. Also consult Ch. 15 of this book.

[26] *Cf.* Stroup, *op. cit.*, Ch. 3.

[27] On protective services generally, *cf.* "Protective services for children," *Social work year book*, 1949 (New York: Russell Sage Foundation, 1949): 354–358; E. de Schweinitz, "Philosophy of protective services," *Welfare*, December, 1947: 4–7. The present discussion is patterned after that in L. J. Carr, *Delinquency control* (New York: Harper and Brothers, 1941), Part III: "The Technology of Control."

child himself, of course, is ordinarily not aware of them. What is most urgently needed here may be described as (a) training people who are daily working with children—teachers, recreational leaders, health workers, physicians, ministers, policemen, and parents of course—in the recognition of the symptoms of behavior difficulties and (b) referring such cases as are noticed to the proper agency—which should be *the court only as a last resort!*—for diagnosis and therapy.[28] A wider use of emotional or behavior diagnostic tests and measurements and their follow-up by conferences with parents, by referral to case-working specialists, and by community teamwork is extremely essential.[29] However, elaborate testing programs cannot replace the insight and judgment of the sensitive parent or teacher or youth leader in the guidance of the child. The point that is being made here is simply that in the interest of the child, once the behavior symptom is spotted, community resources should be mobilized in his behalf.

Assisting children with behavior problems may employ, as Rogers has pointed out,[30] one of three different methods. The child may be removed from the offending environment. An attempt may be made to change substantially the environment itself, or some frustrating element in it. Finally, efforts may be made to change the child's attitude toward his life situation. These activities describe the circumference of the psychological and sociological aids for disturbed children. It is better, wherever it is at all possible, that community agencies and the family co-operate in such work. Indeed, an almost sure defeat awaits any program which does not contemplate a co-ordination of actions here. Too often a problem is dumped in the lap of a case-working agency, or the responsibility is delegated fatalistically and prematurely to the machinery of the law. The child's world is not so starkly segmented as all this. How easy it is in such programs of assistance to cut the child's world into unrelated fragments, a world which for the child himself all along has been

[28] *Cf.* C. R. Rogers, *Counselling and psychotherapy: Newer concepts in practice* (Boston: Houghton Mifflin Company, 1942); Stroup, *op. cit.*, Ch. 6; W. V. Kvaraceus, *Juvenile delinquency and the school* (Yonkers: World Book Company, 1945); C. M. Louttit, *Clinical psychology: Handbook of children's behavior problems* (New York: Harper and Brothers, 1936).

[29] *Cf.* Wayne McMillen, *Community organization for social welfare* (Chicago: University of Chicago Press, 1945); Baylor and Monachesi, *op. cit.*, Chs. 3–5.

[30] C. R. Rogers, *Clinical treatment of the problem child* (Boston: Houghton Mifflin Company, 1939).

intimately though confusedly interrelated! A social worker or a judge in court alone cannot "solve" a child's behavior problems; but if ever a solution is reached, the co-operative behavior of a number of people who belong to the daily-contact world of the child is absolutely essential.[31]

In the next place, there is the need for providing some kind of "screen" for the child surrounded by high-risk situations. Professor Carr has included in the latter: (a) deviant homes, (b) culture-conflict areas, (c) substandard areas, (d) delinquency-tradition areas, (e) street trades and domestic services, (f) some commercialized recreations.[32] Unhappily, there is no "sure-fire" formula here. However, the enormous success which has come from organized community endeavors throughout the nation is impressive: slum-clearance projects, family-life education programs, the leadership role of neighborhood centers and settlement houses, community councils, community recreation, parent-teacher associations, and adequate inspection and enforcement of existing laws.[33]

"Keeping the normals normal" as Professor Carr's apt phrase has it, is a task whose difficulty increases with the multiplication of our cultural stresses and social strains.[34] Child psychologists and psychiatrists have been pointing out for years the way in which collective anxieties and tensions are communicated to the child and become incorporated in his own psychological economy.[35] A part of the general program of child welfare necessarily involves a cultural re-enforcement of the family, along lines described in the preceding chapter. A part of it is involved in the campaign against the exploitation of children

[31] Of strategic importance in this general responsibility is the community utilization of the child-guidance clinic. For further discussion, cf. Gordon Hamilton, *Psychotherapy in child guidance* (New York: Columbia University Press, 1947); D. and W. I. Thomas, *Child in America* (New York: Alfred A. Knopf, 1928), Ch. 3; R. P. Truitt, et al, *Child guidance clinic and the community* (New York: Commonwealth Fund, 1928).

[32] Carr, *op. cit.*, Ch. 10.

[33] For a survey of community programs, cf. Arthur Hillman, *Community organization and planning* (New York: The Macmillan Company, 1950), Parts II–III.

[34] For example, cf. Karen Horney, *Neurotic personality of our time* (New York: W. W. Norton and Company, 1937).

[35] For example, cf. Susan Isaacs, *Childhood and after* (New York: International Universities Press, 1949); Anna Freud, and Dorothy Burlingham, *War and children* (New York: International Universities Press, 1944); Gardner and Lois Murphy, and T. M. Newcomb, *Experimental social psychology* (New York: Harper and Brothers, 1937), pp. 239–241, 371–372, 898–901.

by commercialized agriculture, industrialized street trades, unsupervised domestic service, and sweat-shop labor.[36] A part of it is bound up with the extension of mental-hygiene programs, within the school and through community agencies. A very large part of it is contained in the extension of democratic philosophy into areas notoriously undemocratic in practice, such as minority-group relations. Not a small part of it is linked with the search for a tensionless peace.

Corrective services. These services refer to the needs of physically and mentally handicapped and delinquent children. Programs for the physically handicapped include provisions for the education and treatment of crippled and other handicapped children through special classes and schools, hospitals, and convalescent homes, and in the child's own home.[37] An outstanding contribution to these children has been made by the National Foundation for Infantile Paralysis, by the National Society for Crippled Children and Adults, the National Society for the Prevention of Blindness, the American Society for Hard-of-Hearing, the American Heart Association, the National Organization of Public Health Nursing, and local children's aid societies. Through the Social Security Act, the federal government makes an annual appropriation for grants-in-aid to the states to assist them in locating and providing diagnostic, hospital, and after-care treatment of handicapped children and those suffering from conditions leading to handicaps. The meaning of the term "handicapped" or "crippled" has undergone a progressive liberalization through the years. This has been a real boon to the formal administration of agency services.

Because it involves the far more delicate and complex problems of emotional adjustment, corrective work with delinquent children cannot point so easily to the dramatic instances of "cures" and "rehabilitation" which characterize the programs for the physically handicapped. Nor does it ordinarily excite anything like the public sympathy which the latter work almost without effort is able to do, for delinquency represents a violation

[36] *Cf.* Mangold, *op. cit.*, Part IV: "Child Labor and Vocational Guidance"; "Child Labor and Youth Employment," *Social work year book*, 1949 (New York: Russell Sage Foundation, 1949): 92–97; K. D. Lumpkin, and D. Wolff, *Child workers in America* (New York: Robert McBride, 1937).

[37] *Cf.* R. G. Barker, et al, *Adjustment to physical handicap and illness* (New York: Social Science Research Council, 1946); A. Gesell, and C. S. Amatruda, *Developmental diagnosis* (New York: Hoeber, 1947); National Council on Rehabilitation, *Process of rehabilitation* (New York, 1947).

of strong moral and economic prohibitions of society and is by definition a legal concept. The history of services for the delinquent shows a muddled, confused picture, in which very slowly the delinquent was separated from both the dependent child and the adult criminal and in which the philosophy of treatment very gradually replaced the dogma of punishment.[38]

Institutions for delinquents began with the European houses of refuge, which were actually workhouses for dependent and neglected children. All the early child-welfare programs were linked with the general problem of preventing pauperism; the New York Society for the Prevention of Pauperism is a typical example. Spurred on by Maconachie's mark system of discipline, by Marsangy's parole system, by Crofton's use of intermediate stages in the Irish prison system, by the instructive example of the Quakers' famed Walnut Street Jail in Philadelphia, authorities and specialists in the field of penology came to question the commitment of juveniles in the older houses of refuge and in the adult prisons. They were encouraged in this thinking by the humane work of the juvenile protective associations, by the work of the English Bostal system, by Demetz's famous cottage system, and by the spreading use of the indeterminate sentence.[39]

These ideas culminated in the present-day "system"—if such it may be called—of management of delinquent youth. This system includes the following essential features: (a) detention homes, for temporary care of children awaiting court action; (b) recourse to a special court, the juvenile court, where "cases" are analyzed and investigated rather than "tried"; (c) probation, as a substitute for institutional commitment; (d) training schools, rather than prisons; (e) indeterminate sentence, subject to parole; and (f) specially trained juvenile workers attached to the court for purposes of investigation and supervision. Central in the system is the juvenile court.

The significance of these developments will be quickly seen if it is recalled that prior to the establishment of juvenile courts in 1899, youthful offenders were treated in adult courts as thoroughly responsible criminals. Relatively little attention was given

[38] Cf. Stroup, op. cit., Ch. 8; National Probation Association, Social correctives for delinquency, 1945 Year Book (New York: National Probation Association, 1945), Part II: "Origins of Social Thinking in Crime Treatment."
[39] On the historical and other aspects of the reformatory system, cf. H. E. Barnes, and N. K. Teeters, New horizons in criminology (New York: Prentice-Hall, 1944), Chs. 24, 37, 38; E. H. Sutherland, Principles of criminology (Philadelphia: J. B. Lippincott Company, 1947), Ch. 21.

to conditioning circumstances since there was little understanding of child nature and the influences of environmental and hereditary factors in behavior. Juvenile courts are now established in practically all cities of 100,000 or more population and in the majority of cities of more than 5000.

However, the extent of juvenile courts gives little indication as to their efficiency. Many such courts in reality are still attached to adult courts. Many are poorly equipped and manned by an inadequate and untrained personnel. This is true especially of the courts in sparsely settled regions and in small communities. One of the writers made a study of juvenile-court practices in 35 cities of 5000 to 20,000 population. Only four of these courts had access to clinical services; and in two of these, clinical treatment rarely went beyond outstanding physical disorders. Yet it is recognized that much delinquency is caused by conditions that can be understood and treated only by clinical methods. Judges often are selected with little regard to their understanding of the forces that shape youthful behavior. There is, furthermore, a wide diversity within and between states as to the age limits of children who come under the jurisdiction of the juvenile courts. The upper age limits vary from 16 in eleven states to 21 in two states. The upper ages in the remaining states are 17 and 18. There is also some variation in the types of delinquencies handled by the juvenile courts. Serious offenses are frequently dealt with by adult courts, even though the offender is well within the juvenile age. Juvenile courts are further handicapped in many places by the fact that they have little or no jurisdiction over the adults who contribute to the juvenile delinquency.

The National Probation Association has advanced seven minimum requirements for a successful juvenile court: (1) private court hearings and informal, noncriminal procedure; (2) exclusive jurisdiction to deal with parents; (3) a judge chosen for his sympathetic understanding of children and parents; (4) probation officers with personal qualifications developed by specialized training; (5) an efficient record and statistical system with adequate clerical help; (6) facilities for physical examinations and psychiatric study of problem children; and (7) a well-equipped detention home or selected boarding homes for temporary care of children. The last-named requirement, in relation to the detention care, recognizes what is one of the most difficult problems in juvenile-court administration.

Juvenile courts generally average far below these standards, but certain promising trends may be mentioned: the tendency (1) to establish entirely separate juvenile courts or to combine them with courts of domestic relations; (2) to increase the age limits for juveniles; (3) to increase the clinical services available to the courts; (4) to improve the probationary service; (5) to place greater emphasis upon special qualifications in the selection of juvenile-court officers.

The professionalization of child-welfare work. One of the most important developments in the field of child-welfare services has been the acceptance of the idea that they should be performed by trained technicians. Although there are still areas for significant contributions to child welfare to be made by interested non-professionals, as in certain youth groups, the problems typically call for insights and judgments which are subtle and intricate and for which training is a prerequisite. Professionalization has taken two directions: generic and specific.[40] In the first case, efforts are made to fill gaps in the so-called normal institutional life of the child: health, recreation, education, family organization, and so forth. In the second case, the intention is assisting individuals in overcoming the obstacles standing in the way of their effective use of institutional services and relationships. The methods here are those of guidance and counseling, social case work, clinical psychology, psychiatry, and so forth.

These two patterns of professional work are interrelated, for the research and understanding developed by the latter form the limitations and possibilities of the former. In the last analysis, the ultimate aim of child welfare is the individualization of the child's need. Appreciation of this fact lies behind and lends significance to Arnold Gesell's comments: "In many respects the most conspicuous and significant feature of the past two decades is the extraordinary increase in the volume of research relating to child development. This increase is the result of the expansion of the fundamental biological sciences and the new interest in the understanding of the mechanism and forces of social organization. The study of child development has become at once a branch of human biology and of social science."[41] Professionalization has operated as a powerful stimulus in the development of child-welfare work.

[40] For the background of this distinction, cf. Arthur Miles, *Introduction to public welfare* (Boston: D. C. Heath and Company, 1949), Part I: "Introduction and Historical Background."

[41] Arnold Gesell, *Guidance of mental growth in infant and child* (New York: The Macmillan Company, 1930), p. 11. Quoted by permission.

Child Welfare and Public Policy

Protecting the heritage of the child.   Unfortunately, childhood is not the quintessence of happiness that our mythology depicts. Not all of the three million babies that are born annually grow to be mature and healthy men and women. The quest of child welfare is not for an antiseptic environment, but one which is meaningful for that third of our population almost completely dependent on adult society. Each child is different, but all children have typical needs. The problem of guiding child development is one of striking a balance between these two facts of childhood. Failure to do so springs from many sources, as Emma Lundberg has pointed out: "(1) agency prerogatives— to whom does this job belong? what can we afford to do? (2) too many resources for certain forms of care, and too few for others; (3) vested interests of certain organizations; (4) muddling along with existing facilities, fearing to face the implications of underlying causes, such as bad housing and industrial conditions which undermine standards of family life; (5) failure to provide new or improved facilities because they will necessitate expenditure of additional funds from taxation or private contributions."[42]

The picture of child-welfare services is by no means uniformly inspiring nor is it hopelessly chaotic. Despite familiar failures, there is ground for optimism in the fact that modern society is generally accepting social ills as social *illth*, and that the mature and healthy child is an essential part of the social wealth of our people. The human being himself is a significant natural resource that needs to be conserved!

The meaning of social welfare.   Modern industrial people are by no means the first historically to be concerned with the protection, correction, and care—in other words, with the well-being—of their members. Historically, the pattern of such concern has been one of philanthropy, or charity. In contemporary society the pattern is of society protecting itself, of insurance of the general interest. There is, moreover, the increasing acceptance of the philosophy that social assistance is a right.[43]

A slow evolution has transferred a large part of this collective responsibility from sectarian and fraternal and interested groups to the state. Individual helpfulness was first privately pooled

---

[42] Lundberg, *op. cit.*, p. 4. Quoted by permission.
[43] *Cf.* Edith Abbott, "Is there a legal right to relief?" *Social Service Review*, XII (June, 1938): 238 ff.

and later publicly organized and supported. Today a large variety of social services seek to achieve the social security and individual enrichment which the term "general welfare" implies. These services are concerned primarily "with aid to or care of those members of society who because of misfortune, incapacity, or industrial or economic conditions in the community are unable to maintain themselves; those who require special care, treatment, or training because of physical or mental handicaps; those whose conduct is anti-social or who are in danger of becoming a menace to society; and those who must be protected from exploitation or mistreatment."[44]

The motives of social welfare services are varied and mixed. Sometimes the underlying theme is religious, regarding the task as a holy duty and opportunity. Often it is pure expediency and strategy which guide the services. Most commonly humanitarianism, mingled with a philosophy of democratic rights, consciously inspires community endeavors. Increasingly the professional ambition of utilizing a craft-conscious skill for a public benefit prevails. The variety of motives bespeaks the heterogeneity of conceptions of social welfare. Specialists in general conceive of it as the promotion and protection of the welfare of the public through both private and public auspices and authority. The range of activities is ordinarily thought to include: "(a) the various types of assistance programs—general assistance, work relief, assistance to special groups; (b) activities for the prevention and treatment of delinquency, physical and mental handicaps, dependency; (c) services for the protection of children such as licensing or operating children's agencies and institutions, adoption programs, training schools; (d) services for the protection of the aged, the chronically ill, the feeble-minded, the administration of probation and parole services; (e) the social insurances; (f) public housing."[45]

Originally stemming from the laudable desire to relieve poverty, social welfare has come to embrace all collective efforts to enrich human personality and human relationships in those situations where frustration and threat yield up present or future personal and social maladjustments. The primary objective is the correction and need and the restoration of self-sufficiency:

---

[44] Lundberg, *op. cit.*, p. 25. Quoted by permission.
[45] *Cf.* E. C. Lindeman, "Public welfare," *Encyclopedia of social sciences*, XII: 687–689; H. L. Russell, "Public welfare," *1945 Social work year book* (New York: Russell Sage Foundation, 1945): 351–363.

the maintenance of a sense of adequacy and security. In long-time perspective, this goal is fused with the aspiration of preserving a healthy and stable social order. Where and as maladjustive situations can be prevented, the task of social welfare is thereby enlarged. The orbit of collective responsibility is, in an industrial culture, inescapably expansive.

Treating the whole child. It necessarily follows from such thinking that the scope of child-welfare services, as part of the over-all program of social welfare, should become increasingly inclusive. Defects in the social fabric and damages to the personality structure form the foci of the widening ellipse of child-welfare work. In concrete terms, this philosophy calls for the treatment of the whole child.

"Too often," reported the 1940 White House Conference, "people have failed to recognize the simple truth that the child cannot be broken up into parts— one for the parent, another for the teacher, one for the public official, another for the playground, and still another for the church. The child is an indivisible whole as he grows from infancy to manhood and must be planned for and served as such."[46] From the standpoint of method, this theory means in actual practice both the individualization of the care of the child and the reconditioning of his life environment. The former suggests, ultimately at least, a clinical orientation for child welfare, the latter suggests what Hamilton has termed a "therapeutically conditioned environment."[47] The keynote of the first is "therapy," of the latter "guidance." The problem of the first is the development of a balance between physical and social restrictions on the one hand and social gratifications on the other. The problem of the second is the provision and maintenance of an environment which will strengthen the social impulses and socialization processes of the child. The former seeks a diagnostic and clinical unit of emotional control, the latter a constructed unit of social adjustment. The one is therapeutic, the other supportive. Obviously, the two have a necessary interrelationship.

The legal basis of public policy. Child welfare by no means rests entirely upon the uncertain foundation of sympathy and good-will. Children must be safeguarded at the same time that

[46] *General report adopted by the White House conference on children in a democracy,* January 19, 1940 (Children's Bureau, 1940): p. 9.
[47] Hamilton, *op. cit.,* pp. 156–173.

sympathy is ensured. Legal protection is needed in order to protect the child against both the careless and the deliberate acts of organizations and individuals. If good-will were alone sufficient to develop the welfare of children, the legislative remedies would not be attempted. Unhappily experience has taught us over the years not to depend too heavily on sympathy.

The legislative re-enforcement of child-welfare work has taken many forms. One of them is the Children's Code movement. The philosophy underlying this project is stated in the following principles of child-welfare legislation adopted by conferences held under the auspices of the Children's Bureau in 1919. "The child-welfare legislation of every state requires careful reconsideration as a whole at reasonable intervals, in order that necessary revision and co-ordination may be made and that new provisions may be incorporated in harmony with the best experience of the day. In states where children's laws have not had careful revision as a whole within recent years, a child-welfare committee or commission should be created for this purpose. Laws enacted by the several states should be in line with national ideals, and uniform so far as desirable, in view of diverse conditions in the several states, Child-welfare legislation should be framed by those who are thoroughly familiar with the conditions and needs of children and with administrative difficulties."[48]

In general, the legal re-enforcement of child welfare finds its sanction in the interrelated concepts of the public interest, the general welfare, the police power of the state, and so forth. Specifically, it is hinged on the doctrine which, formulated in connection with the law of guardianship, holds that the state can and must act *in loco parentis:* the doctrine of *parens patriae.* As expressed in law and interpreted by the courts, this doctrine has been able, through administrative practice, to throw a strong hedge around the rights and duties of parents.[49] It is increasingly bringing rights and status to the non-wedlocked child (or, as the Russians say, "the extra-marital child"). It has, in sum, come to be the sanction and the inspiration for most of the services now being made available to handicapped,

[48] *Minimum standards for child welfare adopted by the Washington and Regional Conferences on Child Welfare,* 1919 (Children's Bureau, Publication No. 62, 1920).

[49] *Cf.* Grace Abbott, *Child and the state* (Chicago: University of Chicago Press, 1938), Vol. I.

dependent, neglected, exploited, and delinquent children. Along with the emerging child sciences, it has become a chief factor in the shaping of public policy in the field of child welfare.[50]

Administrative aspects of child welfare. However, it would be a serious failure to hold, as has sometimes been the case, that government has the sole responsibility for the welfare of children. Private responsibility through individual, group, and community action is likewise essential. "Wherever," according to Sidney and Beatrice Webb, "there is reason for its intervention, it (the public authority) must have all the cases on its books. The prescribed national minimum has to be insured and enforced, at all times, as regards every case. . . . On the other hand, though the public authority concerned must be responsible for the adequate treatment of all the cases needing attention, this does not mean that it need do, for all cases, everything that needs to be done. There is . . . an enormous part of the work which voluntary agencies can do better than the public authorities, in which they can bring to bear their specific advantages on particular cases or classes of cases, or in particular parts of the treatment of all cases."[51] Child welfare, then, is a partnership between the people and their government; the primary beneficiary, it must always be borne in mind, is after all the child.

QUESTIONS

1. Outline the history of the successive White House conferences.
2. Describe the successive stages in the child-welfare movement.
3. Distinguish between child-saving and child-development.
4. What are the significant consequences for the child-welfare movement of the changing social composition of the American population?
5. Point out some of the difficulties in classifying children in need. What are some of the advantages in attempting to classify them?
6. Under what circumstances should a child be placed in an institution? in a home? kept in his own home?
7. Distinguish between protective and corrective services for children. Illustrate.
8. Identify the various ways of helping children with behavior problems.
9. Account for the extensive professionalization of child care in our day. Are all childhood services necessarily professional? Explain.
10. Describe some of the legal aspects of child-welfare services.

[50] *Cf.* Lundberg, *op. cit.*, Ch. 13.
[51] Quoted by Wayne McMillen, *op. cit.*, p. 111.

REFERENCES

ABBOTT, G., *Child and the state*. Chicago: University of Chicago Press, 1938.

BOSSARD, J. H. S., *Sociology of child development*. New York: Harper and Brothers, 1948.

CARR, L. J., *Delinquency control*. New York: Harper and Brothers, 1941.

Community Service Society of New York, *Family in a democratic society*. New York: Columbia University Press, 1949.

FREUD, A., and BURLINGHAM, D., *Infants without families*. New York: International Universities Press, 1944.

HAMILTON, G., *Psychotherapy in child guidance*. New York: Columbia University Press, 1947.

HEALY, W., et al, *Reconstruction of behavior in youth*. New York: Alfred A. Knopf, 1936.

HOPKIRK, H. W., *Institutions serving children*. New York: Russell Sage Foundation, 1944.

KESSLER, H. H., *Rehabilitation of the physically handicapped*. New York: Columbia University Press, 1947.

LOUTTIT, C. M., *Clinical psychology: A handbook of children's behavior problems*. New York: Harper and Brothers, 1936.

LUMPKIN, K. D., and DOUGLAS, D. S., *Child workers in America*. New York: Medill McBride Company, 1937.

LUNDBERG, EMMA, *Unto the least of these*. New York: Appleton-Century-Crofts, 1947.

ROGERS, C. R., *Clinical treatment of the problem child*. Boston: Houghton Mifflin Company, 1939.

STROUP, H. H., *Social work*. New York: American Book Company, 1948.

THOMAS, D. S. and W. I., *Child in America*. New York: Alfred A. Knopf, 1928.

CHAPTER 12

Education and the Social Interest

Learning and the Culture Pattern

The cultural expectations. Every society has some type of social arrangements for the socialization of its young.[1] These arrangements may be highly specialized, as in contemporary America, or somewhat informal and diffused throughout the society, as in preliterate cultures. In either case, however, their primary function is to acquaint the new members of the society with the social heritage and skills of the culture. The extent to which functions other than these may be performed depends largely upon the degree of specialization and differentiation of the culture. Eventually, the emergence of a highly differentiated economy brings a specialization of the enculturation process, predominantly in the school.

The responsibility of the process of socialization—or learning or education or enculturation—is to perfect in the individual skills in meeting the problems and expectations of his culture. There are three types of skills which must be developed: activity-skills, fact-skills, value-skills. Thus, physical, social, and economic roles must be learned. The individual must be introduced to the fund of knowledge of the society. And the sentimental, esthetic, religious, moral, political, and other values must be known. Throughout, however, the individual is expected to become skillful in his knowledge and use of each of these three aspects of his culture. As he becomes skilled, he becomes—as we say in our day—"educated." "General" or "liberal" education, in our society at least, denotes an adequate mastery of all three types of skills. Specialized—or vocationalized or profes-

[1] For further development of the concept of enculturation, see M. J. Herskovits, *Man and his works* (New York: Alfred A. Knopf, 1948), Ch. 4.

sionalized—education refers to the narrowing of the range of these skills, usually in the interest of some occupational activity. This occupational bias is a selective influence, limiting or circumscribing the field of learning experience. It is, of course, not the only limiting factor, as we shall see.

This inevitable vocationalizing of the learning process in a differentiated society points to one of the major problems of education. It is obviously impossible to develop mastery of all the areas of skill in our culture. It is necessary to specialize to some extent. Yet the young must be brought into a living relationship with the total range of their culture, much of which represents extensive borrowing from previous societies. Here, then, is a problem of modern education: how to cultivate the totality of relevant culture, on the one hand, and how to perfect mastery of economically and socially useful segments of it, on the other. By no means is the question one of either-or; it is one of proportion or balance. Since the present-day educational system in America can hardly claim to have achieved such a balance, it is indeed fortunate that there are other institutions which specialize in some phases of the three types of skills. In a sense, industry, government, religion, and mass-communication agencies are also educational institutions. However, it would be difficult to prove that even with their aid we have managed to achieve a balance of general and special education which the social interest seems to demand.[2]

Intrinsic and extrinsic features of education. Education, then, may be said to have a center of gravity: culturally demanded skills which must be transmitted to the young and perfected in them.[3] The individual must be taught, trained, and inspired in the knowledge and use of these skills. However, this process is not merely one of transmission, save perhaps in fairly stable or static cultures. In dynamic societies, the maturing of these skills must be oriented around the creative enhancement and enrichment of both the individual and his society. The individual and the culture must not only be "maintained," they must be "improved." This requirement is the extrinsic feature of education, one which grows out of the interactions of a society in

[2] For example, see Ralph Borsodi, *Education and living* (Suffern: School of Living, 1948), 2 vols.; also Alexander Meiklejohn, *Education between two worlds* (New York: Harper and Brothers, 1942).

[3] This distinction between "intrinsic and extrinsic features" is adapted from Educational Policies Commission, *Policies for education in American democracy* (Washington, D.C.: National Education Association, 1946), p. 55.

change. Here again is an important problem of education in the modern world: how to achieve a balance between its intrinsic function of developing skill and its extrinsic function of directing skill creatively.

In static cultures the extrinsic features of education remain undeveloped, for the philosophy which dictates the learning process is essentially a conservative one and centers on the culture as received. The situation is reversed in changing societies. To be sure, there are many theorists in modern educational circles who insist on an "essentialist" position, stressing the acquisition and transmission of received knowledge. Others, starting from the observation that ours is a changing culture, seek to direct the learning process toward creative adaptation to change, both in the individual and in the society. Here again the problem may be seen as one of balance between "essential" aspects of the heritage and "imperative" innovations.[4]

Learning is a cultural process. This discussion of the intrinsic and extrinsic features of the learning process should underscore a thesis, suggested earlier, that it is a cultural process. Unhappily, the great store of books on educational psychology will usually give another picture: that of the individual learner with all his aptitudes and capacities, his habit mechanisms and motivations. The point which anthropological investigations have made with such outstanding success is usually missed.[5] Learning inevitably occurs in a cultural setting, at a particular place and in a particular time. The prevailing culture formulates what is expected as the end-product of the learning process. It defines what shall be learned, who shall teach and who shall learn, where and under what circumstances learning shall take place. The learning process is and always has been the handmaiden of the total culture of a people. It is not expected to take place in a vacuum, as indeed it does not. It may be well to say that "education has obligations to truth itself and for its own sake—obligations to seek it, defend it, or make humane use of it."[6] But "truth" becomes a shadowy substance when it is remembered that it "means" one thing to a Trobriand Islander and another to a New Yorker. The learning process in societies around the world

---

[4] This controversy will be reviewed later in this chapter.

[5] For example, see C. Kluckhohn, and H. A. Murray, eds., *Personality in nature, society, and culture* (New York: Alfred A. Knopf, 1948); R. Linton, *Cultural background of personality* (New York: Appleton-Century-Crofts, 1945); N. E. Miller, and J. Dollard, *Social learning and imitation* (New Haven: Yale University Press, 1941); A. Kardiner, *Individual and his society* (New York: Columbia University Press, 1939).

[6] Educational Policies Commission, *op. cit.*, p. 56.

does not deal in "truth" but in culturally patterned and expected activities, facts, and values. What is expected is not "truth" *per se* —whatever that is—but mastery of such activities, facts, and values as the particular culture happens to prize and promote.

The culture of a given people in a given place, then, is the significant framework of the learning process. Americans are not educated to be Hottentots (though the latter may in time, it seems, learn how to be Americans). The young everywhere the world over are educated for and in terms of their own culture. They may acquire information—not to mention understanding and wisdom—about the cultures of other people. But the "learned" individual, in America and in Samoa, is one who knows how to "deal" with the contact-world of his daily life. Such information as he may acquire about other societies may illuminate, humanize, facilitate—as indeed it often does—his daily experience; it may render it more enjoyable and meaningful. But it is not the primary concern of the learning process. This, then, is another problem of the educational process: how to balance the culturally demanded learning of the individual's own society with a useful (and perhaps necessary) experience of other cultures.[7]

Each society has its own pattern of activities, facts, and values: its "culture pattern." The underlying problem of education in relatively static societies is to produce in successive generations conformity to this pattern.[8] It is only in relatively dynamic societies that the possibility of nonconformity to, even of deliberate change of, the pattern of the culture is considered. Yet in as changeful a society as our own the problem of a challenging nonconformity or redirection is a sore point in educational administration. Can education challenge the American culture pattern? Is it "free" to question it or draw questioning conclusions about it? When does criticism become disloyalty?

These questions cannot be answered by reviewing any particular controversy. For an answer we must return to the thesis that learning is a cultural process. Education—or learning—is always free, but free within the pattern of the culture itself.[9] A culture which itself has grown by challenging the past may continue to

[7] This idea is the motivation behind what is sometimes called social education or intercultural education; one finds it ordinarily in discussions of liberal education.

[8] *Cf.* M. Mead, "Education, primitive," *Encyclopedia of social sciences* (New York: The Macmillan Company, 1931), V: 402 ff.; also, N. Miller, *Child in primitive society* (New York: Coward-McCann, 1928).

[9] For a fuller development of this theme, *cf.* H. F. Simon, *Revolution, whither bound?* (New York: Rinehart and Company, 1936).

encourage challenges of both the past and the present. Even so, there will be many in such societies who are wedded to either the past or the present and who hate and fight any criticisms. A culture which has long since ceased to challenge its past will brook no questioning of its present. Occasionally, even a revolutionary culture finds it wise to silence its critics, as Europe in both the interwar and postwar periods has discovered. Everywhere, in preliterate and in industrial societies, people are free —within the ideology, within the pattern of their culture. No society permits unlimited criticism or nonconformity, and no society is without criticism or nonconformity. The general rule seems to be that so long as the ideology or pattern of the culture is basically accepted, its people are free to question and to challenge. Ironically, even the refusal to accept the pattern becomes in itself a binding frame of values: The rejection of ideology becomes ideological. Here, then, is another problem of the learning process: how to achieve and accept a conditional freedom of learning!

Every society organizes the learning behavior of its young in terms of its own "social interest," whatever that may be and however it may be defined by a given society. The young must learn, there must be some kind of organization for learning, and the "social interest" must be protected and promoted. We shall, therefore, inquire into the nature of the organization of education in America. We shall attempt to describe the social interest of America in its educational system. We shall try to outline the ways in which this interest is being served, or not being served, by this system.

The American Educational System

Education as major economic and social enterprise. It is necessary for a highly differentiated economy such as that of the United States to specialize or formalize ("institutionalize") its learning processes. The result is that education is one of our biggest industries, operated on a public and private basis, enrolling over 32 million full-time students and employing over a million teachers. Investment in close to a quarter of a million schools totals over 12 billion dollars. Annual expenditures for public education average close to 5 billion dollars.

Educational administration as social policy. The American system of education is both public and private. Important features of public education, which is the primary interest in this chapter, include: (1) decentralization of administration on a state and local basis; (2) formulation of policy and operation of educational programs at the local level by publicly elected school boards; (3) free, compulsory, universal attendance; (4) gradation of students into classes and levels of schooling ("the educational ladder"); (5) the philosophy of equal educational opportunity; (6) separation of church and state; (7) a corps of professionally trained teachers and administrators; (8) financing by public funds.[10]

This system is based on the philosophy that education is an indispensable tool of the democratic way of life. A democratic people must be literate and informed. In a sense, American education has been a faith akin to religion. Democracy in America is a social faith, whatever else it may be. American education is part and parcel of that faith. Democracy as a social faith has been described as holding the following beliefs about human beings:[11]

First, the individual human being is of surpassing worth.
Second, the earth and human culture belong to all men.
Third, men can and should rule themselves.
Fourth, the human mind can be trusted and should be set free.
Fifth, the method of peace is superior to that of war.
Sixth, racial, cultural, and political minorities should be tolerated, respected, and valued.

These doctrines of public faith outline some of the social interest which American people have in their educational system.

Recent growth and development of American public education. However much the American people fail to measure up to their social creed, their practices at least push in that direction. Table 20 (p. 304) illustrates this attempt to translate an ideal into reality.

American school enrollments. The total picture of American public- and private-school populations is given in the data made available by the Office of Education of the Federal Security Agency as shown in Table 21.

Educational objectives. What is the social policy toward our schools? What are our expectations?

The answer must not get too far from the fact that the social

[10] *Cf.* A. E. Meyer, *Development of education in the twentieth century,* 2nd ed. (New York: Prentice-Hall, 1949), p. 357.

[11] Formulated by the Educational Policies Commission of the National Education Association, *op. cit.*, pp. 103–104.

policy of America is democracy. This fact means, concretely, the protection of the civil liberties of the people, government by their consent, appeal to their reasonableness, the promotion of their general welfare, and the pursuit of individual happiness.

TABLE 20*
Measures of Educational Expansion and Improvement: 1890–1940

Year	1	2	3	4	5	6
1890	43.97	52.90	134.70	17.23	7.58	21.03
1900	49.68	71.80	144.30	20.21	10.40	27.12
1910	52.65	82.92	157.50	33.23	17.50	40.44
1930	67.35	116.06	172.25	63.98	43.09	69.36
1940	73.95	129.40	175.00	105.74	79.65	130.36

1. Per cent of population, 5–17, attending school daily.
2. Average days attended by each child of school age (5-17).
3. Average number of days school kept open.
4. Average annual expenditures per child attending.
5. Average annual expenditures per child, 5–17 years of age.
6. Average monthly salary (12 months) of teachers.

* Adapted from L. P. Ayres, *Index number for state school systems* (New York: Russell Sage Foundation, 1920); F. M. Phillips, "Educational rank of states, 1930," *American School Board Journal*, (1932) 84: 25 ff.; U. S. Office of Education, "Statistical summary of education, 1941–1942," *Biennial survey of education in the United States* (Washington, D.C.: Government Printing Office, 1944), II, Ch. 2. Data for 1920 not given.

Translating these phases of American democratic practice into educational life, American educators have defined their tasks in terms of the following objectives:

1. Promoting the self-realization of the individual.
2. Sensitizing him to his civic responsibility.
3. Socializing his human relations.
4. Developing his economic efficiency.[12]

The education of free men. Looking at the obligations of education in a democracy even more broadly, we may summarize them in this way: to maintain and improve a society of free men. Such an educational achievement begins with a highly socialized conception of the human being. For the free man,

[12] Adapted from the Educational Policies Commission, *op. cit.*, p. 186.

TABLE 21

School Enrollments: 1948–1950*

Type of School	1949–1950 (estimated)	1948–1949
Elementary schools:		
Public	20,584,000	20,034,000
Private and parochial	2,652,000	2,620,000
Residential schools for exceptional children	61,500	61,000
Model and practice schools in teacher-training institutions	50,000	53,000
Federal schools for Indians	30,000	29,000
Total elementary	23,377,500	22,797,000
Secondary schools:		
Public	5,885,000	5,633,000
Private and parochial	575,000	566,000
Residential schools for exceptional children	20,000	19,000
Model and practice schools in teacher-training institutions and preparatory departments of colleges	47,000	46,000
Federal schools for Indians	6,000	6,000
Total secondary	6,533,000	6,270,000
Higher education:		
Universities, colleges, professional schools including junior colleges and normal schools	2,456,000	2,408,000
Total higher education	2,456,000	2,408,000
Other schools:		
Private commercial schools	270,000	300,000
Nurse-training schools (not affiliated with colleges and universities)	91,000	113,000
Total other schools	361,000	413,000
Grand totals	32,727,000	31,888,000

* Source: *The American Teacher*, January, 1950: 160.

as the Educational Policies Commission has said, is a human being loyal:

First, to himself as a human being of dignity and worth;
Second, to the principle of human equality and brotherhood;
Third, to the process of untrammelled discussion, criticism, and group decision;

Fourth, to the ideal of honesty, fair-mindedness, and scientific spirit in the conduct of this process;

Fifth, to the ideal of respect for and appreciation of talent, training, character, and excellence in all fields of socially useful endeavor;

Sixth, to the obligation and the right to work;

Seventh, to the supremacy of the common good;

Eighth, to the obligation to be socially informed and intelligent.[13]

Such thinking is obviously a product of the philosophy that a society of free men is also one of informed men. Thus, the Commission goes on to say: "The free man today is familiar with certain great patterns or bodies of social knowledge and thought:

First, he has knowledge of the nature of man in society;

Second, he has knowledge of the history of mankind;

Third, he has knowledge of the long struggle to liberate and civilize the human heart;

Fourth, he has knowledge of the present crisis;

Fifth, he has knowledge of the totalitarian movements;

Sixth, he has knowledge of the weaknesses of American democracy;

Seventh, he has knowledge of the resources, achievements, and promise of American democracy."[14]

Responsibilities of government, teachers, and people. These imposing responsibilities call for a governmental support which will maintain conditions favorable to the satisfaction of these expectations. Concretely, they require that government in a democracy shall:

First, establish a special authority for the general conduct of the public school;

Second, provide generous and sustained financial support of the educational undertaking;

Third, insure the broad, thorough, and democratic training of the teacher;

Fourth, safeguard the integrity of the teacher;

Fifth, refuse deliberately to make full use of its own power over the school.[15]

Educational enterprise in a democracy is no less exacting on the teacher and administrator. They must:

First, maintain a steadfast loyalty to the democratic faith;

Second, achieve and sustain high professional competence;

[13] *Ibid.*, p. 113.
[14] *Ibid.*, p. 122.
[15] *Ibid.*, p. 147.

Third, participate actively and intelligently in shaping educational policy;

Fourth, establish and maintain a condition of mutual trust, understanding, and sympathy with the people.[16]

Finally, democratic education demands of the people themselves that they should seek:

First, to achieve a more adequate understanding of the nature of democratic education;

Second, to guard public education against attack;

Third, to establish and maintain a condition of mutual trust, understanding, and sympathy with the teacher.[17]

Some Unfinished Business: Public Support

Deficits in American education. Surveying the American educational scene at the close of the Second World War, two American educators called attention to several glaring failures to make good with the expectations and requirements of education in a democracy. They found that:

1. 3,000,000 adults living in the United States have never attended any kind of school.
2. 10,000,000 adult Americans have had so little schooling that they are virtually illiterate.
3. Half of the brightest and most talented youth of the nation leave school prematurely—before they have had the kind and amount of schooling which would be justified by both their ability and the demands of our way of life.
4. 2,000,000 children, 6–15, were not in any kind of school in 1940.
5. The schooling provided millions of American children who are in school is so inferior and brief that it leaves them unprepared to meet the demands made upon them as citizens and as individuals.[18]

Failure of public support. A large share of these deficits can be laid at the door of public support of education. Thus, Norton and Lawler noted a tremendous range in variation in the financing of American public schools. The best-financed school systems spend $6000 or more per classroom unit (as of 1939–1940), the poorest spend less than $100: a range of 60 to 1. Sorting average expenditures into deciles, they found the following distribution:

[16] *Ibid.*, p. 150.
[17] *Ibid.*, p. 153.
[18] J. K. Norton, and E. S. Lawler, *Unfinished business in American education* (Washington, D.C.: American Council on Education, 1946), p. 3.

TABLE 22*
Expenditures per Classroom Unit in the United States: 1939–1940

Percentage of Classroom Units	Expenditure
Highest 10%	$4115
Next 10	3180
Next 10	2587
Next 10	2147
Next 10	1796
Next 10	1519
Next 10	1263
Next 10	1007
Next 10	779
Lowest 10	470

* Source: Norton and Lawler, *op. cit.*, p. 8.

Norton and Lawler comment that "the poorest schools are generally found in poverty communities. . . . In other words, the children who most need good schools usually get the poorest schools."[19]

Public spending for American schools, while sizable in gross, is unimpressive when compared with some other items of the American budget. Thus, Benjamin Fine, Education Editor of the *New York Times*, reports that the American people spend less for education than for liquor or tobacco. In 1945 the educational expenditure was $17.76 per capita; expenditure that year for tobacco came to $21.69 and for alcohol $55.65. "Ironically enough," writes Fine, "the United States spent a greater percentage of its national income for education during the depression than it does today."[20]

The explanation for the variations, over the years and for different regions, in America's support of its schools lies in its method of financing them. The public school system in this country is local in operation and support. It is financed largely out of the general property tax, which is, as economist Seymour

[19] Norton and Lawler, *op. cit.*, p. 9. However, they are quick to stress the fact—usually ignored—that "the poor states try harder than the rich. . . . The ten states with lowest expenditures as a group devote a larger percentage of the income of their people to the support of schools than the 10 highest-expenditure states." If the average effort of the whole country equals 100, the 10 highest would rate 91 per cent, the 10 lowest 106 per cent. *Ibid.*, p. 22.

[20] From *Our children are cheated* by Benjamin Fine. Reproduced by permission of Henry Holt and Company, Inc. Copyright, 1947, by Benjamin Fine.

Harris points out, "inelastic, inequitable, and depressive."[21] Revenues from this source in 1932 totaled a little over 4 billion dollars. In 1945 they were 2 per cent less than in 1932; and if the shrinking purchasing power of the dollar is taken into account, this meant a revenue for public education of about 3 billion dollars. Yet national income during this same period rose 300 per cent. Consumption increased during the same period by about 100 billion dollars per year.

Financing American education, thus, depends on local governmental units which have the smallest revenue system. The difficulties of these units are made immeasurably worse by the failure on the part of the federal government over the years to stop either depression or inflation and by the manner in which the federal government exploits the most lucrative forms of taxation. Professor Harris ties these facts into a strong conclusion:

> It is necessary now to realize that the distribution of responsibilities which obtained 50 or 100 years ago is no longer appropriate. The country is now highly industrialized; geographical variations in capacity to finance education have increased greatly; migration from state to state is increasingly popular; and, therefore, the costs of inadequate education fall on the nation, not on the state offering the education; new burdens have fallen on local and even state governments hamstrung by relatively inelastic fiscal systems.[22]

These arguments constitute the nucleus of the case for federal support of education.

Some consequences of failure of support. A number of consequences flow from this failure in financing. One of them is the presence of pronounced regional inequalities. Thus, 13 per cent of all school-age children are in the southeastern states which have, however, only 2 per cent of the national income. On the other hand, the urban population of the northeastern states, where 27 per cent of all school-age children live, have 42 per cent of the national income. A similar inequality in demand for education and power to support exists in various size-classes of American communities. This fact is brought out by the report of the National Resources Committee that for 1940 the number of children under 5 years of age per 1000 women varied markedly in size of community. When such inequalities exist, children

---

[21] Seymour Harris, *How shall we pay for education?* (New York: Harper and Brothers, 1948), p. 19. Quoted by permission.
[22] *Ibid.*, p. 208.

simply do not—and cannot—receive uniformly good education, nor does the nation develop its intellectual potential.

TABLE 23*

Distribution of Children per 1000 Women, by Community: 1940

Community	No. per 1000
Towns and Cities	310
Villages	497
Rural-farm	648
Urban Northeast	293
Rural Southeast	722

* Source: Fine, *op. cit.*, p. 130. Quoted by permission.

Another consequence of this failure in public support is the underpaid and substandard conditions of the teaching profession. Reports Editor Fine: "Teachers get less money for cultivating the minds of children than garbage collectors do for picking up waste or street cleaners for keeping the streets tidy."[23] This situation causes the teaching profession to lose some of its abler members and to attract many less-qualified persons into its ranks. Teacher turnover is very high. Annually the profession loses about a tenth of its members; during the recent postwar years it has lost close to 20 per cent. There is a constant demand for teacher replacements; recently over 10 per cent of such replacements have been individuals with emergency or substandard certificates. In 1947 one of every seven teachers in America could not meet the minimum requirements for regular certification. Adequate pay attracts adequate personnel. One index of the inadequacy of teachers' salaries is contained in the following data (as of 1947):

 61,191 teachers have not gone beyond high school.
 101,698 teachers have had one year of college.
 198,224 teachers have had two years of college.
 96,527 teachers have had three years of college.
 290,442 teachers have had four years of college.
 113,764 teachers have had more than four years of college.[24]

Summarily stated, about 40 per cent of our public-school teachers have not gone beyond the sophomore year in college.

[23] *Ibid.*, p. 43. Quoted by permission.
[24] *Ibid.*, p. 25.

Salary inequities form only one part of the problem confronting professional teachers. The full scope of their needs may be seen in the following recommendations made by the nation's top-ranking officials to Benjamin Fine in his national circuit of American schools.[25]

1. Greater financial support of the public schools.
2. Increase in teachers' salaries.
3. Higher requirements and standards in the teaching profession.
4. Federal aid to education.
5. Single-salary schedules.
6. Better working conditions for teachers.
7. Tenure and retirement laws.
8. Elimination of community restriction and meddling.
9. Improvement of teacher-training institutions.
10. Improvement in school facilities.
11. Improvement in rural schools.
12. Introduction of modern teaching methods.
13. Greater teacher participation in school programs.
14. A better recruitment program.
15. Greater public interest in the nation's schools.
16. Expansion of higher-education facilities.

Some Unfinished Business: The Dual System

The American school system has been described as being both public and private. It is a dual system, however, in yet another sense: it is also, in effect, a Negro-White school system. Seventeen of the states have, by state law, biracial, segregated schools. Despite the recent Supreme Court decisions invalidating dual establishments at the level of higher education, it continues in point of daily fact to be a dual system at the elementary and secondary levels. A gross violation of the American creed, as Gunnar Myrdal has showed,[26] its consequences extend far beyond the political and moral "dilemma" which it purportedly creates. A review of some statistical data should quickly demonstrate this fact.

Average public-school expenditures in 1943–1944, in the midst of a great war for democracy, were $116.99 per child for the country as a whole. In 31 states having nonsegregating systems average expenditures totaled $131.36. In the 17 states which practice school segregation, the figure was $84.79. In

[25] *Ibid.*, p. 227 ff.
[26] Gunnar Myrdal, *American dilemma: The Negro problem and modern democracy* (New York: Harper and Brothers, 1944).

these same states the sum for each Negro child was $36.98: less than a third of the national average, less than half of the average for the segregating states.

Similar ratios obtain with respect to other aspects of educational opportunities. Thus, Norton and Lawler found that 69 per cent of all classroom units costing less than $600 annually were being operated in 1939–1940 for Negro children in the 17 dual-system states, whereas only 23 per cent were being operated for white children in these same states.[27] In tabular form the contrast in support for the two racial groups appears as follows:

TABLE 24*

Average Public-School Expenditures per Child per Year in 10 States with Segregated Systems: 1943–1944

State	White	Negro
Alabama	$70.20	$25.65
Arkansas	61.03	25.81
Florida	95.96	47.44
Georgia	73.79	23.63
Louisiana	121.32	40.25
Maryland	115.52	90.82
Mississippi	71.65	11.96
North Carolina	71.60	50.07
South Carolina	82.43	26.85
Texas	92.69	63.12

* Source: Fine, op. cit., p. 152.

A telltale consequence of the dual system, suggesting much of the whole sorry train of results which it creates, is indicated in Army reports on the education attainments of American soldiers in two wars. American Negroes do not receive as much schooling as American whites in the South or elsewhere; the financial data cited above indicate that they cannot possibly receive the same quality of education.

It must be recalled that the segregating states are characterized by a heavy concentration of both Negro and white children of school age and that they likewise compare very unfavorably in the percentage of national income available for education. These states typically try harder to maintain high standards of education than the other states. To be sure, the dual system immeasura-

[27] Norton and Lawler, op. cit., p. 24.

bly worsens their condition in this respect, for even the wealthiest states could hardly maintain two separate systems on a basis of actual equality.

TABLE 25*

Amount of Negro and White Schooling: World Wars I and II

Amount of Schooling	World War I	World War II		
	All Negroes	Negroes of 12 Southern States	Other Negroes	Whites (U.S.)
1–8 years grade school	95%	64%	40%	26%
1–4 years high school	5	32	53	62
1 or more years of college	(few)	4	7	12

* Source: Fine, *op. cit.*, p. 144.

In a careful and sympathetic study of the socio-economic problems of higher education for American Negroes, made as a part of the National Survey of Higher Education conducted by the U.S. Office of Education, Ina Corinne Brown found an answer to the general problem of the dual system in federal leadership and participation. This suggestion, it was noted, rests upon two basic arguments: "(a) simple justice demands that reasonably equal opportunity be assured to the citizens of the United States, regardless of race or place of birth; and (b) national welfare demands that human resources be conserved and developed by affording men and women of ability without regard to race a chance to make their maximum contribution to social progress."[28] The case against a dual system, particularly in a democracy, could not be made in any stronger terms.

Some Unfinished Business: Policy by Pressure

In a democracy the public educational system is necessarily influenced by public behavior: by public opinion and sentiment. Unfortunately, "the public" in a differentiated economy is not one but infinitely numerous: democracy is a pluriverse.[29] Education in a democracy is naturally sensitive to many currents of demands and expectations. On the other hand, it is extremely

[28] Ina Corinne Brown, *Socio-economic approach to educational problems* (Washington, D.C.: U. S. Office of Education, 1942), p. xi.

[29] This point is discussed at greater length in Chs. 2 and 15.

urgent that a democratic educational system maintain an adequate autonomy, a relative independence of partisan pressure. This necessity is recognized in those American governmental practices which provide public functions with constitutional, legislative, and executive safeguards from attack and exploitation. Within education itself there are certain special grounds for pleading independence.[30] Thus, scientific instruction has no peculiar affinity with partisan politics. Preparation for citizenship transcends partisanship. Enhancement of individual economic efficiency does not call for ideologically goose-stepping the young. If controversial questions can be handled with judicial discretion in the courts, they might reasonably be expected to be treated in like manner in the classroom.

The public school, then, is irretrievably caught in a crossfire of partisan pressures and professional demands for autonomy. Any other definition of the education situation is mythological.[31] Indeed, a public school system, logically enough, must be and must remain a *public* system. Pressures are inevitable.

However, the organized interests which turn to the school for indoctrination and promotion are not equal, either in power, intensity, or purpose. Raup, in a well-documented study of 86 organized interests, noted four varieties of group reactions to issues in American public life:[32]

1. Uncompromising absolutism;
2. Compromising absolutism;
3. Melioristic reformism;
4. Uncommitted or undogmatic tolerance.

So far as handling differences of opinion is concerned, these groups split along four different lines: those seeking

1. Suppression of differences of opinion;
2. Co-operation with differences (but hoping to propagandize and convert);
3. Co-operation with differences (but trying to assimilate them);
4. Co-operation with differences (but trying to integrate them).

[30] *Cf.* Educational Policies Commission, *op. cit.,* p. 83 ff.

[31] For example, on this point, *cf.* M. E. Curti, *Social ideas of American secondary education* (New York: Charles Scribner's Sons, 1935); H. B. Alberty, and B. H. Bode, eds., *Educational freedom and democracy,* 2nd Yearbook John Dewey Society (New York: Appleton-Century-Crofts, 1938).

[32] B. Raup, *Education and organized interests in America* (New York: G. P. Putnam's Sons, 1936), pp. 225–227.

These groups manifested another important trait. In a time of severe crisis (*e.g.*, depression, war), suppressive or uncompromising absolutists tend to overwhelm the other pressures: in such times the kingdom of God most certainly does not belong to the open-minded.

The situation is made even more confusing by the fact that not only do these groups have views; they publish them, promote them, and bring "pressure"—on either the teacher or the administration—for the use and adoption of their materials. Thus, the classroom teacher has four alternatives, to: (a) collect materials on specific issues from all groups; (b) select a sample of such materials for illustrative purposes; (c) reject the use of all of them; (d) utilize those which, for one reason or another, may be congenial. The first two alternatives require considerable additional work, the latter considerable courage or diplomacy. In any case, the classroom teacher will in all likelihood be criticized for any course of action he adopts.[33]

We are far from having arrived at a firm policy in American educational circles toward the role and scope of organized interest groups in American public education. Indeed, a highly decentralized, local system such as we have may never be able to develop such a policy. Obligation to the ideal of "truth" is exceedingly hazardous and harrowing in a society whose many interest groups separately claim a monopoly on "truth." Moreover, in periods of crisis, when conformity itself is the test of truth, educational policy tends to be made by men with an ear to the ground. Unhappily, a Biblical narrative serves as an ironic reminder that a babble of tongues is followed by an epidemic of blindness!

Some Unfinished Business: Philosophies in Conflict

Mirroring the Great Society itself, modern theory of education is by no means in agreement as to its purposes, methods, or bases. The differences go far beyond the more practical controversies over traditional versus progressive methods, general versus specialized education, core curriculum versus uniform subject-matter curriculum, and so forth.[34] The different points of view basically revolve around the problem of the relationship of the

---

[33] For further discussion of this question, see Royce H. Knapp, "Social education and citizens' organizations," *Social Education* (1950), XIV: 166 ff.

[34] *Cf.* Report of the Harvard Committee, *General education in a free society* (Cambridge: Harvard University Press, 1943).

schools to a changing culture. Three philosophies of education, sharply marked off from each other, may be noted: reconstructionism, traditionalism, and what may be called adjustmentalism.[35]

The first group, among whom should be listed such writers on educational theory as W. H. Kilpatrick, John Dewey, Harold Rugg, J. H. Newlon, G. S. Counts, B. H. Bode, start from the commonplace observation that modern American society has undergone extensive and rapid change in the last half-century or so. "The crucial concepts of American culture," writes Rugg, "are those of the Great Technology."[36] These men are impressed by the tremendous impact on American life of the industrial revolution, of the rise of the scientific attitude, and of democracy as an ethical idea. They feel that the concept of change must enter into the philosophy and practice of education. Specifically, education "must itself assume increasing responsibility for projecting ideas of social change and taking part in their execution in order to be educative."[37] More emphatic is the assertion by Bode that the "primary concern of a democratic educational procedure is to stimulate a reconstruction of our beliefs and habits in the light of their mutual relationships. . . . " The goal of such a quest "has to do precisely with the remaking of standards; and if this fact is ignored, education becomes an instrument for maintaining the status quo."[38]

Traditionalism is not opposed to education for change but would discover the standards for reconstruction in tested experiences of the past. There is a traditionalism that finds the methodology of social change in the cultivation of eternal or perennial truth. Thus, Robert Maynard Hutchins argues syllogistically: (a) education is a process of imparting truth; (b) truth is absolute and universal; (c) education should be everywhere the same; it must draw its purposes out of the common elements in our common human nature.[39] Another type of traditionalism observes that since the schools are part of their environment, they are

---

[35] This discussion is based on I. B. Berkson, *Education faces the future* (New York: Harper and Brothers, 1943).

[36] Harold Rugg, *Culture and education in America* (New York: Harcourt, Brace and Company, 1931), p. 20.

[37] John Dewey, in W. H. Kilpatrick, ed., *Educational frontier* (New York: Appleton-Century-Crofts, 1933), p. 319.

[38] Bode, in *ibid.*, p. 19.

[39] *Cf.* Hutchins, *Higher learning in America* (New Haven: Yale University Press, 1936); Mortimer Adler, "God and the professors," *Vital Speeches* (1940), VII: 98 ff.; J. Maritain, *True humanism* (New York: Charles Scribner's Sons, 1938).

neither autonomous nor insulated: the environment changes first, education follows. The problem, therefore, is to reproduce so far as possible the norms and patterns of the prevailing social experience.[40]

A third philosophic view of modern education is premised on the psycho-biological observation that life-forms must, in order to survive, adjust to their environments. They must learn how to get on in their world. Education, then, must strive for adjustability to change, not for the latest change to be observed. Not preconceived patterns of reconstruction, but flexibility for a changing culture is the theme of such educational theorists as Morrison, Russell, Judd.[41]

In a moving and wise appraisal of the educational scene, Alexander Meiklejohn has summarized the situation of education in a world in transition.[42] His study has the virtue of being an organic or integrative philosophy of educational responsibilities. Discounting the traditional appeal to authoritarianism, he points out that a differentiated society has and insists on having many cultural authorities. A culture in change increases divisive interests. Yet men must find ways and means of living together in an ordered society. This task calls for an education in reasonableness; people who have, he says, common values to measure must find a common mode of measurement. It is not education for social change but for social *agreement* that a dynamic culture really needs. This philosophy does not have the reassuring certitude of the Hutchins-Adler medievalism nor the exciting fluidity of the Dewey-Rugg school. It does, however, have the value of pressing close to the outstanding problem of modern society: how to develop democratically a human community in an age of explosive and tyrannizing disunity.

QUESTIONS

1. What are the cultural expectations which shape the education of American youth?
2. Explain what is meant by the proposition that education in every society is free within the ideology of that society. Evaluate this proposition.

[40] *Cf.* I. L. Kandel, *Conflicting theories of education* (New York: The Macmillan Company, 1938).

[41] *Cf.* H. C. Morrison, *Curriculum of the common school* (Chicago: University of Chicago Press, 1940); J. D. Russell, and C. H. Judd, *American educational system* (Boston: Houghton Mifflin Company, 1940).

[42] Alexander Meiklejohn, *Education between two worlds* (New York: Harper and Brothers, 1942).

3. Identify the important features of public education in America.
4. Should educational policy be formulated primarily by professional people? Why?
5. What is the primary source of the financial difficulty of American schools? What are the various alternatives?
6. What are some of the outstanding consequences of the failure in public support of American education?
7. In terms of the democratic doctrine, outline the case against the dual system.
8. Should the schools use as teaching aids materials prepared by special-interest groups? Explain.
9. Outline the differences between the educational philosophies of reconstructionism, traditionalism, and adjustmentalism.
10. Evaluate these three philosophies of education in terms of the thesis that every culture imposes its own expectations upon the learning process.

REFERENCES

ALBERTY, H. B., and BODE, B. H., eds., *Educational freedom and democracy*. New York: Appleton-Century-Crofts, 1938.

BERKSON, I. B. *Education faces the future*. New York: Harper and Brothers, 1943.

BORSODI, R., *Education and living*. Suffern: School of Living, 1948.

CURTI, M. E., *Social ideas of American educators*. New York: Charles Scribner's Sons, 1935.

Educational Policies Commission, *Policies for education in American democracy*. Washington, D.C.: National Education Association, 1946.

FINE, B., *Our children are cheated*. New York: Henry Holt and Company, 1947.

HARRIS, S. E., *How shall we pay for education?* New York: Harper and Brothers, 1948.

HUTCHINS, R. M., *Higher learning in America*. New Haven: Yale University Press, 1936.

KARDINER, A., *Individual and his society*. New York: Columbia University Press, 1939.

MEYER, A. E., *Development of education in the twentieth century*. New York: Prentice-Hall, 1949.

MEIKLEJOHN, A., *Education between two worlds*. New York: Harper and Brothers, 1942.

MILLER, N. E., and DOLLARD, J., *Social learning and imitation*. New Haven: Yale University Press, 1941.

MORRISON, H. C., *Curriculum of the common school*. Chicago: University of Chicago Press, 1940.

CHAPTER 13

Racial Minorities and National Policy

What Is a Race?

Strictly speaking, the term *race* denotes a group of people set apart from all other groups by certain inherited physical traits. The term has nothing to do with culture, social status, or achievement. Cultural attainments and practices may differ among different races, but these are not criteria of race.

Difficulty of definition. The significance of defining the term *race* depends upon how many and what kinds of characteristics one wishes to include. If head shape is taken as a basis for racial distinction, then the white peoples might be classified roughly according to two racial types: the narrow-headed, comprising the Mediterranean peoples and the Nordic or North Europeans, and the broad-headed Alpines. This method of classification would also place the Hindu and the majority of pure Negro types in the racial category of the North European. There would be a very large number of individuals, furthermore, who could be placed as logically in one group as in another. The use of a different trait or set of traits would change the racial status of a large number of individuals. For example, if one selected texture of hair as the sole criterion of race, it would result in placing many light-skinned and dark-skinned persons in the same race. The difficulty arises as a result of the biological changes that people undergo, due to environmental pressures and the mixing of various types. Race mixture is by no means a strictly recent phenomenon, though it has been facilitated by modern means of trade and travel. As a consequence of long-continued intermingling of various peoples the world over, individual differences are frequently greater than the average differences between the so-called races. Thus, a strict adherence to certain biological traits as a basis for race determination would result in placing some members of the same family in different races. "The ideal arrangement would be to classify according to traits in which all the members of one group participate, and which are not shared by any individuals outside. Such a classification, however, is impossible since no trait is at one and the same time participated in by all the group and by no one outside."[1] The best that can be done, therefore, is to take a number of outstanding traits most common to one group and least common to all others. Such traits most commonly observed include hair texture, shape of nose, thickness of lips, and pigmentation. We should keep in mind that no race classification is rigid. Roughly, races fall into three major types: Negroid, or "black"; Mongoloids, or "yellow"; and Caucasoid, or "white." These may be divided further into subracial types, and there are still many peoples who cannot be classified with any of them, as, for example, the Papuans, the Australians, the Polynesians, and the Semi-Mongoloids.

Confusion of race and culture. Ordinarily people are not in the habit of looking at questions of race scientifically. The term is frequently charged with a psychological meaning which may have little connection with actual biological traits. Thus, one speaks of the Anglo-Saxon race, the Italian race, and the Germanic race. Equally unscientific is the tendency to classify as Negroes all Americans who are suspected of possessing the slightest strain of Negroid blood. As a matter of fact, Herskovits has shown that the traits of the average American Negro are as far removed from those of the pure Negroid types as they are from the Nordic type.[2] While biological changes have been going on in the case of the Negro, the various elements in the white population have been blending in the direction of new characteristics. The evidence is not absolutely conclusive, but it strongly suggests that the darker elements in the total population are tending to become lighter, while the lighter constituents are gradually becoming darker. Nevertheless, the old patterns of race prejudice persist, and peoples are classified not on the basis of actual biological traits but by preconceived notions about racial capacities. These notions have their origin in ethnocentricisms

[1] J. M. Reinhardt, and G. R. Davies, *Principles and methods of sociology* (New York: Prentice-Hall, 1932), p. 317.

[2] Melville Herskovits, *American Negro* (New York: Alfred A. Knopf, 1928), Ch. 3.

or feelings of race superiority, supported by limited observations of the cultural achievements of other peoples.

Racial Attitudes and Racial Intelligence

It is observed that race attitudes differ considerably with different racial groups. Wide variations in this respect are also found among members of the same race living under varying circumstances. In all cases, however, there appears to be a close relation between the degree of intensity of the antagonistic attitudes and the immediacy and directness of the economic competition between the two groups.

Expression of racial attitudes. The studies of Bogardus and others show that in general the attitudes of the dominant group seem to find expression along three major lines: first, there is a feeling of friendly interest in the new arrivals. Some degree of co-operation is likely to be developed, and the spirit of tolerance and good-will is in evidence. As the newcomers increase rapidly and competition becomes intensified, threatening to force the native workers out of employment, or to lower their standards of living, hostile attitudes arise. Various indirect means may be employed to undermine the strength of the new arrivals. The most successful of these is through legislation designed to limit the economic activities of the "minority" group. It may be done by a denial of citizenship rights, which carries with it certain limitations with respect to property ownership, education, mobility, and tenure. Whether or not satisfactory legislation can be secured, the native population generally seeks an advantage by means of local rules and customs. In all cases, also, nonlegal means are employed. The newcomers are described as a menace to native traditions, a threat to native standards of living and morality, and as "clannish and deceitful."

The third phase or line of activity is open conflict in which actual riots are staged, threats and warnings declared, property destroyed, and individuals murdered. Hostilities may not reach this extreme stage. It all depends upon the success of other methods to effect a satisfactory adjustment. Ordinarily, however, the final stage of activity is characterized by attitudes of relative indifference. This situation may be produced in several ways. Legislation and treaty arrangements may reduce the immigration to the point where tension is removed; the invaders may eliminate the aspects of conflict in the relationship by confining their activities to a restricted field; if of the same racial type as the native stock, a minority group may become merged in the general population. It is this last form of adjustment that places the racial group at a tremendous disadvantage. It cannot become merged in the general population because of differences in physical traits. Because of this distinction of physical traits the personalities of the racial group in a minority situation tend to conform to a type which oftentimes supports the unwarranted assumption of inherited mental traits on which the discriminatory attitudes are based. Such is the situation wherever slavery and caste prevail, except that in a rigid caste system personal relationships between some castes do not exist at all.

A similar pattern of behavior may be observed wherever large numbers of workers with relatively low standards of living are recruited to meet a demand for a type of labor considered too menial or dangerous for the native stock. Examples may be noted in the White-Mexican relations in certain seasonal industries in the United States. The individuals in such a group may assume an attitude of submissiveness on the basis of which a definite "superiority-inferiority" pattern is established. Ordinarily this is sufficient to maintain peaceful relations in the absence of abnormal disturbances. Sometimes the members of the invading race seek to develop business and occupational activities that serve their own group primarily and thus tend to reduce the contacts with the dominant group. Again, they may assume an attitude of restrained arrogance which often means a temporary peace.

Mr. Gonzolo describes the adjustment process of a Filipino immigrant in America as generally characterized by three attitudes. The first is a sense of adventurous optimism. America appears as the land of promise; then comes a period of inner conflict. East and West meet for the first time in his experience, and he is forcibly conscious of his color—custom plays against custom, tradition against tradition. "The frowning awnings of Chinatown—the allurements of sex, the fascination of the dance hall" offer release from the inner tension. Finally, if he belongs to the laboring class of Filipinos, as contrasted to the student group, the inner conflicts and repeated failures have "reduced to ashes" the enthusiasm of the earlier days. He settles down into a state of bewilderment, and his philosophy may be expressed in three words: "What of it?"[3] The history of race contacts in the

[3] D. F. Gonzolo, "Social adjustments of Filipinos in America," *Sociology and Social Research*, XIV: 166.

United States furnishes numerous examples of the characteristic attitudes summarized in the foregoing discussion. We shall now consider some of the more important factors in the race problems of the United States.

Relative capacities of races. Many people believe that some races are superior to other races in native ability. Those who hold this position account for differences in achievement between races in terms of differences in racial inheritance. There is, on the other hand, a growing number of students, particularly in the fields of sociology and anthropology, who hold that if differences in native capacity between races exist at all, there is not enough scientific evidence accumulated on the subject to prove it.

Unfortunately, people have rarely been in the habit of dealing with the problems of race in a scientific way. In this matter, as in many others that affect human relations, emotions run high and prejudices are keen. Consequently, what people think about each other is mainly determined by the strength of individual and group egotism and not by the painful accumulation of facts bearing upon the situation. It is extremely difficult to prove or to disprove satisfactorily that one race of people is superior in native ability to another, mainly for the reason that there is no way of completely isolating cultural influences and studying them apart from biological inheritance. The cultural disadvantages are especially difficult to measure in the case of the Negro in America, because the influences that operate against him are so subtle as to be easily overlooked entirely by the untrained observer and by no means fully appreciated by the experienced investigator. Let us examine briefly some of the arguments that have been used in support of the theory of racial differences in native ability.

Measurements of intelligence. The results of intelligence tests have been widely interpreted as indicating fundamental differences in the native capacities of different races. An examination of a large number of intelligence scores of whites and Negroes tends, on the whole, to give the whites a superior showing. Do these scores, however, prove superior racial inheritance? There are a number of factors that must be considered before such a conclusion is warranted.

In the first place, the definition of race is largely psychological. The tests have generally not been correlated with actual racial traits as determined by anthropological measurements. A number of investigators, particularly Estabrook, Garth, Klineberg, and Herskovits,[4] have emphasized this point. An attempt to correlate intelligence with racial traits without knowing the extent of such traits may seem to strengthen existing notions about racial superiorities and inferiorities, but it is not science. Furthermore, a definite correlation between physical traits and the results of intelligence measurements does not establish a necessary causal relation between them. Other factors that are not evaluated in the tests may be important. For example, we know that racial discrimination affects seriously the physical and mental status of a people. It limits opportunity in practically all directions which, according to the standards of the "superior" or dominant race, indicate exceptional merit. The ideal test situation would be to have two or more groups distinguished by racial traits that in no sense cause discrimination. Such a situation does not exist in the United States or, completely, anywhere else.

Klineberg reports median IQ scores, from a number of students, for racial and national groups as follows: American Indian, 78; American Negro, 84; Mexican, 85; Italian, 85; Chinese, 97; Japanese, 99.[5] The upper score in the IQ range followed the median score, though the highest score for the Mexican and Italian groups was 96; it was 97 for the American Indian, 99 for the American Negro, and 114 for the Japanese. In all cases, however, the range from lowest to highest score was wide.

Cultural factors and intelligence ratings. Superior and inferior individuals are found in all groups. Garth reported an Indian girl of twelve in a southwestern school who had an IQ of 142; a Mexican child in San Antonio scored 144, while four Negroes in Dallas ranged from 125 to 129. Garth concluded that differences in the average intelligence of races as suggested by the tests "can be easily explained by influences of nurture and of selection. The low IQ's of such racial groups as the Negroes and the Indians are undoubtedly due to these factors."[6] This statement seems warranted, especially in view of the fact that some Negroes have made higher ratings than some whites. These

---

[4] G. H. Estabrook, "Proposed technique for the investigation of racial differences in intelligence," *American Naturalist*, 1928, CXII: 76–87; T. R. Garth, *Race psychology* (New York: McGraw-Hill Book Company, 1931); Melville Herskovits, *American Negro* (New York: Alfred A. Knopf, 1928); Otto Klineberg, "Mental testing of racial and national groups," Ch. 6 in: H. S. Jennings, et al, *Scientific aspects of the race problem* (Washington, D.C.: Catholic University of America, 1941).

[5] Jennings, et al, *op. cit.*, p. 25.

[6] *Ibid.*, pp. 83–85.

ratings, furthermore, have been correlated with school standards, language difficulties, conditions surrounding the tests, physical well-being, and various indexes of cultural opportunity.

Aside from the obvious fact that the education of these so-called "inferior" types has never really been seriously undertaken on a magnificent scale, there is the more potent factor of race prejudice, which operates in numerous ways to keep the doors of opportunity closed against them. It should be noted, furthermore, that the complex of traits comprising the cultural backgrounds of the relatively retarded racial groups in the United States differs widely from that of the whites. As a consequence of these factors, the values as well as the means of achieving them will differ also.

People the world over seek to attain desirable ends by whatever means they have. Both the means and the ends desired are parts of the social heritage. If we could measure accurately the weight of these factors, we might be able to account for differences in reactions to the white man's tests without resorting to fundamental differences in native ability. The Negro lives side by side with the white man and under the same government. Nevertheless, the social distances based largely upon consideration of status (*i.e.*, feelings of inequality, of superiority and inferiority) arising out of prejudice and original advantage are so great as to account for almost any amount of difference in intelligence. Generally, white people are ready to accept physical isolation as sufficient to explain the relative backwardness of members of their own race. This explanation has been offered with respect to the cultural lags in some mountainous parts of the United States. The studies of Park, Burgess, Bogardus, and others confirm the view long held by some sociologists that "social distance" is a fundamental factor in the development of the personality.

The relations between the white people and other races in the United States are maintained largely through economic inter-dependencies that are not accompanied by a mutual interest in each other's well-being. This is particularly true of the native whites and the Negroes. The racial attitudes are based upon feelings of "superiority" and "inferiority." In general, it may be said that the achievements in culture and finance that contribute to white prestige tend to lower the standing of the Negro in the estimation of the whites. The prevalent attitudes toward colored peoples influence the administrative policies of business and education to an extent hardly realized. Department stores, for instance, dare not put colored girls behind the counters, regardless of the particular attitudes of the manager. In some cities Negroes may be motormen on streetcars, but not conductors. School administrators where various races attend the same schools are aware of the complex and delicate problems that arise out of racial attitudes among students.

In view of the results of experimental studies it can no longer be doubted that slight changes in environment affecting the social and economic status of the individual, the food supply, accessibility to medical care, and so on may produce significant changes in intellectual ability. Professor Freeman and his associates showed by one of the most careful studies yet made that changes in environment are reflected in changes in intelligence scores[7] and, also, that the influences of the environment tend to vary with the age of the individual. The younger the child when subjected to the new environment, the greater the effect upon his personality and capacity. Burks concluded from an experimental study of 204 foster children that hereditary factors were by far the more important; nevertheless, she felt that "home environment contributes about 17 per cent of the IQ."[8] While Burks does not attach so much importance to environment as Freeman and his co-workers, even so, a variance of 17 per cent attributable by her to family influence might easily account for the difference between a moron and a normal individual. It should be observed, furthermore, that a statement of family influences upon the intelligence of children—assuming that both the intelligence and the weight of the family environment have been accurately measured, which seems unwarranted—by no means explains the effects of environment upon intelligence limitations. Racial environments are not family environments.

Recent experimental work has tended to make untenable efforts to explain mental achievement in terms of specifically measurable quantities of heredity and environment. Achievement is viewed as an emergent product of an interactional system.[9]

[7] F. M. Freeman, et al, "Influence of environment on the intelligence, school achievement, and conduct of foster children," *27th year book national society for the study of education*, 1928, Part I, pp. 103–217.

[8] Barbara Stoddard Burks, "Relative influence of nature and nurture upon mental development: A comparative study of foster parent-foster child resemblance and true parent-child resemblance," *ibid.*, pp. 219–309.

[9] See Gardner Murphy, *Personality: A bio-cultural approach* (New York: Harper and Brothers, 1947).

Intelligence correlated with racial traits. It often has been asserted as evidence of racial superiorities and inferiorities that the degree of intelligence is inversely proportionate to the extent of Negroid characteristics. The relatively superior achievements of those with white skins have been cited as an example. In order to test this claim Melville Herskovits correlated the intelligence-test scores of 115 college students with Negroid traits as determined by anthropometric measurements supplemented by genealogical histories. Herskovits divided the individuals into four classes according to: width of nostril; thickness of lips; white element in skin color; black element in skin color.[10] The correlation of these traits with the results of intelligence tests should have significance, though it must be admitted that obvious differences in degrees of pigmentation do affect one's social and business standing in his own group, as well as his chances for relatively successful contact with the whites. Herskovits and other students of Negro life have demonstrated this fact beyond doubt. Nevertheless, the individuals comprising the groups studied had at least one significant cultural advantage in common: they were all college students. Test scores were correlated with each trait and the same number of individuals, 115, were represented in each correlation. In no case were the correlations significant as showing a lower degree of intelligence with greater degree of Negroid traits. Herskovits concludes:

> We are forced to recognize, therefore, that the relationship between test scores and physical traits denoting greater or less amounts of Negro blood is so tenuous as to be of no value in drawing conclusions as to the comparative native ability or relative intelligence of the Negro when compared to the white. This leads us to recognize further that general conclusions of this type which have been made have resulted from insufficient analyses of the data in hand, or from lack of proper genealogical data.
>
> If, then, we draw our conclusions from the material discussed above, we may say:
> 1. That the hypothesis of less Negro intelligence and social efficiency when compared to whites, which has been generally accepted from results in psychological tests, must be further tested by the acceptability of its logical corollaries.
> 2. That the first of these, that in mixture, a group of those individuals having more white blood is innately superior to a

[10] Melville J. Herskovits, *Negro and the intelligence tests* (Hanover: Sociological Press, 1928).

group of those having more Negro blood, is to be severely questioned in the light of the correlations computed in this study.

3. That the second of these, that it is possible to place individuals on the bases of anthropological traits, such as skin color, with sufficient accuracy to bring groups together to study the problem of effects of intermixture in varying degree, without the use of genealogies, is also to be gravely doubted because of the large overlapping in any traits which may be selected as criteria.

4. That the assumption that there is not sufficient discrimination within the Negro group against those individuals showing emphasized Negroid traits, particularly skin color, to cause differences in social environment which would affect the mean standings of groups selected on the basis of these traits is also to be highly questioned.

That in the light of the findings in this paper, the basic hypothesis of white superiority in general social efficiency and innate intelligence is to be gravely doubted, and that the results obtained by Ferguson are sufficiently contradicted by the results in this paper to render them subject to the most searching criticism and thorough further checking up before they may be utilized.[11]

We conclude, therefore, that at the present time the results of the intelligence tests have not established beyond doubt the innate inferiority of any race. The results of Garth's comprehensive studies strongly support this conclusion. Garth and his students administered the national intelligence test to 1004 Mexicans, 1313 full-blood Indians, 942 mixed-blood Indians, and 1272 Southern Negroes. Garth concluded from these studies that intelligence-test scores can be changed by authentic measures and also that further experimental studies—similar to those conducted by Freeman and his associates—are necessary among children of the colored peoples before any group may be branded as "inferior."[12]

The ebb and flow of cultural achievement. As Dr. Ruth Benedict has so strikingly pointed out, racial achievements in particular directions rise and fall from age to age and do not follow consistently any particular race over a vast stretch of time. It was the vikings who were the aggressors on the seas in the ninth century. The Japanese were a peaceful, subdued people during more than a thousand years of recorded history. Prior to Japan's

---

[11] *Ibid.*
[12] See also J. M. Reinhardt, and G. R. Davies, *Principles and methods of sociology* (New York: Prentice-Hall, 1932), Ch. 12, for a summary of data on intelligence tests and race.

entry into world commerce, ocean-going boats were even forbidden by imperial decree. The long-subdued traits of the Japanese were accepted by the more aggressive peoples of the West as qualities of race.[13] These people, the Japanese, have engaged in six international conflicts of arms since 1853, and interestingly enough, according to a radio report December 12, 1941, the leader of one of the late Axis partners in Europe explained that the Japanese were "yellow Aryans."

It should be noted also that the builders of the same cultures have certainly not always been of the same race, and, as Benedict points out, the same races have not always shared the same cultures. If one follows any great complex of culture traits, on which our modern civilization depends, through its long history, he will find its origins and developmental stages in other races than his own. This is true of mathematics, the processing of steel, the printing press, and the cultivation and use of grains, as of many other complexes. It is essential, if we are going to understand and appreciate the possibilities of race, and of a co-operative social order where different races live together, that we approach the problem historically and with the objectivity of the anthropologist. From this point of view we should find, as Benedict has emphasized, that the devotees of race "superiority" make no attempt to justify their claims by the "civilizing" influences of *all* the members of their own race, wherever found. They point only to those who exemplify their ideals. In the long history of human achievement and failure, the spokesmen of every race have been in position at some time or other to ask legitimately: "Little man, what now?"

The Negro Population of the United States

Race problems in the United States are affected by the extent and distribution of the various racial groups in the total population. This may be noted in the changing racial attitudes of whites in regions where an increase in the colored population has produced keen competition between races along various lines. Racial antagonisms may be intensified also by attempts of minority races to rise in the social and economic scale. This is seen in the increased attempts on the part of whites in some sections to limit the occupational status of colored people through legal and other means. The nature of these antagonisms, the basis on which they rest, and some important social consequences will be dis-

[13] Ruth Benedict, *Race: Science and politics* (New York: The Viking Press, 1940).

cussed in the following pages. Let us first study the Negro population in this country.

Trends in Negro population. During the ninety years from 1860 to 1950, the Negro population in the United States increased from 4,441,830 to almost 13,000,000. This growth has been due mainly to the increase of births over deaths. The fact that the births outnumbered the deaths was not so much due to a low death rate as to a high birth rate. In spite of the tremendous growth in the Negro population, the actual rate of increase has not kept pace with the growth of the white population.

Whereas the white population has increased more than fourfold, the Negro population has made a gain of hardly threefold. In 1790 the Negro population comprised about 20 per cent of the total population, in 1860 slightly more than 13 per cent, and in 1950 about 10 per cent. The greater increase of whites as compared to the Negro population is explained partly by the lower mortality rate among white people, due to better health conditions, better education, and better economic standing. The difference is also to be accounted for in part by the influx of white immigrants from Europe during the period. It is noteworthy that while the rate of increase for whites was somewhat higher than that for colored during the half-century prior to 1914, one result of immigration restriction has been to give the total colored population a slightly advantageous position with respect to rate of increase. The bearing of immigration restriction laws on the problem is suggested by the fact that in the first four years of the period the white increases more than kept pace with the colored.[14]

Distribution and migration. The way Negroes are distributed throws light on where the race problem is likely to be most intense.

First, the Old South has the most Negroes, but the proportion is decreasing. That proportion was 92.2 per cent of the nation's Negroes in 1860, but it has decreased to about 70 (estimated) per cent in 1950. The 10 million Negroes of the South are distributed approximately as follows: the eight South Atlantic states (Delaware to Florida, including West Virginia) have about 48 per cent, nearly half; the four East South Central states, about 28 per cent; and the four West South Central states, 24 per cent.

Second, the ratio of Negroes in the population of the South is

[14] T. J. Woofter, "Racial and ethnic groups," in: President's Research Committee on Social Trends, *Recent social trends in the United States* (New York: McGraw-Hill Book Company, 1933), Vol. I, pp. 553–554.

comparatively very large. In 1950 Negroes comprised approximately 27 per cent of the inhabitants of the South Atlantic division; 23.8 per cent of those of the East South Central; and 18 per cent of those of the West South Central states, but only about 10 per cent of the national population. The Negro population is relatively dense in certain Southern states and sections. One state, Mississippi, is slightly over 50 per cent Negro; South Carolina nearly 46 per cent Negro; and three states (Georgia, Louisiana, and Alabama) have a Negro percentage of between 35 and 40. One county in Mississippi is about 86 per cent Negro, while many others in the "Black Belt," which extends from Texas to Virginia in the richer agricultural parts of intervening states, run as much as 65 to 70 per cent. In about one fourth of the area of Mississippi the population is almost three fourths Negroes.

Third, there is a large migration of Negroes out of the Old South, especially out of the east Mississippi region. In 1920, there were only five Northern states with 100,000 or more Negroes, while thirty years later there were eight. Four Northern states—New York, Illinois, Ohio, and Pennsylvania—had more than a quarter million Negroes each in 1850. The Negro increase in the Northern states between 1920 and 1950 was more than 66 per cent, while the gain in the South amounted to close to 8 per cent. The fact that the industrialized areas are absorbing an increasing number of the Negro population raises new points of racial tension and throws problems of racial adjustment into the arena of industrial conflict.

Discriminatory Attitudes and Treatment

Attitude of whites following Civil War. The close of the War Between the States left the Negro bound by a slave culture which could not be thrown off by an executive decree. Moreover, the outcome of the war did not change the attitude of the white people toward the Negro in a way favorable to his economic and social progress. The white people continued to think of the Negro as incapable of any real cultural and economic achievement. Consequently he was not given the opportunity to learn how to participate in the affairs of community and state. His ultimate advance was further impeded by the attitudes of the North following the Civil War. As in the case of all postwar periods, emotions ran high. The people of the North had little confidence in the humanitarian motives of the South; they suspected that the Negro was being intimidated and suppressed. Having little practical understanding of the Negro's actual situation, they could see no other reason for his failure to participate at once in the affairs of state. They therefore set about forcing the hand of the Southern whites through political pressure. This behavior on the part of the North intensified the hatred between the two sections, and it increased the Southern fear of Negro dominance. It is, of course, impossible to evaluate adequately the far-reaching handicaps resulting from these cultural influences. We know, however, that they are important.

Discriminatory treatment of racial groups. Discrimination against the minority racial groups manifests itself in numerous, and oftentimes subtle, forms. It is reflected in the relatively poor schools, short terms, and low-paid teachers in sections where the races are educated separately and in the attitudes of white children toward Negroes where they attend the same schools. It may be observed in the efforts to prevent Negroes, for example, from expanding into desirable residential sections in cities. New residential subdivisions are sometimes sold under contracts that no person of African descent shall be permitted to occupy the area; property owners frequently sign agreements not to rent or sell to Negroes. As a consequence of these attitudes, the Negroes are often crowded into undesirable sections regardless of the family's cultural or economic status. The fact that property values rise when Negroes seek entrance to a new residential section and fall rapidly when the invasion begins is to a large extent a reflection of discrimination.

Many industries of the South and businesses of the North do not hire Negroes except in the lowest-paying jobs, such as janitors, cleaners, and porters. This discrimination rests upon prejudice rather than ability, as indicated by the fact that some industries that regularly hire Negroes in the North refuse to hire them for similar jobs in the South. These firms simply reflect the current attitudes of the dominant group in the territory in which they operate. Since the Negro is forced to seek employment from white men, he must accept it on the white man's terms. The terms may indicate the racial prejudice of the employer, and they are almost certain to reflect the attitudes of those who patronize his business.

It is still a common practice to bar Negroes from all athletic games engaged in between Northern and Southern institutions. There is hardly a single field of activity, military, professional, cultural, occupational, financial, or social, in which Negroes are not the objects of discrimination. These discriminations are important factors in the economic and cultural status of the Negro. All over the United States, ambitious Negroes seem to have relatively little chance to succeed in business or professional life except in largely segregated and comparatively self-sufficient Negro groups and communities. Elsewhere, the strong tendency is to limit them to inferior positions. Their finest lawyers, doctors, teachers, and nurses cannot obtain a clientele among white people.

Negro Education and Illiteracy

It has long been held by many people that Negroes are incapable of a high degree of intellectual achievement. Such claims frequently have been matched by regulations and rules which prevented the Negro from getting what it was claimed he did not have the brains to acquire.

Attitudes previous to the Civil War.   As early as 1740, South Carolina passed a law forbidding anyone to teach or cause to be taught any slave or to employ one as a "scribe in any manner of writing whatever." Later Georgia, in addition to punishing the teacher, imposed a fine of $500, imprisonment, and whipping on the Negro—free or slave—so instructed. Laws of similar character were passed in other states up to the middle of the 19th century. In 1835 North Carolina abolished its schools for free Negroes and decreed that descendants from Negroes to the fourth generation should not share its public school system.[15] The hostility toward Negro education was by no means confined to the South. The border states restricted the facilities for the education of "blacks." According to Johnson, Negroes in some Northern states frequently received such harsh treatment that they petitioned for separate schools. In one Northern state, attempts to maintain a school for Negroes resulted in mob violence, arrest of the teacher, and final legislation against the enterprise.[16]

Attitudes following the Civil War.   Following the Civil War the South was placed in a tremendously difficult position with reference to Negro education. A considerable proportion of the Southern citizenry felt the need for extending some sort of education to the Negroes, though there was general disbelief in their native capacity to become educated according to white standards.

[15] C. S. Johnson, *Patterns of Negro segregation*, p. 225, in: Myrdal, et al, *Negro in American life* series (New York: Harper and Brothers, 1944).
[16] *Ibid.*, p. 225.

It was also felt by many whites in the South that such education as could be attained would be wholly undesirable. Among the oppressed classes there was generally bitter opposition to any sort of education for the Negro. The objection was usually sustained on the grounds of racial incapacity. It was argued that the Negro could only imitate, he could never really become educated. Attempts to educate him would simply "spoil him." Underneath these expressed reasons was probably real fear of Negro competition. These poorer elements in the white population, long held down by competition with slave labor, saw a chance to rise by denying to their old competitors privileges which they claimed for themselves. Other factors hindered the extension of education to the Negro.

The data presented on intelligence tests and racial abilities suggest strongly that prolonged educational discrimination against the Negro may have a profound bearing upon the intelligence showing, as indicated by the tests. Since some writers have overlooked these cultural influences in interpreting the results of test measurements, it may well be that in many instances they have served to bolster the existing prejudices and to increase, in a relative sense at least, the discrimination against the Negro.

As noted above, the North failed utterly to see the Southern point of view and fully to appreciate the magnitude of the South's problem. It sought to force its own standards of education upon the Negro and to assign him responsibilities which he was in no position to meet. As a consequence, the first attempts to educate the Negro were discouraging. He was given a smattering of theological and classical literature—superficial knowledge which did not help him very much to make a living, but which did tend to confirm the claims of some Southerners that "trying to educate a Negro was a waste of time." These results dampened whatever interest had existed in Negro education in the South and increased suspicions between the two sections of the country. The situation was rendered still more tense because of the financial burdens left to the South by the Civil War.

Pioneer work and present status.   The pioneer work in Negro education came in the years between 1854 and 1870. During these years eighteen colleges were established by white leaders from the North. These represented to a large extent the cooperative enterprises of churches, missionary organizations, and philanthropists. States had little interest in such education at this time.

When the hand of the North was lifted following the "Reconstruction," Southern hostility began to manifest itself in the abandonment of the North's educational program. Largely as a result of the abandonment of the policies instituted by the North, the Freedman's Bureau, together with private philanthropy, assumed a large share of the responsibility for Negro education which had originally been intended for the states. The Freedmen's Bureau was created in 1865 mainly to assist the Negro in the adjustment process. It contributed largely to the establishment of Negro public schools. Its most outstanding adventure, however, was the establishing of Howard University in Washington, D.C. in 1867. Between 1870 and 1890 nine land-grant colleges for Negroes were established, besides thirteen Negro denominational colleges.

The most important period in the evolution of Negro education, however, runs from 1890 to the present time. During this period numerous teachers' colleges and state normal schools have been established, both by public effort and by private agencies. Moreover, several recent Supreme Court decisions have affirmed the Negro's rights to absolute equality of educational opportunity in public institutions for advanced study.

Within the past two decades there has been a shift of about 20 per cent of Negro children of school age to the North. This fact has contributed largely to raising the average level of Negro education. The effects of poor schooling upon the retardation of Negro children is indicated by statistics showing that from 15 to more than 20 per cent of the pupils transferred to the schools of the North from Southern states were retarded three or more years.

There has been a gradual tendency for the state to assume more and more responsibility with respect to Negro education, especially in the elementary branches. This has been due largely, no doubt, to the increasing interest in public education and to the activities of various agencies such as the General Education Board and the Julius Rosenwald Fund. The General Education Board has made some direct appropriations for Negro education in the South. It has also raised the general level of Negro education through subsidizing Negro school supervisors in all of the Southern states. The Julius Rosenwald Fund was established in 1917. A large proportion of this fund has been used to improve educational opportunities for Negroes in the South. By 1936 over 5000 Rosenwald school units had been built in the South at a total cost of more than thirty million dollars. Approximately 44 per cent of this amount was raised by the Negroes themselves. Contributions from white individuals and public money made up 40 per cent, and the Fund gave 16 per cent.

Discrimination and school achievement. The illiteracy rate is relatively high among Negroes. The rate is higher also in the rural districts than in the cities. The highest rates of Negro illiteracy are found in the Southern states which maintain separate schools for Negroes. This is not surprising when one remembers that the Southern states in which a segregated school system prevails are as a whole far below the national average in per capita wealth and income. It is significant, moreover, that with its relatively low level of income and the practice of maintaining two school systems instead of one the proportion of children of school age in the Southern states is larger than the national average. Seventeen Southern states, and the District of Columbia, with less than 35 per cent of the national population and with hardly more than 30 per cent of the nation's income, have almost 40 per cent of the nation's school children. It is perhaps not realized generally that the South spends a greater proportion of its total income on public education than do the more wealthy states. Mississippi, for instance, was recently spending 3.41 per cent of its income for education as compared with an expenditure of 2.61 per cent by New York state. Nevertheless, this meant $400 per class unit in Mississippi and $4100 in New York.[17]

Hence it may be seen that while both white and colored children in the South suffer educational disadvantages, the handicaps fall heavier upon the Negro children because of discrimination in a segregated school system. The President's Committee on Civil Rights found evidences of discrimination against the colored children by every comparison. Whether the test was expenditure per pupil, teachers' salaries, number of pupils per teacher, school transportation facilities, buildings and equipment, school term, or curricula offerings, the colored children were at a marked disadvantage.

It should be noted, however, that the South recognized these discrepancies, their causal conditions, and the problems which they help to create. The progress made in the South during the past two decades toward reducing the educational inequalities between white and colored children has been encouraging. For

---

[17] The President's Committee on Civil Rights, *Right to education*, Oct. 29, 1947 (Washington, D.C.: Government Printing Office), pp. 62–67, 166–167.

instance, in the four years between 1940 and 1944 alone, the average difference in length of school terms was cut from about 15 days to less than 10 days. In the same period the excess colored-pupil load was reduced from almost 9 to 6.

The racial inequalities that prevail in the public school systems are to be found, also, in private schools and in institutions of higher learning whether public or private.

As already observed, racial inequalities of educational opportunity lie deeply imbedded in the structure and character of racial prejudice. They are related to social and economic discriminatory attitudes. They have profound and far-reaching effects upon the physical and mental health of individuals and upon the total strength and security of the nation. They thus become matters of national policy.

It was the opinion of the President's committee that the problem of educational opportunity in the South is not one that the South alone can solve adequately. It is not merely a matter of overcoming prejudice. Even if segregation were abolished, there would remain the reality of an inadequate economic base. This fact will continue to be reflected in unequal educational opportunities, regardless of race, until the national government takes effective steps to remedy the situation through some extension of systems of federal grants-in-aid for educational purposes. A measure designed to attack the problem through federal assistance came before the 81st Congress but did not secure passage.

It is seen that discrimination manifests itself in numerous ways in the Northern states where school segregation is not practiced. It is shown, for instance, in the relative ease by which Negro children can secure work permits, the differential attitudes toward the enforcement of truancy laws, and inside the schoolroom in the way individual recognition is apportioned.

Much of the difficulty lies deep in the economic and social strata of our cultural life. Poverty and wealth are always selective forces. The Negroes have far more of their share of poverty and hence feel its sifting influences in school as elsewhere. Moreover, the difficulties of finding full use of educational skills is greater for Negroes than for whites, and surely these difficulties affect the attitude and counsel of the teacher and the *maturation* of the student.

Higher Education for Negroes

The general public has been comparatively slow in the support of higher education for Negroes by taxation. In the North,

Negroes are admitted to state-supported schools with the whites. In the South, where a separate system of schools prevails, Negroes have depended mainly upon privately supported colleges. A few private institutions, such as Tuskegee in Alabama and Hampton in Virginia, are heavily endowed and well equipped. The great majority of Negro colleges, however, and particularly those under denominational control, are poverty-stricken institutions with inadequately trained teachers and poor equipment.

Financial status of Negro colleges. Federal Supreme Court decisions have established the right of Negroes to have as good public provisions for higher education as are enjoyed by whites in the same jurisdictions. Actual attainment of this right, however, depends largely on local sentiment and hence is rarely enjoyed. A few endowed colleges for Negroes provide good facilities, but even these are far below the standards that prevail for whites. In 1940 only three endowed institutions for higher learning for Negroes had endowments of two million dollars or more, and their combined endowments amounted to hardly more than twenty million dollars. These three institutions—Fisk, Hampton, and Tuskegee—are all in the South, where Negroes are not admitted to schools with whites. In that general area, Duke University alone had almost thirty-five million dollars of endowment, and there are at least nineteen other privately supported colleges for whites with endowments of more than two million dollars each, three of them having more than ten million dollars each and one having more than twenty-five million dollars. While Negroes comprise close to 30 per cent of the total population in the area considered, they do not comprise a similar proportion of potential students under existing economic conditions.

About 70 per cent of the appropriations of the General Education Board for Negro schools and colleges up to June 30, 1935 went to the five major educational centers: Atlanta University and co-operating colleges, in Georgia; Fisk University and Meharry Medical College, Nashville, Tennessee; Hampton Institute, in Virginia; Howard University, in Washington, D.C.; and Tuskegee Institute, in Alabama.[18] Among these institutions, Hampton has an endowment of ten million dollars, Tuskegee about seven millions, Atlanta over five, and Fisk about four and a half.[19] An effort is being made to distribute the money among strategically located schools, able to render regional service.

[18] *Negro year book*, 1937–1938: 193–194.
[19] *World almanac*, 1951, p. 577.

Needs and possibilities in Negro health. The Negro death rate is higher than that for whites in the country as a whole. In the cities it is almost twice as high and approximately one and a half times as high in the rural districts. Nevertheless, the Negro life expectancy has increased from 33 to better than 50 within the past forty years. This is a remarkable accomplishment and tends to confirm the view that the problem of Negro health is mainly a question of scientific disease control in the same sense as is recognized for the white people.

If it be assumed that the Negro, because of racial traits, is handicapped in the fight against disease, it must be remembered that in this country the term "Negro" includes all people with any trace of Negro blood. A large proportion, variously estimated to be from 20 to 70 per cent of American Negroes, have white blood. Many of these have more white blood than Negro blood. Some are almost totally white. Some investigators in this field are inclined to the position that it is not correct to speak of the American Negro as an African. One study showed that the Negro in America represents a blending of all the traits that characterize a diverse ancestry and that on the whole his combined traits are about halfway between the averages for the white population and the African.[20]

Any program of adjustment adopted on the theory that the susceptibility to disease of the Negro differs fundamentally from that of whites will necessarily be applied to large numbers of people who are more white than Negro. Moreover, the value of social measures for health protection as applied to any race in the United States has been demonstrated, and we know that the Negroes have not shared this sort of protection equally with whites.

Among the causes of the relatively high death rate among Negroes must be listed extreme poverty. Poverty does many injurious things to children. It sends mothers to factory and field, it generates ignorance, and creates inability to pay doctors and to provide proper care for children, including food and other physical necessities. Rickets, a hunger disease, is much higher among Negro children than among white children. The poverty factor in the Negro's health status is emphasized in a study by Charles Johnson which showed that in 1929 when 9 per cent of the white employables were without work, 15.7 per cent of the Negroes were unemployed. During the depression years the

[20] Melville J. Herskovits, *American Negro, op. cit.*

Negro's economic problem became even more acute, as evidenced by the following unemployment percentages: whites, 39.7 per cent; and Negroes, 56 per cent.[21]

The infant mortality rate among Negroes accounts in part for their high mortality rate. Everywhere in the country both infant and maternal death rates are higher for Negroes than for whites.

Until the economic and cultural status of the masses of Negroes is brought up to the level of the masses of whites, their health may be expected to remain relatively low. At any rate, this is what may be expected unless fundamental changes are made in the administration of public-health service or in the individual use of economic and cultural advantages for the preservation of health.

The Economic Status and Progress of the Negro

Negroes live in low-income areas. In 1946 the average per capita income in ten Southern states was about $750, the lowest of any major section in the country and lower than any state outside the South. In fact, the highest per capita income state among the ten Southern states was lower than the lowest per capita income state outside the South. It is not necessary to resort to differences in native abilities to explain the relatively lower average income of the Negro population. The Negro population has been concentrated in the Southern states which were left impoverished at the close of the Civil War and never have shared equally with other sections in the fruits of industrial expansion.

It hardly can be argued that low wages in the South are due alone to the low earning capacity of Negroes, since the lowest-paying industry outside agriculture is textile manufacture, which employs almost no Negroes. The figures on national wealth show that the states of the Old South with the exception of Florida have the lowest per capita wealth of any state in the country. Thus, it is observed that the majority of Negroes live in the section of the country which has received the smallest share of the nation's accumulated wealth, and, also, that the great majority of Negroes in this section are engaged in the form of industry, namely agriculture, which has received the lowest incomes and retained the smallest per capita wealth of all the important industries of the South.[22]

[21] Charles S. Johnson, *Economic status of the Negro* (Nashville: Fisk University Press, 1933), p. 19.
[22] *Statistical abstract of the U. S.*, 1948, pp. 278–291.

Historic background of the South's economy. It may be argued that the economic lag of agriculture in the South is due to the inferior native ability of the Negro, which has retarded progress in that section. This position seems difficult to support in the light of the facts.

The fundamental factors of opportunity are not taken into account. The agricultural system of the South early discouraged manufacturing in that region. In 1800 New England manufactured only 500 bales of Southern-grown cotton; fifteen years later, her mills were requiring 90,000 bales a year. Before 1830 Massachusetts alone was operating more than 250 mills, and New England had more than $100,000,000 invested in manufacturing establishments. By 1840 New England produced three fourths of all cotton goods manufactured in the United States. Nor was Northern industry confined to textile goods. Most of the food, clothing, and equipment used by Southern planters came from the North or through Northern cities. In this way "King Cotton" enriched Northern cities and attracted a large proportion of poor, but energetic, free laborers to that section. On the eve of the War Between the States, New York was importing twice as much as she was exporting, while port cities in the Old South were exporting from two to five times as much as they were importing. Nevertheless, the North held a favorable balance. Less than one third of the returns on cotton that went through New Orleans was lodged in the banks of that city. On the other hand, port cities in the North always showed deposits in excess of the value of their exports. In 1850 the total bank deposits of the cotton states amounted to only $20,000,000. Yet in the same year the South's agricultural products sold for almost $120,000,-000.[23] The fact that half the population in the South was considered property made the per capita wealth of that section appear huge in comparison with the North. As a matter of fact, this enormous investment in human beings represented fictitious wealth. In reality it was unemployed capital, since free men, under conditions that provide for the expression of inventive genius and skill, are more valuable to society that are men held in bondage. The rapid spread of the plantation system in the Old South depleted the soil and concentrated incomes by forcing the landless and small-propertied classes to lower economic levels. In 1850 one thousand families received almost as much in-

[23] William E. Dodd, *Cotton kingdom* (New Haven: Yale University Press), pp. 10, 11, 28, 29, 109.

come as the combined incomes of the remaining 660,000 white families.[24]

Thus, intense poverty was an established fact for the vast majority of whites in the South prior to 1861. The Emancipation Proclamation added almost 4,000,000 free propertyless persons to the Southland. The resources of the South had been drained by the Civil War. Thus, we may picture the Negro population starting, theoretically at least, "on its own," only three short generations ago, utterly without property, in an impoverished land, handicapped by a slave culture, and beset by the prejudices of the whites. Hitherto the Negro had never learned to acquire for himself or provide for his future. His status in the economic order was marked by generations of bondage. He might work in the fields or in the kitchen, he might wait on table and, under certain circumstances, be a barber, but the odds against him in the managerial, professional, and skilled pursuits were insurmountable. Even today, Negroes who seek work in competition with whites face difficulties. They may do the work of whites in department stores, but they must wear the dress of a porter and receive a porter's wage. Similar practices apply in other vocations and callings, including school teaching, farm labor, and other work.

Present causes of poverty in the South. Among the present causes of poverty in the rural sections of the South may be mentioned illiteracy, excessive farm tenancy, and deficiency diseases.

Economic progress in the rural South is retarded further by the extent of "cropper" tenancy. A large proportion of Southern farm tenants are croppers, or share tenants. Illiteracy, cropper tenancy, and poverty go hand in hand, all contributing to deficiency diseases, such as pellagra, tuberculosis, hookworm, and malaria. Under the weight of these conditions, both races suffer together. Farm organization on a large scale for mutual benefit is rendered more difficult to attain by the prejudices that exist between the races.

In 1940 the median year of school completed by Negroes aged 25 years or more in the Southern states was 5, while for native whites in the South it was about 8.5. For the rest of the country it was almost 10 for native whites and close to 8 for Negroes.[25]

In 1946 slightly more than 40 per cent of farm operators in the South were tenants as against about 22 per cent for the rest of the country. Moreover, the Southern tenants lived on less pro-

[24] *Ibid.*, p. 25.
[25] *Statistical abstract of the U. S.*, 1948, p. 125.

ductive and less valuable land than tenants in other areas. In 1947 the average value of Southern farmland was $37 per acre as compared to about $67 for the rest of the country.[26]

Negroes work in a restricted field. While the Negro has made progress in certain occupational lines, he has been waging a losing struggle in others. Surprisingly, the greatest handicaps to the economic ambitions of the Negro often have occurred in the occupational fields formerly regarded as the particular domain of the Negro. Even in the sections of the country where his opportunities have been limited most definitely by prejudice and custom, the Negro was "all right in his place." Such occupations as agriculture, road labor, and section work were regarded as his particular domain. He also was free to compete with his own fellows in such activities as waiting on tables, cooking, housekeeping, and to some extent barbering. During the depression years, however, he lost ground in these callings and seems not to have recovered it.[27]

Negro workers in industry. The success of Negro workmen in Northern industrial centers since 1918 indicates that the race is quite able to do the same kinds of work as is done by whites, under conditions that offer equal opportunities. In spite of the fact that the opportunities have rarely been equal, many employers report that the Negro's services are as satisfactory as are those of any other employees. A study in Chicago as early as 1920 by the Chicago Commission on Race Relations showed considerable variation in the opinions of employers, yet the majority indicated that the Negro was readily adaptable to the demands of modern industry.[28] After a careful review of various studies of Negro industrial workers, Kennedy concluded that " . . . the majority of employers consider the Negroes' labor to be as satisfactory as that of the white man, especially as that of European immigrants whose place he has been taking." Some employers, nevertheless, regard him as a failure, though "employers of the largest groups of colored workers are found in the class of those who express themselves as satisfied with the work of the newcomers (Negroes)."[29]

It sometimes is maintained that Negroes will work only until

[26] *Ibid.*, p. 506.

[27] T. J. Woofter, *Races and ethnic groups in American life*, President's Research Committee on Social Trends, 1934.

[28] Chicago Commission on Race Relations, *Negro in Chicago* (Chicago: University of Chicago Press, 1922).

[29] Louise V. Kennedy, *Negro peasant turns cityward* (New York: Columbia University Press, 1930), p. 115.

they get enough money to loaf. If this is true at all, it appears to be so only under circumstances that would produce similar results among whites. An analysis of the employment situation in Detroit revealed that the largest labor turnover among Negroes was in those plants that paid the lowest wages.[30]

The Chicago Race Commission reported that of 137 establishments 118 had found Negro labor satisfactory as against 19 which had not. The commission's conclusion was that: "Despite occasional statements that the Negro is slow or shiftless, the volume of evidence before the commission shows that Negroes are satisfactory employees and compare favorably with other racial groups."[31] A later study in 1926 in Detroit, conducted by the Detroit Bureau of Governmental Research, showed results similar to those produced by the Chicago Commission and revealed also a larger proportion of satisfied employers than was found in the survey in 1918 in the same city.

The Urban League found 66 per cent of the employers interviewed in eight Northern cities "entirely satisfied with Negro employees." In a number of instances where Negro labor was not entirely satisfactory, it had a connection with the type of "boss." The Negroes' cultural background appeared to be a factor in some cases.[32] The satisfaction that the Negro gives appears to vary somewhat from one city to another and from one industry to another. These variations may be largely, if not entirely, accounted for by differences in the attitudes of whites and by cultural factors that have no basis in racial inheritance, except as obvious racial traits determine the attitudes of the dominant group.

The Negro is still a marginal worker. He was the first to be affected by and the last to recover from the depression. About two out of three are unskilled. Semi-skilled and clerical workers among Negroes are few in comparison with both native and foreign-born whites. In the North, Negroes are employed largely in domestic and personal service and in manufacturing and mechanical industries, while in the South they are in domestic and personal service and in agriculture. Among male Negro workers, the percentage in agriculture is 40.7; in manufacturing and mechanical industries, 25.2; in domestic and personal serv-

[30] *National conference of social work* (Chicago: University of Chicago Press, 1928), p. 461.

[31] Chicago Commission on Race Relations, *op. cit.*, pp. 373–374.

[32] "How the Negro fits in northern industry," *Industrial Psychology*, 1926, I: 399–412.

ice, 11.6; and in transportation and communication, 10.8. Females are employed mainly in domestic and personal service and in agriculture. For every 1000 Negro workers 361, as compared with 214 native and 91 foreign-born whites, are in agriculture; 287 per 1000 Negro workers, as compared with 66 native and 127 foreign-born whites, are occupied in domestic and personal service.[33]

To what extent the relatively poorer living conditions of the Negroes have affected their success in industry is not known, but it may reasonably be assumed that they have tended to lessen their efficiency. Certainly the morbidity rate among urban Negroes has been steadily higher than among white workers, and all the data reviewed show that the housing and neighborhood conditions of Negroes averaged far below the whites'. This was especially true during the early years of the Negro migrations. They frequently were in "cellars, attics, sheds, and old store buildings."

Forester B. Washington observed that the great depression in the 1930's produced unusual disorganization in Negro communities. Many organizational and agency activities established by Negroes prior to the depression crumbled. Some of the most important agencies for the promotion of an intelligent interest in their own problems were allowed to die for lack of funds. No group in America was so adversely affected by economic disaster as the Negro group in the decade following 1929. The Negro was first to lose his job; he was pushed into the worst houses; government aid reached him last and in the smallest amounts. Consequently disease, already relatively high, hit him hardest, and, as Washington points out, the death rate in some neglected Negro areas reversed the trend downward and started to rise again.[34]

The exceptional difficulty found by the Negro during the depression was by no means due solely to prejudice against him and certainly not primarily to discriminatory action inherent in the national emergency programs. As was noted, the Negro was at a tremendous disadvantage to begin with. This was due largely to prolonged discriminations on the part of the dominant group but partly, also, to the tremendous distance that the Negro had come, socially and racially, in the relatively short period since the Civil War. There was certainly local prejudice in the administration of some national emergency relief projects. More impor-

[33] *Statistical abstract of the U. S.*, 1948, p. 173.
[34] *Social work year book*, 1941: 371.

tant, perhaps, were the petty prejudices of many white workers on the projects. Nevertheless, such agencies as the WPA and the NYA not only did serve as sources of income for unemployed Negroes, inadequate though it was for both whites and Negroes, but they also provided centers of community life and social activity that probably could not, and certainly would not, have been maintained by the local communities.

Other Racial Minorities: Orientals

Whenever Orientals in large numbers have come in contact with whites, the individual attitudes toward them have tended to follow the same general outlines as those toward the Negro. Owing to the fact that they are immigrant races, the overt expressions of these attitudes have differed in some important respects. A fundamental difference has been the extended use of treaty powers and legislative enactments, designed to limit the numbers and power of Orientals in this country. The actual number of Orientals in the United States has never been large. In 1940 there were less than 80,000 Chinese and about 127,000 Japanese in the entire country, as compared to 334,000 native Indians; 1,600,000 Mexicans; 13,000,000 Negroes; and nearly 119,000,000 whites.[35] The concentration of the Chinese and Japanese along the Pacific coast has intensified the problem in that region.

From the point of view of the national policy and the general welfare, the problems relating to the presence of minority groups of Orientals in the general population are of the same sort as those associated with other minority groups. They have their roots in misunderstanding and prejudice and are related to ego-involvements and feelings of personal security. The remedy lies partly in an unqualified extension of legal protections to minority individuals and groups in the exercise of their rights and privileges under the law and partly in the encouragement of co-operative understanding and mutual appreciation by the appropriate use of educational, religious, and other agencies. Where individuals of a minority group are frustrated because of failure to achieve recognition and personal satisfactions due to barriers imposed by a dominant majority, such individuals often tend to seek refuge or escape by unapproved and illegal forms of behavior or by living in some abnormal degree in a fantasy world. In any case, such individuals can be, in practice at least,

[35] *Statistical abstract of the U. S.*, 1948, p. 19.

never more than part-citizens. As Lee[36] suggests, some such persons seek to adjust to the cultures and life of a "faraway hometown," others may join subversive organizations. Such as these may provide agitators and repeated disturbers of the social order. More often, restrained and hemmed-in minority groups live in ghettoes, carrying on their own restricted ways apart from the sweep of American social life. This is true, as in the instance of many Mexican, Chinese, and Negro settlements, even where the numbers, spending habits, and services of the minority group make them indispensable to the accustomed life of the dominant group. Gamio points up this fact in the case of the Mexicans in some areas.[37] So important are the Mexicans in some sections that business is conducted almost solely in the Spanish language. These Mexicans, even those in positions of authority, while nominally American in sentiment and tradition are in reality "one with the Mexicans on the other side of the Rio Grande."

The need for a sense of unity and of mutual belongingness is most sharply defined in times of great emergency, when the united strength of the community or the nation is required. The need for a united front, made secure by the happy experiences of unqualified citizenship, was perhaps never more felt than during the years immediately following the Pearl Harbor attack, when it seemed advisable to forcibly withdraw thousands of Japanese citizens from the Pacific Coast area.

The American Indian

The American Indian is the oldest race on the continent, perhaps by twelve or more thousand years. Yet there were less than 350,000 Indians in continental United States, including all degrees of blood, in 1940. There were, moreover, hardly more than 170,000,000 full-bloods in the total American Indian population. The population growth of the Indian, however, in recent years has been greater than that of any other group in the United States, with an increase of 0.8 per cent per year, while the general population increase is slightly over 0.5 per cent per year. The Indian has never competed with the white man in the same sense as the other races described. Owing to the character and

[36] A. McClung Lee, "Ethnic minority subversives," *The Annals*, Sept. 1942: 168–169.

[37] Manuel Gamio, *Mexican immigration to the United States* (Chicago: University of Chicago Press, 1930), p. 56.

rigidity of his habit patterns, he resisted the white man's culture. The early white settlers rarely understood why this was so. They wanted his land, and the methods used to acquire it were not such as to inspire confidence. "The status of the American Indian today is the result of three hundred years of contact and conflict between an advanced and a retarded race."[38]

Indian status and tribal culture. It is doubtful if any considerable proportion of the full-blood Indians will ever become thoroughly assimilated, though many individuals reared and educated apart from tribal culture have shown good abilities. The general feeling among the anthropologists seems to be that the relatively meager achievements of the Indians are due to lack of opportunity, the retarding effects of their tribal culture, and to physical and mental deterioration rather than to innate characteristics of a purely racial origin. What has happened to the American Indian might as readily happen to any race under the same prolonged conditions.

Basic life goals come largely as a result of early experience, and also may be determined to a very great extent by the attitudes of one's associates, particularly if they belong to a minority group. It is noteworthy that Blackmar's study revealed that the cultural distinctions between Indians of different tribes were greater than the distinctions prevailing between educated Indians and educated whites.

The attachments of the Indian to the tribe and the tribal culture seem often to stand in the way of vocational success. The Indian youth finds little opportunity to appropriate the white man's skills among his own people, while to appropriate them outside means a partial or complete break with his own. The process of transition appears to present a twofold problem, *viz.*, that of injecting elements of American culture into the tribal life of the Indians and also the problem of drawing the Indians, through education and economic opportunity, into gradual participation in American life.

In 1924 American citizenship was conferred upon Indians; and in 1934 the Indian Reorganization Act was passed. The act was an attempt, only partially successful, to restore to the Indian the management of his own affairs, to protect his material resources, to improve his economy, and to give the Indian cultural freedom. There are still states in which Indians are not al-

[38] F. W. Blackmar, "American Indian and status," *Sociology and Social Research,* XIV: 221.

lowed to vote; and in general the Indian tribal societies still live in essential cultural isolation.

According to the 1945 report of the Office of Indian Affairs 25,000 Indians served in the armed forces of the United States during World War II, and 40,000 more were employed in war industries. The wartime experiences of a large proportion of the Indian population had a disorganizing effect in family and tribal life and sharpened the necessity of helping the Indians to find economic and educational opportunity so that they may find acceptance in the cultural life of the country.

Mexicans in the United States

As a result of three centuries of Spanish invasion of Mexico and later migrations from other parts of the world, the Mexican population is to some extent a mixed type, though the native or Indian blood is generally predominant.

Cultural distinctions. The cultural backgrounds and outlooks of Mexicans and native whites in the United States are as distinct as one could expect to find in the Western Hemisphere. Relatively few Mexicans ever become American citizens. These people generally take little or no part in the political and social life of the community. In the Southwest, where the largest number are concentrated, the Spanish language is still spoken and the old customs followed, even among those who are the descendants of Mexicans living in the territories when they were annexed to the United States. In the cities they live in little colonies apart from the currents of American culture. This situation is quite agreeable to both Americans and Mexicans. In general it may be said that the Mexicans are an exploited but not a conflict group.

Amalgamation is slowly taking place in some areas. A number of eugenists regard this tendency with alarm. Leaving out of account the problem of its effects upon the biology of the race stock, which is a moot question, there are objections on cultural grounds. The mixed bloods find great difficulty in becoming adjusted to the higher culture, and usually they do not. They remain attached to the Mexican group, increasing the volume of problems. One way to approach the problem would be to prevent this class of immigration. Some steps have been taken in this direction. Such a policy is difficult to carry out owing to the demand of American farmers for cheap Mexican labor and the pressure of these people to cross the extended border.

Numbers in the United States. The total "Mexican" population in the United States in 1940 was approximately 10,770,000, of which almost 700,000 were born in the United States of Mexican parentage. The greatest annual increases began with the passage of the immigration-restriction laws of 1924. For instance, Mexican immigration jumped from about 20,000 in 1920 to almost 90,000 in 1924. The great increases were due to legislation reducing the number of persons admitted from other countries. The Oriental Exclusion Law really placed Mexicans in a preferred class as cheap labor.

Occupational and economic status of Mexican immigrants. The professional and skilled occupations among Mexican immigrants is about one third the proportion found among eleven other immigrant groups considered together. Less than 10 per cent of Mexican immigrants above 16 years of age belong to the skilled and professional occupations, as compared to 28.5 per cent among all other immigrant groups.

Surveys reveal that the Mexican occupies a lower economic level than do other immigrant groups, and considerably below the average Negro living standard. A survey in Chicago revealed that the Mexicans were living in dilapidated dwellings left by Slavs and Italians. Twenty-eight per cent of the families were living three or more persons per room. In Denver they were found living seven and more per room. A study in Tucson showed housing conditions averaging about one third as good as those of white laborers, and their living costs were half those of the white laboring classes.

Large numbers live in boxcars along the railroads, others in automobiles or camp tents. The latter are comparatively new types of slum areas, presenting new problems of health and sanitation. In localities where the Mexican children from squalid camps attend the same schools as the whites who are permanently located in the community, problems of health are serious, since Mexicans have been found to be a source of infection. The California Commission of Immigration and Housing quotes the attendance officer: "During the past three weeks, I have had under close observation the migratory labor brought into . . . county. We are able to put the children into school and supply them with a migratory teacher; but yesterday the school nurse was obliged to send them home to clean up because of head lice. . . . This head condition has developed because of the dirty condition of these camps." The Mexican problem is to some extent the migratory problem, but as noted above, it is intensified by factors of race and cultural background.

Illiteracy among Mexican immigrants. The Mexican aliens admitted to the United States show an exceptionally high illiteracy rate, and this is generally true of children in Mexican settlements. The school provisions for Mexican children are frequently poorer than for whites. In some communities there is a difference of four months in the length of the school year, and the amount spent on the education of the Mexican child is often less than half the amount spent on the white child. T. R. Garth, K. Young, W. H. Sheldon, and others have studied the mental capacity of Mexican children and found them averaging lower than most other elements in the population, though their achievement varies widely from place to place and rises with improved living and educational conditions. Mexicans in the United States usually live in squalid segregation, and they generally have high morbidity and crime rates.

Geographical distribution of Mexicans in the United States. The fact that large numbers of the Mexican population are constantly on the move makes it impossible to classify them definitely according to residence.

The Mexican population is highly concentrated geographically. Approximately 90 per cent of all Mexicans in the United States live in the West, South Central, and Mountain and Pacific divisions of the country. Within these sections they are further concentrated. For example, about 85 per cent of the Mexicans coming to this country settle in Texas, California, Arizona, and New Mexico. These are the states also that have a large percentage of native Mexicans in the population. Nevertheless, large numbers of Mexicans are found during the spring and summer months in the beet fields of Colorado, Minnesota, and Wisconsin, and some of them have established permanent residence in the larger cities, such as St. Louis, Chicago, and Detroit.

Thus, while the Mexican population has been largely a rural problem, there has been within recent years a fairly steady drift toward the city. Mexicans have taken the place of South Europeans in the steel mills, automobile factories, foundries, and elsewhere.

Mexican standards and social conflict. Mexican standards conflict with those of American workmen and produce tensions between the native laborer and the Mexican, and between the native worker and the employer. Not unusually, employers prefer Mexican labor in the fields, because, as they have claimed, "they are a more tractable group, less likely to object to poor living conditions and long hours." It may be added, also, that their wives and children do a larger share of work than do the families of white laborers. One employer comparing Mexican with white labor said, " . . . the Mexicans have bigger families and more labor to get out a big crop. If the Mexicans learn English, they don't work so well; if they get educated a little they don't make such good farm hands."[39]

The present magnitude of the Mexican situation in the United States suggests strongly the need of restricting labor immigration from Mexico. Until the influx of Mexicans is decidedly reduced, little headway can be made in the direction of economic and social improvement among Mexicans who are citizens of the United States. It probably would be unwise, and perhaps futile, to attempt to assimilate the Mexican population by direct means. It seems fundamentally important, however, that Mexican children who are citizens of the United States be given the same protection as that afforded white children. It is doubtful if such protection can be given through the ordinary socialization programs. The various states which have large native-born Mexican populations need to develop special programs which take into account the peculiar needs and culture of the Mexican population.

Race Problems National in Scope

The personal and social effects of racial discrimination cannot be localized. They are manifested in the attitudes of other nations toward American governmental policy and in the downward pull that such discriminatory treatment exerts upon the total strength of the nation. Moreover, the national government by its constitutional commitments is obligated to provide equal protection to its citizens without regard to race or cultural background. The split of the Democratic party at the 1948 national convention and the formation of the so-called "Dixiecrat" wing was an expression of the futility of attempts to hold the problems of race and race relations within specifically defined areas of the United States.

Within recent years the Supreme Court of the United States and the national Congress have shown decided tendencies to

[39] Paul S. Taylor, "Mexicans north of the Rio Grande," *Survey Graphic*, May, 1931: 136.

recognize the obligations of the national government to protect its racial minorities against discriminatory treatment. On May 3, 1948, for example, the Supreme Court ruled that the familiar covenants designed to prevent certain racial or nationality groups from living in "restricted" residential areas are not enforceable by law. Several recent decisions have clearly established the Negroes' legal right to be admitted to state-supported universities and colleges on the same terms as whites, and to travel by interstate public conveyance without being denied accommodations and facilities available to other passengers. A number of states have adopted statutes designed to protect its minority groups against discrimination by eating places, hotels, places of amusement, and so on, and a few states have sought to equalize economic opportunities under law by the passage of the Fair Employment Practices Act, the purpose of which is to outlaw the practice of refusing to hire individuals merely because of race.[40]

While these and other measures have been taken to outlaw racial discrimination, numerous local, private, and public agencies have voluntarily removed formerly existing discriminatory practices and many organized political, religious, economic, and other groups have formally protested racial and nationality discriminations of every sort. Moreover, there exists a considerable number of permanent agencies supported primarily by volunteer gifts whose services are available to minority-group citizens whose legal rights have been denied. Among such organizations are the Civil Liberties Union and the National Association for the Advancement of Colored People.

Nevertheless, racial discrimination continues to exist, and racial minorities almost everywhere suffer handicaps in varying degrees imposed by racial prejudice. Numerous examples are afforded in the report of the President's Committee on Civil Rights. In many instances and over relatively wide areas of the population these prejudices are fatal to the developmental and achievement potentials of individuals and groups.[41]

Proposed Remedies Considered

It is no longer possible to think of race problems purely as a sectional matter. Any policy looking toward the improvement

[40] Since World War II various attempts have been made to pass a FEPC law for peacetime.

[41] President's Committee on Civil Rights, *To secure these rights* (Washington, D.C.: Government Printing Office, 1947).

of race relations cannot fail, in some way, to affect people in all parts of the country. Furthermore, racial minorities, like other population groups, are on the move. With the rise in economic and social status, they are traveling more freely and are settling down in places hitherto pre-empted by whites. The migrations cityward have been noted; some of the worst racial conflicts in the history of the country have risen in these industrial centers. It is perhaps more important now than ever before that the whole question of race relations be approached as a national problem. The problem needs to be approached also with sanity and caution. In spite of tremendous obstacles, minority groups are gaining in education and in economic standing. Already some of them have developed leaders of national and international reputation. They are rapidly becoming conscious of their capacities and are demanding a respectable place in the economic and cultural life of the nation. A refusal to recognize this demand willingly is an appeal to prejudice, and to condemn such an aspiration is to place a premium on ignorance and superstition.

Some major aspects of the problem. From a scientific point of view, the questions which present themselves are: First, what are the innate capacities of these various groups for education and achievement? Second, what are the best ways of helping them toward a realization of these capabilities so that they may make the largest possible contribution to themselves, individually and racially, and also American life? A final answer to the first question cannot be made at once; it must be tested in the field of experience. The actual achievements of colored peoples in the face of tremendous obstacles have gone a long way to establish the fact of their ability to rise. The more nearly the economic and cultural barriers to their progress are removed, the more we shall know about their capacities for achievement.

The second question involves a consideration of all the objective factors that might block the progress of a race in a given field of activity. It is to some extent a matter of vocational guidance applied on a large scale. For example, ever so many Negroes may have the capacity for securing graduate and professional degrees, but to encourage unlimited numbers to do so at the expense of other lines of activity that offer larger returns to the race would be injurious.

The status of minority races affects general progress. Regardless of differences as to detail, it is becoming evident to a growing number of people that racial groups comprising so large a proportion of the nation's population cannot be held down permanently without ultimate injury to society generally. Any policy which makes the colored peoples more intelligent, more productive, and law-abiding will be an advantage not only to them but to society as a whole. From this point of view, it will be recognized that the improvement of health and enlarged opportunities for practical education for these races is a step in the right direction. Just what is the best practical method of bringing this about is a matter on which there is considerable argument. There are certain great difficulties, one of which is the fact, pointed out above, that the colored populations are so unevenly distributed. In the first place, increased numbers alone make new demands on the social organization; and in the second place, the attitudes of various races toward each other are by no means the same in regions where one race comprises the vast majority as in sections where the races are more nearly equal in numbers. Furthermore, sectional points of view differ widely, on account of the peculiar racial history of the section.

Negroes divided in loyalties. Race problems as applied to Negroes in the United States are rendered difficult to deal with for the further reason that Negroes themselves are divided in their loyalties. A policy which might be hopeful of a solution of the problem with reference to the backward Negroes in the cities or rural sections of the South might not so readily be applied to the more advanced and economically efficient Negroes in the industrial areas of the North. Many of them would resent bitterly policies that would be readily adaptable to the more depressed classes in both the North and the South. In fact, there appear to be lines of prejudice within the race itself. Some Negroes feel themselves "superior" to other members of their race. Many of these have acquired economic security and show little practical interest in the ultimate welfare of the race. This sort of attitude is by no means peculiar to the colored people. It is a characteristic of some individuals in all races, but it nevertheless increases the difficulties of the problem.

Amalgamation. Another tendency which may have a decided bearing on racial problems in the United States is that of amalgamation. In spite of the social barriers which custom and law have set up between the races, amalgamation has taken place rather widely; so much so that probably more than one third, some authorities say two thirds, of the Negro population in the United States is of mixed blood. Amalgamation is also taking place among all the races where social contacts are somewhat continuous.

Partly because of this amalgamation process there appears to be taking place in the United States a discriminatory system, especially within the Negro population. The mulattoes sometimes tend to hold themselves aloof from those who have no evident mixture of white blood. Just what the final result of this amalgamation process will be it is impossible to foretell. One result, already noticeable, is the passing of whites with Negro blood out of the pure Negro group. The census figures are not absolutely reliable, on account of the difficulties involved in getting the data, but they tend to show a preponderance in the mulatto rate of increase over the rate of increase among pure blacks.

Some people look upon the amalgamation process as the ultimate solution of race problems in America. Obviously such an attitude does not meet the pressing problems confronting the races today. In spite of the fact that mixtures of blood are taking place, there are keen objections to it on the part of all races. The filtering of the colored populations into the white is a tremendously slow and, in the opinion of many people, hazardous process, and always there is the colored population on the outside. Furthermore, in some sections the colored outnumber the whites, which condition gives the problem of amalgamation a new aspect.

Migration.   Many representatives of various races have looked to migration as a way out of the difficulty. There are two factors in the situation, however, which make the problem more serious than the actual numbers would indicate. In the first place, there is enough prejudice against colored peoples to make their presence a problem almost regardless of the numbers. For instance, in one of the schools at Gary, Indiana, some years ago, only 3 per cent of the enrollment was colored. Yet that 3 per cent attracted so much attention that the white children demanded a separation of the two races in the schoolroom. In the second place, if one could hope that migration would remove social prejudice, it would be futile to expect that migration would take place in a way to result in an even and scattered distribution of the minority races, at least within any reasonable length of time. Thus, the race problems remain and call for some scientific and positive approach.

Segregation.   Complete segregation, advocated by some, presents the difficulty of maintaining the kind of co-operative understanding so necessary to the ultimate progress of all races. If complete segregation or separation of the races could take place, it might tend toward an exaggeration of prejudices and misunderstandings which might give rise very easily to greater conflicts than ever. Furthermore, in the case of retarded minority groups it is important to have the co-operation and help of the more advanced race. It is extremely doubtful if anything like absolute separation could be made practicable in modern complex society.

In spite of the difficulties, some progress in race relations is being made. Much along this line is being done through the work of various interracial associations throughout the country. One point needs to be thoroughly recognized, namely, that any human capacity for greater achievement which is not developed is a loss not only to the individual but also to the whole society. An efficient and productive citizen is worth more than one who is inefficient. The workman who takes pride in his work and knows how to improve it is more desirable than the ignorant worker who is unable to develop a practical interest in his vocation or enterprise. These principles are true regardless of color. Thus, the fields of education and health offer especial opportunity for the development of co-operative effort in race relations. It is through education, wisely applied, and the control of disease, which really is an aspect of education, that the possibilities of the individuals and the race are opened up.

QUESTIONS

1. What is the true basis of race distinctions?
2. Why is it often difficult to define a race scientifically?
3. (a) What factors and conditions determine one's attitude toward a race? (b) Give examples.
4. Discuss the relative native intelligence trends of different races in the light of the results of various studies.
5. Why is assimilation especially difficult in the case of a minority racial group?
6. (a) How do people's prejudices affect their understanding of race problems and race relations? (b) Give examples.
7. (a) How are the Negro-White relationships in the United States affected by the distribution of the Negro population? (b) by Negro migration to cities?
8. Account for the relatively slow increase in the Negro population in the United States since the Civil War.

9. (a) To what extent are Negroes handicapped socially and economically by discriminatory attitudes of the whites? (b) Illustrate.
10. Discuss the various factors that probably affect Negro disease and crime rates.
11. Trace the development of Negro education in the United States.
12. Discuss recent tendencies with respect to Negro education.
13. What do these tendencies suggest with respect to the abilities of the Negro people?
14. What are the chief weaknesses in Negro education?
15. What changes should be made?
16. Suggest a program for (a) the general improvement of Negro health; (b) reduction of Negro crime.
17. Evaluate the following possible factors in relation to the low economic status of the American Negro: native ability; race prejudice; cultural backgrounds; geographical location; lack of technical and professional training (may be due to some of the other factors); lack of business and professional experience.
18. What conclusions and possible methods of adjusting the Negro-White relations are suggested by the foregoing discussion?
19. What other plans can you offer?
20. (a) What characteristic attitudes are typified in these relations?
21. In what respects do the Oriental and Mexican problems in this country differ from the problems presented by Negro-White relations?
22. What peculiar problems are presented by the Mexican population in the United States?
23. Propose plans for adjusting the Mexican situation in the United States.
24. How does the American Indian situation differ from that created by other racial groups in America?
25. What general conclusions are warranted with respect to race problems in the United States?

REFERENCES

BOAS, FRANZ, *Anthropology and modern life* (revised ed.). New York: W. W. Norton and Company, 1932.

BOAS, FRANZ, *Race, language, and culture*. New York: The Macmillan Company, 1940.

BOGARDUS, EMORY S., *Immigration and race attitudes*. Boston: D. C. Heath and Company, 1928.

COON, C. S., *Races of Europe*. New York: The Macmillan Company, 1939.

CRISWELL, MRS. JOAN (HENNING), *Sociometric study of race cleavage in the classroom*. New York: Archives of Psychology, Columbia University Press, 1939.

GARTH, T. R., *Race psychology*. New York: McGraw-Hill Book Company, 1931.

HERMAN, A. P., *Approach to social problems*, Ch. 10. Boston: Ginn and Company, 1949.

HERSKOVITS, M. J., *American Negro*. New York: Alfred A. Knopf, 1928.

HOOTON, E. A., *Twilight of man*. New York: G. P. Putnam's Sons, 1939.

JOHNSON, CHARLES S., *Negro in American civilization*. New York: Henry Holt and Company, 1930.

LASKER, BRUNO, *Race attitudes in children*. New York: Henry Holt and Company, 1929.

MOTON, R. R., *What the Negro thinks*. New York: Doubleday and Company, 1929.

NEARING, SCOTT, *Black America*. New York: Vanguard Press, 1929.

SPERO, S. D., and HARRIS, A. L., *Black worker*. New York: Columbia University Press, 1931.

CHAPTER 14

Criminality and Its Control

What Is Crime?

Concept and definition. There is relatively little confusion in the minds of people "on the street" as to what constitutes a criminal act. It is one for which a penalty is assessed by a court of law. Ordinarily the average man thinks of a criminal as one who has been jailed or committed to a reformatory or a penitentiary. One hundred people, about evenly distributed as to sex and representing various occupations, were asked to give a definition of "a criminal." Seventy-five per cent made commitment to a penal institution an essential condition. Fifteen of these included . . . *fine*. Not one attempted to define the criminal in terms of the *character* of the individual or the act apart from a penalty assessment. Indeed, it is difficult to argue with this view. It is supported by the facts of common experience. Men are arrested. They are convicted. They are fined, incarcerated, and released on parole. Such men are obviously criminals. They would be criminals, or some equivalent in the popular mind, even if there were no legal definitions to make them so.

This restricted concept of criminality has practical value. It provides a sure-fire way to separate the goats from the sheep. It tends to remove the sting of inexperience, ignorance, and inexpertness, for here the unlettered man is as good as the scientist.

From a scientific point of view, however, this easy classification on the basis of conviction alone presents certain difficulties. The most obvious difficulty is that it rules out all those who are not convicted. This is important. Common-sense observation and scientific research tell us that numerous factors other than the nature of the *act* or of the *actor* operate to tip the scales to the advantage of one and the disadvantage of another. Sometimes these factors are of such profound significance as to serve unwittingly or otherwise to promote the interests of a whole class of predatory operators whose acts under less favorable environs would inevitably result in penitentiary sentences or the electric chair.

Sutherland's documented study of "white-collar criminality"[1] suggested not only rather widespread criminal intent but showed that such criminal acts as commercial bribery, bribery of public officials, embezzlement and misapplication of funds, short weights and measures, tax frauds, misgrading of commodities, misrepresentation in financial statements, illegal sales of alcohol and narcotics, services to underworld criminals, and many others were engaged in repeatedly without court conviction or penalty.

Fred J. Murphy reported that of a total of some 6000 offenses admitted by youths investigated, less than 2 per cent were actually brought to public attention by arrests or juvenile-court hearings. Austin J. Porterfield compared college students with a group of juvenile-court cases ranging in seriousness from church disturbances to homicide. He found that the students received little or no attention from public authorities. One student in training for the ministry got away with 27 and another with 28 offenses in the list of those for which the "delinquent" group had been hailed into a juvenile court.[2] Wallerstein and Wyle found that 99 per cent of a group of "law-abiding" citizens in New York state had by their own admissions broken one or more of forty-nine criminal laws in that state. These offenses included perjury, falsification, fraud and tax evasion, indecency, criminal libel, and gambling, larcency, burglary, and robbery.[3]

Wilber has called attention to the scientific difficulties of relying upon the restricted legal definition of the "criminal." "Crime should be defined," he says, "in such a manner that questions as to whether a certain kind of behavior is criminal or something else are . . . automatically eliminated . . . " and " . . . to be of greatest value crime must be defined in terms of the universal and intrinsic elements of the subject matter. . . . "[4]

[1] E. H. Sutherland, "White-collar criminality," *American Sociological Review*, Vol. 5 (1940): 1–12.

[2] Austin J. Porterfield, *Youth in trouble* (Fort Worth: Leo Potishman Foundation, Texas Christian University).

[3] J. S. Wallerstein, and C. J. Wyle, *Our law-abiding law-breakers* (New York: National Probation Association, 1948).

[4] George Wilber, "Scientific adequacy of criminological concepts," *Social Forces* (Dec. 1949): 165–174.

Theories of Crime and Punishment

There have been many attempts to explain crime and justify punishment. In primitive societies the general disposition is to attribute life and purpose to material objects. Accordingly, an object by which a person is injured is either punished or protected, depending upon the reasoning that the primitive mind reads into the situation. If the thing is regarded as possessing some occult or divine power, it may be worshiped. If it is believed to be dominated by evil spirits, it may be punished or utterly destroyed. This disposition to attribute evil designs to inanimate objects is extended to the lower animals as well as to human beings. The history of crime and punishment is replete with accounts of the trials and executions of the lower animals. In the same way any person who fails to follow the accustomed ways of the group is assumed to be "possessed."

The demon theory. The demon theory or, as sometimes called, "demonological theory" has been one of the most nearly universal explanations ever invented and in a modified form has been the accepted theory throughout most of the period of recorded history. Whenever the established rules were believed to be creations of the gods or the "Great Spirits," there was little or no distinction between crime and sin. Whatever outraged the group also outraged the gods. Hence there was all the more reason why the offender should be dealt with severely. This submergence of the idea of crime by the prevailing concepts of sin was in evidence during most of the Middle Ages. The theory of "possession" tended to become identified with the Christian concept of original sin or, as it was later explained, "natural depravity." It was inevitable that these theories of crime should find expression in legal codes and should color the practices of courts for many generations. A formal indictment in England in the nineteenth century accused the criminal of "being prompted and instigated by the devil . . . " and the supreme court of one of our own states declared, in 1862, that "to know the right and still the wrong pursue proceeds from a perverse will brought about by the seduction of the Evil One." We may now briefly consider some of the historic *schools* of criminology.

The classical school. Perhaps the most important of the earlier attempts to interpret crime was made in the last half of the eighteenth century and came to be known as the *classical school*. The man who perhaps did most to formulate this theory was an

Italian, Cesare Beccaria (1738–1794), whose chief work, *On crimes and punishments*, appeared in 1764. Beccaria's explanation of crime rests primarily upon a concept of "pleasure seeking," that is, crime is one of the results of the desire for pleasure. The human being, he believed, contemplates in advance the consequences of his actions; if the promise of pleasure outweighs the promise of pain, the act will be performed. In order to prevent crime, therefore, it is necessary to maintain a system of punishments graduated according to the seriousness and nature of offenses, with little regard for the intent of the individual or the circumstances under which the act was committed. There are some inconsistencies in this classical school. While it rests fundamentally upon a belief in the "freedom of the will," Beccaria himself showed some understanding of the deterministic character of human behavior. He maintained that there are no spontaneous or superfluous sentiments "in the heart of man"; they are all results of impressions on the senses. He held also that the "surest, but most difficult, means of preventing crime is to improve education."

The classical school really represented a reaction against the harsh punishments of an earlier time. Society was viewed as the result of a social contract, according to which each individual by his presence in the group agrees to exercise restraints in the interests of social order. Haynes enumerates three fundamental principles which characterize the classical school. The first principle is that the rights and liberties of the individual must be conserved; the second is that crime is a "juridical abstraction and, consequently, each crime has attached to it a definite penalty." A third fundamental principle is that the severity of the punishment should be determined by the social need.[5]

The neo-classical school. The classical school was followed by the *neo-classical*. The adherents of this latter school also believed in individual responsibility but sought to temper the doctrine somewhat by making allowances for those whose wills are immature or warped by conditions beyond their control. Classes subject to special consideration include young children, insane people, and those with little mentality. This theory of crime and punishment profoundly influenced the development of penal codes and methods of legal procedure during the nineteenth century. The chief weakness of the theory inheres in the fact

[5] F. E. Haynes, *Criminology* (New York: McGraw-Hill Book Company, 1930), p. 24.

that the major emphasis was placed upon the character of the offense rather than upon the individual offender.

The positive school. In 1872 the so-called *positive school* of criminology began to challenge attention. The best-known exponent of this school was an Italian, Cesare Lombroso (1836–1909), whose chief investigative work was done between 1854 and 1878. While most of Lombroso's conclusions have been discredited by more recent studies, his name deserves a place of honor among the pioneers of criminological science. He was one of the first criminologists to employ an objective method of investigation, and he introduced a relatively new approach to the problem by centering attention upon the individual criminal rather than upon the nature of the offense.

Lombroso's investigations led him to the conclusion that criminality is not due to the exercise of "free will," but fundamentally to certain inherited abnormalities. These abnormal physical and mental conditions, he thought, are the result of arrested development caused by a reversion to an earlier and more primitive type (atavism) and to diseases that produce degeneracy of the organism. According to this theory, the habitual criminal can be recognized by the presence of certain stigmata, such as long ears, sloping forehead, unusually large frontal sinuses and jaws, projecting chin, and other traits not only of the head but also of other body parts. Since some of these physical anomalies are found among peaceful citizens, Lombroso defined the "born-criminal" type largely in terms of the number and extent of the characteristics.

Lombroso worked out a rather detailed classification of criminals, which included some types that were not physical anomalies at all, and who were highly intelligent, such as the political criminal. Nevertheless he held that the problem of crime is basically a problem of dealing with "born types"; and that segregation, not punishment, must be employed. Lombroso's great contribution to criminological science lies in the fact that his investigations were objective and also that he forced attention upon the individual criminal rather than the crime.

Comparative studies of English prisoners. In order to check further on Lombroso's conclusions with reference to physical types in the criminal population, Dr. Griffiths, an English prison official, in 1901 conceived the idea of measuring various traits of a large number of prison inmates. Owing to changes in the medical staff of the prison, the actual work of measurement fell to Dr. Charles Goring and assistants. The investigators confined their measurements to the recidivists, since it was believed that they would be most likely to conform to criminal types, if any exist. Three thousand criminals were measured, and the results compared with the results of similar measurements of one thousand students at Cambridge University. Other comparisons were made between the prisoners and a group of noncommissioned officers and naval engineers. Certain physical characteristics of the prisoners were compared with those of a group of English schoolboys. Furthermore, the prisoners were classified on the basis of the offense committed, as, for instance, burglary, forgery, and thievery, and compared as to physical traits in the attempt to discover any possible correlation between types of offense and physical anomalies. None of these comparisons offered any substantial proof of the claim that criminals belong to a definite physical type, or that particular kinds of criminals may be differentiated on the basis of certain stigmata. Goring found that the prisoners tended to be smaller in stature and lighter in weight than the general adult population. This difference might easily be accounted for on the basis of differences in occupation and social standing. The criminal classes as a rule came from the more economically insecure elements in the population and hence would apparently not be so well fed and well groomed as a large proportion of the nonprison population.

Modern Explanations of Crime

Recent advances in the physical and social sciences, particularly sociology, psychology, biology, and physiological chemistry, have profoundly affected the theories and explanations of crime. In the light of discoveries made in these various fields, the older notion that crime is due to the presence of specific traits or to deliberate choice is no longer tenable. Many people who are very critical of older views still insist upon generalizing about crime conditions in terms of some single factor, such as mental deficiency, poverty, the broken home, the decay of religion, or the foreign-born. These generalizations are likely to be based upon somewhat narrowly restricted studies or upon prejudice. Such single-cause explanations may have far-reaching influences upon public opinion and have no doubt resulted in the application of unscientific and wasteful measures of control.

Crime arises in a complex of factors. The present tendency among criminologists is to account for criminal behavior in terms of a combination of factors, the removal of any one of which might alter the entire situation. Individual case studies together with careful statistical analyses of criminal rates under varying conditions have shown how inadequate single-cause explanations are.

Satisfactory explanations must be sought through an examination of total situations—including such factors as changes in the age and sex groupings of the population; nationality and cultural backgrounds; economic status; growth and shifting of population centers; world disturbances, wars, business depressions, famines, and political upheavals; the passage of new legislation. Any number of these factors, and many more, playing upon each other might account for increases or decreases in the crime rate. A famine or a political upheaval in an old country might raise the crime rate in a new country by sending large numbers of strangers into its territory. The raising of immigration barriers might result in a rapid increase of crime in the old country by forcing restless people to remain in a restrictive environment.

Problem of accurate interpretation of data. There are no techniques at the present time which make it possible to know all the factors responsible for variations in the rates of crime. It is possible, however, to work out some concurrency between crime rates and other factors. Such a concurrency does not in itself prove that the two sets of phenomenon have an immediate causal relation, but it is nevertheless suggestive.

Watts, in his study of crime rates in Canada, was able, by statistical method, to show a concurrency between the crime conditions and a number of factors which one may believe were significant. He found, for instance, that the depression in the crime rate beginning with 1914 was confined mainly to certain age groups, from which were drawn men for the army and from which immigrants were taken by the calls of their various countries. There is also the fact that the war period created jobs at fairly high wages for those who stayed at home. This not only challenged the full time and attention of the worker but also gave him economic security. Watts's analysis confirms studies made in this country showing that crime rates vary according to the mobility of the population and also its density. For instance, he found that the rate per 100,000 of the population in the districts containing urban centers was about 500 as compared to a rate of only 90 in the least densely populated areas.[6]

[6] R. E. Watts, "Influence of population density on crime," *Journal American Statistical Association* (March, 1931): Vol. 26, 11–20.

It is an easy matter to interpret these statistics so as to run the risk of grave error. One might conclude that density of population is the prime cause of crime. It should be remembered, however, that these centers of population, especially in the newer parts of the world, are likely to be centers of high mobility as well as contact centers for a vast variety of human and cultural types. Furthermore, there is usually a larger proportion of people within the age groups most likely to commit crimes in cities than in the country. Numerous other factors, especially economic, should be studied and compared before one would dare make the assumption that crime in one place is caused by any one or two factors. It is possible, also, that the most important conditioning facts may be the most difficult to recognize and study. The early experiences of the individual or group as related to family, neighborhood, nationality, culture, race, occupation, income, and modes of living might be fundamentally important. But such facts are not only easy to overlook entirely but extremely difficult to evaluate after their possible significance has been admitted.

It is significant that the year 1949 showed an increase in the crime rate of 4.5 per cent as compared to 1948. This was approximately three times as great as the total increase for 1948 over 1947. According to estimates based on reports of more than 4000 police agencies representing about 100,000,000 inhabitants in continental United States, there were 1,763,290 major crimes committed in continental United States during the year 1949. This means that on the average there was a major crime committed in this country every eighteen seconds—better than three a minute. This is a conservative estimate since, while it does include some relatively small larceny offenses, it does not include crimes of arson, carrying concealed weapons, embezzlement, and fraud.[7] Of the offenders, over 240,000 were between the ages of 16 and 24. (See Figure 8, p. 368.)

Increases were shown for every class of offense except criminal homicide and auto theft. Burglaries and robberies showed increases of 8.4 per cent and 7.5 per cent respectively. Larcenies rose 4.8 per cent, and rape went up slightly more than 1 per cent as compared to the previous year. (See Figure 9.) Specifically, 2293 persons were feloniously killed or assaulted, 162 robberies were committed, more than 1100 places were bur-

[7] *Uniform crime reports* issued by the Federal Bureau of Investigation, U. S. Department of Justice (Washington, D. C.: Government Printing Office, 1950), Vol. 20.

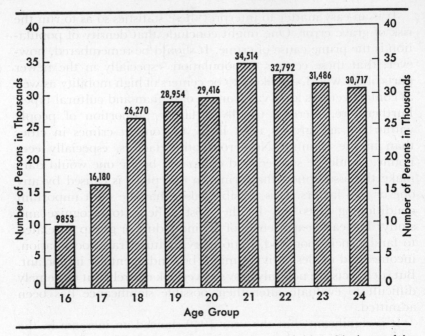

Figure 8. Number of Persons, Male and Female, Aged 16 to 24, Arrested in Calendar Year 1949

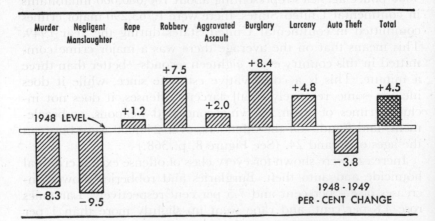

Figure 9. Crime Trends, Urban and Rural, Based on Estimated Number of Major Crimes in the United States

glarized, almost 150 cars were stolen, and 2800 "general larceny" thefts were committed, on the average, for every day of the year 1949. It is worth noting that 1949 showed a decrease in crimes of murder and manslaughter, of 8.3 per cent and 9.5 per cent respectively as compared to 1948. Auto theft decreased 3.8 per cent.

In general, the national crime rate has shown an increase for every year since 1944, but the rates have shown marked varia-

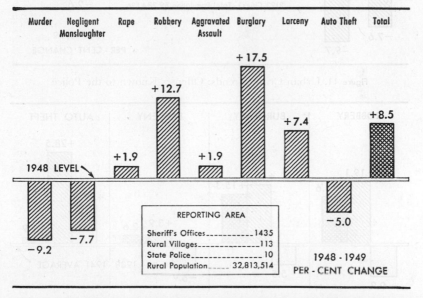

Figure 10. Rural Crime Trends: Offenses Known to the Police

tions according to class of offense and on the basis of geographic and population areas. For instance, the urban crime rate in 1948 was hardly 1 per cent higher than in 1947, while for the same period rural crime rose almost 5 per cent. The figures for 1949 as compared to 1948 show that rural crime went up 8.5 per cent while the increase for urban crime was 4.2 per cent.[8]

There were similar variations according to classes of offenses in both urban and rural areas with increases in rates for burglary, robbery, larceny, and rape tending to run higher in the rural than in the urban areas throughout the period. (See Figures 10 and 11.) The relative rates of increase provide no information

[8] See *Uniform crime reports, 1946, 1947, 1948, 1949,* F. B. I., U. S. Department of Justice (Washington, D.C.: Government Printing Office). All charts in this chapter are taken from the F.B.I. report of January, 1950.

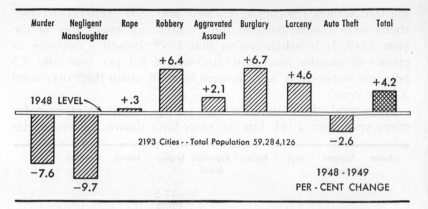

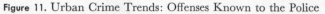

Figure 11. Urban Crime Trends: Offenses Known to the Police

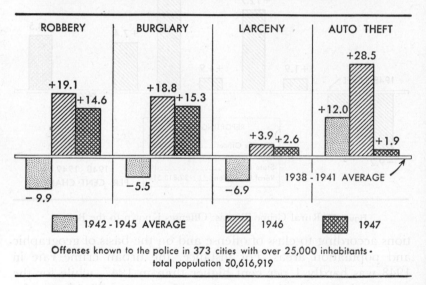

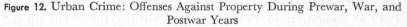

Offenses known to the police in 373 cities with over 25,000 inhabitants -
total population 50,616,919

Figure 12. Urban Crime: Offenses Against Property During Prewar, War, and
Postwar Years

as to the actual number of offenses committed. On the basis of population, urban crime rates run considerably higher than do rural rates. For 1949 the estimated rural offenses for a population of almost 33,000,000 numbered less than 175,000 as compared to more than 1,000,000 urban offenses in a population totaling slightly less than 60,000,000 people.

Figures 12 and 13 show the urban trends for offenses against person and against property over a longer period and reflect the influences of the war and postwar years upon crime rates. It is observed that the period of actual hostilities showed a rate lower than the average for the years 1938–1941 for all but three of the eight major offenses. The years immediately following the war, however, showed rapid increases in the rates for all eight of these major offenses. The rates of increase are seen to be especially marked for the crimes of rape and aggravated assault.

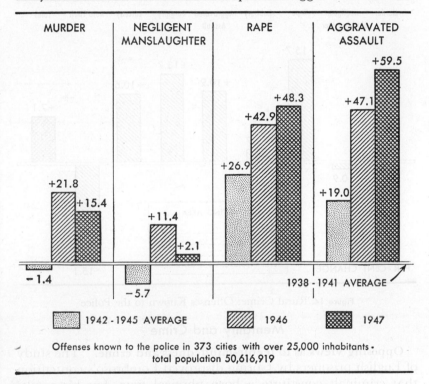

Figure 13. Urban Crime: Offenses Against the Person During Prewar, War, and Postwar Years

Note also, the sharp increases for certain offenses, including rape, in the rural areas for the years immediately following the termination of active hostilities. (See Figure 14, p. 372.)

Crime rates, moreover, show variations with changing seasons and conditions of weather. Certain crimes against property run highest in winter while, in general, offenses against persons show greatest frequency in summer months. For instance, rape and aggravated assault appear to reach peaks in June and July, with the lowest frequencies in December and January. (See

Figure 15.) Here again seasonal variations do not always follow the same trend for rural and urban territories. All of this suggests the importance of a multiplicity of influencing factors outside the personality and dispositional make-up of the individual criminal.[9] We shall now consider some of the factors that seem to have a bearing upon criminal behavior.

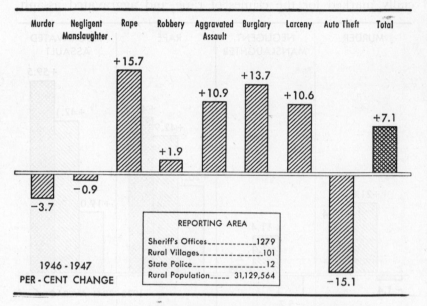

Figure 14. Rural Crime: Offenses Known to the Police

Mentality and Crime

Opposing views as to feeble-mindedness and crime.   The study of English prisoners by Goring disproved Lombroso's contention that criminals constitute a born physical type, but his results tended strongly to identify criminality with mental deficiency. The belief that mental defectiveness is a leading cause of crime gained wide acceptance in the United States early in the present century, and many people today believe that practically all habitual criminals are of low mentality.

A study of 500 criminal careers by the Gluecks indicated that about 21 per cent of the offenders were classed as feeble-minded, and about 50 per cent as dull or borderline cases.[10] Other inves-

[9] Data from *Uniform crime reports, op. cit.*

[10] Sheldon and Eleanor Glueck, *500 criminal careers* (New York: Alfred A. Knopf, 1930).

tigations have shown smaller rates of mental defectiveness in the criminal population.

Murchison found on the basis of results obtained from the use of the Army Alpha test in several state prisons that the prisoners averaged well up to drafted men in the army.[11] Dr. Herman

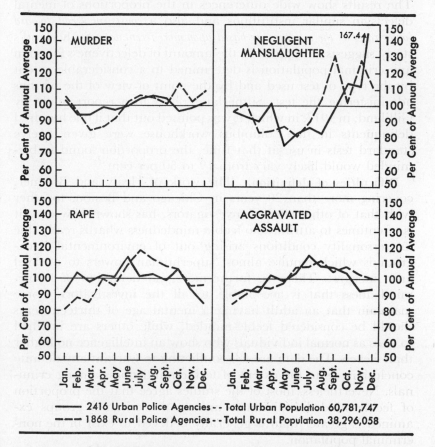

Figure 15. Monthly Variations in Offenses Known to the Police: 1949

M. Adler concluded from examinations of the Illinois penal and reformatory populations that the proportion of inferior intelligence in the prison population is no greater than is found outside. His examinations led to the conclusion that the percentage of youth of inferior intelligence, in the Pontiac institution, from Cook County was lower than the percentage of army men from

[11] Carl Murchison, *Criminal intelligence* (Worcester: Clark University Press, 1926).

the same county examined during World War I.[12] Adler also found that repeaters had on the average a higher intelligence than the first offenders.

E. H. Sutherland has summarized the results of 350 studies on this subject involving 175,000 offenders in various institutions. The results show wide differences in the proportions of mental defects in similar institutions and also a *consistent trend toward lower rates as the results were based upon more recent data.* Sutherland's study suggests strongly that the amount of defectiveness found in any criminal population is determined to a considerable extent by the type of test used and by the point of view of the persons administering the test. Sutherland refers to a report made by Gilliland, in 1917, in which it was pointed out that if one hundred delinquents in the Columbus workhouse were given twelve standard tests in use at that time, the proportion found feeble-minded would likely vary from 19 to 50 per cent.[13]

Difficulties of definition. The work of Healy and Bronner, covering more than 20 years in Chicago and Boston, together with that of other clinical investigators, has shown how easy it is oftentimes to attribute to feeble-mindedness what is really due to personality conditions arising out of environmental backgrounds which require almost superhuman powers to unravel and interpret. There is, furthermore, no definition of feeble-mindedness that is acceptable to all the investigators. Some maintain that an adult having a mental age of thirteen years should be considered feeble-minded, while others are inclined to class as normal individuals who show an intelligence no higher than eleven. The data are too conflicting to warrant any definite conclusions as to the extent of feeble-mindedness among criminals. Nevertheless, most of the studies agree that the proportion of feeble-minded individuals among the criminal groups examined is greater than is generally believed to exist in the non-criminal population.

Investigation confined to prisoners. It should be noted that most of the studies of criminals have been conducted among prisoners and by no means included all of the criminals; besides, the inmates of prisons are likely to be a selected group. There is no conclusive proof that those who are caught and convicted average

---

[12] Dr. H. M. Adler, *Parole and the indeterminate sentence* (Cleveland: Cleveland Foundation, 1928), p. 231.

[13] E. H. Sutherland, "Mental deficiency and crime," Ch. 15 in Kimball Young, ed., *Social attitudes* (New York: Henry Holt and Company, 1931).

lower in intelligence than the criminals who escape, but common sense and the evidence point in that direction. All along the line from the first antisocial act to final commitment, the chances of escape seem to increase with intelligence and the possession of wealth. The evidence, furthermore, indicates strongly that those who have good intelligence are more likely also to be secure economically. Thus, poverty and lack of intelligence probably work hand in hand to produce arrests, convictions, and final commitments. Malzburg[14] found that among 574 persons brought before the Court of General Sessions of New York, 11.9 per cent were diagnosed as mentally defective. Of those found guilty, 16.2 per cent were mentally defective. These figures take no account of those who, because of superior intelligence, may have been able to evade arrest. This interpretation seems justified in the light of common observation. Malzburg also found that 35.2 per cent of all the felons received a suspended sentence as compared to only 18 per cent of the defective felons. In other words, 64 per cent of all those found guilty were sentenced to institutions as compared to almost 82 per cent of the defectives. Other studies have shown that mental defectives are less likely to be paroled than normal individuals as judged by the intelligence-test results.

There is evidence that low mentality in our modern society predisposes individuals to certain classes of offenses. For instance, various studies have indicated that crimes of acquisition, such as fraud, embezzlement, and forgery, are committed by people who show a higher average intelligence than those who commit sex crimes, while most of the crimes of violence are committed by persons averaging in intelligence somewhere between the other groups of offenders.[15]

Emotional factors. The importance of emotional factors is emphasized by a large number of clinical investigators in the field of juvenile delinquency. Such factors appear not only to be more common among criminals and delinquents than among noncriminals, but also to have an important bearing upon the reformation of the individual. Healy and Bronner and associates found that mentally defective delinquents did better when placed in foster homes than other abnormal groups, though

[14] Benjamin Malzburg, "Relation of mental defect to delinquency," *Journal of Criminal Law and Criminology*, August, 1929: 218–221.

[15] E. H. Sutherland, *op. cit.*, p. 372. Also *Report of national commission on law observance and enforcement*, No. 13, 1931: Ch. 3.

neither the mental defectives nor those with emotional and mental disturbances did as well as the normal individuals.

Definition and interpretation. Some of the same difficulties that stand in the way of evaluating feeble-mindedness as a cause of crime are present in attempts to decide what constitutes mental abnormality.

In the first place, there is no clear-cut distinction between normal and abnormal personalities; they are largely a matter of degree and circumstances. An individual may be quite normal in one situation and abnormal in another. It is largely a matter of creating conditions that encourage or discourage the particular traits that lead to antisocial behavior. Some people are better equipped emotionally and mentally than others to measure up to the demands of modern society. In the second place, there is considerable lack of uniformity in the results of various studies of personality among prisoners. For example, 3 per cent of a group of prisoners in Georgia were found to be psychopathics as compared to 9 per cent in South Carolina and 45 per cent in Kentucky. It is hard to believe that such differences actually exist among criminals in states so similar in population and in their economic and social life. In the third place, the studies have been concerned mainly with convicted criminals. Such emotional and mental deviations as are found among prison populations might be contributory factors in their conviction and commitment.[16] Furthermore, we may believe that the incidents connected with the crime and the subsequent trial and commitment, together with the prison experience, are themselves causative factors in the development of abnormal personalities. This opinion is held by a number of court and prison officials. In other cases both crime and the abnormality may be resultants of antecedent conditions which are not revealed by the ordinary methods of investigation, while in still other instances the abnormality may have contributed directly to the commission of the crime.

The assumption on the part of some investigators that a "perfectly healthy mind does not originate conduct that is criminal"[17] rests logically upon the assumption that the social order is in a state of perfect health, and that the individual is the only factor out of adjustment whenever a crime is committed. Indeed, it is

[16] *Report of national commission* . . . , *op. cit.*, "Causes of crime," Vol. 1.

[17] *Arizona mental hygiene*, Survey, p. 47. For comprehensive criticism, see *Report of national commission* . . . , *op. cit.*, No. 13, Vol. I.

asserted that "mental health entails socialization and therefore precludes antisocial conduct."[18] A subcommittee of the National Crime Commission quoted the views of the American Medical Association as follows:

> The behavior shown by persons who follow a career of crime is founded also on defects of bodily constitution, faulty training, or both and may equally be labeled mental disease. *This conclusion is permissible even when the criminal has shown no evidence of mental disease other than his criminal behavior.*[19]

This view, less popular today though still held by many who try to speak with authority, would apparently define as mentally diseased any person convicted of crime regardless of circumstances under which the offense was committed or of the nature of the law. Accordingly, a person who falls repeatedly into the clutches of the law in an environment which provides no adequate outlet for normal human tendencies would thereby be classed as mentally diseased. Moreover, as the commission points out, "if crime itself is understood as mental disease, the statement that mental disease is a cause of crime is meaningless." It is equivalent to saying that mental disease is a cause of mental abnormality.

In view of the evidence one may conclude that mental deviations and diseases are causal factors when considered in the light of other conditions, but the claim that such abnormalities produce crime directly seems hardly justified.

Conclusions as to mentality and crime. In view of the conflicting nature of the results of a number of studies and the various possible interpretations of the data at hand, one is hardly justified in saying that any one factor discussed in the foregoing is in itself a cause of crime. There is, however, considerable evidence to indicate that these and other factors working together and constituting the total situation lead to criminality. This view is supported not only by experimentation but also by common sense. Bernard Glueck has expressed the logic of this view admirably.[20]

---

[18] Quoted by National Crime Commission, *op. cit.*, p. 56.

[19] Quoted in *Report of national commission . . .* , *op. cit.*, from an editorial, "Psychiatry in relation to crime," in the *American Medical Association Journal*, Aug. 2, 1930.

[20] Quoted in *Report of national commission . . .* , *op. cit.*, pp. 58–59, from *First annual report of the psychiatric clinic*, Sing Sing, p. 12.

In any psychopathological study of the offender, the error must be avoided of seeing the cause of the criminal act entirely in the constitutional make-up of the individual. That such is not the case does not require much proof. The criminal act in every instance is the resultant of the interaction between a particularly constituted personality and a particular environment. Because 59 per cent of the total number of cases examined were classifiable in psychopathological terms, it does not at all mean that these individuals were predestined to commit crime. In fact, there are, in all probability, many more psychopathologically classifiable people outside of prison than there are within prison. That more of them do not get into prison is due to the fact that they have had the many benefits of suitable environment and the protection which goes with these benefits, a protection of which those who do get into prison have been deprived to a greater or lesser extent.

Social Factors and Crime

The foregoing discussion suggests that any explanation of crime that fails to take into account the social and cultural setting in which the criminality develops is likely to be inadequate. Nevertheless, those who try to explain crime in terms of some particular environmental condition, such as poverty, a broken home, or illiteracy, also find certain difficulties in the way. Again, the results of various studies are not in agreement. Besides, no matter what social condition is selected for study, all classes, criminals and noncriminals, will be found subjected to it.

For instance, Healy and others have found that other factors, such as personality disturbances, parental attitudes, gang connections, and so on, tend to affect conditions of crime and delinquency more significantly than does poverty alone. Blanchard concluded, on the basis of a study of two groups of problem children—one in Philadelphia and one in Los Angeles—that poverty is comparatively unimportant as a cause of antisocial behavior among children, provided the proper psychological relationships exist in the family circle.[21]

There is rather general agreement that the great majority of criminal careers begin in childhood. If this is true, then it may be assumed that whatever conditions produce antisocial or delinquent behavior among children are causal with respect to adult criminality. The effects of poverty may be easily misinterpreted because it is often found with other conditions, such as

[21] Phyllis Blanchard, *Child and society* (New York: Longmans, Green and Company, 1928), pp. 269–270.

emotional and mental abnormalities, and defectiveness, illiteracy, physical handicaps, the broken home, and strained family relationships. An examination of delinquency areas in a large city tends to reveal that a preponderance of delinquencies are committed in the environments where all of these conditions prevail together to a greater extent than in other parts of the community. Under such conditions any single factor might appear to stand out significantly in a particular situation, yet a comprehensive understanding of the total situation might show this as a result of other conditions, among which poverty might conceivably be the most important. Certainly no one familiar with the facts doubts that extreme poverty contributes to ill health, mental retardation, family disturbances, physical handicaps, and, under some circumstances, to the general breakdown of the moral strength and equilibrium of the family and the neighborhood.

Similarly, attempts to evaluate the deterrent influences of formal education and the "good" home may be very misleading. Superior environmental conditions that make the second five or eight years of schooling possible may far outweigh the values of additional schooling. It may be exactly these factors that keep one secure economically and socially. The fact that a considerable proportion of this group was retarded one or more years probably reflects the conditions under which they went to school as well as lack of school attendance. The advantages of education in some respects are like income: one must have a certain amount of it to get along. The last year of training in a technical or vocational course is often the one that secures the individual against disaster.

It may be assumed also that the advantages of formal education, together with the superior social standing that often is both a cause and a consequence of such education, might aid the individual in the evasion of the law. Hence, as in the case of other conditions already discussed, illiteracy, while accounting partly for the individual's failure to make an acceptable adjustment, is no doubt a contributing factor to arrest and conviction. There is need for further study along this line, but investigations already made point clearly to the combinations of factors revealed by this study of the Gluecks as vital with respect to crime.

Shaw and McKay found a slightly greater percentage of broken homes among a group of public-school boys than among

a group of delinquents from an Italian area characterized by a
high rate of delinquency. But we are confronted again with the
difficulties presented by somewhat conflicting data which tend
to throw doubt upon attempts to define delinquency and crime
in terms of "broken homes" without considering other factors.

General family conditions of delinquents. While there is no
conclusive evidence that crime rates are determined directly by
any single family condition considered alone, the data available
suggest that the preponderance of families from which delinquents and criminals come are below the average standards of
efficiency with respect to a number of factors regarded as important in the development of socialized personality. By a
process of elimination on the basis of undesirable conditions,
such as extreme poverty, unsanitary surroundings, overcrowding, parental neglect, alcoholism, obscenity, immorality, crimi-
nalism, and mentally diseased parents, Healy and Bronner found
that less than 8 per cent of 2000 young offenders were living in
what could be called "reasonably good conditions for the up-
bringing of a child."[22]

The Gluecks reported an abnormal or unhealthy family situation in 60 per cent of the 510 cases studied, due largely to the
long or complete absence of one or both parents. In 71 per cent
of the cases where the home was broken, the rift occurred at the
time the offender was at the "formative and impressionable age
of 14 or under," and in 29 per cent of the cases the family disruption came when the offender was in adolescence. Abnormal
home situations appeared in 84 per cent of the entire group.
Death broke the family in 60 per cent of the cases of disrupted
homes; and there was divorce or desertion in 25 per cent of the
broken families. The investigators felt that this was an under-
statement of fact, since it was impossible to secure adequate information on this point due to the sporadic nature of many
desertions.

Court records in families of criminals. The Gluecks[23] found,
among 402 families of men who had served time in the Massachusetts Reformatory, court records for other members of the
family in 207, or 51.5 per cent, of the cases. These records included brothers, sisters, parents, and in nine cases near relatives.
An additional 118 families, 29.4 per cent, showed delinquencies,

---

[22] W. Healy, and A. F. Bronner, *Delinquents and criminals: Their making and unmaking* (New York: The Macmillan Company, 1926), pp. 128–129.
[23] Glueck, *op. cit.*

such as drunkenness and immorality, which were not recorded
by police courts. Thus, almost 81 per cent of the families who
furnished the group of prisoners studied had other criminal or
delinquent members. It is significant, also, that the offenses in
slightly more than 75 per cent of the 402 families were more
serious than drunkenness or other delinquencies not recognized
by the police.

Delinquency areas. It has long been maintained that the
rates of crime and delinquency vary widely between local areas.
The investigations of Shaw, McKay, and others have thrown
considerable light upon the character of these delinquency areas.
These studies tend to show that the highest rates of delinquency
and crime occur in certain types of transition zones in the immediate vicinities of the commercial centers of large cities and
in the slum areas surrounding or adjacent to large industrial
plants. The families in such areas are characterized by the unfortunate conditions already discussed. Such areas are marked
by a relative absence of parks, playgrounds, boys' clubs, and
other effects of organized social intelligence. Gang life, through
which individuals find some form of expression, springs up and
criminal careers develop. In such situations traditions of lawlessness are established which serve as a further stimulus to
crime. Among the 510 ex-prisoners studied by the Gluecks, less
than 16 per cent had membership in any "social club or organization for the constructive use of leisure." The great majority
of investigators are agreed that habitual criminality generally
is traceable in part to the experiences of childhood. Healy and
Bronner emphasize this point: "The moral spirit of a community
is easily reflected in the conduct of its children. Where such
general spirit is poor, there is very ready imitation of the predatory tendencies of public officials and other adults who were
allowed to persist in evil-doing."[24]

Similarly Van Waters remarks, "Almost all the delinquencies
of youth are the expressed social standards of a part of the adult
community which is under no indictment and which flourishes
without condemnation."[25]

The tremendous importance of the local environmental factors
is further indicated by the work of Shaw and McKay, who note
that ". . . while the relative rates of delinquency in these
high-rate areas remained more or less constant over a period of

[24] Healy and Bronner, *op. cit.*, p. 128.
[25] Miriam Van Waters, *Youth in conflict* (New York: New Republic, 1926), p. 128.

20 years, the nationality composition of the population changed almost completely in this interval."[26]

Companions and associates. The importance of companions and associates in the development of criminality is suggested by practically all of the scientific literature on the subject. Thrasher's study of the gang[27] throws this whole matter of companionship and behavior into clear relief. It should be noted that Thrasher does not conclude that gang life is in itself a cause of crime but, rather, is one of the factors in a total situation and reflects to a large extent the prevalent behavior codes and standards of the community. Shaw and Myers found that more than 90 per cent of 6000 cases of stealing were committed in groups of two or more.[28] Breckinridge and Abbott concluded that " . . . there is scarcely a type of delinquent boy who is not associated with others in his wrongdoing."[29]

The facts presented here point to a concurrency between certain environmental and subjective factors and crime. It is important, however, to remember that all the studies deserve careful interpretation to avoid an overemphasis of any one factor. The "broken home" and poverty may be inevitable consequences of antecedent conditions which are also largely responsible for the antisocial behavior. For instance, continued unemployment of the chief breadwinner of a family might pave the way for both crime and the broken home. Similarly, mental deficiency is apparently a factor in broken homes and also in criminality. Hence, to speak of causes of crime without some conception of the nature of the intercausal relations may be very misleading.

Crime and the Law

Legal rights and duties. The legal rights and duties of people cover a wide range of interests, including obligations to the state; to the public in general, as defined by policies concerning health, education, morality, economy, the public peace and welfare; to public justice, such as would be involved by aiding a criminal to escape, perjury, and bribery; and obligations with reference to persons and property.[30]

[26] *Report of national crime commission, op. cit.*, p. 81.

[27] Frederick M. Thrasher, *Gang: A study of 1313 gangs in Chicago* (Chicago: University of Chicago Press, 1927).

[28] *Juvenile delinquent*, Illinois Crime Survey, 1929.

[29] S. P. Breckinridge, and E. Abbott, *Delinquent child and the home* (New York: Russell Sage Foundation, 1928), p. 35.

[30] John S. Bradway, *Law and social work* (Chicago: University of Chicago Press, 1929).

Legal rights have been classified by Thomas E. Holland according to three major categories:[31]

1. The rights of an individual with reference to himself, such as personal security, reputation, ownership, and exercise of one's professional or vocational calling.

2. Rights arising from contract or the terms of a particular contract. These rights may include a very wide range of relationships, particularly in the fields of exchange and labor.

3. Rights that arise out of certain relationships to which the law attaches rules, such as those existing between members of a family, between trustee and beneficiary, between public officials and citizens, and between certain professional and occupational classes and the public.

Holland presents also a classification of the laws creating legal rights. The first concerns the functional aspects of law, including the substantive law, which declares rights and duties, and the administrative law, which defines the method of expressing rights already declared.

The second elemental phase of law concerns the way by which it came into existence. Here we have: (1) the common law, which arose originally out of customs, usage, and precedent, and finally came to be written in the form of court decisions; (2) the statute law, written by legislatures and parliaments; and (3) the constitutional law, embodying the fundamental principles of the state as related to general welfare. Constitutional law takes precedence over statutes, and the statute law over the common law, wherever these conflict in the judgment of the courts.

Crime is inseparable from the legal guarantees established with reference to certain enjoyments and privileges. Every legal right implies also an obligation. Furthermore, the failure to meet a legal obligation usually results in the invasion of a right. For instance, if a father refuses to support his children, their right to be supported has been invaded. On the other hand, the attempt to exercise one's rights may at times infringe upon the rights of others. For instance, the exercise of "free" speech sometimes infringes upon the right of another to enjoy a good reputation. Crime results from failure to reach a proper balancing of legal rights and obligations.

Law as compromise. An examination of the processes involved in the making of law reveals that it is not a uniform system arising

[31] Thomas E. Holland, *Elements of jurisprudence* (New York: Oxford University Press, 1924). See also Bradway, *op. cit.*, p. 43.

primarily out of established principles of universal justice but more often represents a form of compromise between conflicting social and economic interests. This process may be easily observed and studied in the legislative enactments of modern times. In earlier periods, when the masses were, to a larger extent than now, the pawns of a comparatively small ruling class, the force of conflicting interests was not so much in evidence. The established rules by which society was governed seem, from a distance, to have been fashioned solely by the wishes of the few. This is not strictly true. Even the few were not always in perfect agreement. Furthermore, since the rules changed slowly and the masses were governed largely by habit, any sudden alterations in the patterns of the group produced disturbances often harmful to the monarchical rulers.

Thus, we find in the very beginnings of law the element of conflict and compromise. This process is revealed particularly in the evolution of modern English and American jurisprudence. Some of the compromises were preceded by rather bitter conflicts, such as the Revolution of 1688 in England and the Civil War in the United States. For the most part, the struggles between groups are confined to such comparatively minor opposition as newspaper and platform attacks and legislative lobbying.

New laws invoke opposition. There always is some opposition to the enactment of new laws; otherwise there would be no reason at all for the law. The most open and serious type of opposition assumes the form of criminal behavior. A person is not a criminal so long as he merely advocates changing the law according to constitutional means. He becomes a criminal only when his behavior contradicts the law. The attempt to harmonize the law with the dominant social interests sometimes leads to variations in its interpretation and application. Accordingly, an act which might be accepted as perfectly legal on one day might be illegal on another. For example, the Federal Constitution embodies a guarantee of free speech, yet, as in the case of Eugene V. Debs during World War I, men have been jailed for exercising it. Here is an instance where a principle is regarded as sufficiently important to warrant legal protection. Yet under certain conditions social interest demands protection against it. In this way the number of arrests in a community might show a sudden increase or decrease depending upon a change in circumstances without any change in law or in the habitual behavior of the individuals arrested.

Furthermore, in spite of the fact that law lags behind the most advanced social thought, it tends, in new and rapidly changing societies, to run ahead of the behavior habits of a considerable proportion of the population. When a law is passed contradicting a customary mode of behavior, the habitual behavior becomes criminal in character. Besides, the social interest nearly always crosses the path of individual interests. The whole history of American social legislation is illustrative of these conflicts and their effects upon crime. Laws affecting hours of labor, food, health, factory conditions, trusts, and the like have all produced conflicts affecting in some way the crime situation in the country.

Law and crisis.   The intensity of the social interest and its demand for protection depend upon circumstances. These usually appear great in times of catastrophe, such as floods, storms, wars, revolutions, economic depressions, and famine. In such times there is likely to be legal interference with the usual conduct of many people. In communities where invasion by new cultural groups is taking place, there is a tendency to tighten the strings of legal protection. Under such circumstances the increased legal defenses tend to cut directly across the accustomed ways of the new arrivals and thus intensify the conflict, which may result in further increases of crime.

Inertia of the law.   Crime is affected also by the inertia of the law. This may be illustrated by the persistence of old laws designed for protection of certain institutional interests which have not changed to meet the altered demands of these institutions. In most cases such laws tend to become obsolete. Laws defining woman's status in the family and "Blue Sunday" laws are examples.[32]

The function of law.   Human behavior is extremely complex. No system of law could hope to regulate the whole of it. The function of law, therefore, is to regulate certain types of behavior which experience has shown are most likely to produce conflict. The vast proportion of social conduct is regulated by custom, tradition, and social approval. Whether or not a customary mode of living becomes obnoxious depends largely upon what people are used to doing and upon the circumstances. What might be perfectly proper in some parts of the world or in the open country might be very unwise in another part of the world or in an urban environment. Differences in habits of conduct that

[32] Fowler V. Harper, "Pragmatist process in law," *The International Journal of Ethics*, April, 1931.

produce conflicts are likely to become matters for the law. In this event, the dominant element in society will likely gain legal expression and force all those whose customary ways have been outlawed either to change their habits and redirect their modes of conduct or to become criminals. This appears to be one reason why crime rates are relatively high in expanding communities fed largely by strange and diverse peoples from outside.

Crime and Inequalities Before the Law

The function of law and its relation to crime have been briefly discussed. It should be noted, however, that law does not operate automatically. Criminal justice involves arrest, indictment, prosecution, and finally sentence, with the possibility of carrying the case to a higher court. At every step there are chances that justice may be thwarted. The chances that justice may miscarry are greatly increased by the possession of wealth and influence. The power of wealth and influence is enhanced by our so-called "sporting theory" of justice, according to which legal procedure assumes something of the proportions of a game, where each side is permitted to make certain "plays and counterplays." Ordinarily, in contests of sport there is an effort to present opposing sides that are fairly evenly matched. Members of the "Big Ten" do not challenge high-school teams. In the administration of justice, however, unequal conflicts often occur. Many men are unable to take advantage of all that the law allows because they are too poor, too ignorant, or too unimportant socially. Added to these, in the case of minority racial groups, is the fact of race prejudice. As we shall see later, these gross inequalities before the law account to a considerable extent for the differential crime rates between various classes, races, and nationality groups. In proportion as one increases his chances of evading or thwarting the law does he also increase his chances to break the law without becoming a criminal.

Rights of the accused. It is a fundamental part of our theory of justice that the accused has an individual right to be represented by counsel. The essential basis of this right is to prevent injustice by giving both the accuser and the accused an equal chance to present their respective cases. It also has been argued that only in this way can the whole truth be ascertained. The motive is a noble one and represents an important step in the direction of humane attitudes toward the accused. Unfortunately, however, the application of the theory has often produced results directly opposed to those intended. The disposition to leave the matter of employing defense counsel entirely to the accused frequently means that those who have money are defended by lawyers thoroughly trained in the "quirks and quibbles" of the law, while the poor and friendless are convicted without any efficient representation. Thus, it may be argued that the theory as actually practiced has tended to give the least protection to those who need it most.

Such guarantees to the accused as the right of freedom from self-incrimination, the right to challenge the composition of the jury, the right to know the names of his own witnesses, the right of presumption of innocence, the right to be excused from cross-examination, the right of appeal, and many other rights which some people have felt give the accused an unwarranted advantage over the state, do not extend in actual practice to the poor person ignorant of these rights.

The person who cannot afford bail has little chance to secure competent witnesses. In the absence of a defense counsel he is oftentimes at the mercy of the police department. Frequently his confession is obtained without a trial, and he is carted off to the penitentiary without ceremony. Even when counsel is provided for him, it frequently is inefficient and begins to operate too late to be of any real assistance. The time when a man needs help is when he is in jail waiting for the wheels of the law to turn. Contrast the situation of the poor and ignorant with that of the accused who has money. In some instances the influential position of the accused prevents a formal arrest from taking place, bail is arranged, excellent counsel is obtained, the trial is postponed if necessary, pending complete preparation for a successful defense. When the trial is called, every possible interest of the accused is guarded; and when, in spite of every precaution against it, conviction is obtained, the defense is ready with an appeal which may mean a complete reversal of the decision.[33]

Attempts to equalize justice before the law. It has been noted that our system of government recognizes an obligation of the state to protect the innocent as well as to convict the guilty. There is a tendency to meet this obligation with reference to the accused by attempting to provide representation for those who cannot pay for it themselves. The pioneer work in this field is being done

[33] See "Lawlessness in law enforcement," pp. 267–347 of *Report of the national commission on law observance and enforcement*, No. 11, 1931, for an excellent statement of this whole problem.

largely by private "legal aid societies," many of which arose to meet the demands for legal aid in connection with social work. By far the major portion of the aid furnished by such organizations is in the form of education as to the rights of the poor under the law, and protection of the poor against various types of swindlers and oppressors.

The practice in many cities and states is to appoint a defender at the time of trial for the accused who appears without a defense. These defenders are frequently young and inexperienced lawyers, or persons who volunteer their services, or who can be secured cheaply. In many cases the accused with little money secures the services of shyster lawyers who make a business of exploiting the poor who are accused of crime. Even where good lawyers are secured, they are hardly expected to expend the same amount of energy and time for a small fee as for a large one.

The public defender.   Perhaps the best move so far made in the direction of equalizing the rights of the poor and the rich before the law is the establishment of the office of Public Defender. This movement started in Los Angeles in 1914, with the appointment of a public defender for the superior court. Since then the movement has spread to a large number of cities, and its establishment and support have been justified. It puts the state on both sides of the issue and gives the court the appearance of a fact-finding body rather than that of a mere referee in an arena. However, it is very doubtful if this provision, even if it were made universally available to the ignorant poor in the United States, would ever be equivalent to the advantages of wealth and influence, without some fundamental changes in our legal procedure and practice.

Recommendations of the Crime Commission.   Certain recommendations of the National Commission on Law Observance and Enforcement[34] may be summarized: 1. A statutory minimum time for the preparation of the defense but allowing the judge discretion in the extension of the time under certain circumstances. 2. Adoption by states of the statutory rule (now established in federal courts) by which a judge is automatically disqualified from sitting when an affidavit filed by the accused gives strong evidence of a bias. 3. The requirement that the state furnish a list of its witnesses to the accused at reasonable times. (This rule already exists in some states.) 4. Representation of the accused by counsel in all except cases with very light

[34] Report No. 11, pp. 340–347.

penalties and where the accused refuses counsel. 5. Jury lists to be made up of qualified persons regardless of color. (This recommendation does not require a statutory change but only one of administrative practice in some parts of the country.) 6. Simplification and classification of the law relating to the admissibility of evidence of offenses for which the accused is not on trial. (Lack of simplification in this respect often subjects the accused to unfairness, especially in cross-examinations.) 7. Comment should be allowed upon failure of the accused to testify. (Some states now permit such comments.) 8. Payment of judges, prosecutors, and court officials should not be made from fines and costs. (In other words, payment of persons concerned with criminal justice should not depend upon conviction.) 9. Empowering the judge to comment upon the weight of the evidence. (The federal courts and the courts of several states now permit such comment. Some arguments in its favor are that the judge would be inclined to take his task more seriously; that the comment of an impartial person experienced in the law would be helpful to the jury; that it would tend to make misconduct in the trial procedure less likely to occur.) 10. Empowering the appellate court in all jurisdictions to reduce sentences without a new trial. 11. Empowering appellate courts to grant new trials in the interest of justice even though no exception was taken in the lower court. (On this point the commission's study showed that convictions carrying the death penalty were affirmed by the higher court because no exceptions had been raised to the unfairness in the courts below.)

Agencies that bring the accused to trial. A great deal of criticism has been leveled at the trial procedure of the courts. As already noted, such criticism has considerable justification. Still greater opportunities for the miscarriage of justice inhere in the agencies created to bring the accused to trial. Analyses of a number of important crime surveys by Alfred Bettman of the Cincinnati bar[35] revealed an enormous difference between the number of arrests made and prosecutions instituted and the number of actual convictions. It was shown that a comparatively small proportion of those who escaped punishment did so by jury acquittal. The explanation is found largely in the administration of the prosecutor's office. Certain facts stand out: 1. The

[35] The analyses were made for the National Commission on Law Observance and Enforcement. See the commission's *Report on prosecution*, No. 4, April 22, 1931, pp. 45–138.

prosecutor has wide discretionary powers in the dismissal of cases without trial. He may decide which cases are to be prosecuted and which laws are to be enforced. This often subjects him to political pressure. 2. The prosecutor's salary is generally small, his term of service short, and his tenure uncertain. 3. The political nature of his office frequently leads him to adopt an ineffective and perfunctory routine with respect to the majority of cases and to play up the sensational and spectacular type of case for publicity purposes. 4. His subordinates are frequently appointed as a matter of political patronage. The staff usually is comprised of inexperienced young persons whose terms of service are short. 5. The equipment, organization, and methods of the prosecutor's office are independent of any adequate system of central control, and there is a notable lack of co-ordination between his office and the work of the policemen and sheriff.

Much depends on the character of men. As the commission suggests, specific changes in legal machinery will help to remove unfairness in prosecutions. Of more importance, perhaps, are the character and training of the men who operate the machinery. The wide differences in individuals and circumstances make it necessary that judges and prosecuting officials be given considerable powers. Such powers may lead to grave injustices except as exercised by highly intelligent persons who not only desire fairness but are sufficiently free from political pressure to demand it. It is therefore important that political considerations be eliminated in the selection of officials concerned with the administration of justice.

Recent years have witnessed decided trends toward classification and individualization in the treatment of prisoners, though overcrowding in the prisons has retarded these tendencies, especially in many of the state prisons.

Parole and Probation

Parole. Parole and individual treatment of prisoners are of comparatively recent date. At the opening of the present century convicts were dealt with *en masse*, and parole and the indeterminate sentence had not even reached the stage of experimentation.[36] Fifty years ago " . . . prisoners were released at the prison door at the expiration of sentence—in some states less

---

[36] Amos W. Butler, "What the courts, the prisons, the employer, and the public should know of the released prisoner," *Journal of Criminal Law and Criminology*, XXI (Feb., 1931): 504–512.

commutation or 'good time'—with no one to get them employment or act as friend and supervisor."

Factors correlated with successful parole. Certain facts seem to have a relation to success or failure of parole. According to the Illinois committee, crimes of robbery, fraud, and forgery show a high proportion of violations. It is interesting to note, also, that the violations tended to be higher for those who committed crimes alone than for those who had three or more associates.

The recommendations of the court were a factor in the success or failure of paroles in Illinois. The violation rate appeared lower for those for whom parole was recommended by the court than for those paroled over the protest of the court. The Illinois study showed a relatively low rate of parole violations among the parolees who had been sentenced for long periods of three to twenty years. Murderers had a small proportion of parole violations. More significant still was the fact that the longer the period actually served, the higher the violation rate. Those with previous reformatory or penitentiary records showed higher rates of violation, while those with no previous record showed low violation rates. The lowest rates of parole violations were found among those with regular employment at the time of arrest, while the highest rates were among those with no work record or those who were casual workers.

Need for better organization and personnel. Investigations of the results of paroling prisoners indicate that failure can be attached not to a weakness in the theory but to inadequacies in organization and use of the parole machinery. Notable is the lack of trained parole officers and of complete and careful follow-up work. There is also a lack of understanding of the individual ex-prisoner.

Parole is found frequently to be based upon facts that have little relation to the prisoner's fitness to make good. Social and mental factors are often given relatively little attention. The opinion of the prosecutors, judges, relatives, friends, and parents often have an undue influence on the attitudes of parole boards. Furthermore, there is an inconsistency in the system that releases hardened criminals without supervision upon expiration of sentence but demands supervision of lesser offenders.[37]

[37] National Commission on Law Observance and Enforcement, *op. cit.*, No. 9, pp. 303–305. Also Earl Sachs, unpublished paper, "Recent criticisms of probation and parole," University of Wisconsin, 1932, pp. 36–37.

It seems inadvisable on the basis of parole experience to give out, generally, information concerning the ex-prisoner, though as a rule such information is entrusted to the employer since his attitude is an important factor in the readjustment of the offender. Employment should be secured, if possible, with employers who are sympathetic with the purpose of the parole officers. Such sympathy is particularly necessary since one of the difficulties in the way of rehabilitation inheres in the inability of the ex-convict to secure satisfactory employment. Out of 476 successful employers interviewed in New York City 312 stated unequivocally that they would never knowingly hire a released offender.[38]

There is also great need for full co-operation between the courts and the prison. Formerly the courts were inclined to feel that their job was finished when the culprit was convicted. There is a growing tendency, however, for the courts and prison officials to regard their work as merely part of a larger program of prevention and reconstruction. Such understanding involves exchanges of records and opinions. It means that the recommendations of the courts to the prisons should go beyond a mere statement of the court's wishes with respect to the term of incarceration and should include recommendations concerning the prisoner's personality, his problems and background, as revealed in the trial investigations. Something along this line has been done. As already suggested, it cannot develop very far except as the courts become adequately equipped with experts in criminology.

The parole confronts society with the problem of investigating the conditions under which the offense was committed. It also imposes the obligation to supervise the activities of the offender after his release. In view of the importance of the parole board, it is very important that it be kept completely out of politics.

Success and failure of parole. The committee for the study of the workings of the indeterminate-sentence law and parole in Illinois, in 1928, studied the successes of 3000 parolees, all of whom had been released at least two and a half years from prison and the majority of whom had been at large in the state from three to five years. Among this number of ex-prisoners 74.3 per cent had not violated their paroles and 25.7 per cent had done so. We should be reminded, however, that merely keeping the terms of the parole is not proof that the criminal is making good. As the Illinois committee points out, "making

[38] Clem J. Wyle, *Employment of released offenders.*

good" should mean a change of attitude, often a change of associates. It means a wholesome participation in the life of the community, including an attachment to legitimate employment. It is the conclusion of the committee that at least 35 per cent of the men paroled from the Illinois State Reformatory failed to "make good," either on parole or within three to five years of the time they were paroled. Those punished in the prison by solitary confinement had unusually high rates of violation. The youngest and oldest parolees had the highest violation rates. It is noteworthy, also, that those of inferior intelligence showed no greater tendency to break the terms of their parole than those of average and superior intelligence. Furthermore, according to Adler's examinations, repeaters showed a higher average intelligence than the first offenders. The study showed the personality factor to be important. Those with "egocentric personality pattern" presented especially difficult problems. Almost as bad were those classed as "socially inadequate." Strangely, those classed as "emotionally unstable" showed a relatively low violation rate.

The Illinois committee found that the operation of the parole system in Illinois had tended to decrease the number of pardons granted by the governor and had lengthened the average period of incarceration in penal institutions.

It is a mistake to hold the parole authorities entirely responsible for the failure of a parolee, since in addition to the variable factors in the individual's background, over which the parole officers have no control, there is also the responsibility of the trial court and the institution from which the individual has been released. The chances of success are largely determined by the work and attitudes of those two agencies.

Recommendations of the Illinois committee. The committee concludes its report by recommending that (1) the system of indeterminate sentence and parole be continued in Illinois; and (2) the parole system be accorded freedom from political influence similar to that generally granted the public schools and our great state universities in the United States. It also urges the necessity of a highly trained group of parole and probation officers and the full co-operation of the courts. The committee found the penal institutions were in no case definitely organized and operated for the preparation of men for successful careers outside. Education was poorly directed, idleness was prevalent, the library facilities were inadequate. Prison guards were often politically appointed and were pawns of political influence.

Recreational facilities were almost nonexistent. The parole staff was too small and, for the most part, not trained to deal adequately with the problems of rehabilitation.

Glueck study of parole. The Gluecks found that about 25 per cent of the parolees studied were either serving time in some penal institution or were fugitives from justice, and almost 80 per cent had committed criminal acts during the postparole period. Only one third of the cases had at some time during the parole or postparole period used the occupations taught them in the reformatory, and in over half of these the men had been in these occupations prior to their commitment and merely continued them following release. While there was a slight decrease in dependency, there was also a decrease in the proportion in economic comfort and an increase in the proportion of those in the marginal economic class. There was slight improvement in the general marital conditions, though the mobility conditions remained essentially unchanged. The Glueck study revealed significant correlations between the criminal conduct of a group of ex-reformatory inmates and various objective and subjective factors, including industrial status, attitudes toward family, and the use of leisure time.

Almost 23 per cent of the parolees were laid off, or had to quit their jobs because they were temporary. Only 2.1 per cent kept their jobs for more than 12 months, and the average time for which the entire group held their jobs was only 3.1 months, though 45.5 per cent of the Massachusetts factory workers held their jobs more than five years and less than 16 per cent less than one year. During the period of the parole, which was in the high-wage period of the war, 73 per cent of the parolees received less than $25 per week. The conditions of supervision were bad. The actual periods of supervision were short. In 80 per cent of the cases the employment of the parolee was secured by himself. Sixty per cent of the parolees held their first jobs for one month or less, if at all. Over half of the parolees were not once seen personally by the parole agent on his own initiative, and in a large proportion of the cases the parolees were not visited once in six or more months, on an average.

It appears, then, that present criticism of parole must be lodged against the unscientific methods under which it has operated rather than against the theory.

Probation. Parole, as already noted, is a form of supervision that follows incarceration. Probation, on the other hand, seeks to prevent the need for prison sentence by supervising the conduct of the individual either in his old neighborhood or in a new one selected by the court. Hardly any state, except Massachusetts, had experimented with probation prior to the establishment of the juvenile courts in Chicago and Denver in 1899. Following that year, both the juvenile court and probation spread rapidly in the United States. At the present time, practically every state has some provision for probation. It has been applied chiefly in the treatment of juvenile delinquents, though most of the states have some provision for adult probation.

The history of probation in this country shows it to be a natural development, in view of the reaction against the earlier emphasis upon harsh punishment. The use of probation among juveniles has been particularly encouraged by investigations in the fields of sociology and psychology, which have tended to place a new emphasis upon the experiences of childhood and adolescence and have called for a re-evaluation of institutional treatment.

Results. The results of probation have varied widely. The great difficulty here, as with parole, is the lack of trained personnel, adequate machinery, and the effective support of public opinion. These deficiencies are particularly in evidence in the smaller cities, where the courts rely upon untrained citizens to do the probationary work. Even in the larger centers, the probation officers are often untrained for the work; and where they have the training, the loads are too heavy to be carried with any degree of efficiency. Some legal handicaps to successful probation work include the limitations placed upon the courts in the application of probation. For example, probation in many states is limited by the type of offense, the length of sentence, whether or not the offender has been previously convicted of a crime, etc.[39]

Individual treatment necessary. Successful probation is not a matter of uniform supervision; it presents a problem of individual adjustment. It is important that selections for probation be made intelligently, and this cannot be done without careful investigation. Here is need for an expert court, personnel, and machinery. Where such needs have been met, probation has been more successful, on the whole, than institutional treatment.

Length of sentence and reform. The curative effects of long sentences seem to have little relation to the seriousness of the offense. The consequences of long sentences may be particularly tragic in the case of mere boys who go to prison and come out

[39] Sachs, *op. cit.*, p. 3.

middle-aged men to find the world changed and their habits of life rigidly fixed by the prison existence. Experience indicates that such cases are never readjusted.

Furthermore, the whole prison system needs to free itself from the concept of punishment for crime. The emphasis must be upon prevention and reconstruction. No one would think of deciding in advance the length of time that a patient should remain in the hospital merely on the basis of the seriousness or acuteness of the disease. Nor would anyone think of giving all the patients the same kind of treatment. A somewhat similar approach must be made with reference to our treatment of criminal classes. With the concept of punishment gone, it becomes necessary to have prisons manned by criminologists who know how to study human motives and limitations. The fact that a prisoner is a good prisoner in the sense of obeying prison rules and befriending the guards is by no means absolute proof that he is ready for citizenship, any more than a correct salute indicates a brave soldier, the opinion of some army officers to the contrary notwithstanding.

Prison labor.   There have been, in general, six different systems of prison labor in the United States. These are:

1. The "lease system," according to which the prisoners are leased for a certain consideration. The lessee must feed and clothe the prisoners. This system has the advantage of relieving the state of the financial problem of providing penitentiaries, but as a humane and reformative system of treatment it is a failure.

2. The "contract system," by which the state supplies the labor of its prisoners by contract. In this case, the state retains custody and also maintains them. The contractor furnishes the machinery and raw materials, oversees the work, and disposes of the product. He pays the state so much for the labor of the prisoner, and the state reserves certain rights with reference to defining conditions of labor. As in the "lease system," this practice has the advantage of freeing the state from certain financial burdens and problems of control, but again the system does not rehabilitate offenders. The emphasis in this case, as in the other, is on financial returns, and consequently the prisoner is first and last a means to an end.

3. The "piece price system," a modified form of the "contract system." In this case the manufacturer pays so much per unit of product instead of a set price for the prisoner's labor. Furthermore, this system permits the state to retain complete control

of its prisoners. The objections to this system are the same, though less serious, as to the first two systems defined.

4. The "public account system," giving the state complete control not only of the prisoners but also of the goods produced. This system frequently brings the state into direct competition with private manufacturers and is sometimes costly, due to the inevitable disadvantages of any manufacturing system which must depend entirely upon a prison class of labor. Here also is the tendency to place the emphasis upon financial returns and to overlook the human aspects of the situation.

5. The "state use system," a restricted form of the "public account system." Here the prison manufactures goods for state use only. In this way the field of competition is reduced. It has usually been more successful than any of the other prison-labor systems and has seemed to offer larger opportunities for experimentation along various lines of rehabilitation and reformation.

6. The "public works system," applying prison labor to the building and upkeep of public utilities and properties such as roads, rivers, and lands. This system has the advantage of keeping the prisoners largely out of doors, though it is difficult to maintain efficient treatment—physical, mental, and moral.

None of these systems of labor seems to have been effective in the reconstruction of criminals, as judged by the large proportion of persons who continue criminal careers. Various studies agree that a relatively small proportion of offenders are ever fitted by prison labor for successful employment outside. The fundamental business of institutions that confine criminals is the reshaping of personalities. From this point of view, labor becomes an agency rather than an end and should be individualized through an efficient program of vocational education.

Some needs and tendencies. One of the difficulties of providing accurate and complete information about the conditions of crime in the United States is due to a lack of proper co-ordination among the numerous local, state, and national law-enforcement agencies. This lack of co-ordination contributes also to inefficiency in other ways.

Every town and city has its local police agency. Some of these are small, as in the village with its constable whose official duties take up relatively little of his time. In the cities, however, the departments are large and frequently characterized by a high degree of specialization in police work. Distinct from the town or city, in most instances, is the county sheriff's office, and almost all the states now have some kind of state police force. The federal government, moreover, has several separate law-enforcement agencies. Perhaps the most familiar one is the Federal Bureau of Investigation. Others include: Secret Service; Immigration and Customs Services; Postal Inspectors; Narcotics Bureau; and the Bureau of Internal Revenue.

The divisions in the federal-government agencies are based for the most part on differences of function. This is not generally true in the case of city, county, and state forces. Here it is a matter of political and geographic jurisdiction. These jurisdictional controls of the police force in interdependent geographic and political areas often give rise to jealousies that interfere with good police work. The evils of the system have been made prominent by modern transportation and communication, which have destroyed the natural boundary lines that prevailed in a pioneer civilization. The conditions that have contributed to police inefficiency in America include insecurity of tenure, low standards, and lack of current public interest in law-enforcement problems.

The F.B.I. National Academy. During recent years, however, numerous improvements have been made in standards of efficiency and in the desire of the public to understand and aid the police in their work. The Federal Bureau of Investigation has done more through its peace-officer training programs to raise the level of law enforcement in this country than has any other agency. It has had the support and co-operation of educational institutions, organizations of businessmen and others, and, above all, the co-operation of the policemen themselves.

The efficiency and effectiveness of the F.B.I. as a law-enforcement agency is known and feared by law-breakers and appreciated by law-abiding citizens. The significant contributions of the agency in the field of state and local law enforcement is generally less well known by the people who depend most immediately upon local officers for protection. When J. Edgar Hoover was made Director of the Federal Bureau of Investigation in 1924, he set out to give the people of this country a maximum of security from the criminal elements. This he wanted to do without disturbing local autonomy and without interfering in the slightest degree with the free democratic processes. Accordingly, the F.B.I. National Academy was established in Washington for the training of state and local law-enforcement officers selected from all parts of continental United States and its insular possessions. Three 12-week sessions are held in Washington each year. The standards are high, and the training program is rigid. Nevertheless, there are many more qualified persons who want to enter every session than can be accommodated. More than 2000 peace officers had received certificates of graduation from the National Academy by the end of 1949. In addition to sending back to local agencies highly trained officers, the F.B.I. is continuously responding to calls from local police agencies for assistance in conducting local training schools. Through local schools, initiated largely by National Academy graduates, more than 100,000 policemen throughout the country had been reached by the Academy by the end of 1949.

These training programs have had a profound influence, not only upon the application of science to law enforcement but also upon the attitudes of police officers toward their work. As a consequence, law enforcement in America has been raised to a level where men now talk about it in a new language, a language that carries the marks of a profession. It would be well, also, to bear in mind that it was this far-sighted police-training program that played an incalculable role in the country's defense against saboteurs and enemy spies during World War II. During the first year of the war alone, the F.B.I. conducted 438 civilian defense and war-traffic schools, attended by almost 40,000 police executives and officers. These represented more than 7000 law-enforcement agencies.

Conclusion. The fact that practically all habitual criminal careers begin in childhood and also that the majority of adult criminals have committed previous offenses is a serious indictment of our methods of dealing with delinquency and crime. Among 510 ex-prisoners studied by the Gluecks, 433 had records of previous offenses. These 433 had 1944 offenses previous to the ones which resulted in sentence to the Massachusetts Reformatory, and 52 per cent of these earlier offenses were classified as major crimes. The history of this group of offenders reveals a continuous and open conflict with society from an early age. In 77 per cent of the cases open conflict with authorities outside the home developed before the age of sixteen.

The data suggest that antisocial behavior inheres to a large extent in the cultural patterns of the group. We should not conclude, however, that the mental and physical conditions of the individual are unimportant. Nevertheless, these individual factors are partly the products of the social and cultural life, and the direction which they take appears to be determined largely by outside influences. Attempts to generalize crime conditions in terms of single causes or sets of conditions are unwarranted in the light of recent investigations in this field. Certain factors studied together are important, and the whole problem needs to be put on a scientific basis. This involves some changes in legal procedure and prison methods, and the education of public opinion.

It is the opinion of the majority of investigators that most criminal careers begin in youth and childhood. The most effective measures, therefore, are likely to be those of prevention, applied to the conditions and circumstances under which children grow up. In the meantime, and always, society must be protected from the criminal even at the expense of unwise and wasteful methods.

QUESTIONS

1. (a) What are the principal characteristics and weaknesses of the "demon theory" of crime? (b) of the classical and neo-classical schools? (c) of the positive school?
2. Show evidences of prescientific attitudes toward crime in the modern-day treatment of offenders.
3. What is the general trend of thought among criminologists today as to causes and disposition of criminals?
4. What are the principal difficulties in the way of ascertaining the fundamental causes of crime in individual cases?
5. How are poverty, family situations, disease, illiteracy, physical handicaps, and mental conditions causally related to crime?
6. What is shown, by the studies of Shaw and McKay in "delinquency areas," as to the relation of early environmental factors to crime?
7. Illustrate the various ways by which the extent and nature of crime may be affected by the law.
8. (a) What factors and conditions make for inequalities before the law in the United States? (b) Suggest remedies.
9. What legal principles are violated by the "third degree"?
10. Why is the "third degree" tolerated in the United States?
11. What is the historic position of the courts with regard to criminal responsibility?
12. Evaluate the recommendations of the National Crime Commission summarized in this chapter.
13. (a) Discuss the chief weaknesses in the American system of prevention. (b) Suggest remedies.
14. What are the arguments against leaving the treatment of offenders entirely in the hands of persons trained only in the law?

15. Evaluate probation, parole, and the indeterminate sentence and suggest ways and means of improvement.
16. What are the principal weaknesses in the American prison system?
17. How do you explain the increases and variations in crime as indicated by prison statistics?
18. (a) What factors and conditions may help to explain the relatively high crime rate among 'Negroes? (b) among children of the foreign-born? (c) the relatively low rate among the foreign-born?

REFERENCES

ALEXANDER, F., and STAUB, H., *Criminal, the judge, and the public.* New York: The Macmillan Company, 1931.

BARNES, H. E., *Story of punishment.* Boston: The Stratford Company, 1930.

BARNES, E. B., and TEETERS, N. K., *New horizons in criminology.* New York: Prentice-Hall, 1949.

BERNARD, WILLIAM, *Jailbait.* New York: Greenberg, 1949.

CAVAN, RUTH S., *Criminology.* New York: T. Y. Crowell Company, 1948.

GLUECK, SHELDON and ELEANOR, *Criminal careers in retrospect.* New York: The Commonwealth Fund, 1943.

HEALY, W., and BRONNER, A. F., *Delinquents and criminals: Their making and unmaking.* New York: The Macmillan Company, 1926.

HEALY, W., et al, *Reconstructing behavior in youth.* New York: Alfred A. Knopf, 1929.

HENTIG, HANS VON, *Crime: Causes and conditions.* New York: McGraw-Hill Book Company, 1947.

LAWES, L. W., *Life and death in Sing Sing.* New York: Doubleday and Company, 1928.

LAWES, L. W., *Twenty thousand years in Sing Sing.* New York: Smith and Haas, 1932.

LINDNER, ROBERT M., *Stonewalls and men.* New York: Odyssey Press, 1946.

National Commission on Law Observance and Enforcement: 1931
  No. 3, Report on criminal statistics.
  No. 4, Report on prosecution.
  No. 6, Report on the child offender in the federal system of justice.
  No. 7, Report on the study of the federal courts.
  No. 8, Report on criminal procedure.
  No. 9, Report on penal institutions, probation, and parole.
  No. 10, Report on crime and the foreign-born.
  No. 11, Report on lawlessness in law enforcement.
  No. 12, Report on cost of crime.
  No. 13, Report on police.

POUND, ROSCOE, *Criminal justice in America*. New York: Henry Holt and Company, 1930.

RECKLESS, W. C., *Crime problem*. New York: Appleton-Century-Crofts, 1950.

SHAW, CLIFFORD, and MOORE, M. E., *Natural history of a delinquent career*. Chicago: University of Chicago Press, 1931.

SHAW, CLIFFORD, *Jack-roller*. Chicago: University of Chicago Press, 1931.

SHAW, CLIFFORD, et al, *Delinquency areas*. Chicago: University of Chicago Press, 1929.

SHELDON, W. H., et al, *Varieties of delinquent youth*. New York: Harper and Brothers, 1949.

CHAPTER 15

The Nation's Health and Social Policy

The Evolution of Modern Medicine

There was comparatively little interest in physical well-being prior to the rise of industrial civilization in the nineteenth and twentieth centuries, except among the Hebrew people and in a limited way among the ancient Greeks and Romans. During the Middle Ages the main emphasis was upon the "soul." A healthy body was sometimes viewed as an impediment to spiritual happiness and ultimate salvation. This attitude toward bodily well-being characterizes a large proportion of the Oriental populations today. In earlier societies the ravages of disease were often regarded as visitations of the gods, angered by the sins of the people. Sometimes they were attributed to sinister powers of evil spirits. Accordingly, people sought to mitigate the plagues by appeasing the gods, or by seeking to enlist their support in the war against the evil spirits. Various techniques were used. The most common religious ones were incantations, sacrifices, prayers, and ceremonies. Frequently efforts were made to ward off the disease by the use of magic words, charms, and fetishes. Similar practices may still be found among some small groups in America.

Early speculations about disease. Prior to the modern scientific era, pestilence was the common lot of man. The mortality rate was high, and the average life span was short. This was often considered a blessing. There were here and there individuals who speculated upon the causes and cures of disease apart from the current superstitions of their time; but superstitious beliefs were too heavily weighted with moral and religious meanings to be uprooted by the experimentations of isolated individuals. Nothing short of a cataclysmic change in the economic and social environment could do it.

The Greeks, and to some extent the Romans, speculated upon the causes of disease, and in some instances it appears as if the age of scientific medicine was almost attained in the classical civilizations of antiquity. These earlier speculations were brought to a premature close with the break-up of the Roman Empire, the rise of Christianity, and the barbarian invasions, and they did not reappear again until toward the close of the medieval period. The forebodings of the germ theory of disease are seen in 1564, when Fracastoro of Vienna suggested that diseases might be spread by particles too minute to be perceived by the eye. In the last half of the eighteenth century, however, Kircher, a Roman Catholic monk, perceived the organisms now called bacteria; and in the following year the germ theory of disease was suggested by an Austrian physician, Plenciz.

The germ theory becomes established fact.   Much of the discussion about diseases during the first half-century following Plenciz was, however, crude speculation. Scientific inquiry frequently met with bitter religious opposition. As a result, the germ theory of disease was not a firmly established fact until after the middle of the nineteenth century. A number of men contributed to the establishment of this fact. The most important of them all, however, was the French chemist Louis Pasteur, whose discoveries laid the foundations for the future development of medical science. The first practical application of the germ theory of disease to human ills was in the prevention of pus formations following surgical operations.

Joseph Lister, a surgeon, demonstrated in 1867 that inflammation of surgical wounds was harmful and could be avoided by preventing the inception of micro-organisms. This was a startling demonstration because it ran counter not only to the prevailing ethical concepts but also to the current beliefs among medical men, who had maintained that these pus formations were necessary to recovery; hence the term "laudable pus." In the meantime, experimentations were being conducted on the lower animals, with the result that by the end of the nineteenth century it was known not only that germs cause disease but that certain types of germs under certain conditions produce particular kinds of diseases. A number of these diseases, including tuberculosis, typhoid, cholera, and diphtheria, had been definitely classified and studied. We may think of the last half of the nineteenth century as the period which, in the main, separates the world of scientific experimentation and treatment in matters of health from that of superstition and magic.

Advances in curative medicine: developments and changing attitudes. The application of the germ theory to disease opened the way to rapid advances in curative and preventive medicine. As a result, tremendous sums of money have been invested in medical laboratories for study and research, specialists have developed along various lines of medical and surgical practice, and the public has gradually assumed more and more responsibility for the health of the people.

The last half-century has witnessed a tremendous change of attitude on the part of the general public with reference to the cultural and economic values of good health. This change of opinion is reflected in city ordinances and in state and federal laws respecting such matters as hours of labor, factory conditions, housing standards, food inspection, recreational facilities, water supply, and sewage disposal. The federal government maintains a Public Health Service at Washington, and all the states and cities carry on some form of health service. Practically all cities of 50,000 or more, and many smaller ones, maintain special departments with considerable legal powers to enforce conditions that contribute to the general physical welfare. Large sums of money are appropriated every year not only for the immediate treatment and prevention of disease but also for study and research. Public health service has been encouraged and augmented by liberal contributions from private agencies.

As a result of these liberal policies on the part of governments and private foundations, new light has been thrown upon the whole problem of physical well-being. It has been discovered that the causal factors of disease are far more complicated and indirect than was formerly believed; furthermore, that the hazards of ill health may be correlated with economic and social failures, with mental deficiency, and with many other undesirable conditions that were once considered as isolated factors.

This growing emphasis upon the values of physical welfare results largely from the rapid growth of urban centers. The highly concentrated populations of modern cities have increased tremendously the hazards of communicable diseases. Added to this is the *efficiency doctrine* of our civilization, which has placed a premium upon physical fitness. Moreover, we should be reminded that men always have attacked the problem of human welfare with whatever agencies and techniques they had. Societies devoid of any adequate means of affording a reasonable measure of happiness on earth have placed the major emphasis on the probabilities of a happier world to come. We are living in a scientific age. It is inevitable that the scientific method should place the major emphasis upon physical well-being, since in this matter conditions can be observed and treated objectively and the results measured and tabulated. This is as natural and as normal as was the tendency of a superstitious age to become absorbed in magical practice.

As suggested above, physical welfare was first welcomed primarily because it met the demand for mechanical efficiency. The humanitarian aspects of the matter came later. It has been discovered, however, and this fact is established scientifically, that personality development and mental growth—qualities once conceived of as mysterious entities—are very largely the functions of a healthy organism.

Recent achievements and present tendencies. According to the United States Public Health Service, the most significant advances in public-health achievement have been manifested among the lower-age groups. Of course, the great sanitary reforms, such as filtration and treatment of water supplies, food inspection, drainage systems, and isolation of communicable diseases, have markedly diminished diseases of certain kinds among all ages and classes of persons; but the actual saving of life has been most pronounced among children, especially little children and infants. This is why the expectation of life at birth, that is, the average length of time all children born at a given time will live, has increased from about 35 years in 1825 to about 65 years in 1950. This is encouraging and shows clearly that many early deaths can be avoided if existing sanitary knowledge is used.

Age structure and health protection. Age trends prior to World War II suggested that by 1970 the proportion of persons in the United States 65 and over would be about twice the proportion in that age group in 1940. The wartime rise in the birth rate has altered somewhat the relative proportions of older persons in the United States, but it has not significantly affected the general trend. It is predicted that by 1975 the proportion of persons in the United States 65 years old or over will be about 11 per cent as compared to about 7 per cent in 1945.[1]

[1] P. K. Whelpton, et al, *Forecasts of the population of the United States, 1945–1975* (Washington, D.C.: Government Printing Office, 1947).

The increasing number of older people in the population requires that more attention be given to the study and treatment of diseases common to the aged and relatively less to diseases common to childhood. If this adjustment of medical interest to advancing age is not made, fewer adults will live to reach 65 and the trend will be altered by a reduction in the average life span of the population. It is conceivable, moreover, that the demands of advancing age may absorb so much of the organized interest and skill of the population that the essential requirements of childhood will be correspondingly neglected. If this should occur, one probable result would be a rise in the mortality rate among infants and children. Such an actuality would exert a downward pull upon the average life span and, unless compensated for by a pronounced increase in the birth rate, would threaten the population by cutting it off at both ends. It has been shown, also, that nonfatal injuries of childhood frequently predispose the individual to diseases of later years, thus reducing the life expectancy of adulthood and impairing the average efficiency of the whole population.

It is significant that, except for the war period, the birth rate has been falling faster than the death rate, which points to a stationery or declining population, even if the lethal significance of a steadily increasing average could be discounted. The faster the birth rate falls in relation to the death rate, however, the more is the population pushed toward the time when old age itself will tend to raise the death rate, assuming that the life span remains high. It is conceivable that a rise in the birth rate may check the trend. The birth rate has been higher every year since 1937 than it was for that year.

Control of Communicable Diseases

Tuberculosis. The greatest gains in health have been made through the control of communicable and endemic diseases such as tuberculosis, typhoid, diphtheria, malaria, pneumonia, and other diseases common to children.

The death rate due to tuberculosis, for the calendar year 1947, reached a new low: 33.5 deaths per 100,000 population as compared with 68.5 in 1930. In 1900 the Bureau of the Census recorded a death rate from tuberculosis of 201.9 per 100,000 population. The reduction in the tuberculosis death rate alone represented a saving in 1947 of more than 200,000 lives as compared to the 1900 rate. While the reduction in the tuberculosis death rate has been greatest among city wage earners, as indicated by industrial policy holders, a reduction has been marked among all classes in both country and city areas, in all parts of the country. The decline of tuberculosis is of particular economic significance, because of the relatively long periods during which the sufferers from this disease are deprived of normal earning power and also because the disease often attacks people in youth and middle age, when earning power would otherwise be at its best and when economic responsibilities are greatest. Thus, the breadwinner is not nearly so likely now as formerly to be cut short by tuberculosis while his children are yet dependent upon him.

Other diseases.   While the decline in the death rate for tuberculosis has been more spectacular than for some other major diseases, it is important to note that the increase in life expectancy at birth has been brought about by a sustained attack upon the contagious and infectious disease front. Approximately 12 per cent of the saving has been due to the increased control of pneumonia alone; and almost 10 per cent to the greater control of four childhood diseases: measles, scarlet fever, whooping cough, and diphtheria. Typhoid fever, diarrheal diseases, and diseases associated with pregnancy and birth have shown similar downward trends.[2]

Increase of some diseases.   The death rate in 1948 was about 10 per 1000 of the population, a slight improvement over 1947. The 1948 death rate was lower than that for any previous year but one, 1946, in American history. In contrast, however, to the steady gains made in the fight against the major communicable diseases such as· measles, typhoid, para-typhoid, diphtheria, malaria, lethargic encephalitis, tuberculosis, nephritis, pneumonia, and diseases peculiar to infancy, we may note the threatening rise of other diseases. Diseases of the heart and cancer caused 460,580 and 189,811 deaths respectively in 1947. The death rate from diseases of the heart was 321.2 and for cancer 132.4. Heart diseases led all others as a major cause of death, while cancer was surpassed only by deaths from diseases of the heart. Furthermore, deaths from accidental and unspecified external causes increased from 94.0 per 100,000 of the population to 125 during the nine years from 1938 to 1947.

[2] Data from Public Health Service Reports, 1949, Office of Vital Statistics, Federal Security Agency, Washington, D.C.

Extent of illnesses. It is estimated that, on the average, 2 per cent of the population of the United States are ill every day of the year. In other words, on an average day approximately 2,500,000 people are sick. Somewhere near 33 per cent of this number are wage earners and salaried employees. About 12 per cent of the total population are disabled for a week or longer during the year. The average worker in the United States loses at least seven days a year on account of sickness or nonindustrial injuries. These figures do not include persons injured by industrial accidents, which would raise the proportion to 13 per cent. The Edison Electric Illuminating Company of Boston found in a survey of 2233 workers that the average worker lost almost nine days' time per year on account of sickness. The rate of illness for women workers, furthermore, was more than twice as high as for men.

Negro mortality rates. United States Public Health Reports issued in 1948 showed higher mortality rates for Negroes in all sections studied. The difference tended to be most marked in the urban areas of the South. However, Negro infant mortality rates in the South were closer to the corresponding rate for whites than in other areas. For the country as a whole, the life expectancy for a Negro infant at birth is 10 years shorter than that for a white baby. The Negro death rate is about 60 per cent higher than for whites. For tuberculosis, pneumonia, syphilis, and several other preventable diseases, Negro death rates range from one and a half to eight times the white rates.[3] It is noted, also, that the decline in the Negro infant death rate after the first month of life is lower than for whites. Pneumonia appears especially high among very young Negro infants.

Clinical studies reported by the United States Children's Bureau support the generally accepted view that rickets is more common among Negro children than among whites. Eighty-one per cent of Negro children and 61 per cent of white children "were diagnosed as rachitic clinically." The difference in the incidence of rickets in Negro and groups of white children, furthermore, was found to be confined largely to the severer forms of the disease. The extreme forms showed a frequency ten times as great among Negroes as among whites. It was observed, also, that whereas active rickets declined rapidly among white children after the first year of life, the disease continued much longer

[3] *United States public health,* Vol. 5, No. 13, Aug., 1948.

among Negro children. It is a matter of significance also that the difference in incidence and prolongation of rickets in these groups of children was no greater than the difference in their economic and social conditions.

Conditions unfavorable to Negro health. According to the Committee on Research in Medical Economics, there are four major difficulties in the way of improving Negro health. These are:

> . . . his inability to pay for adequate medical care on the usual fee-for-service basis; the shortage of doctors, hospitals, and other personnel and facilities in many areas in which many Negroes live; the restricted use of available personnel and facilities due to discrimination against Negro patients and Negro physicians; and, finally, insufficient health education to utilize personnel and facilities advantageously.[4]

About three fourths of all Negroes in the United States live in those states where the per capita income is around $1000 or less. Thus, inadequacy of the Negro income to cover medical care becomes sharply apparent.[5] With respect to hospital facilities for Negroes the committee says:

> . . . a hospital survey in Arkansas shows that 72 general hospitals allocated a total of 458 beds to Negroes, who comprise one fourth of the state population; that is a ratio of one bed for 1000.
>
> In Mississippi, the state with the largest proportionate Negro population, there are 0.5 beds per 1000 Negroes, as compared to 2.3 beds per 1000 whites.[6]

Conditions Affecting General Health

Economic status and disease. In 1939 the United States Public Health Service published the results of a study of economic status and the incidence of illness. A house-to-house canvass was made of 740,000 urban families in 19 states, and 36,000 rural families in 3 states, over the period from October 1, 1935 to March 30, 1936.[7] The results were gone over carefully. The families were classified according to economic status into four categories: "under $1000," "under $1500," "under $2000,"

[4] M. M. Davis, and H. H. Smythe, *Providing adequate health service to Negroes* (New York: Committee on Research in Medical Economics, 1949).
[5] *Ibid.*
[6] *Ibid.*
[7] Public Affairs Committee, "Who can afford health?", *Public Affairs Pamphlet No. 27* (1939): 7–10.

and "above $2000." Of the 2,300,000 city dwellers canvassed in the course of the survey, about 40 per cent were members of families with incomes under $1000; 65 per cent of families with incomes under $1500; 80 per cent with incomes under $2000; one in five was in the group with an annual income of over $2000. Almost half of the lowest-income group had received relief in some form during the year 1935.

The major objectives of this study were to find the relationship between sickness and such social and economic conditions as income, occupation, employment, unemployment, housing, and education; to determine what kinds of disabling illnesses strike the population during the year, how long they last, what medical care the sick receive, the permanent results of accidents, and the kinds and amount of prevailing chronic illnesses.

Differential morbidity rates and economic status. The effects of poor housing, inadequate diet, insufficient clothing, and unstable income, which were evident in an earlier study (1933)[8] of 11,500 wage earners' families in eight large cities and two groups of villages, were confirmed in the 1935–1936 survey. The earlier study revealed 57 per cent more chronic illnesses in the lowest- than in the highest-income group. Families just "above relief" but with incomes under $1000 suffered less frequent illness than those on relief but were ill 17 per cent oftener than the highest-income group and had a 42 per cent higher frequency of chronic illnesses. Both studies show less difference in frequency and duration of illness between the relief group and those just above relief than between either of these and the highest-income group. The small difference in incidence of disease is what might be expected in view of the absence of "sharply differentiated economic extremes." The fact, however, that such differences prevail and are correlated with general living conditions even in a small city reveals with striking force an intimate connection between economic status and health.

It is noteworthy that the incidence of certain kinds of diseases showed a somewhat higher rate among the better-situated families than among the poorer classes. This was particularly true with respect to infectious diseases such as whooping cough and chicken pox among the children. We should note, also, that the families in the upper economic levels employed physicians to a much greater extent than the poorer classes. There were also

[8] *Ibid.*, p. 11; also H. E. Barnes, *Society in transition* (New York: Prentice-Hall 1939), p. 437.

more minor operations, like tonsillectomy, performed among the children in the upper groups. This fact would tend to raise the statistical incidence of disease in these groups, since without a physician many ailments among the poor would not be recorded. It is clear that illness rates are higher for the poor than for those economically better off, and that families above the average in economic condition have more medical attention than the poor, as a rule.

An earlier publication (1927) of the United States Public Health Service on the incidence of disease and economic status showed the rates of morbidity and mortality to be in inverse proportion to the family earnings, wherever the data could be compared. The mortality rates among both adults and infants were from 150 to 250 per cent higher in the lowest-income groups than in the most well-to-do groups. Families of the unemployed had about 50 per cent more cases of disabling illness than was found in families having a full-time worker. The figures show consistently that as the wages of adult male wage earners in the family decreased, the incidence of illness increased; also, the periods of illness were longer in the lower-income groups than among those in more favorable economic circumstances. It is noteworthy, also, that in 1918 the deaths from influenza among a group of 100,000 persons studied were 3.8 per 1000—adjusted for age—among those classed as "well-to-do" and 10 among the families classed as "very poor."

Health and regional income. Nowhere, perhaps, is the relation of low economic status to health better shown than by a comparison of the conditions in the South with those prevailing in other parts of the country. Says the Committee on Research in Medical Economics:

> The South has fewer hospitals and higher sickness rates than any other region of this country. Yet, despite the great need, the limited medical facilities and personnel are not used to maximum capacity. The proportion of vacant beds in hospitals in the South is actually higher than in any other region of the country. This is due to the people's inability to pay for these services.
>
> Per capita income, the clearest index of a region's wealth, correlates with surprising accuracy with almost any selected index of a region's health . . . statistical data . . . will show an almost uniform relationship between the number of doctors and hospital beds to population in a given state and the state's rating in per capita income. Approximately the same ratio is reflected

in relationships of dentists to population, infant mortality rate, hospital days per capita, and other health indices included herein.

Unnecessary death, misery, and ill health are revealed clearly in the infant and maternal mortality rates in the South. These figures reflect the desperate shortages of medical personnel and facilities. Nine of the ten states with the highest maternal death rate in 1946 were Southern states. The reason: only five out of ten Southern mothers could afford and had available the protection they needed in childbirth. But outside of the South, almost nine out of ten mothers had such protection. Of fourteen states with the fewest hospital beds per population, eleven were Southern states.

One of every two Southern youths—in the prime of life—was unable to meet the minimum physical or mental requirements for military service. These rejections included educational as well as health deficiencies. The rest of the nation furnished 65 eligible soldiers from every 100 men examined. The Southern states averaged less than 50 out of 100 men examined.[9]

It should be noted here that the Southern states have been among the first in the nation to recognize their own health needs and to take advantage of the provisions of the Hill-Burton Hospital Construction Act. Mississippi, which is next to last in the number of hospital beds per 1000 population, was the first state to build a hospital under the Hill-Burton Act. Said Fielding Wright, the Governor of Mississippi, "Mississippians have long recognized the great health need of better hospital care. We are seeing our plans come true under the great statewide hospital building program now under way."

In 1945 the Mississippi legislature appropriated $5,000,000 to supplement the federal grants, for the first two years of a long-range hospital-construction program with the ultimate goal of 4 hospital beds per 1000 population.

But even such state actions are not an answer to the health dilemma "unless the people can afford to pay for the use of those hospital beds once they are in existence."[10]

The committee believes that the Truman National Health Insurance proposal would provide the following benefits:

1. Sickness costs would be spread over the nation as a whole; allocating health-insurance funds to the states would increase the amount of money available in the poorer states to pay for

---

[9] Committee on Research in Medical Economics, *op. cit.*, pp. 3–4.
[10] *Ibid.*, p. 5.

physicians and hospital services. The money would actually be spent by the states and localities.

2. Purchasing power for medical care of middle- and low-income families would be increased.

3. Doctors would be attracted to many towns and rural areas from which they have been kept away by the low-paying power of the people.

4. Hospitals could be maintained in such areas, because they would be insured payment from the health-insurance fund for the cost of the treatment of insured persons and their dependents.

5. Because the South has an especially large number of low-income families, the South would derive particular benefits.

6. People would feel free to consult their doctors early in the course of a disease instead of waiting until it becomes serious. They would be able to go to their doctors for regular, needed check-ups, even though they were not sick. These preventive measures reduce disability of workers and lessen the costs of ill health.

7. Doctors would be free to prescribe whatever their patients need in the way of laboratory tests, X rays, expensive medicines, and consultations with specialists. Today, doctors are often unable to do their best for their patients because they know their patients cannot afford the cost.

8. The South would benefit from the special provisions of the national health-insurance bill for rural areas. Any state would be empowered to use part of the health-insurance fund to assist localities to provide such services as ambulances, travel expenses for patients and for physicians, nurses, dentists, and other professional workers.[11]

The Committee on Medical Research in Medical Economics describes the National Health Insurance proposal as follows:

The national health-insurance bill would provide health insurance for people regardless of residence, race, creed, or color. About 85 per cent of the population would be covered, self-employed persons being included along with salaried workers and wage earners and their families.

People would be entitled to full services from physicians, both general practitioners and specialists, hospital care, laboratory service, X rays, expensive prescribed medicines, eye-glasses, and special appliances. Limited dental and home-nursing service are included.

There would be free choice of physician or dentist and freedom to change one's choice. Physicians and dentists would be free to participate in the health-insurance system, or not, as they desire.

[11] *Ibid.*, pp. 6–7.

They could continue to have private-practice patients. They would be free to accept or reject patients, as they are now.

Physicians would not be employees of government, but as individuals, or through medical groups or medical societies, would make contracts with the health-insurance agency of the locality or the state, to serve insured persons.

These guarantees apply to organized groups of practitioners, clinics, consumer co-operatives, and similar health-service plans as well as to individuals. Every hospital that participates is guaranteed freedom from governmental supervision or control.

Physicians would be paid according to a method to be chosen by a majority of physicians in any given area: on a fee-for-service, salary, or capitation basis; or by any combination of these methods. Minority groups of physicians could negotiate the methods which they preferred.

The services would be financed mainly by payment of $1\frac{1}{2}$ per cent of earnings, by regular payroll deductions from employed persons, into the national health-insurance fund, an equal amount to be paid by the employer. The $1\frac{1}{2}$ per cent is calculated on annual earnings only up to $4800. Supplementary appropriations to the fund might be made by Congress out of general revenue.[12]

Medical costs. Numerous factors have contributed to the rising costs of medical care. Among these may be mentioned the following: 1. The increasing life expectancy of the American people. This fact has given more people more years in which to be sick; it has brought a larger proportion of the population within striking range of the disabling adult diseases; it has increased the number of people who suffer the ailments of the aged, many of whom require months and even years of medical care before the "final hour" comes. 2. Medical costs have been increased by the growing number of high-priced medical specialists and the tendency of general practitioners to take on the role of the specialist. 3. The expansion of hospitals and the preference of physicians for hospital rather than home-bedside practice have contributed to increasing medical costs. The hospital is certainly better equipped to provide good medical care than the home, but it costs the patient more. The hospital, moreover, is essential to a high degree of specialization. It is a point of medical centralization. Consultations are easy here, and daily visits by the physician may be matters of routine. Hospitalization tends in a sense to put the patient in a financially defenseless position. He is automatically brought under hospital rules. These rules, designed

12 *Ibid.*, p. 23.

albeit for his own physical good, are made without his consent. 4. We should not overlook the costs of the concentration of physicians in high-rent office buildings; and the costs of medical technicians, nurses, receptionists, as well as of modern medical equipment. These increasing costs of medical care have not been totally unrelated to the fact that the American people have become more conscious of the need for good medical care.

Unfortunately, the advances in the field of medicine have not been followed by commensurate means of meeting the costs. Hence, many people do not get the care they need. This fact, perhaps more than any other, accounts for the tremendous interest in various forms of health insurance. Many of the health-insurance schemes now available are good as far as they go, but they do not go far enough. Most such schemes are highly restrictive, in the sense that those most likely to need protection against the costs of illnesses are either too poor to pay the premiums or too sick to be admitted to benefits.

There are several reasons why this is so: 1. The extent and nature of illnesses cannot be predicted. 2. The greatest need for protection generally occurs among low-income groups least able to pay the insurance costs. 3. Even if the nature and extent of disease could be predicted, there is no way under present conditions of medical practice to calculate the cost. The writers found the costs of appendectomies in one city ranging from $75 to $400 without any relation to the nature of the case. One man with health insurance that contributed $50 toward the fee for a minor operation was charged $100, while an uninsured man paid $50 for the same kind of operation. One well-to-do farmer was asked to pay $800 for the removal of a skin cancer but protested and settled for $100. There is, moreover, the unpredictable cost of consultations that show variations often unassociated with the specific nature of the ailment; and there are errors of diagnosis which often necessitate a sort of trial-and-error sampling of one physician after another.

Thus, much of the cost of medical care builds up with no real benefit to the patient. The writers have checked instances in one community where patients tried as many as three to seven different physicians with half, or more, as many diagnoses. There is not intention here to imply a criticism of the physician for making an honest error, but to suggest some reasons why health insurance in the ordinary sense of that term does not and cannot exist for the vast majority of Americans. The best that can be offered, within reach of most citizens, is a money guarantee, not a guarantee to meet medical costs or to provide medical care. Even on this basis most of the sample policies examined by the writers reserve the right to discontinue the policy at the end of the contractual period, usually one year, without regard to the need of the insured at that time.

The staff of the Committee on Research in Medical Economics, under the chairmanship of Michael M. Davis, states: "In the past fifty years medical science has made great advances, but with these advances have come vastly greater expenses for adequate medical care. Unpredictable sickness costs bring financial difficulty or distress to many families and cause many more to delay or forego needed medical service."[13]

This report presents evidence to show that the medical profession acting through its national and local societies has exerted effective pressure to control and restrict health insurance in the United States. The committee says:[14]

> The medical societies affiliated with the American Medical Association have induced their legislatures to enact laws in 22 states which would prevent anyone but physicians from forming medical insurance plans.
>
> These states are:

Alabama	Louisiana	New Mexico
California	Maine	North Dakota
Florida	Massachusetts	Ohio
Illinois	Michigan	Pennsylvania
Iowa	Minnesota	Rhode Island
Kansas	Montana	South Carolina
Kentucky	New Hampshire	Tennessee
	New Jersey	

> The report points out that such laws restrict " . . . the right of free enterprise in medicine in two ways. The managers and workers of an industry, the members of a labor union, the people in any other group who receive health services and pay the bills cannot establish a health-insurance plan with the doctors of their choice. Plans sponsored by such nonmedical society groups have usually been designed to provide comprehensive medical service, preventive and curative, whereas the plans set up by medical

[13] Committee on Research in Medical Economics, *Restriction of free enterprise in medicine,*, p. 3.
[14] *Ibid.*, p. 4.

societies, with few exceptions, provide a limited scope of service—usually only surgery and obstetrics.

Such laws also restrict professional freedoms on the part of the doctor.

Group practice is based on the principle of selectivity, developed in the staff organization of voluntary hospitals and in private group clinics. Physicians who are invited to join the staff of a group, as of a hospital staff, must measure up to the professional standards set by the particular organization. These professional requirements thus may be much more rigorous than the state licensure. But the New Jersey law, and the laws of practically all the other states listed above, require that *every* licensed physician must be permitted to take part in the health-insurance plan if he wishes to do so.

Thus organized hospital staffs and other group-practice units could not institute insurance arrangements for their patients, even though their standards might be higher than the general level of practice in the locality. These laws thus constitute a direct impediment to the freedom of professional organization, just as would laws requiring hospitals to grant staff privileges to every licensed physician in the state.

These efforts to stifle free enterprise in medicine are new or recent manifestations of the medical societies' antagonism to progressive change in this area. In 1929, Dr. Michael Shadid, together with a group of farm people at Elk City, Oklahoma, began the organization of an ultimately very successful co-operative hospital and insurance plan. The local and state medical societies retaliated with a fierce personal onslaught upon Dr. Shadid, culminating in an attempt to have his license to practice revoked.[15]

A number of legal actions have been instituted for the purpose of regulating the activities of medical societies in what has been conceived to be a field of public interest. Two questions will illustrate the nature of the conflict. The first from the charges made in a complaint filed by the Attorney General of the United States against the Oregon Medical Society et al, October 18, 1948; the second from a Declaration of the United States Court of Appeals in January, 1943 in affirmation of the conviction of the American Medical Association et al on a charge of violating the Sherman Anti-Trust Act. The charge in the Oregon case read:

> a. Hindered and obstructed prepaid medical care organizations in their attempts to procure and retain qualified doctors to co-operate with them;

[15] *Ibid.*, pp. 5–6, 9.

b. Expelled, threatened, and incited the expulsion from medical societies of doctors co-operating in prepaid medical care plans other than those sponsored or approved by the defendants;

c. Formed and promoted their own prepaid medical care plans with the intent to drive out, hinder and obstruct other commercial medical care plans operating in the state of Oregon;

d. Interfered with commercial prepaid medical care organizations other than those sponsored or approved by them in obtaining hospital facilities for their members;

e. Refused to treat patients and have caused others to refuse to treat patients who are members of a prepaid medical care plan not endorsed by defendants unless the patient pays cash;

f. Refused and encouraged other doctors to refuse to give patients who are members of a prepaid medical care plan not endorsed by the defendants itemized statements that will enable the patient to be reimbursed under the plan to which he has subscribed;

g. Refused to consult or assist and have encouraged others not to consult or assist doctors who treat members of a prepaid medical care plan not endorsed by them;

h. Spread false propaganda among doctors, hospitals, and the general public for the purpose of discrediting any prepaid medical care plan not endorsed by them;

i. Agreed among themselves and with others not to compete with each other for prepaid medical care business or with other similar organizations approved by or affiliated with them; and

j. Succeeded in making hospital facilities in Oregon available only to members of defendant Oregon Medical Society and its component county medical societies, and have restricted and excluded other qualified doctors co-operating in prepaid medical plans other than those sponsored or approved by the defendants from access to such facilities.[16]

In the District of Columbia case the Court declared:

The situation which confronts appellants (AMA, etc.), and which they have sought to control, is not confined to the medical profession alone. Profound changes in social and economic conditions have forced members of all professional groups to make readjustments. The fact that these changes may result even in depriving professional people of opportunities formerly open to them does not justify or excuse their use of criminal methods to prevent changes or to destroy new institutions. Lawyers, too, have seen, during recent decades, large-scale changes in their professional work. There was a time when lawyers worked entirely

[16] U.S.A. v. Oregon Medical Society, 1948, quoted in ibid., p. 10.

on fee or retainer in particular cases and controversies; now many of them are salaried employees on the staffs of large corporate industrial and financial organizations. . . .

There are some who regret and some who resent these changes. Over the years, as individuals and as members of professional associations, they have labored to prevent or minimize them. But they would not suggest that criminal conduct, as individuals or associations, would be proper for such a purpose.

Professions exist because the people believe they will be better served by licensing especially prepared experts to minister to their needs. The licensed monopolies which professions enjoy consti-tute, in themselves, severe restraints upon competition. But they are restraints which depend upon capacity and training, not special privilege. Neither do they justify concerted criminal action to prevent the people from developing new methods of serving their needs. There is sufficient historical evidence of professional inadequacy to justify occasional popular protests. . . . The people give the privilege of professional monopoly and the people may take it away.

In some instances professional groups have been charged by legislative fiat with powers and duties concerning professional education, licensure, discipline, removal of licensees from prac-tice, and other related subjects. In such cases they act as agencies of government. Although some similar delegations of power have been made to the organized medical profession, there is no evi-dence of delegation of power to appellants, sufficient to authorize the conduct for which they have been convicted. In the absence thereof professional groups must abide by the general laws just as scrupulously as any private citizen or private corporation. It is in this setting that appellants were permitted to organize, to estab-lish standards of professional conduct, to effect agreements for self-discipline and control. There is a very real difference between the use of such self-discipline and an effort upon the part of such associations to destroy competing professional or business groups or organizations.

Except for their size, their prestige, and their otherwise com-mendable activities, their conduct in the present case differs not at all from that of any other extra-governmental agency which assumes power to challenge alleged wrongdoing by taking the law into its own hands.[17]

The following from Dr. Roscoe L. Sensenich, then chairman and later president of the board of trustees of the American

[17] "Restrictions on free enterprise in medicine," *ibid.*, pp. 13–14; also U.S. *v.* AMA et al, D.C.D.D. Criminal No. #63221, 1939.

Medical Association, presumably expresses the official view of the profession:

> The reason . . . [that voluntary insurance plans must] . . . be acceptable to the [AMA's] Council on Medical Service and to authoritative bodies of state medical associations . . . [is] . . . to prevent the entrance into the picture of insurance plans of a kind that were *not sound and not consistent or in any way fair or honest to the subscribers to such funds.*[18]

The AMA's code of ethics, moreover, defines as *unethical* contract practice when, among other things, "the contract because of any of its provisions or practical results is *contrary to sound public policy.*" It is observed that the concept of ethical obligation and duty, on the part of the AMA, reaches into the field of political interest and social policy. Here is defined the arena of conflict between the assumed right of the people to determine "social public policy" and that of an organized "interest" group to determine it for them.

National medical bill difficult to determine. Costs of medical care for the American people are difficult to evaluate for the reason that much that is spent by individuals and families for medical resources is incalculable. In round numbers, three billion dollars is close to the estimates that were accepted by students in the field in 1941, and this figure was used by Davis.[19] This amount went to physicians, dentists, nurses, administrators, medical social workers, dietitians, physical therapeutists, and technicians. It included also costs of maintaining other employees in offices, hospitals, clinics, and allied institutions, as well as money spent for help on sectarian and irregular practitioners and for the maintenance of buildings, equipment, medicines, and supplies. The amounts spent for medical care, as indicated, were about the same as total expenditures for education. As Davis points out, however, the proportions of personal and community outlays are reversed. Only about 17 per cent of the costs of education is paid by individuals directly for services received, while for medical expenditures 70 per cent is personal. In other words, about 30 per cent of the total outlay for medical services was paid by local, state, and national governments and other agencies.

[18] *Ibid.*, p. 2. Italics not in the original.
[19] M. M. Davis, *America organizes medicine* (New York: Harper and Brothers, 1941), p. 45.

The costs of medical care rest preponderantly upon the sick, and incomes are far more uneven among those who are sick than are medical costs. According to the National Resources Committee, the top tenth of the population received about 36 per cent of the national income during 1935–1936, while the lowest tenth received but 2 per cent; and at least one third of the working population had individual incomes of less than $800. Moreover, hardly more than 2 per cent had incomes of over $5000.[20]

"Free care" and the marginal family.   It is not easy to appreciate the burdens of emergency medical care upon the mass of low-income families. These live close to a marginal existence level even when well, and, because they are not on relief, they are generally not eligible for "free care" in the great majority of communities. "Free care," moreover, is avoided by self-respecting people because of its association with charity. This is not the case with education, where the responsibility of the state for general education has come to be popularly accepted out of social experience. To say that medical care costs the average American family about 4 per cent of its annual budget is misleading because of the inequitable distribution of this cost. For some families it is 50 per cent or more of the annual income for a particular year. We should note, also, that the proportion of the family income expended for medical care increases as the income decreases, and the increase approaches a geometric ratio as we move down toward the marginal-income family.

"Free adjustment" fallacy.   It is often asserted, even by men of the medical profession, that doctors adjust their fees to the economic abilities of the family and the individual to pay. As Davis suggests, this puts the physician in "an invidious position." Who is the man to say exactly what each individual is able to pay or should pay for so needful a service? This matter of discriminatory payments for essential services is one that requires some special training in investigation and analyses unrelated to medical practice. Even if this were not true and if it could be justified on democratic grounds, which is difficult to imagine, it would still rest on the assumption that every practicing physician is absolutely honest in his determination of the ability of the patient to pay. Moreover, such a system could hardly be harmonized with arguments in defense of "free choice" of physician.

[20] National Resources Committee, *Consumer incomes in the United States* (Washington, D.C.: Government Printing Office, 1938), pp. 1–5.

Distribution of costs. It has been noted that the calculable costs of medical care in the United States amounted to approximately three billion dollars in 1941. They have risen sharply since that year.

The proportion of this which went to medical practitioners is paid by patients, and these share medical costs very unevenly. Davis has pointed out that about 30 per cent of physicians' incomes in the United States is paid by 10 per cent of the population. These are the people with substantial incomes. From this "good income" group, physicians derive almost as much through fees and other medical charges as from the lowest 50 per cent of the population. Davis presents data to show that this tendency is much more marked in dentistry. Specifically, dental practitioners get 40 per cent of their combined income from the upper tenth and barely 20 per cent from the lower half of the population. The top tenth pays 70 per cent of the income derived by private nurses. This tendency of service groups to derive the larger proportions of their incomes from the top levels of the population is not unique for practitioners in the medical services, but its social effects are likely to be much more profound because of the personal and social import of these services. Some years ago a survey of 9000 families revealed that the services of specialists were employed ten times more often among families with incomes above $5000 than among families with incomes below $1200. [21]

Selecting a doctor in the city. Harold S. Frum interviewed 200 families in Columbus, Ohio in an effort to find out what motives determined their selection of a physician and their attitudes toward physicians. Briefly, his general conclusions were: (1) Economic considerations loomed large as an influence upon the family's use of a physician. (2) There was indicated very little real understanding of the quality of the physician used. (3) More often opinions of relatives, friends, neighbors, and associates determined the choice where the individual himself did not have some personal basis for the selection. (4) In few cases was there any apparent knowledge as to the medical competence of the physician in the selection. Frequent changes were made by families, primarily due to personal dissatisfaction with the physician, the advice of others, and the considerations of cost. [22]

[21] Davis, *op. cit.*, p. 58.
[22] Harold S. Frum, *Choice and change of medical service* (New York: Committee on Medical Economics, 1939), mimeographed.

In an earlier study, Gladys Swackhamer found that families make numerous and unco-ordinated choice of physicians as well as of other medical resources in times of illness. "The family doctor is a vanished ideal among two thirds of the families and is very imperfectly represented among the remaining third." Swackhamer reports that while many families clung to the idea of a family doctor, not one third of them thought they had such a doctor; and even among those who professed to have a family doctor there was by no means any exclusive use of him, and in some instances continuity of relationship was not even kept up. The doctor was called as a rule for "acute and special" needs only. For the most part, the patients went without care or doctored themselves. Among 365 families interviewed for this study, informed choice of physician was rare. Not only was the information lacking on the part of the family, but the cost and difficulty of securing good advice were prohibitive for most of these families since they belonged in moderate-income or low-income groups, 81 per cent having incomes below $2000.

As in Frum's study, the economic factor often caused delay in securing care and caused numerous changes of physician. One important psychological cause given for change of physician was failure to give the patient "desired information and reassurance." Swackhamer concludes that so-called "freedom of choice" resulted in a confusion of choices and in the necessity of seeking medical resources without co-ordination.[23]

On this subject Dr. Michael M. Davis, chairman of the Committee on Research in Medical Economics, reports from his own wide experience with middle-class families who have come to him seeking advice as to how to secure the right physician. He says that parents with two or three children have within a year or two employed from three to five different physicians, "each a specialist for some age or disease group."[24]

Selecting a doctor in the country. The problem of securing a physician in rural areas is an economic one for many families but does not present the complexities and confusions characteristic of urban environments. Here is oftentimes the difficulty of securing a physician at all, because of the scarcity of physicians in rural areas.

A study by Harold Maslow covering the period from 1912 to

[23] Gladys Swackhamer, *Choice and change of doctor* (New York: Committee on Research in Medical Economics, 1939), p. 44.
[24] Davis, *op. cit.*, p. 29.

1936 for six rural Wisconsin counties showed a decline of 33 doctors during the period, although the population had remained practically the same. It would have been impossible, moreover, for very many families to maintain continuity in the use of medical resources since the doctors who were available were moving in and out of the community more or less continuously over the period. More than one sixth of the physicians in these counties changed during an average year. Furthermore, specialists are not available in rural areas unless secured from cities.

Reinhardt and Schroeder completed a study of the distribution and adequacy of certain types of medical services in Nebraska in 1941. It was found that Nebraska had fewer physicians in 1940 than a smaller population in the state had had thirty-four years earlier. Significant, also, was the marked tendency toward concentration of physicians in urban areas. In 1940 less than 40 per cent of Nebraska's population lived in urban areas, whereas these areas contained approximately 80 per cent of the physicians. This would not be serious, perhaps, except for the fact that vast stretches of the state are separated from cities by distance and climatic and road difficulties during the winter months. Two cities, located on the eastern border of the state, and their immediate environs had 40 per cent of the physicians, though they had less than 25 per cent of the state's population.

This study showed also that the older physicians practice in the country. Twenty-seven per cent of the rural physicians, in 1938, were sixty-five or older, and only 18 per cent of the urban physicians were in that age group. Significant is the fact that the proportion of practitioners about seventy years of age was one third greater in the rural than in the city areas. At least five rural counties had no physician at all.[25]

Davis quotes a physician writing to a medical magazine as follows: "In the state of Missouri, 37 per cent of all the doctors who live in the state live in St. Louis, and St. Louis has only 18 per cent of the population. In 982 towns of 5000 population or less, there is not an M.D. under the age of fifty; and 38 per cent of these towns have no M.D. at all. In Delaware County in the state of Oklahoma, there are only two M.D.'s in the county, and one of these is sixty-eight years old."[26]

[25] James M. Reinhardt, and Martin H. Schroeder, "Physicians and hospitals in rural Nebraska," *Medical Care* (Oct., 1941), I: 332–343.

[26] B. F. Collins, "What has disrupted the profession," *Modern Medicine*, March, 1940: 12.

Dental practitioners are more inequitably distributed geographically than physicians. There are approximately 2100 people per dentist for the total population, but in some heavily populated areas, as in New York and Pennsylvania, the proportion ranges from about 1500 to 1900, while for thinly populated areas and some poor rural districts the proportion rises to nearly 6500.

"Free choice" for whom? We have seen that "free choice" of a physician, so often insisted upon, hardly exists in practical reality for a large proportion of the population. Davis refers to interviews in which some forty physicians practicing in New York City reported that they had family practice. They named numerous families whose medical interests they had been serving for years. Yet in these same areas Swackhamer found families who claimed to have a family physician but who shopped around here and there when in need of medical service. It may be noted that many physicians object to "free choice" when a group of men agree on the same physician and wish to distribute the cost of securing his services equitably over the group.

It seems obvious that the "sacred personal relation" so often employed in the past in opposition to consumer organization for medical care does not in reality exist in any prolonged and intimate sense for the great majority of people. One of the reasons discovered by Dr. Robert P. Knight[27] for the use of "cultists" by so many patients was the lack of intimate and sympathetic interest in the patient on the part of the physician.

Welfare obligations of the state. There is also a question of justice involved. We have long recognized the need for public education. The importance of education has been so thoroughly accepted that the obligation of the state to provide it takes precedence over the right of the parent. The obligations of the state with respect to health have not yet been so generally admitted. The opposition to public health programs is oftentimes strong and includes not only those who fear an increase in tax burdens but also a considerable proportion of the medical profession. It has been argued that public health services, except within certain limits, are an invasion of individual rights and a "definite step toward socialism." The objection is sometimes based upon the exceptional character of the service rendered by the private practitioner and the high cost of medical education.

[27] Robert P. Knight, "Why people go to cultists," *Bulletin of the Meninger Clinic,* Sept., 1939: 139–147.

With respect to these claims, it may be stated that there is nothing mysterious or necessarily untouchable about medical practice. Moreover, to maintain that a state has no right to inaugurate any measures or programs for the protection of the health and well-being of the people is, of course, to say that the state has no rights at all and therefore does not exist in reality. Accordingly, lawyers might claim, as in fact they have, that the state should provide no paid defense for the accused; teachers might claim that the state has no right to provide public education. As a matter of fact, a state has a right to do anything that the people demand of it. The question that presents itself to the student of social problems is not, What can a state do, or, What are the peculiar privileges that should be accorded any profession or interest group, but, How can the highest degree of well-being be secured? We have long since accepted without difficulty the obligation of the state to provide medical education.

It has been noted how such diseases as tuberculosis, malaria, trachoma, hookworm, and typhoid yielded under the pressure of highly organized and persistent attacks. There seems little reason to believe that cancer, heart disease, diabetes and other diseases that appear to be increasing may not be brought under control in the same way. It will probably make little difference whether prevention is applied through private or public means, but it may be admitted that in order to be effective it must apply equally to rich and poor. Experience has shown that good preventive work involves not merely attacking the disease early but removing the causes. The inception of many diseases is extremely difficult to detect without careful examination. Nevertheless, relatively few well-to-do persons and apparently no poor persons ever engage a private physician before they themselves suspect disease, and then it is often too late.

Education and medical care.   Programs of education with respect to the care of health and the importance of medical advice are necessary. It has been demonstrated, however, that health education is most effective under conditions where medical care is available. As suggested already, the situation in regard to dental care appears no better by comparison. Physicians and dentists are generally agreed that dental neglect may seriously impair the individual's general health and may often cause severe disease. Yet Dr. James A. Brady, lecturer on dental economics, estimated that approximately 75 per cent of the people in the United States received little if any dental care.

It has been observed that health education, in so far as it emphasizes the importance of making use of medical facilities, is of little value to those who, because of economic circumstances or geographic location, cannot reach these facilities. The one urgent question at this point is, Who is going to put these facilities in reach of these people?

The Social and Economic Costs of Disease

It is impossible to calculate the social and economic costs of disease. Value is a relative matter. In societies where population pressure is intense and disease the common lot of most people, life is likely to be held cheap. Under such circumstances early death may be regarded as an economic gain. On the other hand, where the demand for individual laborers exceeds the supply and where the labor of each individual contributes to the enjoyment of all, life is valuable and precautions are taken by society to preserve it.

The economic values which society attaches to the individual under conditions of inadequate labor supply tend to create social values that do not develop where the cost of rearing children is greater than the amount that their labor will ever be worth. Historically speaking, keen population pressure has been accompanied by high birth rates, high death rates, and miserably low standards of living for the masses, as well as by general illiteracy and vassalage. The sad lot on earth has been compensated for, somewhat, by the hope of future reward.

Disease and social values.   We saw in the chapter on poverty and social well-being how the material inventions and discoveries of the eighteenth and nineteenth centuries increased the bargaining powers of the common man. In the New World, where resources were abundant and the labor supply relatively small, individual life tended to assume new values. Living standards were raised, and general good health came to be viewed as a social and economic asset. Out of this situation arose numerous organizations and agencies, public and private, for the prevention and cure of disease. The problem of disease became a moral issue, and health campaigns were weighted with both sentiment and science. Both factors have contributed to the modern point of view with reference to the costs of disease.

Arguments about the economic worth of man, stated in terms of his earning power, may have little weight in times of general unemployment. Nevertheless, the health machinery is kept operating. Disease strikes at the moral fiber of our society. Its moral effects appear to be far greater among families suddenly reduced to dependency than otherwise. Every additional case of disease in the community, furthermore, increases the chances that another will occur, unless immediate preventive measures are taken. This is a plain problem in statistics. Disease also lowers the total amount of available human energy and consequently the productive powers of society. It has been observed that the highest levels of intelligence, of literacy, and of economic security are found in those areas of greatest human energy and general health. While the relatively low economic and cultural status of the masses who live in areas infested by such diseases as malaria, trachoma, and hookworm can be stated in statistical units, the exact costs of disease in this complex of factors cannot be reduced to definite terms. Its direct and immediate effects, however, may be observed in many demoralized and bankrupt families.

Effects of disease on social progress and war.   According to Lieutenant Colonel Keefer of the United States Army, writing before World War I, in practically all of the wars of history more lives were taken by diseases than by the enemies' guns. Such preventable diseases as cholera, plague, typhoid, smallpox, malaria, and yellow fever have spoiled many a well-planned campaign. Smallpox and dysentery defeated the armies of Arnold and Montgomery in Canada in 1775. Napoleon's plans to carve out an empire in the southern part of North America were wrecked by yellow fever in Santo Domingo.[28] Bossard reminds us that half of the Allied strength in Macedonia during World War I was out of action because of malaria, a fact which was no doubt responsible for the relatively poor showing of the forces in that region. Binder regards health as the "greatest factor in the history of man, since it is the strong and healthy nations which have in the end conquered their richer and, sometimes, more civilized neighbors."[29] It is the strong and healthy who have built roads, spanned streams, tunneled mountains, and built cities.

Health and changing habits of life.   It has been noted that most of the communicable diseases once so terrifying in this

[28] Lieut. Colonel Keefer, in *Military hygiene and sanitation*, cited by J. H. S. Bossard, *Problems of social well-being* (New York: Harper and Brothers, 1927), pp. 128–129.

[29] Rudolph Binder, *Health and social progress* (New York: Harper and Brothers, 1920), pp. 5–9.

country have been declining year by year. It is by no means time to cease the fight against these diseases. Adequate facilities for their control are not within reach of all. Besides, strange as it may seem, there are still many people actually unwilling to apply the most simple preventive measures with respect to some of these ills. The price of health, like the proverbial "price of liberty," is "eternal vigilance." We may, nevertheless, feel fairly hopeful that, in proportion as man is willing to submit the control of his environment and his person to the agencies of good health, such diseases as are caused by bad sanitation, insects, pests, and contaminated water and food supplies will be largely abolished. Modern urban existence, however, tends to put new and heavier burdens upon the organism. The rigid and relentless pressure of competitive enterprise; the steady strains that large numbers of people live under because of uncertainty of status or financial security; rapid material changes that tug almost incessantly at the habit patterns of the individual; high rates of population mobility and fluidity that make it impossible for masses of people ever to become securely attached to anybody or any place— these and other characteristics of moden life, together with a relatively sedentary existence, tend to affect directly the functional aspects of the human constitution. At any rate, many leading authorities regard combinations of these factors as probably fundamental in the spectacular increases of such diseases as cancer, heart disease, diabetes, and various forms of nervous disorders.

Man is not historically a sedentary creature. So long as his work involved the use of his limbs and body in the open he could eat liberally of heavy foods and sugars without serious consequences. Furthermore, such diseases as are now fairly well under the control of science then cut his days relatively short, on the average. As a consequence, the burdens of repair and elimination in old age were not so keenly felt as now. In other words, the problem is still the age-old one of adjustment, but the adjustments have to be made over a longer range of years and to a far more complex set of environmental factors than before.

Some recommendations.   Recommendations of the Committee on the Costs of Medical Care made in 1939 include the following:

1. A program for the eradication of tuberculosis, venereal diseases, malaria; more aggressive control of pneumonia and cancer; extension of public health programs for mental and industrial

hygiene; extension of services to mothers and children of all income groups throughout the country.

2. Expansion of number of beds in tuberculosis, mental, and general hospitals, as well as health and diagnostic centers in areas inaccessible to hospitals.

3. Implement provisions of public medical care for two broad groups of the population through federal grants-in-aid to the states. (The groups referred to are those for whom local, state, and federal governments have accepted some responsibility under the Social Security Act or through other federal programs and those who, though not on direct or work relief, are unable to procure necessary medical care.)

4. Reduction of sickness costs to the individual by provisions for their distribution among groups and over periods of time through a program to increase and improve medical services, to be supported either by some form of taxation or some system of insurance contributions.

5. Assurance of continuity of income to wage earners by a temporary disability insurance somewhat analogous to unemployment compensation and permanent-disability insurance through the old-age insurance system.

The National Health Committee recommended further that definite funds be appropriated for carrying out these proposals. The late Senator Wagner of New York followed the committee's recommendations with a proposed national health bill in 1939. Though the proposed Wagner bill was not enacted, it was followed in 1948 by the President's National Health Insurance proposal which has not reached (in 1951) the floor of the Senate.

The majority report of the Committee on the Costs of Medical Care, in which more than two thirds of its members and all but nine of the twenty-four physicians concur, recommended:

1. Group organization of physicians, dentists, nurses, pharmacists, and other associated personnel for rendering complete home, office, and hospital care, including both preventive and curative services.

2. Extension of all basic public health services to the entire population, according to its needs, by increasing financial support for official health departments and for full-time trained and competent personnel.

3. Establishment of a group-payment basis of costs of medical care through the use of insurance or taxation.

4. Establishment of agencies for the study, evaluation, and

co-ordination of medical service for every state and local community.

5. Emphasis in professional education on training in disease prevention, public health, and the social aspects of the medical profession.

In 1949 a subcommittee on Medical Care of the American Public Health Association issued a rather exhaustive statement on the quality of medical care. Among other things the subcommittee hypothesized the following needs:

> Greater emphasis seems also needed upon the extra-hospital phases of medical education. The graduate should have experience in outpatient service, home care, social service, public-health practice, rehabilitation, and rural and small community hospitals.
>
> The greatest single deterrent to good service is the isolation of the individual practitioner from his colleagues. The patterns of practice should, therefore, be such as to enable practitioners to utilize readily the skills of consultants and other specialized personnel, and to benefit from the stimulation of continuing professional contacts.
>
> . . . elimination of those financial factors which promote "fee splitting" and rebate practices on the one hand, and those, on the other, which deter the family practitioner from calling in a consultant because of additional cost to the patient or fear of "losing his patient," is necessary.
>
> Increased rates of payment for specialists' services in an organized medical-care program should, in the interests of quality, be limited to physicians who meet objectively established standards of special qualification.
>
> Group medical practice facilitates co-ordination of the personnel and facilities essential to medicine of high standard. It provides ready access to consultants and the technical services of trained auxiliary personnel, and permits full use of complex laboratory, X-ray, electrocardiographic and other diagnostic facilities.
>
> Services of professional and practical nurses form the third essential of the modern medical team. Nursing education programs should be planned in conjunction with known and predicted community needs for all phases of nursing service.
>
> The influence of social factors in the production of disease and in restoration of health is of great significance. No medical-service plan can achieve high standards without the well-integrated services of fully qualified medical and psychiatric social workers.
>
> To insure the successful use of these therapeutic agents in a national medical-care plan, competent and scientifically trained pharmacists should be component parts of the medical-service

team, and should be active participants in the organized medical-care program.

Many factors have combined to encourage the appearance of large numbers of sectarian practitioners, quacks, and charlatans and their use in the provision of care to the American public. To the extent that these partially trained and untrained individuals render service to patients, the quality of the system of care degenerates. Factors which underlie the existence of such practitioners include: (1) shortages of medical practitioners, (2) maldistribution of professional personnel, (3) high cost of modern medical care, (4) inability of medical science to cope adequately with many problems of chronic and social factors in medicine, (6) discriminatory practices which prevent minority population groups from receiving adequate medical services, (7) looseness of many state laws governing medical licensure, and (8) inadequacy of health education.

A major criterion of medical adequacy is that the services rendered be comprehensive, balanced, and afford the patient a maximum continuity of care.

A most significant criterion of medical care of high quality is the degree of emphasis placed upon prevention of disease. The unfortunate separation of preventive and curative medicine—historically developed in the independent activities of public-health officers and private practitioners—is incompatible with the highest standards of modern medicine.

It is now widely recognized that treatment is not completed when the clinical disorder is eliminated or stabilized. Wherever possible the patient must be restored to a useful and self-sufficient place in society. This involves the co-ordination of medical, psychiatric, physiotherapeutic, educational, vocational, and social services.

An intelligent, co-operative, and sensitized population is quick to detect flaws in standards of service and can make real contributions to the program by timely and judicious comments on quality of care received.

An essential factor in medical care of good quality is that of sound and adequate financing—so designed that no economic barriers restrict the provision of needed medical services, and that fair and adequate remuneration is provided to all those furnishing the care.

If social insurance is utilized, the maximum financial stability and adequacy is obtained by substantial supplementation with general tax funds and by coverage which assures the broadest possible spread of risk and the widest possible sharing of costs. Differential selection of the best risks by private insurance agencies (so-called "contracting out") should not be permitted because it would leave the national plan in an adverse financial position, greatly complicate administration and public participation, and expose the program to commercial exploitation.

In order to promote medical services of high quality, the use of the means test as a criterion of eligibility should be eliminated in a national health program. The personal indignity of financial investigations prevents many individuals in serious need of medical service from seeking care under means-test programs. A basic requisite for good medical service is a healthy relationship between providers and consumers; recipients of charity medicine are not in a position to insist on a high quality of care.

Good medical care is not promoted when services are rendered on the basis of a double standard—one for "paying patients" and one for "charity cases." Recipients of public assistance should be included in the national medical-care program, and the welfare status of such persons should be unknown to those providing the care.

Professional personnel should retain the right to accept or reject patients, with the provision that the professional participants in an area are collectively responsible for rendering needed services to all persons who do not elect or who are not accepted by a specific physician.

The proper discharge of administrative responsibilities includes the right of the operating agency to ascertain the caliber of the services for which it is paying.

The fee-for-service method puts emphasis upon sickness rather than health and upon quantity rather than quality. It hinders appropriate referral of patients because it provides an economic incentive for the physician to retain his patient. This factor, in addition, seriously limits the effectiveness of regional centers for necessary consultant services. In an organized plan, fee-for-service is cumbersome, requiring itemized billing and auditing and thus a great deal of paper work. It is also the most difficult method under which to control use of service either quantitatively or qualitatively and is therefore the most expensive method to administer in a medical-care program.

By removing or minimizing the incentive for quantity inherent in fee-for-service, the program could make careful, deliberate work, rather than the multiplication of services, the principal motivation for a physician to improve his professional and economic status.[30]

The five-point program approved by the National Health Conference. The National Health Conference, made up of repre-

[30] Subcommittee on Medical Care, *Quality of medical care in a national health program* (Washington, D.C.: American Public Health Association, 1949), p. 900 ff.

sentatives from various organizations of the people and the medical profession, met in Washington in July, 1938 at the call of the President and adopted a five-point program for the improvement of public health, The program included:

1. Expansion of our public health, maternal and child health services, with a special emphasis on preventing sickness.

2. Extension of hospital facilities, especially in small towns and rural areas where fee or low-cost hospital service is practically unobtainable.

3. Provision for medical care at public expense for the one third of the population in the lower-income levels unable to pay for adequate private care.

4. Measures for spreading the cost of medical care either by state systems of medical insurance or further extension of state medical service with the aid of federal subsidies.

5. Protection against the loss of wages during sickness by insurance. Temporary-disability insurance should be set up as was unemployment insurance, on a federal-state basis; permanent-disability insurance should be set up by amending the federal old-age insurance to pay benefits to workers who become disabled before the age of 65.[31]

The National Health Conference program, with the exception of point 4, was later approved by the American Public Health Association and representatives of the American Medical Association.

General conclusions. We should be reminded that an advancing science of medicine is not unrelated to changes in medical practice, which may or may not keep pace with the advancing needs and requirements of the people.

The mortality rate was comparatively high in the days of the proverbial "country doctor." We know why: the doctor did not know much, and the people did not know much either, and so they did not demand much. People wanted to go on living then as now, but comparative ignorance of the means for the prevention and control of disease tended to create a sort of fatalistic view of life and death. Advances in the science of medicine have profoundly altered that view.[32] The masses know now that diseases that once killed great numbers of people in childhood and later life can be prevented or cured. They have witnessed a phenomenal decline in mortality rates, especially among children,

[31] Beulah Amidon, "Who can afford health?", *Public Affairs Pamphlet No. 27* (1939): 28–29.

[32] "Medicine" as used here denotes all forms of disease prevention and control.

and an increase in the buoyant years of adulthood. These facts, together with knowledge of medical potentialities and existing facilities, have tremendously enhanced the demands for medical services.

Significant as have been advances in the general health over the past forty years, they have not kept pace with achievement in the knowledge of the causes, prevention, and treatment of disease. This statement is perhaps less true in the field of sanitary engineering than in any other area of health protection. The exceptional gains in health attributable to the application of knowledge in the field of sanitary engineering have been due largely to the obvious necessity of preventing recurring ravages in urban areas by undiscriminating communicable diseases.[33] The universality of the dangers from these diseases encouraged public support of practical measures of prevention. Similarly, programs of inoculation against certain spectacular and terrifying diseases such as smallpox and diphtheria have been made effective not alone because of existing knowledge but also by means of public support.

No one will assume, of course, that these measures have been appropriated up to capacity. There is still a large proportion of the population, especially in rural areas, which has received relatively little direct benefit from these achievements.

In the matter of individual medical treatment, however, as also in that of prevention through the use of adequate diets, knowledge has gone far ahead of general application. This *lag* in the general use of existing knowledge is serious because herein is probably one of the major internal threats, at the moment, to the happiness and efficiency of the American people as a whole. This has been indicated by numerous local health surveys and by the proportion of rejections for military service during two major military emergencies within the past thirty years.

It is unfortunate that problems of disease prevention and control have so often been approached in an atmosphere of heat and with "bad" language. Questions relating to the distribution of medical services, the manner of payment, the forms and extent of state participation are questions to be dealt with on a broad co-operative plane and in the interest of human need and social efficiency. There is nothing "un-American" about this way of

---

[33] The term "sanitary engineering" is used broadly to include measures for protecting the health not only against infection from water supplies and the disposal of refuse, but also against other common sources of infection.

dealing with social problems. It seems clear that any proposed measures for the protection of the people's health must provide for the security of those who render medical services. It is, moreover, of paramount importance that such persons be left free to use their special skills and knowledge unhampered by outside interferences. Beyond this it is not a matter of how much or how little state participation is "American," or of free enterprise *vs.* socialism, so long as the problems are handled in a democratic manner, which means the preservation of the rights of free public discussion and decision.

QUESTIONS

1. Trace the outstanding steps in the evolution of modern medicine.
2. What was the chief contribution of Louis Pasteur to present-day understanding of disease?
3. How did the "germ theory" affect the prevention and control of disease?
4. What principal factors have determined modern attitudes and developments in the field of health?
5. What new problems in the field of health have developed with the increasing control of communicable diseases?
6. How do you account for the tremendous rise in the number of deaths from cancer and heart disease?
7. What measures should be taken to check these and other diseases that are increasing among adults?
8. Account for the different mortality rates among Negroes and whites.
9. What conclusions may be drawn from the foregoing discussion with reference to economic status and health?
10. What do the studies of health and occupation tend to show as to the causes of disease?
11. Why is adequate care not accessible to a larger number of people in both rural and urban territories?
12. Suggest ways and means by which such care may be made more general in the United States.
13. What are the principal difficulties in the way of a wider extension of health protection?
14. Discuss the advantages and disadvantages of such forms of health insurance as are provided by insurance companies, industrial concerns, and mutual benefit societies.
15. Discuss the social consequences of disease and the stake that the public has in general good health.
16. (a) What are the principal weaknesses and advantages in the present system of medical care? (b) Suggest remedies.

17. If it is not possible under the present system to make adequate medical care accessible to all classes, what changes, if any, would you suggest?
18. What economic interest has the general public in the prevention of disease?
19. (a) Give data showing the relation between disease and economic status. (b) How is health affected by occupation?
20. In the light of Question 19, discuss the obligation of the state with respect to health.
21. Discuss the social and economic costs of disease in the United States.
22. What practical measures may be suggested for improving conditions of health in the United States?

REFERENCES

ARMSTRONG, D. B., *Study of sickness cost and private medical practice*. New York: Metropolitan Life Insurance Company, 1932.

CARPENTER, NILES, "Social costs of illness," *American Labor Legislation Review* (June, 1929), XIX: 115–162.

Committee on the Costs of Medical Care, *Medical care for the American people*, Final Report, Oct., 1932.

DAVIS, M. M., "Blunderbuss of sickness," *Survey* (Jan. 1, 1928), LIX: 435–438, 468–470.

GOLDBERG, J. A., "Medical and dental care as affected by wages and cost of living in New York City," *Hospital Social Service* (May, 1929), X: 169–179.

NEWSHOLM, A., *Story of modern preventive medicine*. Baltimore: Williams and Wilkins, 1929.

PEARL, R., and ROENKHAM, T., "Studies in human longevity," *Human Biology* (Feb., 1932), IV: 80–118.

REED, L. S., *Ability to pay for medical care*, Abstract of Pub. No. 25, Committee on the Costs of Medical Care.

Survey. Practically the entire issues for Jan. 1, 1930 and Nov., 1932 are devoted to articles on various aspects of health costs, by a number of eminent students of the subject.

SYDENSTRICKER, E., "Vitality of the American people," *Recent Social Trends*, I: 12.

CHAPTER *16*

Care and Control of the Defective Classes

The Problem in General

Defectives a problem. During the past half-century, Western society in particular has become solicitous regarding certain types of persons who, because of physical or mental handicaps, create problems for their families, friends, and society in general. These may be included under the heading "defective classes." However, the term does not imply that any social stigma is placed upon those who are so classified.

There is sufficient justification for regarding these classes as social problems. As classes, these defectives are both biological and social products. Even some biological traits may be the outcome of social contacts. Like most other social problems, this particular problem emerges out of a complex of causative factors, and consequently it involves the whole of society.

It is well known that some of the causes of acquired deficiency in practically all kinds of defectives can be prevented by the exercise of sufficient social foresight. As illustrations, we may think of preventable accidents and illnesses which in some degree are producing agents in many defectives. Only a small percentage of the causes of hereditary deficiency in all classes of defectives is understood and consequently within the range of control. The methods of prevention are limited thereby, and actual prevention is greatly impeded. Such being the case, the nature of the problem may be portrayed by outlining its chief features.

Number of defectives. There is no way of ascertaining the exact number of persons classified as defectives. They do not appear as a part of the schedules of census takers. Consequently the extent of these classes can only be estimated from the results of various questionnaires and surveys. In order to obtain a preliminary view of the whole deficiency situation, it will be useful to suggest the approximate number and the total of deficients.

The United States Public Health Service estimated that during 1947 more than 1,000,000 persons in the United States were receiving treatment in hospitals or other institutions offering treatment for psychiatric patients. Almost 700,000 or about 473 out of every 100,000 of the civilian population were resident patients in mental hospitals. Of this number, more than 125,000 or about 87 per 100,000 of the civilan population were in institutions for mental defectives and epileptics. Slightly more than 6000 of the total number were receiving psychiatric services of general hospitals. According to the Health Service report, the patient population of mental institutions increased by about 2 per cent during the year 1947.[1]

It is worth noting that of the entire number of resident patients with mental disorders, more than 87 per cent were in public

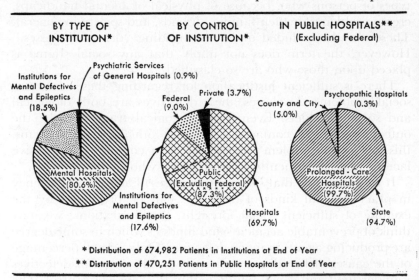

* Distribution of 674,982 Patients in Institutions at End of Year
** Distribution of 470,251 Patients in Public Hospitals at End of Year

Figure 16. Patients in Mental Institutions: United States, 1947

institutions other than federal, and 9 per cent were in federal hospitals, while less than 4 per cent were in privately operated institutions. Figure 16 from the Public Health Service report shows the distribution of patients in mental institutions for the

[1] Data from Mental Health Statistics, Federal Security Agency, Public Health Service, Washington, D.C., Sept., 1949.

year 1947. Figure 17 shows the distribution of about 464,000 resident patients in state mental hospitals according to states. The distribution picture is similar to that shown by states in 1947. These figures do not include the large number of mentally

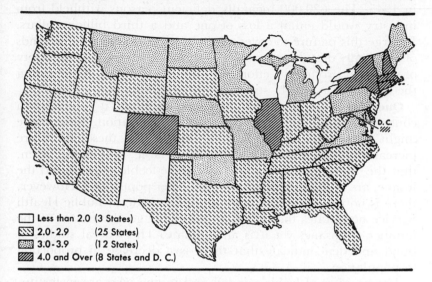

Less than 2.0 (3 States)
2.0-2.9 (25 States)
3.0-3.9 (12 States)
4.0 and Over (8 States and D. C.)

Figure 17. Average Daily Resident Patients in State Hospitals for Mental Disease, per 1000 Civilian Population: 1948

disordered people in the general population who because of their handicaps are unable to take a responsible and self-sustaining place in society. Many of the mental deviates both in and out of institutions require a great deal of special care. The safety of others demands the close confinement of many of the institutional charges. It is observed that the dependent sick and aged are not included in the foregoing classes.

Economic loss. A great burden is created by these defectives in terms of monetary values: cost to support and care for them and loss sustained by their withdrawal from productive enterprises. The average annual per capita cost of maintaining public mental hospitals in 1947 was almost $400. This figure contrasts with the Veterans' Administration expenditure of $2133 per patient in neuropsychiatric hospitals. As the Public Health Service report suggests, this difference probably reflects variations in the type of care received. For treatment in private mental hospitals the per capita cost was $2500. Besides the maintenance costs for public institutions there are capital investments in plants and lands, interest on which probably amounts to $75 to $100 per capita.

The average annual wages of combined male and female workers in manufacturing industries was approximately $2100 in 1945. The 620,000 mentally deficient persons withheld from industry would entail a loss of one and a third billion dollars. Enlarge this picture to cover all the other hundreds of thousands of physically defective persons not employable: the cost to society of withheld productive effort runs into the billions. Recognizing the estimates as rough, still the result is impressive.

Question of increase.   If a real menace exists, it is seen when considering each of three aspects of the situation. First, there might be a menace if it could be proved that these classes are increasing faster than the population at large. It is stated, often, that the "defective classes," meaning the feeble-minded and the insane, are increasing faster than the other population. However, there is no proof for such assertions. The Federal Public Health Service now states that it has a reasonably good estimate of the number of insane, yet it is an estimate. The federal studies of blind and deaf indicate that there is a decrease in proportion to population.

The number of feeble-minded and insane who are in institutions is increasing, and some conclude that this proves these classes are increasing faster than the population. However, in the case of the feeble-minded, it means only that our people are taking larger advantage of the public and private facilities for the care of such persons. It is thought by the Federal Bureau of the Census that the increase of insane persons is partly real, due to increase in mental disease, but also partly due to greater readiness of friends and relatives to send the insane to the hospitals provided for them.

Effect on race stock.   A second possible danger from these multitudes of defectives is their supposed biological effect on the quality of our stock. Is humanity breaking down mentally and physically, deteriorating under this load? We have volumes of lurid statements and warnings to that effect. If the defects were of a hereditary nature, and if the defectives were increasing faster than the population, society might be threatened with collapse. It cannot be proved that all classes of defectives have increased, and there is no reason for being stampeded by assertions of impending menace from increase.

We not only do not know exactly how many there are of any

defective class of persons, but, further, we do not know how many of any class are hereditary and what proportion are so by accident, toxins, or sickness. In the present state of our knowledge, it is presumptuous and superficial to proclaim a great menace from the increase of hereditary defectives of any or all classes. Without reference to the matter of heredity, the problem of our defective class is serious enough.

Effect on family. A third angle is found in the effect on their families of the presence of defectives. There are defective persons in families that are impoverished, in those with few or many developing children, and in those where mothers and heads of families are overworked and without sufficient assistance. The defective person may be loved deeply, yet he is a burden that can scarcely be borne, in spite of the affection. Many families are weighted down, made to function inefficiently, and suffer the pangs of anxiety and strain, as the result of the intimate closeness of these defectives. By all odds, this is probably the greatest menace, burden, and injustice in the whole situation. It is not abstract or remote but very present and concrete.

The Feeble-Minded

Nature of feeble-mindedness. There is a tendency to think of feeble-mindedness as representing a class of persons who are mentally deficient by birth or accident. However, the kinds of feeble-minded are many and merge into each other without dividing lines. According to many psychologists, the intelligence quotients in the successive sections of the curve of distribution for large populations, from highest to lowest levels, run as follows: genius or "near" genius, above 140; very superior intelligence, 120–140; superior intelligence, 110–120; normal or average intelligence, 90–110; dullness, rarely classified as dullness, often as feeble-mindedness, 70–80; definitely feeble-minded, below 70. The feeble-minded are usually graded into (a) morons, 50–70; (b) imbeciles, 20–50; and (c) idiots, below 20. The mental ages of the feeble-minded are: 8 to 12 for morons, 3 to 7 for imbeciles, and under 3 for idiots.[2]

Thus, the feeble-minded occupy one extreme section of the curve of distribution of intellectual capacity, the talented class

[2] L. M. Terman, *Measurement of intelligence* (Boston: Houghton Mifflin Company, 1916), pp. 66, 79; and V. E. Fisher, *Introduction to abnormal psychology* (New York: The Macmillan Company, 1929), Ch. 18. See also F. E. Merrill, et al, *Social problems* (New York: Alfred A. Knopf, 1950), pp. 91–142.

being at the other extreme. As L. M. Terman says, the percentage of the curve given to the feeble-minded depends on the standards arbitrarily determined as to what constitutes feeble-mindedness. The total curve of distribution, according to L. S. Hollingworth, conforms to the normal or probability curve. For both practical and scientific purposes, it is important to understand that the distribution of idiots, imbeciles, and morons falls within the feeble-minded population.[3]

Those we call "insane" are mentally deficient, or ill. But their deficiency is due to the derangement of some of the functions of a previously normal mind. The deficiency of the feeble-minded is caused by arrested development, which in turn may be provoked by numerous conditions. Thus, the feeble-minded have never had normal minds, at least since the time when the deficiency appeared.

One can also see that feeble-mindedness may be relative to situations. A person who is unable to function successfully in a complicated society may be able to adjust his life without injury to himself or others in a simple community. A French physician said he knew a man who was feeble-minded in Paris but quite normal in the country.

If we seek to discover the feeble-minded, we really have to set up some other criterion than mere intelligence. The Presseys think we should have at least four criteria: (a) educational inadequacy, (b) economic inefficiency, (c) social inadequacy, and (d) low-intelligence grading in a series of tests.[4] This pragmatic side to feeble-mindedness appears in the laws for commitment of feeble-minded persons. Social tests have been worked out to measure the social competency and adjustability of persons. It is possible that some of our talented leaders would grade lower by such a test than some of the feeble-minded.

Our former ideas about Mendelian expectancy regarding feeble-mindedness have had to be modified. Earlier it was believed that the occurrence of feeble-mindedness so closely agreed with the percentage expectancy in family stocks afflicted with that misfortune that its hereditary nature was established. Now we know the argument proved faulty because there were no means of establishing the proportion produced by disease, acci-

---

[3] Merrill, *op. cit.*, Part II, pp. 91–142.
[4] See S. L. and L. W. Pressey, *Mental abnormality and deficiency* (New York: The Macmillan Company, 1926), Ch. 10; and Merrill, et al, *op. cit.*, pp. 120–136 for the nature and difficulties of problems of mental inadequacy.

dent, and the like. The figures covered both the hereditary and the nonhereditary cases, and hence there was a correlation of culture and parentage quite as much as one of hereditary feeble-mindedness and parentage.

Certainly feeble-mindedness is no longer regarded as a unit character which is determined by a definite and unitary determiner. The old view was expressed by H. H. Goddard: "It is clear . . . that feeble-mindedness is hereditary in a large percentage of cases, and that it is transmitted in accordance with the Mendelian formula."[5] Previously C. B. Davenport had indicated that feeble-mindedness follows the same law, "is determined by the presence of recessives."[6]

In addition, the importance attached to feeble-mindedness as a factor in the production of many of the problem classes of society has been much reduced. Until recently the estimated percentages of the various problem classes who were feeble-minded ran about as follows: prostitutes, 44; children in orphanages, 29; juvenile delinquents committed by juvenile courts, 25–50; prisoners in penitentiaries, 25–50; inmates of almshouses, 40–50. Healy and Bronner believe that not more than 13 or 14 per cent of delinquents are mentally deficient. Cyril Burt, in England, rates the percentage to be 12 or 13. Some social case workers believe that mental deficiency of some sort accounts for perhaps 15 per cent of their cases. These are generally highly selective cases and cannot be considered as representative of the general population.

The larger proportion of feeble-minded found among delinquents and criminals—as compared with normal persons—is largely due to the fact that their lower level of intelligence increases the liability of their being caught rather than to any inherent meanness or predisposition to being antisocial. The difficulty the feeble-minded have in learning to make successful social adjustments is also a considerable cause.

Pseudofeeble-mindedness. Many years ago William H. Burnham called attention to a kind of feeble-mindedness which is not real but only apparent; that is, if taken when the child is young, it is fictitious; but if let go, it will develop into a serious condition. The mental capacity is there, but it may be inhibited by many

[5] H. H. Goddard, *Feeble-mindedness: Its causes and consequences* (New York: The Macmillan Company, 1914), pp. 437–438.

[6] C. B. Davenport, *Heredity in relation to eugenics* (New York: Henry Holt and Company, 1911), pp. 66–67.

sets of conditions so that it does not develop, and the person remains hopelessly arrested in mind. This form of feeble-mindedness is acquired, just as is that resulting from sickness or the malfunctioning of some gland or glands. It is a form of acquired mental deficiency of which we have hitherto not been aware. It is most important to have it analyzed and revealed to us for at least two reasons. First, it may be that a considerable number of feeble-minded cases are of this kind and that the minds may be reached and brought to normal condition. Second, it throws light on the nature of feeble-mindedness and helps us realize that the line dividing hereditary and acquired mental deficiency cannot be definitely drawn, and that probably the proportion of feeble-mindedness that is hereditary is even smaller than many of our psychologists and biologists believe.

Any one or several of the following conditions may cause pseudofeeble-mindedness: (1) *physical defect*, such as defective vision; (2) *disease*, such as hookworm; (3) *fear*, that may get hold early because of unfortunate experiences; (4) *lack of stimulation* in the home during the early formative period; (5) *overstimulation* that develops mental fruitage too early and undermines mental vitality; (6) *inhibition of the will* in various ways, such as overtaxing the child's powers by too heavy tasks; (7) *unconventional education*, making it impossible for the child to respond in customary fashion; (8) *emotional arrest*, keeping the person at the egoistic and predatory stage and preventing the development of the altruistic sentiments; and (9) *emotional complexes*, breeding introversion, inferiority attitudes, and day dreaming.

The discovery and cure of cases of pseudofeeble-mindedness are extraordinarily difficult and usually require the attention of an expert psychiatrist. There are numerous examples of recovery known, persons "resurrected" to full mental life and personality who otherwise would have remained in life-long blight. It is likely that there are untold thousands of persons in this country rated as idiots and imbeciles who might have been normal, useful people if chance or scientific insight had revealed the true situation.[7]

The nonhereditary feeble-minded. The environmental causes of feeble-mindedness that operate before birth are largely due to the condition of the mother, since the mother is then the child's environment. The more important causes are: (a) *toxins*, such as

[7] W. H. Burnham, *Normal mind* (New York: Appleton-Century-Crofts, 1924), Ch. 18; also Merrill, et al, *op. cit.*

alcohol and other drugs, syphilitic germs, and poisons from maternal disease or occupation. Toxins are believed to produce most biological monstrosities, the technique for the production of which has been worked out by experimentation. Failure of brain development resulting in feeble-mindedness may be of this nature. (b) *Accidents* to the mother which may injure the foetus and cause brain derangement. (c) The *malfunctioning of organs* of the child before birth, affecting the mental development. The malfunctioning of one of the endocrine glands, the thyroid gland, is known to produce that form of idiocy known as cretinism, and this may begin before birth. Physical growth, bodily proportions, and sex are controlled by these glands, all of which might have a bearing on mental development.

Postnatal conditions resulting in feeble-mindedness are many. Accidents at birth may injure the skull and so the brain. The malfunctioning of the endocrine glands begun before or after birth may produce cretinism and probably other types of brain and mental abnormalities. Various children's diseases sometimes have a deadening effect on the mind. Malnutrition is also thought to be a conditioning factor of mental development, but its influence in this direction is not yet accurately determined. In view of the nature of the causes of nonhereditary feeble-mindedness, it is evident that a number of different preventive efforts are called for. Education and care of expectant mothers so that they will understand the effects of their own condition upon the unborn, and care of indigent mothers so that the infants and young children shall secure adequate food, care, and medical attention; better control of drug and liquor traffic and protection of women and men against their use; training and protection against venereal diseases—these are essential features of a preventive program. Some efforts on the part of federal, state, and city governments and by private agencies in all these directions are made, but they are inadequate as yet to reach the masses of people requiring protection and assistance.

Extent and Increase of Feeble-Mindedness

Number of feeble-minded. The United States has never taken a complete census of feeble-minded persons, and in the light of prevalent attitudes it is doubtful if a competent census could be taken. Published estimates vary from about 0.5 to 3 and even 5 per cent of the population. But the latter estimates include many borderline and some higher IQ persons and, in the opinion of the authors, are much too high.

In attempting to establish a reliable estimate of the number of mentally deficient persons in the United States we encounter certain difficulties. We call attention to the following.

1. There is an entire absence of a system of registration of the feeble-minded living outside public institutions. Had we such a system in effect, it would be comparatively easy to collect data that would be as accurate as the method of testing and discovering those who were registered.

2. There is lack of any uniform and standardized procedure in the application of tests by which the feeble-minded are discovered and estimates made. Our "authorities" make use of different criteria in the establishment of their definitions of feeble-mindedness. Surveyors must reach different results in measuring the same boundary line if their chains are of different lengths. Until we know what feeble-mindedness is, and its certain symptoms are, we cannot agree on our estimates of its extent.

3. No boundary lines can be set up between the various stages of mental growth as measured by mental age or IQ. There is no definite and fixed point to denote where the idiots, imbeciles, morons, and borderline cases begin and end. Some estimates doubtless include a much larger portion of the borderline individuals than others, with the result that they yield a larger mentally defective population.

4. In as much as some students base their estimates on the idea that feeble-mindedness is a unitary state, while others base their estimates on the idea that it is a polymorphic or multiple affair, their results will be far apart. To apply an intelligence test alone is a unilateral procedure. But to make use of the IQ plus the measurement of social adjustability is conceiving mental deficiency as a polymorphic matter.

Is feeble-mindedness increasing?   A comparison of the institutional population over the last twenty years shows a rate of increase in the portion of feeble-minded of about 7 to 1. This fact, however, can be very misleading, since there has been an increasing tendency to institutionalize feeble-minded persons. In order to determine whether the feeble-minded increase faster than the general population, we should proceed thus:

1. Accurate recurring censuses of the feeble-minded should be made, so as to reckon gains or losses. We have never had these, nor are we likely to realize them soon, because (a) many families

would conceal, not report, their defectives to enumerators; (b) we lack the great army of trained experts needed to give mental tests; (c) we lack governmental finances for training and maintaining such a corps of experts. At present we prefer to invest our billions in war.

2. Both widespread and comprehensive mental testing should be given, with all methods everywhere on the same basis and comprehending the same range of mental quotients. This would avoid the present confusion in estimates brought about by some "experts," including as feeble-minded only those with an IQ under 70, while others may include all with an IQ under 90. Tests should be made in a completely representative manner of all classes, races, and nationalities living throughout the United States.

3. The birth rates and the death rates among the feeble-minded should be recorded, in order to compare their rate of natural increase with that of the general population.

4. To the same end we should know the proportion of the feeble-minded who are married as compared to people generally.

Since we have realized none of these requirements, we are compelled to judge the comparative rate of increase among the feeble-minded in other ways. Our judgment is that the feeble-minded are increasing no faster than, if as fast as, the general population, for the following reasons:

1. Practically all idiots and lower-type imbeciles are impotent and therefore sterile. This reduces the number of possible fertile feeble-minded to some 90 per cent of all, and pares down the birth rate accordingly. In the opinion of Myerson, the feeble-minded of genetic origin (hereditary) are of so low grade mentally and physically that the males are incapable of sexual intercourse, and the fertility of females is doubtful. As to the latter, he doubts whether, if fertile, they would be subjected to either rape or seduction.[8] At least half of all feeble-minded are genetic, calling for another large reduction of the birth rate.

2. It is probable that what we think is a high birth rate for the feeble-minded generally should be associated with only a section of them. Walter Fernald, who dealt with that class of persons for over thirty years and is recognized as one of the greatest experts we have had, said that what we talk about regarding the "fertility of the feeble-minded is the fertility of people of low

[8] Abraham Myerson, *Inheritance of mental diseases* (Baltimore: Williams and Wilkins, 1925), pp. 74–76.

cultural level, of low economic status, or else unsophisticated in the trends of modern society."[9] Myerson and H. B. Elkind studied the feeble-minded inmates of the Waverly and Wrentham institutions of Massachusetts. Excluding stillbirths, they found a birth rate of only 3.8 at Waverly and 4.5 at Wrentham. Myerson thinks the slightly higher birth rate at Wrentham was due to the fact that the inmates came from a lower cutural level than those of the other institution.

3. There is good reason to believe that the death rate among the feeble-minded is much higher than among normal persons. N. A. Dayton studied the death rate in the schools for the feeble-minded of Massachusetts for a period of fourteen years. The high death rate suggested two things: the feeble-minded are highly susceptible to disease, and they are very short-lived. Their death rate from specific causes was higher than among normal persons the following times: epilepsy, 24; diarrhea, 19; broncho-pneumonia, 14; measles, 9; influenza, 8; lobar pneumonia, 3, etc.[10] The death rate of feeble-minded and epileptics in state institutions in 1934 was 26.8 compared with a general death rate of 11.2.[11]

We are warranted in concluding as follows regarding feeble-minded increase: with a birth rate that probably is lower than that of the population at large, and with a death rate that is much higher, it appears that the feeble-minded do not threaten to submerge the normal population by a higher rate of natural increase. It is further probable that the hereditary feeble-minded are inferior physically, that their vitality is so low that they tend not to marry or mate, and that they die comparatively early. It is also true that idiots, almost wholly, and imbeciles considerably, who together constitute about one fourth of all feeble-minded, are little likely to reproduce because of unattractiveness and impotency.

Care and Control of the Feeble-Minded

General attitudes. Until the present time, our nation has followed two general attitudes for the care of the feeble-minded. First, the attitude of *laissez faire;* that is, leaving them alone. This, evidently, is still the dominant attitude, since we have not

[9] Myerson, *loc. cit.*, p. 82.

[10] N. A. Dayton, "Mortality in mental deficiency over a 14-year period in Massachusetts," *Thirty-sixth proceedings and addresses of the fifty-fifth annual session of the American Association for the Study of the Feeble-Minded* (1931–1932), XXXVI: 127–212.

[11] U. S. Census, 1934, p. 18.

taken the trouble to learn how many persons there are of that kind, and so do not seek to control large portions of them, even of those who are known. This is the easier method, but it may prove to be the more costly one.

Second, nearly all our states have taken some steps toward caring for the feeble-minded. They have passed some regulative laws, and most states have established special institutions where a portion of these people may be segregated permanently or temporarily. Some states have passed sterilization and "eugenic marriage" laws, although few have put them rigorously into effect.

Social control of the feeble-minded should rest on a knowledge of their nature, their variations and classification, and on a comparison of the various classes on the basis of their being a possible social menace. The method of disposal should then be adjusted appropriately to the different classes.

In so far as society has sought to control this situation, several steps have been taken, namely: institutionalization, colonization, parole, and community supervision. These steps are not all clearly defined in any one community and in only a few states. Most of the foregoing methods are more or less definitely in operation in most states.

Appropriate treatment according to class. The first step toward a scientific treatment of the sick is the identification and diagnosis of bodily ailments by the medical practitioner. Efforts to place the feeble-minded will be greatly misapplied until a scientific diagnosis of each individual case is made. This is a large undertaking in any population and seems tremendous in our populous country. Mechanical mental tests administered by untrained, or partly trained, persons are insufficient and unjust to those tested.

These tests should not be attempted until resort can be made to clinical laboratories in charge of men and women with competent clinical training in mental and social testing and diagnosis. Such laboratories have been established at some large universities, but they reach only a few individuals. A few large cities, such as Newark, Chicago, Cleveland, St. Louis, Cincinnati, Oakland, and Los Angeles, have clinics as a part of their educational systems. However, most of our city, village, and farm populations are wholly without any such facilities. Well-equipped clinical laboratories need to be extended as rapidly as funds will permit and thoroughly trained persons can be provided. Traveling clinics might be made available for sparse populations. A diagnostic examination made in a competent clinical laboratory would discover the proper classification of the feeble-minded person so that the appropriate treatment could be provided.

Colonization. This is a form of institutionalization, since colonies are commonly established in connection with special institutions. It has some advantages of economy and education. The earlier custom was to place the supposedly most dangerous or burdensome classes, the idiots and imbeciles, in institutions. It was found that many morons were greater social menaces than the lower type of feeble-minded. It also was costly and wasteful to segregate and support individuals, many of whom are physically competent to make their own way. Accordingly, New York and Indiana instituted farm colonies, in the 80's and 90's of the last century, the industrial colony appearing a little later. Such a colony is "any group of inmates living together under supervision outside the parent institution, while remaining under its jurisdiction and contributing to a greater or less degree by labor to their own support."[12] Probably the State School for Mental Defectives, Rome, New York exemplifies the most extreme development of the colony idea. In 1923 it consisted of 36 colonies, 22 for boys and 14 for girls. Industrial colonies in towns for both men and women, besides farm colonies for men and domestic colonies for women, were a new departure. There the colony exercises a twofold function, training for life and serving as a halfway station between the institution and parole. The plan has proved both economically feasible and socially desirable. Several states now maintain colonies, and other states are beginning to organize them.

Parole. Parole of the feeble-minded from institutions is confined almost wholly to the morons. It is found safe to place the better-class persons on parole after they have been trained to good industrial and social habits. This has been a gradual development recently in the United States and is now practiced to some degree by a large number of states. Dr. Fernald found, as a result of his investigation in Massachusetts, that adult morons, who have had good training, usually lead a normal life and are self-supporting. It appears that they learn with difficulty, and they unlearn with equally great resistance. There is more irregularity among the women than the men, but comparatively

---

[12] S. P. Davies, *Social control of the feeble-minded* (New York: State Charities Aid Association, 1928), p. 109.

few of the former go wrong, marry, or have children. Where the proper training can be given in the home, institutionalization is not required. Since morons are the largest class of feeble-minded, proper home or institutional training obviates the necessity of permanently institutionalizing all feeble-minded persons.

In the case of those paroled from institutions, supervision by social workers or responsible members of the locality until the paroled are socially adjusted and stabilized is necessary. Those trained at home will have their relatives to advise them. All morons in the population at large should have the benefit of friendly counsel by responsible and friendly individuals.[13]

Special schools and classes. This form of education of feeble-minded children has become a significant method of benefiting the class in question. The things seemingly necessary for the success of special classes are:

1. Appropriate equipment and school materials. Since the children are different in some respects from normal children, the materials must be adjusted nicely to their needs.

2. Teachers trained especially to teach this kind of children. Normal schools might give sufficient training for disciplining and teaching purposes, but—and this is a weak point at present—the special schools are deficient in these requisites.

3. Definite selection of those to be trained in special classes. This is a further recognition of the need for proper diagnosis. Many schools have made the special classes a dumping ground for all sorts of children, such as retarded, truants, blind, and deaf, besides all classes of feeble-minded youth. Where large numbers are present in classes, insufficient personal attention can be given by the teacher to make her efforts successful with any of these kinds of unfortunates.

The following case shows what may be accomplished by special classes in our public schools. This child certainly had the indications of feeble-mindedness and social maladjustment.

A greatly retarded boy of 14 entered a city school and was placed in the third grade. Here he gave his teachers much trouble and was severely treated by his parents because of his failure. He was handicapped by deafness in one ear and was mortified by having to sit along in school with younger and smaller children. He had come to doubt his own ability, was sullen, and took revenge

[13] W. E. Fernald, "State program for the care of the mental defectives," *Mental Hygiene*, Oct. 4, 1919: 566–567; and J. H. S. Bossard, *Problems of social well-being* (New York: Harper and Brothers, 1927), pp. 515–517.

by mistreating younger children. The psychologist who visited him found him hard and morose, but he brightened up when he found she was interested in what he could do and not in what he had failed to do. His mental grade was 72, and he was placed in a Special Class. He showed interest in and considerable capacity for industrial work and was given jobs of making rabbit boxes and similar things. His class studies began to receive diligent attention in order that he might be given more time for the manual work he loved. From being a problem and scourge to his teachers he developed into a happy, well-behaved boy. He hung around school after hours to be allowed to do extra manual-training work. His family developed a warm appreciation for what the school was doing for him and manifested pathetic love and loyalty to the teacher who so largely had brought about the change.[14]

Epilepsy

Nature and gravity.   Records of epilepsy go back to the time of Hippocrates (born 460 B.C.). It is proper now to speak of epilepsies, or better, seizures. Seizures are neuro-muscular in nature, ranging from light, momentary muscular spasms with little loss of consciousness (*petit mal*) to prolonged, intense convulsions with entire loss of conciousness (*gran mal*). The presence of the malady can now be detected definitely by means of a new invention, the electrocephalograph, which records brain waves: the normal and those of the various kinds of seizures.[15] The type of wave pattern is the key to the nature of the seizure. Only one side of the brain manifests the wave pattern, while the other side of the body expresses muscular convulsions. Not all normal brain waves are alike, about one in ten being different. But only about one in 200 of these persons manifesting one-in-ten divergencies are subject to seizures.

There are various preconditions of seizure. (1) Injury to brain, before or after birth; infection from some disease settling in the brain; injury to the head; tumor in or on the brain. (2) Bodily disorders, such as those of the kidneys or the glands influencing sex and maturity. (3) Emotional upsets, as may occur during adolescence. Seventy per cent of seizures are reported to occur before the age of 20. The peak age is the first two years of life. The period of adolescence is also prominent in this respect. The age distribution of seizure patients in the institu-

---

[14] "Special classes in the public schools," Bulletin No. 4 of The Committee on Provision for the Feeble-Minded, Philadelphia.
[15] See *Life*, June 3, 1946: 129 for reproductions of such waves.

tions of the United States in 1938 were (in percentage): under five, 3; under ten, 15.2; ten to twenty-four, 58.8; twenty-five to fifty-four, 17.3; over fifty-five, 5.7. Since there were only about 19,000 in institutions, this age distribution cannot represent that of the hundreds of thousands who are at large.

Seizures are likely to be developmentally progressive. Unless checked, the tendency to become more intensive is present, and *petit mal* may develop into *gran mal* ultimately. The seizures also become more frequent.

Prophylactic aspects. Formerly there was little hope of recovery or cure for persons afflicted with seizure. Now, however, the outlook is decidedly hopeful. Regarding *gran mal*, (1) medication is helpful, as this statement shows: the attacks of a patient, 20 a month, were reduced to 10 by the use of bromide, to 7 by phenobarbital, and to 2.5 a month by dilantin sodium. Triodine cures a percentage of cases of *petit mal* and greatly reduces seizures in other cases.[16] (2) Diets are useful to some children. One of fatty foods, such as heavy cream, butter, egg yolk, olive oil, and bacon may gradually produce ketone acids in the blood which have a soothing effect on nerves. (3) Early and continuous training of children and the young into self-expression in following out their own interest-activities is conducive to establishing and strengthening the organic paths for the outlet and expression of energy. Blocking of paths may result in seizure. The establishment and maintenance of colonies for the victims of seizure find their great value as an education in free self-expression of interest and energy.

Number and provisions. From the point of view of numbers, we can form no adequate idea of the epileptic problem. Estimates of current writers state that there are a half million, or 600,000. That such statements are uninformed is deduced from an accompanying statement that a tenth of the 600,000 are in institutions. But since only about 20,000 are institutionalized, the total number would be only some 200,000. Until the national government makes an objective and inclusive study, we will not know the number. From the few institutionalized, especially in some regions, it is evident that public provisions for the epileptic are inadequate. The increase of the ratio of patients from 46.7 per 100,000 population in 1923 to 79.1 in 1938 expresses growing public provision as well as an excess of admissions to discharges.

[16] Milton Silverman, "We can lick epilepsy," *Saturday Evening Post*, September 17, 1948.

A better method for caring for epileptics who are institution-alized is being developed. The older method placed epileptics in institutions for the insane, the feeble-minded, and the depend-ent. Considering the character of epilepsy, such a method has evident disadvantages. The violent epileptic paroxysms demor-alize associated inmates, especially certain classes of the insane. During lucid intervals, most of the epileptics are capable of work of a curative, helpful, and self-supporting nature. They should be placed where these capacities can be utilized.

During the last forty years there has been a gradual trend toward establishing special institutions for epileptics. There is an apparent tendency toward departmental rather than toward special institutions. Institutions with separate departments for insane and epileptics, or for feeble-minded and epileptics, have increased in number during the last few years. It may be that separate institutions and that specialized attention which is equally satisfactory can be given each class of patients.

Several states have established colonies for epileptics, and the newer institutions or departments are mostly of that form. Colonies may be separate institutions or connected with institu-tions. Craig Colony, New York, is one of the most notable examples of this form of care. It comprises a large area of about 2000 acres and carries on farming, gardening, brick making, and domestic economy. Its wards are largely self-supporting.

Craig Colony illustrates the advantages of this method of care, as shown by the following provisions: (1) Simple home life and the individuality of the wards. (2) Education and recreation and amusements suitable to needs. (3) Vocations, outdoor life, and a large measure of self-support. (4) The special methods of care and treatment required for epileptics. (5) Eugenic segrega-tion. (6) Avoidance of humiliation of forced association of those who are normal-minded, much of the time, with the feeble-minded and the insane.

Special educational facilities for the epileptic could be main-tained by the public schools of great cities at least. This is proved by the fact that a special school for that class of unfortunates is a going institution in the city of Detroit, with an attendance of 185. The average number of seizures per day is only five.

Nature and Treatment of Insanity

There are few matters concerning which the public is in greater need of scientific information than insanity. Insanity generally is determined on a legal and not on a strictly scientific basis. It refers to the legal commitment of persons to hospitals for the insane. In most states, counties have insanity boards before which persons charged with insanity are brought and hearings held. If the person is deemed insane, he is committed. The person's variation from customary behavior in one or more particulars must be great and behavior menacing before the charge is sustained and the person committed. In other words, the person must have become "chronically" insane before attention is devoted to the case. Consequently we need to look into the scientific nature of what is legally and popularly called insanity.

Insanities vs. insanity. Insanity does not correspond to just one type of mental illness. The term "insanity," used to mean mental disease, does not signify insanity alone but many insanities. The first attempt to detect definite forms of mental disease in this country for census purposes was made in 1910, when special data were sought on alcoholic psychosis and general paralysis. Previous to that date, scientific knowledge was lacking, and the insane were viewed as a homogeneous group. By 1917 sufficient scientific gains had been made to warrant a classification. In 1917, through the joint efforts of the National Committee for Mental Hygiene and the American Psychiatric Association, a standard classification of mental diseases was adopted and introduced into most of the state hospitals of the country. Later, it was adopted by the United States Public Health Service and the United States Census Bureau and by nearly all of the public and private hospitals for mental disease that had not introduced it in 1917.

This standard classification divides mental disorders into twenty-two principal groups, twenty of which are more or less clearly defined groups of psychoses, while one group is provided for undiagnosed psychoses and another for patients without a psychosis.[17]

Developmental ideas and treatment. The mental-hygiene conception of insanity is recent. Before that movement there had been a long evolution regarding the concept of insanity.

Nearly all primitive peoples ascribe insanity to some form of demoniacal possession. This is natural and inevitable at that stage of cultural development in which there is no scientific body of knowledge about nature or man and no naturalistic

---

[17] "Patients in hospitals for mental disease," U. S. Census, 1923: 40; also Merrill, et al, *op. cit.*, pp. 90–142.

psychology. Human and natural events are explained in terms of demons or spirits in the stage of animism. An event happens because a demon causes it. People act "queer" because a spirit takes possession of them. This conception holds until higher, also prescientific, religions arrive and displace it by a new conception.

During the earlier stages of Christianity insanity, like other human misfortunes, was attributed to sinfulness. In this case, the deity is offended because the afflicted person has "sinned" against some divine ordinance, and the affliction is in the nature of a penalty imposed by the divine ruler and judge. The conception of insanity as "possession" was also current. During the Middle Ages, insanity was explained chiefly as possession by evil powers or evil spirits. Only with the rise and spread of the scientific psychological conception of mind and personality could there be a grasp of the true nature of insanity. Gradually this true idea makes headway until only the ignorant and superstitious think of mental illness otherwise.

Naturally the treatment of the insane follows and is colored by the idea of insanity. Until very recently the insane have been treated brutally. Chaining, imprisoning in the vilest quarters, abandonment to filth and vermin, beating, and torturing were the common lot of the insane. Domesticated animals received a degree of humane and adequate treatment, generally, that was not accorded the mentally afflicted. Mary Brown Stephenson writes: "In Illinois, in about 1900, a woman named Rhoda Dery was discovered locked in a room in the Adams County almshouse. For forty years she had been kept in a rough box bed, with about such toilet facilities as are provided for animals in captivity. She had scratched out her eyes." At what is now the Peoria State Hospital, to which she was taken, "she had expert care, and she became such a pet of the institution that when she died, the nurses cried."[18]

Medical theory and practice of even the late eighteenth and early nineteenth centuries were opaque and unscientific. Insanity was attributed to "yellow and black bile," "increased secretion of the nervous fluid," and "torpor of brain and nerves." Garrison illustrates medical practice as follows:

> Melancholia was treated by quinine pills, excited states by camphor . . . mustard plaster on the head, venesection at the forehead and both thumbs, clysters and plasters of Spanish fly. . . . A melancholic woman was treated with a volley of oaths and

[18] *Welfare Bulletin*, Dec., 1931.

a douche of cold water as she lay in bed. . . . A sensitive, self-conscious patient was confined in a cold, damp, gloomy, mephitic cell, fed on perpetual hard bread, and otherwise treated as a criminal.[19]

Mental illness a natural condition. Today scientific thinking and practice regard insanity and the various psychoses as natural in the same sense as physical disease is natural. This is seen from three bases of consideration:

1. From the causes assigned. (a) Some are doubtless hereditary, the percentage being as yet undetermined. (b) Some come from certain physical conditions, such as focal infections, proportion of water in the brain, and paresis. (c) A large portion arise from psychological conditions such as disturbances due to strains and stresses of life and maladjustments due to other causes. All these causes are a normal part of nature and society. The first and third factors are well-known causes and account for a considerable proportion of mental illness. The second factor is new and experimental.

2. From the fact that everyone is at times *in*sane (not sane). The dividing line between insanity and sanity is so uncertain and vague that often it is hard to determine who is sane and who insane.

3. From the fact that insanity and mental illness rise up out of the normal life and mental activities. Exaggeration of and exclusive concentration on any one mental activity may easily constitute mental illness. For example, if a person broods over a "wrong," the brooding singles out certain factors or ideas, gradually isolates them from support and checking by other mental elements or ideas, and elevates and magnifies them accordingly to a place of dominance in the person's mind. Mental perspective is lost, the wrong is seen to the exclusion of other things, and the mind has become unbalanced.

Mental hygiene and personality. Mental hygiene centers on personality. We defined personality as the expression or function of the psychophysical organism at any given stage of individual and social development. Here we think more particularly of the psychical factors resting on a background of conditioning physical organs. Anyway, the person is the whole complex of physical and mental attributes in action. Personality must be valid, unified,

---

[19] F. H. Garrison, *Introduction to the history of medicine*, p. 106, quoted by Groves and Blanchard, *Introduction to mental hygiene* (New York: Henry Holt and Company, 1930), pp. 18–19.

balanced, in order to function properly. Divisions and disintegrations cripple and disqualify for executing life activities. Manias and emotionalisms interfere with smooth and efficient adjustments to others. Bad habits of mind, morals, or body are exaggerations of ordinarily valid activities, and they disturb social relationships and cause further maladjustments.

Society is a relationship and adjustment of personalities to one another. We do not live for society in itself, but we make use of it as an instrument of service for realizing our personal satisfactions and objectives. We have society in order that we may all live. The smoothness of its operations is determined by the nicety or awkwardness of the adjustment of persons constituting it. The way persons are adjusted is, in turn, determined in large part by the ingredients of personality and especially by the way in which those ingredients are joined together. The person with a grouch or a grievance, the one-idea man, and the eccentric individual are hard to get along with, and they are usually avoided. The insanities are only such exaggerated traits carried a little farther. Moreover, all the clashes of minds and wills, interests and motives, center in personalities and disturb social articulations and modes of operating. It is the business of mental hygiene to reshape morbid personalities, adjust jarring ones, and secure smoother functioning of persons in their group life.

Extent of the problem.   Insanity is a problem of the individual, family, locality, and nation, and it is of first-rate importance. It incapacitates individuals for prosecuting a career or a livelihood. It burdens and disrupts families, burdens localities, and is a menace and a burden to states and nations. Beyond the insanities are the various mental illnesses which handicap individuals and render them inefficient in performing their functions in home, neighborhood, and society generally. We may see the size of the problem by recalling a few facts.

First, there were 601,493 patients on the books of hospitals for mentally ill persons at the end of 1945—87.6 per cent in state, county, city, veterans, and private institutions, 0.4 per cent in family care, and 12 per cent in other outside care. This is a population larger than that of any of ten states, or of any except eleven of our great cities. Besides those are multitudes of unidentified mentally ill persons, enough to make a million or more in all. The number of patients on hospital books increased 12,719, or 2.5 per cent, over the previous year.[20] Hospitalization and the

<hr>

[20] "Patients in mental hospitals," U. S. Census, 1945.

withdrawal of hospitalized insane persons from economic activity runs about $1,650,000,000 yearly.

Fostering conditions. There are several sets of conditions which, if they do not produce insanity, seem to be favorable to it. They are as follows.

1. Cultural conditions. The rate of the insane hospitalized in urban districts is twice that in rural districts. This may mean (a) that urbanism stimulates insanity by increased stress and complexity of adjustment; (b) that insanity is more frequent in cities because life contains the complex of all the causes of insanity; (c) that insanity is a matter of relativity, in that minds too unbalanced for adjustment in a complex society are sufficiently adaptable in a simpler situation; or (d) that relatively fewer of the insane are committed in rural districts. It is difficult to explain why the rate varies so much among states, especially as between New York and Pennsylvania, 376 and 130, or Utah 168 and Nevada 266, states of similar cultural levels.

2. Psychic pressure. We might expect that any disturbed social conditions would exert a psychic pressure which could produce both functional and constitutional insanity, by hastening the time of attack. Even in hereditary insanity, it is logical to suppose the time of arrival of attack could be hastened. We offer a few evidences that such is the case.

Dr. Miner of the University of Michigan disturbed the jumping conditions of his experimental rats so that they failed to attain their shelves, became confused, overcome with nervous shock, sank into a coma, and showed every symptom of "insanity." V. Aaserude drew curves of population and admissions to the North Dakota state hospital for mental patients for the years 1892 to 1938 and found that during periods of drought, depression, and World War I the admission rates accelerated and afterward declined irrespective of population rates of change.[21] The ratio of first admissions to the institutions for mental patients of the United States underwent a great increase during World War II, advancing from a level of about 60 in 1938 to one of 85 in 1941 and 89 in 1942. Tables of frequency of schizophrenia among socio-economic classes of Germany and the United States shows that the ratio between the two varies inversely with group level, the higher the level the lower the ratio.[22]

[21] *Medical service available in North Dakota with special reference to indigent population,* Master's Thesis at the University of North Dakota.

[22] "Schizophrenia, manic-depressive psychosis, and social-economic status," *American Journal of Sociology,* Sept., 1941: 167 ff.

On the other hand, Associated Press reports from Great Britain for 1941 state that nervous disorders did not increase during the great bombardment. C. W. Schroeder found that insanity varies inversely with socio-economic levels in cities, but that there are zone patterns of occurrence which prevent a complete correlation between the two.[23]

Curability and Treatment of Insanity

Recovery and elimination. The elimination of insanity as a social phenomenon and problem is dependent on the control of the causative conditions. A consideration of the fostering conditions mentioned above will reveal that many of them are subject to regulation. Cultural conditions can be improved by means of applying enlightened socio-economic policies. The prevention and cure of syphilis have come about gradually, and it may be expected to be removed as an influence. Theoretically we should be able to remove drug addiction and alcoholism; practically it is difficult to accomplish this. In so far as heredity is a factor in insanity, we have to admit that we are not yet in sight of controlling it. Whether we shall be able to do so in the future is also problematical. Our later discussion of heredity and eugenics should make this position clear. Admittedly, we cannot hope to control sex or age. Probably there is little inherent reason why one sex more than the other is given to insanity. The age factors may be mitigated under a more equitable economic regime.

Mental complexes are significant in normal life, in determining later courses of action and in promoting concord and discord in society. They play a fundamental part in producing and maintaining certain forms of insanity. It was pointed out previously that much mental illness begins with the formation of such complexes. Evidently, then, the problem relative to the "complex" revolves about consideration of its prevention. As to complexes producing insanity, the social cure lies in building a society in which conditions favorable to the formation of complexes will be minimized. Results will be most effective when attention is directed along the following lines:

1. Psychiatry should be developed to such a point that personality difficulties are understood and competently treated.

[23] *Cf.* "Mental disorders in urban areas," *American Journal of Sociology*, July, 1942: 40–47; also, Faris and Dunham, *Mental disorders in urban areas* (Chicago: University of Chicago Press, 1939).

Specialists should be distributed sufficiently widely so that those needing such help are able to receive it.

2. A mental-hygiene attitude should be developed by means of all the educational agencies. This supposes that people will come to understand that personality difficulties and conditions breeding personality conflicts and stresses are vitally important. Should this be realized, situations which invite and promote personality disturbances would be avoided and inhibited, and when they did arise they would secure an adequate specialized attention, as our physical ailments now receive.

3. Family life needs to be placed on a happier and a more agreeable plane. Family conflicts and disagreements, lack of co-operation between parents, stupid and unsympathetic management of children are fruitful soil in which personality troubles grow. The results of psychoanalysis testify amply to the stubborn complexes developed early in child life, which survive later to drive individuals into hospitals or prisons. A revolution in the field of family training would go far to cut down the incidence of insanity.

4. Many now are impressed by the fact that great gains in the direction of mental health of the nation would accrue by instituting a better-conditioned society in which worry about jobs and incomes for tomorrow and the longer future are reduced to the minimum. We would all be saner and have a greater personal vigor to invest in our work and life if we had the assurance that our families would not be threatened by homelessness and starvation on the break-down of our industrial and financial system. Dr. F. E. Williams visited Russia and found an astonishingly sound mental health and a conception of mental hygiene different from ours. Russians believe that "mental hygiene must have to do with *keeping well people well*, of so organizing life and the emotional development of the individual that the anxieties and fears that lead to defensive reactions on his part and which end in inefficiency, unhappiness—and often illness and antisocial conduct—be minimized, so that he may be in a position to contribute of his best."[24] Landis and Page doubt that "psychic pressure" due to social crises causes insanity, but their evidence appears insufficient and further research is desirable.[25]

[24] *Cf.* "Those crazy Russians," *Survey Graphic* (Jan., 1932), Vol. XX: 341–345; also, Kimball Young, *Social psychology*, 2nd ed. (New York: Appleton-Century-Crofts, 1944), Ch. 10.

[25] *Cf.* Landis and Page, *Modern society and mental disease* (New York: Farrar, Straus and Company, 1938), Ch. 13.

Curability of insanity. The degree of curability of insanity in general is difficult to demonstrate because it is so variable in its nature and is so much a matter of development. Some of the many kinds of psychoses are more amenable to treatment than are others. Every form of insanity tends to become more difficult to regulate and relieve in its later developmental stages. Authorities and census reports seem meticulously to avoid stating what percentage of insanity can be cured.

At the beginning of the year 1945 there were 601,493 patients on the books, with the following dispositions: 87.6 per cent in hospitals, 12.0 per cent on parole, 0.4 per cent in family care. Admissions during the year were 295,715. Of these, 67.7 per cent were first admissions, 18.7 per cent re-admissions, 13.6 transfers. There were 282,996 separations from hospitals. Of these, 67.4 per cent were discharged, 19.9 per cent transferred, 12.7 per cent died, the death rate being 95 as compared with a national rate of about 11.

The condition of those discharged from state hospitals during that year who had psychoses when admitted and whose condition was reported was as follows: "recovered," 31.8 per cent; "improved," 56.4 per cent; "unimproved," 11.8 per cent. The gain in number of patients by the end of the year was 12,719, or 2.4 per cent. If "recovered" means cured, then about one third of the patients were cured. It is doubtful if all of them became completely and permanently normal. Evidently not all of those discharged as "improved" are cured, for many relapse and are re-admitted, about 23 per cent during 1938. Roughly, we may think that somewhere between 30 and 40 per cent of the psychotic committed to hospitals are "cured." We confess it is a rough estimate. Nevertheless it approximates the real situation.

The longer the stay in the hospital, the smaller the proportion recovering or being discharged. For the year 1922, 55 per cent were in hospitals less than 5 months; 75 per cent less than one year; and only 1.5 per cent had been in 10 years or more. Over half of the "improved" had been inmates less than 5 months. The majority of those discharged as "unimproved" had been inmates less than 5 months. The reports do not indicate why they were discharged. The import of the objective facts is that unless a cure is effected early, it is almost impossible to accomplish it. Of course, it may be that the long-termers were originally incurable.

Methods of treatment. In discussing the disposition of insanity it is to be understood that insanities are the culminations of mental disease, and that adequate treatment must begin with the mental diseases. Society has made marked advance in its conception and treatment of the insane, and yet a satisfactory system of disposal has not been devised. There have been several stages in the development and treatment of the insane. (a) The primitive conception was that insanity is the result of a magical or supernatural visitation, and therefore the insane are either unreal or dangerous, with consequent ostracism and probable death. (b) It was thought that the insane were dangerous to society, hence their consequent inhuman confinement in poorhouses and jails, the violent and turbulent being chained, straitjacketed, and otherwise harshly restricted with little thought for their welfare. (c) Humanitarianism at first developed with little understanding or thought of cure. The insane should not be placed in jails or almshouses or be harshly treated but should be placed in the custody of institutions and as happily situated as possible. (d) And finally there arose the idea of restoration if possible and, if not possible, then custody. Insanity is regarded as a "disease," which, if given timely and adequate attention, often may be cured.

To realize the curative idea, it is imperative that several principles and practices be observed. All of these are being realized now in particular places.

1. Adequate equipment for the disposal and the treatment of the insane. In institutions this involves ample room for the proper separation of certain classes of inmates; provisions for applying the most effective remedies, such as hydrotherapy, dry therapy, electrotherapy, and heat and other ray treatments; re-education through industrial or other occupations; an adequate staff of physicians trained in psychiatry; a corps of professional nurses and attendants, and provisions for amusements and recreation which not only minister to enjoyment but are effective agencies in restoration.

2. Early recognition and treatment. The prevalent system of treating mental disorders is to await the complete manifestation, the application of formal legal methods of examination for deciding as to insanity, and the commitment to a distant state hospital. This practice violates scientific and humane principles in several respects. (a) Adequate investigation and treatment are delayed too long. Promptness in recognizing and treating the trouble is as essential to recovery as it is in the case of pneumonia or infantile paralysis. (b) The legal process of deciding the case

and commitment to the state hospital attaches a stigma to the afflicted person by branding him insane. This is unnecessary, unjust, and very harmful to the person committed. No one should be pronounced insane if it can possibly be avoided. The handicap to the person who has been pronounced insane, committed, and paroled or discharged is inconceivably undermining and paralyzing. It is a courageous person who can live down the unfair label. Insanity is as respectable a disease as the physical diseases, and a system should be adopted under which afflicted persons may enter and pass out of institutions with the same freedom from stigma as they now have for physical ailments. (c) Commitment to state hospitals often means association with violent and noisy persons, which may further provoke and stimulate the mental trouble. This is unnecessary if the disease is taken in its incipient stages.

3. Placing competent psychiatric and psychoanalytic provisions within easy reach of people. The average medical practitioner cannot be fitted easily to understand mental diseases, especially those due to mental complexes. Specialized experts in the mental field are alone competent to do this work.

4. Making abundant psychopathic provisions available for the earlier stages of mental trouble. This is accomplished at present by establishing psychopathic hospitals, psychopathic wards in general hospitals, and psychopathic departments in hospitals for the insane. But the bulk of the population of the nation is, as yet, without adequate provisions of this nature. Formal legal commitment to state hospitals for the insane and the remoteness of such hospitals from the masses of people defeat adequate attention to initial cases. Such a plan as the county system of hospitals obtaining in Wisconsin provides for a proper distribution of psychopathic care, but even there the county hospitals take chiefly old and incurable cases rather than younger and more promising ones.

5. Developing both out-patient and parole provisions. The growth of the parole system for milder cases of insanity has demonstrated that such cases of mental trouble may be taken care of outside institutions. To attain this end successfully requires distributed psychopathic and psychiatric provisions and trained social workers. This serves to take care of incipient and mild cases and relieves hospitals of undue congestion. Either voluntary associations or the state may carry on this work.

6. Universalizing voluntary commitment of the insane and the

mentally ill. For the most part, the individual can now secure commitment to institutions to receive adequate treatment only after he has become chronically insane. This reduces chances of recovery. With voluntary commitment, the ailing person or his friends may ask his admission for treatment and have him admitted; he may then be discharged privately and quietly when relieved. The needed immediate attention is secured, and unnecessary stigma is avoided. This form of commitment is now provided by a number of states.

The Blind

Nature and extent of blindness. Although blindness constitutes a minor problem as compared with feeble-mindedness or mental disease, it is important. It handicaps the lives of thousands of persons, is accompanied by unhappiness and degeneracy, accounts for a large number of dependent persons, requires the establishment and support of public institutions of a special nature for the education of the blind, militates against proper support and rearing of children by blind parents, and in so far as it is hereditary it tends to reproduce itself.

We accept the definition of blindness set down by the United States Bureau of the Census in its task of collecting data relative to the blind: A blind person is one who cannot see well enough to read even with glasses, whether literate or not. "The test in the case of infants must be whether they can apparently distinguish forms and objects."[26]

The extent of blindness in the United States is largely a matter of conjecture. Since 1930 when 63,489 blind persons were reported by the census, no national census count of the blind has been published. Eye tests have never been given to more than a small proportion of the population. Our information is derived mainly from samplings of and the estimates of specialists. It should be recognized, also, that a tendency to minimize the degree of eye defectiveness by many persons probably reduces the number of cases reported in the enumerations made. According to census reports, there was a decrease in the proportion of blind persons in the population from almost 98 per 100,000 of the population in 1880 to less than 52 per 100,000 in 1930.[27]

The Census Bureau recognizes the incompleteness of its returns. Its corrections for 1920 found 76,000 blind persons and a

[26] "Blind in the United States," Bureau of the Census, 1920, p. 7.
[27] *Social work year book*, 1947, p. 56.

ratio of 72.6 blind per 100,000 inhabitants. The National Institute of Public Health, from a check-up of census returns in various areas, estimated that there were about 117,000 blind in 1930, or over 95 per 100,000 inhabitants.[28] Probably similar corrections are needed for previous estimates. However, conclusions about increase of blindness must rest on census data.

It therefore seems as though blindness may be decreasing. While the number of blind persons has increased, the ratio of the blind in the population has decreased except for the last check-up. Probably the decrease is not so great as the printed ratios denote, because the corrected ratios for 1910 and 1920, while indicating a decrease, show that it is slight. The preventive and prophylactic measures discussed below no doubt account for the decrease.

It is important to observe the distribution of blindness according to race, nativity, and sex. Of the 63,489 persons for whom special schedules were returned in the census of 1930, 57.5 per cent were males and 42.5 per cent were females. Nearly 81 per cent were native whites, and about 10.5 per cent were Negroes.

Causes of blindness. Statistics on the causes of blindness are not always consistent. It is difficult to know how much weight to give them in analyzing reasons for this handicap. Even the national government publications for the same dates present variations, though not of serious import. According to a study published in 1934, the percentage distribution of causes of blindness was as follows: disease, 54.4; accident or other injury, 16.5; other known causes, 3.6; causes indefinitely reported, 25.5.[29]

All the causes except the congenital, atrophy of the nerve, and accidental injury are classed as theoretically preventable though probably not wholly preventable. No doubt, also, a large percentage of the accidental and congenital causes could be avoided. A rough approximation would place far over half the causes of blindness in the preventable list. Since prevention is certain and cure is uncertain and costly, wisdom would point to prevention as the most desirable method. A portion of the unpreventable cases is susceptible to partial or complete reparation. But the blindness which comes with advanced age is difficult to prevent or cure.

It is impossible to determine what part heredity plays in producing blindness. Our national census bureau collects data on

---

[28] National Institute of Public Health, *National health survey*, Bulletin 10, 1935–1936: 102.

[29] *Social work year book*, 1947, p. 56.

blindness and blood kinship of several degrees. We use the statistics relating to first cousinships of the parents of the blind, as they are entirely pertinent and easy to handle.

Table 26 shows that there is little difference between the offspring of first-cousin parents and of those who are not kin, as far as blindness is concerned. The slight differences might easily be due to the small number of cases involved. Further, it is well to note that much of the blindness involved is due to nonhereditary conditions.

TABLE 26

The Blind and the Status of Their Parents

	Offspring of Parents Who Are First Cousins		Offspring of Parents Who Are Not First Cousins	
	Number	Per Cent	Number	Per Cent
Total	821	100.0	38,363	100.0
Both parents reported blind	1	0.1	50	0.2
One parent reported blind	35	4.3	1,507	3.9
Neither parent reported blind	780	95.0	36,654	95.5
Not reporting	5	0.6	152	0.4

Percentages estimated: Census Report on the Blind in the United States 1920, p. 50.

Occupations of the blind.   Of the 3000 blind persons who were engaged in manufacturing industries, over 28 per cent were broom makers, about 15 per cent piano tuners, 8 per cent seamstresses and fancy workers. Blindness leads to unemployment and dependency. Only 10 per cent of the blind who were 10 years old and over were gainfully employed in contrast to 50 per cent of the population. A fifth were on public relief. Evidently in order to be most helpful, vocational training should stress those vocations which the blind usually enter. New devices helpful to the blind promise to make them more independent. Such is the British stenographic machine, which enables the blind to write Braille rapidly, opening up secretarial work to them. A recent American invention, the electric reading pencil, enables the blind to read the printed page.[30]

[30] "Aids for the blind," *Life*, March 8, 1948; "For blind typists," *New York Times*, March 28, 1948.

Prevention of blindness. Society should make an effort to stamp out preventable blindness. To do this, attention must be directed against spreading, by means of contact and use of common articles such as towels, the infectious eye diseases, such as ophthalmia neonatorum, conjunctivitis, trachoma, and ulcer of the eye. Children should be protected against diseases such as measles and scarlet fever, which may result in blindness. Greater care in preventing eye strain and correcting cross-eye and near-sightedness is important. Children should also be kept out of situations in which their eyesight might be endangered. States are legislating in most of these directions. That such measures result in gains is proved by the decrease in the prevalence of ophthalmia neonatorum manyfold. Now the replacement of defective corneas by good ones has caused many blind persons to see. Depositories called Eye Banks are being established where normal corneas may be obtained.[31]

Deaf-Mutes

According to instructions to census enumerators, deaf persons include persons who cannot hear ordinary conversation save when it is shouted or when a hearing device is used. They constitute a defective class, since one of the important organs of sense-perception does not function. This is an undoubted handicap, as is seen in surveying occupations from certain of which they are largely barred and in recalling their limits in making social contacts. With the exception of hearing, they are normal people. They are far less handicapped than the blind, for the eyes are the chief organs of adaptation to external conditions. We also suspect they are, in part, a hereditary class, although this is not easy to establish. However, this claim must be considered.

Prevention of deafness. Could the cases of deafness be exactly determined, a foundation for prevention and cure could be laid. The census ascribes over half of all deafness to "congenital." It covers both hereditary and prenatal conditions, such as accidents and toxic influences which affect the embryo by way of the mother. Most of the other causes listed conceivably could be controlled.

Recent studies distinguish three forms of deafness. These are (1) the conductive, in which infections in the middle ear impair the passage of sound waves, the auditory nerve remaining nor-

[31] Daniel Scware, "They see again," *New York Times Magazine*, April 28, 1946: 18–19.

mal; (2) the perceptive, in which the auditory nerve is degenerated or intoxicated; (3) otosclerosis, initially a lesion in the bones of the middle ear. Helpful drugs have been found to improve hearing, especially in the first form of deafness mentioned above.

Education of the deaf. Table 27 exhibits the nature of the schooling of the deaf in the United States.

TABLE 27
Schooling of the Deaf and the Hard-of-Hearing

Year	Number of Schools Reporting			Number of Pupils
	State	City	Private	
1910	57	53	19	19,324
1922	16	74		2,911
1940	30	168		13,478

Source: U. S. Statistical Abstract, 1935 and 1947.

Most of the pupils are now in public schools or institutions. Those who favor day schools do so because they prevent institutionalizing the deaf and also promote oral speech instead of the sign language. But only large cities can afford to have day schools and classes sufficiently specialized in equipment and teachers to make them effective. Teaching oral speech to those who have never heard a sound and have no idea of the connection of sound with speech organs and muscles is a most difficult task. Relatively few persons who are congenitally deaf or became deaf in infancy obtain an effective use of oral speech. The state schools for the deaf are doing a great work. Many deaf-mutes are housed, fed, clothed, and educated and receive prompt medical care and many uplifting advantages in good institutions.

One of the greatest drawbacks in the education of the deaf is the almost insuperable difficulty of conveying to the deaf, who have never heard a sound or have heard only for a short time, the idea of sound and of the method of producing vocal sounds. A modern invention called "bone-conduction" equipment promises much in this direction. This machine sets the labyrinthine fluid of the inner ear in vibration, so that sounds are reported to the brain just as in normal life. In reporting the invention, George Barton French says: "Recently the writer, using a special bone-conduction receiver, was able in less than a half hour to teach a boy, who never before had heard the sound of a human voice, how to pronounce correctly the entire alphabet, also several short sentences, including intonation of the latter."[32]

The Crippled

Volume of disabilities. Disabilities arising from accidents vary from temporary to permanent and from slight to total. The gravity of the problem of the disabled is seen from several angles. (1) In its incidence. It burdens individuals, families, and the public. (2) Permanent disability is cumulative, the volume being incremented annually. (3) The volume is enormous and appalling. During a recent year (1947), 99,579 of our inhabitants were killed; ten times as many were injured.[33] The number killed was nearly twice that of our forces killed during World War I, and the volume of injured was several times that of the wounded during that war. The number killed by accidents was over 87 per cent that of our men killed in World War II, and the volume of injured was over 42 times that of our forces wounded during that war. The National Safety Council estimated that 365,000 persons were permanently disabled in accidents during 1935. Twenty-nine per cent of those compensated for injuries received in industrial accidents in New York State during 1940 were permanent disabilities, a considerable share of which were total. Some idea of the causes of accidents may be gained from sources of accidental deaths. In 1935 the Federal Rehabilitation Service estimated 55,000 of the disabled annually need vocational rehabilitation. Leading causes of the accidental deaths occurring in the United States during 1947 of which information was given were, by percentages, as follows: motor vehicle, 22.8; falls, 16.7; drowning, 4.0; burns, 3.3; railway, 1.9; firearms, 1.7; air transport, 1.4; poison gas, 1.4; other poisons, 1.0.

In these facts we see the conditions to be controlled, if accidents are to be eliminated. Accidents in mining, agriculture, conflagrations, food poisoning, and some others are not included in this account.[34]

Causes of children's disabilities. Multitudes of causes inevitably account for the disabilities of crippled children. It is now possible to obtain a fairly accurate picture of the national situa-

[32] "Hearing without ears," *Scientific American*, Jan., 1930: 17.
[33] *World almanac*, 1950, p. 479; and Forney and Johnson, in *Encyclopedia Americana*, 1944 ed., I: 74.
[34] *World almanac*, 1950, p. 479.

tion. Figure 18 represents the cases reported to the U. S. Children's Bureau during a recent year by all but four states. It is reproduced from the *Statistical bulletin* of the Metropolitan Life Insurance Company for May, 1948.

	Prevalence Rate per 10,000
Poliomyelitis	13.9
Cerebral palsy	7.4
Trauma	6.3
Clubfoot	6.2
Osteomyelitis	3.5
Rickets	3.0
Scoliosis	2.3
Tuberculosis of bones and joints	1.8
Paralysis due to birth injury (exclusive of cerebral palsy)	1.7

Figure 18. Leading Causes of Orthopedic Impairments Among Children Under Age 21: United States, 1945.*

* Excludes Delaware, Montana, Pennsylvania, and Virginia.

Source: "Crippled children on state registers," reported to the U. S. Children's Bureau.

Poliomyelitis is seen to be the leading cause. It accounts for about 3 of each 10 afflicted children. Much has been done to prevent and relieve such cases. Cerebral palsy afflicts about half as many children. The average community is not equipped to do much about it yet, although proper treatment, education, and physical rehabilitation could make about half the victims able to adjust and support themselves. The other disabilities can be removed or slightly mitigated, if taken early. The various kinds of attacks vary with age and must be treated accordingly.

The causes of disability among adults would include proportionally more industrial and mechanical accidents and would encompass millions of permanently and partially injured. Safety devices for dangerous machines, abolition of grade crossings, better traffic control, licensing automobile drivers, and the like will do much for increased safety. But machines break, humans err, and many fools are at large. However, we should be able to accomplish much toward paring down accidents and making life safer.

Control of producing conditions. A solution of the problem of crippled and disabled individuals is dependent on the control of all the conditions which produce them. An inspection of the causes accounting for disabled children brings inference that the larger portion are or will be preventable. The development of medical science may be expected to take care of that. As yet, most of the congenital deformities are not understood, but they may be in time. Theoretically the disabilities arising from industry in all its ramifications and from transportation and communication are preventable. We can conceive a society in which such disasters would not occur. The invention and adoption of safety devices in connection with all dangerous machinery, abolition of grade crossings, licensing of all automobile drivers, and adoption of stringent safety rules are suggestive of the direction future developments may take.

Practically, it is probable that some accidents always will take place. However, it should be possible to pare accidents to such a small number that resulting human wreckages will become relatively infrequent. Certainly one of the most important tasks society confronts is the development of methods of prevention and control of industrial, public, and domestic or personal accidents.

The care of the crippled and disabled is an intricate matter, and we shall discuss only its major features. It is evident that our treatment of these persons has grown up in a hit-or-miss fashion and that it is unsystematic, fragmentary, and generally inadequate, although there are certain localities which have handled the problem in competent fashion.

The following agencies indicate the nature of the efforts made to meet the situation: (1) State hospitals and schools, such as obtain in Minnesota, Massachusetts, Michigan, and Iowa, where disabled children go for treatment and schooling. (2) Private hospitals and homes, such as the Widener Hospital in Philadelphia and the series of orthopedic hospitals established by the Order of Elks, performing about the same functions as the state hospitals. (3) Municipal hospitals or wards in hospitals; for example, the Chicago Municipal Tuberculosis Sanitarium. (4) Co-operation of various agencies, juvenile courts, and state boards of charities with local homes for disabled children, as in Ohio. (5) Public special schools and classes, together with orthopedic care as needed, as in Chicago, Detroit, and some other large cities. (6) Industrial rehabilitation, as carried on by the United States Board for Vocational Education. (7) Workmen's compensation systems of various states, providing some sort of insurance against accidents in certain trades and industries.

Care of crippled children. Our great need now is to discover cripples and provide for their care. Relative to crippled children, there are several things that should be done in a prevalent and competent manner, assuming that most of the disabled children are mentally normal. (The percentage of the normal-minded is practically the same as for the general population.) (1) There is need for a survey of all the localities to discover the disabled. (2) Immediate attention should be given to cases which may be relieved by orthopedic care, such as straightening deformed feet and limbs. This should be begun with infants and very young children as it is then that physical re-adjustments are most easily made. (3) State, municipal, or district hospitals for the indigent and chronic cases should be provided. Most village and rural districts are remote from hospital resources, hence the need of near-by provisions. A large portion of deformed and disabled children come from poor homes, and so must receive attention elsewhere for a time. It was found at the Gillette State Hospital in Minnesota that 11 per cent of the children were without homes or families, 65 per cent were from homes where the parents were too poor or too indifferent to co-operate in educating and rehabilitating their children, and only 24 per cent had parents who showed a hopeful, co-operative attitude. (4) Special schools and classes should be established for crippled children where the city is large enough to provide buildings or rooms adapted to cripples and the various equipment and facilities they require. Teachers trained to deal with crippled children, orthopedic and physiotherapy attendants, accessible hospital facilities, and transportation for school and hospital purposes should be provided. Such large cities as Chicago and Detroit are doing remarkable things in these directions. The present tendency is toward state legislation for authorizing special schools or classes. A number of states provide funds to be applied locally or authorize local school boards to furnish home instruction for children detained in their homes, and seven states authorize local boards to provide transportation. This legislation is in the right direction, but certainly many localities are not prepared to carry it out effectively.

Care of adult cripples.   Most adult cripples are permanently disabled. They have lost their capital in skill and technique and are helpless unless re-equipped for work. Systematic social effort should be directed toward accomplishing several things. (1) The prevention of accidents. (2) Expansion of rehabilitation work now being carried on by national and state governments. Of the approximately 60,000 persons disabled a year by accident, only about 10 per cent are restored to industrial competency. The other 90 per cent are as needy and deserving. (3) The extension of compulsory accident insurance. This may help remove the disability, and it insures them against dependency. The state need not enter insurance itself, but it should compel employers to carry proper insurance in private companies.

Those afflicted with stiff joints may soon hope to find relief. Dr. S. S. Hudack of New York has developed a surgical technique in which the diseased parts of bones are removed and plastic parts substituted for them. The restored bodily activities are painless and approximate normality.[35]

In conclusion, we should call attention to the medical program of the Veterans' Administration. This program has demonstrated what can be done to rehabilitate certain classes of handicapped persons. One of the first steps designed to increase the extent and nature of medical care in the veterans' hospitals was made in January, 1946, when President Truman signed a bill providing for an independent Department of Medicine and Surgery for the Veterans' Administration.

Since that time, the treatment of physically handicapped veterans has expanded into a variety of medical, surgical, and occupational therapies. Such hospital activities as manual arts and educational therapy are linked up with post-hospital vocational guidance and counseling services. A post-hospital guidance program has made use of the co-operative efforts of private enterprises, such as the International Business Machines, Eastman Kodak Company, Bausch-Lomb, Bulova Watch Company, the Radio Corporation of America, and others. Moreover, the co-operative efforts between certain industries and the Veterans' Administration in the rehabilitation program has had a profound educational influence upon other employers and interested persons.

[35] *Life*, Jan. 12, 1948 (illustrated).

An outstanding example of what a good rehabilitation program can do is afforded in the work done at "Independence Hall" at Kennedy Hospital in Memphis, Tennessee. Attention is given not alone to the correction of physical difficulties but also to a restoration of the will to achieve.

A study of the program at "Independence Hall" is well worth while. It points the way toward a new level of thought and achievement in the field of human relations.[36]

One problem to which more interested students and instructors are turning attention is that of the aged. Here again the Veterans' Administration is pointing the way. This problem has been made especially acute for the Veterans' Administration because of the large number of aging World War I veterans who have sought help in the veterans' hospitals. A study of 128 World War I chronic patients in the V.A. hospital in Minneapolis in 1947 revealed that about twenty-five were able to take employment after nine months, and about forty others were discharged to their homes and were able to do light work. About half of those remaining at the hospital had achieved ability to do some self care, while the other half were ambulatory patients undergoing advanced rehabilitation.

These facts appear significant when we understand that many of these 128 patients had been hospitalized continuously for more than ten years and some had been bedfast for two years or more. According to the report, all but ten of the entire group had shown some "worth-while permanent improvement." This experience has both humanitarian and economic values. Rusk and Taylor point out that the rehabilitation of 65 patients discharged from the hospital has amounted to an economic saving to the government of $1,250,000. Other studies confirm the Minneapolis experience. Rusk and Taylor have supplied facts to emphasize the importance of the great untapped potentials that are undeveloped and unused in large numbers of our handicapped people.[37] The public, moreover, needs to be educated as to the employability of certain classes of handicapped persons whose physical difficulties are not curable.

During the war, more than 11,000 physically handicapped people were successfully employed by the Ford River Rouge

[36] For a full description of the V.A. rehabilitation program, see H. A. Rusk, and E. J. Taylor, *New hope for the handicapped* (New York: Harper and Brothers, 1949).

[37] *Ibid.*, pp. 56–61.

Plant alone. Among these were more than 1000 individuals with serious defects of vision, more than 100 deaf-mutes, more than 100 epileptics, and many others with organic heart ailments and other marked physical deformities. These people were employed because of their abilities, and their performance measured up to high standards. This experience in the River Rouge Plant has been duplicated in many other industries. Moreover, the effect upon the personalities of these people was significant. As Morrison has pointed out, " . . . physique is one of the raw materials of personality, disability is also a psychological problem. . . . "[38]

QUESTIONS

1. What evidence is there that the defective classes constitute a social problem?
2. Can you offer scientific proof that these classes actually are lowering the average of physical and mental efficiency of our total population?
3. What are their effects on the family?
4. (a) Is there more than one kind of feeble-mindedness? (b) What is their position in a curve of distribution of "intelligence" as determined by mental tests? (c) Differentiate between feeble-mindedness and insanity.
5. Discuss these points indicating a changed view about feeble-mindedness in accounting for poverty, crime, and prostitution.
6. On what should adequate social control and treatment of the feeble-minded rest?
7. (a) How would you go about securing scientific identification and classification of the feeble-minded in order to effect a competent disposal? (b) How far is such a program practiced?
8. (a) What class of feeble-minded may be paroled? (b) How do men and women compare as to availability for parole? (c) How should the paroled be looked after?
9. (a) Who should be educated in the special schools and classes for the feeble-minded of the public-school system? (b) In what way should equipment and teachers be specially adapted to the needs? (c) What does the case study represent?
10. What is epilepsy? (b) Is it a particular disease? (c) Do we know its cause or causes?
11. (a) What are the advantages of colonies for epileptics? (b) Is there a trend toward establishing colonies?
12. What is the common meaning of "insanity"?
13. (a) What is meant by "mental complexes"? (b) Are they normal occurrences? (c) What is their relation to insanity? (d) What kinds of procedure might reduce their abnormal development?

[38] Morrison, *Time*, June 7, 1948.

14. Does the fact that the city has a higher ratio of insanity than rural districts or one section of the nation than another prove that the former populations are inherently more prone to become insane?

15. What light do the following factors throw on the curability of the insane: (a) relation of admissions to discharged, paroled, and deceased; (b) percentage of "recovered," "improved," "unimproved"; (c) length of stay in institutions, and the length of stay of those cured and improved?

16. What provisions for the treatment of the insane should be made in hospitals for the insane?

17. (a) Why is early treatment of mental illness so essential? (b) In what ways does the present system of legal commitment and distribution of specialized hospitals defeat this requirement?

18. (a) Why is the average medical practitioner scientifically incompetent to care for the insane? (b) What is the corrective for this?

19. Compare the handicaps which blindness and deafness place on individuals.

20. Compare the advantages of institutional schools and special schools and classes in the public schools for the blind and the deaf.

21. (a) What are the chief causes of disabilities among crippled children? (b) Would they be the chief causes of disabilities among adults?

22. What would a complete solution of the problem of the crippled by society involve?

23. What advantages would the following provisions regarding crippled children have: (a) complete census; (b) early orthopedic attention; (c) hospital facilities; (d) special schools and classes? (e) Do any of them have disadvantages?

24. Could it be established that the blindness and deafness of certain persons were hereditary, would you advocate including them in the scope of "eugenic marriage" and sterilization laws?

REFERENCES

BEERS, CLIFFORD W., *Mind that found itself*, rev. ed. New York: Doubleday and Company, 1948.

DAVIES, STANLEY P., *Social control of the mentally deficient*. New York: Thomas Y. Crowell Company, 1930.

DEUTSCH, ALBERT, *Mentally ill in America*. New York: Columbia University Press, 1946.

FARIS, R. E. L., and DUNHAM, H. W., *Mental disorders in urban areas*. Chicago: University of Chicago Press, 1939.

FARIS, R. E. L., *Social disorganization*. New York: Ronald Press, 1948.

JOHNSTONE, E. L., "What shall we do with the mentally deficient?", *Mental Hygiene*, 30 (1946): 296–302.

KAPLAN, OSCAR, ed., *Mental disorders in later life*. Stanford: Stanford University Press, 1945.

MENNINGER, KARL A., *Man against himself*. New York: Harcourt, Brace and Company, 1938.

Mental health statistics, Federal Security Agency, Public Health Service, Sept., 1949. Washington, D.C.: Government Printing Office, 1949.

MERRILL, F. E., et al, *Social problems*. New York: Alfred A. Knopf, 1950. Part II.

REES, JOHN R., *Shaping of psychiatry by war*. New York: W. W. Norton and Company, 1945.

ROSANOFF, A. J., *Manual of psychiatry and mental hygiene*. New York: W. W. Norton and Company, 1938.

RUSK, H. A., and TAYLOR, E. J., *New hope for the handicapped*. New York: Harper and Brothers, 1949.

SARASON, E. K. and S. B., "Problem in diagnosing feeble-mindedness," *Journal of Abnormal and Social Psychology*, 40 (1945): 323–329.

STERN, EDITH M., "Family care for the mentally ill," *Survey Graphic*, 31 (1942): 31–32, 42–44.

SULLIVAN, HARRY STACK, "Mental disorders," *Encyclopedia of the social sciences*, 10 (1933): 313–319.

WALKER, HELEN M., and SCHAUFFLER, MARY C., *Social adjustment of the feeble-minded*. Cleveland: Western Reserve University Press, 1930.

CHAPTER 17

Eugenics and Public Policy

The Need for Eugenics

Meaning of the term. It was Sir Francis Galton, cousin of Charles Darwin, who made popular the ideal concerning the eugenic control and improvement of the human stock. Eugenists commonly believe that society will be improved by regulating and controlling heredity. The term "eugenics" literally means "producing the fit or 'good' race." Galton coined the word to mean the application of the known laws of heredity to the production of human beings who thereby become free from defects and have desirable characteristics. In 1904, he said, "Eugenics is the science which deals with all influences that improve the inborn qualities of a race; also with those that develop them to the utmost advantage."[1]

However, despite Galton's recognition of possible environmental factors, eugenics continues to center its attention on the elimination of the hereditary defectives by means of suitable methods. In a state of nature, this is done by natural selection. The fittest animals and plants survive, and the unfit are eliminated in the competitive struggle for existence. In society, this is not permitted to take place so freely. Social selection, the synthesis of all the factors and forces at work in the social situation, determines who shall survive. Many unfit are protected, some of whom reproduce, often perpetuating, no doubt, their own unfit kind. Because nature is slow to work out its results and more especially because the social environment has come into existence to check the effects of natural selection, eugenists desire to interfere with and assist the selective process. They would not withhold the protection of the weak and unfit by society, but they would seek to prevent reproduction by the

[1] Sir Francis Galton, *Sociological papers* (New York: The Macmillan Company, 1904), p. 45.

unfit. Hence, they would have society, the social environment, take control of heredity and regulate and direct it. This assumes, of course, that the environment is the ultimate and decisive factor, since heredity cannot solve its problems by itself.

The eugenic problem.   Such being the need for eugenics, the problem of its realization arises. The solution of this problem must come out of a thorough scientific understanding of the basic facts of heredity and of methods for controlling it. Until such knowledge is attained, efforts to improve the human stock by an application of so-called "eugenic methods" are more likely to prove harmful than beneficial. Competent scientific knowledge, necessary to make a useful working eugenic program, involves several things.

1. It requires full knowledge and full understanding of the processes and results of heredity among human beings, as a background to the understanding of the problem of defectives. This cannot be realized until inheritance among people is fully known in all its phases. It must be known how the hereditary determiners combine to produce results, and what characteristics are to be traced to ancestral traits.

2. Such a program requires demonstrated and exact information regarding the hereditary genesis of each of the defective classes. The following items are essential to such a complete understanding: (a) a complete enumeration of persons belonging to each of these classes; (b) the ability to determine scientifically which persons are made defective by heredity and which by the accidents of life and the environment; (c) the ability, also, to determine who among normal persons are "carriers" of deficiencies and hence likely to bear defective offspring. These constitute the minimum of necessary scientific knowledge and insight to make possible any effective and safe eugenic undertakings.

3. It necessitates a scientific understanding of how personality is produced so far as it is determined by heredity. It is obvious that the content of personality is built up from the social-environmental side and exists as habits, beliefs, sentiments, and overt behavior patterns. Behind this, of course, is a hereditary structure, the constituents of which are almost infinitely numerous. In terms of heredity, the type of person in any given case is the result of combinations of gene determiners. In human beings, these genes may combine in millions of ways and so may result in many different types of persons. If there are better and worse, poorer and richer, defective and normal types of personalities by

inheritance, then the eugenic problem becomes one of understanding how each type is produced. The solution of this problem, obviously, is a tremendous and seemingly hopeless undertaking.

Heredity and environment.   Eugenics proposes to control the processes of inheritance by making use of environment. This leads one to inquire into the relationships which these two factors sustain toward each other. The term "heredity" implies that certain human traits are determined by means of, and through, the germ cells as distinct from body cells; the term "environment" includes all objects and activities that lie outside the germ cell and organism. Ordinarily these factors maintain fairly stable relations with each other. Let us review that relationship.

1. These factors are mutual and reciprocal. They are not independent and cannot operate without each other. It is a case of one *and* the other, not of one *or* the other. There can be no organisms and no heredity without environment, and the term "environment" has no significance without organisms with their hereditary features. They are partners in the reproductive and development enterprise, each with its particular functions.

2. Each factor has its limitations and each factor sets limitations on the other factor. Heredity cannot make and develop an individual without an environment to furnish food, warmth, and so on. Arrested development arises because the environment withholds something that the growing organism requires. Thus, cretinism comes, Jennings says, because the mother's thyroid glands are not functioning properly. On the other hand, the environment depends on heredity for many things it could not do alone. Under nature, it cannot make giants of pygmies nor blacks of whites, save in pathological cases. The limits of stature of racial and family stocks, on the average, are set by heredity. Heredity cannot much exceed the bounds set by environment, and environment cannot exceed very far the limits set by heredity.

3. The natural relationship obtaining between the two may be upset by human interference. Human control and intelligence build up an environment of ideas, techniques, mechanisms, chemicals, and medicines, which can be used to interfere with reproductive processes. In the case of lower organisms under experimentation, the genes may be so manipulated and reordered in reproduction that the most ridiculous and seemingly irrational traits in individual organisms are secured. Nature originally furnished only a few types of dogs, horses, cattle, fowls,

and other animals which man has domesticated. Today we have many sorts of such animals because man has interfered with the natural hereditary processes. Were man allowed to experiment with human genes in the same fashion as he does with plants and animals, doubtless he could produce many new and strange traits in human beings.

In some cases it is seen that he does interfere either purposively or undesignedly. It is fairly certain that toxic poisons, such as those derived from alcoholism and venereal disease, often produce disastrous effects in offspring. It is generally held, also, that cretinism is hereditary. But Jennings states that, if a cretin is taken in time and is given thyroxin, he outgrows cretinism and becomes a normal individual. Evidently we must accept this with some reservation. For example, the writer has a letter from A. R. T. Wylie, Superintendent of the Institution for Feeble-Minded of North Dakota, concerning the use of thyroxin. He indicates that if the results are to be beneficial, several requirements must be met. The child must be treated very early in life, the age of 8 or 10 years being too late. The treatment must occur continuously. Otherwise the person relapses into the condition of dullness. Good results are secured in hypothyroid cases, which are lighter in nature than cretinism, but even here the administration of the drug must be continuous.

Regarding the possibility of producing new forms of human beings were experimentation allowed, a suggestion comes from the use of radio-activity in producing new varieties of lower organisms. This now is done experimentally. It is conceivable that, if it could be applied appropriately in the genesis of human beings, mutations might be secured. However, two objections or difficulties at once present themselves. First, the new type probably would appear to be a monstrosity and allowed to default in development or be put in a dime museum for commercial reasons. Second, since no one can foresee what types would appear, the chances of producing malignant and beneficent types of personalities are equal. Such speculative possibilities need only critical consideration to demonstrate their fruitlessness.

Possibility of Eugenic Control

The possibility of eugenics is bound to rest on our scientific understanding of heredity and its control. If such knowledge is lacking or defective, there can be either no eugenic results or insufficient ones. We therefore need to take an inventory of our scientific knowledge in order to determine to what extent a eugenic program is possible.

Our knowledge of genetics. Genetics is that branch of biological science which investigates the processes, factors, causes, and principles of transmission of inherited characteristics. Its chief field of investigation is with lower animals, but more experimentation has been done on the fruit fly, *Drosophila,* than on any other form of life. Most of what we know about heredity comes from those studies. We assume that what obtains there also obtains among human beings, so far as mere heredity itself is concerned. But we must remember that the social environment of human beings begins to influence persons so early in life, and does this so increasingly, that it is difficult to know what is transmitted through the germ plasm and what through social inheritance.

Man is so surrounded and enmeshed by the cultural medium, his society, with its profound influence from the very moment of birth, that its results may easily be set down as being hereditary. Inborn tendencies, impulses, instincts, predispositions are molded, impressed, disciplined, inhibited, or stimulated from the very first by parents and other human beings about the child. Society has thousands of ideas embedded in customs, manners, tastes, attitudes, organizations, and institutions which are brought to bear on the child by its parents, teachers, and associates. The reordering of reflexes and instincts begins so early and proceeds so fast that the results are similar to inborn patterns and are likely to be mistaken for them. This socio-cultural medium stands between all civilized persons and the natural environment and mitigates or inhibits the forces of natural selection. In the realm of ideas and purposes which distinguish human beings, the social environment is bound to be the commanding agent.

Ideas about heredity have been revolutionized during the last few years. Much of what was taught about it has been repudiated or greatly modified. Generally accepted notions of eugenics earlier than 1930 were of little practical value. What we shall have to say about heredity rests primarily upon more recent ideas and evaluations of the *laws* of hereditary transmission.

Hereditary transmission. The reproductive cells are composed of nucleus and cytoplasm. The nucleus contains the microscopic chromosomes, the conveyors of hereditary characteristics. The chromosomes are constituted of bundles of genes, chemical elements, strung together like beads on a string. Every offspring receives two strings of these genes, one from each parent. Each string contains a bundle of characteristics, one string representing one physical type, the other another physical type of individual. The offspring receive some traits of each bundle and so become composite, reproducing some of the traits of each parent. The two strings of genes, usually lying side by side, consist of pairs. Each pair of genes may have particular functions in heredity, such as laying the foundations of an eye, producing color of the eye, or affecting the growth of the body. Each gene produces its results in its own way.

The relation of the two sets of genes is illustrated by means of letters in Figure 19. Letters above the line represent the series of genes in each germ plasm received from one parent, and those below represent those received from the other parent.

(a)	(b)	(c)
ABCDEFGH..Z	ABCDEFGH..Z	ABcDEFgH..Z
ABCDEFGH..Z	abcdefgh..z	abcdefgh..z

Figure 19. The Gene Determiners in Heredity

We may suppose that each pair of genes relates to the same trait in the production of offspring. In (a) all gene pairs have a similar bearing on each trait that they supposedly determine. In (b) the genes of all the pairs are in contrast and do not co-operate in determining hereditary traits. In (c) some of the pairs are in contrast and some in agreement. Thus, in type (c) A tends to counteract a, and B to counteract b, while c and c co-operate and reinforce the work of each other. Under the simplest form of the Mendelian law we may think of A as dominant for eye color, and a as recessive for that color. Since dark is a dominant for eyes and light is a recessive, the eye color in this case will appear as dark. If it were a case of $\frac{a}{a}$, a light eye would be the result. This, however, represents only simplest case of combination and is mainly illustrative.

In so far as Mendel's law obtains, double parentage is seen to have advantages, for since each parent bequeaths a string of genes to the offspring and since each gene in each pair of genes has a different function from its partner, if one gene of a pair is defective, its bad influence may be overcome by the normal character of its associate. If one character is dominant and the other is recessive, the dominant will likely prevail, this being dependent on the relation of the genes in one parent to those in the other. If the recessive is a defect, then it will not appear in the offspring. But if both genes of a pair are defective, the offspring is certain to be defective unless environmental influences are used to offset the deficiency.

For purposes of convenience, the following brief summary is given of some of the more important points concerning heredity as established by genetic research.

Conclusions regarding inheritance. (1) The genes are the determiners of transmitted characters. No other factors convey such traits. (2) In only a relatively small proportion of cases does one gene or one pair of genes transmit a character. Generally a plurality of genes contributes to or fixes a trait. "The conception of unit characters dependent on single representative particles is revealed as based upon a logical and material fallacy."[2]

(3) The Mendelian law is only one of many laws of inheritance. This law holds that "when parents that are unlike with respect to any character are crossed, the progeny of the first generation will apparently be like one of the parents with respect to the character in question." This parent is called the dominant. "When, however, the hybrid offspring of this first generation are in turn crossed with each other, they will produce a mixed progeny, 25 per cent of which will be like the dominant grandparent, 25 per cent like the other grandparent (recessive), and 50 per cent like the parent resembling the dominant grandparent."[3] This is "character inheritance" and occurs only "when the two parents differ in only a single pair of genes $\left(\text{as } \dfrac{A}{a} \right)$ affecting the characteristic we are examining." But parents may differ in two or more pairs of genes. This is multiple-factor inheritance, for which there are other than Mendelian laws.[4]

[2] H. S. Jennings, *Biological basis of human nature* (New York: W. W. Norton and Company, 1930), p. 197; see also C. Stern, *Principles of human genetics* (San Francisco: W. H. Freeman and Company, 1949); F. Osborn, *Preface to eugenics* (New York: Harper and Brothers, 1940).

[3] H. E. Walter, *Genetics* (New York: The Macmillan Company, 1922), p. 123; see also H. H. Newman, ed., *Nature of the world and of man* (Chicago: University of Chicago Press), p. 388 ff.; Stern, *op. cit.;* Osborn, *op. cit.*

[4] Jennings, *op. cit.*, pp. 196–197; also R. R. Gates, *Human genetics*, Vols. I and II (New York: The Macmillan Company, 1946).

(4) Even among lower organisms, other than hereditary influences may shape individuals; and it is assumed that the same is true of human beings. It is supposed that genes are chemical packets and that by their chemical interaction they determine characters in offspring step by step during their development. So a change in one of these genes may result in a change in one or several traits. Many traits that are inherited "in typical Mendelian or sex-linked fashion" are readily modifiable by environmental changes. This is true of certain traits of the fruit fly, the color of corn, the eye in fish, sex in different organisms, and many others.

(5) Like usually produces like, but by manipulation of the environment of the growing organism geneticists get unlike from like. A fish with one eye located in the forehead obtained from the ordinary two-eyed fish is only one of numerous examples.[5]

(6) There are two sources of variations in individuals bred from the same parents. The first is the synthesis of characteristics produced by mingling the unmodified genes inherited from the parents. The above discussion pertains to these. These variations are static, repetitious, recurrent generation after generation. Second, variations in individuals may be due to gene mutation. Such changes are dynamic, specie-producing, causative of developmental changes. Occasionally a change occurs in the constitution of a gene which transforms its function so that it bestows new characteristics on the offspring. In lower forms of life this is estimated to happen in the ratio of about one to thirteen genes. The changes occasioned by gene mutation range all the way from very slight to large ones, the former being very much the more numerous. Experiment has demonstrated that such changes may be produced by radio-activity, such as the X ray and radiations from radium. It is believed that, in nature, radiation and the cosmic ray may be producing similar transformations. It is conceivable that among human beings racial change might occur without racial crossing.

(7) While we suppose there are laws of inheritance governing human characteristics, there are very few that have been demonstrated beyond a doubt. One can find lists of traits for which hereditary determinism is claimed, but the informed scientist is very skeptical about them. In the field of mental characteristics, we know next to nothing about how, and to what degree, they

[5] See Kimball Young, *Social psychology* (New York: Appleton-Century-Crofts, 1930), pp. 39–40 for a discussion of this point.

are transmitted from parents to offspring. We find plenty of assertions and a paucity of evidence to support the same. As we have already stated, the assumed proof that feeble-mindedness is transmitted according to Mendel's law, in which occurrence and expectancy so closely agree, is clearly beside the point, since knowledge is insufficient to be able to exclude from consideration persons whose deficiency is acquired.

Limits to knowledge of defective classes. Eugenic undertakings must be limited necessarily to the degree of our certain information concerning the inheritance of physical and mental deficiencies. And here we are faced by limited knowledge about two very important considerations.

1. We have very uncertain knowledge in regard to what the hereditary defects are. We have already faced some of the facts in this connection. What proportion of feeble-mindedness is due to heredity is a matter of estimate rather than of certitude. What individuals among those in institutions for the feeble-minded or outside are mentally deficient by heredity cannot be determined definitely. It is not inevitable that even hereditarily feeble-minded parents shall produce feeble-minded children, because a larger percentage of the offspring of parents both of whom are feeble-minded are not mentally deficient. Myerson and Elkind found that "68 per cent of such parents had practically no feeble-minded children and only 5 per cent had only the one feeble-minded child."[6] We saw from our statistical analysis of blind and deaf offspring of kinship defective parentage that heredity plays almost a negligible part.

2. We are unable to discover and to control the greatest source of mental deficiency. Jennings and Fisher state that not more than 10 or 11 per cent of such deficiency comes from the known feeble-minded.[7] The remainder springs from individuals of the normal population, estimated at 12 or 15 millions. These persons are not defectives but are carriers of defective traits. Which of us normals are carriers cannot be determined, for we all "look alike." Prunett figured it would require 2700 years to reduce the feeble-minded from 1 in 100, say, to 1 in 10,000 by operating on the known source, the 10 per cent. Fisher figured more critically that greater gains could be made but still the far

---

[6] Stanley P. Davies, *Social control of the mentally deficient* (New York: T. Y. Crowell Company, 1930), pp. 155–156.

[7] Jennings, *op. cit.*, p. 241; R. A. Fisher, "Elimination of mental defects," *Journal of Heredity.*

greater proportion would be uncontrolled. Obviously, these things being true, the problem of eliminating hereditary feeble-mindedness is an insuperable one.

Limited knowledge of hereditary control. Extant knowledge of methods of controlling the hereditary process accounting for defective persons conditions and limits any eugenic efforts. Our knowledge of causes and determining processes always limits the means and power to exercise social control. We are able to control no further than we have certain knowledge. We have just reviewed the limitation upon this knowledge and now seek to apply it by enumerating what we cannot control.

1. We cannot control hereditary production of defectives by defectives until we know who are hereditarily defective and to what extent like begets like in that particular. So much we do not certainly know.

2. We cannot control the production of defectives by carriers of deficiency until we are able to lay hands on them and know to what extent they are responsible for mental and other kinds of deficiency. As yet there is scarcely an embryonic criterion to guide in the detection of such persons. When they are located, we do not know how to treat them and dispose of them. Shall we prevent their marriage, institutionalize them, sterilize them, or what? Think also of dealing with 10 or 15 million people in any of these ways!

3. There are some matters of another nature, too, the control over which is bound to be difficult. (a) Much reproduction comes as a consequence of "falling in love." If we are to improve the human stock by eugenic methods we must learn how to control falling in love. Until that and marriage are regulated, normal and defective persons are likely to meet, fall in love, and mate. We might regulate, but we have not begun to do it, and it looks like a big job. (b) There is strong public sentiment against certain so-called "eugenic measures," such as "eugenic marriage laws" and human sterilization, especially against the latter. These have been found almost insuperable obstacles to enforcing whatever legislation of such character has been enacted by our states.

Methods of Eugenic Realization

We have passed in review the scientific foundations and limitations to eugenic undertakings. Now we shall consider critically the scientific basis of general and special eugenic methods.

Positive eugenics. Those who discuss eugenics speak of two kinds, positive and negative. These two aim at dissimilar objectives. In taking up positive eugenics, we find two varieties.

First, there is the attempt to improve the human stock by securing the mating of fit with fit. This means obtaining marriage between those who are free from defects. If only such would marry, it is clear that the level or mean of human efficiency would be heightened. Let us note a few things about the possibility of this undertaking.

(a) It is now impossible to determine who are the fit. Those who are fit in body may be unfit in that the germ plasm carries deficiencies, which means that the offspring may have defects.

(b) The fit may not want to mate with the fit. Of course, we can conceive that various educational devices, rewards, honors, and appeals to pride of stock might have some influence toward such mating. However, so long as carriers of deficiency are present in a population, the program is likely to be defeated.

(c) The seeming superiors may not want to bear children when married. A large percentage of such marriages are childless, and the "higher" the social class, the lower the birth rate, as shown in Chapter 8. We do not say that nothing of a desirable nature would come of such attempts. We are satisfied that, on the average, such mating is desirable. Only we must avoid thinking it will secure greater results than are possible.

Second is the effort to secure a more superior human stock by selective mating than we now have. This is a captivating thought which has lulled many intellectuals to false optimism. It needs examination.

(a) We are ignorant of traits that would constitute superior personalities. Shall we magnify proportionately all the powers and traits we now have? Or shall we select some trait and aim to modify that? Or shall we try to introduce into the human constitution a characteristic or characteristics now unknown to and unpossessed by us? Do we really need "superior" powers? Could we conceive of so improving our strength, speed, sense-perception, and even mental skill as to compete with the machines and mechanisms we can make, such as automobiles and airplanes, diggers and lifters, telescopes and microscopes, and computing machines?

(b) We do not know the connection between the traits we now have and determiners, therefore we cannot make improvements by the use of what we have. Then it is perhaps absurd to contemplate trying to work out superior, nonexistent characteristics. According to computations of geneticists, the number of different individuals possible as the result of genes going into combination with each other in different ways runs into the millions of billions. This means that you and I are just one of a million billion kinds or types of personalities we might have been, had the parental genes combined differently. We cannot begin to think scientifically about how any of the many potential personalities might be produced under controlled conditions.

Negative eugenics.   The improvement of the human stock by the prevention of mating and reproduction by defective persons is what is meant by negative eugenics. Nature in the jungle eliminates the unfit forms of life by means of the struggle for existence. Altruistic human society must accomplish it by some means of social control. Eugenists propose various methods of social control: sterilization, segregation, and eugenic marriage laws. In so far as they are workable and effective, all would help prevent the production of human defectives. However, segregation of defectives is used for persons with acquired deficiencies as well as for the hereditary sort. We shall therefore consider sterilization and the eugenic marriage laws as eugenic measures particularly aimed at the hereditary deficiencies.

Sterilization: laws and practices.   Both males and females may be sterilized by means of surgical operations. The one performed on males is vasectomy and that on females salpingectomy. That of the male consists of tying the reproductive tubes, and so is not destructive of fertility, which may easily be restored.

Acceptance of sterilization has been slow, and perhaps justifiably so. As early as 1899 a Dr. H. C. Sharp performed an illegal sterilization operation upon a woman inmate of the Jeffersonville, Indiana Reformatory. In 1897 the Michigan legislature introduced a sterilization law, but it failed passage. About the same time the Pennsylvania legislature passed such a law, but it was vetoed by the governor. Indiana was the first state to get a sterilization law on the statute books. That was in 1907. Three other states passed sterilization laws, in 1909; namely, California, Connecticut, and Washington. Reckoning bills introduced and laws passed for sterilization as activities, 1913 and 1925 appear to have been years of greatest activity. Nearly one third of all such legislation between 1905 and 1925 occurred in those years.

By 1949 some 34 states had passed sterilization laws. In a

number of instances the state supreme courts have declared the laws or some parts of them invalid. In 1927 the constitutionality of a Virginia sterilization law was upheld by the Supreme Court of the United States. Nevertheless, the states have continued to be conservative in the wording of such laws and in their enforcement.

The practical usefulness of sterilization laws as a means of controlling hereditary defectives is open to serious question. Professor Samuel J. Holmes has suggested that a reasonably successful control through sterilization would require that approximately 10 per cent of the total population would have to be sterilized.[8]

An examination of the preambles of the sterilization laws, obtaining in 1930, which have apparently changed little since that time, reveals that the following purposes are announced as motives of such laws, as a group: (1) Prevention of hereditary diseases or traits. (2) Improvement of the health of the individual. (3) Protection of society from burdens of support and care of the families of incompetent parents. (4) Protection of society against the consequences of syphilitic individuals. (5) Punishment of the individual, as in a number of states beginning as far back as 1909. At the present time punishment is a minor consideration and is generally incidental to other forms of control, such as institutionalization. Laws providing for sterilization of "incompetent" individuals are made to operate only on the inmates of certain state institutions, such as those for the feeble-minded, the insane, epileptics, and criminals.

In states declaring sterilization laws unconstitutional, the various reasons assigned by the courts are: (1) invading the rights of the individual; (2) class legislation; (3) denying equal protection of the law; (4) denial of due process of law. But the Supreme Court of the United States has declared the Virginia sterilization law constitutional, thus obviously approving the sterilization motive to protect society against menacing individuals. It suggests that if sterilization laws are carefully defined and drawn, they will be considered constitutional, at least by enlightened courts.[9]

[8] Samuel J. Holmes, *Eugenic predicament* (New York: Harcourt, Brace and Company, 1933).

[9] For a fuller discussion of this subject, see N. K. Teeters, and J. O. Reineman, *Challenge of delinquency* (New York: Prentice-Hall, 1950), pp. 95–97; also Arthur E. Fink, *Causes of crime* (Philadelphia: University of Pennsylvania Press, 1938), Ch. IX; L. C. Dunn, and T. Dobzhansky, *Heredity, race and society* (New York: Mentor Books, 1946).

Sterilization as experiment.   Sterilization as a means of control is yet in the experimental stage. Nevertheless, it appears that there is a definite tendency toward legalized sterilization. This is seen in the increase in the number of states passing such laws. It is observed also in the increase of operations performed. Between 1925 and 1941 there were 29,626. For the same period these operations in California alone were 4636 and 9932, or 74 and 35 per cent of all. Prior to 1925 only three states had had 300 or more cases; by 1941 nine states each had 1000 or more. In California, marriage of a considerable proportion of sterilized feeble-minded women from institutions takes place. A study of 125 of these marriages discloses that two thirds of them are "successful"; that is, the married couples are "monogamous, law-abiding, self-supporting or supported from some legitimate source, and reasonably happy." This is a rather high percentage of marital success, as marriages go today. But to assign its accomplishment to sterilization is questionable.

Those who favor sterilization may justify it on two grounds of social policy. First, it is protective against deterioration of human stock by the hereditary transmission of defective traits. Second, mental defectives, whatever the cause of deficiency, are not fit to undertake the rearing of families. They represent a low level as to mentality, culture, and economic efficiency. Their families are likely to become public burdens. Let us consider the first ground of justification.

Method overrated.   Sterilization offers a less promising solution of the problem it proposes to solve than is generally believed. Our statistics of sterilization indicate its narrow range of application in actual practice.

1. It is limited to persons in institutions. This is only about 18 per cent of the probable number of feeble-minded persons in our country, although it would represent, perhaps, the larger portion of other defectives. Since about half of these are reckoned to be so by heredity, the reach of sterilization is only 18 per cent of all hereditary feeble-minded. It is not proposed to apply it to the blind, the deaf, or the deformed. Its application to the mentally defective would very likely exclude idiots and imbeciles, due to their sexual impotency and their unattractiveness. It is being applied, to some extent, to psychotics or the mentally ill.

2. The difficulty of detecting the hereditary defectives is very great. In most cases the only criterion lies in family and parental deficiency, but, as we know, this is not first-class proof.

It offers evidence merely of the suggestive kind. Since sterilization is aimed at them as a prevention from reproduction, justice requires that accurate knowledge shall be present.

3. Sterilization does not reach the many carriers of mental deficiency among the normal population. Since this is the great supply house, furnishing an approximate 90 per cent of all hereditary cases according to various estimates, sterilization falls far short of being a "cure" of hereditary mental deficiency.

4. It is doubtful if we have any authentic proof that sterilization of defectives, such as the feeble-minded and psychotics, accomplishes what it aims at. It purposes to socialize the afflicted persons, to make them able to adjust themselves to others in society more successfully. But its practice is confined almost wholly to those in institutions, and the life in these places in itself is curative and socializing. The record of dismissed and paroled feeble-minded persons from the institutions at Waverly and Wrentham, Massachusetts, and Letchworth Village, New York, where rehabilitation and routinization without sterilization obtain, reveals just about as large a percentage of successful adjustments to society as is found among those dismissed and paroled from the institutions of California after sterilization.[10]

Eugenic marriage laws. The idea that society can safeguard itself and prevent deterioration of the human stock by blocking marriage of certain kinds of individuals has taken root in the United States. Vaguely worded legislation against marriages between incompetents has existed for years. In 1930, twenty-one states prohibited "marriages of the 'insane'; 19 include the term 'idiots'; 15 specify 'imbeciles'; 11 cover those who are 'feeble-minded'; 8 cover persons of 'unsound mind'; 7 mention 'lunatics'; and 2 refer to persons 'unable to contract.'"[11] This unscientific nomenclature together with the absence of examination of applicants for marriage renders such legislation incompetent.

Great Britain and most European countries have been adverse to establishing compulsory examinations for persons making application to marry. The matter has been discussed widely, but, so far, opinion has been generally against it. Only two countries, Norway and Turkey, had such enactments down to 1925. By

[10] J. H. Landman, *Human sterilization* (New York: The Macmillan Company, 1932), pp. 263–268.

[11] C. G. Vernier, *American family laws* (Stanford: Stanford University Press, 1938), p. 190.

that date, seven of our states had passed such laws: Alabama, Louisiana, North Carolina, North Dakota, Oregon, Wisconsin, and Wyoming. Five of these states required examination of male applicants alone, and only one state required examination of both contracting parties. Five states required certification of males for venereal diseases and for both parties for feeble-mindedness, imbecility, epilepsy, insanity, pulmonary tuberculosis, and common drunkenness. In all seven states the certificate of satisfactory condition is issued by a licensed physician. Wisconsin provides for free state laboratory service, but requires clinical and laboratory tests only at the discretion of the examining physician. Penalties for violation of law by physicians or officers issuing marriage licenses are commonly provided.

Limitations to eugenic marriage laws. So-called "eugenic marriage laws" are chiefly records of optimistic aspirations on the part of those who initiated them. Their accomplishments are so small that we must seek the reasons for that fact. It is well to inspect their chief limitations.

1. The results of studies which have been made in Wisconsin and North Dakota regarding the working of eugenic marriage laws pertaining to venereal disease indicate a lax and inefficient administration. The efficiency of such laws depends on the thoroughness of the examinations made by physicians. In the two states above mentioned, the following statements manifest the kind of attention the laws receive from physicians called on to make the legal examination. (a) The laws are discredited or are not observed by nearly half of the physicians. (b) The laws are observed by a majority of the physicians called on to pass on candidates for marriage, but by most of them in a perfunctory manner. Often the test is only oral for men and practically always so for women. (c) A considerable minority of physicians believe the laws of value if carried out faithfully. (d) Some physicians think the presence of the laws has some educational value and deterrent effect.[12] That such laws have some deterrent effect locally is shown by the fact that a good many young people cross state lines to be married in other states or Canada to escape the legal requirements.

2. The provisions requiring examination for other conditions than venereal disease cannot be administered. The North Dakota law requires physicians to examine for and pronounce on the

[12] F. S. Hall, *Medical certification of marriage* (New York: Russell Sage Foundation, 1925).

presence or absence in applicants for marriage of the following things: feeble-mindedness, imbecility, insanity, common drunkenness, pulmonary tuberculosis, and venereal disease in males. The larger percentage of doctors, asked about their methods of examination, gave an examination for tuberculosis, chiefly by stethoscope. Pulmonary tuberculosis is not inherited, although some predisposing conditions may be. Oral examination or knowledge of applicants' habits regarding drunkenness was made by about half the physicians questioned. Again, this affliction is not hereditary, whatever we may say about constitutional predispositions. As to mental deficiency, physicians satisfied themselves by giving oral tests and by their general knowledge about applicants. Of course, anything like a scientific test as to the presence of hereditary mental deficiency, which is the object of eugenic marriage laws, ostensibly, is beyond the average practitioner, since he has no special training for it. Furthermore, so much time would be required to perform scientifically and thoroughly all the tests required that few physicians could afford to make them for the small fees allowed by law. If such laws were to be administered adequately, supposing we had the requisite scientific foundation for conducting the various examinations, there would need to be a wide distribution of competently equipped laboratories manned by highly trained specialists.

3. It ought to be obvious that it is senseless and also useless to pass laws regulating marriage conditions and qualifications until we have worked out the knowledge and standardized tests for putting them into effect. Such laws should be limited to one condition for a long time; namely, venereal disease. It is possible that a state, in time, might be in a position where such a law could be administered.

4. The regulation of sex is about the most difficult of all matters of social control. If we go too far in attempts to regulate marriage, we defeat our purpose, for nature will find its own outlet by way of natural marriage or prostitution. There are some virtues that cannot be forced into existence by legal means. Probably the results desired are to be realized only by the slow and long process of educating our youth to higher levels and standards regarding marriage and having families.

QUESTIONS

1. (a) What is eugenics? (b) How does eugenics differ from natural selection? (c) What is its relation to social control?

2. What scientific knowledge must there be in order that eugenics may do its part?

3. (a) Why is it foolish to discuss whether heredity or environment is the more important? (b) If environment is a negligible factor in race improvement, why should eugenists call on the environment to control heredity?

4. Is heredity or environment the more determinative (a) of mental and physical capacity? (b) of cultural ability and possession of technique? (c) of what language we speak?

5. (a) Why is it easy to refer a result of social environment to heredity? (b) In what culture field is the influence of social environment likely to be predominant?

6. (a) What is the law of Mendel? (b) What proportion of cases would it apply to? (c) Are characteristics in offspring determined by one or many genes, generally?

7. (a) Distinguish between assumption and proof that human traits are transmitted according to laws of inheritance found to obtain among subhuman animals. (b) How far should we go in building regulatory and social-control programs on assumptions?

8. (a) What are the deficiencies in our information about who are hereditary defectives? (b) Are all offspring of feeble-minded parents feeble-minded? (c) Are the feeble-minded also physically deficient?

9. (a) Who are "carriers" of mental deficiency? (b) What proportion of feeble-mindedness do they account for?

10. (a) What are the difficulties involved in trying to control transmission of defects? (b) If you knew the carriers, how would you deal with them? (c) What of "falling in love" and adverse public sentiment?

11. (a) What two meanings of positive eugenics are there? (b) What are the handicaps to controlling mating of fit with fit? (c) What obstacles are there to the effort to conceive and build an entirely new and superior type of human being? (d) Do we really need such a type? (e) How many different personalities might you have been?

12. (a) What is meant by negative eugenics? (b) Why should we confine our attention, our eugenic attention, to the hereditary defectives?

13. (a) How old is legal sterilization? (b) How extensive is it? (c) What purposes do state laws assign to their enactment? (d) Are they constitutional? (e) How do believers in legal sterilization justify it? (f) How extensively is it practiced?

14. (a) What defectives is it proposed to sterilize legally? (b) What portion of the feeble-minded would it reach? (c) Would it touch carriers of deficiency?

15. (a) How extensive are eugenic marriage laws? (b) What is their aim? (c) What objects do they comprehend?

16. (a) Do the Wisconsin and North Dakota studies of eugenic marriage laws indicate a considerable degree of success? (b) What agents or agency is responsible for success?

REFERENCES

American Journal of Sociology, May, 1927: A symposium on the relationship between psychiatry and sociology.

American Neurological Association, *Eugenical sterilization*, 1926, Report of the committee.

BIRKELO, C. P., "Operation of the North Dakota eugenic marriage law," *Quarterly Journal of the University of North Dakota*, XXII (1932): 303–309.

BOSSARD, J. H. S., *Problems of social well-being*. New York: Harper and Brothers, 1927.

BROMLEY, D. D., *Birth control: Its use and misuse*. New York: Harper and Brothers, 1934.

BROWNE, F. W. S., et al, *Abortion*. London: G. Allen and Unwin, 1937.

BURLINGAME, L. L., *Heredity and social problems*. New York: McGraw-Hill Book Company, 1939.

FREEMAN, FRANK N., "Heredity and environment in the light of the study of identical twins," *Scientific Monthly*, Jan., 1937: 13–19.

HIMES, N. E., *Medical history of contraception*. Baltimore: Williams and Wilkins, 1936.

HORNEY, KAREN, *Neurotic personality of our time*. New York: W. W. Norton and Company, 1937.

JELIFFE, S. E., and WHITE, W. A., *Diseases of the nervous system*. Philadelphia: Lea and Febiger, 1935.

JENNINGS, H. S., *Biological basis of human nature*. New York: W. W. Norton and Company, 1930.

JENNINGS, H. S., *Genetics*. New York: W. W. Norton and Company, 1935.

OSBORN, F., *Preface to eugenics*. New York: Harper and Brothers, 1940.

ROGERS, C. R., *Clinical treatment of the problem child*. Boston: Houghton Mifflin Company, 1939.

STERN, C., *Principles of human genetics*. San Francisco: W. H. Freeman and Company, 1949.

TEETERS, N. K., and REINEMAN, J. O., *Challenge of delinquency*. New York: Prentice-Hall, 1950.

United States Bureau of the Census, *Patients in mental institutions*. Washington, D.C.: Government Printing Office, 1938.

YAHRAES, H., *Epilepsy: The ghost is out of the closet*. New York: Public Affairs Committee, Inc., 1944.

ZUBIN, JOSEPH, ed., *Trends of mental disease*. New York: Columbia University Press, 1946.

CHAPTER 18

Alcoholic Beverages and the
Social Welfare

The Liquor Problem

Aspects of the problems. The liquor problem emerges when injuries and abuses arising in connection with the consumption of alcoholic beverages demand the attention of organized society. Some aspects of the problem in our country may be noticed.

1. The great diversity of plans for control is illustrated by this fact: When W. C. Durant offered a prize of $25,000 for the best plan for making national prohibition effective, it was found difficult to reduce the kinds of plans received to as few as eight very wide and general classes.

2. While we had national liquor prohibition, its administration and enforcement became a vast and complicated problem. The difficulties of enforcement, especially in great cities, were overwhelming. Opposition was really nothing new, for efforts to control the liquor traffic by every law passed—national, state, local—and by every system of regulation that was ever set up anywhere have met widespread evasion and violation.

3. Many and varied systems of regulation have been tried in the United States. Thousands of legal restrictions have been enacted, nationwide, statewide, and local. Licensed saloons, high licenses, local option of various kinds, and state dispensary systems have been tried. Thousands of restrictive laws are still on the statute books. All of which attests two things. Our liquor problem is tough and complicated. The many and persistent efforts to regulate and control it demonstrate past all doubt that the problem is here, it is real, and it still faces us and demands solution.

4. Divergent attitudes have developed regarding liquor con-

sumption. As always, when efforts at regulation of conduct arise, there are those who want to let things alone. They are numerous and powerful, but this *laissez-faire* view does not work, and the liquor problem keeps cropping up. Then there are advocates of "personal liberty," who seem to believe that drinking and even excessive drinking is an ordinance of nature. At the opposite extreme, some prohibitionists would completely eliminate the traffic in liquor. To them liquor is ruinous individually and collectively. This attitude has proven historically impractical. Yet drinking is a man-made habit, subject to regulation as are all such things.

Extent and nature of alcoholism. The term "alcoholism" refers to intoxicating and excessive drinking in the psychological and sociological sense. It is estimated that 50 million of our inhabitants consume alcoholic liquor, that 3 million drink excessively, and that 750,000 become chronic drunkards. Excessive drinkers are potential drunkards, since excessive drinkers are given to repeated heavy drinking and hence intoxication.

Where the alcohol in the blood amounts to 0.15 per cent or more of blood content, drinking is merely physiological. It is social-economic when the socio-economic results are bad; namely, when dependents suffer neglect because income is spent on the selfish gratification of the drinker. Often both parents are offenders.

Numerous questions arise regarding the effects of alcohol as a beverage. Practically everything in the situation centers in the effects. If all the effects are good, then of course there is no social problem at all. Some of the more important of the many effects are the following: (a) the influence of alcohol as a chemical substance on the physiological organs and functions of the body; (b) the psychological effect by way of the nervous organization, whether that of stimulation or depression; (c) since the use of alcohol may affect the offspring of users in some way, the character of such effects, whether detrimental or beneficial, and whether inheritable or otherwise; and (d) the consequence of drink in many social situations, appearing as a factor in family disorganization and the production of crime, pauperism, insanity, and the break-down of political and governmental organization. There is a question regarding the influence of the use of alcoholic beverages on the death rate, and the close association between vending places and vice and crime suggests a causal relationship.

Why men drink alcohol. Human beings have made alcohol and used it as a beverage from very primitive times. How far down among pre-industrial peoples it extends is uncertain, but we know that many backward primitive tribes ferment various juices of fruits and other liquids for beverages. The drinking of liquor is undoubtedly older than human records, and it is worth inquiring as to why men drink.

1. It makes them "feel good." It is a shortcut to short-lived happiness. In his article "The alcoholic motive,"[1] G. T. W. Patrick studied the psychology of relaxation and classed drinking as a means of relaxation. Our society, he thinks, demands regularity, order, industry, conventional procedure of all of us daily and yearly. Alcoholic beverages furnish a temporary release from this grind. Moderate drinking may keep consciousness actively on the job to enjoy it. Drunkenness is oblivion.[2]

2. It relieves the nerves and brain from the feeling of strain. In advanced societies this strain becomes very apparent, and an opportunity for release is tempting. Alcohol artificially seems to accomplish what nature accomplishes by play and sports. Patrick says: "Normal forms of relaxation, such as play and sport, relieve the brain by calling into exercise only the older and more stable brain patterns, those associated with ancient forms of muscular activity and with relatively simple kinds of mental activity. . . . Alcohol relieves the overtaxed brain by the slug-shot method, putting to sleep to a greater or less extent the overtaxed part."[3] Some people have so emphasized this resort from strain as to appear to elevate it into an alibi for liquor drinking.

3. It gives a "feeling of inner power and importance; it stirs the emotions; it accentuates the ego; it increases the intensity of consciousness." William James, the great psychologist who was also educated for medicine, wrote: "The reason for craving alcohol is that it is an anesthetic, even in moderate quantities. It obliterates a part of the field of consciousness."[4] It suppresses timidity and the sense of inferiority and thus expands and accentuates the feeling of free and unrestrained existence. One comes to feel himself "as good as anybody."

4. Further drinking helps restore normality after the decided

---

[1] *Forum*, April, 1928: 546–556.

[2] *Cf.* also W. R. Miles, in Haven Emerson, et al, *Alcohol: Its effects on man* (New York: Appleton-Century-Crofts, 1934), pp. 266–270.

[3] *Loc. cit.*

[4] H. S. Warner, *Social welfare and the liquor problem* (New York: Board of Temperance, 1929), p. 49.

slump and sense of inferiority following upon previous drinking. This if the effect of narcotics and narcotic drugs. A series of drinks and doses paves the way for succeeding drinks and doses because normalcy is not restored until they are partaken. The drinking habit and the drug habit are firmly established in this very manner and for this reason.

5. Probably the one greatest cause of drinking is the pressure and coercion of social custom. Much drinking is merely following example. But there is a powerful drive of social coercion present. It is good form to drink, "the best people," all our associates, See pg. 520 indulge. We fear to seem peculiar, if we do not drink. Few are brave enough to withstand this coercive pressure. Widespread drinking promotes widespread drinking.

6. Drinking is not inherited, biologically. Of this scientists are now certain. This comes out repeatedly in the most authoritative sources on the effects of the consumption of liquor.

Psychophysical Effects of Alcohol

In discussing the effects of alcohol, we are concerned only with ethyl alcohol, the form that is available for beverages. It is produced chiefly by the work of the yeast fungus in saccharine substances. As a result of fermentation the various alcoholic beverages produced range in their percentage of alcoholic content from 2 to 12 per cent in beer and "natural wine" to the 35 to 75 per cent in distilled spiritous liquors.

Alcohol and the physiological process. Like other substances which the body ingests for food and some poisons never taken for food, alcohol goes through the stages of absorption, oxidation, and elimination. About a third of this process occurs in the stomach, the remainder in the intestines. Alcohol does not require digestion, but it goes at once into the blood, is then carried to the liver, where it is oxidized, as are all foods, thence is borne by the blood to the heart, thence through the blood to all tissues of the body. These tissues appropriate it according to their water content. Blood is 90 per cent water, the body is 72 per cent water. An 0.05 per cent alcoholic content in the blood would mean an 0.04 per cent content in the body generally. Scientific tests show that 0.15 per cent concentration in the blood is proof of intoxication, a greater percentage spelling greater intoxication. A concentration of 0.5 to 0.7 per cent in the blood is lethal, means death.

Several factors determine the rate of absorption of alcohol by the body, and the latter determines the inception of intoxication. The following factors regulate the rate of absorption. First, the per cent of alcohol in the beverage hastens or retards the rate of absorption. The greater the concentration of alcohol, the more rapid is the absorption. Second, the presence of other materials, especially of fat in the stomach, is a retarding influence. This is especially true in the case of habitual drinkers, in whom the presence of fat retards absorption.

The distribution of alcohol to the various organs of the body is summarized by G. B. Wallace as follows:

> Miles has shown that after taking alcohol, the maximal blood concentration occurs in 60 to 90 minutes after ingestion. In the organs of a man dead from alcoholic poisoning Juckenack found alcohol distributed in the following proportion: blood, 0.53 per cent; heart, lungs, and liver and gall bladder, 0.24 per cent; brain, 0.42 per cent; and urine, 0.42 per cent. In an extensive study, Gettler and Tiber found that the brain tissue of intoxicated persons dying in Bellevue Hospital a few hours after admission contained from 0.27 to 0.51 per cent of alcohol.[5]

It is clear from this that the various organs of the body appropriate differing amounts of the ingested alcohol.

Alcohol as food. In order to understand in what way alcohol is a food, let us compare the feature of our regular food that mankind has lived on for ages with alcoholic beverages. (1) Natural food supplies energy, the living, working force of the body. (2) It repairs bodily tissues by replacing their wastes resulting from the metabolic process. (3) Constant use of food up to the limit required does not injure the organism. Overfeeding may, of course, do so. (4) The amount of food ingested by adults does not have to be increased in order to secure the desired results. (5) Excess food energy can be stored in the body without injury, a great advantage in times of emergency.

In contrast, the following effects are assigned by scientists to beverage alcohol: (1) Alcohol is oxidized in the body and during oxidation its contained energy is set free and becomes part of the body's energy supply. During this time the oxidized alcohol exerts its narcotic effects. (2) It can impart only a limited supply of energy, since the capacity of the organism to oxidize alcohol cannot exceed 5 to 10 grams per hour, irrespective of the degree of concentration of the alcohol or the requirements of the

[5] G. B. Wallace, in *Alcohol: Its effects on man, op. cit.*, p. 28.

organism for food.[6] (3) It cannot be stored for future use, as are foods, when needed or take part in the restoration of wastage due to the wear and tear of life. (4) In order to secure the desired effects from alcoholic consumption, users must constantly increase the amount ingested. It is quite different in this respect, also, from natural food, where a regulated diet of the same proportions insures the maximal results. (5) Alcohol is a habit-forming beverage, aside from its food value. Although it can supply only a small percentage of the food energy required by the human body, in the course of time alcohol comes to be demanded to satisfy the cultivated cravings. In this respect it can be put in the same classification as opiate drugs.

Alcohol, anesthetic or stimulant? This was long a moot question, but now, so far as nerve and mental effects go, physiologists seem to have settled it. Popularly it is regarded as a stimulant. A high-school student, unconvinced by scientific explanation, said, "But, papa, it peps you up." (1) If sense and feeling were the basis of judgment, liquor would be a stimulant. (2) If energy given the body by its food calories were the basis of judgment, it has the strength-giving quality of food fats. Its calories may substitute up to about 50 per cent of total food calories. But here is the catch. In time the drinking of liquor may bring nutritional diseases because alcohol does not provide calorie variety. The body requires fats, carbohydrates, minerals, and vitamins. Alcohol supplies only one kind, fats. There is just one short-lived physiological reaction in which temporarily alcohol is a stimulant. Given for fainting, the contact of strong alcohol on nerve endings of gullet and throat produces a brief reflex action before the alcohol is absorbed by the body. It runs up the heart rate and increases blood pressure.

(3) When the brain is the basis of judgment, alcohol loses all claim to being a stimulant. Authoritative physiologists agree that it is an anesthetic, a sedative, a depressant. The blood containing alcohol passes quickly from liver to cortex and, with sufficient dosage, speedily reduces its power as a directing and control agent. An anesthetic "induces a progressive descending depression of the central nervous system. . . . To this group belong ether, chloroform, and alcohol." "The action of an anesthetic starts at the top of the brain, and with increasing doses, it progresses deeper and deeper, with correspondingly more powerful effects on those parts" affected by earlier doses. Thus, alcohol

[6] *Ibid.*, pp. 11, 30.

deranges the highest mental faculty. Small alcoholic dosages may seem to be stimulative, but large ingestions always exhibit narcotic effects.[7]

The narcotic nature of alcohol is denoted by its chemical nature. By distilling ethyl alcohol (C_2H_5OH) with sulphuric acid, ether $(C_2H_5)_2O$ is obtained. Thus, the most-used anesthetic, perhaps, is the concentration of the ether radical of grain alcohol.

Therapeutic value of alcohol.   Alcohol in various forms, especially as whisky, brandy, and wine, has been resorted to for a long time as medicine for many different ailments, from colds to tuberculosis, and from chills and fever to snake bites. Since, as we have seen, the function of alcohol is only slightly stimulative, its therapeutic value, so far as one exists, must be based on its narcotic and its energy-giving properties. Let us review how alcohol might act as a therapeutic agent.

First, because its energy and heat reach the blood quickly, it is used in cases of exposure, shock, and chill, although many physicians prefer other remedies that have no depressive effect.

Second, because of its narcotic effects, some pharmacologists recommend light doses of alcohol to relieve anxiety and strain and to ameliorate sleeplessness under conditions of worry. Heavy doses might be used to counteract pain, but the best medical experience shows that there are much better drugs for this purpose.

Third, there are a few practitioners and "authorities" who recommend light doses of alcohol for the feeble aged, who cannot get about for amusements and find time weighing heavily upon them. The difficulty in the last two cases, of course, is that light doses have temporary effects, necessitating more frequent potions, heavier doses, or both.

In summarizing the therapeutic uses of alcohol, Dr. Haven Emerson writes:

> As a *solvent* for various medicaments alcohol performs a useful, perhaps indispensable function and the pharmacist requires it to compound many of our widely used therapeutic preparations. [But] the *therapeutic* part played by alcohol in these preparations is very limited. As therapeutic agents alcoholic beverages have a place in rendering more comfortable and peaceful the disturbances of chronic disease and old age. Sometimes it is useful to increase appetite. Beyond this there are very few conditions needing alcohol and alcoholic beverages in their treatment. Many of the uses of

[7] D. M. Whipple, in *ibid.*, pp. 94, 130, 184, 242.

. . . alcoholic beverages of the past no longer exist, for better therapeutic measures have replaced them. It seems a fact that in both private and hospital practice the utilization of alcohol and alcoholic beverages by the better-trained physicians has decreased greatly and is continuing to decrease.[8]

Alcohol as a cause of disease. The use of alcohol as a medicine by doctors and hospitals has greatly declined. The hospitals of Britain and the United States report such decline. Norman Joliffe reviews the situation relating to alcohol as a causative agent in diseases; specifically relative to polyneuropathy, pellagra, encephalitis, cirrhosis of the liver, alcoholic convulsions, and epilepsy. "Hobnail liver" occurs more frequently among heavy drinkers than nondrinkers. It is not due to the direct effect of alcohol on the liver but to some nutritional deficiency, the exact kind having not yet been discovered. Oriental beriberi (polybeuropathy) and pellagra are both dietary deficiency diseases, and alcohol may cause either by deranging the diet. Encephalitis is not caused by alcohol consumption. It is not known how liquor drinking is related to so-called "alcoholic convulsions," but it is probably an irritant or a pre-existing brain condition. Alcohol does not produce epilepsy but may make the condition of an epileptic worse. Alcohol does bring on nutritional diseases by substituting "bad" food calories for "good" ones. A good dietary maintains a "vitamin-calorie ratio" of 1:7 or more. Alcohol food calories are of one kind, fat. If half the food calories are those supplied by alcohol, in spite of the fact that total food calories consumed daily are normal or above normal in amount, the vitamin-calorie ratio in a predominating proportion of cases remains below 1:7. Hence, the drinker becomes nutritionally diseased. Dr. A. M. Snell of the Mayo Clinic found that alcohol produces from 20 to 30 per cent of clinical cases of pneumonia.[9]

The decline in the use of alcohol in hospitals is an excellent negative index of its value as a medicine. Reports from a large number of British hospitals indicate a reduction during the last thirty years to nothing or to a small percentage of the amount formerly used. The records of scores of United States institutions show an equivalent decline.

Famed Dr. William Osler said that 53 per cent of pneumonia fatalities occur among drunkards. Dr. K. L. L. Picknell of

[8] *Ibid.*, p. 176.
[9] *Ibid.*, p. 334.

Johns Hopkins Hospital, experimenting on rabbits, discovered why this is true. It is because ethyl alcohol, in intoxicating amounts, paralyzes the blood vessels so that white corpuscles, leucocytes, cannot travel to the point of contagion. Consequently, there is a greatly diminished antipneumococcus defense against the disease. Intoxicated immunized rabbits could not resist the disease and so died, while nonintoxicated immunized rabbits could do so and lived.[10]

General physical effects. Multitudes of experiments have shown that alcohol reduces capacity for work where co-operation or skill is required for sustained strain; it reduces endurance for prolonged feats of mountain climbing, racing, and exposure to cold. Arctic explorers do not depend on it for food or warmth, and athletic and pugilistic trainers withhold alcohol from the diets of those under training, since both scientific tests and experience have demonstrated that abstainers have more reliable and enduring nerves and muscles than those who use it.

Is the thirst for liquor hereditary? E. M. Jellinek answers the question, Is the thirst for liquor hereditary? He distinguishes between social and biological heredity, the latter being through the germ plasm and the other by way of social environment. Also, he notes that to be congenital is not to be hereditary, since it is prenatal and postconception.

There is no evidence of the inheritance of a drive to drink. Many authors assert there is, but none have offered objective proof. Three of those asserting it vigorously have never made an objective investigation. Studies were excluded which could not be made to bear directly and clearly on the inheritance of alcoholic psychosis as distinct from other kinds of psychosis. Since a biological craving for intoxication cannot be assumed (since it is to be proven, if possible), this gives evidence of the great risks to which the offspring of alcoholics are exposed through example and neglect.

Sixteen pieces of research by as many researchers as to the inheritance of alcoholism were studied and analyzed, covering 5294 cases. Among these, the incidence of alcoholic taint did not exceed 35 per cent, about a third. That is, a heredity of some sort was indicated, but it was not biological heredity. The only permissible conclusion is that not a disposition toward alcoholism is inherited but rather a constitution involving such instability as does not offer sufficient resistance to the social risks of inebriety.

[10] K. L. L. Picknell, "Alcohol and pneumonia," *Time*, Nov. 11, 1938.

In other words, their inherited constitution is too weak to resist the drink example set them by their associates.

Some of the parents of alcoholics may have both alcoholic and other kinds of psychosis. Some of the other psychoses may be transmitted by biological heredity, but such is not the case with alcoholism. If children of alcoholic parents are tainted with alcoholism it is because they got it by imitating the pattern set them by the drinking persons about them, not by way of the germ plasm.[11]

Are the effects of alcohol hereditary? Many pieces of research have been performed on lower animals to discover whether alcohol affects the germ plasm or only the developing offspring. A review of these by C. R. Stockard is found in *Alcohol: Its effects on man*, Chapter 5. Wilson Gee researched on the germ cells of sea minnows and concluded that "unless human germ cells are far more susceptible than those of the fish (and the same will hold of the others), which withstood about 20 per cent, they are safe from alcoholic injury on account of the lethal limits to alcoholic content in the human blood." The lethal limit for humans is 0.7 to 1.0 per cent, which usually spells death.

Experiments by Stockard on guinea pigs, by MacDowell and Hanson and Heys on rats, by Agnes Bluhm on 30,000 white mice, and by Pearl on fowl regarding the effects of alcohol on animal offspring, in the main, confirm one another. A control group was used against which to check the results of the treated group. The following are the effects on the progeny Stockard got from his treated guinea pigs: (a) Average litter size was somewhat smaller in treated series. (b) The size of the offspring at birth in both series was about the same. (c) The mortality rate under maturity was 80 per cent greater in offspring of alcoholized parents than in those of the control. (d) The prenatal death rate in the treated series was two and a half times that of the early postnatal, in the control series it was a case of 50–50. Thus, the evidence is that "more of the weaker embryos are eliminated from the alcoholic stock, and a higher proportion of resistant or strong individuals survive among the fewer offspring." (e) The high mortality rate among descendants of the alcoholized series affects even the third generation. It is 80 per cent higher in the first generation, 64 per cent in the second, and 40 per cent higher in the third generation than in the control series. (f) This last generation of the alcoholized series "produce off-

[11] E. M. Jellinek, in *Alcohol: Its effects on man, op. cit.*, p. 108.

spring that actually average better than those of the control stock." By this time, it appears, all the weak strains have been eliminated. Alcohol has exercised a selective influence and eliminated the unfit embryos while reducing the rate of increase.

The conclusion of Stockard and that of C. B. Davenport regarding the effect of alcohol on offspring agree in this: the effects take place in the embryo but not on the germ cells. It is not a case of securing results by hereditary but by postconception selective processes. The hardier strains are selected for survival; the weaker go to the wall and become eliminated.[12]

The application of these findings to human beings is purely theoretical. To say that alcoholic consumption during generations of human beings has exercised a selective or eliminative effect, with the result that the weak have been eliminated and the strong chosen for survival, is to assert something which conceivably may be true but which would require extended (and probably impossible) investigations to prove. It must also be noted that in these experiments on lower animals, the animals were alcoholized far more than any human being ever is. Some of the guinea pigs used were kept under the influence of alcohol for 4 years out of the 5 years they were permitted to survive. In addition, often, they were forced to breathe alcoholic fumes, a thing unheard of among human beings. To propose that we adopt alcoholism as a eugenic device to refine and improve the human stock implies unfortunate social consequences which more than counterbalance any good that theoretically might be derived.

Neurological consequences of alcoholism. Recent scientific research by Carl C. Speidel reveals how alcoholization causes nerve degeneration. Tadpoles were placed in alcoholic solutions of varying strengths. In weak solutions of not over 0.5 per cent there was little nerve injury. Solutions of 2 to 2.5 per cent brought on serious degeneration of nerves. In the degenerative process, the effects begin at nerve terminals and proceed toward the center. Where tadpoles were kept in a 2.5 per cent solution for five hours, myelinated nerves broke up into segments, and some continued the process after the tadpoles were put in pond water. In heavy human drinking, it is probable that nerves swell and degenerate. Headaches the next day after heavy drinking are probably due to pressure on swollen nerves. Since alcohol affects nerve endings, synapses must be affected. Swelling and

[12] C. R. Stockard, in *ibid.*, pp. 112–123.

retraction of nerve endings at synapses are likely. This, of course, must interfere with the transmission of impulses between nerve cells vital to brain processes. Bodily balance, proper focusing of eyes, the function of speech, and various mental or brain activities are disturbed.[13]

Psychological effects. The psychological effects of alcohol arise out of its effects on the brain. It appears to be established scientifically that the amount of alcohol in the brain (rather than in the blood and other organs) determines the degree to which a person is influenced by alcohol. A five-year study of 6000 brains exposed to alcohol concludes that the given percentages of alcohol in the brain accompany the following effects, on the average: (a) Normal condition under 0.1 per cent. (b) "Aggressiveness," but not generally unbalanced, with 0.1 to 0.25 per cent. (c) "Loss of equilibrium," intoxicated, with 0.25 to 0.4 per cent. (d) "Unbalanced," intoxicated, with 0.4 to 0.6 per cent.[14]

H. S. Martland, who writes on "Pathology of acute and chronic alcoholism" and who reports the above figures, says: "I have frequently encountered cases in which the alcohol content of the brain has been low (0.2 plus), yet death had occurred as the result of acute alcoholic poisoning. . . . Gettler and Tiber state that the degree to which any person is affected does not depend on the quantity consumed but on the amount of alcohol present in the brain at the time.[15]

It is pretty certain that whatever influences the body fundamentally has a correlative influence on the mind. A. R. Cushny states the psychological effects of alcohol as follows, remarking that it varies a good deal with individuals:

> In small quantities it generally produces a feeling of well-being and good fellowship, along with increased confidence in the powers, mental and physical, of the subject of the experiment. Larger quantities are followed by a certain amount of excitement, marked by laughter, loquacity, and gesticulation. The face becomes flushed and hot, the eyes brighter and livelier, the pulse accelerated. Even at this stage self-control is partly lost and the will-power is weakened. The speech may be brilliant but it often betrays the speaker; the movements are more lively but they are

[13] Carl C. Speidel, "Changes in nerve fibers during alcoholic intoxication and recovery," *Scientific Monthly*, Feb., 1937: 178–185.

[14] Findings of Gettler and Tiber, 1927, reported in *Alcohol: Its effects on man, op. cit.*, p. 204.

[15] *Ibid.*, p. 204.

often undignified. The loss of self-control is often indicated further by furious outbursts of anger and unreasonableness, or by indulgences in maudlin sentimentality and sensual fancies. The sense of responsibility and the power of discrimination between the trivial and the important are lost and the individual has no regard for the feelings of others, or the ordinary conventions of life. If the bout be further continued, the movements become uncertain, the speech becomes difficult and stammering, the walk becomes a stagger, and a torpid slumber follows."[16]

Sometimes death results from the paralysis of bodily functions. Thus, there are at least three well-marked psychological stages which can best be understood by recalling the stages by which the mind appears and is built up.

Alcohol attacks first the highest mental functions, those last acquired by the race and the individual, the most valuable because the most critical and productive of an ordered life. The intoxicated man loses poise and dignity because values and the ability to see himself in perspective are lost. He sinks to lower levels. He becomes less than a little child in the second stage. He may be dangerous to society because he retains the sense and cunning and, having lost the sense of values, is unscrupulous. Automatisms and impulses replace critical intelligence. In the last stage, all co-ordination disappears and man becomes an infant, without its dignity of nature and promise of developing potentialities.

Effect on the mental functions.   What we call "mind" exercises its functions by means of nerve cells and fibers, and these must be maintained in a healthy integral condition. Recent research finds that heavy doses of alcohol cause the disintegration of the nerve body, and that from extra heavy doses the nerves do not recover completely. Since the tops of nerves are immediately involved in the functioning of the synapses of the brain, nerve disintegration impairs the transmission of nerve impulses between brain cells. This is the basis of the disturbances of balance, proper functioning of eyes, speech, and various mental activities.[17]

A number of studies report reactions which have significance for industry, social behavior, and personality adjustments. They concern threading needles, marksmanship, typewriting, motor control of the speech mechanism, and the like. The alcoholic

---

[16] A. R. Cushny, *Textbook of pharmacology and therapeutics* (Philadelphia: Lea and Febiger, 1924), pp. 176–177.

[17] C. C. Speidel, "Changes in nerve fibers during alcoholic intoxication and recovery," *op. cit.*, pp. 178–185.

dosages used range from 5 cc. to 30 cc. alcohol. The effects are uniformly depressant and deterrent on functions. The percentages of reduction of efficiency run from 6 to 100.

Various tests bearing on the effects of alcohol on the learning and memory processes indicate a retarding influence varying from a slight percentage to 13 per cent following dosages ranging from light to heavy.

The power of association has also been investigated. A 30 cc. dosage of alcohol impaired the ability of male students regarding word association by percentages ranging from a slight 1 to 20 per cent. Imbibing wine retarded the mathematical processes of a large number of students some 15 per cent.

The tests regarding the sensory threshold relate to the ability to discern when a stimulus such as sound or light begins to affect ear or eye, and to the power to discriminate between sensory phenomena. Those reported by Miles on hearing, sight, and detection of the effects of an electrical current applied to the finger indicate a general lowering of efficiency. Sometimes in cases of sound and sight the threshold is lowered, but it is invariably the discriminatory ability between stimuli that is impaired. In the electric-current experiment there was just one case where sense-perception was improved.

The power to concentrate and sustain attention is vital in mental and social pursuits. The studies of the influence of alcohol on this function indicate that it is almost always that of impairment. In one experiment the reduction ran as high as 50 per cent in some cases. In another the average reduction was 14 per cent, but there was one heavy drinker whose attention was improved 6 per cent by the small amount of alcohol administered.

Our modern world places a large premium on thinking and reasoning. They are central to business, the professions, statesmanship, science, and other important phases of life. Consequently, it is important to know how they are affected by the use of alcohol. Cattell conducted an elaborate experiment (1930) on a large group of young people to find how alcohol affected their intelligence. He found that a 10-gram dosage had no apparent effect, but that one of 20 grams lowered the thinking power slightly, some 1 per cent. Hollingworth also has administered a test and finds that a dosage of 2.75 beer retards the action of intelligence from 15 to 25 per cent.

The effect of alcohol on the mental activities of children has been investigated many times during the last thirty years.

Erlacher gave an arithmetical test (1926) to 26 boys and 26 girls, half of each being 10 and 14 years of age. The alcoholic potion was the strength of sweet wine. There was an average retardation of computing ability of 5 to 7 per cent. For boys the percentage of retardation ran from 5.8 to 10.1 per cent, and for girls from 2.8 to 8.0 per cent. The younger children were influenced by it more than the older ones.[18]

Insanity and alcohol. Insanity is a general term for scores of different psychoses. A psychosis may be temporary or permanent, occasional or continuous. Liquor causes several psychoses, delirium tremens and some six others. Many chronic drunkards have delirium tremens, a violent, intensive hallucinatory condition. These alcoholic psychoses are as real and incapacitating while they last as many other psychoses and must be thought of as insanities, the proper scientific term for so-called "insanity." They are a small percentage of all, but they have tragic and devastating effects.

The percentage of patients with alcoholic psychosis in hospitals for the insane varies directly with the consumption of alcohol at large, creating the probability of a causal relation between alcoholism and insanity. The admission of such patients to the civil state hospitals of New York ranged, in per cent of all patients admitted, from 10.8 in 1909 to 8.6 in 1917; 4.0 in 1919; 1.9 in 1920; 3.2 in 1922; 7.0 in 1927; and 6.0 in 1930.[19] The great decline was during prohibition, beginning in 1919, and in the first year of the Volstead Act. When administration slackened, the percentage increased. The figures for the Vienna hospital "Am Steinhof," Austria, from 1910 to 1926 ran in a similar manner. The percentage of inmates with alcoholic psychosis ranged above 9 previous to 1914, then fell to 5.6 in 1915, sank to 1.4 in 1917, rose to 2.7 in 1920, to 9.8 in 1922, and has been above 20 since 1925.[20] The proportion was very small during World War I and immediately after, when restrictions on alcoholic consumption were in force. Somewhat similar data for Belgium and Switzerland are obtainable.[21]

There has been a tendency to explain alcoholic insanity and alcoholism as products of a previous morbidity or hereditary defect. It is held that morbidity provokes the thirst and the ulti-

[18] W. R. Miles, "Psychological effects of alcohol on man," in *Alcohol: Its effects on man, op. cit.*, pp. 224–256.
[19] H. M. Pollock, in *ibid.*, p. 355.
[20] *Ibid.*, p. 421.
[21] *Ibid.*, p. 422.

mate insanity and that, therefore, alcohol does not produce insanity. However, the facts presented are against this view. The correlation of alcoholic insanity and liquor consumption in various countries, as shown previously, indicates a causal relationship. It would be extreme to think that all who drink habitually are pathological cases. It explains too much. Many persons drink because of associations, as we have previously pointed out. Habitual drinking develops normally out of such associations. It fluctuates according to laws, law enforcement, and associations. Insanity fluctuates accordingly. The cause of most of the drinking lies in the social rather than in the hereditary field.

General Social Effects of Alcoholism

Because it modifies the behavior of users and those with whom they come in contact, and conditions human relationships in many directions, the alcoholic complex demands consideration. We do not allude to occasional light resort to liquor but to habitual and heavy potation. Occasional light use may be deleterious only in its habit-forming tendency. Habitual or heavy occasional use brings direct consequences which may socially be a fundamental detriment.

Mortality rate. The great insurance companies are our best authorities as to the effect of alcoholism on the length of life. They all believe that alcoholic addiction shortens life and so increases the death rate. Since policy holders number millions, the statistical conclusions have a firm basis. The actuarial experience of the British companies is to the effect that abstainers have a mortality rate 35 per cent lower than that of drinkers. The experiences of 41 insurance companies of the United States, with over 20,000,000 policy holders, is to the effect that the mortality rate among drinkers ranges from 18 per cent in the group of moderate occasional users to 86 per cent in that of moderate steady drinkers who are accepted for insurance purposes above that for policy holders in general.

The Northwestern Mutual Life Insurance Company studied the mortality record of 286,000 policy holders regarding the class of liquor used and compared it with that of abstainers. It found that the death rate among moderate occasional drinkers was 19 per cent higher, that of daily users of beer was 33 per cent higher, and that of daily imbibers of spirits was 66 per cent higher than that of abstainers. The study of a few thousand cases by occasional investigators with somewhat favorable conclusions are statistically unimportant in comparison with the above finding covering millions of cases.

That alcoholism affects the death rate is demonstrated by Figure 20. The figure presents the death rate per 100,000 white

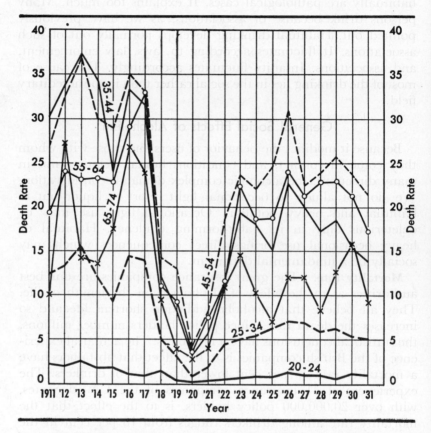

Figure 20. Death Rate from Alcoholism Among White Males in the United States

males in the United States for each year from 1911 to 1931 as found among policy holders of the Metropolitan Life Insurance Company. The lines represent the various age groups. We note that there is a great variety in the variations of the different curves on each side of the u-loop, but that there is great uniformity in the movement downward in the years 1918 to 1922. This is the period of war prohibition and the beginning of constitutional prohibition. There is a comparatively high death rate from alcoholism both before and after that period and a very low one within those years for all age groups presented. There was little liquor dispensed during 1918–1922, with a consequent low rate of mortality from alcoholism. There are other factors than alcohol entering into the situation as a cause; but they are minor ones, and no one can seriously doubt that the data afford competent evidence regarding the effect of alcohol on mortality.

The data for six countries other than the United States— England and Wales, Scotland, New Zealand, Australia, Norway, and Denmark—during equivalent periods related to World War I are to the same effect.[22]

Alcohol and poverty. The idea that drinking makes for poverty is traditional and well accepted. Society has seen so much of it for ages that it does not require statistical demonstration to prove it. The force of alcohol as a causative factor in producing poverty may be overrated, but the social judgment is good for practical purposes.

Just what exact causative force liquor drinking has in producing poverty cannot be determined. It is only one among many causal factors, and it is impossible to assign to each of the interlaced conditions its degree of productiveness. The Committee of Fifty, which made an extensive study of the liquor question in the 1890's, reported some suggestive findings. It found as follows:

Alcohol was a direct or indirect cause of 25 per cent of the dependency relieved by charity organizations, 18 per cent being direct—the effect of drinking on the drinker—and 9 per cent indirect—the effect of drinking on others. Regarding almshouse paupers, the total causative force of alcohol was 37 per cent, the direct being 32 and the indirect 8. Forty-five per cent of the destitution of children was assigned to alcoholism of parents and other responsible persons. The direct and indirect effects for males and females differed from each other. Thus, among those relieved by charity organizations the direct and indirect effects among males were 22.7 and 3.8 per cent, while among females they were 12.4 and 17, the males, of course, being the chief drinkers.[23] Charles Booth in London found that 25 per cent of dependency was due to liquor. The extensive figures of Massachusetts run somewhat higher.

[22] *Cf.* Dublin's tables and graphs, in *ibid.*, pp. 385–395.
[23] Committee of Fifty, *Liquor problem* (Boston: Houghton Mifflin Company, 1905), pp. 108–115.

Estimates of the 1890's by Warner (which covered hundreds of thousands of cases in many nations and a hundred great cities) as to the weight of alcohol as a contributory cause of poverty ranged from a percentage of 2 to one of over 20. The average for great cities of this country was about 12 or 13.[24]

According to John Koren, the study of recipients of relief in Norway in 1910 showed drink as a cause of dependency in only 8.6 per cent of the cases. Whether conditions were the same in the United States at that time he thinks is problematical.[25]

According to social workers, alcohol ranks high as a cause of poverty. Thus, R. W. Kelso says, "Of the personal causes of poverty it is undoubtedly the greatest."[26] The National Conference of Social Workers, at the Pittsburgh meeting, 1917, passed a unanimous resolution urging Congress to enact the Eighteenth Amendment.

Alcohol and accidents. We should expect that the use of alcohol would lead to accidents, since our review of the psychological effects shows that it lowers mental and motor efficiency. Whatever acts as an anesthetic on our highest rational and critical factors, which determine the quality of our perceptions, judgments, and executions, is bound to be detrimental to individual and social performance. There is an undoubted conflict between worker's and driver's feeling of superior efficiency under the influence of alcohol, and the results measured by objective reactions. It is the latter that must serve as the criterion of efficiency.

Nothing is more certain than that whatever undermines human neuro-muscular control will multiply accidents. We have had abundant evidence that intoxication does this by unseating critical intelligence, judgment, and caution. The exact amount of accidents due to liquor and intoxication is indeterminable. Laws vary, and their interpretation and enforcement personnel vary from state to state. Many other factors are present which make exactitude in estimates impossible. But we still have a rather reliable picture of the situation.

Business makes rules against intoxication among its responsible workers. Sobriety is demanded of such workers as trainmen, busmen, enginemen, and the like. Accident rates in factories and

[24] A. G. Warner, *American charities*, revised by M. R. Coolege (New York: T. Y. Crowell Company, 1908), Ch. 2.

[25] John Koren, *Alcohol and society* (New York: Henry Holt and Company, 1916), p. 44.

[26] R. W. Kelso, *Poverty* (New York: Longmans, Green and Company, 1929).

mines are higher on "blue Mondays" than on other days. Motor-vehicle-accident rates are higher among drinking drivers and pedestrians than among "normal" persons. Slightly intoxicated drivers are more dangerous than those heavily "under the influence," because the latter are usually unable to drive. The Motor Vehicle Commissioner of Connecticut says that the really dangerous driver is the man who has had one or two drinks only, who still thinks he is in possession of his faculties, but whose driving judgment is impaired. A prominent distiller offered $100,000 to teach the danger of drinking. He said, "Liquor has no place in the front seat of an auto. . . . Alcohol and gasoline do not mix."[27]

A. S. Berry, Director, Traffic and Transportation Division, National Safety Council, centers his study on fatal accidents in which intoxication figures because the whole field of accidents is too confused. From figures for the whole country, which are not too good, he finds that 6 per cent of drivers were "under the influence." In five widely located great cities, 10.8 per cent of drivers and 13 per cent of pedestrians "had been drinking." In the four states which require blood-concentration tests (1939), 86 per cent of traffic accidents were at night and week ends. About a third of the cases reported drinking drivers or pedestrians. A chemical test in four cities found these percentages of drivers who "had been drinking" or were "under the influence" in that order: Evanston, 38 and 21; Uniontown, 48 and 27; Cleveland, 56 and 38; New York, 51 and 42. The per cent of drivers who had been drinking was four times that of normal drivers.

The alcoholometer is a device for testing the amount of alcohol in the blood by the use of the breath. It is so simple and its results so scientifically accurate and certain that it is coming into rapid use in states and cities. Some persons with an alcohol content of 0.05 to 0.15 per cent in blood would be "under the influence." Every driver with a percentage concentration above 0.15 is definitely "under the influence," intoxicated. A concentration of 0.15 is a sure evidence of intoxication.

The advantages of chemical-test legislation are "(1) It is easier to get the evidence admitted in court. (2) It avoids the need for expert testimony in most cases. (3) It usually results in a marked increase in the number of cases in which there are pleas of guilty. (4) Since the number of contest cases is reduced, court

[27] *International Student*, Jan., 1936: 43.

costs are lower. (5) It provides for greater uniformity within the states in the enforcement of drunken driving legislation."

Michigan is using an alcoholometer called an "intoximeter" for roadside testing of drivers. The claim is that it has eliminated miscarriage of justice by discriminating between sick, injured, or drugged persons and alcoholized ones; and that it provides the police with a "foolproof" method of proving intoxication.[28]

Alcohol and crime.   From previous discussions we should expect alcohol to act as a predisposing cause of criminal behavior. In intoxicating amounts, it undermines critical acumen, balanced judgment, caution, social and moral restraints. It unloosens the so-called "lower" impulses and propensities, dulls the conscience, and weakens moral control. It is no accident that the moral defenses of women are lowered by it and that drinking and vice most often are associated.

Difficulties meet us in seeking to weigh the force of alcohol as a criminal causative. (1) Of dozens of factors which may promote crime, it is only one. How to disassociate it from all the others and measure its real force objectively is so far an insurmountable scientific problem. (2) Crime is also a legal affair, a product of law. In a sense, crimes multiply in proportion to the number of conduct actions set aside as illegal. The number of laws, the import of laws, the interpretation and administration of laws vary from state to state and region to region. What is criminal here may not be criminal there, or if it is, it has a different value and interpretation. The psychopathic factor is bound to be vague because the term "psychopathic" is a kind of catch-all for leftovers from "instinctive," "pathological," etc. Because of this, attempts to make psychopathic factors the parent of the crime in which intoxication appears operate in a fog of obscurity. No doubt there are cases where "psychopathic" factors in the criminal" account for his drinking, which eventuates in criminal acts. But to make some such cases serve as a general law to cover all criminal behavior where alcohol is an associated factor is to far exceed good scientific judgment.

Table 28 is reproduced from the *Yale lectures* and shows the proportion of both inebriate and noninebriate convicts in Sing Sing Prison, New York, for the years 1938–1940. The study was made under the "direction of trained investigators and scientists" and probably is the best representation we have. It is seen that in the first three classes the incidence is higher among inebriates.

[28] Associated Press Report, Dec., 12, 1946.

Our caution is that this is a study of one criminal population and may not be true throughout the nation. However, the chances are that it is fairly representative.

TABLE 28

Incidence of Selected Crimes Among Inebriate and Noninebriate Prisoners
Committed to Sing Sing Prison: 1938–1940

Class of Crime	Inebriate Prisoners		Noninebriate Prisoners	
	Number	Per Cent	Number	Per Cent
Sex Crimes	53	8	122	5
Homicide	61	29	192	8
Assault	149	15	313	13
Grand Larceny	106	19	544	22
Robbery	131	21	504	21
Burglary	146	7	336	14
All Other Crimes	51	1	427	17
Totals	697	100	2438	100

Source: *Yale lectures*, 147.

Habitual crime appears to be stimulated by liquor. Aschaffenburg and Healy believed that the elimination of alcohol would reduce crime by one fifth. They were competent students, and their judgment is worth a good deal. Saloons, gambling, vice are historic associates, and crime lurks near by.

The family. It is a historical commonplace that drink undermines and impairs the family and home. Its effects are much greater qualitatively than quantitatively. Drunkenness registers its effects on the family through divorce records. But habitual alcoholism without drunkenness may not appear in such records and yet produce far greater deteriorating results. Impoverishment, the lowering of the family tone through dulled senses, selfish gratification, lack of co-operation, and the creation of shame, distrust, disapproval, disdain, and contempt in other members of the family may all occur without family disruption.

According to the records of the charity organizations operating in 25 cities, drink was associated with desertion in one fourth of the cases. The Associated Charities of Boston reported in 1910 that out of 352 able-bodied men who failed to support their families 69 per cent were drunkards. Drunkenness is a legal ground for divorce in many states, but intemperance may be a factor in the case without being a legal ground. For the five-year period 1881–1886, drunkenness was the legal ground assigned in 4.5 per cent of all divorces granted in the United States, of 6.1 per cent of those given to wives and of 1.3 per cent of those granted to men. In 1916, 3.4 per cent of all divorces were granted for drunkenness, as were 4.5 per cent of those granted to women and 0.8 per cent of those granted to men. In 1922, the percentages in the order named were 1.0, 1.4, and 0.3; and in 1930, they were 1.7, 2.2, and 0.4, But investigations of courts of domestic relations in such cities as Chicago and Brooklyn find that much larger percentages of separations are due to intemperance, the percentage in Chicago being 46 and in Brooklyn 45.8.[29] The economic costs of caring for families unsupported because of drink must be considerable.

Child life. We need to pity the unfortunate children of the world whose lives are broken and made miserable by the parents' use of alcohol. The daily outlay for drink by many parents constitutes a large part of the meager income, all of which is needed by the family for legitimate purposes. Besides, the coarseness and insensitive selfishness of a "soaked" if not drunken parent robs the child in the home of an immeasurably valuable element of parenthood.

Drinking and drunkenness undoubtedly have a strong influence toward the production of dependent and neglected children. According to the figures of the Committee of Fifty, alcohol was a causal factor in about 46 per cent of the cases investigated. The Chicago Juveniles Protective Association studied the records of about 1400 dependent and neglected children it cared for during the first six months of 1910 and concluded that 75 per cent of the cases had drunkenness of parents or guardians as the leading cause. Healy did not find alcohol to be the chief productive factor in his series of a thousand cases of juvenile delinquency in Chicago, but he did find that one or both parents of 31 per cent of the children in one of his series of a thousand drank to excess, of 26.5 per cent in another series, and of 51 per cent in a Boston series.

Immorality. Sex immorality, vice, and prostitution have always been intimately associated with the use of liquor. The influence of alcohol on the personality releases the restraints of social codes and conventions because it sets the individual free

[29] G. E. Howard, *American Journal of Sociology*, XXIV: 74.

from the critical scrutiny of his own consciousness. The findings of vice commissions of various cities a decade or two ago generally testified to the depressing effect of the saloons and commercial liquor traffic on morals.

The report of the Chicago Vice Commission may be taken as a telling sample of the others. It found that grills were a fertile source of vice, especially for young girls, and that houses of prostitution were agents and sales places for liquor. On the other hand, saloons were effective promoters of prostitution. Many saloons had rear rooms which were frequented by prostitutes who solicited trade and sold drinks on commission. Bartenders and waiters in saloons were regularly connected with prostitution and would engage to find a girl and room for a patron. Saloons were found to be places where careers in vice often began. Cadets, seducers, and procurers used the associations and drink as agencies to work upon young girls and overcome their conventional scruples. Vulgarity in language and especially in bodily posture and exposure abounded. The saloons protected their recognized prostitutes when they got into legal difficulty, paid their fines, bailed them out, and performed whatever was needful.

Methods of Liquor Control

By now we should be able to see and understand the need for liquor control. The need might exist without the desire and ability on the part of the public to exercise control. A view of long-time trends in the field of control is edifying. This list of brief statements without discussion will have to suffice.

Historic trends in liquor control. (1) Growth of control legislation through the centuries. (2) Development of organizations to exercise control of the sale of liquor. (3) Extension of police powers over liquor distribution to promote public welfare. (4) Development of court options that liquor control and control acts, including outright prohibition, are constitutional as acts by sovereign peoples to protect their common welfare. (5) Growth of United States Supreme Court validation of public-welfare legislation and practice of reviewing liquor-case judgments of state courts. Trend in laws and courts toward viewing intoxication and drunken acts as antisocial. (7) Growth in number of acts involving liquor control. (8) Increasing enmeshment of liquor use with rapidly expanding and differentiating culture. (9) Shifts in meaning of liquor laws and concepts, such as drunkenness and prohibition in the exercise of police powers and court interpretations. (10) Development of increasingly democratic methods in determining public policies toward liquor matters.

Present national symptoms.   Efforts to control and limit the use of liquor as a beverage have taken many forms. At present there are four types of agencies employed by civilized nations.

1. *License and regulation.*   Great Britain, France, Italy, Belgium, Denmark, Chile, Soviet Russia, and other countries license and regulate liquor.

Prior to 1928 Great Britain reduced drunkenness by a rigid license system, but a recent youth propaganda by the liquor interests has greatly increased drinking. In Germany the Nazi government took over the temperance movement. Temperance was encouraged, drunken auto drivers were severely punished, liquor ads were regulated, and chronic alcoholics were sometimes sterilized.[30]

2. *Governmental importation, distribution, and sale,* as seen in the various Canadian provinces, except Prince Edward Island. The government is chiefly vendor for private corporations. Permits to purchase liquor are general, save in Quebec. Ontario requires home consumption after purchase. Other provinces provide drinking places or permit their establishment.

3. *Government control through corporations,* as in Sweden and Norway. Corporations' manufacture, importation, and sale are regulated by a governmental commission. The Bratt System obtains in Sweden. That country maintains a national corporation for wholesale purposes and local corporations for retailing liquor, the majority of the directors of each being selected by central and local governments respectively. Individuals purchase by permits only, although beer of low alcoholic content is freely made and sold. There is local option, but individuals may bring in liquor by permit. Norway's system is somewhat similar but less stringent.

4. *Absolute prohibition* as a national system, as formerly obtained in Finland, Norway, and the United States.

Our experiments with control systems.   The people of the United States have conducted a vast and varied experiment in the field of liquor control during the last hundred years. Almost every known system has been tried by national, state, county,

[30] Robert Nercord, "Germany and liquor today," *The International Student,* Jan., 1940: 74–78.

or city government during that time. Various states have rather rapidly cycled from system to system. Thus, Ohio established nine different systems of liquor regulation between 1851 and 1915. No doubt some of these trials were too short to be convincing as tests.

State prohibition began to make its appearance as early as 1845. There were 24 prohibition states in 1915, and 28 by the time of national prohibition. The number had been reduced to 3 by June, 1944. Interspersed during that period was nearly every conceivable system of licensing, also local option and state dispensary.

National prohibition. Our nation conducted an extensive experiment in prohibition between 1917 and 1933. Congress enacted "war prohibition" legislation to be in effect during World War I. In 1919 it validated the Eighteenth Amendment to the federal Consitution over the veto of President Wilson, who believed the nation was not ready for it. Since it had been approved by the legislatures of 46 states, it was democratically sanctioned. However, within a short time, popular currents ran against it, and the Eighteenth Amendment was scuttled in 1933.

Some of the influences that caused this reversal were: (1) A colossal propaganda against the prohibition system by liquor forces of both this country and Europe. It was unscrupulous and bitter and shook the faith of even some supporters of it. (2) The invention and multiplication of "easy devices" for making liquor at home. (3) The quick spread of a black market for liquor run by bootleggers, highjackers like Capone, thugs, gunmen, corner groceries, and drugstores. (4) Return of war veterans, many of whom had become addicted to drinking during service. (5) Failure of state and local governments to loyally co-operate with federal enforcement agencies.

While national prohibition failed because it could not be enforced, its advocates pointed to certain virtues they claimed it possessed.

1. It was adopted as a war-emergency measure because it would check national weakening by the insidious influences liquor inevitably exercises. If national health should be protected against such forces during war, all the more it should be protected against them in time of peace. Pneumonia or malaria are no more deadly to public health during war than during peace.

2. There are certain evident socio-economic gains. If what was previously said concerning the causal relation of alcoholic con-

sumption to industry, mortality, insanity, feeble-mindedness, child life, crime, vice, and the like was true, then it was assumed that, in so far as prohibition succeeded, the pathological conditions ought to have been diminished. There are indications that prohibition did promote thrift, increase savings, reduce mortality, advance the life of children and youth by improved home conditions and educational opportunities, and cut down the rates of certain kinds of insanity.

3. It removed young children from contact with open saloons and the degenerating influences of public drinking places.

Social changes following the repeal of prohibition. Certain significant social changes closely related to the liquor traffic have taken place since repeal.

1. The consumption of alcohol greatly increased between the prohibition year 1930 and the postprohibition year 1946, as shown by the following facts. Production of distilled spirits, in millions of gallons, for the two separated years was respectively 197 and 275; of still wines, 3.2 and 390; of sparkling wines, 0.5 and 41; of rectified spirits and wines, .03 and 151; of fermented malt liquors, 9.2 and 85 (million barrels); of ethyl alcohol withdrawn from warehouses for denaturing, 183 and 277 million gallons.[31] The national drink bill has risen from less than 2 to about 8 million dollars.

2. In Chicago, the Juveniles Protective Association found that juvenile delinquency has been greatly promoted by violation by liquor vendors of laws aimed to protect parental association and child care in homes.[32]

3. Increase of alcoholism has brought increased rejection of applicants for insurance by life-insurance companies. The rejections by the Northwestern Life Insurance Company of Minneapolis increased 24 per cent between repeal and 1936.[33] According to President G. B. Cutting of Colgate University, rejection of applicants between 1932 and 1936 increased 75 per cent.[34]

4. Drinking and intoxication have made for more motor casualties. In 1933 there were 22,943 such casualties in which drinking was a factor; in 1936 there were 47,828. If we regard the first as 100, the second becomes 208. The National Safety Council studied highway casualties during the nine months

[31] *U. S. statistical abstracts,* 1931 and 1947.
[32] W. O. Cromwell, *Liquor and juvenile delinquency,* 1940.
[33] Special report by that company, 1939.
[34] G. B. Cutting, "Meet a Prohibitionist," convocation address, Sept. 20, 1939.

before repeal and during nine months of 1934 in 12 states of large population and in 33 cities having populations of 60,000. It found drinking drivers involved increased 29 per cent and drinking pedestrians 53 per cent.[35]

5. A severe strain has been put on courts, penal institutions, and enforcement machinery because of the great number of arrests for violation of traffic laws, and there is corruption of courts.

Shift in public attitude. Governmental action and political policies are the outcome professedly of the pressure desires of the public, "public opinion." In turn, public opinion of any but the most deep-seated and permanent kind undergoes shifts and transformations from time to time. Such a shift took place between the time of the adoption of war prohibition and the Eighteenth Amendment in the late 1920's and early 1930's, culminating in the repeal of that amendment. Hornell Hart's study of periodical literature to discover shifts in reform movements seems to show that such movements reached their zenith between 1905 and 1915 and then declined to a lower level down to 1930. Obviously, the public had lost much of its interest in reform movements in general.[36] The decline in prohibition sentiment was a part of this shift, evidently.

New type of saloon. Today we witness the development of a saloon that, while it is minus some of the undesirable features of the old, has added undesirable traits of its own. One of these traits is the association of women and girls with the liquor traffic. The employment of hostesses and barmaids is widespread. This practice is intended by the dealers to promote sales and undoubtedly accomplishes its purpose with male patrons. It also associates women, especially young girls, with conditions which are also doing their utmost to widen the patronage of liquor-sales places among women and girls. Their success is attested by the growing number of females who patronize liquor shops.

Another trait of the new saloon in a more threatening form than it assumed in the old saloon is check cashing across the bar. Saloons are assuming the functions of banks and undermining the trade of mercantile establishments by absorbing money in drink that would otherwise go to trade at the stores for the necessaries of life. This seeming gratuity service of the saloon entails certain results. It fosters "courtesy" drinking, the

[35] National Safety Council, *Public safety*, Feb., 1935.
[36] Hornell Hart, in *Recent social trends*, I (1933): 427–430.

recipient of the courtesy extended by the saloon paying for it by buying another drink. The drink often multiplies into drinks. An even more serious abuse by the saloon in this connection is the practice of holding back a part of the check. This leads to frequent visits by those to whom payments are due, more frequent drinking, and the absorption of a large amount of the face of the check in payment.

What the Next Steps Should Be

Control necessary. If recent American and world historical changes and trends in the field of liquor control mean anything, it is that (a) prohibition breaks down because people will make, smuggle, and use liquor in spite of prohibitory laws; (b) nations cast it out because they dislike it or regard it as a failure. So we must follow either of two courses relative to the liquor business: (1) practice *laissez faire* or (2) adopt some other regulatory and control plan. What that should be is a matter of discussion.

All in favor of temperance, including many users of liquor, agree that *laissez faire* will not do because the excesses and evils of an unregulated traffic would constitute such a paramount menace to civilization. Ultimately, the public would be driven to seek some form of control. If history proves that prohibition is a failure, it much more overwhelmingly demonstrates that a let-alone policy regarding making and vending liquor is a colossal failure. The "wettest" populations are driven inevitably to some form of regulation.

Basic principles of control. Considering the experience of our states, our nation, and other nations with systems of control of intoxicants, it appears wise to caution against placing complete trust in any one system. The final test of successful control is general social welfare seen as improved standards of living, health, decency, character, disposal of leisure time, economic condition, and other things. Crime rates are often used as a criterion of success of systems of liquor control. Recognizing that it is only one criterion, we do find that criminal rates have been reduced almost equally under such contrasted systems as that of Sweden, whose chief principle is the elimination of private profit; that of Denmark, with its high license system; and that of England, combining licensing with strict limitation of night sales and maintaining periods of nonsales in both forenoon and afternoon.

There are principles recognized in various systems which

appear to be helpful as regulatory devices in liquor dispensing. The following are probably as useful as any and deserve consideration of thoughtful students of the subject of control.

1. Placing dispensing places on as nearly a purely sales basis as possible, like stores and shops. This means they should be well lighted, open public places free from loafing, amusements, and carousing.

2. Placing a graduated tax on liquors according to alcoholic content. Thus, beer and light wines would bear little or no tax, while heavy wines and spiritous liquors would carry heavier ones. This is a fundamental principle of the Bratt System of Sweden, and our states have partially recognized it in placing lower license fees on nonintoxicating beverage-sales places than on those dealing with intoxicants.

3. Limiting the annual amount dispensing places may sell and the amount of profit or dividends the liquor producers and dispensers may derive. Under the Bratt System, dividends are limited to five or five and a half per cent, and limits are set on annual sales. In case more is sold, all profits are taken by the government.

4. Substituting general social welfare as a motive of governmental tax for the revenue-raising motive. To treat liquor regulation as a revenue matter entirely is to make government further liquor production and sale as a business. In Sweden, revenue collected from liquor sales cannot go into general funds and be used to defray expenses of government. It is used for temperance education, reduction of the national debt, and the like.

5. Restricting dispensing establishments to strictly business districts, and away from all kinds of residential districts, schools, and churches. This is particularly needed where the saloon system is allowed to exist, with its associations of vice, gambling, and drunkenness.

6. Excluding minors from places of manufacture and sale of intoxicating beverages. The Swedish system prohibits issuing passbooks to persons under 24 years of age or to irresponsible parties.

7. Strictly enforcing the laws regulating the liquor business. We suspect that the recent efficacy of the English licensing system was largely due to rigid enforcement of the limitations imposed. Contrasted with this is the notorious violation of liquor laws permitted in the cities of this country.

8. Restricting motor-vehicle driving to sober persons. This

can be done by licensing only drivers of proved sobriety and depriving violators of their rights to drive for a year or more. This would perhaps do much to induce sobriety and temperance.

The British Medical Association investigated the effect of light drinking on the driving of motor vehicles and found that "two or three ounces of whisky are sufficient to impair a driver's faculties, inspiring him with overconfidence in himself and disturbing the co-ordination between eye, hand, and foot; further, that the effect of even moderate doses is prolonged over several hours." [37]

Substitutes for liquor. The people of our nation developed from a stage of pretty nearly general drinking in the early part of the last century to one, until recently, where a large portion of our people did not use beer, wine, or spirituous liquor. This large percentage of our inhabitants found substitutes for strong drink. Conceivably we can look forward to a time when a larger proportion will be self-imposed prohibitionists. Let us set down briefly the points indicating why recreation of all kinds might be thought of as possible substitutes for liquor drinking.

1. It is a well-known fact that athletes in training consume little or no liquor. Pugilists, football and baseball players in league teams, track men, contenders for championships in golf and other games live the lives of teetotalers, at least while they are in training or competition, and appear thoroughly to enjoy life meanwhile. For the time at least they find competent substitutes.

2. A large portion of drinking is done in leisure time. Recreation and other forms of amusement are also leisure-time activities, and they might well be made competitors of drinking. Along with drinking often go gambling and vice. If recreation could supplant these, it might also supplant their associate, liquor.

3. Various forms of amusement and recreation—used by the saloons as decoys—are employed to attract people with the hope that they will become patrons of the bar. It is possible, then, to conceive of them as substitutes for public drinking.

Educating about alcoholic properties and effects. In the long run, we have to depend upon a knowledge of the various life situations to save us from error and its bad consequences. Great systems of error have worked in the past, but they gradually gave way to a more competently understood and consequently better

[37] Nercord, *The International Student, op. cit.*, Feb., 1936: 52.

way of making adjustments in living. The growth of temperance in our country has been partly due to temperance teaching in and out of schools and to the development of more adequate ways to enjoy life and to have a good time. When military and later constitutional prohibition was established, prohibition was regarded as a panacea by temperance people, temperance movements largely died, and their efforts to secure scientific temperance teaching in the schools declined. During national prohibition a violent propaganda arose against it, and an extreme public hysteria was developed which resulted in repeal of the Eighteenth Amendment.

Now the abuses, excesses, and tragedies which always accompany a widespread use of liquor have reappeared, and a portion of the public is again becoming mindful of the need of placing John Barleycorn on leash. The public might well consider reestablishing temperance teaching in the schools. The public schools are the education agencies of society and the state for developing and promoting the general welfare, and the public has a right to expect them to perform their functions wherever possible. There is now adequate and dependable scientific information about ethyl alcohol and its consequences, and there are agencies interested in putting it into the form which is usable for schools.

The friends of temperance, be they "wet" or "dry," must now realize that the liquor question is a persistent and so far a baffling problem, and that any sort of "solution" must depend upon the use of all our resources of science, sanity, and devoted co-operation. It is a situation in which the nation must have recourse to all the wisdom it can muster. If Congress and the legislatures are to legislate wisely, they must be in possession of the results of disinterested research into all the ramifications of the effects of the use of alcohol on the individual and on society, and also into the different methods of regulating the manufacture and sale of alcohol and alcoholic beverages, together with an evaluation of their results as control agencies. It must be realized that scientific research has become a great business that requires technologists who are trained and disciplined in methods and techniques of research. We therefore submit that the most likely mode of procedure lies in the establishment of a great national commission of research technologists who shall follow out the broad lines of research suggested and such others as they deem necessary, and in the publication of their findings for the education of our citizens and the instruction of our legislative bodies.

QUESTIONS

1. Give your statement of the liquor problem and compare it with that of the text.
2. What have the following to do with the problem of liquor control: (a) "personal liberty" theory? (b) plan of control? (c) administrative difficulties? (d) physical effects? (e) social effects?
3. Distinguish between physiological and social aspects of the problem.
4. How extensive is alcoholism, as the text defines it, in the United States, physiologically and socially?
5. How many persons in this country drink alcoholic beverages? What is the annual cost in billions of dollars? How does the cost compare with our national education bill?
6. Is the drinking thirst hereditary or due to social pressure, association? What do experiments of lower animals show as to the hereditary effects of alcohol?
7. Trace the course of alcohol consumed from the stomach to the tissues of the body. What determines the rate of absorption of alcohol consumed by the body?
8. In terms of blood content, what is an intoxicating per cent of alcohol? What is a lethal dose? Does alcohol in the brain or in the body at large intoxicate?
9. Distinguish between usual foods and alcohol as a food. Why cannot alcohol alone be used as a food? Relate it to food chemistry.
10. Give scientific findings regarding alcohol as a narcotic or as a stimulant. Relate if to the body and the brain.
11. (a) On what does the therapeutic value of alcohol rest? (b) Is it general or restricted? (c) Have hospitals increased or decreased their use of alcohol as a medicine? (d) Does alcohol warm the body or only seem to do so? (e) Explain.
12. Why does heavy drinking produce nutritional diseases? What other diseases may it produce?
13. What insanities (psychoses) may result from heavy drinking? Describe the narcotic effects of alcohol on the highest and the lower nerve centers.
14. (a) Knowing the physical and the psychological effects of alcohol on man, what would we anticipate its social effects to be? (b) Would you expect it to make for crime and accidents?
15. What are the important items on which the economic results of inebriety have been estimated? Is the total monetary cost impressive?

16. Is a considerable per cent of traffic accidents due to intoxication?
17. Could a chemical test of the blood detect intoxication? What device makes this available for detecting drunken drivers in traffic accidents? Do any states or cities use it?
18. What facts indicate that drinking may lead to crime?
19. Discuss the effects of alcoholism on family, divorce, child life, vice, and sex morals.
20. What historic trends in liquor control have occurred in the United States?
21. What regulatory legal systems have been used in attempts at control? Weigh prohibition as one attempt.

REFERENCES

(*Yale lectures* refer to *Alcohol, science and society*, studies of alcohol, Summer School Lectures on Alcoholism, 1945. New Haven: Yale University Press, 1945.)

ANDERSON, DWIGHT, *Analysis of wet and dry propaganda.* Yale lecture 23.

BACON, A. D., *Inebriates, social disintegration and marriage.* Yale lecture 45.

BAIRD, E. G., *Controlled consumption of alcohol.* Yale lecture 21.

BAKER, SYBIL M., *Social case work with inebriates.* Yale lecture 7.

BERRY, D. S., *Alcohol and traffic.* Yale lecture 18.

CARROLL, R. S. (M.D.), *What price alcohol?* New York: The Macmillan Company, 1941.

CHILDS, M. W., "Liquor control that works" in *Sweden, the middle way.* New Haven: Yale University Press, 1936.

CORBIN, JOHN, "Liquor here and in England," *New York Times*, Feb. 21, 1932.

CUSHNY, A. R., *Textbook of pharmacology and therapeutics.* Philadelphia: Lea and Febiger, 1924.

DOLLARD, JOHN, *Drinking mores of social classes.* Yale lecture 8.

EMERSON, HAVEN (M.D.), et al, *Alcohol: Its effects on man.* New York: Appleton-Century-Crofts, 1934.

FISHER, IRVING, and BROUGHAM, H. B., *Noble experiment.* New York: Alcohol Information Committee, 1930.

FLEMING, ROBERT, *Medical treatment of inebriates.* Yale lecture 25.

FORD, JAMES, "First farm colony for drunkards," *Survey*, Oct. 1, 1910: 46–55.

FOSDICK, R. B., *Liquor laws.* New York: Harper and Brothers, 1933.

JELLINEK, E. M., ed., *Alcohol addiction and chronic alcoholism.* New Haven: Yale University Press, 1942.

KELSO, R. W., *Poverty.* New York: Longmans, Green and Company, 1929.

KOREN, JOHN, *Alcohol and society.* New York: Henry Holt and Company, 1916.

LANDIS, B. Y., *Some economic aspects of alcoholism.* Yale lecture 15.

LANDIS, CARNEY, *Theories of alcoholic personality.* Yale lecture 11.

National Woman's Temperance Union, free publications. Evanston, Illinois.

NEWMAN, H. W., *Acute alcoholic intoxication.* Stanford: Stanford University Press, 1944.

SMITH, W. H., *Alcohol: Physiological effects.* Boston: Little, Brown and Company, 1940.

SPEIDEL, CARL C., "Changes in nerve fibers during alcoholic intoxication and recovery," *Scientific Monthly,* Feb., 1937.

WARNER, H. S., *Social welfare and the liquor problem.* New York: Board of Temperance, 1929.

CHAPTER 19

Public Opinion and Social Control

The Emergence of a Mass Society

A historic sequence of maps of the globe displays enlarging size and perspective: the globe has literally expanded as human contacts and knowledge have been extended. If we possessed maps of the social world of man, they too would show an expanding universe. And in a historic series of such maps the most pronounced, even revolutionary, shift would appear in those for the last hundred years. In that time human beings, and particularly Euro-Americans, have moved from localized and isolated communities to large-scale and interactive mass societies. The industrial culture of the Western world has in the last century produced a mass age.

The mass society of modern man is a product of four major technologies. The *industrial* technology of massed mechanization evolved a new human productive organization: industrialism. The *political* technology of centralized government brought a new state organization: the nation-state system. The *social* technology of urbanization and commercialization, building on the decline of the folk culture, erected a new form of social organization: urban, contractualistic, secondary society. The *psychological* technology of mass-mediated communication has molded a new organization of human interests and involvements: an age of mass communication and movements.

Conceptions of mass culture. What has been created is unquestionably a historic novelty: modern mass society. The modern man, particularly in the industrial West and increasingly in the rest of the world, lives in a mass age. This new mass culture may be described in many different ways. One view calls attention to the predominance in our day of huge masses of human beings, aggregated, conglomerated, and more or less organized. Thus, Kimball Young writes of contemporary society as "a vast mass of segregated, isolated individuals, interdependent in all sorts of specialized ways, yet lacking in any central unifying value or purpose. . . . The interconnections and the totality rest chiefly on external, more or less mechanical relationships of persons and groups."[1]

Another view emphasizes the crowd-like nature of modern society. Thus, Emil Lederer stresses the role of masses of men, acting as crowds, integrated by a leader who is skilled in evoking "hidden qualities" in the crowd upon the occasion of some crowd-sensed crisis.[2] This magical relationship between mass and leader is the basis of the mass state of our time.

A third view is impressed with the manner in which modern technologies have brought together great networks of collective habits, interests, and organizations: what Robert MacIver calls the "multi-group" society.[3] These networks of human associations and purposes are power units which compete and struggle with one another for common values and for the control of the social order.

The multi-group society and its social control.   Modern mass culture, for present purposes, must not be regarded as an undifferentiated lump of human beings. It is an intricate network of interlocking patterns of group interests, often competing, often conflicting, sometimes working together. The structure of modern society contains many "institutional complexes" which exist or come into existence "wherever diverse organized interests are institutionally co-ordinated into a unified functional system."[4] Contemporary society is a moving equilibrium of functions structuralized around human interests. These interests, as Dean Pound has noted, are "the claims or demands or desires which human beings, either individually or in groups or in associations or in relations seek to satisfy. . . . "[5] The outstanding problem

---

[1] Kimball Young, *Sociology*, 2nd ed. (New York: American Book Company, 1949), p. 24.

[2] Emil Lederer, *State of the masses: The threat of a classless society* (New York: W. W. Norton and Company, 1940), p. 31. Much earlier Sigmund Freud developed this theme; *cf.* Appendix I, "On group psychology and magical thinking," in *Group psychology and the analysis of the ego*, translated by James Strachey (London: International Psycho-analytical Press, 1922), pp. 44–45.

[3] R. M. MacIver, *Web of government* (New York: The Macmillan Company, 1947), p. 51.

[4] R. M. MacIver, *Society: Its structure and change* (New York: Farrar and Rinehart, 1937), p. 269.

[5] Roscoe Pound, "Survey of social interests," *Harvard Law Review*, LVII (1943): 1–39.

of social order, therefore, is how to bring these groups into satisfying adjustment with one another.

This is no simple task. For one thing, people belong not to one group but to several at the same time. Again, any given individual is never wholly concerned with his society or responsive to it. Moreover, whatever unity may occur in society arises from the unity, even if temporary and tentative, of the things various groups happen to want. Finally, the process of decision-making has been so thoroughly removed from the reach of the individual that he achieves his ends only in groups. The levers of social decision are group levers. Social order is a balancing, a compromising, a struggle of group interests.

The nature of social control. Social control refers to the process by which groups exert influence for the purpose of regimenting or directing human beings along the line of the values of the group. Its purpose, thus, is the achievement of conformity, solidarity, continuity—in other words, social order as conceived by the group or the groups. Social control requires the conditioning of human responses in accordance with group ends. Concretely, it means manipulating and directing the stimulations which play upon human beings in such a manner that they will be persuaded, encouraged, coerced into conformity. This process calls for the use of the major institutions of society: the use of religion, education, government, economic organization. It utilizes the positive methods of praise, flattery, suggestion, slogans, propaganda. It resorts to the negative methods of gossip, satire, name-calling, threats, commands. It both rewards and punishes. How social control in a changing multi-group society works may be illustrated by an examination of the processes and problems of public opinion.

Public Opinion and the Process of Social Control

The nature of the public. Modern society has many publics. Industrial-urban culture has fostered an endless number of indirect-contact groups, formed around common problems, preserving common values, promoting common interests. Public opinion, therefore, is a phrase which describes the problem-solving behavior of a public.[6] Existing as verbalizations, or as

---

[6] The background for this discussion of the concept "public" may be found in R. T. LaPiere, *Collective behavior* (New York: McGraw-Hill Book Company, 1938), Chs. XII–XIII; D. Katz, and R. L. Schanck, *Social psychology* (New York: John Wiley and Sons, 1938), Ch. XVIII; G. A. Lundberg, "Public opinion from a

actions, or as readiness for action, the thinking of any public may turn successively to criticism, to discussion, to the formation of a collective judgment, to the selection of leadership, to social action. This is the process of public behavior. Individuals select their publics (or are selected by them), participate in many of them, are often torn to confusion by them as a result of their counterclaims on their loyalties.

We may distinguish between general and special public behavior, between that of many or all publics concerned with the same interest and that of special publics concerned with particular issues. If there is no majority opinion, there is no public opinion in the general sense. In a democracy the majority is the public. If the opinion of the general public is murky and hazy, that is the kind of opinion it then is; but it may become clarified later by thought, discussion, and public events that affect the situation in question. Mature thought and discussion-struggle, as well as situational changes, especially of an emotion-provoking kind, result in the most intense, deep-seated, and dynamic type of opinion. This kind of opinion is also likely to exhibit great tenacity and be prolonged throughout much time without great change. Polls of different kinds are now placing before the general public results of their sampling of opinions about various matters. There is even projected an international public-opinion polling program.

Public opinion as a control agency. Public opinion is an influence in every kind and extent of social group: family, locality, commonwealth, city, nation, and international group. Careers are made and broken by it, institutions thrive and fail under it, governments seek its favor and try to determine and direct it, and international arbiters seek to mold it or divert it. Its value as control may be illustrated by reference to government.

In a democracy, voting and direction of governmental policies are fundamental, and in both activities public attitudes and opinions are large factors. Votes on men and issues are expressions of mass opinion, and office seekers and holders so view them. By every means, usually legitimately but not necessarily so, they solicit the favor of voters and also seek to mold their views. Governmental policies expressed in legislation have a poor chance of becoming effective if a strong current of disfavor is

---

behavioristic viewpoint," *American Journal of Sociology*, XXXVI (1930): 383–405; P. H. Odegard, "Social dynamics and public opinion," *Public Opinion Quarterly*, III (1939): 239–250.

generally prevalent. Adverse public opinion, even if held only by a few strong special publics, can practically dam the operation of any measure.

The case is not absolutely different in totalitarian countries, but the governmental mechanism is loaded against effective public thought. The fact that such governments keep up the machinery of voting and submitting men and measures to ballots is an index of the power of mass thought and favor even there. The one-party system is a machine for drafting popular leaders and stimulating and molding the minds of the masses toward objectives sought by the dominant public.

The competence of public opinion. Public opinion has its limits, and in order to function effectively it must observe them. First, it cannot decide technical and expert matters, such as building the Golden Gate Bridge, the method of operating TVA, planning and taking a census, or determining what tariff schedule should be instituted. Those, like thousands of other cases, are fields for experts and technicians. Second, it cannot carry out executive affairs, such as directing any one of the great policies government may undertake. Only trained administrators fit in there. Third, it cannot anticipate coming events and try to shape public affairs so that the public shall receive the greatest benefits or the least injury from them.

But there are some things public opinion is capable of undertaking. First, it is suited to determine great issues, or to be aided to do so. Shall we have war or peace? Shall we undertake national soil conservation, or provide forestry, or build a system of national parks? Such great questions can be grasped and settled on principle by the public. Second, the issues presented to the public at one time should be few, simply and clearly stated, and time should be given for consideration. Political-party platforms which follow this model would not bewilder and confuse.

Mass Communication and Public Opinion[7]

One of the major problems of social control in modern society is the fact that the process of public opinion depends upon the mechanisms of mass communication.

The media of communication. About the time of the First World War it became clear to Graham Wallas, an English social

[7] The following discussion of mass communication is adapted from Paul Meadows, "Age of mass communication," *Psychiatry*, X (1947): 405–411 and from *Culture of industrial man* (Lincoln: University of Nebraska Press, 1950) and is used by permission of the editors.

theorist, that modern industrial civilization had created a new type of social organization, which he called the "Great Society."[8] This new system of human relationships is a historic product of the successive industrial revolutions. Small, self-sufficient communities were replaced, or at least dwarfed, by metropolitan interdependent cities; handicraft production by factory and machine production; provincial government by national states; local trade by world trade. Such a society would not have evolved without the implementation of newer devices and types of communication. The Great Society is, whatever else it may be, a society of secondary contacts.

These new systems of communication may be classified into two groups, the mediated, or point-to-point, and the mass impression.[9] Among the former are postal service, the telegraph, cable, and wire services and the telephone. Among the latter are newspapers and periodicals, movies, radio, and television. In both cases, during the last century an amazingly extensive and intricate network of technics and agencies has evolved. The outstanding result has been a gigantic increase in the number of human contacts. Thus, for example, during the first thirty years of the present century the number of post offices increased sixfold, telegraph messages threefold, cable messages 1900 per cent, commercial wireless messages about 2400 per cent, and telephone calls fivefold. In the field of mass-impression agencies, a similar record has been made. Between 1916 and 1930 trans-Atlantic dispatches increased 300 per cent. Movie houses in the United States more than doubled between 1910 and 1931. The first radio station was established in 1920; by 1930 there were 612 of all types, and the development of FM broadcasting and television will greatly swell this number. In 1940 about 95 per cent of American families owned a receiving set. Industrial man has established for himself the right to talk, and to listen, and with television to see.

A widened range of intercourse is the more obvious consequence of this evolution. The flow of interest and attention is worldwide and impersonal. Writing for the Hoover Committee series of reports on social change, M. Willey and S. A. Rice have commented on this mechanical mobilization of communication:

[8] Graham Wallas, *Great society* (New York: The Macmillan Company, 1914).

[9] *Cf.* W. Willey, and S. Rice, *Communication agencies and social life* (New York: McGraw-Hill Book Company, 1933); J. W. Albig, *Public opinion* (New York: McGraw-Hill Book Company, 1939); S. M. and L. Rosten, *Technology and society* (New York: The Macmillan Company, 1941).

"These new agencies unite individuals in concerted responses to common stimuli. Social mechanisms now exist whereby it is possible to impress the people of an entire country simultaneously. A communication system fraught with greater possibilities for evil and for good has never before existed on so vast a scale."[10]

The next and current phase in the evolution of the communication system in the United States was the appearance of concentrations or integrations of the agencies. This development was naturally inevitable in the mediated or point-to-point systems for reasons of economy and efficiency; free competitive enterprise here was virtually impossible from the beginning. American public policy in this area has been to recognize the fact of natural monopoly and to regulate such monopolies. However, the agencies of mass impression have not needed and do not yet need this kind of treatment. Because they are mass media, it is highly desirable that they should remain competitive and diversification should prevail.

Unfortunately, the mass-impression agencies are beginning to undergo the same process of integration and concentration.[11] In the case of the press, ten states no longer have a single city with competing daily papers. Fourteen companies owning eighteen papers control about a fourth of the total daily circulation. Thirty-two hundred weekly newspapers have disappeared. One company actually owns over 3200 weeklies. In the field of broadcasting, one notes that four networks (before 1941) had control of 95 per cent of all nighttime broadcasting power. One third of all regular radio stations are interlocked with newspapers. Ninety-seven per cent of all network income is accounted for by 144 advertisers. The key theaters of the nation are controlled by five movie-producing companies, which also receive over three fourths of all movie tickets. Two companies produce 90 per cent of all the raw film stock in this country.

The one shining exception to the prevailing trends in mass impression is book publishing. Since 1920 the number of firms publishing five or more books annually has risen from 89 to 302. But this particular increase must be viewed in terms of a similar increase in the number of chains of newspapers: from 31

[10] Willey and Rice, *op. cit.*, p. 209. Quoted by permission.
[11] *Cf.* R. B. Dixon, "Concentration and absenteeism in daily newspaper ownership," *Journalism Quarterly*, XXII (1945): 97 ff.; C. J. Durr, "Freedom of speech for whom?", *Public Opinion Quarterly*, VIII (1944): 391 ff.; M. L. Ernst, *First freedom* (New York: The Macmillan Company, 1946); A. M. Lee, *Daily newspaper in America* (New York: The Macmillan Company, 1937).

in 1923 to 60 in 1940. The chains own about two fifths of the
daily and about one half of the Sunday newspaper circulation
of this country. R. B. Dixon, editor of the *Journalism Quarterly*,
has commented on this situation: "Daily newspaper competition,
certainly in the full economic meaning of the word, has become
eliminated from all but 117 American cities."[12]

An age of mass communication.   Today is an age of mass communication. This means that mechanical media create an
audience whose size is without defined boundaries and for which
physical assemblage is not essential.[13] It means, moreover, a set
of networks blanketing the entire country, disseminating news,
opinion, information. By means of volume, repetition, and other
audience-appeal techniques, the stimulation played upon the
average person has been intensified. It means, in addition, the
enlargement of the spheres of experience for the average man;
indeed, he has an almost limitless variety of "worlds" in which
to participate, even if only as an interested wish-fulfilling
spectator.

Mass communication is rather like a great flow of attention
and interest, and the flow is easily capable of being diverted by
persons or groups of persons for ends which do not have to be
disclosed and by means which are not necessarily the same in
every instance: the very essence of propaganda.[14] The ease with
which this flow of attention-events can be captured has been one
of the sources of power of recent social and political movements.
Indeed, it is doubtful if the economic and political life of the
great nations of the industrial world could retain even a sem-
blance of their structures as we know them without this skill.
Mass society means mass business, mass government, mass
education. The scale of modern American living is massive. And
whether the average man wills it or not, he is wittingly or unwittingly a member of countless social groups. In a real sense,
mass communication represents a chain reaction far more explosive than the atomic bomb.

The mass patterns of experience as shared communicatively by
modern technology, contain within them unfathomed possibilities
of personal anonymity and irresponsibility. One can share in

---

[12] Dixon, *op. cit.*, p. 101.

[13] *Cf.* M. Willey, "Communication agencies and the volume of propaganda,"
Annals, 185 (1936): 194.

[14] Not all writers so conceive propaganda; however, *cf.* L. L. Bernard, *Social
control* (New York: The Macmillan Company, 1939); F. E. Lumley, *Propaganda
menace* (New York: Appleton-Century-Crofts, 1933).

world events and can contribute to them without in the least bit bearing any responsibility for that vicarious participation. Howard Odum's study of race[15] brings out the fact that the most cruel injuries to a minority can be perpetuated by the "nicest" people through the rumour process, by people who under more restricted circumstances would not dream of engaging in reprehensible behavior. Perhaps this is another way of saying that mass communication makes possible the flow of ideas across many boundaries. Like the flow of people which modern transportation has made possible, the new technological mediation of ideas on a mass basis is the ground for much friction. Modern communication, therefore, because of its mass character, may be said to facilitate social conflict in modern society.

Mass communication has come to mean also the pyramiding of the "acceptance factors" of audience appeal. An age of mass audiences must learn how to talk in a mass language. This rule is the guiding maxim of the art and possibly the science of public relations. It is of vital concern to the public-contact organizations—broadcasting companies, advertising firms, business corporations, political parties, and churches. The public-relations expert, or counsel, is a person supposedly learned in the arts of reader or audience appeal. Public relations becomes a strategy in a general campaign aimed at capturing a public. It is no accident that the literature of the field shows a remarkable resemblance to the literature of military strategy and tactics.[16]

Finally, mass communication tends to create a horizontal world in which experience moves swiftly but is shallow. There are many interests, and they come in a rapid succession of attention spans, more rapidly than ever before in the history of human society. Yet they tend to lack social depth. They do not sink their roots in the soil of individual human life. The average modern man is never alone, for many mass events impinge upon his consciousness. His sociality is not necessarily the richer because of it. The screen of the movie theater is a fine symbol of the experience-world of the average man as he lives his life in an age of mass communication. The figures of action are made to be captivating, but they do not come alive in his own private world.

[15] Howard Odum, *Race and rumours of race* (Chapel Hill: University of North Carolina Press, 1943).

[16] *Cf.* H. L. Baus, *Publicity: How to plan, produce and place it* (New York: Harper and Brothers, 1942); R. F. Harlow, *Public relations in war and peace* (New York: Harper and Brothers, 1942); M. Wright, *Public relations for business* (New York: McGraw-Hill Book Company, 1939).

They are two-dimensional; they have depth neither in social space nor social time.

Some consequences of mass communication. These statements about an age of mass communication seem to point to one consequence, the uniformity and standardization of human experience. This condition is apt to seem very desirable to partisans of a totalitarian society. But to liberals, such as the American people by tradition and practice have tried to be, it is a condition which is very likely to arouse great apprehension. Liberal Justice Holmes is often remembered for his comment in a famous case. "The ultimate good desired is better reached by free trade in ideas. . . . The test of truth is the power of thought to get itself accepted in the competition of the market. . . . "[17]

Liberals are very much afraid that the emergence of mass communication spells the doom of the free market-place of ideas, so indispensable to the democratic process. They feel that mere exaggerated size carries with it the presumption of antisocial power.[18] The arguments against large-scaleness in the field of mass communication point to standardization of thought and feeling and often to concealed and ill-concealed conspiracies of silence. Liberal democracies likewise have iron curtains which drop over important and little-understood events. An age of mass communications can easily, as Europe has unhappily discovered, bring masses to life: mass action and mob behavior. Liberals can, therefore, make only the most guarded statements about the mass production of ideas. Just as the mass production of goods often leads under conditions of monopoly to increased prices and loss of flexibility, not to mention inferior quality, so the mass production of opinion may carry with it an asking price which is too high, as judged by liberals. An example may be found in the nationalism of the nineteenth and twentieth centuries. The nationalization of thought, proceeding *pari passu* with the nationalization of industry, can be just as lethal as modern warfare, which nationalized industry has made possible.[19]

Certainly the newer and more attractive methods of mass communication are causing no end of readjustment by the older and more institutionalized agencies of society, notably by the school and the church. They likewise promise to be revolutionary

---

[17] Quoted by Ernst, *op. cit.*, p. 8. Quoted by permission.

[18] *Ibid.*, p. 45.

[19] *Cf.* E. H. Carr, *Propaganda in international politics* (London: Oxford University Press, 1939), p. 9.

in their influence upon the folkways and *mores* of society. The average person is inevitably bound up in the uncertainties and tensions engendered by the competing suggestions of mass communication.[20] It is true that these resultants of the newer technology of communication are not in themselves antisocial. But the liberal knows that the mass forces which the selfsame technology has set in motion can exploit these situations for the destruction of the whole structure of liberal industrialism. The first freedom, that of expression, is not only empty but also dangerous when the only persons really free are those who stand near the top of the pyramid of ownership and control of the media of mass communication.

Mass communication and freedom of expression. Freedom of expression for the few can hardly mean freedom of expression for the many. Such a situation now exists among the nation's weeklies. Some 9000 country editors receive from a single syndicate, the Western News Union, 100-odd canned features— comics, news pictures, columns, and editorials. This practice, known as boiler-plating, enables editors who cannot bother with writing their own editorials to publish ready-made columns; it even supplies "ready-print" pages, complete with Lydia Pinkham ads.[21]

This example is perhaps extreme. Yet it is no less disturbing than the lack of free enterprise in the field of communications as a whole. For instance, the newspaper industry is big business. In 1895 when William Allen White bought the *Emporia Gazette*, he paid $3000 for it. "Today," according to White, "if a man were starting a paper, the machinery alone would cost him $75,000 and he would have to get some of it second-hand."[22] The *Wall Street Journal* has commented editorially: "A newspaper is a private enterprise, owing nothing to the public, which grants it no franchise. It is, therefore, 'affected' with no public interest."[23] In the same manner the issue of bigness versus freedom of enterprise has become no less critical. Morris Ernst has said, "The high price of network time and of stations and the squatter sovereignty of frequencies are removing standard broadcasting, if not yet FM, from the reach of new enterprise or the average

---

[20] *Cf.* Willey, *op. cit.*, pp. 198–199.
[21] *Cf.* story in *Time* for June 24, 1946.
[22] Quoted by H. L. Ickes, in *America's House of Lords* (New York: Harcourt, Brace and Company, 1939), p. 10.
[23] Quoted by Ickes, *ibid.*, p. 10.

man."[24] The absence of free enterprise and competition is equally marked in the movie industry. A two-billion-dollar business, it is dominated by five major theater-owning companies and three satellites. The five majors control more than 80 per cent of all first-run metropolitan theaters, and 70 per cent of the total rental of film goes to them. Nearly one half of the entire number of theaters has no competition. Independent producers reach a considerable public only if and as they have the sufferance of these five majors. Whatever else it may mean, freedom of expression signifies something different from freedom of enterprise to express.

Mass communication is cut on the bias. The exception is for one to receive news without a slant. Leo Rosten has wisely remarked that "the freedom of the press does not mean freedom of the news."[25] This fact becomes apparent if the structure of interests of the news industry is laid bare.[26] For instance, newspapers are not only properties, they are investments for profit; moreover, publishers often have, in the local community or elsewhere, vested interests in nonjournalistic enterprises. Publishers are human beings, with human preferences and inhibitions. They are, for example, employers. They have their own social set. Although they may not tell an editor what to print, the editors whom they employ know what the publisher wants printed. The larger part of the publisher's income is derived from advertising, not circulation. Freedom of the press inevitably means, therefore, something a little different to the publisher from what it may mean to the general reader.

Lack of bias is a slogan, not a practice, in mass communication. Ernst, surveying the presentation of controversial issues by the radio industry, concluded: "We are faced with the fact that several large sectors of society cannot, generally speaking, get through the bottlenecks of the air. . . . Radio has not given listeners that diversity of points of view to which a democratic society is entitled."[27] Durr, quoting the Code Manual of the National Association of Broadcasters, makes the point that labor is just such an unrepresented sector. "Employers, as a rule," according to the manual, "won't discuss their labor problems on the air and are inclined to frown on those stations, especially

[24] Ernst, *op. cit.*, p. 157.
[25] *Cf.* Leo Rosten, *Washington correspondents* (New York: Harcourt, Brace and Company, 1937), p. 303.
[26] *Cf. ibid*, pp. 278–291.
[27] Ernst, *op. cit.*, p. 147.

in smaller communities, which open their facilities to labor unions."[28] Moreover, the Code Manual, a voluntary agreement, forbids the sale of time for "the presentation of controversial issues," except for campaign speeches. On the other hand, radio commentators deal with controversial issues with doubtful impunity. A content analysis has been made of the scripts of one commentator, Fulton Lewis, Jr., between May 1, 1944 and July 19, 1944.[29] Labor was discussed in nearly two thirds of the broadcasts; three tenths of all space in the scripts was devoted to labor, and 44 per cent was unfavorable, 33 per cent neutral, and 14 per cent favorable.[30]

Mass communication and propaganda. Mass media are very easily mobilized for the promotion of opinion or any other value. Dr. C. H. Rowell, former editor and administrator, has described an instance of this promotional use of mass media. "When the Tugwell Food and Drugs Act was first before Congress, the newspaper opposition to it was directly and openly organized by advertising agencies, acting through the advertising departments of newspapers. They relied, not on arguments in the public interest—though such arguments might have been well justified as to some features of the original Bill—but on direct pressure politics, conducted by agencies handling the accounts of medicine and cosmetic advertisers, and communicating with editors and publishers through their advertising departments."[31] This illustration makes even more significant William Allen White's comment as a guest editor of the Chicago *Times:* "The most serious danger that menaces the freedom of the American press is the obvious anxiety of rich publishers about the freedom of the press."[32]

Mass media of communication have a peculiar fascination for the political monopolists. Every dictator has, or is, his own "Minister of Enlightenment"—or "Culture." Mass communication is an inestimable source of power for any promotional group. The political monopolists have long known this fact, perhaps far better than any other group. For it means, concretely, mass output for mass consumption. Propaganda is the strategy of mass output.

[28] Durr, *op. cit.*, p. 400.

[29] *Cf.* "Mass media," *Common Sense*, XIV (1945): 32 ff.

[30] Content analysis is being used increasingly by students of radio and the press, with excellent results. *Cf.* the files of *Public Opinion Quarterly*.

[31] "Freedom of the press," *Annals*, 185 (1936): 85.

[32] In newspaper issue for July 2, 1934; quoted by Ickes, *op. cit.*, p. 135.

"Propaganda" implies that certain facts are concealed. It is promotion with concealment. For this reason, any statement of a promotional group has elements of a lie.[33] Propaganda is conspiracy in broad daylight. Thus, the nationalism of the last hundred years has inevitably turned to the arts and crafts of propaganda as the most effective tool of the promotion of "the national interest." It is no accident that the media of mass communication are nationalistic in structure and spirit. There is no government in the world which hesitates to "weight" the news in its own interest.[34] Press associations know very well that if they are favorably disposed they can enjoy favorable terms, financial or otherwise. Yet it should not be forgotten that nationalistic propaganda is only one of the many collective uses of mass communication.

Propaganda and opinion control. Propaganda makes use of many kinds of agencies to influence and control the minds of the masses. Thus, sometimes history, including biography, becomes an undertaking for special pleading. Writings which, by design or mere bias, give undue emphasis and approbation to doctrines, systems, parties, or practices come very close to being propaganda. It has often been pointed out that publishers must have United States histories edited and censored to meet the views and doctrines of certain sections of the nation. It is well known that science textbooks have been emasculated of all references to the evolution of man to satisfy the views of certain sectional constituencies.

Again, literature may be invaded by propaganda motives and used as a vehicle to influence people in support of certain views and prejudices. It is nicely suited to such an undertaking because its real motives may be subtly hidden in the interesting narrative, buried in the midst of captivating esthetic adornment, and made effective by the force of emotional appeal. Some of the most persuasive works for and against the Negro in the United States have appeared in the form of fictional literature. Two notable samples are Mrs. Stowe's *Uncle Tom's Cabin* and Thomas Dixon's *The Clansmen.*

Third, whenever the persuasive human voice is heard from the public rostrum, propaganda is likely to be uttered. Some of the

---

[33] *Cf.* A. Koyré, "Political function of the modern lie," *Contemporary Jewish Record,* June, 1943: 290 ff.

[34] *Cf.* R. W. Desmond, *Press and world affairs* (New York: Appleton-Century-Crofts, 1937).

most vicious and unprincipled appeals to prejudice—class, race, or national—emanate from some pulpits of the nation. Political-party campaigns are loaded with suppressions and misrepresentations of issues and opponents. Diametrically opposed principles and positions are presented as undoubted truths; fictitious and ingenious arguments are formulated to support them; and facts and events are invented or distorted to bolster up the arguments.

Fourth, pictures, especially cartoons, are one of the most effective forms of propaganda. By means of an exaggerated appeal to the eye, situations which lengthy articles and addresses could not equal are portrayed vividly at a glance. Ridicule eclipses argument as an agency of persuasion and conversion, and the cartoon is singly the most effective means of ridicule. The skillful cartoonist can make the saint appear a demon and the righteous man a sinner and a grafter. The movie film also may be an effective agent of propaganda. Like the cartoon, it may make the worse appear the better and develop situations which most unjustly represent individuals and causes. For example, it is probable that "The Birth of the Nation" did more to create race prejudice against the Negro than all the other factors combined since World War I.

Finally, the radio, like the press, has its possibilities for mass output of strategic ideas. The public ear is stormed and abused when it is not cajoled by singing commercials—by advertising, and the public is unable to help itself. Since broadcasting, like the press, is on a commercial basis, there is little to prevent any group or individual with capital from presenting propaganda in behalf of its interests.

Techniques and methods. Propaganda has developed very effective ways to influence those it wants to reach.[35] (1) A careful selection is made of just the facts and ideas which will serve its purposes. Those are used which it wants to have believed. Opposing facts and evidence are ignored and suppressed.

(2) The chief appeal is made to both sentiment and prejudice, and the main effort is to foster illusions. The basis of this effective appeal is the emotions. The desired results can be achieved much more quickly by presenting statements so as to arouse fear, envy, revenge, and hate than by using rational argument and detailed evidence. The latter, however, may be employed as foils and as sops to intelligence.

[35] For example, cf. A. M. and E. B. Lee, eds., *Fine art of propaganda* (New York: Harcourt, Brace and Company, 1939).

(3) The group which is employing propaganda always assumes the possession of the primary virtues of honesty, righteousness, idealism, and any other virtues needed. To the opposition are assigned dishonesty, trickery, debased motives, and other vices needed to make a strong case.

(4) The diversion of public attention from the central or important issue raises false or subsidiary issues. Thus, in the early 1930's there was a concerted attempt made to divert attention from the need of unemployment insurance, which many students of the labor situation then regarded as the most-needed piece of legislation, by raising the issue of stabilization. Something like this was practiced several years ago when accident insurance was first proposed. Its opponents tried to produce a smoke screen in the form of pressure for the prevention of accidents.

Of course, propaganda has results satisfactory to its users or else it would not be employed. Some of the most conspicuous results are these. It brings confusion. The floods of falsehoods and halftruths are bewildering except to those of wide knowledge and deep understanding. It promotes crowd-mindedness and mob action. Promoters seek to reduce the individuals constituting their public to a condition of sheer gregariousness, so that they will, sheeplike, follow their leaders blindly. It breeds suspicion and indifference. Many persons who have been misled in crowd-like fashion settle down in listless stolidity and blackball all further public affairs.

Interests, Pressure, and Social Control

The mass culture of our times has been described in these pages as a vast network of interlocking, competing, conflicting interest groups. They organize about themselves attention publics. They have at their disposal the mechanisms and agencies of opinion-formation and decision-making. And they turn to that ultimate reservoir of authority and influence in our society, government, for the implementation of their needs.

The uses of government. "Engineering consent" is not confined to appeals to "the public." It is a practical, even scientific, enterprise, to which government is ideally suited. Great and wide-ranging powers over all phases of society belong to the various departments of government. Laws can be selectively enforced, discriminatingly chosen for particular enforcement purposes, and judicially interpreted for specific ends. Public funds, public education, and taxing power have endless possibilities for organized interest groups. Patriotism and nationalistic sentiments are an ever-present bandwagon available for all groups. Deals and understandings which will advance one group interest while blocking another are the stock in trade of legislatures.

The "pressure boys," as Stuart Chase has called the lobbyists, are well aware of these possibilities. In a provocative study, Chase has summarized the activities of these "massed battalions" of pressure.[36] Utilizing data assembled by the Temporary National Economic Committee, Chase classified the 400 pressure groups operating in Washington as follows:[37]

> *The Big Three*—official business, labor, and farm organizations . . .
>
> *Specialized producers*, such as cattlemen, publishers, citrus growers, broadcasting stations, telephone interests.
> *Professional and occupational groups*, such as the bankers, insurance companies, advertisers, real-estate men, exporters and importers, doctors, teachers, lawyers.
> *Reformers*, such as the conservationists and the birth controllers.
> *The governments in exile*, who are now protesting loudly against actual or anticipated injustices to Ruritania.

What do these groups really want? Tunneling under "the exalted verbiage," Chase notes some very simple wants:[38]

> Shoe manufacturers want a higher tariff.
> Farmers want parity prices.
> The merchant marine wants subsidies.
> So do the airlines.
> The silver bloc wants 71 cents an ounce, and would take $1.00.
> Teachers want federal aid.
> Unions want a closed shop.
> Dairymen want a prohibitive tax on oleomargerine.
> Railways want to weaken the waterways and the bus lines.
> Cattlemen want Argentine beef plainly labeled "not fit to eat."
> Insurance men do not want too much social security.
> Medical men want to scuttle socialized medicine.
> Coal operators want hydroelectric projects halted.
> Drug men would like food and drug reformers quietly chloroformed—which would not displease the publishers either.

[36] Stuart Chase, *Democracy under pressure: Special interests* vs. *the public welfare* (New York: Twentieth Century Fund, 1945).
[37] *Ibid.*, p. 22.
[38] *Ibid.*, p. 23.

The aluminum interests want no nonsense at all about competitors getting hold of new government plants.

One could continue the list until it became a saga. The objective behind these wants is usually a direct subsidy for the interest itself, or a hand grenade for a competitor.

Activities such as these must not be publicly presented as selfish grabs. They must be glorified in terms of "Free Enterprise," "The Amerian Way," "The American Standard of Living." The opponents of the measures being pushed by the pressure boys are stigmatized as "communistic," "bureaucratic," "chiselers," "fascists," "clericals." It has the style and cast of characters of a medieval morality play.

But words are never sufficient in themselves. Strategy and tactics, scientifically studied and professionally employed, must be utilized. They have been described by Chase as follows:[39]

First, get the "right" Congressman elected . . .

Second, turn the heat on Congressmen already elected.

Third, influence an administrative agency to interpret the bills in the "right" way . . .

Fourth, fight the constitutionality of unfavorable bills through the courts, right up to the Supreme Court.

The uses of the schools. A mass culture lives apparently by promotion. We not only promote the sale of goods but of ideas as well. Mass media and mass promotion are the Siamese twins of mass strategy. The rule seems to be that if it is a mass agency, it must therefore be used, and none should be overlooked. A case in point is the promotional use of the American school system. After a careful survey of citizens' organizations, Royce Knapp made the following report on group promotion in American education:[40]

A study of recent textbooks, films, and other teaching materials used in the social studies reveals that considerable attention is given to some of the aims and ideas of citizens' organzations. Moreover, at national and state meetings of social-studies teachers one will find these groups presenting their ideas and objectives. At the 1949 meeting of the National Council for the Social Studies, the American Association for the United Nations, the American Federation of Labor, and the National Retail Dry Goods Association presented speakers. In the recent past the American Legion

---

[39] *Ibid.*, p. 25.

[40] Royce Knapp, "Social education and citizens' organizations," *Special Education*, XIV (1950): 166 ff.

and the Bureau for Intercultural Education had their speakers available for National Council meetings. The fact that some groups get a hearing for their programs undoubtedly stirs other groups to action.

Another indication of the success of some groups in influencing the teaching of the social studies is seen in the wide use that is made of some of the teaching materials which they prepare and make available to schools. . . .

Citizens' organizations often collaborate with social-studies groups in the production and distribution of teaching aids. . . . The United States Government has also worked closely with social-studies teachers in numerous ways. . . .

Thousands of teachers belong to citizens' organizations such as the American Legion, the Anti-Defamation League, and the American Association for the United Nations. Moreover, to the public at large the teachers are in themselves a group with policies and programs. . . .

This same set of findings can, in all likelihood, be duplicated with reference to churches, lodges, civic study and action groups, and other organizations devoted to the cause of general education.

Mass Culture and Improved Control

We must assume the possibility of some measure of social control over human affairs. Certain aspects of society favor the view that it is possible. (1) Since society is a human structure largely, it should be within man's power to control it to the extent that it is a made thing. (2) Social control is possible because men practice social planning and direct social activities so as to realize the plans.

What form the problem of social control will take and the extent to which one exists are determined by the culture of the group at the time. In times of autocracy, the objective of control is discovered in the whims and interests of the ruler, whether party secretary or industrial magnate. In democratic systems, whether in state, ecclesiastical organization, the family, or industry, the objective of control is the well-being of the masses of the membership of the group.

Until the recent rise of totalitarianism, there had been a manifest development in Western civilization toward a more democratic constitution of the social order. It evinced itself in a universalization of political rights and duties, the extension of public education to all, the substitution of free labor contract and movement for slavery and serfdom, the widening of religious toleration, the improving of standards of living, and the institution of governmental programs for social security. This evolutionary drift warranted our thinking that the great objective of social control and direction is the realization of a social order in which humanity can realize its rights, satisfy its needs, and become the heir of all past achievements, irrespective of faith, race, nationality, or class. Developments during the interwar and the current postwar periods indicate that our thinking was too optimistic. It may or may not be true that, as H. G. Wells said, democracy dies five miles from the parish pump, but it is unquestionably true that it dies when people in a democratic social order find the control of their own decisions at a considerable distance from their reach.

Controlling the process of social decision. Our danger lies in having the mind of the general public made up by self-interested and exploitive agencies. What might be done to improve the situation is very problematical. We dare not place our trust in any panacea or pet remedy. It does not seem to be a matter for direct legislative effort, not in every case certainly. What does need to be done is to recall the possibilities available to the people themselves.

Thus, in the field of propaganda, certain steps can easily be taken. A critical intelligence among people, a thoughtful, penetrating approach capable of evaluating issues can be developed.[41] A healthy skepticism as to the infallibility of human agencies can be cultivated. Experts, trained specialists, and technologists must be trusted with technical matters and technical administrative tasks. Methods of identifying prejudiced partisans and financially interested parties must be devised.[42] Organs of expression of unprivileged and unrepresented groups must be developed and protected.

In the field of mass communication, there must be a general acceptance that mass media can become tools of a vigorous democracy.[43] The publics of a liberal society must be protected in their expressions; just as they must be protected from one another, so likewise the general public must be protected from

---

[41] *Cf.* the informative and highly useful analysis by Paul Hutchinson, "How to read a newspaper," *Social Action*, III (Dec. 15, 1937): *passim*.

[42] An important step in this direction were the laws enacted by the Congress requiring the registration of all lobbyists and of all persons being paid by foreign governments.

[43] These two paragraphs adapted from Meadows, *op. cit.*, and used by permission of the editors.

any specific public. This work plainly requires some fundamental democratization of the media of communication.

Such democratization of mass media depends upon the recognition and bold use of the fact that every step in the concentration of control of the material apparatus of communication is a threat to a liberal democracy. The freedom of enterprise and competition in communication must be protected and promoted wherever and as necessary. But in all cases public regulation in "the public interest" is essential. Unsocialized monopoly of the media of communication, whether public or private, must be broken up. In so far as democracies have "ministry of enlightenment" the work must take this form and this direction. This responsibility has perhaps nowhere been described so succinctly as in the following statement by Walter Lippman. "The task of liberty, therefore, falls roughly under three heads, protection of the sources of the news, organization of the news so as to make it comprehensible, and education of human response."[44]

Finally, in an age of mass culture, when social action and realization must necessarily occur through group identification and activity, it would be foolish to diminish the role of interest groups. Yet in the interest of public welfare—that is, of values shared by all publics!—an extension of the theory of checks and balances as developed within government into social life outside government seems to be urgent. Power units must be balanced, and the pyramiding of power by one unit must be prevented. To that end, interest groups must be identified as such, their ideologies understood as such, their methods tagged as such, and their opportunities for the promotion and protection of their interests fully equated with one another. A democracy is a pluriverse, and it must maintain the liberty and equality of groups with the same integrity and vigor as it seeks to maintain the liberty and equality of individuals.

QUESTIONS

1. In order to insure freedom of expression in our age of mass communication, should government require a definite percentage of space and time in the press and radio for the use of opposing groups on any issue? Is this democratic?
2. Would a demand by the public through social legislation to require accuracy and honesty in advertising be detrimental to democratic

[44] Walter Lippman, *Liberty and the news* (New York: Harcourt, Brace and Company, 1920), p. 72. Quoted by permission of The Macmillan Company.

government and free communication? What are some of the practical difficulties of such a requirement?

3. Sex morals are the principal point of censorship in radio and the movies. Are there other issues which should also be censored? Evaluate censorship in terms of democratic theory.

4. Have mass communication systems tended to distort one culture in the eyes of the others? How? Why?

5. Show how mass communication changes the character of the institutional agencies of modern society.

6. What are the consequences for the various publics in our society of the system of mass communication? Describe the relative position of the labor, religious, educational, and other publics in an age of mass communication.

7. Discuss the various ways in which mass communication can be made "the tool of a vigorous democracy." Should it?

8. Is there a distinction between propaganda and advertising? Explain.

9. Should pressure groups be "outlawed"? Explain.

10. How would you describe the over-all system of social control in the United States?

REFERENCES

ALBIG, J. W., *Public opinion*. New York: McGraw-Hill Book Company, 1939.

CARR, E. H., *Propaganda in international politics*. New York: Oxford University Press, 1939.

CHASE, STUART, *Democracy under pressure*. New York: Twentieth Century Fund, 1945.

DESMOND, R. W., *Press and world affairs*. New York: Appleton-Century-Crofts, 1937.

ERNST, M. L., and LORENTZ, P., *Censored: The private life of the movie*. New York: Cape and Smith, 1930.

ERNST, M. L., *First freedom*. New York: The Macmillan Company, 1946.

GALLUP, G., and RAE, S. F., *Pulse of democracy*. New York: Simon and Schuster, 1940.

HARLOW, R. F., *Public relations in war and peace*. New York: Harper and Brothers, 1942.

ICKES, H. L., *America's House of Lords*. New York: Harcourt, Brace and Company, 1939.

LAPIERE, R. T., *Collective behavior*. New York: McGraw-Hill Book Company, 1938.

LEDERER, E., *State of the masses*. New York: W. W. Norton and Company, 1940.

LEE, A. M., *Daily newspaper in America*. New York: The Macmillan Company, 1937.

LEE, A. M. and E. B., eds., *Fine art of propaganda*. New York: Harcourt, Brace and Company, 1939.

LUMLEY, F. E., *Propaganda menace*. New York: Appleton-Century-Crofts, 1933.

MACIVER, R. M., *Web of government*. New York: The Macmillan Company, 1947.

MEADOWS, PAUL, *Culture of industrial man*. Lincoln: University of Nebraska Press, 1950.

ROSTEN, L., *Washington correspondents*. New York: Harcourt, Brace and Company, 1937.

WILLEY, M., and RICE, S., *Communication agencies and social life*. New York: McGraw-Hill Book Company, 1933.

CHAPTER 20

National Policy and World Social Order

Significance of Social Order

The influential position which the United States has come to occupy in international affairs not only has altered the character and relative importance of international problems but has given rise to new problems that compel new patterns of thought and action. The problems that arise in connection with international relations are undoubtedly among the gravest ones for civilization. They are many and varied, and their full consideration requires voluminous treatises in the fields of international relations and international law. We can only hope to notice some of the important features which have a bearing on our central problem of war and peace. As a fitting introduction and point of vantage from which to view the international situation, let us give brief attention to the import of social order and disorganization.

A sociological consideration of society falls into two main divisions: social order and social change; a study of both divisions is essential to an understanding of society. Let us briefly review the situation concerning the social order.

The role of social order. The business of living in all its many phases requires stability. Were conditions continually changing, life would be impossible. We must know what to expect in the home, the neighborhood, in the nation, in government, in business. A stable social order is also necessary to conserve and perpetuate the cultural surplus, the accumulated achievements of the past. Our present and future are capitalized by past accomplishments.

This is not to deny the necessity of social change. The perpetuation of a given social order results in petrifaction. Social development and progress are requisites of improved conditions of life. All of our great societies have grown out of previous lower and narrower cultural stages. Change and innovation have been requisites to accomplish this. A wholesome society must be a happy combination of conservation and change, of stable order and fortunate readjustment.

The growth of nations has come about by establishing social order. Nations have arisen through the co-ordination of jostling, conflicting elements. The elements co-ordinated may have been kinship tribes, feudal realms, or small nations. Whether the agency of co-ordination was coercive or pacific coalescence, a larger social order eventuated that was propitious for life, because it emancipated it from the threat of ruthless uprooting and destruction. It is rather manifest that life is more secure, freer from disturbance and disruption within the area comprised by the United States or Canada as a nation than it would have been had the same area contained many nations.

Slow emergence of a world-order. One can think of a time when the world was made up of thousands of small societies, separate, inarticulated with one another, often hostile. Nothing like a world-order was perceptible. At a later period embryonic nations were forming; history reports long periods of feuds, of pillage and plunder, of restricted commercial and diplomatic intercourse, of piracy on the high seas—a piracy to which nations even paid tribute in order to secure immunity for their ships. Today, in contrast, there are many varieties of pacific international ties: political, economic, literary, scientific, religious— and international associations exist to promote them. Travel, trade, and communication are normally safe everywhere. This emerging world-society is very imperfect and especially weak in certain respects. Disputes and collisions between some of the many nations are possible and frequent. The problem is concerned with building a more co-operative and pacific order. But a perfect, frictionless world-order need not be expected.

War as a Historic Fact

Evolution of war. Much is learned by glimpsing war as a historic occurrence. Like other social institutions, it has grown apace with, and participated in, the evolution of society. A large part of human energy is spent in and on war. We now know that there is "hot," or active, and "cold," or nonfighting, war. "Cold" war is a long-drawn-out, nonfighting bellicose attitude between nations. It evokes much diplomatic fencing and counter-fencing, propaganda on both sides, dispositioning of fighting forces, and expansion of air, land, and sea forces. The cold war between soviet and capitalistic countries which arose after World War II illustrates the intensity and dynamism of conditions that have repeatedly led to conflict in the past.

Regarding its active aspects, war calls for some reckoning. There were 24 wars and 600 campaigns between 1900 and 1941. According to an index of wars, the volume of war of this century, prior to World War II, was ten times that of all preceding centuries. War consumed 55 out of every 100 dollars of our national income during World War II. The cost of killing a man has increased greatly. In Caesar's time it is estimated at 75 cents, in Napoleon's at $3000, in the Civil War at $5000, in World War I at $25,000, and in World War II at $50,000. War has become a highly specialized undertaking. In primitive times, all the men went to fight the enemy with their farming or hunting implements, returning afterwards to peacetime pursuits. Now highly specialized forces on land, sea, and in air carry on war by means of thousands of different kinds of mechanical devices. A considerable part of the fighters now consist of "standing armies." War weapons have evolved from tools through swords, battle axes, spears, crossbows, armor for fighters, gunpowder, cannon, hand bombs, jet-propelled bombs, atomic bombs. Fighting was first by land, then by land and sea, later by land, sea, and air. Now there looms distant bombing by radar-directed projectiles, in addition to other means of fighting. Atomic and bacteriological warfare threatens to destroy continental populations. The civilian population is brought within the range of war by taxation, rationing, regimentation for military assistance, and by enemy attack. All ages and classes are subject to direct attack.

In seeming contradiction to all this, hot war is being humanized. The death rate due to fighting in our last war was only a half or a fourth of that of the previous war. We fight to kill and destroy but treat our captured enemies humanely, giving them the best of treatment, food, and medical care. Military medical care has made great strides. Almost immediate attention to our wounded on the field of battle is given. Motorized hospitals appear near the fighting front. Suffering is reduced and healing speeded by new wonderful drugs, such as the sulfas and penicillin and the use of blood plasma. Surgery has made great advances, anesthetics improved, demoralized fighters have psychiatric treatment. There is blood-donor service; community recreation is furnished at large camps with a profusion of Hollywood stars giving their services; and there are ample contingents of technologists and dietitians. Nevertheless, war still remains the "hell" General Sherman called it.

Present pointings. It is inadvisable to be too optimistic about terminating war. The trend we have reviewed was toward larger and more frequent wars. The accomplishments of the United Nations to date are not thrillingly hopeful. Our own nation votes larger and larger funds for war purposes because of the threatening outlook, and men everywhere in the West profoundly fear war will come. Now our nation is to maintain bases and war forces in Europe.

Yet we have some grounds of hope. A high moral civilization should be able to preclude war, as being bad and inconsistent. War is a man-made institution and, as such, should be amenable to transformation and elimination. Men do not get angry and fight in war because they are mad. Nation-states incite and conduct war as matters of policy, aggression, safety. The fighting men may not feel angry at all while making war. Logically, theoretically, we should internationally be able to eliminate war. We have yet to bring all nations to a sense and agreement of the desirability.

A cold war may easily become a hot war. Each of two great nations leads a bloc in the United Nations almost constantly antagonistic. It is largely a contest between ideologies. Russia leads and promotes totalitarianism while the United States is the leading exponent of Western capitalism. Various Western nations have modified their capitalism toward considerable socialism. These opposing and fundamentally different politico-economic ideologies face each other and contend in United Nations' deliberations. The United States is apt to view some Russian acts and demands as belligerent, such as moves toward securing military bases in Iceland and Spitzbergen, demand for joint control of Japan (although the United States had conquered that nation before Russia entered the war against it), penetrating China by way of Korea and Manchuria, reaching out toward Japan through the Kurile and Hokkaido islands, sovietizing east-European satellite states, seeking to dominate and Russianize Germany and Korea, and demanding the right to fortify the Dardenelles, free transit through which it already has. Russia seeks a foothold in southeastern Europe by means of which it could control the Mediterranean and western Europe. The United States has entered two European wars to keep western Europe free from totalitarianism and views these Russian moves with suspicion. On the other hand, Russia regards our possession of the Panama Canal as monopolistic and unfair, our insistence on maintaining democratic government in the Balkan states as an invasion of its backyard, our instigation of the Atlantic Alliance, and our control of Japan and Pacific island bases and our interference in Chinese affairs as inimical to its eastern interests.

It is difficult to find a criterion by which to determine whether Russia's seemingly aggressive acts are only efforts to promote its national security or really denote an aggressive national expansion. The same is true of the acts of the United States or other nations. This exhibits one crying need of such a neutral tribunal as we hoped the United Nations would be, where situations are weighed and judged fairly and the grounds of war removed.

Some historic causes of war.   War is a group or mass affair and is motivated by group instead of mere individual concern. Individuals get angry at each other and fight as individuals. Groups develop desires regarding other groups and their property and may resort to mass action against them. This is war. War is organized mass action of a national or other large group against another. The causes of war are almost innumerable, and a nation may elevate almost any event into an excuse for making war on another nation. We are able to notice only some of the more outstanding historic causes of war.

Exploitation.   Organized warfare began with mass attack of one primitive group of people to exploit another primitive group of its hunting land or its agricultural resources. Early wars were about all of that kind. But the exploiting motive has continued until now. Fascistic Italy under Mussolini made war on Ethiopia to secure its land and resources. Germany under Hitler made war on all surrounding European nations for the same purpose, and so began World War II. Today several nations are rivals to secure the rich oil beds of the Near East nations.

Ambitious men.   Unprincipled rulers of nations have often warred on neighbor nations to satisfy their ambition. Napoleon was an outstanding example in his day. He kept Europe in turmoil for many years, engaged in a series of wars in order to make himself master of the world. His methods of false propaganda against friendly nations, concealed under the guise of friendly co-operation, made glaring copy which Hitler could and probably did follow. Hitler undertook to do the same and exceeded Napoleon only in executing the massacre of helpless peoples inside and outside Germany.

Aggressive nationalism. Nationalism has its virtues, such as the co-ordination and advancement of the interests of the people of a nation. But when driven to the extreme, it becomes the foe of mankind and of its own people ultimately. Ambitious men commonly conduct wide and vicious propaganda within their nation as a means of developing fictitious ideas of national claims and prejudices against the defensive claims of other nations. Germany over all, Italy over all, even America over all have been rallying cries to incite inhabitants and involve them in wars of aggression.

Struggle for markets. Nations compete with other nations for possession of the natural resources of weaker peoples and may overrun the latter to secure those resources. They also compete with each other to gain access to and monopolize, if possible, the rich markets of more backward and weaker peoples. This is likely one motive for maintaining the Monroe Doctrine by the United States. It certainly has been the dominating reason for our national foreign policy of the Open Door in China. Britain's sea power helped us make the earlier doctrine a working concern. But we never had the strength, sea power, to implement the latter policy. Consequently Japan invaded China, closed its markets to us, and so laid the basis for World War II in the Far East. Free Chinese markets remain a bone of contention between the United States and Soviet Russia and bode ill for pacific relations in that area. Even the maintenance of tariffs as national concerns may lead to friction and could lead to war.

Armaments and militarism. Rivalry among nations to build armaments and maintain fighting forces against the threat of attack by each other is a prolific cause of international strain, irritation, and trouble. Militarism exists wherever the war motive is elevated to the rank of first importance and the great aim of society and government is viewed as that of getting ready for war. Whatever emphasizes the superimportance of preparedness, the inevitability of war, and warriors as a superior or privileged class smacks of militarism. Constant emphasis on preparedness breeds militarism. There are several factors that encourage it. One is the presence of an aristocratic class which originated in force and exploitation and survives by fostering its privileges.

It has favored large armaments and fighting forces because, being in control of government, it could command force to keep its place of privilege. It has also favored secret diplomacy, something in harmony with privilege.

Professional military classes promote militarism almost as a matter of course. Military affairs is their business, and every vocation values itself highly. Army and navy officers like to see their business thrive, to equal or outrank such businesses of other nations. Advancement and success are more assured if preparation for war is increasing. That they tend to exaggerate the importance and necessity of increased preparedness may be viewed as a quite logical and natural consequence of their vocation. Sometimes war and navy departments overstep their place and seek to subvert the peaceful policies their governments have adopted.

Cultural difference. The customs, manners, institutions, modes of living, dressing, and eating of peoples are liable to differ. In primitive times these cultural differences were regarded as basic and were taken as signs of inferiority. People fought to destroy other groups having different ways of life. This situation has been mitigated among advanced peoples. We may look down on others because of their mode of reaction, but we scarcely think of them as enemies on that account.

However, there are certain cultural matters which may still provide friction, such as language and religion. It has been the practice of some European nations to suppress differences of language within their confines. The language and literature of the minorities were very precious to them, and they struggled to preserve them. These old conflicts were among the fruitful causes of the Great War, and new notions were established afterward somewhat along cultural lines of difference. Those who lived during World War I cannot forget the propaganda of the Allies against the superior *Kultur* claimed by the Germans. Cultural superiority was also claimed by the Nazis and was the basis of their contempt for conquered nations and the nations against whom they fought in World War II. Of course, history is full of illustrations of conflict over religious matters, such as the long-drawn-out wars between Christianity and Mohammedanism and the Thirty Years' War.

Private manufacture of armaments. Since the outlay by nations in armaments of all kinds is enormous, and because the manufacture of armaments is a private undertaking and the profits derived therefrom are great, armament companies become powerful promoters of preparedness and war alarms. Some of the things armament companies have been known to do in order to boost their business are worth recalling. Some time prior to war, German companies established or subsidized French papers to create war scares in France against Germany. The Krupp Armament Company of Germany in 1913 was discovered to have bribed governmental officials to divulge government armament secrets and specifications. In 1914 Japanese officials were punished for accepting bribes from German armament companies. During 1929 W. B. Shearer sued several American shipbuilding companies for over a quarter million dollars for his services as their representative to defeat disarmament efforts at Geneva, Switzerland, during the three years 1926–1929. Stockholders and owners of armament companies sit in parliaments and use their influence in favor of preparedness. "Before the World War, the British executive committee of the National Service League was composed of nine men who were at the same time officers in armament firms."[1] In promoting preparedness campaigns and war scares, these companies often make use of so-called patriotic organizations to further their purposes.

War propaganda. Direct propaganda for war creates war fever and has been known to provoke war. Every great power involved in World War I had a publicity organization which "educated" its people as to the righteousness of its military undertakings and as to the perfidious character of the aims and methods of its antagonists. Great Britain and Germany made use of the same pictures of vessels being sunk by submarines, the other nation being conveniently designated in either case as the enemy. Both those nations likewise conducted a mighty propaganda in the United States prior to the declaration of war by the latter, each seeking to commit our country to its cause. On its part the United States established a propaganda organization which did much to fan war fever in our nation, to create high but incidental war motives such as "a war for democracy" and "a war to end war," and even to flood Germany behind the fighting front with statements of the iniquitous aims of the German rulers.

Ideological differences. Differences in national and economic ideologies have assumed great importance in recognition as

---

[1] R. L. Buell, *International relations* (New York: Henry Holt and Company, 1929), p. 520.

causes of international conflict. Perhaps they have been important in causing many collisions in the past, but now they have assumed impressive importance. Just how important they are is difficult to judge, but their presence and force at the present time cannot be denied. Popularly expressed, the tussle between the Eastern and Western powers is between democratic capitalism and autarchal or oligarchic totalitarianism. The latter is accused and suspected of attempting to spread its system over the whole world, to dominate and rule the world. The former claims to stand for international justice, for large freedom of the individual within national life, and to further the right of every nation to maintain its independent existence. How the conflict between the two systems is to be abated, what measures of compromise and adjustment are to be found to assure national security and maintain peace remain for future discovery.

World Danger Spots

Revolution. A survey of world conditions reveals some real danger spots. Without question we are in a revolutionary period. Great revolutionary areas exist, as in India, which has broken away from British rule; Indonesia, which is seeking freedom from the colonial systems of Britain and Holland; Indo-China, which is in revolt against French rule. Within each area there are sub-revolutions, such as in India between Hindus and Mohammedans. In various European nations the change is from capitalistic economies and Western democratic governments to nationalized economies and "communistic" states. France is moving toward nationalization and "socialism," and Great Britain has rapidly nationalized a great deal of its economic system. Other European nations are in transit toward greater socialization. A recent majority communistic vote in certain Brazilian cities frightened Brazilians out of their political composure. Nationalization of the various economies under Peron in Argentina savors of Nazism and autarchy. Rapid change is in process in several other South American countries. It is doubtful if there has ever been a period characterized by so many expansive and radical politico-economic movements and changes. They exhort us to alertness and vigilance.

What future international and intranational situations are to be is highly problematical. Some exploratory discussion may be helpful for clarification purposes.

Various "scientific guesses" during the last war were made as to the future. It was professedly a war in favor of freedoms, and men were troubled about its significance. Some regarded it as an expression of an "inevitable revolution." If fascistic totalitarianism was defeated, there would be a redistribution of world territory between the "haves" and the "have nots." The great national landholders, such as France and Great Britain, would have to disgorge in favor of exploited peoples. Then, also, within the conquering nations, a revolution would have to take place in favor of the great suppressed classes, since it was a war against exploitation. Of course, a peaceful revolution had been in process in northern and western European nations and Great Britain. In Great Britain, for example, the revolution has been resumed since the close of the war. A "democratic socialization" is taking place. The laboring masses have undertaken to transform the social-economic system so that it will be more responsive and better adjusted to the needs of the lower classes. The industrial and financial systems are undergoing nationalization. The coal industry and the financial systems are undergoing nationalization. The coal industry and the financial system have been taken over by the national government, and the steel industry is in process of nationalization. The socialization aims also to include many welfare matters. Social security through unemployment compensation has long been in practice. Medical care for the masses has become free for all and compulsory for health agencies. Pensions for the aged, widows, and orphans are provided, etc. State "democratic socialism" has gone far there. Sweden has much of the same thing. It is quite different from the totalitarian socialism of nations farther to the east.

Is revolution inevitable? The occurrence of seasons, storms, and earthquakes, the movements of glaciers, the revolution of the earth on its axis, and the cyclical appearance of sun spots are inevitable. Is the "inevitable revolution" like that? What is meant by revolution? A radical departure in any sphere of society is thought of as a revolution. Let us consider three cases:

Industrially, a revolution implies radical changes in manufacture, such as the displacement of the houschold system of manufacture by the factory system; rise of great industrial cities; substitution of steam, gas, and electric power for horse and hand power.

Politically, a revolution usually is the transfer of power from a monarch or an oligarchy to the masses, such as the universalizing of voting and education. Such were the French and English revolutions, the Communist revolution of Russia, and the freeing and enfranchisement of slaves in the United States. Or the movement may be in the other direction, from control by the masses to bureaucratic control.

Socially, even "inevitable revolution" is conditioned by other societal factors. In order to happen it must be preceded by favoring causes. That dictatorships should dominate the world and redistribute political and economic power is being tested. This contingency does not look as probable as it did. The co-operation of non-dictator nations and evidences of sharp rifts within the dictator countries offers grounds for hope that assumed "inevitability" may be conditional. World War II smashed the chief fascist aggressors. The predominant problem now is to liquidate communistic dictatorships without the necessity of a World War III.

Russia and the West.   Since World War II, disturbing differences have appeared between Soviet Russia and its Western allies and the whole Western world. The "Western nations" comprise all European nations that are not satellites of Soviet Russia, together with the nations of the Western Hemisphere, South Africa, Australia, and New Zealand. These Western nations are similar in having a capitalistic economy and a republican form of government, so-called "democracy." Soviet Russia is characterized by state socialism. Practically all land and productive property and business are owned and operated by the state. Private ownership is almost wholly in personal property and wages. There is no opportunity to make "profits" by doing business as an individual. There is a one-party system for political purposes, the membership of which is confined to not much over three per cent of the population. These members are hand-picked by the organization; they do the voting, political administering, and office-holding. Great central committees and syndicates really run national affairs, and the one party largely registers their decisions. What the West prizes as free speech, free press, and free political activity is almost unknown. News from the outside world is censored. The freedoms of the Western world do not exist. Russia is the expression of extreme, intensive totalitarianism and the corporate state. It is highly suspicious of Western capitalistic nations and has vetoed or rebuffed almost every proposition made by them in the United Nations. It has asked that decisions go its way almost entirely. Should it develop a conciliatory attitude and freely co-operate, the chance of United Nations success would be greatly enhanced. So far as Western democracy goes, this is the crux of our international security organization.

Russia and world dominance. Potentially Russia is the strongest nation of the world. Just now, to be sure, the United States stands first in actual wealth and military power in terms of recent modes of making war. But Russia is leading in jet-propelled aviation and bomb devices and may have developed the atomic bomb. It owns and controls the great expanse of Eurasia called the "Heartland" by Sir Halford Mackinder, who laid the basis of geopolitics. Russia comprises 16 per cent of world land area, 23.6 per cent as much as that of all other members of the United Nations and 76 per cent of all Eurasia. Together with its satellites, it comprises 17 per cent of the world area and 24.9 per cent as much as all other United Nations members. It possesses vast agricultural and mineral resources and, with a rapidly growing national population of about 190,000,000 and well-developed science and technology, together with great climatic reaches and products, it may become almost self-sufficing.

With its vast resources, population, and position it could become the dominant world power and go far toward dictating the world course of events. Its fundamental ideological differences from those of the West and its zeal in propagating them throughout the world make for a test of military strength. In a war, Russia could be reached by bombing but scarcely by land armies necessary for a conquest. The Western world must watch in gravity its attitudes, demands, and concessions. We may have to organize a world government of free nations to promote national security.

Preparedness: Security and Economy

Until an international organization can guarantee our national security, we must maintain a reasonable amount of military preparedness. A reasonable amount would be a military personnel and equipment sufficient to protect our national interests throughout the world and to provide national security. Let us consider some associated things.

Security of the national objective. It may be thought that we maintain armaments or organize internationally to secure *peace*. We do, but much more, we do those things to secure *national security*, which means our own individual and family security.

If we can gain security, we likely will have peace. But peace as pacifism could prove deadly. It could head us into a vicious circle. It could lead us to disarm so that we become a weak prey to a greedy and aggressive enemy. We have tried it twice with costly results, namely in pre-World War I days and in pre-World War II days. We allowed our armaments to decline and then became involved in world wars. Had it not been for British sea power in each case, we would have been defeated before we could build aggressive military forces. It is better to have peace through security than risk having security through a defenseless pacifism.

Our great disarmament.   Under President Harding we held a world naval disarmament conference at Washington in 1921 and 1922. We and our then recent allies agreed to disarm. Our own nation led in the disarmament race. We not only disarmed but forced our allies to do the same. Then we got Great Britain to outlaw its alliance with Japan, which ultimately drove that ambitious nation to become a member in the Axis agreement. Then we and Britain promised Japan not to fortify Guam and the Philippines. By these acts we and Britain so weakened our sea power in the Pacific that both nations were caught defenseless and lost their possessions when war came. Because of our naval weakness, we were able to do no more than make protests to Japan for seizing Manchuria and invading China, in spite of our long-standing commitment to maintain the Open Door policy in China. Germany forced the war in Europe because it believed the United States was too weak militarily to enter the war. Our interests demand preparedness until an effective international organization can guarantee security.

Disarmament not economical now.   Some have maintained that we could save money by disarming between wars. A rough calculation will show the fallacy of the claim. About twenty-four years elapsed between World Wars I and II. Our average annual expenditure for military purposes (excluding pensions and payments on war debts) was about 2.5 billion dollars, or a total for the period of some 60 billion dollars. This total amount is to be compared with the amount we spent for promoting World War II, 336 billion dollars, nearly six times what our annual military outlay had been. Our economizing on preparedness cost us some 275 billion dollars outright. Beyond the money outlay are other great costs of aggressive war, such as national demoralization, general social and economic disorganization, loss of education by the draftees, loss of life, distracted and ruined careers on the part of millions, etc. Reasonable preparedness would likely have prevented most of those tragic wastes.

Again, it is asserted that since we maintain our military establishment largely to protect our foreign commerce and since that foreign trade amounts to only about ten per cent of our total commerce, it would be economical to let foreign trade take its chances and save money by disarming. That looks like something, but it is less than it seems. Here is the twofold answer: The loss of all foreign trade would amount to more in dollars than the upkeep of our military establishment; and we have got to keep up foreign trade because we are not self-sufficient as a nation. For the whole period 1927–1939, the value of our national exports was 7.9 per cent of that of our total national production, the average annual value of our exports being $3,340,000,000. The average annual value of imports equals about 2.8 billion dollars, making a total foreign-trade value of something over 6 billion dollars. Our average annual military upkeep we saw was about 2.5 billion dollars or less than half as much. To permit foreign trade to lapse totally in order to save the cost of military upkeep would be to lose 6.1 billion dollars in order to save 2.5 billion.

Our nation not self-sufficient. The idea is often expressed that, since our nation is self-sufficient, we are not in need of imports from abroad. But that does not square with the facts. We consume a great many kinds of imports per year. For the above period of years, 1927–1939, the average annual value of all imports was 2.8 billion dollars. Many of these imports are necessities which we do not produce. Just recall some of the important things we must ship in from abroad yearly, such as rubber, sugar, tea, coffee, spices, tin, besides a number of indispensable metals, our supply of which is practically exhausted or nonexistent. Our demand for foreign uranium from which atomic energy comes is now great, our present supply of that element being limited. We must import important products even for manufacturing our military armament. It will be well to recall in this connection what was said in discussing natural resources. It was discovered that while we still have, as a nation, an abundance of certain minerals, such as coal, iron, oil, and gas, and a very few others, our other mineral resources are practically "exhausted." We must depend on outside sources for our supplies of them.

Efforts Toward International Organization

During modern times, much thought has been devoted to ways to bring about international harmony, and various devices have been legalized by international agreement to effectuate it. It has been a long record of hope and disappointment, but still hope survives and brings new undertakings. Visions of world peace and security haunt us.

The pith of nationalism is the universal claim of nation-states to sovereign independence—that is, the absolute right to settle their "own national affairs" in their own way. This involves not only all internal domestic matters but a large measure of those touching other nations. It also includes upholding "national dignity" and resenting all "insults to national honor," even at the cost of armed action. These claims make it difficult under provocative conditions for nations to get along with one another peacefully and to maintain any sort of international agreement which in any way affects those sensitive and touchy questions of sovereignty. The League of Nations failed because in itself it possessed no power of a restraining or coercive nature over the nations. Until nations become willing to limit their national sovereignty out of consideration of world good, which is also national good, there can be little hope of abolishing war and securing permanent peace.

The civilized world today confronts the fact that the nations are only points of emphasis and individualization in a world-wide social order. The connecting cables of commercial, political, and general cultural relations are so numerous and gripping that no nation can escape the consequences of the acts of other nations. There are no longer any such things as complete national independence and aloofness. We cannot keep out of the great international tidal ebb and flow. We can no longer strictly "mind our own business" and let other nations mind theirs. The asserted *sovereignty* and independence of a nation are now seen to be *conditional*. The world society, the first great world-order, has arrived and the demand is that nations learn to act as constituent interdependencies of that order.

There is now instantaneous interchange of news. Transit of the Atlantic has been reduced from three months to as many days by water and to a few hours by air, and there exists the prophetic possibility of a crossing in less time by means of rocket ships navigating the stratosphere. World-wide trade and world markets dominate commerce. There is such a vital dependence of great populations on the daily arrival of foods and other necessities from all over the world that one day's disruption is almost fatal. The interlocking interdependence of nations has become so close and vital that leading nations have at times co-operated to secure the financial stability of one or more of their number.

Basic requirements for international co-operation. When individuals in any situation come into recurrent contact with one another and find it desirable or necessary to co-operate in order to avoid inconvenience or disaster, they discover that they cannot co-operate until they have worked out mutually satisfactory plans and agencies of co-operation. Co-operation requires planning, agreement, organizational mechanism. The plan must be sufficiently comprehensive and detailed to provide for recurring needs for teamwork, it must be sufficiently elastic to meet the needs of emergencies and crises as they arise, and it must be mutually satisfactory so as to command the loyal support of all associates. Every partnership or corporative business represents such a plan. So does every city, state, or other governmental entity.

Specific requisites of internationalism. There are certain specific requisites which an international co-operative organization possesses. *First*, it must be constantly available for legislation,

TABLE 29
Pre-United Nations Attempts at Internationalism

Kind	Shortcomings or Merits
Embassies	Entirely nationalistic. Partial. Mitigative.
Arbitration	Nationalistic. Partial. Mitigative.
Hague Tribunal	Continuous adjudication. Voluntary. Partial and mitigative. Only 19 cases heard in 30 years.
International congresses and conferences	Voluntary. Nationalistic. Mitigative. Partial: 75 conventions in 70 years.
International law	Multitudes of laws, through centuries. Mitigative. Enforcement voluntary with nation.
Treaties	Nationalistic. Mitigative. May become "mere scraps of paper."
League of Nations	Grand attempt: 55 national members at height. Fairly democratic. Lacked coercive power to retain national members and enforce rulings. United States probably killed it by refusing membership.

making international regulations and laws covering ordinary pacific matters. *Second*, it must provide a continuous system for administering these laws. *Third*, it must maintain agencies for settling ordinary disputes as they arise and also methods of anticipating these occasions by formulated regulations or laws which will prevent friction. *Fourth*, this mechanism must realize international democracy. As such it will recognize two principles: (a) the right of all national members to a voice and a vote in the proceedings; (b) the difference in the weight of nations by some method of proportional representation, thus assigning to a nation of a hundred million people greater deciding potency than one of a million people. *Fifth*, the wholesomeness and safety resident in publicity of international proceedings must be recognized. Democracy, safety, and justice are all dependent on a wide diffusion of information concerning the proposals and discussions in international considerations.

United Nations. The United Nations was organized at a world conference held in San Francisco, April-June, 1945, in which most of the nations of the world participated. Two houses exercise discussion and legislative functions: the Assembly, where only discussion and voting opinion take place, and the Security Council, where discussion and final decisions are exercised. The assembly is open to all nations, equal voting weight being given to the one representative member of each nation. A representative from each of eleven nations sits in the Security Council, only five of whom have a deciding vote—those of China, France, Great Britain, Russia, and the United States. These five nations waged the war for the Allies. Each has veto power on decisions they object to. The opinions of the Assembly go to the Security Council, which is, however, not bound by them.

Besides these two houses, there is an international court of justice, an economic and social council, and many international organizations for conferences on labor, agriculture, monetary affairs, etc. There is also a committee on military affairs and a secretariat. United Nations is empowered to use military forces to prevent war or suppress aggressions. The final form of its military functions has not yet been worked out.

Merits of the United Nations.   1. The United Nations is an important effort in the right direction. It may not be a perfect plan, but, given time, experience may discover and correct the defects. While very similar to the League of Nations, it possesses some advantages over that plan.

2. It affords a world forum where free discussion can converge attention on troublesome international problems and build a world opinion and a world sense of justice about them. A stubborn nation may defy world opinion, to be sure, but even the most obdurate is likely to be affected by it finally, since it must live with member nations.

3. It provides a meeting place for nations where patterns of international conduct are being fashioned and agreements arrived at to realize them. Nations, like strange dogs meeting, have to look each other over and feel each other out before deciding whether to fight, run a big bluff, or go along with the others peacefully. In time, these patterns of conduct may become conventionalized and regulative of international conduct as a matter of course. It is not possible now to maintain an assembly line, which can build up and deliver prefabricated judgments on international conduct without any friction.

4. The United Nations was greeted with world-wide acceptance and enthusiasm on the part of the nations everywhere. The magnitude and devastating effects of World War II were sufficient mainsprings of this reception. Over 50 nations have become members, and there is a waiting list of applicants. The universal need for security is a working cause of loyal support. If the big nations do not wreck the enterprise, this loyalty may be expected to endure.

Weaknesses in the United Nations. Some of the following defects, recognized in the United Nations, are perhaps necessary at the present juncture. Many observers would question the necessity, however.

1. *No Bill of Rights.* Our own national Constitution could not get adopted until such a bill was included. The United Nations appointed a committee to prepare such a measure but no action has been taken, so far as we can learn.

2. *Veto power by any of the Big Five.* Veto of a measure affecting it by one of the Big Five is now absolute, blocking international action on vital matters. Could veto power be amended out of the Charter, the nation most frequently using it would probably withdraw from the United Nations. Such disruption might bring into existence something better.

3. *Importance of small nations.* Small nations have full voice and vote in the Assembly but have only representative discussion, no vote, in the Security Council, where final decisions are made. They are almost powerless in determining vital issues.

Probably they should not be made equal to great nations in all respects. Power and responsibility of the two are unequal.

4. *Impotency in employing coercive military force.* No provision has yet been made by the United Nations to employ collective military force to carry out decisions. No individual nation dares assume coercive power, since other nations could charge motives of aggression. At some such point the League of Nations failed. The Atlantic Alliance seeks to remedy this weakness within its jurisdiction.

5. *Representatives of member nations undemocratically chosen.* Governments of member nations appoint their representatives in Assembly and Security Council. Critics of this say that such appointees represent only the ruling *cliques* and not people at large. However, there are evident weaknesses in devices proposed to execute choice by popular vote. One criticism is of the fact that the larger and more powerful nations which have to bear the major burden of carrying out United Nations' policies have no more voting power than the small nations. The United States, for instance, has no more votes than Afghanistan. It may be countered, however, that actual voting power is not measured by the number of votes which a nation is allowed to cast. The influence that a nation is able to exert upon other nations on vital issues is likely to be far more important, in the long run, than mere voting privilege. This is to a larger degree a matter of moral and political philosophy, geographic position, economic power, and the art of persuasion. However, whether a large and powerful nation has more at stake than a small nation depends upon the point of view. A weak nation like a weak individual has its existence at stake in vital situations that threaten it. A large nation can risk no more than its life. It has been argued with apparent justification that a major test of the ability of nations to work out an effective basis for international co-operation under rules of order is in the capacity for mutual trust. A voting system calculated to protect the interests of the strong by a concentration of voting power might well remove the conditions essential to mutual trust.

QUESTIONS

1. Give an operational statement of social order. (a) Was there social order during World War II? (b) Distinguish between peaceful and conflict social order.
2. Have recent boundary and governmental changes among nations promoted or retarded world-order?

3. Distinguish between fascistic and communistic totalitarianism. Would you like to live under either regime?
4. What is a social institution? (a) Is war a social institution? (b) If it is, can it be modified or eliminated like other institutions?
5. (a) Evaluate the weight of the causes of war discussed in the text. (b) Add other causes you regard as important. (c) Which causes would be least responsive to control?
6. (a) Did racial differences enter as a cause of the last war to any great extent? (b) Was the Nazi attack on the Jews war or something else?
7. Is war as a phenomenon exactly like sun spots and storms as natural events? Are wars biological or sociological occurrences wholly or chiefly?
8. (a) Do the evolutionary steps in war denote steps in "social progress"? (b) If another war comes, will it likely promote human welfare (progress)?
9. Could war be so humanized that it would be desirable? Why?
10. Are Russia and the United States inevitably leaders in the "next war"?
11. Make five propositions you can objectively defend on each of the following: (a) the virtues of war, (b) the evils of war.
12. Defend in three propositions each: (a) Military preparedness. (b) Disarmament.
13. Were we self-sufficient as a nation, would it be desirable to make less outlay for "preparedness" than if we were not? Can we be really isolated as a nation today?
14. Would you say that the series of attempts at internationalism the world has made represents an evolution which reflects a definite objective?
15. Investigate and report whether the United Nations is a better charter to bring security and peace than was the League of Nations.
16. Discuss the defects of the United Nations and indicate "sure" remedies.
17. Evaluate Russia's attitude and acts in United Nations procedure so far as to whether it arises from self-consciousness, suspicion, efforts at obtaining its security, desire for expansion, or pure bluff. On the same points, is the record of the United States better?
18. Toward what objective does the present revolutionary period trend?
19. What could prevent Russia from dominating the world, were it so minded, considering its extent of domain, location, natural resources, if it could develop to the technological and scientific level of the best Western nations?
20. (a) Could it set up a world totalitarian state? (b) Do we have to think of such possibilities, and that there could be no recourse? (c) Or would it supply a desirable peaceful and secure world-order?

REFERENCES

ALSOP, J. and S., "Can we protect the country against atomic warfare?", *Saturday Evening Post*, July 13, 1946.

ALSOP, J. and S., "Must America save the world?", *Saturday Evening Post*, Feb. 21, 1948.

BARTLETT, R. J., *League to enforce peace*. New York: United Nations Press, 1944.

BERNSTEIN, G. A., "World government progress," *The Nation*, June 5, 1948 and June 12, 1948.

BOYD, A. K. H., *United Nations organizational handbook*. London: Pilot Press, 1946.

BRYSON, LYMAN, *Which way America—communism, fascism, or democracy?* New York: The Macmillan Company, 1939.

BUELL, R. L., *International relations*. New York: Henry Holt and Company, 1929.

BUELL, R. L., and ALEXANDER, R. C., *War drums and peace plans*. New York: Grosset and Dunlap, 1936.

BUTLER, SMEDLEY D., *War is a racket*. New York: Round Table Press, 1935.

CARR, E. H., *Nationalism and after*. New York: The Macmillan Company, 1944.

CHAMBERLAIN, W. H., *World order or chaos*. London: Gerald Duckworth and Company, 1946.

CHANDLER, A. R., *Clash of political ideals*. New York: Appleton-Century-Crofts, 1940.

CHASE, STUART, *For this we fought*. New York: Twentieth Century Fund, 1946.

CLARK, FREDERICK, *Our food problem: Study of national security*. New York: Penguin Books, 1939.

CULBERTSON, ELY, "How to win the atomic peace," *New Leader*, Jan. 12, 1946.

DULLES, J. F., et al, *Three years of United Nations*. New York: Carnegie Endowment for International Peace, 1948.

EAGLETON, CLYDE, *Analysis of the problem of war*. New York: Ronald Press, 1937.

EBENSTEIN, WILLIAM, *Nazi state*. New York: Farrar and Straus, 1945.

FISCHER, LOUIS, *Great challenge*. New York: Duell, Sloan and Pearce, 1948.

FOX, W. T. R., *Super-power*. New York: Harcourt, Brace and Company, 1944.

GRABOWSKE, Z., *Creative peace*. New York: The Macmillan Company, 1944.

HANSEN, A. H., *American role in world economy*. New York: W. W. Norton and Company, 1945.

HAZLITT, HENRY, "Will dollars save the world?", *Readers Digest*, Feb., 1948.

HEIMANN, EDWARD, *Communism, fascism, or democracy*. New York: W. W. Norton and Company, 1938.

HUTCHINS, R. M., "Atomic bomb versus civilization," *NEA Journal*, March, 1946: 114–117.

JESSUP, P. C., *Modern law of nations*. New York: The Macmillan Company, 1948.

LASKI, H. J., *Where do we go from here?* New York: Viking Press, 1940.

LIPPMAN, WALTER, *United States foreign policy*. Boston: Little, Brown and Company, 1941.

LYONS, EUGENE, *Assignment in Utopia*. New York: Harcourt, Brace and Company, 1937.

MORGENTHAU, H. J., *Scientific man versus power policies*. Chicago: University of Chicago Press, 1946.

NORTHROP, F. S. C., *Meeting of the East and West*. New York: The Macmillan Company, 1947.

RIDER, FREMONT, *Great dilemma of world organization*. New York: Reynal and Hitchcock, 1946.

SHOTWELL, J. T., *Great decision*. New York: The Macmillan Company, 1944.

"Social conflict and war," *Publications American Sociological Society*, vols. 10 and 25.

"War," symposium on various aspects, *American Journal of Sociology*, March, 1946: 350–487.

WELLS, SUMNER, *Where are we heading?* New York: Harper and Brothers, 1946.

Index of Authors

Index of Subjects